The ULTIMATE BOOK OF TOP 10 LISTS

A MIND-BOGGLING COLLECTION OF FUN,
FASCINATING AND BIZARRE FACTS ON MOVIES,
MUSIC, SPORTS, CRIME, CELEBRITIES,
HISTORY, TRIVIA AND MORE

The ULTIMATE BOOK OF TOP 10 LISTS

A MIND-BOGGLING COLLECTION OF FUN, FASCINATING AND BIZARRE FACTS ON MOVIES, MUSIC, SPORTS, CRIME, CELEBRITIES, HISTORY, TRIVIA AND MORE

THE BEST OF LISTVERSE.COM

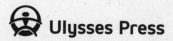 Ulysses Press

Published by:
ULYSSES PRESS
P.O. Box 3440
Berkeley, CA 94703
www.ulyssespress.com

ISBN: 978-1-56975-715-4
Library of Congress Control Number: 2009902010

Acquisitions Editor: Nick Denton-Brown
Managing Editor: Claire Chun
Project Manager: Karma Bennett
Editorial staff: Jennifer Privateer, Lauren Harrison, Elyce Petker, Kate Kellogg
Production: Judith Metzener
Design: what!design @ whatweb.com
Interior photos: see page 705

10 9 8 7 6 5 4 3 2

Printed in Canada by Transcontinental Printing

Distributed by Publishers Group West

Table of Contents

Acknowledgments

I would like to acknowledge the hard work of the Listverse administrators, Cynthia, Judy, and Dan. Their tireless work keeps Listverse running smoothly. Thanks also to Elsa, Trigun472, Randall, and warrrreagl for last minute finishing touches.

I would also like to thank Karma Bennett and the staff at Ulysses Press for allowing me to realize my dream of writing this book and for helping me every step of the way.

Thank you to each and every contributor of lists to the site or this book. The following is a non-exhaustive list of contributors:

downhighway61
Tempyra
Diogenes
JT
damien_karras
Blogball
StewWriter
Rushfan
Rolo Tomasi
Jimmy Burke
Abhishek
Tamala
Nicosia
Jono
Stevenh
Trigun472
The Anachronism
Heroajax
Grubthrower
Antmansbigxmas
Brotherman
MT

Kutuup
Kreachure
Dazednconfused
alextenn
Peter B-P
STL Mo
Steeveedee
F. McClure
SteveD
Randall
The Bed-headed
Stranger
TiffanyH
Tequila Mockingbird
Randy
Kazorek
Satori
Simon Arms
Kowzilla
Apepper
Vakattack91
Deletetechnique

Dangorironhide
B.C.
Cedestra
Hope
Patholdenmd
KGB99
Astraya
ChrisF
Dana
Mystern
Spanner-In-The-Works
Crubel
BishopWhiteT
DentShop
Bucslim
Skydiver
Jason Hirschhorn
Mathilda
Flibbertigibbet
Maman
JediMoonShyne
Gringo Joe

CHAPTER ONE

Bizarre Stuff

1. Top 10 Unsolved Mysteries
2. Top 10 Urban Legends—Debunked
3. Top 10 Bizarre Medical Anomalies
4. Top 10 Unfortunate or Embarrassing Deaths
5. Top 10 Bizarre Beauty Products
6. Top 10 Macabre Collectibles
7. Top 10 Bizarre Museums
8. Top 10 Bizarre Things You Can Buy on Amazon.com
9. Top 10 Bizarre Relationships
10. Top 10 Bizarre Eating Habits
11. Top 10 Bizarre Patents
12. Top 10 Amazing Coincidences
13. Top 10 Bizarre Mental Disorders
14. Top 10 Bizarre Curses
15. Top 10 Bizarre Surgical Procedures
16. Top 10 Bizarre Fetishes
17. Top 10 Most Haunted Places
18. Top 10 Bizarre Phobias
19. Top 10 Bizarre Traditions
20. Top 10 Truly Bizarre Deaths
21. Top 10 Bizarre Death-Related Facts
22. Top 10 Bizarre or Frivolous Lawsuits
23. Top 10 Bizarre Afterlife Experiments
24. Top 10 Bizarre Festivals
25. Top 10 Incredibly Eccentric People

TOP 10 UNSOLVED MYSTERIES

10 THE BABUSHKA LADY

After the assassination of President John F. Kennedy, film footage that had been provided by a witness was carefully checked for clues to the killer's identity. Unexpectedly, the film also showed a woman standing on a grassy knoll wearing a brown overcoat and scarf. Because she looked like a Russian grandmother (babushka) she was labeled "The Babushka Lady." She appeared to be filming the scene and she continued to do so even as the majority of the crowd fled after the shooting. She eventually walked away to the east up Elm Street where she disappeared from history forever. The FBI requested that the woman come forward but she never did. Her true identity and perhaps her involvement in the crime are unknown to this day.

9 THE ZODIAC KILLER

The Zodiac Killer was a serial killer who was active in Northern California for ten months in the late 1960s. He is believed to have killed at least five people and injured two. After one of the killings, the police received a phone call from a man claiming to be the killer—he admitted to two previous killings. The man eventually sent a series of letters to the press that included ciphers that he claimed would lead to his identity. While the majority of the codes were broken, eighteen letters remain unsolved. The ciphers did not help the police and the identity of the killer has never been determined. The prime suspect, Arthur Leigh Allen, was never convicted despite an enormous amount of circumstantial evidence against him.

8 JACK THE RIPPER

Jack the Ripper is probably the most famous serial killer in history. He was active in the later half of 1888 in London. He committed his crimes mostly in the poor Whitechapel area and his victims were typically prostitutes. In some cases the bodies of the victims were discovered only minutes after the Ripper had left the scene. Despite a large list of suspects, the police have never been able to uncover the identity of the notorious murderer.

7 THE VOYNICH MANUSCRIPT

The Voynich Manuscript is a book written in the Middle Ages in an unknown language using an unknown alphabet system. Attempts have been made to interpret the document for over one hundred years but there has not been a single breakthrough. The book includes illustrations of plants (some unknown to modern botanists) and astronomical information. It is possible that the book was the work of an alchemist who used codes to keep his discoveries private but, until the book is decoded, no one really knows for sure.

6 COMTE DE SAINT-GERMAIN

The Count of St. Germain was a mysterious man from the eighteenth century who was skilled in music, art, and alchemy. His origin was unknown and he eventually disappeared without a trace. There were rumors that he had discovered an elixir of youth and several people in recent years have claimed to be him. Some people also believe that he appeared through history as various historical figures such as St. Joseph, Plato, and Roger Bacon (under whose guise some claim he wrote the complete works of Shakespeare).

5 THE BLACK DAHLIA

In 1947, the body of Elizabeth Short was discovered cut into two pieces in a parking lot in Los Angeles. The press dubbed the then-unidentified woman "The Black Dahlia"—after a movie playing called *The Blue Dahlia*. The investigation into Short's murder was one of the largest in the history of the city, however, despite this, the motivation and identity of the killer have never been uncovered.

4 THE TAOS HUM

The Taos Hum is a low-pitched sound that can be heard in various parts of the world, but especially in the United States and Europe. It is described as sounding like a distant engine and it is undetectable by microphones and other electronic monitoring equipment. It is most famous for its occurrence in Taos, New Mexico—the town from which it takes its name. In 1997, the United States Congress asked scientists and observers to find the source of the sound—they were unable to do so.

3 THE MARY CELESTE

Mary Celeste was a 280-ton ship launched in Nova Scotia in 1860. When the ship was ten years old, she was purchased from a salvage yard for three thousand dollars and put to use carrying alcohol from the United States to Genoa, Italy. The ship was eventually discovered floating in the middle of the Strait of Gibraltar with no one onboard and no sign of struggle. All documents except the captain's log (which gave no clue to the mystery) were missing. In 1973 two lifeboats containing six bodies and an American flag were found on the coast of Spain—the bodies were never identified but there is some speculation that they may have been the members of the *Mary Celeste*'s crew.

2 THE BERMUDA TRIANGLE

The Bermuda Triangle is a large area of ocean in the North Atlantic that has been the source of many plane and boat disappearances. A number of explanations (many are not particularly credible) have been offered for the mystery, which include bad weather, time warps, and alien abductions. There is substantial documentation to show that many of the disappearances have been exaggerated, but even if those are excluded from the total count, the odds of vanishing are higher in the triangle than anywhere else.

1 THE SHROUD OF TURIN

The Shroud of Turin is allegedly the burial shroud of Jesus Christ mentioned in John 20:6-7, which bears the image of a crucified man. Despite many scientific investigations, no explanation exists for how the image could have been imprinted on the cloth. No attempts to replicate the image have been successful. Radiocarbon tests date it to the Middle Ages, but its existence has been known since at least the fourth century, and pollen and weave testing put it at the time of Jesus. Interestingly, both the shroud and another cloth (the Sudarium of Oviedo) appear to have been placed on the same man and contain traces of the same blood type (AB)—rare in Europeans in the Middle Ages but common in Middle Eastern people.

✳✳✳✳✳✳

TOP 10 URBAN LEGENDS—DEBUNKED

10 MADE IN USA, JAPAN

Apparently the Japanese renamed a town in Japan to USA so they could legally export goods to the U.S. and conceal their place of origin. This legend was spurred on by the fact that in postwar America, "Made in Japan" became synonymous with cheap, poorly made goods. It is, of course, ludicrous to think that American customs officials would simply ignore the import of products that are clearly labeled to mislead.

An interesting addition to this tale is that Sony Corporation intentionally made their "Made in Japan" labels small so that American people would not realize that it was a Japanese company. A large number of Sony shipments were turned away by customs officials because the labels were smaller than regulations required them to be.

9 WHO INVENTED THE TOILET?

Contrary to popular belief, it was not Thomas Crapper. Crapper is known to most as an ingenious Victorian plumber who came up with the idea of a flushing lavatory. The majority of this deceit comes from a book written in 1969 by Wallace Reyburn, *Flushed with Pride: The Story of Thomas Crapper*. This author also wrote Bust Up: *The Uplifting Tale of Otto Titzling* and *The Development of the Bra*. Crapper was in fact a plumber, and he did take out a number of plumbing related patents in his time, but none for the flush toilet.

In reality, Alexander Cummings is generally credited as being the inventor of this illustrious gadget, in 1775 (fifty years before Crapper was born). Joseph Bramah and Thomas Twyford improved upon Cummings's design by adding the ballcock. Finally, the use of the word "crapper" for a lavatory is of unknown origin but is believed to have started out in America.

8 THE DADDY LONG-LEGS

For quite some time there has been a rumor spreading that the daddy long-legs spider is the most poisonous spider but is unable to kill humans simply because its fangs are not strong enough to pierce our skin. In fact, there is a small twist here—it is not possible for us to test the toxicity of the spider because of international codes of ethics and Amnesty International (for some bizarre reason) which prevent the inevitable harming of the spider during testing.

In reality, the most poisonous spiders are the brown recluse and the funnel web spiders.

7 LEMMINGS OCCASIONALLY THROW THEMSELVES FROM CLIFFS

This urban legend has quite an awful beginning; in the 1958 Disney documentary *White Wilderness*, a camera crew forced a group of lemmings off a cliff to document their supposed suicidal behavior. The film was made in Canada and lemmings were brought in for the film after they were purchased from Eskimo children. The lemmings were filmed in a variety of artificial situations and then herded to a cliff where they were pushed to the edge to simulate a migration.

It is unknown whether Disney was aware of the behavior of the film crew, but the fact remains, lemmings do not throw themselves from cliffs.

6 KENTUCKY FRIED CHICKEN NAME CHANGE

The legend is that Kentucky Fried Chicken changed its name to KFC because they feared the word "fried" had negative connotations not good for marketing. There was also another ludicrous legend that surely no one would believe: it claimed that KFC was breeding super chickens to get more meat from them and by law they could not refer to them as chickens because they were a new breed of animal.

As it turns out, Kentucky Fried Chicken was not concerned about bad publicity at all—in fact, the company has not given a specific reason for the name change. You may be interested to know that the company is now once again beginning to use the original name of Kentucky Fried Chicken.

5 THE MOST HOLY RELIGION OF JEDI

Some years ago a strange rumor started to pass around the Internet—the claim that if enough people wrote "Jedi" as their religion on a census form, the government would be compelled to include it as an official religion on the next census. This first started with an English census in 2001, followed by an Australian one, and a New Zealand one in the same year.

Not only is it entirely false, in Australia and New Zealand you can be fined a thousand dollars for falsifying your census results. Not only do you risk a fine, the census information is used to determine allocation of tax funds, so by lying people are doing other members of society a disservice.

4 SNUFF FILMS

Snuff films are movies of people being killed. Most rumors claim they are made to order due to the high risks involved in distribution. The legend surrounding snuff films often piggybacks on other rumored films of cannibalism, necrophagia (eating human carrion), and necrophilia. This myth has been helped along in recent years by films such as *8MM* (starring Nicholas Cage), which treats the subject as if it were fact.

In reality, there has not once been a snuff film found. Every time there is a report in the press about one, upon investigation it turns out to be false. There is even a one-million-dollar reward for anyone that can come forward with a commercially sold snuff film. The reward has been offered for many years now with no one ever attempting to claim it (though perhaps that is understandable).

3 MCDONALD'S SHAKES ARE MADE FROM RECONSTITUTED ANIMAL FAT

This rumor has been very popular on the Internet and I even remember it from my own childhood. The belief was that the liquid poured into the milkshake machine (and the ice cream machine) at McDonald's was reconstituted fat—either from pigs or chickens.

Nowadays, fast-food restaurants like McDonald's are required by law to make the full nutritional information of their products available to consumers. This is the complete list of ingredients in a McDonald's shake: whole milk, sucrose, cream, nonfat milk solids, corn syrup solids, mono and diglycerides, guar gum, vanilla flavor, carrageenan, cellulose gum, vitamin A palmitate. Admittedly some of these things sound a little weird, but they are all perfectly safe for human consumption and, aside from the milk, are not animal byproducts. Carrageenan is a type of seaweed (also called Irish Moss) used to control freezing in the shakes; if it were excluded, the milkshake would be a solid block of ice.

2 SANTA CLAUS WAS INVENTED BY COCA-COLA

In the 1930s, Coca-Cola was looking for ways to spread their burgeoning empire during the winter months—traditionally slow for soft drink sales. They hired Haddon Sundblom, a highly regarded commercial illustrator who proceeded to create a series of images of Santa Claus associating him with Coke. His drawings became a regular annual sight for the Coca-Cola corporation, which helped spur on the idea they had conceived the image.

In fact, the red-suited jolly man was already a well-established depiction of Santa Claus by the 1920s. *The New York Times* reported this in 1927: "A standardized Santa Claus appears to New York children. Height, weight, stature are almost exactly standardized, as are the red garments, the hood, and the white whiskers. The pack full of toys, ruddy cheeks and nose, bushy eyebrows, and a jolly, paunchy effect are also inevitable parts of the requisite makeup."

1 WALT DISNEY'S BODY IS CRYOGENICALLY FROZEN
The rumor tells us that Walt Disney, who was well-known for being a technical innovator, had his body put into a vat of liquid nitrogen upon his death so he could be reanimated when scientists discovered the means. Some versions of the tale even tell us that Walt's cryo-vat is hidden under the Pirates of the Caribbean attraction in Disneyland!

And the reality? This rumor is entirely false. On December 15, 1966, Walt Disney died of complications from the treatment he was receiving for lung cancer. Following Disney's wishes, his family had him cremated (they have since confirmed this fact) and his ashes were interred at the Forest Lawn Memorial Park in Glendale, which you can visit to this day.

✳✳✳✳✳✳

TOP 10 BIZARRE MEDICAL ANOMALIES

10 DIPROSOPUS
Diprospus (sometimes called "craniofacial duplication") is a rare disorder in which the face is duplicated on the head. This is not to be confused with fetus in fetu (number 9), which is a joining of two separate fetuses; diprosopus is caused by a protein called, believe it or not, "sonic hedgehog homolog." The odd name is due to a controversial tradition in molecular biology to use unusual names for genes. The protein determines the makeup of the face,

and when there is too much of it, you get a second face in a mirror image. If you do not have enough of the protein, you can end up with underdeveloped facial features. Children with this defect are normally stillborn, but a girl, Lali Singh, born in 2008, survived for two full months before dying of a heart attack.

9 FETUS IN FETU

The most famous recent case of fetus in fetu was Sanju Bhagat, thirty-six years old, from India. He became fully pregnant with his own twin. Because Sanju lacked a placenta, the fetus inside him attached directly to his blood supply. Doctors delivered the twin, which was severely malformed and did not survive. Fetus in fetu is an extremely rare disorder in  which a twin somehow becomes connected (internally or partly externally) to its twin while still in the mother's womb. In some cases the fetus in fetu will remain unknown inside the host twin until it begins to cause problems. In more common cases, the signs are visible from the outset and are often initially confused with cysts or cancers.

8 PROTEUS SYNDROME

The Elephant Man, Joseph Merrick, is the most famous case of proteus syndrome. The disease causes excessive bone and skin growth, and frequently comes with tumors. Only two hundred cases have been confirmed worldwide since the disease was officially discovered in 1979 It is possible to have a minor form of this disease, which can go undiagnosed. The case of the Elephant Man has been the sole reason that this disease is so widely known. Sufferers have normal brain function and intelligence.

7 MÖBIUS SYNDROME

Möbius syndrome is a rare disorder in which the facial muscles are paralyzed. In most cases the eyes are also unable to move from side to side. The disease prevents a sufferer from having any facial expressions, which can make them appear to be uninterested or "dull"—sometimes leading people to think they are rude. Sufferers have completely normal mental development. The causes are not fully understood and there is no treatment aside from addressing the symptoms (such as an inability to feed as a baby).

6 HUTCHINSON-GILFORD PROGERIA SYNDROME

Hutchinson-Gilford progeria syndrome (progeria) will be familiar to people old enough to remember the television program *That's Incredible* from the '80s in which a young sufferer of the disorder appeared. The disease causes premature aging—so rapidly that a young child can look like a very old person. The disease is especially interesting for scientists as it may lend clues to the natural aging process in man. The disease is caused by a genetic mutation, and does not pass from parent to child. There is no known cure and most children with the disease do not live beyond the age of thirteen—usually dying of stroke or heart attack (diseases usually associated with old age).

5 CUTANEOUS PORPHYRIA

Cutaneous porphyria is a disorder that causes blisters, excess hair, swelling, and rotting of the skin. It can cause red-colored teeth and fingernails, and after exposure to sun, urine can turn purple, pink, brown, or black. The disease is thought to be connected to the many werewolf and vampire legends of the past, where a sufferer (who would have lived hidden away from society) might have been confused for a monster. The disease is part of the more general group of disorders called porphyrias, which cover a range of mental and physical disorders due to the overproduction of certain enzymes in the body. The disease gets its name from the Greek word *porphura* meaning "purple pigment."

4 ELEPHANTIASIS

First off, note the spelling—it is elephant-iasis, not elephant-itis, as many people wrongly think. Elephantiasis is a thickening of the skin (as opposed to proteus syndrome which is a thickening of the bones as well as the skin). Unfortunately, this is a disease any one of us can get as it is caused by parasitic worms passed on through mosquito bites. It is, consequently, not uncommon in tropical regions and in Africa. A slightly different form of the disease is caused through contact with certain types of soil. In some parts of Ethiopia, up to 6 percent of the population suffers from the disorder. It is one of the most common disabilities in the world. Efforts to eradicate the disease are well underway and it is hoped that it will be successfully relegated to the annals of history by 2020.

3 FIBRODYSPLASIA OSSIFICANS PROGRESSIVA

Fibrodysplasia ossificans progressiva (FOP for short) is a very rare disease that causes parts of the body (muscles, tendons, and ligaments) to turn to bone when they are damaged. This can often cause damaged joints to fuse together, preventing movement. Unfortunately, surgical removal of the bone growths is ineffective as the body "heals" itself by recreating the removed bone. To make matters worse, the disease is so rare that it is often misdiagnosed as cancer, leading doctors to perform biopsies, which can spark worse growth of these bone-like lumps. The most famous case is Harry Eastlack whose body was so ossified by his death that he could only move his lips. His skeleton is now on display at the Mütter Museum. There is no cure.

2 LEWANDOWSKY-LUTZ DYSPLASIA

Lewandowsky-Lutz dysplasia (also known as epidermodysplasia verruciformis) is an extremely rare inheritable disorder in which masses of warts form on the skin. It normally affects the hands and feet and while it can start in middle age, it normally begins between the ages of one and twenty. There is no known effective treatment for the disease though surgery can be used to remove the warts. Unfortunately, after surgery the warts begin to return and it is estimated that a sufferer would need at least two surgeries per year to remove the warts each time they grow back. In 2007 a sufferer had surgery for the disease and 95 percent (thirteen pounds in this case) of warts were removed.

1 DIPHALLIA

Diphallia (also known as penile duplication) is a condition in which a male is born with two penises. It is a rare disorder with only one thousand cases recorded. Sufferers are also at a higher risk of spina bifida than men with one penis. A person with diphallia can urinate from one or both of his penises. In most cases, both penises are side by side and the same size, but occasionally one smaller penis will sit atop another larger one. One in 5.5 million men in the United States have two penises.

✳✳✳✳✳✳

TOP 10 UNFORTUNATE OR EMBARRASSING DEATHS

10 EMPEDOCLES—DIED 430 BC

Manner of death: Threw himself into a volcano to become immortal.

Empedocles was a Greek philosopher probably best remembered for his classical theory of the four elements. He was the last Greek philosopher to write his theories down in verse form. Legend has it that Empedocles threw himself into the active volcano Mount Etna in Sicily in order to fool his followers into believing that his body had vanished and that he would return as a god. Unfortunately for Empedocles, one of his sandals survived the fury of the volcano and his followers discovered it—revealing their leader's deceit.

9 PYRRHUS OF EPIRUS—DIED 272 BC

Manner of death: Killed when he was stunned by a tile thrown by an old lady.

Pyrrhus of Epirus was one of the greatest conquerors, although heavy losses in one campaign led to the term "pyrrhic victory" being coined in his honor. Pyrrhus was such a great warrior that a Spartan royal (Cleonymus) asked him to defeat Sparta and put him on the throne. Pyrrhus was defeated—having underestimated the strength of the Spartan warriors, so he moved on to his next campaign in Argos. As he entered the city through the narrow streets on the back of an elephant, an old woman (unhappy with the conflict) threw a roof tile at him from her balcony. The tile stunned Pyrrhus, which allowed a common foot soldier to stab him—killing him.

8 ELEAZAR MACCABEUS—DIED 162 BC

Manner of death: Killed by the elephant he killed.

Eleazar Maccabeus's death is told in the Old Testament book of I Maccabees. During the Battle of Beth-zechariah, Eleazar thought he saw the enemy, King Antiochus V, riding an elephant nearby. Thinking he would perform a heroic act by killing the elephant and king, Eleazar jumped under the elephant and stabbed it in the stomach with his spear. The dead elephant fell right on top of Eleazar killing him instantly. To add insult to injury, it was not even the king's elephant.

7 EMPEROR VALERIAN—DIED 260 AD

Manner of death: Used as a footstool then skinned.

Valerian was a Roman nobleman who became Emperor Valerian I. During his disastrous reign, the western empire fell into total disrepair. In 260 AD, Valerian was defeated in the Battle of Edessa and taken captive by the Persian King Shapur I. In order to humiliate the Emperor, Shapur used him as a footstool. When he grew tired of his footstool, Shapur had Valerian skinned and had his skin stuffed with dung and straw and put on display in one of the large Persian temples.

6 HUMPHREY DE BOHUN—DIED 1322 AD

Manner of death: Speared through the anus.

Humphrey de Bohun was a member of a very powerful Anglo-Norman family in England. He spoke out against the excesses of the King, Edward II. While leading troops at the Battle of Boroughbridge, Humphrey de Bohun, 4th Earl of Hereford, met with a rather unpleasant end:

> *"[Humphrey de Bohun] led the fight on the bridge, but he and his men were caught in the arrow fire. Then one of de Harclay's pikemen, concealed beneath the bridge, thrust upwards between the planks and skewered the Earl of Hereford through the anus, twisting the head of the iron pike into his intestines. His dying screams turned the advance into a panic."*

Strangely, death via anal insertion was not entirely uncommon during this period of the Middle Ages, as the next item will attest.

5 KING EDWARD II—DIED 1327 AD

Manner of death: Speared through the anus with a hot poker.

Edward II was King of England for twenty years (1307–1327). Edward greatly upset the nobility in England because he preferred low-born citizens and had many "special" male friends, who received extravagant and expensive gifts. After he abdicated the throne and was imprisoned, his wife Isabella, disturbed by the close relationship the king had shared with a young man in the Royal Court, brought about his execution in secret:

> *"On the night of 11 October while lying in on a bed [the king] was suddenly seized and, while a great mattress... weighed him down and*

suffocated him, a plumber's iron, heated intensely hot, was introduced through a tube into his secret private parts so that it burned the inner portions beyond the intestines."

4 HUMAYUN—DIED 1556 AD

Manner of death: Tripped over his skirts and fell down some stairs. Humayun was a Mughal Emperor who ruled modern Afghanistan, Pakistan, and parts of northern India from 1530–1540 and again from 1555–1556. He was a great lover of the arts and astronomy and left behind a great legacy as a consequence. He was also very religious and this is what led to his downfall (literally). As he was carrying books from the library, Humayun heard the Muslim call to prayer. It was his habit to kneel on one knee when the call was made, and as he bent his knee, his foot got caught in the folds of his long robes. He happened to be standing at the top of a small flight of stairs. He fell all the way down and hit his temple on a jagged rock, killing him.

3 ARTHUR ASTON—DIED 1649 AD

Manner of death: Beaten to death with his wooden leg. Sir Arthur Aston was a lifelong professional soldier, most noted for his support for King Charles I in the English Civil War. He was a great soldier who saw a great deal of action during his lifetime. In September 1644, he fell from a horse and ended up with a wooden leg, which was later used in his murder. In 1649, Oliver Cromwell's forces attacked his town in the Siege of Drogheda and ordered everyone be executed. Aston offered to surrender but the soldiers who captured him believed he was hiding gold in his leg. They ripped it off and beat him to break open the leg. Unfortunately, it was solid wood and it killed Aston.

2 JULIEN OFFRAY DE LA METTRIE—DIED 1751 AD

Manner of death: Ironically ate himself to death. Julien Offray de La Mettrie was a French doctor, philosopher, and potentially the founder of cognitive science. He believed that sensual pleasures, such as eating, sex, and play were the sole reason for life, and so he decided to live his life by that principle. Julien was an atheist and believed that life on earth was just a farce to be lived and ended in self-gratification. Ironically, he died rather painfully after eating too much truffle pâté at a feast held in his honor by a man he cured of an illness.

1 BANDŌ MITSUGORŌ VIII—DIED 1975 AD

Manner of death: Died after eating pufferfish, which he claimed to be immune to.

Bandō Mitsugorō VIII was one of Japan's most highly regarded Kabuki (a type of dance/drama) actors, so much so that he was declared a national treasure. On the 16th of January, the natural treasure decided to dine out on fugu liver (highly toxic) claiming that he was immune to it. The fugu chef who served him said that he simply could not refuse to serve the deadly livers to such an esteemed gentleman. Needless to say, Mitsugoro died within seven hours.

✳✳✳✳✳✳

TOP 10 BIZARRE BEAUTY PRODUCTS

10 HUMAN-DERIVED COLLAGEN INJECTIONS

Collagen injections are used to smooth out frown lines, crows feet wrinkles, and smile lines, as well as to give the appearance of full lips. Like Botox, this procedure is quite common but the main ingredient is just bizarre. There are two main sources of collagen, a protein responsible for skin strength and elasticity, bovine (cow) and… human. About three in a hundred people experience an allergic reaction to bovine-derived collagen which has prompted manufacturers to source collagen from aborted fetuses, placentas, and donated cadavers as the probability of an allergic reaction is virtually nonexistent. Possibly the most morally outrageous source of collagen is the rumored harvesting of collagen from executed prisoners in China, taken without the consent of the prisoners or their families and exported worldwide for socialites to shoot into their faces.

9 BOTOX INJECTIONS

While the Botox procedure to prevent frown lines and wrinkles may sound fairly normal, what you are having injected into your skin is quite bizarre. Botulinum toxin (bo + tox = botox) is one of the most poisonous naturally occurring substances on the planet and the single most toxic protein. Eating food contaminated with Clostridium botulinum can lead to serious food poisoning (the fatality rate is 5–10 percent). One microgram (1/1000000 of a gram) is lethal to humans. The amounts used in cosmetic procedures are consequently very small.

8 SNAKE VENOM CREAM

The neurotoxins produced by members of the cobra family of snakes (and some vipers and rattlesnakes) act on prey by blocking the nerve impulses to the muscles and inducing paralysis. Realizing that snake venom could produce a similar effect to that of Botox, the beauty industry has come up with a synthetic form of snake venom that is applied to the face as a cream rather than injected. It is meant to be safer and less invasive. The venom that was used to create the synthetic version comes from "snake farms" in Brazil where thousands of snakes are "milked" for their venom.

7 PLACENTA WRINKLE CREAM

According to manufacturers of the product, placenta wrinkle cream derived from bovine placentas can slow down the appearance of visible signs of aging by moisturizing skin and combating wrinkles. Some companies also use plant placenta (yes, flowering plants have placentas!) and even human. Claims were first made in the 1940s (when this idea was first marketed) that the nutrient-rich placenta gave off the benefits of hormones and stimulated cell growth. Since the FDA quickly decided that this constituted a medical claim, the manufacturers changed their claims to say that the proteins present in the placenta moisturize one's skin and hair.

6 BULL SEMEN HAIR TREATMENT

How dedicated are you to having smooth, shiny hair? If you're serious enough there's the option (in the UK at least) to have a hairdresser massage bull semen into your scalp. The reasoning behind this revolting idea? Hair is made up of protein, although essentially your hair is dead, and some proteins can help form a protective layer around the hair. Some people thought it would be a good idea to market protein treatments as a way of keeping your hair healthy. The supposedly ultimate source of concentrated protein? Bull semen.

5 BIRD POOP FACIAL TREATMENT

There is an old Japanese beauty secret making its way over to the Western world. It's called *uguisu no fun* or sterilized nightingale droppings. An enzyme called guanine (also added to various makeup products for its pearly sheen) found in the nightingale's droppings apparently does a good job of bleaching and exfoliating skin. Kabuki actors and geishas have been using *uguisu no fun* for hundreds of years to remove makeup and to keep their skin soft. The joy of spreading bird excrement on your face doesn't come as cheap as a jar of Olay though. It's around twenty U.S. dollars for one ounce. If you'd rather have someone else do the smearing, you can go to the Shizuka Day Spa in New York and $180 later your face will be smooth and soft.

4 LEECH THERAPY

Letting blood-sucking parasites attach their slimy bodies to you as a "detox" sounds like a questionable idea. However, leech therapy, or hirudotherapy, has been practiced since 1020 AD for treating skin disease and helping patients recover from surgery. These days, leeches can be used in the treatment of varicose veins, reducing blood coagulation, and helping stimulate blood circulation in reattached organs that require critical blood flow. If you are more adventurous you can follow in the footsteps of celebrities, such as Demi Moore, and make your way to Austria to have your blood feasted on by the medicinal species of leech, Hirudo medicinalis.

3 FISH PEDICURE

If you're willing to give the leeches a go, you might also be interested in letting a school of small fish nibble the dead skin cells off your toes. The idea is that you put your feet into a tank containing a species of carp (doctor fish) and wait 15–30 minutes while they feast on your calluses. Because the fish are toothless, the process is meant to be very safe, as they can only suck off pieces of dead, flaking skin. In Turkey, where the treatment originated, the fish live in natural hot springs and are a popular skincare option for the people who bathe there.

2 PIGS' FEET DIET

This odd treatment isn't plastered on your face, or combed through your hair, but eaten instead. Pigs' feet are being marketed as an edible way to combat wrinkles, by the owner of Hakata Tonton, a New York restaurant.

He figures that since the tootsies of the pig contain a high amount of collagen (which is used in anti-wrinkle creams and lip injections) a person might as well eat them to gain similar benefits. Although collagen is one of the major proteins involved in maintaining skin and muscle tone, consuming a meal of pig trotters is almost certainly a less effective method of keeping the scalpel away than simply maintaining a healthy diet, exercising regularly, and staying out of the sun.

1 SNAIL SLIME CREAM

Because snails can heal and regenerate their shells using the slime they secrete, the beauty industry is now using the slime of the common garden snail species (Helix aspersa) in beauty products. The myriad of claims for the slime's efficacy range from getting rid of acne to improving stretch marks and scarring. The snail secretion, which is also used by the snail to reduce friction as it moves, seems to have antibacterial in addition to antioxidant qualities. If it works for the snail, why not put it on your face?

✳✳✳✳✳✳

TOP 10 MACABRE COLLECTIBLES

10 TATTOOS

With over a hundred skinned masterpieces of the tattooed deceased variety, you won't see any new age "Celtic/tribal" bands or Warner Bros. cartoons here. Dr. Katsunari Fukushi's full-body inked skins are traditional Japanese *tebori* (hand-applied). With a goal to preserve and study, Fukushi's collection includes one-of-a-kind Yakuza skins dating as far back as the 1920s. They can be viewed, on request, at the University of Tokyo.

9 BONES

The "Bone Palace" of Ray Bandar is home to seven thousand skulls. The only place free of this biologist's collection is in the bedroom (at his wife's demand). Seventy-nine-year-old Bender has been collecting skulls and bones for more than fifty years! That's dedication! With official permits in hand, he has been able to get his skulls from virtually anywhere around the globe. His specimens come from zoos, beaches, and even off the road.

8 MEDICAL PHOTOS
The Dr. Stanley B. Burns Collection has a most revered historical photographic collection, with operating room images, depictions of diseases and the effects of war on the body, post-mortem photos and malformations or anomalies, along with criminal behaviors depicted in public lynching and executions. It is the largest of its kind in the U.S., with more than sixty thousand images.

7 FREAKS
Peter the Great's "Kunstkammer" is the result of fifteen years of collecting the oddities and rarities of Russia and the world, before making it available to the public in 1719. Animals with two heads or multiple legs or pickled punks are among Frederik Ruysch's amazing anatomical dioramas (which included fetal skeletons surrounded by "trees" of their own preserved circulatory systems) and in the early days of the museum, live "freaks" were on display.

6 DEATH MASKS
Interested in obtaining a true likeness of great men, Laurence Hutton (1843–1904) set out to acquire death masks of historical or well-known figures. Some in his collection include Napoleon, Beethoven, Shakespeare, Goethe, Newton, and Charles XII, who was killed in battle (the bullet's entry is visible above his right brow). Today the Hutton collection is housed at Princeton University and is available for viewing online.

5 GENITAL CASTS
What began in 1968 as a way to "meet awesome men" and to fulfill a college assignment led to Cynthia Plaster Caster (yes, that is her name) casting famous (and not so famous) penises. Rock stars and road managers make up most of her subjects. In the early days, Cynthia's casting partner would permit appropriate oral contact—in order to make a good impression. More recently she has included women in her collection. Jimmy Hendrix, Jello Biafra, and Karen O are among her better-known donors.

4 MURDERABILIA

While the "killer clown," John Wayne Gacy, was spending the rest of his life in jail, Rick Staton became his exclusive art dealer, becoming one of the first of America's top collectors of murderabilia. Some well-known murderabilia buyers include painter Joe Coleman, Lux Interior and Poison Ivy from The Cramps, and shock rock performer Marilyn Manson. The Son of Sam Law does not allow a killer to profit from his crimes (i.e., movies or books), but murderabilia has become an Internet phenomenon and new laws have been difficult to pass, as first amendment rights are contested, so buying and selling is likely to continue. One proposal is the "Stop the Sale of Murderabillia to Protect the Dignity of Crime Victims Act."

3 HAIR COLLECTION

They can be sold down to the follicle and by the inch! Lincoln, Kennedy, Monroe, Einstein, Lennon, and Presley are among John Reznikoff's hair reps. When Britney shaved her head, guess who was super eager to get her locks? Reznikoff became more widely known for his small donation of Beethoven's hair to LifeGem, a memorial service company that made three synthetic diamonds from the resulting carbon.

2 PRESERVED HEADS

For more than a year, General Horatio Gordon Robley (1840–1930) made detailed drawings, from life, of the early Maori (New Zealand's earliest settlers) and their face and body tattoos. He also collected as many of their heads as he could, seeing them as works of art. When later searching for a buyer, the New Zealand government turned him down and all but the best five ended up in New York's American Museum of Natural History. In more recent years, New Zealand has been trying to get Robley's collection back (along with other moko heads in different institutions), with varying success.

1 STUFFED ANIMALS

Walter Potter (1835–1918), a self-taught taxidermist, created strange tableaux of small dead animals that he arranged in unnatural or humanlike situations. These include gambling rats being caught offguard in a raid, a couple of robins surrounding a tiny coffin in a funeral procession, and a yard filled with exercising toads. The collection was unfortunately broken up and sold at auction to different buyers in 2003.

TOP 10 BIZARRE MUSEUMS

10 MUSEUM OF JURASSIC TECHNOLOGY
Address: 9341 Venice Boulevard, Culver City, California 90232

The Museum of Jurassic Technology is, in a sense, a living work of art. It claims to be a repository of technological artifacts and relics from the Lower Jurassic, despite the fact that hominoids did not exist for another 150 million years. The museum houses a decomposing set of antique dice, a collection based on trailer-park culture, and a group of micro-miniature sculptures card from a single human hair.

9 BRITISH LAWNMOWER MUSEUM
Address: 106-114 Shakespeare Street, Southport, Lancashire PR8 5AJ, England

This thrilling museum is home to hundreds of vintage lawnmowers. It also includes experimental mowers such as solar powered and super-fast mowers. Many of the exhibits are from the Victorian and Edwardian eras and you can find names normally not associated with garden equipment, such as Rolls Royce, Daimler, and Diesel.

8 KANSAS BARBED WIRE MUSEUM
Address: 120 West 1st Street, LaCrosse, Kansas 67548

Another thrilling museum, the Kansas Barbed Wire Museum is dedicated to one thing and one thing only: barbed wire. Over two thousand types of barbed wire can be seen there, including antique samples from the nineteenth century. In fairness to the museum, we should say that it is at least contributing to the preservation of a seldom considered aspect of the early Midwest.

7 GLORE PSYCHIATRIC MUSEUM

Address: 3408 Frederick Avenue, St. Joseph, Missouri 64506 (Be mindful not to drive into the entrance for the prison next door—they're a little jumpy.) The Glore Psychiatric Museum exhibits the checkered history of psychiatric treatment through history. Fortunately for those of us in the modern world, we are no longer subject to some of the more unusual methods of "curing" psychological illness on display there, including ice baths, vibrating chairs, and bleeding.

6 CREATION MUSEUM

Address: 2800 Bullittsburg Church Road, Petersburg, Kentucky 41080
The Creation Museum was created to promote young Earth creationism. It presents an account of the origins of life and the universe using literal interpretations of the Biblical book of Genesis. The museum rejects evolution and contains fossils that "prove" man and dinosaur coexisted. The British newspaper *The Guardian* called the museum, "quite possibly ... one of the weirdest museums in the world."

5 MUSEUM OF EROTICISM

Address: 72 Bd de Clichy, 75018 Paris, France
The Museum of Eroticism in Paris is dedicated to erotic art collections. It was founded in 1997 and contains religious art of India, Japan, and Africa. The five-story museum has one floor especially devoted to brothers of the nineteenth and twentieth centuries.

4 ICELANDIC PHALLOLOGICAL MUSEUM

Address: Hedinsbraut 3a, 640 Husavik, Iceland
The Phallological Museum is a museum of penises and penis parts belonging to all mammals. You can view thirty types of whale penis, and a polar bear penis. There are, in all, over one hundred types of penises on display and a benefactor has left his own penis to the museum for inclusion upon his death.

3 SULABH MUSEUM OF TOILETS

Address: Mahavir Enclave, Palam Dabri Road, New Delhi, India
If you are fascinated with toilets and wish to learn the history of the useful appliance, head on down to the Sulabh Museum of Toilets. There you can find everything you could ever want to know about the subject. The museum was

founded by Dr. Bindeshwar Pathak, the head of a non-profit organization, in the field of sanitation.

2 MÜTTER MUSEUM
Address: 19 South 22nd Street, Philadelphia, Pennsylvania, 19103
This museum contains a multitude of bizarre and fascinating objects, including a model of a woman with a human horn, the tallest skeleton in the U.S., the petrified body of the "soap woman," and the malignant tumor removed from President Grover Cleveland's mouth. This is a must-see museum for people interested in the bizarre.

1 ANTIQUE VIBRATOR MUSEUM
Address: 603 Valencia Street, San Francisco, California 94110
Believe it or not, vibrators were once used as a treatment for hysteria in women. Hysteria simply meant mental or emotional distress. A variety of the prescribed vibrators can be found at the Antique Vibrator Museum along with an array of modern devices designed less for therapy than pleasure.

✳✳✳✳✳✳

TOP 10 BIZARRE THINGS YOU CAN BUY ON AMAZON.COM

10 WOLF URINE
100 percent pure wolf pee. Use this pee to deter unwanted creatures from your home. Its effectiveness is vouched for by one Amazon reviewer who said:

> *"My Uncle Jared had been under the weather since his wife passed away. He was also in a lot of debt and doing drugs. So one day he bought this Wolf Lure, apparently covered his body in it, and went into the forest. We held his funeral last Thursday, but there was no body to place in a casket so we just remembered him the way he was, and placed*

flowers by the forest where his mauled clothing and remnants of teeth and flesh lay in eternal slumber. The local news ran a report of him, and we all wish him well with his wife."

Please note: this product cannot be shipped to California due to state regulations on the importing of animal pee.

9 STOP EATING POOP!

From the product review: "Stop Eating Poop contains Glutamic Acid to deter dogs from eating their own stool. Yucca helps control stool and urine odor. Peppermint and parsley help to eliminate bad breath." The peppermint and parsley are clearly essential for the dog that enjoys an occasional meal of poo. This product is not fit for human consumption.

8 GAY ATTRACTION BODY MIST

According to the product review, "Man to Man was created after years of study to naturally help gays attract other gays." I thought tighty whiteys and cosmos were already doing that!

7 DR. JOHN'S FAMOUS PEE PEE

Are you about to take a drug test at work and you know you are going to fail? Dr. John to the rescue! This synthetic pee tests within normal ranges in standard urine tests. Avoid workplace discrimination by carrying a bottle of Dr. John's Pee with you at all times!

6 TANK

For only $19,995 you can own your very own battle tank. This tank carries a crew of up to five internally and one externally. Includes head/tail lights and a 400-watt premium PA system. If you are unsure whether this tank is the one for you, check out this excerpt from one of the reviews on Amazon:

> *"I'll admit it. Shopping for a personal tank can be a bit daunting. Many times in the past I've purchased overpriced, so-called battle tanks then driven them into battle only to be wrecked in ten minutes by the first blow off of some insurgents home-made mortar. But not this baby, no way."*

It looks like a great deal to me!

5 LIQUID ASS FART SPRAY

There must be a market somewhere for a product of this type. Here is an excerpt from the product description: "Liquid ASS is an overwhelming, stinky, funny prank product. Once unleashed, this powerpacked, superconcentrated liquid begins to evaporate filling the air with a genuine, foul buttcrack smell with hints of dead animal and fresh poo."

4 UFO DETECTOR

Over the years many UFO sightings have reported magnetic and electromagnetic disturbances. The UFO detector will beep and flash in situations like this, warning you of an impending alien visit. Now you can be the first to arrive on the scene of alien landings or crashes!

3 ROSWELL SOIL SAMPLE

For those of you who have no luck with your UFO detectors, you can still experience part of the UFO/alien phenomenon by buying soil from Roswell—the crash site of an alien spacecraft some years ago.

2 DEER'S BUTT

This is a genuine whitetail deer rear. Perfect for the lover of taxidermy or bottoms. Use this in combination with number 5 on the list for many evenings of entertainment!

1 URANIUM

Yes, it is true, you can actually buy a can of real uranium! According to Amazon, the uranium sample is for "educational and scientific use only" so please don't buy this product if you have any other plans in mind; we cannot guarantee that you will not end up on an FBI watchlist.

✳✳✳✳✳✳

TOP 10 BIZARRE RELATIONSHIPS

10 ALLEN AND PREVIN

In 1978, at the age of eight, Soon-Yi Previn was adopted by Mia Farrow and her then-husband Andre Previn who were on vacation in Korea. In 1980, when Soon-Yi was ten, Farrow began a long-term relationship with Woody Allen, which lasted twelve years. In 1992, Farrow found naked photographs of Soon-Yi in Allen's apartment and subsequently discovered that the two had been having a romantic relationship (at the time she was twenty-two and Allen was fifty-six). Allen parted ways with Farrow and married Soon-Yi in 1997. Both of Allen's biological children refused to see him. Allen and Previn have two adopted daughters.

9 WILDE AND DOUGLAS

In 1891, Oscar Wilde was introduced to the twenty-two-year-old Lord Alfred Douglas, an undergraduate at Oxford at the time and son of the 9th Marquess of Queensberry. The two began an intimate relationship, which may have involved sexual relations, though Douglas later denied that this was the case. In the course of the relationship, for sexual satisfaction, Wilde would look on while Douglas entertained other young men for his pleasure. The Marquess eventually found out about this "scandalous" relationship and sued Wilde and after a series of arguments between the two, Wilde took him to court. The case failed and Wilde was eventually charged with gross indecency and sentenced to two years of hard labor. After he was released on May 19, 1897, he spent his last three years penniless, in self-imposed exile from society and artistic circles.

8 CALIGULA AND DRUSILLA

Drusilla was Emperor Caligula's favorite sister. When he became Emperor it is believed that he ordered her to divorce her husband, after which she became his lover. She most likely had a great deal of influence over Caligula. When she died in 38 AD, he never recovered from the loss. He buried his sister with the honors of an Augusta, acted as a grieving widower, and had the Roman Senate declare her a Goddess as "Diva Drusilla," deifying her as a representation of the goddess Venus or Aphrodite. Drusilla was consecrated as Panthea, most likely on the anniversary of the birthday of Augustus.

7 LINCOLN AND SPEED

In 1837, Abraham Lincoln (age twenty-eight) met Joshua Fry Speed (age twenty-three) when Lincoln moved to Springfield, Illinois, to set himself up as a lawyer. Lincoln tried to buy a bed from Speed's store on credit, but Speed offered to share his room and bed instead. Previously Speed had heard the young Lincoln speak on the stump when Lincoln was running for election to the Illinois legislature, but the two men had exchanged only bits of conversation. The two ended up having a lifelong friendship, and upon the death of Lincoln, Speed and other members of his family put up funding to create a Lincoln Memorial. The bizarre nature of this relationship is not that the two shared a bed, but that it is an example of a now extinct version of "romantic friendship"—a term that described an intimate, but non-sexual relationship between two people. Romantic friendships were very common until the mid to late nineteenth century when homosexuality was beginning to be defined. Other famous examples of romantic friendship are William Shakespeare and his "Fair Lord," and Emily Dickinson and Sue Gilbert.

6 THE TOMAINIS

Al Tomaini was a human giant who was eight-feet, four-inches tall. He weighed 356 pounds and wore size 27 shoes. He spent the majority of his life working in circuses as a sideshow attraction. In 1936 he met Jeanie, who was to become his wife. Jeanie was only two-feet, six-inches tall because she was born without legs. They both retired from circus life and moved to Gibsonton, Florida.

5 VERLAINE AND RIMBAUD

In 1871, at age sixteen, Arthur Rimbaud—a budding young poet—traveled to Paris at the invitation of Paul Verlaine (a highly regarded French Symbolist Poet). When Rimbaud arrived in Paris, Verlaine fell in love with him and the two began a turbulent relationship that lead to the breakup of Verlaine's marriage. During absinthe and hashish influenced nights, the two scandalized Paris with their obscene behavior and violence. At one point, while drunk on absinthe, Rimbaud stabbed Verlaine in the hand. The two moved to England and eventually Brussels. On the morning of July 10th, Verlaine bought a revolver and ammunition. That afternoon, "in a drunken rage," Verlaine fired two shots at Rimbaud, one of them wounding the eighteen-year-old in the left wrist. Eventually Rimbaud asked the police to arrest Verlaine, and he was sent to jail for two years. The two met again only once and at age twenty-one, Rimbaud stopped writing. He is now considered to be one of the most influential French poets in history.

4 STUEBING AND KAROLEWSKI

Patrick Stuebing and his biological sister Susan Karolewski are a German couple who have been involved in an incestuous relationship since 2001. When the couple met they did not know that they were related, as Patrick had been adopted. After they discovered their blood ties, they continued in their relationship and had four children, only one of whom is still with the parents due to incest laws in Germany. Stuebing spent two years in jail for incest.

3 THE BUNKERS AND THE YATESES

Chang and Eng Bunker were conjoined twins born in Siam (their condition and place of birth created the term "Siamese twins"). They were joined at the sternum by a small piece of cartilage. Their livers were fused but independently complete. Although nineteenth-century medicine did not have the means to do so, modern surgical techniques would have easily allowed them to be separated today. The two became American citizens and respected members of the community, owning a plantation and slaves. On April 13, 1843, they married two sisters: Chang to Adelaide Yates and Eng to Sarah Anne Yates. Chang and his wife had ten children; Eng and his wife had twelve. In time, the wives squabbled and eventually two separate households were set up just west of Mount Airy, North Carolina, in the community of White Plains—the twins would alternate spending three days at each home. The twins died on the same day in 1874.

2 NERO AND SPORUS

Suetonius (c. 69 AD–130 AD) wrote that the Emperor Nero fell in love with a young boy, Sporus, and loved him so deeply that he tried to make a woman of him:

> "He castrated the boy Sporus and actually tried to make a woman of him; and he married him with all the usual ceremonies, including a dowry and a bridal veil, took him to his home attended by a great throng, and treated him as his wife. And the witty jest that someone made is

still current, that it would have been well for the world if Nero's father Domitius had that kind of wife. This Sporus, decked out with the finery of the empresses and riding in a litter, he took with him to the courts and marts of Greece, and later at Rome through the Street of the Images, fondly kissing him from time to time."

As bizarre as that sounds, there is another even more bizarre relationship:

1 DUMAS AND DOS SANTOS

Jean (or Juan) Baptista dos Santos is said to have been a "Gypsy," born in Faro, Portugal, around 1843, to normal parents with two other normal children. He possessed two functioning penises and three scrota, the outer two of which each contained a single testis. Dos Santos claimed that the central scrotum had also contained a pair of fully formed testes, but that these had retreated into his abdomen when he was ten years old. He also had a third leg. Fortunately for dos Santos, at the same time there lived in Paris a woman named Blanche Dumas who had four breasts and two vaginas (and also a third leg). Dumas was working as a high-class prostitute. Dos Santos traveled to Paris and it is believed that the two had a torrid affair.

✳✳✳✳✳✳

TOP 10 BIZARRE EATING HABITS

10 ORTHOREXIA

Characterized by the obsession with eating healthy foods, this disease can be confused with and/or diagnosed as anorexia, the main difference being the reasoning behind the eating habits. Anorexics are obsessed with losing weight, while orthorexics feel a need for healthy or "pure" foods. Orthorexia is not recognized by the DSM IV and in general will not be diagnosed, but it is seeing an increasing stronghold across the U.S.

9 ANOREXIA

Anorexia is self-starvation and is often associated with other bizarre habits such as drinking orange juice laced with cotton wool in order to give a false sense of satiety. This is a serious eating disorder that causes many deaths every year around the world.

8 XYLOPHAGIA

Xylophagia is the disorder in which a person eats wood. Sufferers will also eat wood-derived products like paper, pencils, and tree bark. It is not entirely uncommon in children where it can be a typical oral fixation.

7 TRICHOPHAGIA

Trichophagia is the compulsive consumption of hair—most often one's own. Frequently a person with long hair will chew the ends while it is still attached to the head. This can be very dangerous, as hair will gather in the gastrointestinal tract. In 2007 an eighteen-year-old girl was found to have a ten-pound hairball in her stomach.

6 HYALOPHAGIA

Hyalophagia is glass eating. It is a pathological illness and is, for obvious reasons, extremely dangerous to humans as glass can cut the stomach, intestines, and throat as it passes through the body.

5 UROPHAGIA

Urophagia is the compulsive drinking of urine—your own or others. It is generally harmless as a healthy person's urine is sterile, but there are always small risks involved due to infections in the genitals of the person whose urine is being consumed.

4 GEOPHAGY

Geophagy is the eating of earth—such as clay and chalk. It can often occur in a person with mineral deficiencies but it can be a mental disorder in healthy people. Scientists have mixed views on this practice, with some believing it harmless and others believing it dangerous.

3 ANTHROPOPHAGY

Anthropophagy is also known as cannibalism; it is the act of eating other members of the human race. Anthropophagy has been practiced throughout history in tribes in the Amazon Basin and South America.

2 AUTOSARCOPHAGY

This is the disorder of self-cannibalism. Sometimes it is a minor disorder, which is quite common—this normally manifests itself as skin nibbling. But sometimes it can be quite serious: On January 13, 2007, Danish artist Marco Evaristti hosted a dinner party for his most intimate friends. The main meal was agnolotti pasta, on which was topped a meatball made with the artist's own fat, removed earlier in the year in a liposuction operation. Bernd Jürgen Armando Brandes had hoped to engage in self-cannibalism before being cannibalized himself in the infamous recent German trial of his murderer, Armin Meiwes. This is an exact quote, taken from usenet, in which Brandes offered himself for consumption:

> "i,m a male who really love's the thought of being on the dinner table, my body is yours to cook anyway you want, i am for real my flesh is yours. fry me,broil me barbacue me i don,t care just as long as you enjoy your meal, i want to be your meal, its my calling an i'm ready. longpig!"

1 COPROPHAGIA

Coprophagia is the practice of consuming feces (poo); it is extremely uncommon in humans. It is generally thought to be the result of the paraphilia known as coprophilia, although it is only diagnosable in extreme cases where it disturbs one's functioning. Consuming other people's feces carries the risk of contracting diseases spread through fecal matter, such as hepatitis, hepatitis A, hepatitis E, pneumonia, and influenza. Vaccinations are generally recommended for those who engage in this practice.

✳✳✳✳✳✳

TOP 10
BIZARRE PATENTS

10 BUTTOCK PARTER—INTERNATIONAL PATENT WO02069773

Yes—you read that right. This patent is meant to part your buttocks while sitting on the toilet. Here is a direct quote from the patent: "The invention relates to a toilet seat comprising a seat surface for the user and an opening limited by the seat surface. The invention aims to facilitate defecation for the user in a simple, comfortable manner and prevent soiling in the area around the anus when defecating. Means which are actuated by the weight of the user are provided for spreading the buttocks of the user during the defecation process." Charming.

9 POOP CATCHER—GERMAN PATENT DE4020440

While we are on the subject of toilets, let me introduce the poop catcher. The device comprises a tube with two apertures, the first of which, insertable in the anus, has a rounded end. It is made of soft to hard plastics. The second end is connected to an all-purpose suction unit. The tube is screwed into the middle of a plastic funnel. The funnel locates correctly against the buttocks, thus preventing any unnecessary staining. Use: For the hygienic removal of feces from dogs. The device can also find application with human patients who suffer from chronic constipation, or are bedridden. I think the inventor of this patent could very nearly be a candidate for the "Top 10 Most Evil Men" list. Your dog or bedridden relatives will really love you if you get them one of these... Not!

8 DOG EAR PROTECTOR—U.S. PATENT US4233942

This invention provides a device for protecting the ears of animals, especially long-haired dogs, from becoming soiled by the animal's food while the animal is eating. The device provides a generally tubular-shaped member for containing and protecting each ear of the animal, and a member to position the tubular member and animal ears away from the mouth and food of the animal while it is eating. I would hate to see the poor dog trying to get through a dog door with this thing on its head.

7 AMUSEMENT URINAL—U.S. PATENT US4773863

A urinal with amusement features. "Discourages the inadvertent or intentional diversion of urine outside the proper receptacle." Pressure and temperature sensors detect the urine and activate a loudspeaker and video screen to give you an audio-visual extravaganza while you pee. The user can modify the sights and sounds by altering the direction of his urine stream.

6 UNICORN MAKER—U.S. PATENT US4429685

This invention relates to a method of growing unicorns in a manner that enhances the overall development of the animal. In order to achieve this quite bizarre creature, the patent describes surgery to join the two horns of a goat together as one central horn. I am sure the SPCA will have something to say about this if anyone actually tries it out.

5 GROIN ENHANCER—UK PATENT GB2301524

This is a special device to make a man's scrotum look bigger than it really is. We have all seen the thousands of spam e-mails for increasing penis size, well here is one for artificially increasing the other part of that region! While this patent may work well when trying to pick someone up, it won't work so well when you drop your pants and all is revealed.

4 SAFE-SEX SUIT—FRENCH PATENT FR2640874

This invention, which looks something like a spacesuit, is designed to protect every aspect of your body from the diseases during the sexual act. Consequently, it works so well, it will also protect you from the joys of the sexual act.

3 KISSING SHIELD—U.S. PATENT US5727565

The kissing shield is designed to spoil any fun you might have while kissing someone. You hold the device in front of your face as a potential lover approaches and you are protected from their lips (and tongue, if they are the passionate type). Never again will you need to suffer the enjoyment of a kiss.

2 SANTA CLAUS DETECTOR—U.S. PATENT US5523741
This is a special device for those children who simply must see Santa on Christmas Eve. Stick this device near the chimney and it will alert you as soon as Santa arrives.

1 HICCUP STOPPER—U.S. PATENT US7062320
This device is shaped like a drinking glass. When you take a sip, it detects your lips and shoots an electric shock at you. The aim is that the electric shock will frighten the hiccups away. A great one if you have annoying kids that hiccup a lot.

✳✳✳✳✳✳

TOP 10 AMAZING COINCIDENCES

10 FALLING BABY
In Detroit in the 1930s, a young man named Joseph Figlock came to the aid of a careless mother twice. On the first occasion, Figlock was walking down the street when the baby fell from a window many stories above. Fortunately, the baby fell on Figlock who managed to catch it—neither was hurt. One year later, the very same baby fell from the very same window; a certain Joseph Figlock (the very same one in fact) happened to be passing beneath the window and, for the second time in his life, he caught the baby as it fell.

9 MYSTERY MONK
In the 1800s in Austria, a well regarded portrait painter, Joseph Aigner, tried to kill himself on a number of occasions. At the age of eighteen, during his first attempt, a Capuchin monk interrupted him. He survived. Four years later the same monk again interrupted Aigner as he tried to hang himself. Eight years later, Aigner was sentenced to hang for treason due to his political activities. His life was saved by the intervention of an unnamed Capuchin monk. At the age of sixty-eight, Aigner committed suicide by shooting himself. The unknown Capuchin monk presided over his funeral service.

8 PHOTOGRAPHIC COINCIDENCE

In 1914, a German mother photographed her infant son. She took the film plates to be developed at a store in Strasbourg but was unable to retrieve them due to the breakout of World War I. Two years later she bought a film plate in Frankfurt, over a hundred miles away, to photograph her newborn daughter. By a bizarre coincidence, she had been sold her original plate, which had been mistakenly marked as unused. When the print developed, both children were in the picture.

7 BOOK FIND

The great actor Anthony Hopkins agreed to appear in a film version of *The Girl from Petrovka* by George Feifer, in 1973. Hopkins was surprised to find a copy of the novel lying on a bench at a train station. He kept the book, which turned out to be Feifer's own copy he had lent to a friend. The book was stolen from his friend's car and eventually found its way to the train station where Hopkins found it.

6 TWINS

Jim Lewis and Jim Springer were twins separated at birth. Both adoptive families named their boys James. Both boys grew up and became law enforcement officers. Both had training in mechanical drawing and carpentry and both ended up marrying women named Linda. They both had sons, one named James Alan and the other James Allan. The twin brothers divorced their wives and remarried—both to women named Better. Both brothers owned dogs named Toy.

5 REVENGE KILLING

In 1883, a young man, Henry Ziegland, broke off a relationship with his girlfriend, which caused her to kill herself. The girl's brother tracked down Ziegland and shot him—then took his own life. Ziegland survived the shooting as the bullet grazed his face and lodged in a tree. Years later, Ziegland decided to cut down the tree with the bullet in it. The tree was so large that he decided to blow it out of the ground with dynamite. The explosion caused the bullet to fly out of the tree and into Ziegland's head—killing him instantly.

4 GOLDEN SCARAB

From *The Structure and Dynamics of the Psyche* by Carl Jung:

"A young woman I was treating had, at a critical moment, a dream in which she was given a golden scarab. While she was telling me this dream I sat with my back to the closed window. Suddenly I heard a noise behind me, like a gentle tapping. I turned round and saw a flying insect knocking against the windowpane from outside. I opened the window and caught the creature in the air as it flew in. It was the nearest analogy to the golden scarab that one finds in our latitudes, a scarabaeid beetle, the common rose-chafer (Cetonia aurata) which contrary to its usual habits had evidently felt an urge to get into a dark room at this particular moment. I must admit that nothing like it ever happened to me before or since, and that the dream of the patient has remained unique in my experience."

3 TAXI

In 1975, a young man riding a moped in Bermuda was struck and killed by a taxi. One year later, his brother was killed in exactly the same way: driving the same moped and by the same taxi with the same driver. To make matters even more bizarre, the taxi was carrying the very same passenger as he had when he killed the first brother.

2 HOTEL DISCOVERY

In 1953, Irv Kupcinet (a television reporter) was covering the Coronation of Queen Elizabeth in London. In the drawer of his hotel room he found some items that had been left by the previous resident, Harry Hannin—a basketball star with the Harlem Globetrotters and, coincidentally, a good friend of the reporter. Two days later, Kupcinet received a letter from Hannin telling him that he had found a tie in the hotel Meurice in Paris with Kupcinet's name on it. Kupcinet had stayed there the previous week.

1 HISTORICAL COINCIDENCE

Thomas Jefferson and John Adams, two of the founders of the United States of America, were involved in the crafting of the Declaration of Independence. On July 4, 1776, the Continental Congress approved the document. Exactly 50 years later (to the day), both Jefferson and Adams died.

TOP 10 BIZARRE MENTAL DISORDERS

10 **STOCKHOLM SYNDROME**
Stockholm syndrome is the name of the disorder in which a person becomes sympathetic to a person harming them in some way. It can appear in people who are sexually abused, raped, or kidnapped. The most famous case is that of Patty Hearst—a millionaire's daughter who was kidnapped in 1974. She not only ended up sympathizing with their cause, she ended up engaging in criminal activities with them.

9 **LIMA SYNDROME**
Lima syndrome is the opposite of Stockholm syndrome in that the captors become sympathetic with the hostages. It is named after a crisis in Peru where several dignitaries were held hostage, including the future president of Peru and his mother. The hostages were released and the terrorists were all captured.

8 **DIOGENES SYNDROME**
Diogenes syndrome is a disorder that leads to extreme self-neglect, compulsive hoarding (often of animals), and reclusion. It is normally found in old people as it is connected in some way with senile dementia.

7 **PARIS SYNDROME**
Paris syndrome is a disorder that affects mostly Japanese people. The disorder is characterized by nervous breakdown when visiting the city of Paris, due to an inability to cope with the culture shock. It is most likely that the tourists are unable to reconcile the perfect image of Paris shown by most films, with the not-so-perfect city that exists in reality. There is even a twenty-four-hour hotline for tourists suffering the syndrome.

6 STENDHAL SYNDROME

Stendhal syndrome is a disorder in which a person experiences hallucinations, confusion, and rapid heartbeat when in the presence of particularly beautiful or famous art. It can also occur occasionally in people when they experience an especially stunning natural landscape.

5 JERUSALEM SYNDROME

Jerusalem syndrome is the name of a disorder in which a person (of any religion) suffers psychosis-like symptoms after visiting the city of Jerusalem. The disorder manifests itself as delusions and obsessions—usually related to religion. The majority of sufferers have been found to have previous histories of mental illness.

4 CAPGRAS DELUSION

The Capgras delusion is a bizarre disorder in which a person believes that someone they know (usually a loved one) has been replaced by an identical imposter. It often occurs in sufferers of schizophrenia, but it can also appear in people suffering brain injury or dementia.

3 FREGOLI DELUSION

The Fregoli delusion is the opposite of the Capgras delusion. In this case, a person believes that different people in their life is the same person who appears in a variety of disguises. It is named after Leopold Fregoli who was able to make quick changes between scenes when acting on stage.

2 REDUPLICATIVE PARAMNESIA

Reduplicative paramnesia is the belief that a location has been duplicated—causing it to appear in two places. Occasionally the sufferer believes an area has been relocated elsewhere. For example, the reduplicative paramnesiac may think the hospital he was admitted to has now been moved to a different part of the country.

1 COTARD DELUSION

The Cotard delusion is an extremely rare disorder in which a person believes they are dead. In some cases they believe they are alive, but lacking vital organs. It is named after Jules Cotard who first described the disorder in 1880.

✳✳✳✳✳✳

TOP 10
BIZARRE CURSES

10 BJÖRKETORP RUNESTONE

This is one of a group of runestones found in Blekinge, Sweden, dating back to the sixth century AD. The stones measure up to 4.2 meters in height. Some of the stones appear in circles while others stand alone. The Björketorp stone bears the following inscription:

> "I, master of the runes(?) conceal here runes of power. Incessantly (plagued by) maleficence, (doomed to) insidious death (is) he who breaks this (monument). I prophesy destruction / prophecy of destruction."

A local legend relates that the curse was once tested and proved. A very long time ago, a man wanted to remove the stone so as to get more land to cultivate. He piled wood around it in order to heat it up and then crack it with water. The weather was dead calm and there was no wind. He had just lit the fire when a sudden gust of wind turned the direction of the flame setting the man's hair on fire. He threw himself on the ground to extinguish it, but it spread to his clothes and the poor man died in terrible agony. However, the fire around the runestone was extinguished as if an enormous hand had enveloped the stone and smothered the fire.

9 CURSE OF THE BAMBINO

The curse of the Bambino refers to the run of bad luck the Boston Red Sox experienced after trading Babe Ruth to the New York Yankees in 1920. Up until that time, the NY Yankees had never won a World Series, and hoped that Ruth would change this for them; he did. After the trade, the Boston Red Sox did not win the World Series again until 2004. During their winning game, a total lunar eclipse occurred—a first for the World Series. Even more dramatic was the fact that the 2004 win was against the New York Yankees.

8 CURSE OF TIPPECANOE

William Harrison won the presidency in 1840 with the slogan "Tippecanoe and Tyler Too," a reference to the Battle of Tippecanoe. He died one year later. From that year through the election of Ronald Reagan in 1980, every president elected in a year ending in a zero died during their term. The years and presidents who suffered this curse were: 1840 (Harrison—natural causes), 1860 (Lincoln—shot), 1880 (Garfield—shot), 1900 (McKinley—shot), 1920 (Harding—natural causes), 1940 (Roosevelt—natural causes), and 1960 (Kennedy—shot). Interestingly, an assassination attempt was aimed at Reagan—had it succeeded, he would have died before the end of his first term.

7 CURSE OF SUPERMAN

The Superman curse refers to the misfortunes that occurred to people involved with the Superman story over the years. Probably the most famous people to have been allegedly afflicted by this curse are George Reeves, who played Superman in the television series, and Christopher Reeve, who played the character in the early movies. George Reeves committed suicide, and Christopher Reeve became paralyzed after falling from his horse. Other victims often named are Jerry Siegel and artist Joe Shuster who created the character but made very little money from it because DC Comics, their employer, held all the rights. Some even say that Jerry and Joe put the curse on the character because of what they believed was unfair compensation for their work. There is even speculation that John F. Kennedy was a victim of the curse. Shortly before his death, his staff approved a Superman story in which the hero touts the president's physical fitness initiatives, and was scheduled to be published with an April 1964 cover date. Because of this curse, many actors have refused to play the role of Superman in the latest movie. Paul Walker was one of these actors, though perhaps in his case it is for the best, as he was more likely to kill the role than to have the role kill him.

6 CURSE OF THE BILLY GOAT

The curse of the billy goat struck the Chicago Cubs after a Greek immigrant, Billy Sianis, was ejected from a game after he tried to parade around the field with his pet goat. When he was thrown out, Sianis cursed the Cubs, saying they would never win another game at Wrigley field. They lost the World Series that year and for twenty more years they remained in the second division. In 1967 the streak ended.

5 JAMES DEAN'S PORSCHE

In 1955, iconic film star James Dean was killed in an accident involving his Porsche Spyder. George Barris purchased the wreck of the car for twenty-five hundred dollars. While his mechanic was trying to repair the car, it slipped and broke both of his legs. In 1956, two cars racing with spare parts from the Porsche were involved in an accident—one of the drivers was killed. The car disappeared in 1960 and its whereabouts is unknown.

4 THE KENNEDY CURSE

The Kennedy family appears to be suffering from a curse, which is now known as the Kennedy Curse. Several members of the family died young—including both John F. Kennedy and his brother Robert (both assassinated while in office), and John F. Kennedy, Jr., who was killed in a plane crash. Other members of the family to have suffered from the curse are JFK's sister Rosemary, Joseph Kennedy, who was killed during World War II, Edward Kennedy, Jr., who had a leg amputated at the age of twelve, and Michael Kennedy, who was killed skiing.

3 THE HOPE DIAMOND

The Hope Diamond has been around since 1642. It is a brilliant blue diamond weighing 45.52 carats. Legend states that the diamond was stolen from a statue in India causing the curse to begin. The thief was ripped apart by dogs in Russia (after selling the diamond). The diamond ended up belonging to King Louis XVI of France, who was murdered by revolutionaries along with his wife, Queen Marie Antoinette. It was eventually donated to the Smithsonian Institute and is now on display as part of the National Gem and Mineral collection in the National Museum of Natural History.

2 THE 27 CLUB

The 27 Club is the name given to the group of highly influential musicians who all died at the age of twenty-seven. There are various lists of members because some dispute the level of influence of some lesser-known members. Accepted names on the list are Jimi Hendrix, James Morrison, Janis Joplin, and Kurt Cobain. Some lists also include Brian Jones (from the Rolling Stones).

1 THE CURSE OF TUTANKHAMEN

A few months after the opening of Tutankhamen's tomb tragedy struck. Lord Carnarvon (the financial backer of the search for Tutankhamen's tomb), fifty-seven, was taken ill and rushed to Cairo. He died a few days later. At the moment of his death, the lights in Cairo went out and his favorite dog began howling on his estate in England. When the mummy was unwrapped in 1925, it was found to have an identical mark in the place where Carnarvon was bitten. Five years later, over eleven people connected with the opening of the tomb had died—some through suicide and unexplained circumstances. One of the victims left a suicide note which read: "I really cannot stand any more horrors and hardly see what good I am going to do here, so I am making my exit."

✖✖✖✖✖✖

TOP 10 BIZARRE SURGICAL PROCEDURES

10 HEMISPHERECTOMY

Believe it or not, this surgical procedure involves removing or disabling an entire half of the brain. The hemispherectomy has been performed since 1923 when Dr. Walter Dandy first used it. It is reserved for cases of extreme seizures that cannot be controlled through medication. All of the people who have this treatment end up with paralysis of the body on the opposite side to the brain hemisphere that was removed. In time, most patients regain some of their previous abilities as the other side of the brain takes over from the missing sections.

9 HEMICORPORECTOMY

Also known as translumbar amputation, this surgery removes the lower half of the body from above the pelvis. The result is that the sexual organs, anus, rectum, legs, pelvis bones, and urinary system are removed. The procedure is only recommended as a last resort for people suffering fatal illnesses. It has only been performed in a small number of cases and it normally takes place in two stages—the first to disconnect the parts of the body to be amputated, and the second to perform the actual amputation.

8 BILATERAL CINGULOTOMY

This is a brain surgery used in pain treatment for severe cases of cancer. It involves disabling the frontal lobes—so in a way it is a less extreme surgery than a lobotomy. It is also sometimes used in surgery for mental disorders, but its use in that area is highly controversial, though it is well supported in the case of pain management.

7 ENDOSCOPIC THORACIC SYMPATHECTOMY

ETS is a surgery in which portions of the sympathetic nerve trunk are dissected. By cutting these nerve sections, the surgeon is able to treat severe cases of hyperhydrosis (excess sweating). What makes this bizarre is a side effect of this treatment is that the person no longer blushes. For that reason it has also become a cosmetic procedure for people who blush excessively. If only one side of the body is treated, a person who has undergone this surgery will have half of their body blushing while the other half remains in its natural state. The treatment is always performed on both sides of the body.

6 VAGINECTOMY

In a vaginectomy, part or all of the vagina is surgically removed. This is normally used as a treatment for various forms of cancer but it also occurs in some sexual reassignment surgeries. It is normal for a surgeon to reconstruct the vagina after this surgery by using other parts of the patient's body.

5 LOBOTOMY

Lobotomy is a very controversial medical treatment in which the frontal lobes of the brain are destroyed. While it is seldom performed nowadays, it does still occur. Lobotomies have been used in the past to treat all manner of mental illnesses, including schizophrenia. This procedure often results in major personality changes and sometimes mental retardation. John F. Kennedy's sister was given a lobotomy against her will.

4 PENECTOMY

A penectomy is the total removal of all, or parts, of the penis. It is normally used as a treatment for cancer, but it sometimes had to be performed after a botched circumcision. Horrifying, penectomies have been performed occasionally on men who wish to use it as a form of extreme body modification. Many doctors consider this use of the surgery as unethical.

3 CIRCUMCISION

Circumcision is a very common procedure performed for religious reasons (among Jews and Muslims) and by many doctors who claim health benefits.

Much controversy surrounds this procedure (in which the foreskin of the penis is surgically removed) as it is a nonessential surgery normally performed on a child that has no say in whether it is performed or not. Some adult men develop psychological issues as a result of circumcision, which leads us to the next bizarre surgery: foreskin restoration.

2 FORESKIN RESTORATION

Foreskin restoration is the process of expanding the skin left behind after a circumcision in order to create a new foreskin. The technique is most often requested by men who have suffered an injury to the area, been circumcised as a child, or who wish to have a larger foreskin. During World War II, some European Jews sought out surgical foreskin restoration treatment in order to avoid Nazi persecution.

1 LINDBERGH OPERATION

The Lindbergh Operation is included here as a special mention. It was the first surgery ever performed entirely with robots being guided by doctors through telecommunications. The surgery occurred in France and was controlled by French doctors in New York. The operation was performed successfully on September 7, 2001, by Professor Jacques Marescaux and his team from the IRCAD (Institute for Research into Cancer of the Digestive System). The operation was to remove a gallbladder and it took a total of forty-five minutes.

✳✳✳✳✳✳

TOP 10 BIZARRE FETISHES

10 FURRY FANDOM

Furry fandom is the classification given to people who like to dress up as anthropomorphic animals, or watch others do so. Members of this fandom watch pornography of people dressed in animal suits, and engage in the sexual acts themselves. Sometimes this can merely involve non-sexual touch and rubbing while in costume.

9 TERATOPHILIA

Teratophilia is being sexually attracted to people who suffer from deformities, such as amputees. There is a great deal of pornography published to cater to this unusual attraction. Some people with an extreme version of this fetish will seek out doctors to perform amputation on them for no reason other than sexual pleasure.

8 UROLAGNIA

Urolagnia is when a person derives sexual pleasure from urinating or watching others urinate. In some cases this can lead to urophagia, the consumption of urine. A great deal of pornography has been created for this fetish. Urolagnia is also known as "watersports" or "golden showers."

7 EMETOPHILIA

This fetish involves vomiting or watching others vomit. This fetish is also known as a "Roman shower" when the participants actively vomit on each other. A website dedicated to this fetish says, "Vomiting was probably something either arousing or frightening to emetophiles at some point … it aroused powerful emotions, and the emetophier called upon these emotions for the purpose of sexual gratification."

6 BLOOD FETISH

This fetish (also known as Renfield's syndrome) is when a person derives satisfaction from watching someone bleed, or simply seeing blood on partly or entirely naked skin. There is a large community around this fetish, however, due to its controversial nature, it tends to remain underground. Blood fetishism is often accompanied by some licking or drinking blood and can also involve menstrual blood, referred to as "Red Wings."

5 COPROPHILIA

Coprophilia is the sexual pleasure derived from feces. The fetish can involve defecating on a partner, called "human toilet." This frequently includes defecating in the mouth of the other person. Coprophilia can also include coprophagia, which is the consumption of fecal matter. This can (obviously) lead to serious health risks.

4 CRUSH FETISH

While illegal in many countries (including the United States and United Kingdom), crush fetish is a quite common desire to see small insects or animals crushed to death. Pornography created for this often involves the killing of an animal beneath the feet of women—this usually includes slow motion replays. Some crush fetishists are content to see inanimate objects crushed (such as cigarettes or fruit).

3 KLISMAPHILIA

Klismaphilia is the fetish in which enemas are given or received for sexual gratification. There is a large amount of pornography available on the Internet for those who have this fetish. The majority of klismaphiles are males and most pornography caters to the heterosexual community.

2 OMORASHI

Omorashi is a fetish found mostly in Japan. It involves sexual gratification around having a full bladder. In most cases, sexual climax coincides with the moment of relief and it is sometimes associated with other urine-related fetishes. Most pornography for this fetish is soft-core and involves clothed women looking uncomfortable as they struggle not to wet themselves.

1 NECROPHILIA

Necrophilia is a sexual attraction to human corpses. This fetish can lead to grave-robbing and sexual activity with the dead body. In the United States, no federal law exists to outlaw this act, but several states regard it as a misdemeanor or felony. It is, therefore, surprising that cases are not more widespread.

✳✳✳✳✳✳

TOP 10 MOST HAUNTED PLACES

10 **THE TOWER OF LONDON, LONDON, ENGLAND**
The Tower of London is a historic monument in Central London. It has been said to be haunted for many centuries. The most famous ghost to reside there is Ann Boleyn—one of King Henry VIII's wives who lost her head to the axe. She is sometimes seen walking the halls carrying her head beneath her arm.

9 **WAVERLY HILLS SANATORIUM, LOUISVILLE, KENTUCKY**
Waverly Hills Sanatorium in Kentucky was a hospital for the quarantine of people suffering from tuberculosis. The hauntings are so famous it has been featured on television repeatedly. The building is home to all manner of strange phenomena such as ethereal screams, isolated cold spots, shadows where there shouldn't be shadows, and occasional apparitions.

8 **THE QUEEN MARY, LONG BEACH, CALIFORNIA**
The RMS *Queen Mary* was an ocean liner that sailed the North Atlantic Ocean for the Cunard White Star Line. When it was decommissioned, it was moved to Long Beach and turned into a hotel. The most haunted part of the ship is an engine room where a seventeen-year-old boy was crushed to death in a fire. Voices are heard throughout the ship and children are said to haunt the pool area.

7 **THE WHITE HOUSE, WASHINGTON, D.C.**
The White House, home to the President of the United States of America, is said to be haunted by President Andrew Jackson. In addition, First Lady Abigail Adams has been spotted, and the ghost of Abraham Lincoln is said to linger. Eleanor Roosevelt believed she witnessed the ghost of Lincoln while she was living at the White House.

6 **EDINBURGH CASTLE, EDINBURGH, SCOTLAND**
Edinburgh Castle, formerly the home of the Scottish Royal Family, is one of the most haunted spots in Scotland, and Edinburgh itself is said to be the

most haunted city in all of Europe. People have witnessed phantom bagpipers, French prisoners, and even a ghostly dog.

5 THE WHALEY HOUSE, SAN DIEGO, CALIFORNIA

Author deTraci Regula relates her experiences with the house:

"Over the years, while dining across the street at the Old Town Mexican Cafe, I became accustomed to noticing that the shutters of the second-story windows [of the Whaley House] would sometimes open while we ate dinner, long after the house was closed for the day. On a recent visit, I could feel the energy in several spots in the house, particularly in the courtroom, where I also smelled the faint scent of a cigar, supposedly Whaley's calling-card. In the hallway, I smelled perfume, initially attributing that to the young woman acting as docent, but some later surreptitious sniffing in her direction as I talked to her about the house revealed her to be scent-free."

4 RAYNHAM HALL, NORFOLK, ENGLAND

Raynham Hall is a country house in Norfolk, England. It has been the home of the Townshend family for over three hundred years and believed to be haunted by the Brown Lady—one of the most famous ghosts in the world. Witnesses who saw her walking down one of the large staircases took a photo of her—the photo is one of the best ghost photos in existence.

3 THE MYRTLES PLANTATION, ST. FRANCISVILLE, LOUISIANA

The Myrtles Plantation is one of the most haunted spots in the United States. Reports of twelve separate ghosts exist and there is a record of at least one murder in the house, though some people believe that up to ten people may have been murdered there. One of the ghosts is said to be that of a female slave named Chloe who was forced to become the mistress of the master of the house.

2 EASTERN STATE PENITENTIARY, PHILADELPHIA, PENNSYLVANIA

The Eastern State Penitentiary, which opened in 1829, is believed to be the world's first true prison. On June 1, 2007, a television show, *Most Haunted*, went live to the penitentiary. Part of the group went to Al Capone's cell where two people passed out while "investigating" it. One member of the team, Yvette, said, "this is the most evil place I have ever been."

1 BORLEY RECTORY, ESSEX, ENGLAND
Borley Rectory was the site of the most famous haunting in Britain during the 1920s and '30s. It was home to an enormous number of sightings and eerie sounds. Virtually every visitor was witness to one bizarre phenomenon or another. Some of the occurrences have been scientifically explained, but the vast majority remains inexplicable.

❋❋❋❋❋

TOP 10
BIZARRE PHOBIAS

10 HEXAKOSIOIHEXEKONTAHEXAPHOBIA—FEAR OF THE NUMBER 666
Hexakosioihexekontahexaphobia is the very unusual phobia that originates with the Biblical verse in Apocalypse (Revelation) 13:18 which states that 666 is the "number of the beast"—referring to Satan or the Antichrist.

9 EPHEBOPHOBIA—FEAR OF YOUTHS
This is the irrational fear of young people. It is often combined with a type of loathing for youth-related concepts.

8 COULROPHOBIA—FEAR OF CLOWNS
Coulrophobia is the exaggerated fear of clowns. It is quite common among children and less so in adults. The fear often comes from a negative portrayal of clowns witnessed by the sufferer in youth.

7 ERGASIOPHOBIA—FEAR OF WORK
Ergasiophobia is a fear that can be so severe as to prevent a person from working. It is frequently just a symptom of another deeper psychological problem, which may not be obvious.

6 GYMNOPHOBIA—FEAR OF NUDITY

The fear of nudity can be quite debilitating as it can affect marriages and relationships by preventing the sufferer from being able to have sexual relations. It is often caused by a lack of confidence in oneself due to the idealized bodies portrayed by the mass media.

5 NEOPHOBIA—FEAR OF NEWNESS

Neophobia is the fear of new things or new experiences. It often manifests itself as an inability to change routine habits. It is often accompanied by frustration and anger. Technophobia (the fear of new technology) is a subset of neophobia.

4 PARASKAVEDEKATRIAPHOBIA—FEAR OF FRIDAY THE 13TH

This fear comes from the fact that historically Friday the thirteenth has been considered a day of bad luck. The word comes from ancient Greek and literally means "Friday thirteen fear." This is a subset of the more general fear of the number thirteen, which is called triskaidekaphobia.

3 PANPHOBIA—FEAR OF EVERYTHING

This is a terrible debilitating fear of nothing in particular. The sufferer is in a constant state of fear without knowing why or knowing what it is they fear. It is often described as a feeling of "persistent dread" and is often a symptom of schizophrenia.

2 TAPHOPHOBIA—FEAR OF BEING BURIED ALIVE

Taphophobia is a fear of being buried alive. It is a fear that is not entirely irrational as few people would be happy with the idea. It has been frequently dealt with in literature—especially in the horror genre. The most famous example is probably "The Premature Burial" by Edgar Allan Poe.

1 PTERONOPHOBIA—FEAR OF BEING TICKLED BY FEATHERS

Pteronophobia is the fear of being tickled with feathers. It can be sparked off by an event in childhood where the person being tickled feels helpless and trapped. It is related to the less-specific fear of being tickled.

✳✳✳✳✳✳

TOP 10 BIZARRE TRADITIONS

10 DUELING

Dueling is an age-old custom in Western societies. A duel would involve two men who would face off in an open field and fire a single shot at each other. Duels were often fought over matters of principle and honor. In earlier years, duels were fought with swords in a one-on-one scenario. It was considered dishonorable for a man to refuse a duel and eventually the concept was condemned by the dominant Christian religions as it almost always lead to death.

9 CONCUBINAGE

A concubine was a person who was put into a quasi-matrimonial state with a man of higher status. The man would often have more than one concubine and they were regarded as lower in the social order than his wives and children. It was often a voluntary state as it ensured economic security for life. Some extreme cases of concubinage involved sexual slavery.

8 GEISHA

The original geisha were highly trained women who were educated in the arts, dancing, conversation, and music. They were extremely skilled and would perform the role of an escort for gentlemen. They were not prostitutes and for many of the girls, this was a way to secure a living when they had no hopes of otherwise escaping a life of poverty. The modern geisha are not trained in quite as rigorous a manner, so many of the original traditions have been lost. It is now entirely a voluntary way of life, whereas in the past many girls were forced to train as geisha.

7 FOOT-BINDING

Foot-binding is a custom that began in China in the tenth century and continued right up to the early twentieth century. Young girls (usually from the age of six) would have their feet bound so tightly that as they grew older, their bones would break—keeping the foot small and delicate. Sometimes the parents intentionally broke the girl's toes in order to facilitate the process.

The practice of foot-binding was usually found in upper-class families who had enough servants to perform the menial tasks that lower-class women had to perform themselves.

6 SELF-MUMMIFICATION

In Northern Japan a group of Buddhist monks called Sokushinbutsu practiced a very extreme form of self-denial that ended in death. For three years, a monk would prepare himself for death by drinking a special type of lacquer while undergoing extreme physical exercise and strict dieting in order to reduce body fat. When the monk was ready for death, he would be sealed in a tomb not much bigger than himself and would remain there until he died. The lacquer that he had been drinking would stop his body from decomposing, thereby mummifying him. Between sixteen and twenty-four self-mummified bodies exist today.

5 EUNUCHS

Eunuchs were men who were castrated in order to fulfill certain roles in society. Castration was used as a punishment in China and also as a means of getting a job at the Royal Palace. Some eunuchs wielded an extreme amount of power. Some eunuchs were castrated before puberty in order to ensure that their voices would not break—enabling them to sing high soprano roles in opera and in choirs. The boys were given no choice and the procedure rendered them unable to have children. It was not until 1912 that the role of the eunuch ended.

4 SATI

Sati is an old Hindu custom, unfortunately still occasionally practiced today, in which the wife of a recently deceased man is expected to jump onto his funeral pyre to be burned alive—thereby joining him in death. In many cases, if the wife would not comply, the family of the husband and even other members of the village would throw her onto the fire. Sati was particularly common among women with no children as they would often have no source of income for the rest of their lives.

3 SEPPUKU

Seppuku was a part of the Samurai code of honor. It involved stabbing oneself in the abdomen with a left-to-right cut. Once the warrior had cut himself, his helper (called a *kaishakunin*) would cut off his head with a sword to prevent undue suffering. Prior to this ritual suicide, the Samurai would write a death poem.

2 HUMAN SACRIFICE
As long as there have been humans, there have been human sacrifices. Originally the sacrifice was intertwined with paganism and various groups around the world, independently of each other, practiced it. Sometimes young children or babies were killed in the hopes that their innocence would make the sacrifice more worthy. Some methods of sacrifice were especially bizarre, as was the case of the vestal virgins of ancient Rome who were entombed until dead.

1 TIBETAN SKY BURIAL
Tibetan sky burial is the method of burial preferred by Tibetan Buddhists. It involves the crushing of a corpse with a variety of hammers and mallets. The bones are powdered and the resulting mixture is combined with barley flour, tea, and yak butter. The remains are then thrown to vultures that consume the entire body. The Buddhists believe that this is the most natural way to rid the earth of an otherwise empty shell because they believe that the soul will be reincarnated.

❋❋❋❋❋❋

TOP 10 TRULY BIZARRE DEATHS

10 KING ADOLF FREDERICK OF SWEDEN, MAY 14, 1710–FEBRUARY 12, 1771

Manner of death: Eating too much pudding

Adolph Frederick was the titular King of Sweden from 1751–1771. The omnipotent *Riksdag*, or senate, held the reins of power despite Adolph's best efforts to wrest it from them.

A victim of personal excess, Adolph Frederick is known by Swedish children as "the king who ate himself to death." On February 12, 1771, after partaking of a banquet consisting of lobster, caviar, sauerkraut, smoked herring, and champagne, he moved on to his favorite dessert, *Semla*, a traditional bun or pastry made from semolina/wheat flour, served in a bowl of hot milk. One or two portions would have been sufficient; fourteen servings were excessive. He died shortly thereafter of digestion problems.

9 HORACE WELLS, JANUARY 21, 1815–JANUARY 24, 1848
Manner of death: Used anesthetics to commit suicide

An American dentist, born in Vermont and educated in Boston, Horace Wells was one of the pioneers in the field of anesthesia. Weary of screaming patients (it was known to upset him terribly, and he often debated leaving the field of dentistry altogether), he was one of the first practitioners to see the value of nitrous oxide or laughing gas as an anesthetic.

After a failed experiment and a falling out with the medical community, Wells became a traveling anesthetic salesman and European expert for his former partner, Gardner Quincy Colton. His "investigations" led to a chloroform addiction that would be his downfall. In 1848, delirious and deranged after a week of self-experimentation, Wells ran into the street and assaulted two prostitutes with sulfuric acid. He was arrested and confined at New York's infamous Tombs Prison. Recovering from the drug-induced psychosis, the true horror of his actions came home to roost. Unable to live with this shame, Wells committed suicide by first inhaling a substantial dose of chloroform and then slitting his femoral artery.

8 TYCHO BRAHE, DECEMBER 14, 1546–OCTOBER 24, 1601
Manner of death: Didn't get to the toilet in time

Famous as an alchemist and astronomer, Brahe's pioneering observations of planetary motion paved the way for Sir Isaac Newton to develop the theory of gravity.

Unfortunately, brilliance and common sense do not always go hand in hand—the manner of his death being the case in point. Knowing that it was very bad form to leave a banquet table before the festivities concluded, Brahe, who was known to have a weak bladder, neglected to relieve himself before dinner. To compound matters, he was known to drink excessively, and this particular banquet was no exception. Too polite to ask to be excused, his bladder strained causing a protracted (eleven-day), agonizing death. Whether he died of a burst bladder or hyponatremia (low levels of sodium in the blood) or mercury poisoning is now debated.

7 GRIGORI RASPUTIN, JANUARY 22, 1869–DECEMBER 29, 1916

Manner of death: Drowning after being poisoned, shot, stabbed, and bludgeoned

The Mad Monk, Grigori Rasputin, was a peasant and mystic healer who found favor with the royal court of Russia by providing relief to Crown Prince Aleksey, a hemophiliac and heir to the throne.

Wielding much influence on the royal court, the unkempt, vulgar, and amazingly resilient Rasputin made many political enemies. He had to go; much easier said than done. The conspirators first tried poison, enough poison to kill a man three times his size, but he seemed unaffected. Next they snuck up behind him and shot him in the head. This should have done it, but no; while one of the assassins was checking his pulse, the mystic grabbed the conspirator by the neck and proceeded to strangle him. Running away, the would-be assassins took up the chase, shooting him three times in the process. The gunshots slowed him down enough to allow his pursuers to catch up. They then proceeded to bludgeon him before throwing him in the icy cold river (in the Russian winter). When his body was recovered an autopsy showed the cause of death was drowning.

6 ISADORA DUNCAN, MAY 27, 1877–SEPTEMBER 14, 1927

Manner of death: Strangulation and a broken neck

Isadora Duncan is widely considered the mother of modern dance. Born in San Francisco, California, Dora Angela Duncan was the product of divorced parents; her father was a disgraced banker and her mother a pianist and music teacher. Her free-form style was never very popular in her home country, but she found great success after immigrating to Paris. She founded three schools of dance and her likeness is carved over the entrance to the Théâtre des Champs-Élysées.

Isadora Duncan died of a broken neck and accidental strangulation when her scarf caught on the wheel of a car she was traveling in. *The New York Times*, succinctly and brutally described it thus:

> *"The automobile was going at full speed when the scarf of strong silk began winding around the wheel and with terrific force dragged Miss Duncan, around whom it was securely wrapped, bodily over the side of the car, precipitating her with violence against the cobblestone street. She was dragged for several yards before the chauffeur halted, attracted by her cries in the street. Medical aid was summoned, but it was stated that she had been strangled and killed instantly."*

5 CHRISTINE CHUBBUCK, AUGUST 24, 1944–JULY 15, 1974

Manner of death: Suicide on live TV

Christine Chubbuck was the host of *Suncoast Digest*, a well-regarded public affairs program on WXLT-TV in Sarasota, Florida. Breaking format, her guest was waiting across the studio at the news anchor's desk; Christine read eight minutes of national news stories before the tape reel malfunctioned while Christine was describing a shooting at the Beef and Bottle restaurant. Seemingly unfazed by the technical glitch, Christine looked into the camera and said:

> *"In keeping with Channel 40's policy of bringing you the latest in blood and guts, and in living color, you are going to see another first: an attempted suicide."*

Taking a revolver out from under her desk, she placed it behind her left ear and pulled the trigger (she learned this was the most effective way to commit suicide from the police while researching a project for her show). She tumbled violently forward as the technical director slowly faded to black. Some viewers called 911 while others called the station to see if it was real. Camerawoman Jean Reed later stated that she didn't believe it to be genuine until she saw Christine's body twitching on the floor.

4 SHARON LOPATKA, SEPTEMBER 20, 1961–OCTOBER 16, 1996

Manner of death: Volunteered to be tortured and murdered

Sharon Lopatka was an Internet entrepreneur and one sick puppy. Living in Hampstead, Maryland, Sharon was killed by Robert Frederick Glass in a case of consensual homicide.

While advertising unusual fetishist pornography on her website, Sharon began her hunt for a partner willing to torture and kill her for their mutual sexual gratification. After many false starts, of course most replies were not serious, she finally found Robert Glass who was more than willing to fulfill her fantasy. They exchanged many messages, culminating in their meeting in North Carolina. Glass tortured her for several days before strangling her with a nylon cord. He was later convicted of voluntary manslaughter and possession of child pornography.

3 FRANCIS BACON, JANUARY 22, 1561–APRIL 9, 1626

Manner of death: Stuffing snow into a chicken

Francis Bacon, statesman, philosopher, creator of the English essay, and advocate for the scientific revolution (he established "The Scientific Method" still used today), was one of very few people to die as a result of one of their own experiments.

In 1626, while gazing out the window at a snowy afternoon, Sir Francis Bacon had an epiphany of sorts. Why would snow not work as preservative of meat in much the same way salt is used? Needing to know and unheeding of the weather, Bacon rushed to town to purchase a chicken, brought it home and began the experiment. Standing outside in the snow, he killed the chicken and tried to stuff it with snow. The experiment was a failure; the chicken didn't freeze, and as a consequence of standing around in the freezing weather, Bacon developed a terminal case of pneumonia. Trying to stave off the inevitable, Bacon roasted and ate the chicken. That too was a failed experiment. He died.

2 ATTILA THE HUN, 406–453
Manner of death: A nosebleed on his wedding night

History's most brilliant tactician, warlord, and notorious villain, Attila the Hun conquered all of Asia by 450 AD. Using a combination of fierce combat and ruthless assimilation, Mongolia, to the very edge of the Russian Empire, fell to Attila and his armies.

Known for his frugal eating and drinking habits, Attila must have thought that his own wedding was an occasion to celebrate. Marrying a young girl named Ildico, in 453 AD, he overindulged in both food and drink. Sometime after retiring for the evening, his nose started to bleed. Too drunk to notice, it continued to bleed, ultimately drowning him in his own blood.

1 AESCHYLUS, 525 BC/524 BC–456 BC
Manner of death: An eagle dropped a tortoise on his head

Considered the founder of tragedy, Aeschylus is the first of the three ancient Greek playwrights whose work still survives. He expanded the characters of a play so that there was conflict between them instead of actors solely interacting with the chorus. Sophocles and Euripides famously followed in his footsteps.

While visiting Gela on the island of Sicily, legend has it that an eagle, mistaking Aeschylus's bald pate for a stone, dropped a tortoise on his head, killing him. Some accounts differ, stating that a stone was dropped on his head, the eagle mistaking his shining crown for an egg. This is not as farfetched as it seems. The Lammergeier, or bearded vulture, is native to the Mediterranean, and is known to drop bones and tortoises on rocks to break them open.

✳✳✳✳✳✳

TOP 10 BIZARRE DEATH-RELATED FACTS

10 EDISON'S DYING BREATH

Bizarre Fact: Thomas Edison's dying breath was captured in a bottle.

Thomas Edison, the well-known inventor who perfected the modern lightbulb, was friends with Henry Ford, founder of the Ford Motor Company, and considered to be a father of modern assembly lines. As Edison lay dying, Ford convinced his son, Charles, to fill a bottle with Edison's dying breath. Charles complied by bottling some of the air in the room. The bottle is on display at the Henry Ford Museum in Greenford, Michigan.

9 ECO-BURIAL

Bizarre Fact: A Swedish company will pulverize your body and bury it in a cornstarch urn, providing a completely biodegradable burial.

Shortly after your death (within one-and-a-half weeks) your corpse is frozen to minus 18 degrees Celsius (64.4°F)—causing the body to become very brittle. It is then subjected to vibrations that render you a frozen powder. This powder is then placed in a vacuum tube, which extracts all the water, resulting in a dry powder. The powder is then put through a metal separator, which removes fillings and other metal objects that have become a part of your body over your lifetime. The powder is then placed in a cornstarch coffin for burial at any time in the future. The organic powder, which is hygienic and odorless, does not decompose when kept dry. The burial takes place in a shallow grave in living soil that turns the coffin and its contents into compost in about six to twelve months time. If you want a more permanent resting place, you might want to look into the next item instead.

8 SKY BURIAL

Bizarre Fact: Tibetan Buddhists cut and beat a dead body (including the bones) to a pulp and leave the results for vultures to eat.

As Tibetan Buddhists believe in reincarnation, they consider the dead body to be an empty vessel that has no further use in life except as food for nature. Coupled with the very hard rocky ground in Tibet, sky burial seemed the most effective method of disposal. While accounts differ slightly from burial to burial, common features exist. Tibetan monks cut the limbs off the body and hack them to pieces. Each piece is handed to an assistant who bashes it to a pulp with rocks and then mixes it with barley flour, tea, and yak butter. This is then left for the vultures. In some places, the vultures are so eager to eat that the monks have to beat them off with sticks until they are ready to feed them.

7 DANCE OF DEATH

Bizarre Fact: In Madagascar, people dig up the bones of their loved ones and dance with them.

Each year, the Malagasy people of Madagascar perform a funeral tradition called Famadihana. The ceremony involves the digging up of the bones of loved ones, dressing them in new clothing, and dancing with them around the tomb to live music. The custom is surprisingly not especially ancient (seventeenth century) and the Catholic Church permits it because it is not a religious but rather a cultural custom. The practice is beginning to decline in modern days due to objections from Protestant groups and the high price of the silk shrouds usually used in the ceremony.

6 DEADLY PORTRAIT

Bizarre Fact: The Victorians photographed their dead because they could seldom afford a picture of them alive.

Photography was still relatively new in the Victorian era, and the difficulty in staying still long enough for a high-quality photograph and the extremely high price of a painted portrait meant that many Victorians would have a photograph taken of a loved one after they died as a memento. This practice (*memento mori*) also meant that photographs could be sent to distant relatives who may never have met a young child who died. It was not uncommon for members of the family to pose with the dead in a kind of macabre family portrait.

5 SIN-EATER

Bizarre Fact: Ancient British people employed a sin-eater to "eat" the sins of the dead.

In ancient England, Scotland, and Wales, each village had a member (usually a beggar) who was the designated "sin-eater." When a person died in the village, the sin-eater would be called in to their home. A relative would place a loaf of bread on the chest of the dead and pass a cup of ale to the sin-eater across it. The sin-eater would drink the ale and eat the bread, thereby eating the sins of the dead person. The origins of this bizarre practice are unknown but it is believed to have continued into modern times in Wales.

4 TOWERS OF SILENCE

Bizarre Fact: Zoroastrians "bury" their dead in circular towers to avoid the demon of the dead.

Zoroastrian tradition says that a dead body is unclean, and that the evil corpse demon would rush to a dead body to contaminate it and anything else it came in to contact with. For this reason, the Zoroastrians built towers with a roof containing three concentric rings (one for men, one for women, and one for children) on which they would place the dead bodies until they were completely destroyed by birds and sun. The remaining bones would then be shoved into a central well where they would remain buried inside the tower. This tradition continues to this day in Parsi communities in India.

3 SOAP PEOPLE

Bizarre Fact: Some humans turn into soap after they die.

In a process known as saponification, some human bodies turn partly or completely into soap (adipocere—also known as grave wax). The fatty tissue of the body, along with other liquids from putrefaction, slowly form into lumps of adipocere; this happens to both embalmed and non-embalmed bodies. It is especially common in people with large fat deposits in their bodies prior to death. The famous Mutter Museum has an exhibit of "The Soap Lady" who is entirely composed of grave wax. On occasion, these deposits can be seen leaking from closed tombs.

2 TO SPACE AND BEYOND

Bizarre Fact: It is now possible to be buried in space!

A company called Memorial Space Flights will now launch your loved one's cremated remains into outer space for a fee. In addition, they will provide you with a memorial service and an excellent spot from which to watch the rocket launch off with the remains. Because of the high price involved in each launch, the company only launches a small portion of the remains—the rest of the ashes are scattered to sea if you wish. Once your loved one is in space, you can go online to view the location of the rocket as it travels in its permanent orbit around the earth. The company offers a variety of different services to suit your budget: brief orbit and return to earth ($695), permanent orbit around earth ($2495), launch to surface of the moon ($9995), and launch into deep space ($12,500).

1 LIFEGEMS

Bizarre Fact: An American company will take your remains and turn them into a diamond that can be used by your loved ones.

The company uses the cremated remains of you or a pet to create synthetic diamonds, which range in weight and price. A full human body can provide sufficient carbon to make up to fifty one-carat diamonds (which cost around $14,000 each). After the carbon from the corpse is purified, it is converted to graphite, which is then used in the synthetic diamond process. The resulting diamond is engraved with the name of the dead and is accompanied by a certificate of authenticity. In 2007 the company used carbon extracted from strands of Ludwig van Beethoven's hair to produce three diamonds for charity. LifeGem retained one diamond, they donated one to John Reznikoff who provided the hair sample, and the third was sold on eBay for $202,700.

✳✳✳✳✳✳

TOP 10 BIZARRE OR FRIVOLOUS LAWSUITS

10 MAN VS. HIMSELF

In 1995 Robert Lee Brock, a prisoner in Virginia, wished to be removed from prison and placed in a mental institution. In order to achieve his goal, he decided to sue himself. He claimed that his crime was committed while he was drunk, which was a violation of his religious beliefs. He claimed that he had violated his own civil liberties. He sued himself for five million but to make matters worse, he claimed that the state should pay as he was behind bars and without an income. Thankfully the case was dismissed and Brock didn't get his transfer.

9 DUKES FAMILY VS. KILLER WHALE

In 1999, Daniel Dukes, a twenty-seven-year-old from Florida, hatched a clever plot so that he could have his lifelong dream of swimming with a whale fulfilled. He hid from the security guards at Sea World and managed to stay in the park after closing. Shortly after, he dived into the tank containing a killer whale— fulfilling his dream. Daniel was killed by the whale. His parents proceeded to sue Sea World because they did not display public warnings that a killer whale (named Tillikum in this instance) could kill people. They also claimed that the whale was wrongly portrayed as friendly because of the stuffed toys sold there.

8 NEW YORKER VS. SUBWAY

A twenty-seven-year-old New Yorker is suing Subway because he took a bite of a sandwich and found a seven-inch knife baked into the bread. The knife did not cut him and he did not swallow it. The reason he is suing is because he was violently ill with "severe stomach issues" for three hours and he claims that he caught food poisoning from the handle of the knife which was plastic and, according to the man, filthy. He is suing for one million dollars.

7 HOLY ROLLER VS. MAGICIANS

This is a true case of believe it or not. Christopher Roller, a resident of Minnesota, sued David Blaine and David Copperfield, demanding they reveal their secret magic tricks to him. He demanded 10 percent of their total income for life. The reason for the suit is that Roller believes that the magicians are defying the laws of physics, and thereby using godly powers. But it gets worse. Roller is suing not just because the magicians are using God's powers—he is suing because he thinks he is God and, therefore, it is his powers they are stealing.

6 MADERA CITY VS. TASERS

Marcy Noriega, a California police officer, decided to tase a suspect in the back of her car when he became uncontrollable and started kicking at the windows. Noriega drew her taser from her belt and fired it at the man. Unfortunately for the crook, the officer had accidentally drawn her gun instead, and she shot him in the chest, killing him. The city is now suing the taser company, arguing that any reasonable officer could mistakenly draw and shoot their gun instead of their taser. They are suing for the full costs of the wrongful death lawsuit that the man's family has filed against the city.

5 TRAFFIC COP VS. UNDERWEAR

This is a recent case in which a fifty-two-year-old traffic officer from Los Angeles sued Victoria's Secret for damage to her eye. The damage was caused, claims the cop, Macrida Patterson, when she was trying on a new thong. The tight fit caused a metal clip to fly off hitting her in the eye. The case was filed on June 9, 2008, and Officer Patterson is seeking unspecified damages. The courts have not yet informed the officer that as a traffic cop, she doesn't need fancy underwear as she is unlikely to ever have a date anyway.

4 PETA VS. DIVISION OF FISH AND WILDLIFE

PETA, the often-insane animal-loving organization, held an anti-hunt protest in 2001—defending the rights of deer to live. On the way home from the protest, two members hit a deer which had run on to the highway. The members informed the New Jersey Division of Fish and Wildlife that they intended to sue for damages and injuries. In their letter they stated that the Division was responsible for the damages "as a result of their deer management program, which includes, in certain circumstances, an affirmative effort to increase deer population."

3 MAN VS. ANHEUSER-BUSCH

For a while in the 1990s, Anheuser-Busch, the producers of Budweiser, ran a series of ads in which two beautiful women come to life in front of two truck drivers. A Michigan man bought a case of the beer, drank it, and failed to see two women materialize. Cue the lawsuit. He sued the company for false advertising, asking for a sum in excess of ten thousand dollars. Thankfully the court dismissed the suit and the man remained penniless and dateless.

2 WOMAN VS. ACT OF GOD

We all know that weather reports are frequently wrong and we take that into account when planning our days, but this was not the case for an Israeli woman who sued a TV station for making an inaccurate prediction. The station predicted good weather but it rained. The woman claimed that the forecast caused her to dress lightly, resulting in her catching the flu, missing a week of work, and spending money on medication. She further claimed that the whole incident caused her stress. She sued for one thousand dollars—and won.

1 COMMON SENSE VS. MCDONALD'S

In 1992, a seventy-nine-year-old Albuquerque woman (Stella Liebeck) bought a coffee from a McDonald's drive through. Her grandson was driving and he parked the car so she could add cream and sugar to the drink. She put the cup between her knees and pulled the lid toward her; inevitably the coffee spilled in her lap. She sued McDonald's for negligence because she claimed the coffee was too hot to be safe. Unbelievably the jury found that McDonald's was 80 percent responsible for the incident and they awarded Liebeck $160,000 in compensatory damages. But it gets worse: they awarded her $2.7 million punitive damages! The decision was appealed and the two parties ultimately ended up settling out of court for a sum less than $600,000.

✳✳✳✳✳✳

TOP 10 BIZARRE AFTERLIFE EXPERIMENTS

10 EVP EXPERIMENTS

EVP (electronic voice phenomena) is a mysterious event in which human-sounding voices from an unknown source are heard on recording tape, in radio station noise, and in other electronic media. Most often, EVPs have been captured on audiotape. The mysterious voices are not heard at the time of recording; it is only when the tape is played back that the voices are heard. Some skeptics say interpreting random sounds into voices in their own language would sound like random noise to a foreign speaker.

Interesting Fact: The 2005 film *White Noise* starring Michael Keaton focuses exclusively on the phenomenon of EVP as the main character attempts to contact his recently deceased wife.

9 DEAD WEIGHT EXPERIMENT

This is not the official name of this experiment, but I thought it had a nice ring to it. In 1907 Dr. Duncan MacDougall of Haverhill, Massachusetts, placed six terminal patients on a specially designed bed built on a scale and weighed them as they took their last breath. Based on results from the experiment, the patients lost approximately three-quarters of an ounce, equal to 21.3 grams. MacDougall also measured fifteen dogs in similar circumstances and reported the results as negative with no perceived change in weight. He took these results as confirmation that the human soul has weight and that dogs do not have souls. MacDougall's experiments were published in *The New York Times* and some medical journals.

Interesting Fact: MacDougall's complaints in his journal about not being able to find dogs dying of the natural causes led to the suspicion he was poisoning dogs to conduct his experiments. Also: These experiments inspired a film called *21 Grams* starring Sean Penn.

8 THE GOD HELMET EXPERIMENT

The God Helmet refers to a controversial experiment in neurotheology (study of correlations of neural phenomena) by Michael Persinger. When a modified snowmobile helmet is placed on the subject's head, magnetic fields start stimulating the brain. Persinger claims that near-death experiences such as bright lights, the presence of God, and seeing dead relatives are reproduced. Richard Dawkins, who is known for his atheistic views and criticism of religion, volunteered to test Persinger's device. Afterward, he admitted on BBC that he was very disappointed he did not experience communion with the universe or some other spiritual sensation. It should also be noted the helmet was also tested by a person that previously experienced a near-death experience and the results failed to duplicate the same sensation.

Interesting Fact: Persinger claims at least 80 percent of his participants experience a presence beside them in the room, which they variously say feels like God or someone they knew who had died.

7 THE PHILLIP EXPERIMENT

The Phillip Experiment was conducted in the early 1970s by the Toronto Society of Psychical Research. The purpose of the experiment was to see if a fictitious historical character could manifest itself through the group's efforts of concentration. They named the ghost Phillip and gave the ghost a personality and a complete background, even drawing a portrait to make him seem more real. The eight members in the group also memorized the fictional biography and studied the period in which Phillip was supposed to have lived. The séances proved nothing for many months until 1973 when Phillip began to communicate. He first came through as a solid rap on the table. In the months that followed, the group discovered that when they asked questions using one knock as "yes" and two as "no," they could actually have an intelligent conversation with their ghost.

Interesting Fact: The experiment came to a strange end when one member of the group broke ranks and stated aloud in a reply to Phillip, "we only made you up, you know." All communications stopped. Once the group denied that Phillip was real, he ceased to exist.

6 GHOST HUNTERS

Ghost Hunters is a reality television series that debuted in 2004. A team of investigators travel to locations reported to be haunted. To locate ghosts the team has experimented with Geiger counters, EMF (electromagnetic field) scanners, infrared and night vision cameras, handheld digital video cameras, digital audio recorders, and laptop computers. The ghost hunters claim to have several good recordings of strange mists, odd lights, moving objects, and shadowy figures that manifest before the camera and disappear quickly.

Interesting Fact: Critics and skeptics of the program point to a lack of scientific methodology and critical examination in their investigations as well as questionable production aspects including editing.

5 HARRY HOUDINI'S SECRET CODE EXPERIMENT

Houdini's training in magic allowed him to expose many mediums as frauds that had successfully fooled many scientists and academics. Fearing that spiritualists would exploit his legacy by pretending to contact him after his death, Houdini left his wife a secret code. Ten words were chosen at random from a letter written by Conan Doyle that he would use to contact her from the afterlife. After Houdini's death on October 31, 1926, a friend of Doyle, Rev. Arthur Ford, claimed to have contacted both Houdini and his deceased mother at a séance through his spirit guide. Ford stated the message received was in the prearranged code worked out by Houdini and his wife before Houdini's death. However, most believe Ford conspired with Doyle and also talked Houdini's wife (who was ill and self-medicating with alcohol) into conspiring to assist him in creating the impression he had contacted Houdini's spirit.

Interesting Fact: Houdini's wife, Bess, held yearly séances on Halloween for ten years after Houdini's death, but Houdini never appeared.

4 THE AFTERLIFE EXPERIMENTS

Gary Schwartz, a professor of psychology at the University of Arizona, wrote a book in 2002 called *The Afterlife Experiments.* In the experiments he used mediums and sitters (someone who had had very close relationships with people now dead) to investigate whether or not there is life after death. The mediums consistently came up with specific facts and names about the sitters' departed friends and relatives that the skeptics have been unable to explain away as fraud, cold reading, or lucky guesses. For the first sitter the results showed the mediums ranged from being 77 to 95 percent accurate. The average hit rate was 83 percent. The hit rate for the second sitter was similar to that of the first sitter. To rule out lucky guesses Schwartz set up a control group of sixty-eight students from the University of Arizona. The hit rate of the control group was just 36 percent.

Interesting Fact: When the 83 percent hit rate of the mediums was compared with the 36 percent of the control group, Schwartz claims the statistical probability of the control group difference occurring by chance is one in ten million.

3 SIR WILLIAM CROOKES'S EXPERIMENTS

Sir William Crookes was an English chemist and physicist and attended the Royal College of Chemistry in London. One of Crookes's accomplishments was the "Crookes Tube," which would lead to the discovery of cathode rays, x-rays, and the electron. Crookes had developed an interest in Spiritualism, possibly by the untimely death of his younger brother in 1867 at the age of twenty-one. In 1870 Crookes decided that science had a duty to experiment with the phenomena associated with Spiritualism. The conditions he imposed on mediums were as follows: "It must be at my own house, and my own selection of friends and spectators, under my own conditions, and I may do whatever I like as regards apparatus." Among the phenomena he said he witnessed were movement of bodies at a distance, changes in the weights of bodies, levitation, appearance of luminous objects, appearance of phantom figures, and the appearance of writing without human circumstances, which would point to the agency of an outside intelligence. His report on this research in 1874 concluded that these phenomena could not be explained and that further research would be useful.

Interesting Fact: Most scientists were convinced that Spiritualism was fraudulent, and Crookes's final report so outraged the scientific establishment that there was talk of depriving him of his Fellowship of the Royal Society.

2 THE REINCARNATION EXPERIMENTS

Australian psychologist Peter Ramster made a documentary in 1983 called *The Reincarnation Experiments*. During the experiments he found very convincing evidence of past lives. One of the individuals featured in the film remembered a life during the French Revolution. When under trance she spoke in French without any trace of an accent, understood and answered questions put to her in French, and knew the names of streets which had changed and were only discoverable on old maps.

Interesting Fact: General George S. Patton was a staunch believer in reincarnation and often claimed to have seen vivid, lifelike visions of his ancestors and also believed he was a reincarnation of Carthaginian General Hannibal.

1 THE SCOLE EXPERIMENT

In 1993 four psychic researchers and observers embarked on a series of experiments in the Norfolk village of Scole, England. For five years, more than five hundred experiments were carried out. During some of the experiments objects materialized, lights danced, and solid beings appeared. Luminous spheres also flew around the room in apparently intelligent manner. Messages were also transmitted on to audiotape. The experiments were repeated in the United States, Ireland, and Spain. In the United States scientists from NASA, the Institute of Noetic Sciences, and Stanford University also took part.

Interesting Fact: James Webster, a professional magician with forty years of experience investigating paranormal phenomena, came to the following conclusion: "I was unable to discover any sign of fraud, and it seems to me that fraud couldn't have been possible, both because of the type of phenomena observed and by the conditions in which they came about."

✻✻✻✻✻✻

TOP 10 BIZARRE FESTIVALS

10 LA TOMATINA

On the last Wednesday of August every year in the town of Buñol in the Valencia region of Spain, nine thousand locals and twenty to forty thousand foreigners descend on the town to throw tomatoes at each other in honor of the Virgin Mary and St. Louis Bertrand. The tradition has been around since the 1940s, though it was briefly suppressed under the reign of Franco. The festival starts with a person attempting to scale a greased pole to capture a cooked ham. Once the ham is taken down from the pole, water cannons are fired at the participants and over a hundred tons of tomatoes are dumped into the streets for throwing. Women are expected to wear white and men to wear no shirts. Anyone caught wearing a shirt inevitably has it ripped off, including women and especially tourists who tend to be the main target of the locals.

9 CHEESE ROLLING FESTIVAL

The Cheese Rolling Festival is held every May in Cooper's Hill, Gloucestershire in the United Kingdom. The festival involves an official tossing a cheese down the extremely steep hill, after which hundreds of people begin to run down the hill (risking life and limb) in order to catch the cheese. Each year the event results in casualties and, for this reason children are not allowed to participate, though oftentimes boys from the local town will join in anyway. For the children, there is an uphill race. Women and men race separately in the main event.

8 BONFIRES OF SAINT JOHN

The Bonfires of Saint John is a popular festival in Spain held on the 19th to the 24th of June. The strange festival involves the lighting of bonfires (frequently fueled by old furniture). The locals share hot chocolate while watching the bonfires. But then it gets weird. The children of the villages then take turns running through the fires. The entire week is filled with festivities including fireworks displays and eighty-six women and eighty-six young girls are elected the "Beauties" of the bonfires. These "Beauties" preside over the festival as queens.

7 GOAT TOSSING FESTIVAL

The Spanish certainly like their odd festivals. Every year on the fourth Sunday in January, the locals of a small town named Manganeses de la Polvorosa gather together for the Goat Tossing Festival, in honor of St. Vincent de Paul, their patron saint. The festival has been around for so long that no one knows when it started. It involves a young man who finds a goat in the village, ties it up, and takes it to the top of the local church belfry. He then tosses the goat over the side and it falls fifty feet to be hopefully caught by villagers holding up a sheet of tarpaulin. The village officials banned the event but it continues regardless. Various animal rights agencies have complained about it, though their complaints have also been ignored.

6 HADAKA MATSURI

Hadaka Matsuri is a Japanese festival in which the participants are all but naked. The festival is celebrated many times throughout the year in various parts of Japan and those involved usually wear a type of traditional loincloth. Some of those involved go completely naked, which is not frowned on at all—in fact it is considered healthy. The festivals often involve the use of mud (for entertainment) and there are often separate women's and men's festivals. In some towns special festivals are held for children as a rite of passage, but sometimes children participate in the adult festival. The festival has its origins as a religious event, but these days the religious aspects are virtually forgotten.

5 EL COLACHO

Dating from 1620, El Colacho (or baby jumping) is a festival in Spain held every year on the feast of Corpus Christi. The festival involves the laying on mattresses all babies born in the previous twelve months. The adult men of the village of Castrillo de Murcia then dress up as devils and take turns jumping over the babies. The festival often results in injuries (usually of the adults) and it is believed that the jumping rids the babies of original sin—a bizarre kind of baptism. Pope Benedict XVI has recently asked the local priests to distance themselves from the festival as it is dangerous and contrary to the Catholic religion.

4 FIESTA DE SANTA MARTA DE RIBARTEME

Every year in Las Nieves, Spain, people who have suffered a near-death experience in the previous year get together to attend Mass in celebration of Saint Marta de Ribarteme, the patron saint of resurrection. But here is the twist: they turn up at Mass carrying a coffin, or being carried in a coffin. After Mass, the coffins all process to the top of a nearby hill with a statue of the saint. Despite the somberness of the event, people light fireworks and shopkeepers fill the streets to sell religious objects.

3 GOOSE CLUBBING FESTIVAL

Until recently, an annual festival was held in Germany in which a goose was tied by its feet to a post and then clubbed by the local men until its head came off. As a result of complaints from animal rights activists, the festivalgoers now hit a goose which has previously been killed. A very similar event occurs in Spain (surprise, surprise) every year in which a man hangs from the goose until the head comes off. Again the goose is killed prior to the event that dates back 350 years. The Spanish festival is called Antzar Eguna.

2 KANAMARA MATSURI

Every year in Spring, the festival of Kanamara Matsuri (The Steel Phallus) is held in Kawasaki, Japan. It is a Shinto fertility festival and, as you would expect, it involves a rather large penis statue. During the festival, people can buy candies, vegetables, and gifts in the shape of a phallus. The festival was very popular among prostitutes who thought participation would help prevent them getting sexually transmitted diseases.

1 THAIPUSAM

Thaipusam is a Hindu festival (celebrated mostly by Tamils) held in January/February each year to celebrate the birth of Murugan (the son of gods Shiva and Parvati). The participants shave their heads and perform a pilgrimage, at the end of which they shove very sharp skewers through their tongues or cheeks. Some of the practitioners put hooks into their backs and pull heavy objects like tractors. The aim is to cause as much pain as possible—the more you endure, the more "blessings" you receive from the gods. The festival is popular in India, but the largest celebrations take place in Singapore and Malaysia, where it is a public holiday.

✳✳✳✳✳✳

TOP 10 INCREDIBLY ECCENTRIC PEOPLE

10 HETTY GREEN, 1834–1916

Hetty Green was an eccentric miser who became known as the "Witch of Wall Street." With her business acumen she accumulated such wealth that she was the richest woman in the world. In order to save money, Hetty would work out of trunks at her local bank so she wouldn't have to pay rent. When her son fell ill, she disguised herself and took him to a charity hospital; when they realized who she was, she fled claiming she would cure her son herself. Unfortunately, he contracted gangrene and had to have his leg amputated. She always wore the same black dress and never changed her underwear unless it wore out. She moved back and forth between New York and New Jersey in order to avoid the taxman.

9 WILLIAM ARCHIBALD SPOONER, 1844–1930

William Archibald Spooner is forever locked into history because the linguistic phenomenon known as a "spoonerism" is named after him. A spoonerism involves the accidental (or sometimes intentional) swapping of letters, words, or vowels in a sentence, for example: "Go and shake a tower" (meaning "go and take a shower"). Spooner was a professor at Oxford and he became so famous for his spoonerisms people would attend his lectures just to hear him make a mistake. He was not pleased about the great publicity that surrounded him but as he neared death his attitude softened and he gave interviews to the press. Spooner not only got his words wrong, he once wrote to a fellow professor to ask him to come immediately to help solve a problem. At the end of the letter he added a postscript that the matter had been resolved and he needn't come. Some spoonerisms attributed to Spooner are:

> *"Mardon me padam, this pie is occupewed. Can I sew you to another sheet?" (Pardon me, madam, this pew is occupied. Can I show you to another seat?)*

> *"Let us glaze our asses to the queer old Dean" (...raise our glasses to the dear old Queen)*

> *"We'll have the hags flung out" (...flags hung out)*

8 SIMEON ELLERTON, 1702–1799

Simeon Ellerton lived in the eighteenth century and was a fitness fanatic. Because he loved to walk long distances, he was often employed to carry out errands or act as a courier for the locals. On his many frequent journeys he would gather up stones from the roadside and carry them on his head. His aim was to gather sufficient stones to build his own house. Eventually he had enough stones and made a little cottage for himself. Having spent so many years carrying extra weight, he felt uncomfortable without it, so for the rest of his life he walked around with a bag of stones on his head.

7 JOHN CHRISTIE, 1882–1962

John Christie and his wife are most well known for starting the Glyndeborne Opera Festival, but John was also a famed British eccentric. One evening while sitting next to the queen during the opera, he removed his glass eye, cleaned it, put it back in its socket, and asked the queen whether it was in straight. If he got too hot, he would cut the arms off his formal jacket, which he would often wear with a pair of old tennis shoes. He owned 180 handkerchiefs, 110 shirts, and despite paying tens of thousands of pounds on an opera production, would travel third class and carry his own luggage to avoid tipping. For a while, Christie would wear nothing but lederhosen and, in 1933, he expected all guests of the opera to do the same.

6 OSCAR WILDE, 1854–1900

Oscar Wilde is undoubtedly the most famous member of this list—and for good reason. During a time of moral conservatism, Wilde managed to survive his youth decked out in flamboyant clothing exuding eccentricity, because of his stunning wit—the true cause of his celebrity. While studying at Oxford University, Oscar would walk through the streets with a lobster on a leash. His room was decorated with bright blue china, sunflowers, and peacock feathers. He was the direct opposite of what Victorian England expected a man to be and he flaunted it for all he was worth. Unfortunately, an affair with Lord Alfred Douglas brought an end to a brilliant career when Wilde was jailed for sodomy.

5 SIR GEORGE SITWELL, 1860–1943

Sir George Sitwell (father of the famous writer Dame Edith Sitwell) was a very bizarre man in many ways. He was a keen gardener (he actually studied garden design) and, annoyed by the wasps in his garden, he invented a pistol for shooting them. After he moved to Italy to avoid taxes in Britain, he refused to pay his new wife's debts, which resulted in her spending three months in prison. He was such an avid reader and collector of books that he had seven libraries in his home. Other eccentricities included paying his son an allowance based on the amount paid by one of his forebears to his son during the Black Death, and trying to pay his son's Eton school fees with produce from his garden. But perhaps most bizarrely, Sir George had the cows on his estate stenciled in a blue and white Chinese willow pattern in order to make them look better. This is the notice that Sir George hung on the gate of his manor in Derbyshire, England: "I must ask anyone entering the house never to contradict me or differ from me in any way, as it interferes with the functioning of my gastric juices and prevents my sleeping at night."

4 GERALD TYRWHITT-WILSON, 1883–1950

Also known as Lord Berners, Gerald Tyrwhitt-Wilson got off to a strange start in life with a super-religious grandmother and a prejudiced mother. When he was nine he was sent to boarding school where he had a relationship with an older boy; the relationship ended when Berners vomited on him. As an adult, Berners became a relatively good composer and writer and an extremely eccentric man. He had the pigeons at his stately home dyed in a variety of colors and kept a pet giraffe with which he would have afternoon tea regularly. His chauffeur had to fit his Rolls Royce out with a harpsichord so Berners could play music while being driven around the countryside. He left his estate to his much younger companion, the equally eccentric Robert Heber-Percy.

3 FRANCIS EGERTON, 1756–1823

Francis Egerton (8th Earl of Bridgewater) inherited his title along with a very large fortune in 1823. He became famous for his unusual dinner parties, which he threw for dogs. All of the invited dogs would be dressed in the finest fashions of the day, including shoes. Another eccentricity was his manner of measuring time; Egerton would wear a pair of shoes only once—when he was done with them, he would line them up in rows in order to count the passing days. He also kept pigeons and partridges which had their wings clipped so he could shoot them for sport even with failing eyesight. When he died, he left a large number of important documents on the subject of French and Italian literature to the British Museum, as well as a large financial donation to the Royal Society.

2 WILLIAM BUCKLAND, 1784–1856

William Buckland is famous for two things: he was the first man to write a full account of a fossil, and he was incredibly eccentric when it came to animals and food. Buckland's love of natural history resulted in his house being something akin to a zoo. He filled it with animals of every kind and he then proceeded to eat them all (and serve them to guests). He claimed to have eaten his way through every animal. The worst-tasting creatures, he said, were bluebottle flies and moles. Various dinner guests describe being served panther, crocodile, and mouse. A famous storyteller at the time (Augustus Hare) told this tale of Buckland: "Talk of strange relics led to mention of the heart of a French King [Louis XIV] preserved at Nuneham in a silver casket. Dr. Buckland, whilst looking at it, exclaimed, 'I have eaten many strange things, but have never eaten the heart of a king before,' and, before anyone could hinder him, he had gobbled it up, and the precious relic was lost for ever."

1 JEMMY HIRST, 1738–1829

If you thought the previous entries were eccentric, you are in for a surprise. Jemmy (James) Hirst was so famous an eccentric in his own time that King George III summoned him to tea. When he received the invitation, Hirst declined, stating he was training an otter to fish. Eventually he did visit the king, and he threw a goblet of water over a courtier who was laughing; Hirst believed the man was having a fit of hysteria. The king gave him a number of bottles of wine from the royal cellar. Jemmy loved animals and he trained his bull to behave like a horse. The bull (named Jupiter) would draw his carriage about the village and Hirst even rode him in foxhunts. Instead of dogs, he used pigs he had trained as hunt dogs. He regularly blew a horn to invite the poor to his home for free food, which was served out of a coffin. When he died, he requested twelve old maids to follow his coffin to the grave, as well as a bagpiper and a fiddler to play happy music.

✳✳✳✳✳✳

CHAPTER TWO

Crime

TOP 10 LESSER-KNOWN SERIAL KILLERS

10 GERARD SCHAEFER

Gerard Schaefer, a policeman, was convicted in 1973 of only two murders, but it is believed he was responsible for more than thirty killings in total. He was a sexual beast who would lure women off the roads with his police badge and eventually rape, torture, mutilate, and murder them. He would leave the women tied to trees while he went to work as a police officer. Parts of his victims' bodies and clothing were found in a trunk in his mother's attic.

9 FRITZ HAARMANN

Fritz Haarmann lived in Germany during a severe economic depression in 1918. He seduced a young runaway named Friedel Roth who had run away from home. Friends of Roth eventually led the police to Haarmann's home. When they entered, they found Haarmann in bed with another young boy for which he was sentenced to nine months in prison. Unfortunately, the police did not search Haarmann's house—if they had done so, they would have found Roth's head stuffed behind the stove wrapped in newspaper. This was not known until Haarmann confessed five years later.

8 JOHN ROBINSON

John Robinson was connected to the murders or disappearances of eleven women. A sadomasochist, Robinson would lure women through the Internet or personal ads to appease his sexual appetite. After sixteen years of killing and cashing in on the Social Security checks of his victims, Robinson was caught when two barrels, each containing a female body, were found on his Kansas property.

7 ARTHUR SHAWCROSS

Arthur Shawcross (also known as the "Genesee River Killer") started his killing rampage when he was fighting in the Vietnam War. He claimed to have murdered and eaten two young Vietnamese girls. When he returned to the United States he murdered a ten-year-old boy and an eight-year-old girl. He was arrested and went to jail for fifteen years for these crimes. After his release he began murdering prostitutes (eleven in total). He was caught when the police saw him masturbating in his car near the spot where one victim had been found.

6 DENNIS NILSEN

Dennis Nilsen was a Scottish serial killer who lived in London. He is unique in that he does not fit the standard serial killer profile. Nilsen killed for friendship and company. He would invite a young man to his home and after sexual relations would kill him out of fear he would be left alone in the morning. He would then leave the corpse in his apartment for days so he could place it in various poses (such as watching television or sleeping in bed) as if the body were his boyfriend. When a local plumber found bones and rotting flesh in the apartment's sewerage system, Nilsen was arrested and ultimately sentenced to life in prison for murdering fifteen young men.

5 BOBBY JOE LONG

Bobby Joe Long had an unusual childhood; until the age of thirteen he shared a bed with his mother and the two frequently traveled from the home of one relative to another. During that time, Bobby Joe suffered many head injuries, which are believed to have been accidental. Between 1980 and 1983, Long terrorized Miami, Ocala, and Fort Lauderdale where he would seek out housewives whose husbands were at work so he could bind and rape them. He strangled and shot at least nine victims, though authorities believe there was a tenth victim. He was sentenced to death for killing nine women and raping fifty.

4 CARL PANZRAM

After suffering years of torture, sexual abuse, and beatings, Carl Panzram became one of America's most violent and hateful serial killers. He committed crimes in Europe, the United States, and South America. In 1920 he committed his first murder—killing sailors in New York he lured from a bar. He also raped and killed two small boys he beat to death with a rock. Speaking of his own life, Panzram said, "my only regret is that I wasn't born dead or not at all."

3 LARRY EYLER

Larry Eyler (the "Highway Killer") began picking men up along highways when he was in his thirties. He would invite the men into his car under the guise of having consensual sex with a little light bondage. He would take the men to a secluded area, handcuff and brutally beat them. Most victims were found disemboweled with their pants pulled down. Eyler was observed dumping eight trash bags found to contain the remains of a fifteen-year-old boy into a dumpster. Eyler was sentenced to die by lethal injection but he died of AIDS before he could be executed. In all, he murdered twenty-one men.

2 PETER SUTCLIFFE
Peter Sutcliffe (the "Yorkshire Ripper") began killing in 1975. He was to ultimately murder thirteen women and attempt to kill another seven. The survivors were left with such emotional scars that psychologists said they would never fully recover. He would usually knock his victims unconscious with a ball-peen hammer and then mutilate them with knives and sometimes a screwdriver. In February 2009, Sutcliffe was declared "fit" to leave Broadmoor high-security prison. It is possible he will be released on "rehabilitation leave."

1 PETER KURTEN
In the summer of 1929, a fresh corpse was found nearly weekly in the German city of Dusseldorf. Most victims were young women—horribly slashed or bludgeoned to death. Peter Kurten (the "Vampire of Dusseldorf") prowled for victims at night—seeking sexual satisfaction by swallowing the blood of his victims as he cut their throats. For eighteen months Kurten was on a rampage. He ultimately killed over thirty people. He was executed by guillotine.

❋❋❋❋❋❋

TOP 10 AMAZING EXECUTION SURVIVAL STORIES

10 ELIZABETH PROCTOR, CIRCA 1652
In 1692 Elizabeth Proctor and her husband John were accused of witchcraft in the Salem Witch Trials. After their arrest the court met to discuss the fate of John and Elizabeth and several others. In spite of the petitions

and testimonies from friends, both John and Elizabeth were found guilty and sentenced to death. Elizabeth, who was pregnant at the time, was granted a stay of execution until after the birth of the baby. John tried to postpone his execution, but failed. On August 19, 1692, he was executed. In January 1693, while still in prison, Elizabeth gave birth to a son. For some reason, Elizabeth was not executed as the court had ordered and then, in 1693, the governor, believing that people were being wrongly convicted without hard evidence, ordered 153 people set free. Elizabeth was among this general release of prisoners.

9 JOHN HENRY GEORGE LEE, 1864–CIRCA 1945

In 1884 at her home at Torquay, England, Miss Emma Keyse was bludgeoned to death with an axe, her throat slashed with a knife, and her house set on fire. John Lee, who was one of the servants at the house, was arrested and convicted of her murder and sentenced to death by hanging. The date for the hanging was set for February 23, 1885, at the Exeter Prison. When Lee was standing at the gallows waiting to die the trapdoor release malfunctioned. Not once, not twice, but three times! Amid the confusion of these botched attempts Lee was returned to his cell and at some later time the Home Secretary reduced his sentence to life imprisonment with the recommendation he never be released.

8 ZOLEYKHAH KADKHODA, BORN 1977

In 1997 in Iran, twenty-year-old Zoleykhah Kadkhoda was arrested and charged with engaging in sexual relations outside marriage. She was immediately sentenced to death by stoning. Kadkhoda was then buried up to her waist in preparation for her execution but soon after the stoning began it prompted a violent reaction among most of the village inhabitants, which caused the stoning to stop. It was first thought the woman had died and she was taken to the morgue but she began to breathe again and was taken to the hospital. Her condition improved and an appeal for amnesty was submitted to the court on her behalf.

7 JOHN SMITH, CIRCA 1690

John Smith, from England, was convicted of robbery and was sentenced to death by hanging at Tyburn. On Christmas Eve, 1705, having been pushed off the back of the cart, he dangled for fifteen minutes until the crowd began to shout, "reprieve." He was then cut down and taken to a nearby house where he soon recovered. When Smith was asked what it had felt like to be hanged, this is what he told his rescuers: "When I was turned off I was, for some time, sensible of very great pain occasioned by the weight of my body and felt my spirits in strange commotion, violently pressing upwards. Having forced their way to my head I saw a great blaze or glaring light that seemed to go out of my eyes in a flash and then I lost all sense of pain. After I was cut down, I began to come to myself and the blood and spirits forcing themselves into their former channels put me by a prickling or shooting into such intolerable pain that I could have wished those hanged who had cut me down."

6 ANNE GREEN, CIRCA 1630

Anne Green was a twenty-two-year-old woman from England who was, most likely, seduced by the grandson of her employer. When Green became pregnant she hid her pregnancy and gave birth to a premature baby boy who died soon after he was born. After trying unsuccessfully to hide the child's body, Green was accused of the murder and sentenced to death by hanging. She hanged for thirty minutes until her body was cut down and placed in a coffin and taken to a local doctor who gave anatomy lectures at the university. When the doctors and others assembled for the dissection opened the coffin, they noticed the corpse was breathing and making noises. After being given hot drinks she opened her eyes. The treatment continued with bloodletting and twelve hours after the execution Anne Green was able to say a few words. After her unique rescue the court usher attending the execution and the prison director of Oxford agreed that Anne Green should be reprieved. Green later married, had three children, and lived for fifteen years after her famous execution.

5 WILLIAM DUELL, 1724

In 1740, sixteen-year-old William Duell was convicted of raping and murdering a girl in the village of Tyburn, London. Duell was sentenced to death by hanging along with four others. During this time period, bodies of criminals were regularly provided to medical training colleges, so after the execution Duell's body was brought to Surgeons' Hall to be anatomized. After he was stripped and laid on the board one of the surgeons noticed he was breathing.

After Duell's breath became quicker and quicker the surgeon took some blood from him and in two hours he was able to sit up in his chair. That evening the authorities decided to grant him a reprieve and reduced his sentence.

4 WENSESLAO MOGUEL, CIRCA 1880

On March 18, 1915, Wenseslao Moguel was captured while fighting in the Mexican Revolution. He was sentenced without trial to execution by firing squad. Moguel was shot nine times, with the final bullet fired close range at his head. Moguel somehow survived and managed to escape. He went on to live a full life after his "execution."

3 JOSEPH SAMUEL, CIRCA 1780

Joseph Samuel was born in England and later transported to Australia after committing a robbery in 1801. He became involved in a gang in Sydney and robbed the home of a wealthy woman. A policeman who was stationed at her home was murdered. The gang was soon caught and at the trial Joseph Samuel confessed to stealing the goods but denied being part of the murder. The leader of the gang was released due to lack of evidence and Joseph Samuel was sentenced to death by hanging. In 1803, Samuel and another criminal were driven in a cart to Parramatta where hundreds of people came to view the event. After praying, the cart on which they were standing drove off, but instead of being hanged, the rope around Samuel's neck snapped! The executioner tried again. This time, the rope slipped and his legs touched the ground. With the crowd in an uproar, the executioner tried for the third time and the rope snapped again. This time, an officer galloped off to tell the governor what had happened and his sentence was commuted to life imprisonment. The governor and others believed that it was a sign from God that Samuel should not be hanged.

2 MAGGIE DICKSON, CIRCA 1700

Maggie Dickson lived in Edinburgh, Scotland, in the early eighteenth century. Her story is remarkably similar to Anne Green's. After her husband deserted her in 1723, she was forced to move further south to Kelso near the Scottish Borders. She worked for an innkeeper in return for basic lodgings and started an affair with the innkeeper's son, which led to her becoming pregnant. Not wanting the innkeeper to discover this because it would lead to her dismissal, she concealed her pregnancy as long as possible. The baby was born prematurely and died within a few days of being born. She then planned to put the baby into the River Tweed but couldn't bring herself to and finally left it on the riverbank. The same day the baby was discovered and traced to Maggie and in 1724 she was charged under the contravention of the Concealment of Pregnancy. Maggie was taken back to Grasssmarket for her public execution by hanging. After the hanging she was pronounced dead and her body was bound for Musselburgh where she was to be buried, however, the journey was interrupted by a knocking and banging from within the wooden coffin. The lid was lifted to find Maggie alive and well. The law saw it as God's will and she was freed to live for another forty years.

1 WILLIE FRANCIS, 1929–1947

In 1945, Willie Francis, age sixteen, was charged with the murder of a drugstore owner in St. Martinville, Louisiana. The murder went unsolved for nine months until Francis was detained due to an unrelated crime. Police claimed he was carrying the wallet of the drugstore owner in his pocket. A short time later, Francis confessed to the murder. He later directed the police to where he had disposed of the holster used to carry the murder weapon. Despite two separate written confessions, Francis pleaded not guilty. The state-appointed defense attorneys offered no objections, called no witnesses, and put up no defense. Two days after the trial began, Francis was convicted of murder and sentenced to death by the electric chair. On May 3, 1946, as the lethal surge of electricity was being applied, witnesses reported hearing the teenager scream, "Take it off! Take it off! Let me breathe!" Another report states that he heard Willie say, "I'm n-not dying!" The electric chair failed to kill Willie Francis. It turned out that an intoxicated prison guard had improperly set up the portable electric chair. After the botched execution, Francis appealed to the Supreme Court citing various violations of his Fifth, Eighth, and Fourteenth Amendment rights. The appeal was rejected and Willie Francis was executed on May 9, 1947, over a year after his first execution.

※※※※※※

TOP 10 AMAZING PRISON ESCAPES

10 MAZE PRISON ESCAPE

In September 1983, thirty-eight Irish Republican Army (IRA) prisoners executed the biggest prison escape in British history. The prisoners were incarcerated at the Maze Prison in County Antrim, Northern Ireland. Using smuggled guns, the prisoners took the guards hostage, stole their clothing, and forced a food delivery truck to drive them out of the prison. All thirty-eight managed to escape the maximum security prison, then considered to be one of the most escape-proof prisons in Europe.

9 ALFRED HINDS

"Alfie" Hinds was a petty criminal, who also happened to be an expert escape artist as he was to prove over the years through his numerous prison escapes. In his most daring escape, Hinds sneaked through the locked doors and a twenty-foot prison wall at Nottingham Prison. For this seemingly miraculous escape, he was dubbed "Houdini Hinds." When he was captured six months later, he sued the authorities for illegal arrest. Needless to say, he lost.

8 THE TEXAS SEVEN

The Texas Seven is a very well-known group of prisoners who escaped from the John Connally Unit in Texas in 2000. The group used the slowest period of the day to escape by overpowering civilian maintenance workers and prison guards. They used a maintenance truck to leave the prison. They were caught a month later thanks to the television show *America's Most Wanted*. Five members of the group remain and are all on death row awaiting execution.

7 ALFRÉD WETZLER

Alfréd Wetzler was a Slovak Jew and one of only a few people who managed to escape from Auschwitz during the war. Thanks to his escape, a detailed report (known as the Vrba-Wetzler report) of the horrors of Auschwitz reached the Allies. It was the first report of the atrocities being committed by the Nazi regime. Wearing stolen suits and overcoats, Wetzler and his friend Rudolf Vrba hid out in a woodpile for four nights until they were able to walk away from the camp uninterrupted. They walked for eighty miles using a map from a child's atlas that Vrba had found in the camp.

6 SŁAWOMIR RAWICZ

Sławomir Rawicz and six other prisoners managed to escape from one of the harshest environments possible—the frozen wasteland of a Siberian prison camp. Rawicz (a Polish national) was sentenced to twenty-five years hard labor for spying on the Soviets. By using a blizzard as cover, the group was able to leave the camp, after which they walked all the way from Siberia to India (four thousand miles) in a journey that took nearly one year. Only four of the group survived the journey.

5 ESCAPE FROM ALCATRAZ

Alcatraz operated as a prison for twenty-nine years, during which there were fourteen escape attempts. Of those attempts, one is especially famous. In 1962, Frank Morris and the Anglin Brothers burrowed from their cells and climbed to the top of the cellblock. They were able to cut through the bars of an air vent and climb onto the open roof. From there they shimmied down a drainpipe and escaped to the edge of the island where they built a raft and vanished. While many people believe that the three died in the San Francisco Bay, they were never found and there is every possibility they survived the journey and are in hiding.

4 LIBBY PRISON ESCAPE

The Libby Prison Escape is one of the most famous prison breaks of the American Civil War. In 1864, 109 Union soldiers escaped from the prison in Richmond, Virginia. Of the escapees, fifty-nine succeeded in reaching Union Lines, while the rest were captured or died in the process. The prisoners escaped by digging a tunnel from the basement of the jail to a nearby warehouse.

3 PASCAL PAYET

There can be no doubt this man deserves a place on this list—he has escaped not once, but twice from high-security prisons in France—each time via hijacked helicopter! He also helped organize the escape of three other prisoners, again with a helicopter. Payet was initially sentenced to a thirty-year jail term for a murder committed while robbing a security van. After his first escape (in 2001) he was captured and given seven more years in jail. He then escaped from Grasse Prison using a helicopter that was hijacked by four of his friends from the nearby airport. The helicopter eventually landed at Brignoles, twenty-four miles northeast of Toulon, France, on the Mediterranean coast. Payet was recaptured on September 21, 2007, in Mataró, Spain, about eighteen miles northeast of Barcelona. He had undergone cosmetic surgery, but was still identified by Spanish police.

2 THE GREAT ESCAPE

The Great Escape is one of the most inspirational and incredible tales of a jailbreak. In 1943, a group of prisoners of war hatched a plot to dig their way out of Stalag Luft III. Over the next year, the prisoners worked together to dig three tunnels thirty feet below the surface of the prison. As the tunnels were so large and deep, the group came up with many innovative tricks, such as building a rail car system for the transportation of soil, electric lighting, and air pumps to keep the tunnel full of fresh oxygen. Eventually seventy-six men were able to escape the prison using one of the tunnels. Of the seventy-six, only three managed to evade capture. The rest were killed or sent back to the prison.

1 COLDITZ ESCAPE

During World War II, two British pilots (Jack Best and Bill Goldfinch) were imprisoned in Colditz Castle. The prison was famously difficult to escape from but Best and Goldfinch came up with a particularly novel approach to the problem; they decided to build a glider and fly away. They assembled the glider from stolen pieces of wood—floorboards, bed slats, and virtually anything they could get their hands on. Because they were building the glider in the attic, the German soldiers (who were used to looking down for tunnels) did not notice them. The two men never had a chance to use the glider as the camp was relieved by the Allies before they finished it, but a model based on their original plan was later proven to have been able to fly.

❋❋❋❋❋❋

TOP 10 GRUESOME ANCIENT METHODS OF EXECUTION

10 BRAZEN BULL

The Brazen Bull was invented by Perilaus of Athens (a Brass worker) in the sixth century BC and offered to Phalaris, Tyrant of Agrigentum, as a gift. It was a large brass bull that was completely hollow inside with a door on the side large enough for a man to enter. Once the man was inside the bull, a fire would be lit beneath it in order to roast him to death. In the head of the bull, Perilaus put a series of tubes and stops that were designed to amplify the screams of the victim and make them sound like the roar of a bull.

Interestingly, Perilaus was the first person to feel the pain of the Brazen Bull. After Perilaus said to Phalaris, "[his screams] will come to you through the pipes as the tenderest, most pathetic, most melodious of bellowings," Phalaris was so disgusted that he tricked Perilaus into entering the bull. Lucian recounts the tale:

> "His words revolted me. I loathed the thought of such ingenious cruelty, and resolved to punish the artificer in kind. 'If this is anything more than an empty boast, Perilaus,' I said to him, 'if your art can really produce this effect, get inside yourself, and pretend to roar; and we will see whether the pipes will make such music as you describe.' He consented; and when he was inside I closed the aperture, and ordered a fire to be kindled. 'Receive,' I cried, 'the due reward of your wondrous art: let the music-master be the first to play.'" (Phalaris I:12)

Perilaus was removed from the Bull before he died and Phalaris had him thrown off a cliff. The Brazen Bull became one of the most common methods of execution in ancient Greece.

9 HANGING, DRAWING, AND QUARTERING

Hanging, drawing, and quartering was the common form of punishment in England for the crime of treason considered the worst crime you could commit. The punishment was only applied to men; women found guilty of treason were burnt at the stake. Unbelievably, this punishment remained in law until 1814.

The first stage of the execution was to be tied to a wooden frame and dragged behind a horse to the place of your death. Following that, the criminal would be hanged until they were nearly dead. The criminal would then be removed from the noose and laid on a table. The executioner would then disembowel and emasculate the victim, and burn the entrails in front of his eyes. He would still be alive at this point. The person would then be beheaded and their body cut in to quarters. Samuel Pepys, in his famous diary, was an eyewitness at one of these executions:

> "To my Lord's in the morning, where I met with Captain Cuttance, but my Lord not being up I went out to Charing Cross, to see Major-general Harrison hanged, drawn, and quartered; which was done there, he looking as cheerful as any man could do in that condition. He was presently cut down, and his head and heart shown to the people, at which there was great shouts of joy. It is said, that he said that he was sure to come shortly at the right hand of Christ to judge them that now had judged him; and that his wife do expect his coming again. Thus it was my chance to see the King beheaded at White Hall, and to see the first blood shed in revenge for the blood of the King at Charing Cross."

The normal practice was to send the five parts of the body to various areas where they would be put on display on a gibbet as a warning to others.

8 BURNING

Burning at the stake was normally done in one of two ways. In the first, the victim would be led to the center of a wall of sticks and straw and tied to the stake, after which the space between the criminal and the wall would be filled with wood, concealing the person. It is believed this is the manner in which St. Joan of Arc was burnt. The other method was to pile sticks and straw up to the level of the calves only.

When performed by a skilled executioner, the person would burn in this sequence: calves, thighs and hands, torso and forearms, breasts, upper chest, face, and then, finally, death. Needless to say this would have been excruciating. If a large number of people were to be burnt at the same time, death could occur through carbon monoxide poisoning before the fire reached you. If the fire was small, you could die of shock, blood loss, or heatstroke.

In later versions of burning at the stake, the criminal would be hanged until dead and then burnt symbolically. This method of execution was used to burn witches in most parts of Europe, but it was not used in England for that purpose.

7 LING CHI

Ling chi—execution by slow cutting—was practiced in China until it was outlawed in 1905. In the execution, the criminal is slowly cut in the arms, legs, and chest, until finally they are beheaded or stabbed in the heart. Many Western accounts of the execution method are largely exaggerated, with some claiming that the execution could take days to perform.

One modern eyewitness report from journalist and politician Henry Norman describes an execution thus:

> "The criminal is fastened to a rough cross, and the executioner, armed with a sharp knife, begins by grasping handfuls from the fleshy parts of the body, such as the thighs and the breasts, and slicing them off. After this he removes the joints and the excrescences of the body one by one—the nose and ears, fingers, and toes. Then the limbs are cut off piecemeal at the wrists and the ankles, the elbows and knees, the shoulders and hips. Finally, the victim is stabbed to the heart and his head cut off."

6 BREAKING WHEEL

The breaking wheel was also known as the Catherine wheel and it was a medieval execution device. The criminal would be attached to a cart wheel and his arms and legs stretched out along the spokes. The wheel would be made to turn while a heavy metal bar or hammer would deliver bone-breaking blows to various parts of the body between the spokes. If a merciful execution had been ordered, after a large number of bones were shattered, fatal blows would be delivered. In cases where mercy was not offered, the criminal would remain on the wheel until they died; this could sometimes take days and the person would die of shock and dehydration.

After the shattering was complete, the limbs of the person would be woven between the spokes and the wheel would be hoisted to the top of a pole for birds to eat the, sometimes still living, body.

In France, a special grace was sometimes offered in which the criminal would be strangled to death before the blows were delivered, or after only two or three.

5 BOILING

In execution by boiling, the condemned is stripped naked and either placed in a vat of boiling liquid, or in a vat of cold liquid which was then heated to boiling. The liquid could be oil, acid, tar, water, or molten lead. During the reign of King Henry VIII it was a punishment especially reserved for poisoners.

> *"The preamble of the statute of Henry VIII (which made poisoning treason) in 1531 recites that one Richard Roose (or Coke), a cook, by putting poison in some food intended for the household of the bishop of Rochester and for the poor of the parish of Lambeth, killed a man and woman. He was found guilty of treason and sentenced to be boiled to death without benefit of clergy. He was publicly boiled at Smithfield. In the same year a maid-servant for poisoning her mistress was boiled at King's Lynn."* (Encyclopedia Britannica, 1911)

The "Chronicle of the Grey Friars of London," published by the Camden Society, has an account of a case at Smithfield, in which a man was fastened to a chain and let down into boiling water several times until he was dead. In modern days, Idi Amin has been accused of using this method of execution on his enemies:

4 FLAYING

Execution by flaying is when the skin of the criminal is removed from their body with the use of a very sharp knife. Attempts are made to keep the skin intact. This is a very ancient method of execution. The apostle Bartholomew was flayed and crucified upside down. His skin and bones are kept in a Cathedral in Sicily.

There are accounts of Assyrians flaying the skin from a captured enemy or rebellious ruler and nailing it to the wall of his city, as warning to all who would defy their power. The Aztecs of Mexico flayed victims of ritual human sacrifice, generally after death.

While this method of execution is not lawful in any country, in 2000, government troops in Myanmar (Burma) allegedly flayed all of the males of a Karenni village.

3 NECKLACING

Necklacing is a type of execution in which a rubber tire is filled with gasoline, forced over the arms and chest of the victim, and set afire. It was a common practice in South Africa during the 1980s and 1990s anti-apartheid struggle. Necklacing has also occurred in Brazil and Haiti, and at least one person was killed by this method in Nigeria during Muslim protests over the Muhammad cartoons.

2 SCAPHISM

Scaphism is an ancient Persian method of execution. According to Wikipedia, a naked person would be firmly fastened within a back-to-back pair of narrow rowboats (or in some variations a hollowed-out tree trunk), the head, hands, and feet protruding from this improvised container. The condemned was forced to ingest milk and honey to the point of developing severe diarrhea, and more honey would be rubbed on his body so as to attract insects to the exposed appendages. They would then be left to float on a stagnant pond (or alternately, simply exposed to the sun somewhere). The defenseless individual's feces accumulated within the container, attracting more insects, which would eat and breed within his exposed (and increasingly gangrenous) flesh. Death, when it eventually occurred, was probably due to a combination of dehydration, starvation, and septic shock.

Plutarch writes that it took Mithridates seventeen days to die by this method of execution. Native American Indians also used a similar method of execution where they would tie the victim to a tree, smear him, and leave him to the ants. Because he was not previously force-fed, he would generally starve in a few days.

1 SAWING

In execution by sawing, the criminal would be hung upside-down and a large saw would be used to cut their body in half, starting with the groin, all the way to the head. Because the person was hanging upside-down, the brain received sufficient blood to keep them alive until the saw finally reached the main blood vessels in the abdomen. In the Asian version of this execution, the victim would stand upright and the sawing would begin at the top of the head.

Some traditions state that the Prophet Isaiah was executed with the saw. It is believed that Saint Paul is making reference to this in his Epistle to the Hebrews 11:37:

> "They were stoned, they were cut asunder, they were tempted, they were put to death by the sword, they wandered about in sheepskins, in goatskins, being in want, distressed, afflicted."

This method of execution was used in the Middle East, Europe, and parts of Asia. It was also used in the Roman Empire and was considered to be the favorite punishment dished out by Emperor Caligula.

✳✳✳✳✳✳

TOP 10
UNSOLVED MURDERS

10 OSCAR ROMERO

Oscar Romero was a well-known archbishop serving the Catholic Church in El Salvador during very turbulent times. Serving during the 1960s and 1970s, he was a very outspoken proponent concerning human rights and the horrific conditions faced by the poor during that country's bloody and vicious civil war. Presiding over his flock left him an open target and after speaking out and encouraging civil disobedience, in particular calling out the injustice of the U.S. in supporting the government during this tumultuous time, his assassins used this as an opportunity to send a message to his supporters by killing him while he said Mass at a small church. While many theories abound, and nothing was ever proven, most believe he was killed by a Salvadorian death squad.

9 OLOF PALME

Palme was Sweden's prime minister (1982–1986) who was shot and killed while walking home with his wife after a night at the movies. A vocal advocate of intense regulation and investigation of his country's nuclear energy program, especially after the incident at Three Mile Island in 1979, he also pushed a number of other political "hot" topics while in office. It may have been his ideas concerning European security, his push for economic reform of a socialist nature, or any other number of items on his political agenda. Which button he pushed or which topic set someone off is not known to this day. It has not even be proven that the murder was politically motivated and may have just been a random act of violence. No one has ever been charged with his murder nor has anyone been able to pinpoint the motive behind the crime.

8 THE BOY IN THE BOX

In 1957, a large cardboard box was found along Susquehanna Road in Philadelphia. While unusual, such a find was not newsworthy. It was what was discovered once the box was opened that set law enforcement officials' hair on end and provoked intense public outrage. Inside the box was the nude body of a young white male aged between four and six. Further complicating the issue was the manner in which the body was found. Horrific bruises showed signs of a brutal beating, but that was juxtaposed against the obvious tenderness someone showed in caring for his remains. He was clean and well kept and wrapped in a blanket in a manner that suggested great care after his death. Despite the public's cry for justice and advancements in DNA testing as an investigative tool, the case remains unsolved to this day.

7 JACK THE STRIPPER

Jack the Stripper was a modern-day serial killer who, it is suggested, modeled himself after the infamous Jack the Ripper. Targeting prostitutes, his body count quickly rose to six during a short span (1964–1965). Other murders during that time were thought to be his handiwork but could not be conclusively linked to the other cases with forensic evidence. The sudden end to the killings left many to believe it was tied in with the abrupt suicide of a young man who died around the time period Jack the Stripper's reign ended. With little or no evidence at the crime scenes, this coincidence of timing, and a cryptic message left to his family in his suicide note concerning his inability to take the stress any longer, made him the lead suspect. No charges were ever filed.

6 THE AXEMAN OF NEW ORLEANS

On May 23, 1918, a bloody and violent murder spree began in New Orleans. The bodies of Joseph Maggio and his wife were found in their apartment over their privately owned grocery store. While robbery was not a motive, concluded by the investigating officers at the scene, a bloody axe left at the home and the brutal nature of the killings sent fear through many in this coastal town. The killer left a single cryptic clue written in chalk. The killer was fond of his weapon of choice and used it with great skill to commit a second string of murders against another grocer and his common-law wife, which also left little or no evidence. All told the "Axeman of New Orleans" left eight dead before ending his killing spree. While the police had a strong suspect in the killings, the lack of scientific advances in police investigation at the turn of the century left them unable to bring charges against anyone.

5 JONBENÉT RAMSEY

JonBenét Ramsey was a six-year-old girl found murdered in the basement of her parents' upscale home in Boulder, Colorado. Many incongruities in the crime scene left investigators baffled. Generating intense media scrutiny, many believed the investigative officers focused on the wrong suspects: members of her own family. Vilified in the press the family moved to another area, all the while vehemently protesting their innocence. Enough DNA was found at the scene to submit to the FBI for a possible match, but no match has been found to date. JonBenét's mother passed away from cancer before hearing the news that the Boulder police conclusively ruled out any family members as possible suspects, but that comes as little comfort to her remaining family as the killer remains on the loose to this day. Her DNA is checked against the database on a regular basis but has yet to be solved.

4 BLACK DAHLIA

On January 15, 1947, police were called to investigate the report of a woman's body found in Leimert Park in Los Angeles. What they found when they arrived sparked a fascination that continues to this day. The carefully mutilated body, or should I say body parts, of Elizabeth Short were found laying out in the open in a most gruesome manner. The ritualistic nature of the disembodiment led to speculation of the manner in which the murder was carried out but did not lead to any solid suspects. Because of the sensational nature of the murder, the LAPD was inundated with false confessions, which also helped to further complicate the case and muddy the investigation. To date no motive or clear suspect has ever been found and no one has ever been charged.

3 ANDREW AND ABBY BORDEN

Unlike most of the cases on this list, the murders of Andrew and Abby Borden quickly brought forth a viable suspect: their daughter Lizzie. A large inheritance and suspicious behavior on her part in the days before

the murder led many to believe she had motive and means to have killed them both. She attempted to buy prussic acid (poison) the day before the murders. While the crime was being investigated it was found she burned a dress in the family wood stove shortly after the murders. No conclusive weapon was found, though they did find an axe that would have created the type of wounds suffered by Lizzie's parents. Lizzie was actually brought to trial, but was acquitted due to the lack of firm evidence. Shunned by her community for the remainder of her years, her brazen act prompted a children's rhyme that is still quoted to this day: "Lizzie Borden took an axe and gave her mother forty whacks, when she'd seen what she had done, she gave her father forty-one." No deathbed confession was given and the case is still considered unsolved.

2 THE ZODIAC KILLER

The Zodiac Killer captured the imagination of the American public during a particularly unsettled time. It was the "Summer of Love," the beginnings of a large and persistent protest of America's involvement in Vietnam and the beginnings of a budding counterculture. It was in this environment of the "public's right to know" that a prolific serial killer decided to play cat and mouse with the press concerning a number of unsolved murders. His use of symbols, cryptic hints, and a code that has yet to be deciphered soon captured the public's fascination. Speculation was rife as to the identity of the Zodiac Killer, with over two thousand leads investigated to no avail. With seven known victims, and numerous others suspected of dying at his hands, the Zodiac Killer has yet to be identified.

1 JACK THE RIPPER

I am sure it comes to no one's surprise that the number one spot is reserved for the ever infamous Jack the Ripper. During a short period in 1888 ol' Jack went about his business of targeting prostitutes by the most heinous methods of mutilation. The rumored surgical like skill and speed with which the crimes were suspected to have been committed led to great speculation that The Ripper was a man of prominence and education that could slip in and out of anywhere without standing out. The notoriety of the crime and the conspiracy theories surrounding it has led to a cult following of the case that is still heatedly debated to this day. No leading suspect or motive has ever been uncovered.

✳✳✳✳✳✳

TOP 10 INFAMOUS CONMEN

10 FRANK ABAGNALE, BORN 1948

Frank Abagnale started taking risks at an early age. Always one to find a new way around the system, Frank escalated the risks with each new scheme. He seemed driven to make each one bolder than the last. One thing that stood out about Frank was his youth and sheer boldness. Frank liked to make a quick turnover, but didn't shy away from the long con. From drafting off of other's banking accounts by forging his own account number on their deposit slip to masquerading as a licensed jetliner pilot, he liked to play it hot and loose. After nearly a year of "playing doctor" as a medical supervisor, he was finally caught in France and did a short stint in the slammer. Very short, it turned out, as he escaped from prison by passing himself off as an officer for the Bureau of Prisons. After being recaptured, he spent five years in prison before agreeing to work for the U.S. Government in training others how to detect fraud. As the head of his own consulting firm, he now makes millions of dollars by trying something completely different: earning his money legitimately.

9 CHARLES PONZI, 1882–1949

Most of us have heard the term "Ponzi scheme." It serves as a cautionary tale. Unmitigated greed on the part of both the conman and the target rarely ends well. Ponzi decided at a young age that his only goal in life was to make money, lots of it. And he didn't care where it came from. Arriving in America with only $2.50 to his name, Ponzi quickly rose through the ranks of shady investment bankers, being so bold as to con the cons. After being busted for check fraud and serving time in prison, Ponzi was more determined than ever to take every dime that would come his way. His biggest con began legitimately, offering devalued stock at an incredible markup, then showing his own profits to potential investors. Promising huge returns and a quick profit, many normally astute investors let the promise of easy money keep them from peeking behind the curtain. But before long people began asking questions and wanted a full accounting. Surprise. There was no money. Those who had invested ended up losing every penny entrusted to Ponzi. Now it was time to pay the piper. After a brief escape from prison, Ponzi served out his term and then was deported back to his native Italy. Life delivered a final ironic twist to the tale of Ponzi the conman. For a man who was driven to ruin others in his pursuit of money, he ended up in exile and died penniless.

8 JOSEPH WEIL, 1877–1975

Joseph "Yellow Kid" Weil was a different breed of conman. While most are motivated by the thrill of the con or the allure of easy money, Weil seemed to be driven by contempt of his fellow man. With a smooth nature and a slick tongue, one day he would be an oil man sharing portions of a company that didn't exist, and the next day he would be a land baron offering to share in his good fortune. In one of his few legitimate jobs he uncovered a scheme by fellow coworkers to skim money from the interest on accounts. Weil's solution was to blackmail them to keep him quiet. Weil enjoyed conning the conman. Weil's drive to crush those he felt were beneath him paid off quite well. He is estimated to have conned over eight million dollars from investors—an unimaginable fortune at the turn of the century.

7 VICTOR LUSTIG, 1890–1947

Ever wish you had a machine that would crank out money as it was needed? Evidently you're not alone because it was that very machine that Lustig sold to numerous investors. Lustig's niche in the con world was the ability to see a need and fill it. He worked wonders at making the impossible seem quite plausible. His most infamous con was selling the Eiffel Tower for scrap metal, not once, but *twice*. The first buyer was too embarrassed to go to the authorities once he realized how gullible he had been, leaving the door wide open for Lustig to return a few years later and revisit his most daring con. Authorities were able to finally catch up with him and charged him with counterfeiting. Lustig was sentenced to twenty years in Alcatraz. After a transfer to Springfield, he died quietly from pneumonia.

6 GEORGE PARKER, 1870–1936

Parker was a conman's conman. His exploits were so outrageous as to defy belief. And yet his cons worked like a charm. He had an uncanny instinct for drawing gullible investors with what would seem like obviously crackpot ideas. He sold the Brooklyn Bridge on a regular basis for years. He seemed to enjoy targeting well-known landmarks during his career. Some of his best "sales" came from conning marks into buying Grant's Tomb, Madison Square Garden, and the Statue of Liberty, as well as other well-known American iconic locations. His audacity led to the commonly used phrase, "And if ya believe that, I've got a bridge to sell ya." Considered one of the best "hoaxers" of all time, he died in prison, quite popular with his fellow inmates who enjoyed his tales of unbelievable scams.

5 SOAPY SMITH, 1860–1898

Soapy Smith was the master of the shill game. By promising something and delivering nothing he helped perfect the art of the street corner con. His signature con was selling bars of soap on a street corner, waiting until a crowd had gathered, and then making a show of wrapping a couple of bars with hundred dollar bills inside. Using a "plant" to find the first bill, he would then use sleight of hand to remove the remaining bill, as the crowd was worked into a frenzy paying for a bar of soap that "might" have the lucky bill in it. At times the crowd grew so rowdy he would auction off the bars of soap to the money-hungry crowd. Though he was a master of manipulation, his shady ways eventually caught up with him. Soapy was shot to death, by a group he tried to swindle while playing cards.

4 EDUARDO DE VALFIERNO

Valfierno was a connoisseur of the long con. His most famous job required a great deal of planning and forethought. He worked with an inside employee at the Louvre in Paris and had him simply walk out the front door with the *Mona Lisa*. Sounds like an audacious act? Well, we're just getting started. Before the theft of perhaps the world's best-known piece of art, he had quietly commissioned a number of forgeries and had them shipped to different points around the world. His main goal was not keeping the actual painting, but to ensure the theft received a great deal of worldwide publicity. He then proceeded to sell the *Mona Lisa* several times over for incredible amounts of money. He was also the personification of the perfect long con artist. He knew when to walk away. After selling the fake paintings he stopped all contact with the museum employee who still had the original in his possession. The employee was eventually caught trying to sell the original and went to prison and the real *Mona Lisa* was restored to its rightful place in the Louvre.

3 JAMES HOGUE, BORN 1959

Hogue's specialty in the con world was the burgeoning art of identity theft. While certainly not the first to try this con, he was certainly one of the most persistent. Using the identity of dead infants he slowly worked his way up the ladder. First he attended Palo Alto High School using the birth information of a child who would have been sixteen years of age. This is while Hogue was actually eleven years older than his claimed identity. You'd think that might have made him stick out. But he had such an affable nature and favored the status of "orphan" that most people simply took him at his word. Emboldened by the ease of his first con, Hogue applied and was accepted to Princeton University posing as a self-educated orphan. He was accepted, granted financial aid, and even made the track team and joined the Ivy Club. Eventually exposed, Hogue spent a short stint in the slammer, but made headlines again shortly after by working for Harvard University as a security guard. It was only after numerous valuables from Harvard's museum turned up missing that his fake identity became known. Using his charm he pleaded down all the charges and only received a ten-year sentence.

2 ROBERT HENDY-FREEGARD, BORN 1971

Hendy-Freegard was an unusual type of con artist. His con was more about the "power play" and manipulating people than aiming for the big money. By claiming to be a secret operative of Britain's famed MI6, he used brainwashing techniques and fear to see if he could make people bend to his will. He would con for money as well, but his main drive seemed to be seeing just how far he could make people go, based on his words alone. His methods were cruel and caused a number of people extreme mental trauma. His favorite bogeyman was the IRA, constantly using the threat of death if they did not behave exactly as he said. His behavior against his marks was riddled with "loyalty" tests. Having them sleep in odd places for days at a time, for example, just to see if they would do it. While most victims of con artists primarily suffered the loss of money, Hendy-Freegard's marks lost their sense of security and piece of mind as well. A counter-sting conducted by Scotland Yard and the FBI finally brought him to justice but it is feared many of his victims never came forward for fear it was another one of his "loyalty" tests, so the full extent of the damage he caused may never be known.

1 BERNARD CORNFELD, 1927–1995

Bernard Cornfeld is considered one of the most dangerous forms of conmen: the conman in the business suit. A natural salesman, he used loopholes in his businesses to make himself a robber baron on a worldwide stage. He utilized loopholes in the laws of different countries and strategically placed his businesses close to borders in case of the need to make a mad dash to a more loophole-friendly environment. While making large profits for his biggest investors, Bernard became emboldened and felt untouchable. With an estimated personal fortune of over a hundred million dollars, Bernard couldn't resist skimming off the top of monies due to his employees. He was charged by Swiss authorities with fraud and spent less than a year in jail. He then returned to Beverly Hills and lived a very comfortable life for the next two decades before dying of a cerebral aneurysm. Men like Bernard Cornfeld led the way for a wave of similar conmen who hid behind a business suit and put their own megalomaniacal egos above all else in the pursuit of power. We owe his business model for Club Fed being populated by the likes of men such as Bernard Madoff.

✳✳✳✳✳✳

TOP 10 ASSASSINS

10 JOHN WILKES BOOTH

John Wilkes Booth assassinated President Abraham Lincoln on April 14, 1865, at Ford's Theatre in Washington, D.C. Booth was an actor and Confederate sympathizer who conspired with several others to kill Lincoln, Vice President Andrew Johnson, and Secretary of State William Seward. It was hoped that the death of Lincoln and his first two successors would cripple the Union government and allow the Confederate government, which had surrendered four days earlier, to continue the war. Lincoln was the first American president to be assassinated. The others since are James Garfield, William McKinley, and John F. Kennedy. Booth used a single-shot .44 caliber Deringer, which he fired into the back of Lincoln's head at point-blank range.

9 BALTHASAR GERARD

Balthasar Gerard killed Prince William I of Orange, Count of Nassau (also known as William the Silent) on July 10, 1584. William was prominent in the Dutch fight for independence from the Spanish crown in the Netherlands. He was directly involved (either financially or as a leader) in the battles that began the Eighty Years' War. Gerard, a Catholic Frenchman and supporter of Phillip II, believed William had betrayed both the Spanish king and the Catholic religion. Gerard shot William in the chest at close range at William's home in Delft. Many historians believe William of Orange to be the first world head of state to be assassinated through use of a handgun.

8 GAVRILO PRINCIP

Called "the shot heard round the world," the death of Archduke Franz Ferdinand of Austria at the hands of Princip sparked the outbreak of World War I. The political goal of the killing was to splinter southern provinces from Austria to form a separate country (Greater Serbia or Yugoslavia). Anywhere from six to twenty-two (depending on which account you read) conspirators lined the route of Ferdinand's motorcade armed with pistols and hand grenades. Despite one car in the motorcade being blown up, Ferdinand made it through unharmed. While trying to leave the city, Ferdinand's driver apparently made a wrong turn and unknowingly drove into Princip's line of fire. Princip fired into the car twice, striking and ultimately killing Ferdinand and his wife, Sophie. Princip's weapon of choice was a 7.65 x 17 mm Fabrique Nationale semi-automatic.

7 JAN KUBIS AND JOZEF GABCIK

Reinhard Tristan Eugen Heydrich was the head of the German Reichssicherheitshauptamt (RSHA), or German secret police, during World War II. The better-known Gestapo was a division of the RSHA. On September 27, 1941, Heydrich was appointed military governor of the Protectorate of Bohemia and Morovia (Czechoslovakia). Heydrich's brutality and cruelty to the Czech people, and Jews in general, earned him the nicknames Butcher of Prague, Blond Beast, and Hangman. Heydrich was so successful in the pacification of the Czech lands that Hitler considered making him governor of Paris. When British intelligence heard this, it was decided that Heydrich had to be eliminated at all costs. Thus was born Operation Anthropoid. Kubis and Gabcik were Czechoslovakian soldiers who had fled the country early in 1941. After being trained by the British, they parachuted in near Prague and set up an ambush for Heydrich as he was driven to Prague Castle on May 27, 1942. After Gabcik's gun jammed, Kubis threw a modified anti-tank grenade at Heydrich's car, spraying Heydrich with shrapnel from the seat of the car. Heydrich died eleven days later from septicemia, probably from horsehair used in the upholstery. This was the only successful Allied assassination of a leading Nazi figure during WWII.

6 CHARLOTTE CORDAY

Corday assassinated Jean-Paul Marat on July 13, 1793. Marat was a key figure in the French Revolution and was held up as a martyr for his cause following his death. He attained almost quasi-sainthood and busts of him actually replaced crucifixes in many churches in Paris. His support of the September

Massacres and hand in starting The Reign of Terror tarnished his reputation and he was seen as something of a revolutionary monster in the Second Empire. For her part, Corday was generally reviled for murdering Marat, although during the Second Empire she was seen as a heroine of France. Marat suffered from an unknown skin disease (possibly dermatitis herpetiformis) from which the only relief he found was sitting in a cold bath. He spent the last three years of his life conducting the majority of his business from his bathtub. After gaining entrance to see Marat (while in his bath) under the auspices of informing on a planned Girondist uprising, Corday stabbed Marat in the chest with a recently purchased dinner knife, piercing his lung, aorta, and left ventricle. I included Corday on this list because of the historical importance of the French Revolution and because she was the only female assassin I found in my research.

5 NATHURAM GODSE

Godse assassinated Mahatma Gandhi on January 30, 1948. Gandhi's actual name was Mohandas Karamchand Gandhi; Mahatma is an Indian honorific similar to "Your Excellency." Godse was a member of the Hindu Mahasabha, a Hindu nationalist organization opposed to the Muslim League and the secular Indian National Congress. The
reason for the assassination is generally attributed to Gandhi's support of the Partition of India and weakening of India by insisting upon a payment to Pakistan. Godse believed Gandhi was sacrificing Hindu interests in an effort to appease minority groups, i.e. Muslims. Godse killed Gandhi during his nightly public walk on the grounds of the Birla House in New Dehli. Godse approached Gandhi, bowed to him, then shot him three times at close range with a Beretta semi-automatic pistol.

4 FELIX YUSUPOV

This is perhaps the most interesting, or bizarre at the very least, assassination in history. On December 16, 1916, a group of nobles lead by Prince Felix Yusupov and Grand Duke Dmitri Pavlovich assassinated Grigori Rasputin. According to legend, Rasputin was poisoned, shot, clubbed, and ultimately thrown into an icy river where he finally succumbed to death. The conspirators, having decided that Rasputin's influence over Tsaritsa Alexandra (wife of Tsar Nicholas II) was too dangerous a threat to the empire, first poisoned Rasputin with "enough cyanide to kill seven men." When unaffected by the poison,

Yusupov shot Rasputin in the back with a revolver. Yusupov then left the body to consult with the others. When they returned to the body, Rasputin grabbed Yusupov by the throat and whispered, "You bad boy," into his ear before hurling him across the room and running out. As he ran out, he was shot three more times. The group followed him out and found him still struggling to carry on. They then clubbed him into submission, wrapped him in a sheet, and threw him into the Neva River. Three days later, the body was pulled from the river and autopsied. The cause of death was found to be hypothermia and his arms were found in an upright position as if he had tried to claw his way through the ice. It should be noted that Rasputin had survived a previous attempt on his life. On June 14, 1914, Khionia Guseva stabbed Rasputin in the abdomen, and his entrails hung out in what seemed a mortal wound. Rasputin recovered after intensive surgery and it was said of his survival, "the soul of this cursed *muzhik* was sown on his body."

3 LEE HARVEY OSWALD

Perhaps the most debated and controversial of all assassinations is Oswald's November 22, 1963, murder of President John F. Kennedy. An avowed Marxist, Oswald was a former Marine who immigrated to the Soviet Union in October of 1959. He later returned to the United States in 1962, finding life in the Soviet Union to be less than the idyllic existence he expected. After drifting through numerous jobs (and one failed assassination attempt upon General Edwin Walker), Oswald ended up in the Dallas/Ft. Worth area where he killed Kennedy. Oswald shot Kennedy from a sixth-floor window of the Texas Schoolbook Depository (where Oswald worked) as the president's motorcade passed through Dealey Plaza in Dallas, Texas. Oswald used a Mannlicher-Caracano rifle purchased via mail order earlier that year. I counted ten separate theories surrounding the Kennedy assassination, including KGB, CIA, and Mafia involvement, multiple gunmen, and imposters for both Oswald and Kennedy.

2 ANDREI LUGOVOI

Lugovoi is the man believed to have poisoned Alexander Valterovick Litvinenko with polonium-210 on November 1, 2006. This is notable because Litvinenko is the first known victim of induced acute radiation syndrome or radiation poisoning, the first "nuclear assassination." Litvinenko is thought to have been poisoned while having tea with Lugovoi and Dmitiri Kovtun. Litvinenko was a harsh critic of the Russian government and Russian president Vladimir

Putin, and was currently investigating the death of Anna Politkovskaya, a Russian journalist known for her opposition to the Putin administration who was found murdered in 2006.

1 MARCUS JULIUS BRUTUS

Brutus, and as many as sixty or more men, stabbed Gaius Julius Caesar to death on March 15, 44 BC, the "Ides of March." Caesar was the military dictator of Rome beginning about 50 BC, but his relationship with the Roman Senate was contentious, to say the least. Brutus, a friend of Julius, but a Senator first, conspired with other Senators to kill Caesar, as they feared his growing power would make the Senate obsolete. Supposedly, Caesar's last words as he lay dying on the steps of the Forum were "*kai su teknon*," which roughly translates from the Greek as "and you my child."

✳✳✳✳✳✳

TOP 10 LESSER-KNOWN MASSACRES

10 GRANADA MASSACRE, 1066

Mob violence against the Jewish people (and early Christians—they were considered Jews) has been occurring for over two thousand years; by the Greeks leading to the Maccabean revolt, and by the Romans in Alexandria during Caligula's rule. Surprisingly, Jews fared much better under Muslim rule; generally treated with tolerance and decency up until the eleventh century. Dispute with an ostentatious Jewish vizier (executive officer) coupled with inflammatory religious writings created an atmosphere ripe for tragedy. On December 30, 1066, a Muslim mob stormed the Royal Palace, crucified Vizier Joseph ibn Naghrela, and murdered four thousand Jewish inhabitants of the city.

This poem of Abu Ishaq, written in Granada in 1066, was considered to be largely instrumental in sparking this massacre. It contains the following lines:

> Do not consider it a breach of faith to kill them, the breach of faith would
> be to let them carry on.

They have violated our covenant with them, so how can you be held guilty against the violators?

How can they have any pact when we are obscure and they are prominent?

Now we are humble, beside them, as if we were wrong and they were right!

9 ST. BARTHOLOMEW'S DAY MASSACRE, 1572

An uneasy peace between the Huguenots (Protestants) and the staunchly Catholic monarchy and general populace of France was torn apart in Paris shortly after the arranged marriage of Marguerite de Valois, daughter of Catherine de Medici, mother of the King, to Protestant Prince Henry of Navarre (the future King Henry V). A failed assassination attempt on Admiral de Coligny, a prominent Huguenot, caused a preemptive strike by the monarchy. Leery of the large Protestant army camped outside the city walls, the gates were ordered closed and the populace armed to prevent uprising. Prominent Huguenots were ordered killed and the mayhem spread first to the city and then to the surrounding countryside. Beginning on August 24, 1572, and lasting for several months, the St. Bartholomew's Day massacre resulted in over five thousand deaths.

8 BATAK MASSACRE, 1876

The Batak massacre was one of the atrocities committed by the Ottoman Empire during the April Uprising of 1876. The emergence of the nation-state, excess taxation, a sense of identity tied to ethnic/geographic borders, religious differences, and a suppressed populace all led to a Bulgarian insurrection against the Ottoman Empire.

The City of Batak declared its independence a few weeks into the uprising. The empire's reaction was swift; soon eight thousand Turkish soldiers, led by Ahmet Aga Barunwere, were camped outside the city. After the first battle the revolutionary committee from Batak decided to negotiate a truce. After laying down their arms, the ruthless Ahmet and his troops attacked a defenseless population. Over five thousand people were slaughtered, most by beheading.

Public outrage in Europe and America over this massacre and others during the April Uprising indirectly led to the formation of Bulgaria as an independent state in 1878 and hastened the fall of the Ottoman Empire.

7 MASSACRE OF THESSALONIKI, 390

The arrest and imprisonment of a charioteer, a revered and honored figure of the day, for seduction of a servant precipitated the massacre of Thessaloniki and the death of thousands. Botheric, a *magister militum*, or top soldier in the emperor's army, sent to detain the charioteer, was inadvertently killed in the melee that ensued when the population protested the arrest. Enraged soldiers are said to have killed seven thousand (likely exaggerated) in the Hippodrome (chariot racing stadium) of Thessaloniki. This tragedy angered the ruling bishop of the time, Ambrose, he in turn forcing the emperor to suffer penance for this transgression. It was important to the church and to the rule of the people—the emperor was not head of the church but limited by it.

6 SREBRENICA MASSACRE, 1995

The Srebrenica massacre was the state-sponsored killing of eight thousand Bosniak men and boys as well as the ethnic cleansing of between twenty-five and thirty thousand refugees.

After declaring independence from Yugoslavia and being recognized as a separate state, Bosnia-Herzegovina fell apart due to territorial struggles between the three major ethnic groups in Bosnia: the Bosniaks—Bosnian Muslims, the Serbs, and the Croats. The area around Srebrenica was tactically important to the Serbs and was their excuse for ethnic cleansing and eventual genocide. Cities were taken by the Serbs; Bosniak men and women were separated; men interned or murdered, women and children forced to flee.

On April 13, 1993, the Serbs told the UNHCR representatives that they would attack Srebrenica within two days unless the Bosniaks surrendered and agreed to be evacuated. The Bosniaks refused. Attack was thwarted on April 16 when the United Nations enacted Resolution 819, declaring Srebrenica a UN-protected zone. Dutch peacekeepers were flown in to enforce the resolution. By early 1995 the situation was critical; fewer and fewer provisions were making it to the city. People were starving, there was no fuel for cooking or vehicles, even UN soldiers were short of rations and forced to patrol on foot. Despite massive efforts to negotiate a peace and international condemnation, the leader of the Serbian army, President Radovan Karadžić, enacted Directive 7:

> "*Complete the physical separation of Srebrenica from Žepa as soon as possible, preventing even communication between individuals in the two enclaves. By planned and well-thought-out combat operations, create an*

unbearable situation of total insecurity with no hope of further survival or life for the inhabitants of Srebrenica."

The directive was horrifyingly effective. Men were shot; women loaded up in trucks that often never reached their destination. Columns of men trying to reach safe areas were strafed from the air and massacred on an unimaginable level. The UN peacekeepers were basically hostages in this situation and could do nothing to help. Women were raped and children murdered. Thus far, over fifty-eight hundred victims have been identified through DNA analysis, and mass graves are still being discovered.

5 MASSACRE OF ELPHINSTONE'S ARMY, 1842

The massacre of forty-five hundred British and Indian troops as well as twelve thousand working personnel was caused by both the treachery of Akbar Khan and the incompetence of Major-General William Elphinstone.

The Afghan people were never comfortable with British rule; it took little effort on the part of Akbar Khan to rouse a guerrilla army from tribesman in surrounding villages. In 1841 Khan declared a general revolt and the citizens of Kabul followed suit. The house of a senior British political officer, Sir Alexander Burns, was stormed and he was murdered. Elphinstone took no action, which served to encourage further revolt. Governor Macnaghten, realizing the precariousness of the situation, made overtures to try and negotiate a withdrawal. Invited for tea by Akbar Khan, Macnaghten and his party were murdered as soon as they arrived; Macnaghten's body dragged through the streets. To the horror of the remaining British troops, not only did Elphinstone ignore the murders, he signed a very unfavorable treaty. The British and their civilian support would be allowed to leave if their newer weapons and extra ammunition was turned over to the Afghans. The aged and ill would be left behind, their safety guaranteed.

The first dangerous pass was just fifteen miles from Kabul; instead of hurrying to reach and secure the pass, Elphinstone ordered a rest after just six miles. With no real leadership the convoy did not reach the pass until two in the morning. The Afghans were waiting for them. Rather than lead his men, Elphinstone and other senior officers offered themselves as hostages, leaving their men to try and fight their way to Jalalabad, only ninety miles away—one man made it. The ill and infirm were already dead; they were killed and their tents set on fire as soon as Elphinstone and his army left the city.

4 KATYN MASSACRE, 1940

Originally referring to the murder of Polish military officers from the Kozelsk POW camp in the Katyn forest of Russia, the Katyn massacre now encompasses the simultaneous execution of 21,768 military and civilian prisoners of war. Proposed by Lavrentiy Beria, Russian Chief of Security, and approved by Stalin and the rest of the Politburo, the Katyn massacre took place in the Katyn Forest, Starobelsk and Ostashkov POW camps, NKVD headquarters in Smolensk, at a Smolensk slaughterhouse, and at prisons in Kharkov, Kalinin, Moscow, and other Soviet cities. Doctors, lawyers, university professors, Boy Scouts, all deemed counter-revolutionaries, were included in the massacre. It was in Stalin's best interest to keep Poland weak. He intended to keep the eastern portion of the country; a strong, vital Poland and Polish military would be a constant threat.

3 BABI YAR MASSACRE, 1941

Babi Yar is the name of a ravine located in the city of Kiev where over the course of two days 33,371 Jewish civilians were summarily executed. Harried by guerrilla attacks, Major-General Friedrich George Bernhard ordered the killing of the Jews on September 26, 1941, as a retaliatory measure. A notice was posted:

> "All Jews of the city of Kiev and its environs must appear on Monday, September 29, 1941, by 8:00 a.m. on the corner of Melonakos and Dokterivsky streets (near the cemetery). You are to take your documents, money, valuables, warm clothes, linen, etc. Whoever of the Jews does not fulfill this order and is found in another place shall be shot. Any citizen who enters the apartments that have been left and takes ownership of items will be shot."

More than thirty thousand people assembled at the cemetery expecting deportation by rail car; the Nazis and Ukrainian collaborators kept up this deception, most victims not realizing their fate until too late. Their clothing and valuables removed along the way, the people were led to the ditch and shot. The atrocity at Babi Yar is considered the largest single massacre in the history of the Holocaust.

2 NKVD PRISONER MASSACRE, 1941

The NKVD prison massacre refers to the mass execution of prisoners by the NKVD, or Russian secret police, in Eastern Europe, Poland, the Baltic States, Romania, the Ukraine, and other parts of Soviet Russia. The number of victims is estimated at over one hundred thousand—more than ten thousand in the Ukraine alone.

On June 22, 1941, the Germans implemented Operation Barbarossa, the invasion of Russia on a grand scale. The Red Army, forced to retreat from Eastern Europe, began the execution of their prisoners almost from the onset of hostilities. Those not murdered outright were evacuated and died on forced death marches. Most of the victims were political prisoners, imprisoned and executed without trial—in Poland one in ten adult males was incarcerated. Most died. Prisoners were shot, bayoneted, had grenades thrown into their cells, or were simply starved to death, left to rot without food or water. After the war more than twenty-five prisons were identified where prisoners were murdered and mass graves continue to be discovered today.

1 NANKING MASSACRE, 1936/37

The Rape of Nanking, lasting for more than six weeks, was committed by the Japanese Army following the fall of Nanking, then the capital city of the Republic of China. Following the war, international tribunals found ample evidence of the atrocities committed by the Japanese Imperial Army; systemic rape, arson, looting, and execution of civilians and POWs on such a scale as to justify a charge of war crimes against Japan.

Ostensibly executing Chinese soldiers in disguise, the death toll soon climbed to over 250,000 people. Civilians trying to flee were shot—in one incident civilians trapped on the eastern shore of the Yangtze River and those trying to swim across were caught by advancing Japanese troops. A Japanese soldier reported the next day he saw an uncountable number of dead bodies of adults and children covering the whole river. He estimated that more than fifty thousand people had been killed.

Rape was widespread and used as a tool of terror. The International Military Tribunal for the Far East stated that eighty thousand women were raped, including children and pregnant women. Many of the rapes were systemized, Japanese soldiers going door to door collecting young girls. Many were killed directly after the assault and in the most degrading and horrifying ways. Women were killed by mutilation, having their breasts cut off or by having bayonets, bamboo stakes, or other sharp instruments stabbed into their vaginas.

Soon after the end of the war the International Military Tribunal of the Far East was convened and some of the primary offenders were put on trial. Ultimately only two people were convicted of war crimes: General Iwani Matsui, commander of the expeditionary forces sent to China, was to bear ultimate responsibility for the massacre. He did nothing, or nothing effective, to abate these horrors. Hirota Koki, Japan's foreign minister, was also convicted for waging a war of aggression against international laws. Both were sentenced to death. The Nanjing War Crimes Tribunal, established by China in 1946, convicted and sentenced four further Japanese soldiers. Only one was still alive; General Hisao Tani was executed by firing squad on March 10, 1947.

Although the Japanese government had acknowledged atrocities were committed, it was not until 1995, on the fiftieth anniversary of the surrender of Japan, that the Prime Minister of Japan gave the first clear and formal apology for the atrocities committed in Nanking. The Emperor joined Prime Minister Tomiichi Murayama offering statements of mourning and offering sincere condolences.

✳✳✳✳✳✳

TOP 10 MOST WANTED FUGITIVES

10 GANGSTER NOEL CUNNINGHAM

He escaped from a prison transportation van in June 2003; he was being taken from Brixton Prison to face charges over a £1.25 million security-van heist in which the driver of the van was shot in the knee after he was ordered to open the door while his colleague was pistol-whipped. His partner in crime was convicted in February 2008 of using a gun to escape from the van. Detectives have vowed that Cunningham will have his day in court.

9 CRIME BOSS JAMES J. BULGER

Linked to eighteen murders, Bulger has evaded the FBI for nine years. Known as "Whitey," the seventy-eight-year-old Boston crook is on the U.S. 10 Most Wanted List for drug dealing, money laundering, extortion, murder, and other organized crimes. He is known to use disguises to visit libraries and historic sites. The FBI is offering one million dollars for information leading to his arrest.

8 DRUG DEALER JOAQUIN GUZMAN LOERA

The top target of American Drug Enforcement Administration, the fifty-four-year-old, also known as "Shorty," heads the Sinaloa Cartel of international drug traffickers. He reputedly pays up to two million dollars to lieutenants to keep him safe and is said to change mobile phones after each conversation. Loera follows the Sinaloan credo of not killing innocent people and is regarded as a Robin Hood–type character.

7 FRAUDSTER ASIL NADIR

In 1990, following the collapse of his Polly Peck business empire, Nadir fled from the UK to northern Cyprus. He was prosecuted on various counts of theft and fraud but failed to appear for trial in 1993, having absconded to the unrecognized Turkish Republic of Northern Cyprus, which has no extradition treaty with the UK. He is wanted on theft charges of £34 million. In 2003 he vowed to return to clear his name but refused until the British government promised not to remand him in jail until his trial.

6 EX-SPY ANDREI LUGOVOI

The former KGB spy, age forty-two, is wanted in the UK for the murder of soldier and spy Alexander Litvinenko, who died in 2006 after being poisoned with radioactive polonium-210 in London. The authorities say they have enough to charge Lugovoi but the Russians refuse to hand him over. He protests his innocence from Moscow and claims MI6 spies, the Russian Mafia, or Kremlin opponent Boris Berezovsky carried out the killing.

5 WAR CHIEF AUGUSTIN BIZIMANA

So far eighty-three people wanted for genocide by the United Nations International Criminal Tribunal for Rwanda (UN-ICTR) have been apprehended. Augustin Bizimana is the most senior of the thirteen remaining still at large. The fifty-four-year-old former defense minister faces charges over the massacre of 800,000 Tutsis and moderate Hutus in 1994. Six years ago the U.S. offered a five-million-dollar reward for his capture but he has evaded capture.

4 DICTATOR OMAR HASSAN AL-BASHIR

The UN says the ethnic cleansing carried out by Sudanese dictator Omar Hassan al-Bashir left 300,000 dead and 2.5 million homeless in the Darfur region, where his regime used rape as an instrument of terror. International Criminal

Court prosecutor Luis Moreno-Ocampo requested a warrant to arrest him on ten charges of genocide, war crimes, and crimes against humanity, but critics said it would make matters worse for the people of Darfur.

3 "DR. DEATH" ARIBERT HEIM

Known as Dr. Death, SS officer Dr. Aribert Heim is accused of the killing and torture of inmates at the Mauthausen concentration camp. Now ninety-four, his methods included injecting toxic compounds into the hearts of victims and performing surgery without anesthetic. He is one of the last major Nazi fugitives still at large. He fled Germany in 1962. The Simon Wiesenthal Centre and German and Austrian governments are offering a $495,000 reward.

2 ARMY CHIEF RATKO MLADIC

Mladic, sixty-six, was Bosnian Serb leader Karadzic's army chief and a key figure in the ethnic cleansing of Croats and Muslims. He was indicted for genocide, by the UN International Criminal Tribunal for the former Yugoslavia (UN-ICTY) at The Hague in 1995. The Serbia government is offering one million dollars for his capture while the U.S. is offering five million. He is one of only two of 161 wanted by the UN-ICTY who remain free. The other is Goran Hadzic who faces fourteen counts of war crimes.

1 TERRORIST OSAMA BIN LADEN

The man allegedly behind the world's worst terror attack has continued to evade justice since 2001 after three thousand people died in 9/11. Saudi Arabian Osama Bin Laden, fifty-one, has also been indicted over the 1998 embassy bombings in Tanzania and Kenya. There is almost fifty-million-dollars of reward on his head. His most likely whereabouts are thought to be around the border of Afghanistan and Pakistan. U.S. intelligence officials believe he no longer uses a cell phone.

✳✳✳✳✳✳

TOP 10 OUTLAWS OF THE WILD WEST

10 WILLIAM "CURLY BILL" BROCIUS, CIRCA 1845– MARCH 24, 1882

"Curly Bill" was so-called because of his head of thick, curly black hair. After the death of "Old Man" Clanton, he became the leader of the "Cowboys" gang of cattle rustlers in Tombstone, Arizona. He also worked for a while as a tax collector for Cochise County Sheriff John Behan. Curly Bill was a heavy drinker who became even more rambunctious when drunk. One night, while drinking with other Cowboys, he was asked by Marshall Fred White to give up his pistol. In handing the gun over to the marshall, it accidentally discharged, hitting White. White, who had been friendly with Curly Bill, made a statement on his deathbed that he believed the shooting was an accident and Brocius was acquitted. Wyatt Earp testified in his defense, but later shot and killed him in retaliation for the murder of his brother, Morgan Earp.

9 SAM BASS, JULY 21, 1851–JULY 21, 1878

Sam Bass started out an honest man. After running away from the abusive uncle who raised him, he went to work in a sawmill in Mississippi. His dream was to be a cowboy and he eventually made his way to Texas. After one season, he decided he didn't like it. In 1876, Bass and a rough character named Joel Collins drove a herd of longhorns up north where the prices for cattle were higher. They were supposed to go back to Texas to pay off the owners of the herd, but instead they took the eight thousand dollars profit for themselves. He and Collins wasted the money from the cattle drive on gambling in Deadwood. A few months later, he and Collins went into another venture—stagecoach robbery. After holding up seven stagecoaches, they didn't make much money. They set their sights on bigger prizes and turned to train robbery. Bass and his gang robbed the Union Pacific gold train from San Francisco, netting over sixty thousand dollars, which is, to this day, the largest single robbery of the Union Pacific. He was wounded by Texas Rangers on the way to rob a small bank in Round Rock, and died two days later on his twenty-seventh birthday.

8 BELLE STARR, FEBRUARY 5, 1848–FEBRUARY 3, 1889

Myra Maybelle Shirley was born in Carthage, Missouri. As a young lady, she attended the Carthage Female Academy where she excelled in all subjects and became an accomplished pianist. She grew up with Cole Younger and later befriended the James brothers. When the outlaws of the James-Younger gang needed to hide out, they often stayed at the Shirley family farm. It wasn't long before Maybelle was introduced to a life of crime and earned the nickname "The Bandit Queen." In 1866, Belle married Jim Reed, a former Confederate Army guerrilla. Jim Reed tried to live the honest life of a farmer, but when that didn't pan out, he fell in with the Starrs, a Cherokee Indian family notorious for stealing horses. Along with his wife's friends, the Jameses and Youngers, they planned and executed many daring heists. Jim was killed while trying to escape from the custody of a deputy sheriff who had arrested him for one such robbery. After the loss of her husband, Belle made her living organizing and planning robberies, as well as fencing stolen goods. When she was unable to bribe the law into looking the other way, she would seduce them to get what she wanted. She married Sam Starr in 1880, and two years later both of them were convicted of stealing horses. They were released a year later and went right back into lawlessness. Belle was murdered on February 3, 1889, two days before she was to turn forty-one. She was shot in the back while riding home from the general store. Her killer has never been identified.

7 THOMAS COLEMAN YOUNGER, JANUARY 15, 1844–MARCH 21, 1916

Cole Younger's life was forever changed when his father was murdered by Union Captain Walley. Mr. Younger had given Walley a severe beating for making advances on his daughter (Cole's sister). Cole was already a member of Quantrill's Raiders but after the murder of his father, he joined the Confederate Army. It is not for certain when he went into banditry, but the first time he was mentioned as a suspect was after the 1868 robbery of Nimrod Long & Co., a bank in Russellville, Kentucky. Cole and his brothers formed a gang with Jesse and Frank James. They robbed stagecoaches, trains, and banks in Missouri, Kentucky, Kansas, and West Virginia. Luck ran out for the Younger boys on September 7, 1876, during a botched bank robbery. Cole and his brothers Jim and Bob pled guilty to avoid the hangman's noose. They were sentenced to life, but were paroled in 1901. Cole toured the nation with Frank James giving speeches about the Wild West. He later became a Christian and renounced his criminal past, dying peacefully four years later, with eleven bullets still embedded in his body.

6 JAMES B. "KILLER" MILLER, OCTOBER 25, 1861–APRIL 19, 1909

James Miller was also known as "Deacon Jim" because he went to church and did not smoke or drink. Despite his piousness, he was actually one of the deadliest guns in the Wild West. He openly stated that he would kill anyone for money, and his rate was reported at anywhere from one-hundred-and-fifty to two thousand dollars. Miller's usual method was to ambush his victims at night using a shotgun and wearing a black frock coat, making him hard to see in the darkness. His coat also concealed a steel plate he wore on his chest to protect him from opposing gunfire, an early version of a bulletproof vest. He is known to have committed fourteen murders, but rumors swelled that number to fifty. He was arrested in Oklahoma, for the murder of A. A. "Gus" Bobbitt. Not wanting to leave it up to a jury, a lynch mob dragged Miller and three others out to an abandoned stable to be hanged. Before he died, he made two requests. He wanted his ring to be given to his wife (who was a cousin of John Wesley Hardin) and to be allowed to wear his hat while being hanged. He went out on his own terms, shouting "Let 'er rip!" before he jumped off his box to his death. His body and the bodies of the other three men lynched that night were left hanging for hours until a photographer could be found to immortalize the event.

5 THE SUNDANCE KID, 1867–NOVEMBER 6, 1908

"The Sundance Kid," Henry Longabaugh, earned his nickname when he was caught and convicted of horse thievery in Sundance, Wyoming. Despite his reputation as a gunfighter, he is not certain to have actually killed anyone. After his release from jail in 1896, he and Robert LeRoy Parker, aka "Butch Cassidy," formed the gang known as the "Wild Bunch." They were responsible for the longest string of successful train and bank robberies in American history. Due to the pressure of the Pinkerton Detective Agency on their trail, Sundance, Butch, and Etta Place left the United States for Argentina to let things cool down. The Sundance Kid is believed to have been killed in a shootout in Bolivia, but several family members claim he actually returned to the U.S., changed his name to William Henry Long, and lived in the small town of Duchesne, Utah, until 1936. Long's body has been exhumed and is undergoing DNA testing to determine the truth.

4 BUTCH CASSIDY, APRIL 13, 1866–CIRCA NOVEMBER 1908

In 1879, at the age of thirteen, Robert LeRoy Parker lived and worked with his family on the ranch of Jim Marshall in Circleville, Utah. It was there he met his friend and mentor, Mike Cassidy, who gave Bob his first gun and taught him how to shoot. Years later, Bob would take his last name, Cassidy, as a tribute. His first run-in with the law occurred when he rode into town to buy a new pair of overalls. The general store was closed, so Bob let himself in, found a pair that fit, and left a note promising he would be back to pay later. The merchant reported him to the sheriff, but he was acquitted of any crime. On June 24, 1889, he and three others robbed the San Miguel Valley Bank in Telluride, Colorado, netting twenty-one thousand dollars. With this money, he bought a ranch near the infamous "Hole-in-the-Wall" outlaw hideout. Parker, by this time "Butch Cassidy," was never a very good rancher, and it is believed to have simply been a cover for his illegal activities. In 1896, he became the leader of the infamous group of criminals known as the Wild Bunch that included some of the most well-known outlaws of the Wild West. As with the Sundance Kid, it is unknown if he really died in Bolivia, or if, as some relatives claim, he returned to America.

3 JOHN WESLEY HARDIN, MAY 26, 1853–AUGUST 19, 1895

The son of a Methodist preacher, Hardin was named after the founder of the Methodist faith. When he was only fourteen years old, he stabbed a boy for taunting him. A year later, he was playfully wrestling with an ex-slave named Mage. He scratched Mage's face, and the next day, Mage hid on a path and attacked Hardin in retaliation. Hardin fired three warning shots, but when Mage didn't back off, Hardin was forced to shoot him in self-defense. Mage died as a result. Since many of the Texas State Police were themselves former slaves, and Hardin was a "Johnny Reb," he didn't stand a chance of a fair trial. He went into hiding and was warned by his brother when the police found out where he was. He did not run, but stayed and fought instead. He killed all three policemen and evaded the law. Several arrests and escapes later, he ended up in Abilene, Kansas, where he befriended "Wild Bill" Hickok. While in Abilene, he stayed at the American House Hotel. When the stranger in the next room wouldn't stop snoring, he fired a gun into the ceiling twice. The first shot woke the man up, and the second one killed him. Hardin made his escape out of the window and left for Texas. Many skirmishes with the law followed, and he was finally captured, convicted, and was incarcerated for seventeen years. During his time in jail, he finished his law degree and practiced as a lawyer upon his release. He died when he was shot in the back of the head while playing dice.

2 JESSE JAMES, SEPTEMBER 5, 1847–APRIL 3, 1882

Jesse James was born in Missouri, and along with his brother, Frank, was a Confederate guerrilla fighter during the Civil War. After the war, the James boys joined the Younger brothers and formed the James-Younger Gang. Together, they robbed banks, stagecoaches, and trains. In 1869, the gang held up the Daviess County Savings Association in Gallatin, Missouri. Jesse shot and killed a clerk, believing him to be someone else. When he realized his terrible mistake, he began a correspondence with John Newman Edwards, editor and founder of the *Kansas City Times*. Edwards had fought for the Confederacy also, and was sympathetic to the James brothers. He ran many admiring articles about the gang and published Jesse James's letters to the public, in which he declared his innocence. These articles raised his public profile and made him a kind of folk hero. Though he was famous while alive, he became even more so in death, when he was shot in the back of the head in his own home by trusted friend Robert Ford. His mother, Zerelda James, chose this epitaph for her son: "In Loving Memory of my Beloved Son, Murdered by a Traitor and Coward Whose Name is not Worthy to Appear Here."

1 BILLY THE KID, NOVEMBER 23, 1859–JULY 14, 1881

There is no outlaw more legendary than Billy the Kid. Countless books, movies, and songs have been written about his life, but the reality was not quite as sensational. Often portrayed as a cold-blooded killer, he entered a life of crime out of necessity, not malice. People who knew him personally called him brave, resourceful, honest, and full of laughter. Under different circumstances, he could have been a successful man. It has been said that he killed twenty-one people, one for each year of his life, but he was probably only responsible for four. In 1877, he went to work as a cattle guard for rancher John Tunstall, who was embroiled in a bitter dispute with the local merchants Lawrence Murphy and James Dolan. On February 18, 1878, Tunstall was murdered by Murphy's workers, while herding his cattle in the open range. He was unarmed and alone. This event started what would be called the "Lincoln County War." Enraged, the ranch hands, including Billy, were deputized and given the warrants to bring in the Murphy men. They called themselves "the Regulators." Due to the corruption of the day, the governor sided with Murphy, and the Regulators became the enemy. After a daring escape from jail, and a few years on the run, he was shot and killed by Sheriff Pat Garrett while hiding out in a friend's home.

Over the years, several people have claimed to be Billy the Kid, but the chance he survived and/or his body was misidentified is highly unlikely.

✳✳✳✳✳✳

TOP 10 MODERN METHODS OF EXECUTION

10 GARROTE

The garrote is one of two methods of execution on this list no longer sanctioned by law in any country though training in its use is still carried out by the French Foreign Legion. The garrote is a device that strangles a person to death. It can also be used to break a person's neck. The device was used in Spain until it was outlawed in 1978 with the abolition of the death penalty. It normally consisted of a seat in which the prisoner was restrained while the executioner tightened a metal band around his neck until he died. Some versions of the garrote incorporated a metal bolt, which pressed into the spinal cord, breaking the neck. This spiked version is known as the Catalan garrote. The last execution by garrote was José Luis Cerveto in October 1977. Andorra was the last country in the world to outlaw its use, doing so in 1990.

9 STONING

Execution by stoning is permitted under Islamic Sharia Law and is practiced in a number of Islamic nations such as Iran and Saudi Arabia. The punishment is used for those convicted of adultery and other serious crimes. Islamic law requires that the stones used in the execution be small enough to prevent death after only two blows but sufficiently large to cause severe injury. This method of execution is protested against by international organizations, though this seems to have had little impact thus far.

8 GUILLOTINE

Contrary to popular belief, Joseph-Ignace Guillotin did not invent the guillotine; he suggested a method of execution be devised that was quick and to be used on all people regardless of class. He sat on the committee that eventually designed the device, but it was actually Antoine Louis who came up with the design then used to build the first functioning guillotine. This is other execution method on this list which is no longer used anywhere in the world.

The device itself is a large timber frame with a space at the bottom for the neck of the prisoner. At the top of the machine is a large angled blade. Once the prisoner is secured, the blade is dropped, severing the head and bringing about immediate death. Much speculation exists as to whether or not the person dies immediately, and one man went so far as to ask a prisoner to blink after his head was cut off if he could. The accounts tell us he did blink, but it is most likely if he did, it would have been a post-mortem twitch.

The last public guillotining in France was secretly filmed, and the scandalous behavior of the onlookers caused the government to ban public executions. It was the official method of execution in France until the death penalty was outlawed in 1981.

7 BEHEADING

In some nations that adhere to Islamic Sharia law, beheadings are still a commonly used method of execution. The most frequently seen cases involve beheading by a curved, single-edged sword. While many nations allow beheading by law, Saudi Arabia uses it most often. The sentence is normally carried out on a Friday night in public outside the main mosque of the city after prayers. The penalty can be dealt for rape, murder, drug-related crimes, and apostasy (rejection of religious beliefs).

Saudi Arabia frequently comes under fire from international agencies because they continue to pass this sentence on minors. Saudi Arabian officials state they are not in breach of international law because the sentence is not carried out until the child has reached the age of eighteen. This was the case with Dhahian Rakan al-Sibai'i who was sentenced at fifteen but executed in 2008 at the age of eighteen.

6 HANGING

Hanging is carried out in a variety of ways: the short drop is when the prisoner is made to stand on an object which is then thrust away—leaving them to die by strangulation. This was a common method of hanging used by the Nazis and was the most common form used before the 1850s. Death is slow and painful. Suspension hanging (very popular in Iran) is when the gallows itself is movable. The prisoner stands on the ground with the noose around their neck and the gallows is then lifted in to the air, taking the prisoner with it. The standard drop was in common use in English nations after the 1850s—it involved tying the noose around the prisoner's neck and then dropping them a short distance (usually four to six feet) to break the neck. This was the method used to execute the Nazi war criminals. The final method is the long drop, devised in 1872, in which the weight of a person was taken into account to determine the correct rope and drop to be used to ensure the breaking of the neck.

The night before the execution, Pierrepoint would visit the condemned man in his cell with the warden. The prisoner was not told that Pierrepoint was his executioner. The purpose of the visit was to size the man up. Pierrepoint would use the information he had gained on the visit to decide what thickness of rope and length of drop to use. He would soak the rope in water and hang a sandbag the weight of the prisoner at the end to prevent stretching during the execution. The next day Pierrepoint would put a cloth over the face of the prisoner and tighten the noose around his neck. He was very careful to ensure the trapdoor beneath the condemned would be opened as soon after the noose went on as possible and would often kick the level with his foot. The person would then drop through the trapdoor and their neck would break, causing death.

There have been some instances where the long drop method has caused decapitation—the most recent of which was the hanging of Saddam Hussein's half brother, Barzan Ibrahim al-Tikriti, in Iraq in 2007.

5 FIRING SQUAD

The firing squad is considered by many to be the most honorable method of execution, and for that reason it was specifically not used on war criminals. While the method differs widely from country to country, generally the condemned is blindfolded and restrained. A group of men then fire a single bullet into the heart of the prisoner. In some cases, one of the shooters is given a blank—so that afterward he will feel less guilt. None of the shooters knows who has a blank or, in fact, if any of them do. In the most recent execution by firing squad in Utah, the brother of the executed man stated there were five bullet holes in his brother's shirt, indicating every shooter fired a live round. Here is an eyewitness account of the execution of William Johnson, a deserter in the Army of the Potomac in 1861:

> "All being ready the Marshal waved his handkerchief as the signal, and the firing party discharged the volley. Johnson did not move, remaining in a sitting posture for several seconds after the rifles were discharged. Then he quivered a little, and fell over beside his coffin. He was still alive, however, and the four reserves were called to complete the work. It was found that two of the firing party, Germans, had not discharged their pieces, and they were immediately put in irons. Johnson was shot several times in the heart by the first volley. Each of the four shots fired by the reserves took effect in his head, and he died instantly. One penetrated his chin, another his left cheek, while two entered the brain just above the left eyebrow. He died at precisely a quarter to four o'clock."

In the United States only two states allow execution by firing squad: Idaho and Oklahoma; though Utah still has four prisoners on death row who were sentenced when it was lawful there and they may be permitted to be executed in this way.

4 SINGLE PERSON SHOOTING

Execution by shooting is the most common method of execution in the world, used in over seventy countries. While most of these countries use the firing squad, single person shooting is still found. In Soviet Russia, a single bullet to the back of the head was the most frequently used method of execution for military and non-military alike. This is still the main method of execution in Communist China though the gunshot can be to either the neck or head. In the past, the Chinese government would ask the family of the executed person to pay the price of the bullet. In Taiwan, the prisoner is first injected with a strong anesthetic to render him senseless and then a bullet is fired into his heart.

3 GAS CHAMBER

The gas chamber has been used for executions for a considerable number of years. It has gained the most notoriety from its use in the German prison camps during World War II where it was used to exterminate millions of people in one of the worst cases of genocide in the twentieth century. All of the five U.S. states that still use the gas chamber allow the prisoner to choose death by lethal injection instead. The last death by gas chamber in the U.S. was in 1999 when German Walter LaGrand was executed in Arizona. There are unconfirmed reports North Korea is using the gas chamber as a method of execution and to test poisonous gases on prisoners.

Prior to the execution, the executioner will enter the chamber and place potassium cyanide (KCN) pellets into a small compartment beneath the execution chair. The prisoner is then brought in and secured to the chair. The chamber is sealed and the executioner pours a quantity of concentrated sulfuric acid (H_2SO_4) through a tube that leads to a holding compartment in the chair. The curtains are drawn back for witnesses to see the execution and the prisoner is asked to make his last statement. After the last statement, a level is thrown by the executioner and the acid mixes with the cyanide pellets generating lethal hydrogen cyanide (HCN) gas. The prisoners will generally have been told to take deep breaths in order to speed up unconsciousness, but in most cases they hold their breath. Death from hydrogen cyanide is painful and unpleasant.

After the prisoner is dead, the chamber is purged of gas and neutralized with anhydrous ammonia (NH_3). Both the ammonia and the acid that must be removed from the chamber are highly dangerous. Guards with oxygen masks then enter the chamber and remove the body so it can be examined by a doctor.

2 THE ELECTRIC CHAIR

The electric chair was invented by Harold P. Brown who was employed by Thomas Edison for the sole purpose of investigating the uses of electricity for execution. Brown, a dentist used to working with people in chairs, used a chair design for his device. At the time there was still competition to see whether Edison's direct current (DC) or Westinghouse's alternating current (AC) would win the current war. Edison was in favor of using his opponent's AC as he thought it would lead people to believe that AC was more dangerous than DC. In fact, it would make little difference which current was used as the voltage needed for an execution. Edison was so keen to alienate Westinghouse he tried to get people to refer to execution by electrocution as "westinghousing" someone. The chair was first adopted in 1889 and the first execution took place in 1890 in New York.

In execution by electric chair, the prisoner is strapped to the chair with metal straps and a wet sponge is placed to his head to aid conductivity. Electrodes are placed on the head and leg to create a closed circuit. Depending on the physical state of the prisoner, two currents of varying level and duration are applied. This is generally 2000 volts for fifteen seconds for the first current to cause unconsciousness and to stop the heart. The second current is usually lowered to 8 amps. The current will normally cause severe damage to internal organs and the body can heat up to 138 degrees. While unconsciousness should occur within the first second or two, there have been occasions where it has taken much longer, leading people to speak out against this method of execution.

The post-execution cleanup is an unpleasant task as skin can melt to the electrodes and the person often loses control over bodily functions. The skin is also often burnt.

1 LETHAL INJECTION

Before an execution by lethal injection, the prisoner is prepared for his death. This can include a change of clothing, a last meal, and a shower. The prisoner is taken to the execution chamber and two IV tubes are inserted into his arms; a saline solution is fed through the tubes. These tubes are then fed through the wall into an anteroom from where the execution will be carried out. The anteroom contains direct telephone connections to officials who have the power to stay the execution. Once the IV tubes are connected, the curtains are drawn back so witnesses may watch the execution, and the prisoner is allowed to make his last statement.

Unless a stay is given, the execution begins. There can be one or more executioners, and sometimes in the case of multiple executioners, the lethal dose is given by only one so that no one knows who delivered it. The executioners are shielded from the view of the prisoner and witnesses. The drugs can be delivered by a machine, but due to the fear of mechanical failure, most states prefer to manually inject the drugs into the IV. The drugs are then administered in the following order:

Sodium thiopental: This drug, also known as Pentathol, is a barbiturate used as a surgical anesthetic. In surgery, a dose of up to 150 mg is used; in execution, up to 5000 mg is used. This is a lethal dose. From this point on if the prisoner is still alive, he should feel nothing.

Pancuronium bromide: Also known as Pavulon, this is a muscle relaxant given in a strong enough dose to paralyze the diaphragm and lungs. This drug takes effect in one to three minutes. A normal medical dose is 40–100 mcg per kilogram; the dose delivered in an execution is up to 100 mg.

Potassium chloride: This is a toxic agent that induces cardiac arrest. Not all states use this as the first two drugs are sufficient to bring about death.

Saline solution is used to flush the IV between each dose. Within a minute of two after the final dose is given, a doctor declares the prisoner dead. The body is then sent to the coroner for verification, and sometimes an autopsy, and then is released to the family or the state for burial.

✳✳✳✳✳✳

CHAPTER THREE
Food and Drink

TOP 10
LUXURY FOODS

10 OYSTERS

The name oyster is used for a number of different groups of mollusks, which grow for the most part in marine or brackish water (water that is saltier than fresh water but not as salty as sea water). All types of oysters (and, indeed, many other shelled mollusks) can secrete pearls, but those from edible oysters have no market value. Oysters are best served raw in their own juices with a slice of lemon. Oysters have, for many years, been considered an aphrodisiac.

9 MATSUTAKE

Matsutake is the common name for a group of mushrooms in Japan. They have been an important part of Japanese cuisine for the last thousand years. The tradition of mushroom giving persists today in Japan's corporate world, and a gift of *matsutake* is considered special and cherished by those who receive it. The annual harvest of *matsutake* in Japan is now less than a thousand tons, and it is partly made up of imports from China, Korea, and Canada; this is due to the difficulty in harvesting the mushrooms. The Japanese *matsutake*, at the beginning of the season, which is the highest grade, can go for up to $2000 per kilogram.

8 LOBSTER

Lobsters form a large family of marine crustaceans that nets $1.8 billion for the seafood industry every year. They have a close family relationship with fresh water crayfish. Lobsters live on rocky, sandy, or muddy bottoms from the shoreline to beyond the edge of the continental shelf. They generally live singly in crevices or in burrows under rocks. The most common preparation of lobster is to drop the living creature into a pot of boiling water, which kills it very quickly. The flesh is then served with melted butter so as to not overpower the subtle flavor of the meat.

7 FOIE GRAS

Second to caviar, foie gras is one of the finest Western foods available. It is the liver of ducks (*foie gras de canard*) or geese (*fois gras d'Oie*). It is produced by a method called *gravage*, which is force-feeding the animal grain via a tube down the throat. Ducks and geese have an anatomy that makes this painless. The liver expands to many times the normal size and contains a great deal of fat. The texture of foie gras is very similar to that of butter with a very earthy flavor. Foie gras is generally eaten as a raw pâté, but it can be lightly cooked to give it a greater depth of flavor. Unfortunately, this delicacy is surrounded by controversy and the sale and consumption is banned in some U.S. cities, such as Chicago. It is freely available in all parts of Europe and the rest of the world.

6 FUGU

Fugu is the Japanese word for pufferfish and is also a Japanese dish prepared from the meat of pufferfish. Pufferfish are deadly and if the fish is prepared incorrectly it can lead to death; in fact, there are numerous deaths reported in Japan each year from the consumption of this delicacy. One pinhead of the pufferfish poison is sufficient to kill a full-grown adult male human. It has become one of the most celebrated Japanese dishes. In order to prepare the fish for human consumption, a Japanese chef must undergo rigorous training and certification. It is normally prepared in such a way that a tiny amount of poison is left in the fish as the poison gives it a slightly numbing and tingling effect.

5 BIRD'S NEST

The nests in question here are produced by a variety of Swifts, specifically Cave Swifts, who produce the nest by spitting a chemical compound that hardens in the air. The nests are considered a delicacy in China and are one of the most expensive animal products consumed by humans. It is generally served as a soup but can also be used as a sweet. When combined with water, the hard nests take on a gelatinous texture. My own experience of bird's nest was in a pudding called Bird's Nest and Almond Soup—the nest was dissolved in almond milk and served as a sweet soup. The nest tasted musty and had the texture of snot.

4 KOBE BEEF

True Kobe beef, raised from the black Tajima-ushi breed of Wagyu cattle, is produced only in Hyōgo Prefecture in Japan. It is bred according to secret and strict traditions. It is fed on beer and grain and produces meat so tender and fatty it rivals foie gras in texture. The beef can cost up to three hundred dollars per pound. This breed of cow is genetically predisposed to intense marbling, and produces a higher percentage of oleaginous, unsaturated fat than any other breed of cattle known in the world. Another special trick in the production of this meat is daily massages by the human owners. I must confess to being a little envious!

3 WHITE TRUFFLES

Truffles are from the underground ascomycetes family (tubers) and are reputed for their high prices. They have an odor similar to deep fried walnuts, which is extremely pungent to some people, causing a reeling effect. Interestingly, some people are unable to detect the odor of truffles (which is possibly to their advantage!). The white truffle is the most expensive of the family. They are generally served sliced into extremely thin slivers on top of other food and are frequently suffused in oil for sale as truffle oil.

2 SAFFRON

Saffron is the most expensive spice in the world, reaching prices beyond two thousand dollars per pound (depending on season). Saffron is the three stigmas and style of the crocus flower. Each stigma and style must be picked by hand and it takes thousands to make a single ounce of the spice. Brightly yellow in color, the spice is used for coloring and subtle flavoring of food. It has a bitter taste and a hay-like fragrance.

1 BELUGA CAVIAR

Beluga caviar is the most expensive food item in the world, costing up to five thousand dollars per kilogram. Caviar is fish roe (eggs) and this particular brand comes from the beluga sturgeon, found mostly in the Caspian Sea. It can take up to twenty years for a beluga sturgeon to reach its maximum size and they can each weigh up to two tons. The eggs are the largest of the fish eggs used for caviar. Beluga usually ranges from purple to black, the palest being the most expensive. Beluga caviar is generally served on its own on small pieces of toast, as it needs no additions of flavor to improve it. If you have not experienced eating caviar, when you bite down each egg pops and releases a slightly salty-fishy flavor.

✳✳✳✳✳✳

TOP 10 UNUSUAL USES FOR BEER

10 BATH SOAK

Beer is an excellent skin conditioner. Next time you want to have a long soak in the bath, tip in a good dark beer before you hop in and just soak in it! This is a nice alternative to adding salt crystals, which soften water, but I see no reason you couldn't combine both for a super-luxurious bath. Just don't be tempted to drink the bathwater! Oh—and be careful if you go outside afterward on a hot day (see number 4).

9 SOOTHE AN UPSET TUMMY

This is my favorite item on the list. If you have a stomach upset, slowly sipping a can of beer can help to settle it down—and the alcohol has an anesthetic effect, which helps to alleviate the pain. As most of us will know, this is also a very effective hangover cure! Just be sure not to use this trick if you have an ulcer or gastritis.

8 POLISH YOUR FURNITURE

Beer is a surprisingly good wood furniture polish. Let a can of beer go completely stale and flat and pour a little onto a polishing cloth. Buff your wood furniture and follow up with a final dry buff. You will be amazed at how brilliant and shiny your furniture will end up looking.

7 MARINATE MEAT

Beer makes an excellent marinade. It really doesn't matter what meat you are preparing—it will benefit almost all types from a few hours (the longer the better) in a marinade of beer. You can get really adventurous too; add any flavors you like to the beer, even things like marmalade or jam. A more common addition would be soy sauce or other Asian sauces. If you are marinating pork, you might want to add some chunks of pineapple and pineapple juice with some ginger for a sweet and sour dish.

6 NATURALLY REMOVE SLUGS

Slugs are terrible pests in a garden, particularly if you are growing for eating. Instead of using chemicals like DDT on your veggies, bury a small saucer up to its lip in the garden and put fresh beer in it each day. The slugs will be attracted to the smell, get drunk, and drown. Be sure to refresh the beer daily. With a little luck you should have a saucer full of slugs and healthy looking cabbages!

5 FERTILIZE YOUR GARDEN

The yeast and other extracts in a can of beer are very good for plants. If you end up with a pile of leftover half-drunk cans or bottles of beer, tip them out onto the garden. Just watch out for cigarette butts if your guests use them for ashtrays; while some plants like nicotine extract, not all do and you could kill your prize plants.

4 DETER BEES

Bees and wasps are attracted to beer. Instead of spending a fortune on citronella oils or candles, try putting a few open beer cans around the yard at your next BBQ. Obviously you should put the cans away from where people will be sitting or standing. Oh—and make sure no one decides to have a swig from one of the cans when they are drunk—it will result in a very unpleasant (and potentially lethal) situation!

3 WASH YOUR HAIR

Beer "shampoo" can add luster and body to dull limp hair. It is also a much more natural alternative than store-bought shampoos which contain a lot of chemicals. Just mix one can of beer with a raw egg and use as you would a normal shampoo. It was quite common in days gone by to use raw eggs for shampoo; it even lathers up like the chemical stuff. Try it—I am sure you will be pleasantly surprised. Just keep in mind that the shampoo will go bad if you don't use it within a couple of days. This is probably best as a once-a-month special treatment. You can also use beer on its own as a conditioner—rinse your hair with it, let it dry off, then rinse it off.

2 MAKE A BATTER

When making a batter, you often add a little rising agent, usually baking powder. In this recipe, you use beer—the bubbles in the drink and the yeast provide the rising. So, here is the recipe: put one-and-a-half cups of flour and half a teaspoon of salt into a bowl. Pour in one twelve-ounce can of beer while mixing. That is it! If the batter is too thick, add more beer. If it is too thin, add a little more flour. If you are planning to use this batter with fish, dredge the fish in flour first, remembering to shake off the excess. This is a great-tasting batter I use all the time.

1 BBQ A CHICKEN

This has to be one of the easiest recipes around. You simply take a full opened can of beer, stand a chicken on it, and throw it on the barbecue (well, don't literally throw it, that could be very messy!). The beer can is inserted in the neck area (where you would normally stuff the chicken) and stood upright. While the chicken cooks, the beer heats up and subtly flavors the meat. You end up with a tasty and surprisingly moist chicken. You should also rub a little olive oil over the chicken and salt and pepper it before starting. If you have a favorite "rub," you can add that too. Make sure you drink half of the can first—it should be half full when starting out. I am sure you will have no trouble finding someone to help you with that part of the recipe. Cook the chicken with the BBQ lid on for approximately one-and-a-quarter hours or until the internal temperature registers 165°F in the breast area and 180°F in the thigh (or the juices run clear if you pierce it with a knife).

✳✳✳✳✳✳

TOP 10 COMMON ERRORS MADE IN COOKING

10 PAN TOO COLD

When you cook in a pan not hot enough, things stick and they don't color. This is a very common mistake made when cooking steak or other meat dishes in a frying pan. Don't be afraid to turn the heat right up; you can always remove the pan from the heat if it looks to be too hot. Don't use a nonstick pan—throw all the nonstick cookware in the garbage and use real pots and pans.

9 FISH OVERCOOKED

Overcooked fish is one of the most revolting things you can eat. It lacks flavor and moisture. When you cook fish properly, it should retain some of the transparency you get with raw fish. Don't fear that it will be raw—the heat can still penetrate to the core without overcooking it. As a side note, when buying fresh fish, make sure the fish eyes are shiny and clear and the gills are still red. Fresh fish should also have no odor (apart from the smell of the sea); if it smells fishy, don't buy it.

8 TOO MUCH INTERFERENCE

When you cook a steak, you must put it in the pan and not touch it again until it is time to turn it over. Moving meat around a pan stops it from browning. Coupled with a cold pan (number 10), you will end up with limp, soggy, and uncolored meat. You should not fall to the temptation to give things a shove or to check for the level of cooking. Cook based on time (for example, one minute either side for steak) and leave it alone!

7 OVERCROWDING

When frying on top of the stove, people tend to try to do everything at once, like putting half a dozen sausages in the pan, or two or three steaks. This only ruins the food—overcrowding the pan causes food to boil, as there is not enough room for the steam to leave the pan, instead of browning. Cook in batches and, if you need to, keep meat in a warmed oven while you continue through the batches.

6 OVERCOOKING MEAT

Most people who have little cooking experience will be familiar with the large cut of meat that has shrivelled up like a prune during cooking. The reason for this is that when you heat meat beyond a certain temperature, the meat proteins begin to contract—forcing the juices (and flavor!) out of the meat. The solution is to make sure that when you roast meat, you do it on a low heat for a long time. The great chef Heston Blumenthal, owner of The Fat Duck, cooks his meat at a maximum of 75°C (~170°F) for many hours, resulting in succulent and flavorful cuts. I strongly recommend you check out his cookbooks. *Family Food* is a particularly good one and includes a section on meat cooking in this manner.

5 NOT ENOUGH SALT

All too frequently people use too little salt in their cooking (or worse still: no salt at all!). Salt is essential in cooking as it provides flavor and, in some cases, texture. You should salt all meat before you cook it, and most of the time you should salt water before cooking vegetables in it. It is not enough to add salt at the last minute as some foods cook better with salt added during the cooking process. I should also mention here that you should immediately throw away any table salt you own and buy proper sea salt (or kosher salt). Table salt contains flowing agents and anti-caking agents. It contains so much of this stuff that if you sniff a container of table salt it smells like metal. Good quality salt should have no smell or a very slight perfume (from the sea).

4 BLUNT KNIVES

Blunt knives are not only bad in the kitchen because they tear at what you are cutting, but they are extremely dangerous. Most accidents involving knives in the kitchen are caused by blunt knives. The reason for this is that the knife is more prone to slipping. I personally prefer Japanese steel in my knives but there are also some excellent quality European knives as well. For those with the big budget I strongly recommend Hattori knives (go for the HD or KD series—they will cost upwards of three hundred dollars a knife).

3 USING DRIED HERBS

Dried herbs have no place in the kitchen. They have little (if any) of the flavor of the herb they are meant to represent. If you cook with dried herbs, you cook with no flavor. The first time you use fresh herbs in your cooking, you will immediately understand the importance of them. This also goes for vegetables. Always buy the freshest vegetables you can, preferably locally grown—buying locally grown means you only get what is in season, and, therefore, the best tasting veggies.

2 USING CHEAP KITCHENWARE

I am sure we are all well acquainted with pots and pans that are as light as a feather and coated with a nonstick coating. Throw. These. Out. Now. You simply cannot get the right feel for heat with these abominable tin pots. A proper cooking pot should have a very heavy base. They need not be cast iron, but they should certainly require a little elbow grease to lift. If you have a budget large enough, you should aim for copper pots as they provide the best conductivity of heat.

1 USING CHEAP WINE

Wine is undoubtedly my favorite thing in the world—I quaff copious amounts of the stuff (in order to improve my palate of course). One of the big "sins" in the kitchen is using "cooking" wine. There is no such thing as special wine for cooking—it is cheap and nasty wine with a dishonest label on it! The golden rule with wine in the kitchen is you must only use wine you would happily drink. The upside to this golden rule is you invariably end up with a lot of spare wine for drinking. Be sure not to keep your "good" wine in the pantry when you are done—drink it and buy a fresh bottle next time you need it.

✳✳✳✳✳✳

TOP 10 FASCINATING FOOD FACTS

10 BUTTER TEA

Fascinating Fact: In Tibet, a common drink is butter tea made from yak butter, salt, and tea.

The average Tibetan can drink fifty to sixty cups of this tea in any one day! It is made by drying Chinese tea in the road for several days (to let it acquire a strong flavor). The tea is then boiled for up to half a day and churned in bamboo churns to which salt, a pinch of soda, and rancid butter have been added. When drinking the tea, you can blow the scum (from the butter) away from the edge of the cup and sip. Some Tibetans add *tsu* and flour to their tea (in much the same way as we add milk and sugar). *Tsu* is a mixture of hardened cheese, butter, and sugar. When you sip the tea, your host will refill your cup, as it should always remain full. We now move on from one drink to another:

9 HOT CHOCOLATE

Fascinating Fact: The ancient Mayans made truly hot chocolate—they added chilies and corn to it!

The first records of chocolate being used for drinking come from residue found in ancient Mayan pots, dating back to the fifth century AD. The drink was made by pounding chocolate beans into a paste, which was then mixed with water, chili peppers, cornmeal, and assorted spices. The drink was then poured back and forth between a cup and a pot, which gave it a foamy head. This was drunk cold, and people of all classes drank it regularly. The drink tasted spicy and bitter, unlike today's hot chocolate. When chocolate finally reached the West, it was very expensive, costing between fifty and seventy dollars per pound in equivalent modern U.S. dollars. If you ever get to Paris, be sure to visit Angelina for the best hot chocolate in the world—try the Chocolat l'Africain.

8 MYSTERIOUS HISTORY OF DONUTS

Fascinating Fact: No one really knows when donuts were invented or who invented them.

Donuts (doughnuts in UK English) were originally made as a long twist of dough, not in the ring form that is most common these days. It was also common in England for donuts to be made in a ball shape and injected with jam after they were cooked; this is still very common. Both methods of cooking involve no human intervention as the ball and twist will turn itself over when the underside is cooked. The ring donut common in the U.S. just seemed to appear; but one Hansen Gregory, an American, claimed to have invented it in 1847 when he was traveling on a steamboat. He was not satisfied with the texture of the center of the donut so he pressed a hole in the center with the ship's pepper box.

7 APPLE, POTATO, OR ONION?

Fascinating Fact: Apples, potatoes, and onions all taste the same when eaten with your nose plugged.

As a child we had a science class in which we were blindfolded, had our noses plugged, and given an apple or onion to eat; we were not told which of the two we would be given. Not one person was able to state which was which. This shows the incredibly important part the nose plays in the sense of taste. The fact that the three items have a similar consistency makes it virtually impossible to tell them apart without the sense of smell. If you try this, I should warn you: once you unblock your nose, you can tell what you have just eaten.

6 FLOATING EGGS

Fascinating Fact: When an egg floats in water, it has gone bad and should not be eaten.

As eggs age, gases build up inside the shell making it more buoyant. This is the best way to test whether an egg has gone rotten without having to break open the shell, risking the foul odor escaping. When an egg is extremely fresh it will lie on its side at the bottom of a glass of water. As it ages, the egg will begin to point upwards, and will finally float completely when it has gone bad. Fresh eggs have a very firm white, while old eggs have a very watery white. This is why it is best to use the freshest eggs possible for poaching and frying. Older eggs are perfectly good for omelets or scrambling.

5 VANILLA JUNKIE

Fascinating Fact: The consumption of natural vanilla causes the body to release catecholamines, including adrenalin, considered to be mildly addictive.

When vanilla plants were first exported from Mexico to other tropical climes, they flowered but wouldn't produce vanilla pods. It was discovered a bee native to Mexico was the only creature that could pollinate vanilla flowers (vanilla comes from a special species of orchid). Attempts to move the bee to other countries failed and it was not until a slave boy discovered a method of artificial pollination that Mexico lost its monopoly on vanilla. As well as being mildly addictive, vanilla has also been found to block bacterial infections.

4 BANANA TREES

Fascinating Fact: Banana trees are not actually trees; they are giant herbs.

The large stem mistaken for a trunk on a banana tree is actually a "pseudostem," meaning "fake stem." Each pseudostem provides a single bunch of yellow, green, or red bananas. This then dies and is replaced by another pseudostem. Smaller bunches of bananas (such as the ones we buy in shops) are actually called "hands," not "bunches," which can weigh up to 110 pounds. The bananas we eat are specially cultivated to exclude seeds; therefore, you can't plant a banana tree from a commercially grown banana. Wild bananas have many large hard seeds.

3 BRAIN FREEZE

Fascinating Fact: The term "brain freeze" was invented by 7-11 to explain the pain one feels when drinking a slurpee too fast.

Believe it or not, there is a real scientific name for "brain freeze": sphenopalatine ganglioneuralgia. Try saying that five times fast! When something very cold (usually ice cream) touches the top palate of the mouth, it causes the blood vessels to constrict. This makes the nerves send a signal to the brain to reopen them. The rapid reopening of the vessels causes a buildup of fluid in the tissues causing a slight swelling in the forehead and, therefore, causing pain. It normally takes thirty to sixty seconds for the fluid to drain, relieving the pain.

2 ANCIENT SAUCE

Fascinating Fact: Ketchup was originally a fish sauce originating in the orient.

Two words from the Fujian region of China were used to describe a fish brine/sauce and a tomato sauce. Both words bear a striking resemblance in sound to the word "ketchup": *ke-tsap* and *kio-chiap*. Early Western ketchups were made with fish and spices, or mushrooms. In fact, mushroom ketchup is still available in the United Kingdom and is prized by some modern chefs for its natural inclusion of monosodium glutamate—the only substance known to stimulate the fifth human taste sense *umami* (savory).

1 FEEL GOOD WITH 7-UP

Fascinating Fact: 7-Up, invented in 1920, contained lithium, the drug now commonly prescribed to sufferers of bipolar disorder.

The drink was originally marketed as a hangover cure, due to the inclusion of lithium citrate. It was released just a few years before the Wall Street crash of the 1920s and marketed under the name "Bib-Label Lithiated Lemon-Lime Soda," quite a mouthful! The name was changed to 7-Up shortly after its release but lithium remained one of the ingredients until 1950. Some popular myths surround the name of the drink, but the name is most likely due to the original recipe containing seven ingredients (with the "up" portion relating to the lithium) or the fact lithium has an atomic mass of seven.

✳✳✳✳✳✳

TOP 10 FOOD MYTHS DEBUNKED

10 FAT FREE—LOSE WEIGHT
The Myth: Fat-free food is calorie free.

This is a very common myth, so common that food manufacturers market to it. The misconception that fat-free is better is the reason so many products are labeled "fat free," "low in fat," "fat reduced," etc. So many people who want to lose weight will chow down on all of these "low-fat" foods thinking they are going to lose weight; even worse, they often tend to eat more of the low-fat food than they would have if it were full-fat. What really matters when trying to reduce weight is calories—eat fewer calories than you burn and you will lose weight. When fat is removed from food a lot of the flavor is removed as well; consequently, extra sugars and chemicals are often added to give back the flavor. Fat-free food can, therefore, be far worse and fattening for you than regular full-fat food.

9 EAT THE SALAD
The Myth: Fast food salads are the "healthy option."

A 2005 report by the *Independent* said: "[a]n investigation of the food sold by the 'big four'—McDonald's, Burger King, KFC, and Pizza Hut—found that [...] five out of eight of the salads used as 'evidence' of their embrace of healthy eating had 'high' salt or fat content." It is all too common to see dieters who crave a little something naughty, ordering salads or other "healthy choices" from fast food joints, but what they usually don't realize is the salads can be as bad as the regular food and they would be more content if they just ate a Big Mac. For the sake of comparison, I looked it up: one Big Mac has 540 calories and 1040 mg of salt; one Premium Southwest Salad with crispy chicken and dressing has 530 calories and 1260 mg of salt. The Mac is healthier.

8 PROTEIN POWER

The Myth: When trying to gain muscle, you should eat copious amounts of protein.

According to the Mayo Clinic, 10 to 35 percent of your daily dietary intake should be protein, whether trying to gain weight, lose weight, or maintain weight. Most of this comes from our regular food and we seldom need to take protein supplements. Even more damning for this myth are two recent studies by independent sport medicine journals in which various people (including bodybuilders) were given varying extra quantities of protein each day; summing one study up, Dr. Richard Krieder from the University of Memphis said: "Although it is important for athletes to get an adequate amount of protein . . . consuming additional amounts of protein does not appear to promote muscle growth."

7 FRESH FRUIT IS BEST

The Myth: Fresh fruit is better than dried fruit.

This myth is true in only one regard: if you are looking for vitamin C, then fresh fruit is best, but other than that, dried fruit contains just as many nutrients and sugar for energy as fresh fruit. If you subscribe to the notion that you should eat five fruits a day, then you only need one tablespoon of dried fruit per portion, so five tablespoons of dried fruit fulfill your daily need. The same is true of canned or frozen fruit. Fruit juice can also be used as a daily fruit portion but only one should be made up of juice only.

6 SIX MINI MEALS ARE BETTER THAN THREE

The Myth: It is better to eat six small meals during the day instead of three larger meals.

First off, this can be okay, but only if you are extremely good at controlling your portion sizes; it is all too easy to turn six small meals into six large meals. This myth again comes down to the whole "calories per day" rule. If your three large meals contain as many calories as your six small meals, there is no difference at all. For the majority of people it is easier to put the time aside for three meals, so this is still the best choice for most. The time of day that you eat does not have a bearing on weight gain or loss.

5 CELERY HAS NEGATIVE CALORIES

The Myth: It takes more calories to eat a stick of celery than are contained in the celery itself, making it a negative calorie food.

This one is so popular even Snopes believes it, and it is rare for Snopes to be wrong. But the problem is, the numbers don't add up. One stick of celery contains around six calories. A female weighing 150 pounds, age thirty-five, and five-feet-five-inches tall burns thirty calories per hour eating while sitting. In the interests of science I ate a stick of celery (which is no mean feat considering I hate raw celery) to see how long it would take: two minutes and fourteen seconds. If the female described above takes as long as I do, that means she can eat just under thirty sticks of celery in one hour, totaling 180 calories. That leaves an excess of 150 calories still not burned. Granted, there is some calorie burning involved in the digestive process as well, but there is no way these numbers allow for negative calories; on average you burn sixty-two calories an hour just existing (this includes digestion). That still leaves an excess calorie count of eighty-eight. No matter which way you look at it, celery does not result in negative calories.

4 DECAF HAS NO CAFFEINE

The Myth: Decaffeinated coffee contains no caffeine.

International standards require decaf to be 97 percent caffeine free (EU standards are a little stricter at 99.9 percent). The process of removing caffeine is a long one and it also means that many other chemicals (up to four hundred, in fact) essential to the taste of coffee are lost. If you have an allergy to caffeine, you should probably keep away from all forms of coffee, decaf included. But for those who can cope with caffeine, unless you really can't stand the slight "high" produced by it, you will have a nicer tasting drink if you just opt for regular coffee. And if that hasn't convinced you, the chemical often used in decaffeinating coffee beans (dichloromethane) is also used as a paint stripper.

3 STARK CRAVING MADNESS

The Myth: Craving is your body telling you it needs something.

When we get a craving for certain foods, such as fruit juice, we often think it is because of a lack in our body of a certain nutrient. Interestingly, scientists who put this idea to the test found out it wasn't true at all. In the study, a person who craved chocolate was given a cocktail of chemicals that contained all of the essential components (minus taste) of chocolate, and another cocktail containing chocolate flavor but no components of chocolate. The craving was satisfied when they took the chocolate-flavored cocktail, but not the essentially flavorless chocolate. This strongly suggests cravings are simply emotional. We crave certain foods because of the memories and emotions relating to that food in our lives.

2 SALT INCREASES BLOOD PRESSURE
The Myth: Excess salt increases your blood pressure.

This is a myth that originated in the 1940s when a professor used salt reduction to treat people with high blood pressure. Science has since found out there is no reason for a person with normal blood pressure to restrict their salt intake. However, if you already have high blood pressure, you may become salt-sensitive, in which case you should reduce salt or increase your potassium intake, as it is the balance of the two that really matters. Furthermore, people who suffer from hypertension should be careful with salt as it can have an impact there. Ultimately, eating more potassium is probably more important than reducing salt. Potassium-rich foods are spinach, broccoli, bananas, white potatoes, and most types of beans.

1 FAST FOOD IS BAD
The Myth: Fast food is bad for you.

A very wise man once said, "all things in moderation." This ancient phrase applies to most things in life, including fast food. A moderate amount of fast food is no worse for you than a moderate amount of home-cooked meat and vegetables. A constant diet of nothing but fast food may not be the healthiest choice you can make, but then again, eating macaroni and cheese every night is not very healthy either. Variety and moderation are the keys to good eating and health. If you feel like a cheeseburger, eat one.

✳✳✳✳✳✳

TOP 10 UNUSUAL USES FOR PEANUT BUTTER

10 LUBE IT UP
Peanut butter is an excellent lubricator. If your lawnmower blades are getting a little tight and rusty, smear on some of the spread and voila—perfect

lubrication. This hint is particularly useful because almost every time I need lube, I don't have any around, but I always have a jar of peanut butter in the cupboard. It can be used for virtually all your lubrication needs.

9 ANIMAL MEDICINE

If you own a cat or a dog, you will know how hard it can be to get them to take their medication, especially when it is in pill form. Fortunately cats and dogs love peanut butter, so next time you have to give them some medication, mix it up with a spoonful and feed it to them. No more struggling with the animal as you hold its mouth open and try to force-feed it a bitter pill.

8 BUTTER REPLACEMENT

Most recipes that use butter can be cooked with peanut butter instead. In cookies and cakes this can make a wonderful and subtle taste difference. Next time you are making fudge brownies, try using peanut butter instead; it will be like eating a huge Reese's Peanut Butter Cup. You can also stir peanut butter into a sauce instead of butter to give it a nutty finish.

7 MOUSETRAP BAIT

Mice are not particularly fond of cheese, so it is strange that it is the first food people go for when they are baiting their mousetraps. What most people don't know is that mice prefer peanut butter; how this has been proven I do not know, but the fact that peanut butter is so much cheaper than cheese

makes this tip a very handy and frugal one. So next time you need to bait a mousetrap, don't bother loading it with Camembert or five-year-aged cheddar, stick on some trusty peanut butter.

6 PRICE TAG REMOVAL

Despite the major advances in science in recent years, no one seems to have managed to invent a label that can be removed easily without leaving any glue behind. Fortunately, we have peanut butter. Rub some of the tasty spread on the label glue and rub with a cloth—it works brilliantly.

5 DE-FISH THE HOUSE

If you have ever fried fish, you will know it leaves behind a rather unpleasant fishy smell in the house. To help eradicate the smell, take a tablespoon of peanut butter after you have finished frying the fish, drop it in the frying pan, and fry it off for a minute or two. The smell of peanut butter in the house is much more enjoyable than stale fish and oil.

4 LEATHER CLEANER

Peanut butter is an excellent cleaner for leather furniture. Just rub a small amount on and work it in with a circular motion. Remove with a buffing cloth and there you have it! The caveat to this tip is peanut-butter smelling furniture. To avoid that you might want to mix a little perfume oil in it, but not too much. Also, if you do add the perfume, make sure you don't mix up your jars or you will end up with a peanut butter and jelly sandwich that tastes like mouthwash.

3 PEANUT BUTTER COOKIES

This one doesn't seem quite so weird, but it is included because these cookies use peanut butter as the main ingredient—there is no flour at all. The cookies are a mix of peanut butter, sugar, egg, and vanilla. You can even throw in a handful of chocolate chips if you wish. The resulting cookies are amazingly tasty and it only takes about twenty minutes from start to finish.

2 GUM REMOVER

While it doesn't happen quite so often to us adults, children often end up with gum in their hair. This would normally be followed by a lot of tugging and pulling with a comb to remove it, and the eventual chopping of the locks. But what most people don't realize is that peanut butter is a perfect "gum remover"—not only will it remove gum from hair, it will remove gum from carpet and any other object tainted with the chewy stuff. Just rub some peanut butter into the gum and you can wipe the whole mess off with a cloth.

1 SHAVE WITH IT

Believe it or not, peanut butter makes a great shaving gel. Just apply it like you would apply the gel, and shave as normal. It works just as well, and anyone that has bought a container of shaving gel will know it is a hell of a lot cheaper. The end result is a very smooth shave and, as a bonus, the oils in the peanut butter are very good for your skin, so you don't need to spend even more money on moisturizer for your legs or face. You might want to remember to use smooth peanut butter though; the chunky stuff doesn't work quite as well.

✳✳✳✳✳✳

TOP 10 BIZARRE INGREDIENTS IN FOOD

10 GOLD

Gold is one of the most popular metals used in jewelry. It is also very useful in electronics. In addition to its more common uses, gold is used as a food additive, usually for decorative purposes in the form of gold leaf (food additive number 175). It is quite popular as an additive to alcoholic drinks and there is a traditional Polish and German liqueur called Goldwasser (Goldwater), which contains thousands of tiny flakes. Gold is inert to body chemistry so it passes through the body unaltered and has no nutritional value.

9 VIRUSES

In August 2006, the U.S. Food and Drug Administration approved the use of bacteriophages in the preparation of food (specifically ready-to-eat meat products). A bacteriophage is a virus that infects bacteria; the point of applying these viruses to food is they will kill any bacteria that might cause food poisoning. Every year, twenty-five hundred Americans get sick from listeriosis; consequently, millions of Americans now regularly chow down on viruses added intentionally to stop those few thousand people getting sick. The FDA does not require that food treated with these viruses should carry a label. Frighteningly, they say, "As long as it [is] used in accordance with the regulations, we have concluded it's safe." Worthwhile? You be the judge.

8 BORAX

Borax: fire retardant, insecticide, treatment for horse thrush, component in glass and detergent, and … food ingredient. Borax is illegal as a food additive in the U.S. in all goods except caviar, but not so in many other nations. In some

Asian countries it is found in noodles, meatballs, and steamed rice. It can have serious toxic effects on humans, particularly affecting the testes.

7 COAL TAR

Once upon a time, amaranth was used as a food coloring (red to be specific) but scientific testing found it to be extremely carcinogenic, so someone came up with a replacement: allura red AC. Allura red AC is made from coal tar (a liquid byproduct of turning coal into coal gas or coke). Coal tar is flammable and is frequently used in medicated shampoos designed to kill head lice. It is also used to make Tylenol. While allura red AC is not carcinogenic, it can cause vomiting and other side effects in some people. Despite this, it is FDA-approved and very common in candy and soft drinks.

6 VARNISH

Okay, to be more exact we are talking about shellac, which was very commonly used as a varnish back in the old days (from around 1880–1930) before it was replaced with lacquer. Shellac is used in baking and in mass-produced candy to give the finished product a nice shine. The most likely source of shellac in most of our readers' diets will be from Skittles, the colorful coated fruit-flavored candies. Now that we know how much we love to eat shellac, we should probably also point out it is made from a secretion of the female lac beetle. She excretes the shellac onto branches in order to help her cocoon stick.

5 BUGS

Cochineal and carmine are two red food colorings derived from bugs, the cochineal bug to be exact. Cochineal is produced by drying and pulverizing the whole body of the cochineal bug; carmine is a derivative of cochineal powder. The bugs are usually killed by immersing them in boiling water—the amount of time they spent in the water determines the level of redness—whether it be a lighter orange color or a vivid red. 155,000 insects are needed to make two pounds of food dye. Cochineal has been used for hundreds of years and it is also a very popular cloth dye.

4 CIGARETTES

You read that right… Cigarette smoking has been banned from bars and pubs all around the world, so someone came up with a brilliant idea: if you can't smoke it, eat it! The trick is to take a fine bottle of spirits (usually vodka but sometimes brandy, etc.) and drop a smoke or two in it (or a cigar in the case of brandy). The nicotine, and other chemicals, seep out of the cigarette and infuse flavor and color into the drink. These concoctions are often called "nicotine tea." I was fortunate (?) enough to try one at a bar recently and I can't say I enjoyed the drink a great deal.

3 BEAVER ASS

Beaver anal juice, castoreum, is not yet able to be synthesized so it is still used in foodstuffs. It is most commonly found as a flavor enhancer in raspberry products; apparently it adds a nice rounded flavor. It is also found in chewing gum and cigarettes. The question is: who the hell discovered beaver poop juice tasted good with raspberries?

2 HUMAN HAIR

L-cysteine is an amino acid commonly used in baked goods because it adds elasticity and helps soften dough. It is also commonly used in hair perm solutions. You can find it in bagels, doughnuts, bread, cookies, and frankly, a hell of a lot of yummy things. The cheapest way to produce it (and therefore the most common source at present) is by a special chemical process using human hair, most of which is sourced (and prepared) in China. Because of this, it has led to some debate over whether eating products containing l-cysteine is a type of cannibalism. In China it was also used in the production of soy sauce:

> "When asking [the soy manufacturer] how the amino acid syrup (or powder) was generated, [he] replied that the powder was generated from human hair. Because the human hair was gathered from salon [sic], barbershop [sic] and hospitals around the country, it was unhygienic and mixed with condom [sic], used hospital cottons, used menstrual cycle pad [sic], used syringe [sic], etc."

1 POOP

A common ingredient found in poop is called skatole. The word comes from the ancient Greek root "skat" meaning "dung"; this is the same root from which we get "scatology," the study of feces. It is derived from mammals (it is produced in their digestive tract) and it smells (not surprisingly) like poop. This delightful ingredient is used in cigarettes, many perfumes and, most importantly for the purposes of this list, strawberry ice cream. Like the beaver ass above, someone discovered strawberry flavor is greatly enhanced with the addition of a little dung. Frankly, I will stick to pepper.

✳✳✳✳✳✳

TOP 10 WAYS TO SAVE MONEY ON FOOD

10 MAKE A LIST

When you are shopping for food, it is important you make a list—this will help avoid buying things you do not need. The highest cost of shopping is almost always the unexpected extras you don't really need. Making a list also helps you to realize just how much food you are buying—you would be surprised how much "deadwood" you can cut out. This is particularly effective when used in conjunction with numbers 6 and 8.

9 STOP USING RECIPES

Cooking from recipes is great if you are not the most confident cook, but if you force yourself to experiment with food, you can use up all the bits and pieces left over in the refrigerator and cupboards that might otherwise just sit there and spoil. If you try to empty your cupboards between shopping you will save a fortune; in some cases you will find you can skip a whole week of shopping. When you are trying to save money you have to give up the idea of luxury meals every day.

8 SHOP ONLINE

When I shop online with a list (see number 10), my grocery bill is more than halved. Supermarkets are designed by specialists who know how to convince you to buy things you don't want. Every item is placed in such a way that it will entice you. The supermarkets have become incredibly good at this, as is evidenced by my half-price shopping bill when I don't go to the store. You usually save so much money that the small delivery fee charged by some online shopping stores is worth paying. Make sure to follow tip 10 and buy only what it is on your list—nothing more.

7 KEEP LEFTOVERS

Supermarkets have a tendency to package items in odd numbers, such as a pack of three steaks when you only want two. This can work to your advantage: buy the three-pack, cook it all, and save one piece for lunch the next day. This is true of all leftovers—they can either be reheated and eaten the next day, frozen for later use, or recycled in another meal (when you cook leftovers it is called *réchauffé*). Leftover chicken from a roast can be turned into a hearty chicken soup, leftover cooked meat can be ground (minced) and made into a pie filling; the list is endless. Just remember (number 9) that recipes are not going to help you to cook with leftovers—you need to just dive in and give it a try.

6 MAKE A CORE MENU

It is a good idea to make a core menu for the week—a menu that doesn't change from week to week. This may include things like sausages and mashed potatoes, fried chicken, Caesar salad, and so on. By adding five regular meals you can control the cost of your shopping, and as time goes on, you can learn ways to make shortcuts and save more money. Furthermore, one large bag of potatoes can be used up in two weeks instead of half a bag sitting around spoiling. Use your extra two days to add a special meal—something that changes every week so you don't get bored with your meals.

5 BUY IN BULK

Buying in bulk is almost always cheaper than buying small portions. It is important to remember, however, this is not an effective shopping tool if you are buying bulk items that you don't normally use. Bulk shopping should be reserved to the items you use regularly and in large quantities. For example, if you bake your own bread, you should buy the largest sack of flour you can, but if you never bake your own bread, you should not buy bulk flour. This seems like an obvious point, but a lot of people get so enthusiastic about the savings they buy unnecessary goods.

4 BUY STORE BRANDS

Not only are store-brand goods almost always cheaper, often they contain the very same food as a label brand. This is true not just of food but also clothing. It is definitely not worth paying twice the price just for a fancy label when the quality of the goods is identical. We certainly wouldn't buy a Kia with a Mercedes logo on it for twice the price as a Kia with the Kia logo. Why do it with food?

3 COOK FROM SCRATCH

Cooking from scratch is one of the best ways to save money in shopping. Pre-packaged and pre-cooked meals are expensive; every step in the process of turning raw food into prepared food adds more to the price. This is true of cuts of meat as well: chicken with the skin and bones intact costs a lot less than skinned and boned chicken breasts. For the two minutes of work you save when buying pre-cut meat, it is hardly worth paying a premium price. Cooking from scratch will not only save you money, it will make you healthier as your food will not contain preservatives and chemicals. Also, you can quite often cook a meal from scratch in the same time as it takes to open and heat a pre-made meal.

2 USE COUPONS

Coupons are an excellent way to save money. Some shops use "loss leaders," when they sell goods at cost or less than cost. The aim of loss leaders is to draw customers into the store. Take advantage of this and shop at a few different places—buying only coupon items. You will be amazed how much money you can save. But be warned—just like bulk buying—do not buy items you do not need just because they are so inexpensive. You are not saving any money when you buy something you don't need.

1 BUY LOCAL PRODUCE

Buying local produce will always be cheaper than transported goods because you are not paying transportation costs, and it is these costs that are growing the most rapidly at present. Furthermore, you get to build up a good relationship with members of your local community and get the freshest fruit and vegetables. This also means you are eating seasonal produce and not something frozen for a year before it hits the shops. Why pay twice the price for last year's apples when you can get apples that have just come off the tree?

✳✳✳✳✳✳

TOP 10 POISONOUS FOODS WE LOVE TO EAT

10 MUSHROOMS

We have all heard of toadstools, and know they are poisonous, but what many people don't know is that a toadstool is actually a mushroom, not a separate type of plant. "Toadstool" is slang for "poisonous mushroom." While there are some useful signs indicating a mushroom is poisonous, they are not consistent and all mushrooms of unknown origin should be considered dangerous to eat. Some of the things you can look for to determine whether a mushroom is poisonous are: a flat cap with no bumps, pink or black gills (poisonous mushrooms often have white gills), and the gills should stay attached to the cap (not the stalk) if you pull it off. But, remember, while this is generally true of many types of mushroom, it is not always true.

9 PUFFERFISH

The fugu (pufferfish) is so poisonous that in Japan, fugu chefs are trained specially for the job and are tested before being given a certificate of practice. The training takes two or three years. In order to pass, the chef must answer a written test then give a demonstration of his cutting abilities. The final part of the test involves the chef eating the pieces of fugu he has cut. Only 30 percent of apprentices pass the test, which is not to say the rest die by eating their fugu; they can fail in earlier parts of the test. Only the flesh of the fugu is consumed, as it is less likely to have high amounts of poison (which causes a slight tingling sensation in the mouth). Fugu is the only food officially illegal for the Emperor of Japan to eat—for his safety.

8 ELDERBERRY

Elderberry trees are very attractive and quite large. They are covered with thousands of tiny flowers, which have a delicate scent. The flowers are used mainly for making elderflower liqueur and soda. Sometimes the flowers are eaten after being battered and deep-fried. But beneath the pretty surface lurks danger! The roots and some other parts of the elderberry tree are highly poisonous and will cause severe stomach problems. So next time you decide to pick some elderberry flowers for eating, be sure to eat just the flowers.

7 CASTOR OIL

Castor oil, the bane of many of our childhoods, is regularly added to candies, chocolate, and other foods. Furthermore, many people still consume a small amount daily or force it on their unwilling children. Fortunately, the castor oil we buy is carefully prepared, because the castor bean is so deadly, it takes just one bean to kill a human, and four to kill a horse. The poison is ricin, which is so toxic that workers who collect the seeds have strict safety guidelines to prevent accidental death. Despite this, many people working in the fields gathering the seeds suffer terrible side effects.

6 ALMONDS

Almonds are one of the most useful and wonderful of seeds (it is not a nut as many people would have you believe). It has a unique taste and its excellent suitability for use in cooking have made it one of the most popular ingredients in pastry kitchens for centuries. The most flavorful almonds are bitter almonds (as opposed to "sweet" almonds). They have the strongest scent and are the most popular in many countries. But there is one problem: they are full of cyanide. Before consumption, bitter almonds must be processed to remove the poison. Despite this requirement, some countries make the sale of bitter almonds illegal. As an alternative, you can use the pip from an apricot stone, which has a similar flavor and poison content. Heating destroys the poison. In fact, you may not know that it is now illegal in the U.S. to sell raw almonds; all almonds sold are now heat-treated to remove traces of poison and bacteria.

5 CHERRIES

Cherries are a very popular fruit used in cooking, liqueur production, or eaten raw. They are from the same family as plums, apricots, and peaches. All of the previously mentioned fruits contain highly poisonous compounds in their leaves and seeds. Almonds are also a member of this family, but they are the only fruit harvested especially for its seeds. When the seeds of cherries are crushed, chewed, or even slightly injured, they produce prussic acid (hydrogen cyanide). Next time you are eating cherries, remember not to suck on or chew the pit.

4 APPLES

Like the previous two items, apple seeds also contain cyanide, but obviously in much smaller doses. Apple seeds are very often eaten accidentally but you would need to chew and consume a fairly high number to get sick. There are not enough seeds in one apple to kill, but it is absolutely possible to eat enough to die. I recommend avoiding apple-eating competitions! Incidentally, if you want to eat an apple and find a worm in it (and hopefully not half a worm), you can drop it in a bowl of saltwater, which will kill the worm.

3 RHUBARB

Rhubarb is a very underrated plant—it produces some of the nicest tasting puddings and is incredibly easy to grow at home. Rhubarb is something of a wonder plant; in addition to an unknown poison in its leaves, they also contain a corrosive acid. If you mix the leaves with water and soda, it becomes even more potent. The stems are edible (and incredibly tasty) and the roots have been used for over five thousand years as a laxative and poop-softener.

2 TOMATOES

First off, a little interesting trivia: in the U.S., thanks to a Supreme Court decision in 1893, tomatoes are vegetables. In the rest of the world they are considered to be fruit (or more accurately, a berry). The reason for this decision was a tax on vegetables but not fruit. You may also be interested to know that technically, a tomato is an ovary. The leaves and stems of the tomato plant contain a chemical called glycoalkaloid which causes extreme nervousness and stomach upsets. Despite this, they can be used in cooking to enhance flavor, but they must be removed before eating. Cooking in this way does not allow enough poison to seep out but can make a huge difference in taste. Finally, to enhance the flavor of tomatoes, sprinkle a little sugar on them. Now we just need to work out whether they are "toe-mah-toes" or "toe-may-toes."

1 POTATOES

Potatoes have appeared in history books since their introduction to Europe in the sixteenth century. Unfortunately, they appear largely due to crop failure and severe famine, but they will be forever the central vegetable of most Western families' daily diet. Potatoes, like tomatoes, contain poison in the stems and leaves—even in the potato itself if left to turn green (the green is due to a high concentration of the glycoalkaloid poison). Potato poisoning is rare, but it does happen from time to time. Death normally comes after a period of weakness and confusion, followed by a coma. The majority of cases of death by potato in the last fifty years in the U.S. have been the result of eating green potatoes or drinking potato leaf tea.

✳✳✳✳✳✳

TOP 10 UNUSUAL COOKING CONCEPTS

10 TRANSGLUTAMINASE

Imagine a bowl of steaming prawn noodles, made almost entirely with prawns and including no flour (the prime ingredient in noodles). This is the type of food you can produce using transglutaminase ("meat glue"). Transglutaminase breaks down the cells of meat and basically turns it to a mush that can be piped or shaped. It is used in commercial food for binding meats together (as in hot dogs and sausages) but it really comes to life in the hands of modern chefs.

9 METHYL CELLULOSE

This is an incredibly exciting product being used in cooking. Methyl cellulose is a compound that turns to a firm gel when it is heated. For this reason, many bakeries mix it into their pie fillings to ensure that they don't spill out of their pastry shells when cooking. But, the molecular gastronomers have found a more exciting use for it in their restaurants: hot ice cream! This is done by mixing a standard ice cream base with methyl cellulose (1.5 percent of the total recipe) and submerging a scoop filled with the liquid into a pot of hot water. The hot water causes the ice cream to go hard. This is served immediately and as the ice cream cools down, it melts!

8 OTHER SENSES

Some restaurants are now experimenting with food via the other senses that we normally don't relate to cuisine, such as darkness and audio. For example, when eating in a pitch black environment, diners are said to have a much greater appreciation of individual flavors in food as they are not distracted by the built-in perceptions of food that come from appearance. Other restaurants use sound to enhance flavor: at the Fat Duck in Bray, England, there is a course called "Sound of the Sea" in which you listen to the sounds of the sea through an iPod while eating powdered baby eels, oysters, pickled onion juice foam, and more. It is an extraordinary experience. Scientists have shown that when a person eats a carrot with the crunch amplified via a microphone and headphones, the consumer believes it to be much fresher and cleaner tasting than a carrot without the audio equipment.

7 POWDERS

Powders are a new addition to modern menus; they are flavors that are dried to a dust and then sprinkled or served alongside food as a garnish. In some restaurants they are served as an entire course on their own. The main method for preparing powders is to mix a liquid of some type with maltodextrin. This is then processed in a food processor until you get a powder of the consistency you prefer. An incredibly tasty powder is made from rendered bacon fat and maltodextrin; it melts in your mouth while filling it with an intense bacon flavor. What more could anyone want to eat?

6 SLOW COOKING

No doubt we are all familiar with the good old slow-cooked stews our parents made. But modern cuisine has to take things further. First, a little science: when cooking meat at a high temperature, the flesh contracts and pushes the liquid out—the end result being a dry lump of hard meat. The solution to this is to cook the meat at the perfect temperature for eating—low enough not to cause constriction of the flesh. Master chef Heston Blumenthal has a recipe that calls for beef to be cooked at 50 degrees for twenty-four hours. When it is done, you sear it with a blowtorch to brown and flavor it. The resulting flesh is so soft it can be cut with a spoon. In his restaurant, The Fat Duck, he roasts a chicken at high temperatures for the juices (and does not serve the meat), and then cooks one at low temperatures for the soft meat. This is served with the juices from the first bird. Expensive, but worth it.

5 SOUS VIDE

In a way this is a rather ancient method of cooking—eggs could be said to be cooked *sous vide* when boiled. *Sous vide* (meaning "under vacuum") is when food is vacuum packed and cooked in a pot of boiling water until it is done. The benefit of this type of cooking is that meat can be cooked for hours without overcooking. For example, beef can be cooked to medium rare by boiling it in a vacuum-sealed bag for one-and-a-half hours at 160 degrees. Oxtail will cook perfectly in eight hours at 165 degrees. Because the water can be kept at a constant temperature (with the use of a thermometer), you cannot overcook the meat. When the meat is done, you can brown it with a blowtorch or in a frying pan—guaranteed perfect results every time—and the most tender meat you could imagine.

4 AIR

In the finest of modern restaurants, gravy and sauce are becoming a thing of the past, being replaced with airs and foams. Airs are produced by using a submersion blender with cooking juices or fruit juices, combined with a stabilizer, usually lecithin. The blender causes the liquid to froth up and the froth is then used on the plated meal. Foams are slightly more dense than airs and they are generally made with a similar liquid, but foamed up in a cream whipping device charged with nitrous oxide. Airs and foams are both used in the same way but for different effects. It should also be noted that in some restaurants, you can be served a course which is made of nothing but air.

3 VAPOR

If you thought airs were unusual, you ain't seen nothin' yet! In many haute cuisine restaurants, all of the senses come into play—and smell (perhaps the most important sense next to taste) can play a significant role. The idea is to bathe the diners in scents that cause a deepening of the flavors of the food. This is achieved in a variety of ways. At the Fat Duck (rated best restaurant in the world in 2007), waiters spray lime scent when serving lime and green tea mousse. At El Bulli (ranked the best restaurant in the world in 2008), diners are given fresh stems of rosemary to smell while they eat, and in some restaurants, bags filled with food scents are stuck with holes and weighted so there is a constant release of odor during the meal. Next time you eat a piece of lamb, try sniffing a stem of rosemary instead of adding it while cooking; you get the flavor of rosemary without overpowering the delicate lamb flavor.

2 ALGINATES

Alginates are a type of gum that cause calcium-based liquids to gel. They are used to create "caviar"—fruit juices in the form of caviar, ravioli without pasta, and much more. The uses are virtually unlimited.

1 LIQUID NITROGEN

Freezing has long been a staple in kitchens and cooking, but it is only recently that it is really coming to the fore, particularly extreme temperature and fast freezing. Liquid nitrogen is especially useful in making ice cream as the rapid freezing prevents ice crystals from forming which prevents an inferior product. Liquid-nitrogen-frozen ice cream is the smoothest, silkiest ice cream you will ever eat and it takes only a few minutes to freeze. You can also use this technique to freeze pure fruit juices into sorbets.

❊❊❊❊❊❊

TOP 10 DISCONTINUED SODAS

10 COKE II

So, back when Coca-Cola started to slump a little in sales to its fiercest competitor, Pepsi-Cola, someone made the executive decision to dink around with Coke's secret formula, thereby making it taste more like, well, Pepsi. It wasn't bad, per se, but it sure as hell wasn't Coke. I remember consuming mass quantities of this stuff by can and the newest form of container: two liters. This was an early '80s disaster and it always managed to make an appearance at our sleepovers keeping us wired for hours. I think it had more sugar as well. I really do miss this stuff, but sadly, when Coke went back to its "Classic" formula permanently, Coke II disappeared into soda oblivion.

9 HUBBA BUBBA

The strongest memory I have of Hubba Bubba Soda is from high school. We used to hold schoolwide contests involving all manner of self-deprecation. One of the "games" was the infamous "Pop Chug." The teaching staff that came up with this gem was sick and evil sadists of the highest degree. Everyone would stand over a beach towel with a "spotter" on one side and commence to gulp as much warm Hubba Bubba Soda as humanly possible. Loads of fun. I was never a big fan of this gum-flavored pop, but it does hold certain high esteem in my clogged memory bank.

8 PEPSI'S WILD BUNCH

Just in case the images aren't clear, we've got: Raging Razzberry, Tropical Chill, and Strawberry Burst. I love how "raspberry" is cleverly misspelled into "cool" territory with the two "z"s. Very nice. Anyway, the deepest memories I have of this particular trio was the chilling innards of my grandparents' ancient refrigerator in their garage. It was one of those "chill chest" types with the giant metal restaurant-freezer-style handle and enough wattage to cause neighborhood brownouts. Yeah, that thing was always chock-full of every conceivable beverage from beer to Bosco. Every time we'd visit we'd try to find the most odd drink we could dig out of there and I quite fondly remember tossing back a few of these guys. Dead and gone now. No, not my grandparents, but the fridge and the soda, for sure.

7 SURGE

Though not out of circulation as long as some of these, Surge has still become a classic. Coca-Cola distributed this green soda for quite some time. I can remember it coming into its own right around 1995 or so, and really building up steam for a few years before succumbing to the popularity of other, weaker, beverages. It had a citrus-like flavor but there was something almost lime-Jell-O-ish in the background that would always leave a little tang phlegm at the back of my throat. But it was pretty tasty and I could knock back a two-liter in a sitting, no problem. Almost, but not quite, melted candy.

6 LEED

Leed was a carbonated lemonade drink sold in some parts of the world during the middle-to-late twentieth century. It was produced and distributed by Coca-Cola Amatil only in New Zealand and Australia. Leed was one of the staple drinks among New Zealand retailers during the 1980s and probably the most common lemonade drink distributed by Coca-Cola Amatil during its life. In 1984, Leed was discontinued and replaced by the more widely known Sprite brand. Accompanying this change was also a new recipe.

5 JOSTA

This was a pretty recent extinction as well. I remember drinking a few of these back when Guarana was the new kid on the beverage block being marketed by Coke as the energy source of choice. Josta was so chock-full of the stuff you could, in fact, taste it. It was a tad medicine-y, but that flavor was nicely buried beneath the strong fruit and spice overtones that assaulted your taste buds moments before. This pop was far different taste-wise than just about anything else out there, and it was pretty decent while it lasted.

4 ORBITZ

Oh yeah, soda with little chewy chunks in it. Outstanding. Somehow, the creators of this beverage managed to thwart the normalcies of science by allowing starch nuggets to suspend themselves ever so beautifully in a super-sweet solution. It was really good, too. I remember Target selling the hell out of this stuff for quite a while. I enjoyed the drinking part, but somehow, coming to the little lumps floating in there was a lot like drinking a glass of gravy… except a lot sweeter. I do miss it.

3 KICK

Kick was a lot like the bastard stepson of Mountain Dew and Mello Yello. It tasted really similar to both, but almost leaning a bit toward Mello Yello with its citrus overtones. I actually preferred it over the others and would go through a case of this stuff during my late-night Dungeons and Dragons marathons.

2 SLICE

Slice was the precursor to Sierra Mist by the Pepsi corporation and for my buck, it tasted a whole lot better. My grandmother, in her massive fridge of holding, used to keep a constant supply of the Mandarin Orange flavor of this stuff. I hate mandarin oranges in any form, so I stuck to the lemon-lime standard and all was good with the world. There was something less overpowering about Slice as compared to 7-Up; not quite as crisp, not quite as effervescent, but certainly just as tasty.

1 CRYSTAL PEPSI

I was in college in 1993 and this soda was a huge hit up at Northern Michigan U. in Marquette, Michigan. My roommate and I loved the stuff. We could get it at the local Circle K for like two dollars for an eight-pack of twentyouncers. I honestly loved this stuff; I would drink the hell out of a few packs per week. I remember one time I tried to be cool by slashing open the plastic yolk that securely held together the octuplets with my X-Acto knife. Bad idea. I ended up cutting two of the bottles and sprayed soda all over our dorm room. Not especially funny. Anyway, there was just something about the non-caramel-colored Pepsi that really appealed to me. I miss this the most of all.

✖✖✖✖✖✖

TOP 10 CHEESES YOU SHOULD TRY

10 PECORINO—ITALY

This cheese was first made roughly two thousand years ago in the countryside surrounding Rome. Most of it was made in the region of Latium in Italy. In 1884, the city council began to prohibit the salting of cheese inside shops, so most of the makers moved to Sardinia. It's made exclusively from Sardinian sheep. To make it, the cheese is curdled, salted, and then pressed into molds, to which it sets. The pressing removes most of the moisture, making it very hard. It's got a great rich flavor that can enhance any meal where you would have used standard cheese. This cheese is great eaten alone, sliced into small cubes, or grated onto pasta. There are a few varieties of this cheese, which differ slightly by region.

9 CAMEMBERT—FRANCE

Camembert and Brie are like brothers, with Brie being the older one. Both cheeses are made from unpasteurized cow's milk, which is then curdled, and placed very carefully into molds. The cheese is then left to set, and turned over without pressing. It's this unique process which gives the cheese a soft texture. The molds penicillum candida and penicillium camamberti then ripen these soft round cheeses for a few weeks. These molds give the cheese a characteristic hard white coating on the outside, while the inside cheese remains soft. Camembert is a bit softer on the inside than Brie. Camembert took the spot on the list, simply because it's ever so slightly more unique.

Marie Harel, a farmer from Normandy, France, first made Camembert in 1791. She heard about a cheese called Brie from a priest who came from that area, and developed her own version. Originally when Camembert was made, the outside was a blue/gray color, but as manufacturing techniques changed to accommodate mass-production, this changed to a pure white mold. This cheese is best eaten on crackers, or my personal favorite, served sliced with spicy steaks.

8 GRUYÈRE—SWITZERLAND

Gruyère is named after the town of Gruyère, in Switzerland. It was first made in the twelfth century. It is made to a fine process, where it's curdled, sliced into tiny pieces, and then agitated. This is then cooked at a low temperature to release some more moisture. The cheese is placed into molds and washed with brine, then left to ripen. The bacteria inside the cheese produce bubbles of carbon dioxide, which give the cheese characteristic holes. This unique process gives the cheese a lovely hard texture, and a nutty flavor. Gruyère was the center of controversy (as far as cheese goes anyway) before 2001, where similarly styled French cheeses were using the Gruyère name. Gruyère is best served sliced thin, or grated with salads or pasta. Its nutty flavor means it's great by itself or as a subtle flavor with other food.

7 MASCARPONE—ITALY

Mascarpone is a cheese originally made around about the turn of the sixteenth century. It's a triple-cream cheese, which means it contains at least 75 percent butterfat. This is something you may not want to replace your other cheese with immediately. Mascarpone is made from heavy cream, which is heated to 85°C, and then tartaric acid is added to it. This mixture thickens, is refrigerated for twelve hours, and then strained to remove further whey. Mascarpone is a spreadable, thick ivory-colored cheese, with a rich flavor similar to that of cream and yogurt. It's one of the main ingredients in tiramisu, but it's overpowered by other flavors mostly. Mascarpone is best served chilled, with a bit of sugar stirred or sprinkled on. Or it can be used in place of cream on desserts.

6 RED WINDSOR CHEESE—ENGLAND

It's red! I actually put this cheese on the list because it's red. I saw it in a shop one day, and I was amazed that someone had decided to make cheese in other colors. Red Windsor Cheese is made very similarly to cheddar cheese. First the milk is curdled, and allowed to set a little bit, then sliced into small cubes. This sits for a period, and then is cooked and stirred for a period of twenty to forty minutes and drained. The curds are made into lumps, and then stacked and left for a while. This is to increase the acidity. Finally, the curds are salted and mixed. At this stage, wine (usually a Bordeaux or Port) is splashed onto the curds. Then they are pressed and left to mature for a short period, shorter than normal cheddar. The cheese is of firm texture, with pink marbling throughout. It has a strong taste, with a hint of wine as the aftertaste. This cheese is best served plain, with crackers, to shock your guests.

5 NETTLE CHEESE—ENGLAND

Nettle cheese is one of those more obscure cheeses. There are two varieties. One is called Yarg and is the older kind. This was originally made in Cornwall in England. The cheese was made normally, but before being left to mature, it is wrapped tightly in nettle leaves. The nettle leaves were originally used to help preserve the cheese. This is then left to mature for a few months. Sometimes it is even left to mature in caves, as caves have a constant humidity and temperature. As the cheese is maturing, the nettle leaves begin to grow mold on them, and they dry out slowly as the air and mold absorbs the moisture. The cheese varies from a creamy to a crumbly texture. The cheese tastes mild and has a strong aftertaste in the mouth, not unlike mushroom. The mold also gives the cheese a hard edible rind on the outside, which also gives its own unique sharp flavor.

The other variety is more recent, and most I've encountered comes from Holland (also other places). Here nettle leaves are ground and added to the cheese curd before it is pressed. Then the cheese is left to mature. The nettles grow a bit of mold, and infuse their unique flavor into the surrounding cheese. What you get afterward is a cheese similar to mild cheddar, with a unique flavor that you've probably never tasted, probably most similar to cabbage. But of course, that's only what it reminded me of. You'll have to try it. Nettle cheese, or Yarg, is best served as a snack, either plain or with crackers or bread. Also great with Alfredo sauces.

4 STILTON—ENGLAND

Stilton first appeared in Stilton, in 1730. A man called Cooper Thornhill sold it to travelers from his inn. He was a cheese lover, and one day after seeing a blue cheese that he particularly loved, he acquired the rights to exclusively market it. He did a great job of marketing it, and today it's now the famous cheese it is. Stilton is a protected cheese, which means it has to be made to strict guidelines, including the location it's made, its shape, and the manufacturing process. Stilton is made from pasteurized milk, which is then curdled with rennet, and the curds left to dry. The curd is salted, and then put into cylindrical molds, and turned every so often. Then, finally, the cheese is pierced with needles, which impregnate the cheese with mold, which grow and form the blue veins inside the flaky white cheese. Stilton is a rich creamy, round-flavored blue cheese, which isn't too strong. It can be enjoyed with crackers, or with salads or soup. My personal favorite way to enjoy Stilton is in a burger. Mmm.

3 DANABLU—DENMARK

This is quite possibly one of my most favorite flavors of cheese. Danablu, or Danish Blue that comes from Denmark, is one of the strongest flavored of the blue cheeses. This cheese is full of blue veins of mold. The cheese is a soft texture (almost spreadable), and also slightly crumbly. This cheese was invented in the early twentieth century by Marius Boel, who was trying to copy Roquefort cheese, a very similar blue cheese that is made exclusively in France. Danablu, from what I have seen, has almost eclipsed it in popularity however, mainly because it's easier to get a hold of. Danablu is made from cow's milk, and before it is left to age, the curds are penetrated with a sample of the mold to create the veins throughout the cheese. The cheese is then left to age for two to three months. Once that wait is over, we have a powerful cheese that has a strong butyric tang to it. Danablu goes best with other food; it's a bit too strong to eat plain, or without other big flavors. My favorite way to enjoy Danablu is melted on top of some crumbed pork schnitzel.

2 EMMENTAL—SWITZERLAND

Emmental. A strange name. The reason it's on this list? Because it's the real Swiss cheese (Gruyère is also). Often when you buy Swiss cheese, too often, you're receiving inferior cheese. Emmental is the real deal, as Erin Brockovich would say. It was first made in about 1293, in a place called Emmental near Berne. It's pretty much the oldest cheese from Switzerland. Emmental is famous for its very large holes (called eyes) that fill the cheese, and produce interesting slices when it's cut up. The cheese is a firm to a hard texture, and has a yellow color. It has a strong flavor best described as cheese flavor. The cheese is full of holes because of a bacteria that metabolizes the lactic acid in the cheese, and releases carbon dioxide bubbles into the cheese, which slowly expand and form the characteristic eyes. The larger the eyes, the stronger the flavor. This is a side effect of longer aging and higher temperatures, which allow the bacteria to produce a stronger flavor, and more time for carbon dioxide to build. Emmental is best served in a sandwich. Then you'll never go back to inferior cheese.

1 HALLOUMI—CYPRUS

Halloumi is quite possibly the strangest of all the cheeses on the list, and quite possibly the most amazing. The thing that makes this cheese special is that it doesn't melt. The reason for this is that the curd is heated before it's placed into brine. The heating denatures the proteins in the cheese to make it into long fibers, which resist melting. It will actually cook instead. Halloumi originated from Middle Eastern Bedouins, or nomads. It was made because it keeps very well. Nowadays, Halloumi is made in Cyprus from goat and sheep milk. There are cheaper varieties made from cow's milk available, but the authentic stuff tastes a lot better. The best way to eat it is to slice it thin and then fry it in a pan. The outside of the cheese will become crispy, and if you sliced it thick enough, the inside will become almost melted. It can also be barbecued. It's great on salads instead of Feta, and it tastes great just plain. It has a strong salty taste, and has an almost greasy feel to it, sort of like eating rubber. The texture is amazing however, and has to be experienced to be understood. This is a really great cheese to have with a nice breakfast meal.

✳✳✳✳✳✳

TOP 10 ODD SUPERSTITIONS ABOUT FOOD

10 HOLLOW BREAD

It was once (and perhaps still is) a superstition that if you found a hole in a loaf of bread you cut, it symbolized a coffin and meant that someone was soon to die. If a person found a loaf in this state, there would be days of discussion to guess who it might be that would be stricken down. Of course, these days we are less likely to cut our own loaves of bread, so this one is likely to die into obscurity.

9 EGGSHELLS

It was once a superstition that if you did not crush the ends of an egg after eating it, a witch would gather the shells and use them to craft a boat that she could use to sail out to sea to raise storms. This is a very ancient superstition, which seems to originate in the 1580s. If you shattered the end of the shell, it

would create enough holes to make it useless as a boat. We won't even go into the logic of how a full-sized human might be able to stand in an eggshell—that was obviously not on the minds of our superstitious forebears.

8 CROSSED BREAD

This innocent old superstition dictated that all loaves of bread must be marked with a sign of the cross before baking. The idea was that the cross would prevent the devil from sitting on the loaf, and thereby prevent him from cursing or spoiling the bread. The upside to this superstition is that bread rises much better in the oven when crossed, though obviously not from the influence (or lack thereof) of the wicked one.

7 SALT

We all know of the superstition surrounding the spilling of salt, but here is a slightly more unusual one. It used to be considered bad if you helped another person to the salt; there was even a little phrase that evolved from the superstition, "help to salt, help to sorry." Salt is such an important part of human life that it is no wonder it appears so frequently in the history of superstition.

6 TEA RITUALS
It used to be considered bad luck for two people to pour tea from the same pot. In addition, if you left the lid off the teapot while brewing tea, it was meant to mean that a stranger would visit soon. There were even a series of small rituals you could perform to determine the exact day, hour, and gender of the visitor by means of tapping the wrist.

5 CHRISTMAS CAKE
Superstitions surrounding Christmas are as numerous as Elizabeth Taylor's husbands. One such superstition says that all members of a family must have a turn stirring the Christmas cake mixture or else bad luck will befall them. Young unmarried girls were especially supposed to have a turn, otherwise they would remain alone for another year.

4 EGGY LUCK
In many parts of Europe, farmers would take a fresh egg into the fields in the hopes that it would bring a good healthy crop. Eggs were also used to tell fortunes: two yolks would mean a marriage was coming up soon, a black spot on a yolk was a bad omen, and an egg with no yolk at all was just about as bad as you could get.

3 GARLIC
In Greece there is an ancient superstition called the Evil Eye. It is believed that when someone gives you the evil eye, bad luck (usually minor) will befall you. Now you may be wondering why this is on a food superstitions list; the reason is that the way to prevent the evil eye from affecting you is to carry around a piece of garlic. This is unlikely to help you when you are having a night out looking for a date!

2 THE WISHBONE
Before we all sit back on our laurels and laugh at the superstitions around the world that would never afflict us, let us remember one of our own most revered superstitions, the pulling of the wishbone. In Western (especially

American and British) tradition, two people use their pinky finger to break the wishbone. The person who wins the longest piece gets good luck and usually makes a wish. We may all say we aren't superstitious, but this is something we have all done at one time or another, which leads us to our last (and equally common) superstition:

1 WEDDING RICE

Throwing rice at a wedding is such a common event that we don't even bat an eyelid when we see it happening. But what most of us don't realize is that this a very superstitious tradition with a very long history. The throwing of rice is meant to bring prosperity, wealth, and happiness to the couple. Frankly though, with the amount of money people spend on weddings these days, it would be more useful to throw wads of cash rather than rice.

✳✳✳✳✳✳

CHAPTER FOUR

History and Politics

TOP 10 FASCINATING FACTS ABOUT SLAVERY

10 **ESTABLISHED IN VIRGINIA**
Slavery was officially established in Virginia in 1654, when Anthony Johnson, a black man, convinced a court that his servant (also black), John Casor, was his for life. Johnson himself had been brought to Virginia some years earlier as an indentured servant (a person who must work to repay a debt, or on contract for so many years in exchange for food and shelter), but he saved enough money to buy out the remainder of his contract and that of his wife. The court ruled in Johnson's favor, and the very first officially state-recognized slave existed in Virginia. Johnson eventually became very wealthy and began importing his own black slaves from Africa, for which he was granted 250 acres (at the time, any person importing a slave would be paid fifty acres per person). Eventually, the unfortunate repercussions of this decision would come back to haunt Johnson when his land was confiscated and given to a white man because Johnson "was a Negroe and by consequence an alien."

9 **DISASTROUS INVENTION**
In the second part of the eighteenth century, slavery was beginning to disappear naturally in the United States as farmers were planting crops that required far less manual work. Many slave owners freed their slaves and it began to look like slavery would die out completely. But things were to change. In 1793, Eli Whitney invented the cotton gin, a device for processing raw cotton. This meant that a single man could process fifty times more cotton in a day than previously, making cotton a huge money-making crop. This caused the almost immediate replacement of many crops with cotton, and slavery became once again firmly entrenched until its modern abolition.

8 **THE WORD**
The word "slave" comes to us from the Byzantine Greek word *sklabos*, which was the name for the Slavic people. The reason for this is that the Vikings used to capture the Slavs and sell them to the Romans as slaves. The term only dates back as far as 580 AD, as the Latin word *servus* was more commonly used before that for all kinds of servants, enslaved or not.

7 THE BIBLE AND SLAVERY

The Bible does not expressly condone or forbid slavery. In the New Testament, Jesus heals a slave and commends his owner for his faith. He does not take the time to condemn the slave owner for having a slave, nor at any point does he try to suggest that slavery is wrong. Saint Paul said this to slave owners: "Do not threaten [your slaves], since you know that He who is both their Master and yours is in heaven, and there is no favoritism with Him" (Ephesians 6:9). The Old Testament goes a little further and reminds people to treat their slaves well. The most likely reason for this apparent moral discrepancy is that the Bible was penned at a time when slavery was not only widespread, but considered perfectly normal and moral; there was no reason to mention it as most people wouldn't have considered it an issue worth thinking about. Slaves at the time were also generally treated much better than the slaves of modern times, and would usually end up being made free after a number of years' servitude.

6 LAND OF THE FREE

Liberia is a small nation on the west coast of Africa, surrounded by Sierra Leone, the Ivory Coast, Guinea, and the Atlantic Ocean. In 1822, Liberia was founded as a colony, by American slaves who had been freed. So thankful were the slaves for the efforts of President James Monroe that they named their new capital city after him (Monrovia). The area was populated by various native ethnic groups and the American slaves had a tendency to look down on them as uncivilized. In 1847, the freed slaves declared independence and the nation was officially born. For its first 133 years, the country was a one-party state dominated by the Americo-Liberians. Ironically, the Americo-Liberians and their children were the only people considered citizens and allowed to vote. Liberia is currently the only (and first) African nation to have an elected woman (Ellen Johnson-Sirleaf) as its head. Liberian English (the official language in Liberia) is a transplanted variant of the English spoken by African-American slaves in the nineteenth century. The freed slaves turned Liberia into a replica of the cities they left in the United States, as can be seen by the now dilapidated Masonic Temple in Monrovia.

5 A MARK OF HONOR

In Africa, prior to the arrival of European slave traders, slavery was a normal part of life. The thing that makes it stand out from European-style slavery was the fact that it was a sign of good reputation and honor if a slave owner treated his slaves with respect and kindness. The better treated your slaves, the more honorable and highly regarded you were. Manhandling a slave (as the Europeans were wont to do) was considered unethical and you risked your reputation if you did not feed, clothe, and provide quality surroundings for your slaves.

4 CHARLES LYNCH

Charles Lynch was a farmer and American revolutionary from Virginia. During the American Revolution, he headed an irregular court, which tried and punished loyalist supporters of the British. The sentences handed down were usually property seizure, flogging, or conscription into the army. After the revolution, Lynch became a member of the Virginia Senate. He is, of course, now famous for the term "lynching" or a "lynch mob." Lynching of slaves initially started out as flogging, but within a short period of time this progressed to summary execution (usually by hanging). Lynchburg in Virginia is named for his brother John.

3 ANCIENT PRACTICE

Slavery is an ancient practice; it is referred to in man's earliest records, such as the Code of Hammurabi (1760 BC), the earliest known law code, from Babylon. It is mentioned in the Bible and some of the ancient philosophers (including Aristotle) believed that some men were born in a natural state of slavery, thereby making it moral to enslave that man (a nice way to justify it if ever there was one). Slavery in those days was often the punishment for debt; once the debt was repaid, the slave might be released.

2 PAPAL PERMISSION AND PROHIBITION

While the Catholic Church has repeatedly condemned the idea of slavery, there was a short period in the fifteenth and sixteenth centuries when it was allowed by special papal permission. The Pope who gave permission was Pope Nicholas V in 1452 when he issued a special bull (a formal letter issued by the Pope) allowing King Afonso V of Portugal to enslave pagans caught during wars. The pertinent text is:

"We grant you [Kings of Spain and Portugal] by these present documents, with our Apostolic Authority, full and free permission to invade, search out, capture, and subjugate the Saracens and pagans and any other unbelievers and enemies of Christ wherever they may be, as well as their kingdoms, duchies, counties, principalities, and other property [...] and to reduce their persons into perpetual slavery."

In 1537, Pope Paul III returned to the traditional anti-slavery view of the church.

1 SLAVERY TODAY

According to studies done by anti-slavery groups, there are currently more slaves today than at any time in history! Three-quarters are female and over half are children. It is believed that there are around twenty-seven million people in slavery right now. Furthermore, this number does not include people who are not technically slaves but are in a form of servitude tantamount to slavery. This is sometimes called "unfree labor." The average slave today costs around ninety dollars, whereas in the past they cost upwards of forty thousand dollars (in today's money). A study done at University of California at Berkeley estimates that there are around ten thousand slaves in the United States at the moment.

❋❋❋❋❋❋

TOP 10 WORST PLAGUES IN HISTORY

10 MOSCOW PLAGUE AND RIOT, 1771

The Moscow Plague progressed from its initial appearance to full-blown epidemic between late 1770 and the spring of 1771. Although city authorities took the usual steps of epidemic control, such as forced quarantines and confiscation/destruction of contaminated property, the city's population reacted with uncontrolled anger, fear, and paranoia. The Moscow economy was hit by instant paralysis due to the forced closings of public and private businesses, which ultimately led to food shortages and a total breakdown of the standard of living. However, wealthier, upper-class citizens were able to escape the plague by leaving Moscow altogether during the outbreak. Finally, on September 17, 1771, a riotous crowd of a thousand confronted the army at the Spasskiye gates and demanded the end of quarantines and the release of rebel prisoners. The army and crowd attacked each other, and the army managed to disperse the crowd, arresting over three hundred demonstrators. One week later, a government commission under Grigory Orlov was created to address the demands of the citizens, providing them with clean food and work, and eventually restoring order.

9 GREAT PLAGUE OF MARSEILLES, 1720–1722

The Great Plague of Marseilles arrived in 1720 and became one of the most significant outbreaks of bubonic plague in the eighteenth century. It spread throughout the city and the surrounding provinces, killing a hundred thousand, yet was nearly controlled through legislation. The Act of Parliament of Aix made it punishable by death for anyone to cross between Marseilles and Provence, and the Mur de la Peste plague wall helped enforce the separation. As a result, the Marseilles economy took only a few years to recover, and its population achieved pre-plague numbers by 1765.

8 ANTONINE PLAGUE, 165–180 AD

The Antonine Plague of the Roman Empire was also called the Plague of Galen. It was likely smallpox or measles, and was probably brought back by returning Roman soldiers from Near East campaigns. The Antonine Plague was so named because it claimed the lives of two Roman Emperors with the family name of Antonine: Lucius Verus in 169 and Marcus Aurelius Antoninus in 180. The plague returned again nine years later and claimed an estimated two thousand lives per day, leading to death estimates upwards of five million among both civilians and a severely decimated Roman Army.

7 PLAGUE OF ATHENS, 430–427 BC

The Plague of Athens struck disastrously when the Athenians, under Pericles, were in the second year of the Peloponnesian War against the Spartans. The full sweep of the plague was felt throughout the eastern Mediterranean (including Sparta), but was particularly devastating inside the walls of Athens, probably entering through the Athens port of Piraeus. In an attempt to protect the city from the advancing Spartans, Pericles ordered all Athenians into the city, and he locked the gates behind them, leading to the deadly and rapid spread of the disease. One of the symptoms of the plague was a burning fever, and many infected Athenians took the unfortunate remedy of sprawling in the city's water supply in a futile attempt to cool off. Even Pericles himself was struck down by the plague in 429 BC, as the plague returned yet again in 427 BC. Although the disease has been historically attributed to be bubonic plague, modern historians have advanced theories based on the reported symptoms that the disease could have been anything from typhus, smallpox, measles, and even toxic-shock syndrome.

6 THE GREAT PLAGUE OF MILAN, 1629–1631

The Italian Plague, or the Great Plague of Milan, was actually a small series of bubonic plague outbreaks in northern Italy covering two years and costing 280,000 lives. The highest death tolls were in Lombardy and Venice, although Milan lost almost half of its 130,000 population. The disease was brought initially to Mantua by German and French troops as part of the Thirty Years War (1618–1648), and then spread rapidly into the Venetian troops, who retreated into northern and central Italy and took the disease with them. This plague is usually considered to be one of the final significant outbreaks of the Black Death, which spread over several centuries throughout Europe.

5 AMERICAN PLAGUES, SIXTEENTH CENTURY

Since indigenous people of North and South America remained isolated from Europe, Asia, and Africa for tens of thousands of years, they had no natural immunities to many common European diseases. Although many of these diseases were minor inconveniences, some of them were devastating, especially measles and smallpox. Frequently, these diseases were passed along to Native Americans by European fishermen and hunters, well ahead of official European contact, resulting in rapid pandemics and cultural/political/military collapse. Many European settlers to the Americas encountered vast areas of cultivation with no people anywhere nearby—they were all dead. The Aztec and Inca civilizations were only weak shadows of their former magnificence by the time substantial European exploration arrived, making their enslavement relatively easy. It was only a small consolation that syphilis was passed from the Native Americans to the Europeans, and subsequently swept throughout Europe.

4 THE GREAT PLAGUE OF LONDON, 1665–1666

The Great Plague of London killed anywhere between 75,000 and 100,000 people, which was fully one-fifth of the total London population of the time. Although the disease causing the fatalities has been historically suggested to be another small outbreak of bubonic plague, or Black Death, others have suggested the symptoms seem more closely related to a viral hemorrhagic fever. This was one of the last widespread pandemic outbreaks in England.

3 PLAGUE OF JUSTINIAN, 541–542

The Plague of Justinian was named after the Byzantine ruler at the time of the initial outbreak, Emperor Justinian I, and it was enormous in scope. The plague, most probably bubonic plague, infected the capitol of Constantinople, and stretched throughout south Asia, north Africa, Arabia, and Europe (as far north as Denmark and as far west as Ireland). The plague also managed to return every generation for almost a hundred more years. At its peak, the pandemic killed five thousand people per day in Constantinople, and eventually claimed approximately 40 percent of the city's inhabitants, including Emperor Justinian himself, and approximately 25 percent of the entire Mediterranean population.

2 THE THIRD PANDEMIC, 1855–1950S

"Third Pandemic" began in the Yunnan Province of China in 1855 and was considered active by the World Health Organization until 1959, when its deaths finally dropped below 200 per year. It was most certainly bubonic plague, and was probably started when large populations encountered infected rodents while fleeing war, famine, political unrest, and drought in central Asia. More than twelve million people in India and China alone were claimed by the Third Pandemic. Advancements in global trade then seemed to carry the disease worldwide.

1 THE BLACK DEATH, 1347–1351

The Black Death, Black Plague, and Bubonic Plague are all names for the same deadly pandemic that claimed approximately seventy-five million people worldwide, including twenty-five to thirty million in Europe alone. It is believed to be caused by the bacterium Yersinia pestis, and spread to humans through the fleas of infected ground rodents. Although the origins of the plague are disputed (either China and central Asia or Russia in the early 1300s), it no doubt leaped into Europe from Crimea in the 1340s. The plague is believed to have returned every generation until the 1700s, causing more than a hundred outbreaks in Europe, and new research suggests that bubonic plague is lying dormant at the present time.

✳✳✳✳✳✳

TOP 10 MYTHS ABOUT THE MIDDLE AGES

10 DEATH PENALTY
Myth: The death penalty was common in the Middle Ages.

Despite what many people believe, the Middle Ages gave birth to the jury system and trials were, in fact, very fair. The death penalty was considered to be extremely severe and was used only in the worst cases of crimes like murder, treason, and arson. It was not until the Middle Ages began to draw to a close that people like Elizabeth I began to use the death penalty as a means to rid their nations of religious opponents. Public beheadings were not as we see in the movies; they were given only to the rich, and were usually not performed in public. The most common method of execution was hanging, and burning was extremely rare (and usually performed after the criminal had been hanged to death first).

9 LOCKED BIBLES
Myth: Bibles were locked away to keep the people from seeing the "true word."

During the Middle Ages (until Gutenberg came along), all books had to be written by hand. This was a painstaking task, which took many months, particularly with a book as large as the Bible. The job of hand-printing books was left to monks tucked away in monasteries. These books were incredibly valuable and they were needed in every church as the Bible was read aloud at mass every day. In order to protect these valuable books, they would be locked away. There was no conspiracy to keep the Bible from the people—the locks meant that the church could guarantee that the people could hear the Bible (many wouldn't have been able to read) every day. And just to show that it wasn't just the Catholic Church that locked up the Bibles for safety, the most famous "chained bible" is the "Great Bible" which Henry VIII had created and ordered to be read in the Protestant churches.

8 STARVING POOR
Myth: The poor were kept in a state of near starvation.

This is completely false. Peasants (those who worked in manual work) would have had fresh porridge and bread daily, with beer to drink. In addition, each day would have an assortment of dried or cured meats, cheeses, and fruits and vegetables from their area. Poultry, chicken, ducks, pigeons, and geese were not uncommon on the peasants' dinner tables. Some peasants also liked to keep bees, to provide honey for their tables. Given the choice between McDonald's and medieval peasant food, I suspect the peasant food would be more nutritious and tasty. The rich of the time had a great choice of meats, such as cattle, and sheep. They would eat more courses for each meal than the poor, and would probably have had a number of spiced dishes; something the poor could not afford.

7 THATCHED ROOFS
Myth: Peasants had thatched roofs with animals living in them.

First of all, the thatched roofs of medieval dwellings were woven into a tight mat; they were not just bundles of straw and sticks thrown on top of the house. Animals would not easily have been able to get inside the roof—and considering how concerned the average Middle Ager was, if an animal did get inside, they would be promptly removed, just as we remove birds or other small creatures that enter our homes today. And, for the record, thatched roofs were not just for the poor—many castles and grander homes had them as well—because they worked so well. There are many homes in English villages today that still have thatched roofs.

6 SMELLY PEOPLE
Myth: People didn't bathe in the Middle Ages; therefore, they smelled bad.

Not only is this a total myth, it is so widely believed that it has given rise to a whole other series of myths, such as the false belief that church incense was designed to hide the stink of so many people in one place. In fact, the incense was part of the church's rituals due to its history coming from the Jewish religion, which also used incense in its sacrifices. This myth has also led to the strange idea that people usually married in May or June because they didn't stink so badly, having had their yearly bath. It is, of course, utter rubbish. People married in those months because marriage was not allowed during Lent (the season of penance). So, back to smelly people. In the Middle Ages, most towns had bathhouses. In fact, cleanliness and hygiene were very highly regarded, so much so that bathing was incorporated into various ceremonies, such as those surrounding knighthood. Some people bathed daily, others less regularly, but most people bathed. Furthermore, they used hot water; they just had to heat it up themselves, unlike us with our modern plumbed hot water. The French put it best in the following Latin statement: *"Venari, ludere, lavari, bibere; Hoc est vivere!"* (To hunt, to play, to wash, to drink; This is to live!)

5 PEASANT LIFE

Myth: Peasants lived a life of drudgery and backbreaking work.

In fact, while peasants in the Middle Ages did work hard (tilling the fields was the only way to ensure you could eat), they had regular festivals (religious and secular), which involved dancing, drinking, games, and tournaments. Many of the games from the time are still played today: chess, checkers, dice, blind man's bluff, and many more. It may not seem as fun as the latest game for the Wii, but it was a great opportunity to enjoy the especially warm weather caused by the Medieval Warming Period.

4 VIOLENCE EVERYWHERE

Myth: The Middle Ages were a time of great violence.

While there was violence in the Middle Ages (just as there had always been), there were no equals to our modern Stalin, Hitler, and Mao. Most people lived their lives without experiencing violence. The Inquisition was not the violent bloodlust that many movies and books have claimed it to be, and most modern historians now admit this readily. Modern times have seen genocide, mass murder, and serial killing—something virtually unheard of before the "enlightenment." In fact, there are really only two serial killers of note from the Middle Ages: Elizabeth Bathory and Gilles de Rais. For those who dispute the fact that the Inquisition resulted in very few deaths, statistics show that there were (at most) 826 recorded executions over a 160-year-period—from 45,000 trials!

3 OPPRESSED WOMEN

Myth: Women were oppressed in the Middle Ages.

In the 1960s and '70s, the idea that women were oppressed in the Middle Ages flourished. In fact, all we need to do is think of a few significant women from the period to see that that is not true at all: St. Joan of Arc was a young woman who was given full control of the French army! Her downfall was political and would have occurred whether she were male or female. Hildegard of Bingen was a polymath in the Middle Ages who was held in such high esteem that kings, popes, and lords all sought her advice. Her music and writing exists to this day. Elizabeth I ruled as a powerful queen in her own right, and many other nations had women leaders. Granted, women did not work on cathedrals but they certainly pulled their weight in the fields and villages. Furthermore, the rules of chivalry meant that women had to be treated with the greatest of dignity. The biggest difference between the concept of feminism in the Middle Ages and now is that in the Middle Ages it was believed that women were "equal in dignity, different in function"; now the concept has been modified to "equal in dignity and function."

2 FLAT EARTH

Myth: People in the Middle Ages believed the earth was flat.

Furthermore, people did not believe the Earth was the center of the universe. The famous monk Copernicus dealt a death blow to that idea (without being punished), well before Galileo was tried for heresy, for claiming that it proved the Bible was wrong. Two modern historians recently published a book in which they say, "there was scarcely a Christian scholar of the Middle Ages who did not acknowledge [Earth's] sphericity and even know its approximate circumference."

1 CRUDE AND IGNORANT

Myth: People of the Middle Ages were crude and ignorant.

Thanks largely to Hollywood movies, many people believe that the Middle Ages were full of religious superstition and ignorance. But, in fact, leading historians deny that there is any evidence of this. Science and philosophy blossomed at the time, partly due to the introduction of universities all over Europe. The Middle Ages produced some of the greatest art, music, and literature in all history. Boethius, Boccaccio, Dante, Petrarch, and Machiavelli are still revered today for their brilliant minds. The cathedrals and castles of Europe are still standing and contain some of the most beautiful artwork and stonework man has been able to create with his bare hands. Medicine at the time was primitive, but it was structured and willing to embrace new ideas when they arose (which is how we have modern medicine).

✳✳✳✳✳✳

TOP 10 FASCINATING SECRETS TAKEN TO THE GRAVE

10 AXEL ERLANDSON, 1884–1964

Erlandson started as an alfalfa farmer and started grafting and shaping tree trunks as a hobby. He would later, over a period of decades, train trees to grow into shapes of his own design. He experimented with birch, ash, elm, and weeping willows, making loops, hearts, chairs, spiral staircases, zigzags, rings, birdcages, towers, picture frames, and ladders. Erlandson found his trees to be a popular amusement and decided to create his "Tree Circus." Erlandson would not tell anyone the secrets of his techniques and would carry out his graftings behind screens to protect against spies. Erlandson died in 1964, along with his amazing secret procedure used to propagate his trees.

Interesting Fact: In 1985, after the Tree Circus went out of business, the trees were bought by millionaire Michael Bonfante and transplanted in his amusement park, Gilroy Gardens in Gilroy, California.

9 "JEROME," 1840–1912

On September 8, 1863, a fair-skinned stranger believed to be in his twenties was found by two fishermen at Sandy Cove in Digby County, Canada. Both of the man's legs had been freshly amputated and a jug of water and some bread had been placed nearby. The man was unable or unwilling to speak and is said to have uttered no more than two or three words after being found. One of the words was thought to have been Jerome and he was soon given that name.

Jerome was filled with rage when certain words were spoken, which led many to believe Jerome was carrying some kind of secret that he was not allowed to say. Jerome conducted himself with dignity and when offered money he would appear humiliated. There are many theories to who Jerome really was but no story has ever been proven. Jerome died April 19, 1912.

Interesting Fact: Jerome continues to be part of the collective psyche of the community where he was found. A residence for the handicapped has been named after him, songs have been written about him, and he has been depicted in paintings and a film.

8 THE FEMALE STRANGER, 1793–1816

During the fall of 1816, in Alexandria, Virginia, two people, a man and his wife, walked into the Gadsby's Tavern Hotel. The woman was ill and it was thought she was suffering from typhoid fever. The woman's condition continued to deteriorate despite being attended by one of Alexandria's doctors. The husband then summoned the doctor and hotel staff and even the owner's wife to the room to ask a very unusual request: He asked that everyone present swear an oath never to reveal their identities. All agreed and each took the secret to the grave. Several days after the oath was taken, the Female Stranger died, and to this day no one knows her identity. Before disappearing, her husband commissioned an extravagant headstone and buried her at St. Paul's Cemetery in Alexandria, Virginia.

Interesting Fact: The engraving on the headstone reads:

To the Memory of a
FEMALE STRANGER
whose mortal sufferings terminated
on the 14th day of October 1816
Aged 23 years and 8 months.
This stone is placed here by her disconsolate
Husband in whose arms she sighed out her
latest breath and who under God
did his utmost even to soothe the cold
dead ear of death.
How loved how valued once avails thee not
To whom related or by whom begot
A heap of dust alone remains of thee
Tis all thou art and all the proud shall be

To him gave all the Prophets witness that
through his name whosoever believeth in
him shall receive remission of sins.
Acts 10:43

7 THE LEATHER MAN, CIRCA 1839–1889

The Leather Man was a wandering vagrant who traveled in an endless 365-mile circle between the Connecticut and Hudson rivers. He was fluent in French but communicated mostly with grunts and gestures and dressed in crudely stitched leather from his hat to his shoes. He picked up cigar butts along his way and gratefully accepted offerings of fresh tobacco or cigars that townsfolk would give him as he walked silently through their villages. When asked of his background he would abruptly end the conversation. He was so reliable in his rounds that people would have extra food ready for him at a certain time every thirty-four days. It is unknown how he earned money, although one store kept a record of his order: "one loaf of bread, a can of sardines, one-pound of fancy crackers, a pie, two quarts of coffee, one gill of brandy and a bottle of beer." After a blizzard in March 1889, the Leather Man's body was found in his Saw Mill woods cave in Sing Sing, New York. He died from cancer of the mouth, most likely due to tobacco use. His bag was found next to him and contained leather-working equipment such as scissors, awls, wedges, and a small axe and a small prayer book in French.

Interesting Fact: The Leather Man's tombstone reads, "Final resting place of Jules Bourglay of Lyons, France, 'The Leather Man.'" However, the story published in the newspaper that claimed to know his real name was later retracted. According to researchers, his identity still remains unknown.

6 ARNE BEURLING, 1905–1986

Arne Beurling was a Swedish mathematician and professor of mathematics. In 1940 he broke the German code used for strategic military communications. This accomplishment is considered by many to be one of the greatest achievements in the history of cryptography. Using only teleprinter tapes and cipher text, he deciphered the code that the Germans believed impossible to crack in just two weeks. Beurling created a device that enabled Sweden to decipher German teleprinter traffic passing through Sweden from Norway on a cable. When Beurling was asked how he broke the code he replied, "A magician does not reveal his secrets."

Interesting Fact: Beurling's code breaking allowed Swedish authorities to know about Operation Barbarossa (the codename for Nazi Germany's invasion of the Soviet Union) before it occurred.

5 JAMES BLACK, 1800–1872

James Black was an Arkansas blacksmith and the creator of the original Bowie knife designed by Jim Bowie. Bowie was already famous for knife fighting from his 1827 sandbar duel. But his killing of three assassins in Texas and his death at the Battle of the Alamo made him, and the blacksmith's knife, legend. Black's knives were known to be exceedingly tough yet flexible. Black kept his methods for creating the knife very secret and did all of his work behind a leather curtain. Many claim that Black rediscovered the secret to producing Damascus steel, which is a type of steel used in Middle Eastern sword making from 1100 to 1700 that could cut through lesser-quality European swords. The original techniques to make James Black's knife cannot be duplicated even today. Black died on June 22, 1872, in Washington, Arkansas.

Interesting Fact: In 1839, shortly after Black's wife's death, he was nearly blinded when his father-in-law and former partner broke into his home and attacked him with a club, having objected to his daughter having married Black years earlier. After the attack, Black was no longer able to continue in his trade.

4 EDWARD LEEDSKALNIN, 1887–1951

Edward Leedskalnin was a Latvian emigrant to the United States and an amateur sculptor. Leedskalnin single-handedly built the monument known as Coral Castle in Florida and is also known for his unusual theories on magnetism. Leedskalnin was only five-feet tall and weighed a hundred pounds. He aligned many of his stones astronomically and integrated them into a grand architectural plan based on mathematical and astronomical data. Leedskalnin used only simple tools to cut, trim, and assemble over three million pounds of dense coral blocks to build his castles. When asked, "How did you build the castle?" he replied, "It's not difficult really, the secret is in knowing how." When Leedskalnin moved his Coral Castle ten miles away to Homestead, Florida, he asked the trucker to look away when it came time to load and unload the coral stones. Leedskalnin died from malnutrition due to stomach cancer in 1951 at the age of sixty-four, without ever revealing his secret.

Interesting Fact: Billy Idol wrote and recorded the song "Sweet Sixteen" and filmed the video in the Coral Castle. The song was inspired by the story of

Leedskalnin's former love, Agnes Scuffs, who is believed to be the main reason Leedskalnin built the Coral Castles.

3 JOHANN BESSLER, 1680–1745

Johann Bessler was born in Zittau, Germany, and built a machine that he claimed was self-moving. By 1717, he had convinced thousands of people, from the ordinary to the most prominent, that he had indeed discovered the secret of a self-sustaining mechanism. The machine underwent numerous tests and passed rigorous inspections. It was made to do heavy work for long periods, and in an official test it ran continuously for fifty-four days. The internal design of the machine was always closely guarded by its inventor. Plagued by paranoia and a nasty temper and with no patent laws to protect him, Bessler destroyed the machines in a fit of anger and took his secret to the grave. The true motive power behind Bessler's demonstrations, and the energy source that moved the wheel's internal weights, still remain unexplained. Obviously a machine like this violates the law of conservation of energy that states energy can never be created nor destroyed, but it should then be asked how did Bessler fool so many people for so many years?

Interesting Fact: Recently, a series of coded features has been discovered among various papers published by Bessler. He constructed a variety of codes from very simple to very complex, which could, in time, be collected together to reveal his secret. Some of these codes have been solved but many others remain undeciphered.

2 BENJAMIN FRANKLIN, 1706–1790

Benjamin Franklin is one of the most well-known Founding Fathers of the United States. Other talents included author, printer, satirist, political theorist, politician, scientist, inventor, civic activist, statesman, and diplomat. In 1730 Franklin acknowledged an illegitimate and only son, William, raised by his father, Ben, and Ben's common law wife, Deborah Rea. Some of the many theories speculated for not disclosing William's mother is the couple was not married when William was born and Franklin wanted to take all of the blame so as not to allow any dishonor to come to Deborah. Other evidence suggests his mother was a prostitute. William's mother's official identity still remains unknown.

Interesting Fact: In 1752, when William was twenty-one, he assisted his father in the famed kite experiment. William later became a steadfast Loyalist throughout the Revolutionary War despite his father's role as one of the most prominent Patriots during the conflict, a difference that tore the two apart.

1 ANTONIO STRADIVARI, 1644–1737

Stradivari was an Italian crafter of stringed instruments such as violins, cellos, guitars, and harps. For centuries scientists and historians have tried to figure out Stradivari's secret to his instrument making. Recently, modern research tools and devices, such as scanning lasers, are aiding researchers in testing the theory that the careful shaping of belly and back plate, in order to "tune" their resonant frequencies, could be an important factor. Glues and varnishes used by Stradivari have also been analyzed extensively and could also attribute for the sound and quality of his instruments. Experts concede there remains no consensus on the single most probable factor to explain the superior sound of the Stradivarius and most likely it is some combination of all, and something not yet recognized.

Interesting Fact: It is estimated that Stradivari made around 1100 instruments. Today only 650 instruments remain, including approximately 500 violins.

✳✳✳✳✳✳

TOP 10 FAMOUS HISTORIC MISQUOTES

10 VOLTAIRE

Quote: "I disapprove of what you say, but I will defend to the death your right to say it." (*"Je désapprouve ce que vous dites, mais je défendrai à la mort votre droit à le dire."*)

What Voltaire actually said was, "Think for yourselves and let others enjoy the privilege to do so too," from Voltaire's "Essay on Tolerance." That certainly doesn't have quite the same ring to it. The misquote actually comes from a 1907 book called *Friends of Voltaire*, by Evelyn Beatrice Hall.

9 GEORGE WASHINGTON

Quote: "I cannot tell a lie. It was I who chopped down the cherry tree."

Washington never said this. In fact, the story was first told in the 1800s by biographer Parson Weems. In Weems's book, the tree was not "chopped down."

8 EDWARD MURPHY

Quote: "Anything that can go wrong, will." (Murphy's Law)
Edward Murphy did not say this. What he most likely did say is something along the lines of, "If there's more than one way to do a job, and one of those ways will result in disaster, then somebody will do it that way."

7 MARK TWAIN

Quote: "The only two certainties in life are death and taxes."
This is more a problem of misattribution rather than misquotation. Mark Twain did not coin this phrase; it was actually coined by Benjamin Franklin in a letter written to Jean-Baptiste Leroy in 1879.

6 WILLIAM SHAKESPEARE

Quote: "Gild the lily."
This is a misquote from Shakespeare's *King John*. The actual quote is, "To gild refined gold, to paint the lily."

5 NICCOLO MACHIAVELLI

Quote: "The ends justify the means."
This is a very liberal interpretation of what Machiavelli actually said: "One must consider the final result." Rather different meanings.

4 WINSTON CHURCHILL

Quote: "The only traditions of the Royal Navy are rum, sodomy, and the lash."
Churchill did not utter this phrase at all; his assistant, Anthony Montague-Brown, did. What Churchill did say later was that he wished he had said it.

3 QUEEN MARIE ANTOINETTE

Quote: "If they have no bread, let them eat cake!" ("*S'ils n'ont plus de pain, qu'ils mangent de la brioche!*")
Queen Marie Antoinette is still much maligned over this quote, and she never even said it! It was actually from the book *Confessions* by Jean-Jacques Rousseau in which he said: "I recalled the make-shift of a great princess who was

told that the peasants had no bread and who replied, 'Let them eat brioche.'"
The attribution to Queen Marie is no doubt anti-royal propaganda during a very troubled time in French history.

2 PAUL REVERE
Quote: "The British are coming!"
Revere's mission depended on secrecy and the countryside was filled with British army patrols; also, most colonial residents at the time considered themselves British. The quotation is more likely based on (although not taken verbatim from) the later famous poem, "Paul Revere's Ride."

1 PHILIP SHERIDAN
Quote: "The only good Indian is a dead Indian."
What General Sheridan is alleged to have said is, "The only good Indians I ever saw were dead." He actually denied saying anything remotely like it.

✳✳✳✳✳✳

TOP 10 THINGS YOU DIDN'T KNOW THE ANCIENTS HAD

10 COSMETICS
Roman women would put metal compounds on their faces in order to enhance their color. Tin-oxide or lead-oxide was used as a paling agent; arsenic (though they knew it was poisonous) as a rouge or blush; and charcoal was used as eyeliner. Romans also were the first to use a pocket mirror.

9 ODOMETER
Although first used effectively by the Greeks in their measurements between cities, the Romans employed a very simple cart odometer that had

four-foot wheels. Each time the wheel completely turned, a pin would engage a cogwheel one notch out of its four hundred teeth. Each time said cogwheel turned, the cart had traveled one Roman mile.

8 FLAMETHROWER

The ancient Byzantines first used flamethrowers as a naval device, usually to set alight the rigging and sails of an enemy vessel. Although handheld devices were cumbersome and dangerous, naval ones were much more efficient. Working on a simple siphon pump concept, they would be pumped, and the action would pull flammable liquid out of a reservoir tank, forcing it past an open flame igniting the spray in a lethal barrage of a panic-inducing inferno.

7 MEDICINES

There is much archeological and historical evidence to support the use of complex medications and medical procedures within the ancient world. Honey was used as a topical antiseptic, honeysuckle often for spleen problems, horsehair for stitches, fine needles for cataract corrective surgery, and maggots for wound cleaning (as they eat dead tissue). Most medical procedures used today haven't changed significantly in several thousand years. Boils are still lanced, drained, cleaned, and closed; bones are still set; and teeth are still pulled, although pain medication has come a long way.

6 BIOLOGICAL WEAPONS

With the increase in medical knowledge through the ages, there has also been a markedly increased reverse engineering of the same knowledge to produce biologically based warfare tactics. In medieval times, besieging armies would hurl rotting carcasses into a city with catapults and trebuchet. Longer ago, there is evidence that plagued prisoners were thrown into rivers and streams leading to a city, poisoning its water supply and demoralizing the defending forces.

5 HEATED INDOOR SWIMMING POOLS

The Baths of Caracalla were one of the largest bathing complexes built in ancient Rome. The baths boasted both heated and cooled rooms, heated and cooled baths, a gymnasium for sports, and a "hat check room" where garments and personal effects were held under guard by a slave. An ingenious network of under-floor rooms and tunnels, coupled with heating furnaces arrayed around the lot, created the marvelous thermal differences used by the patrons.

4 POSTAL SYSTEM

Ancient postal systems were normally used either for official business conducted by the government or by the military. They were often the fastest form of information conductivity available.

3 CONCRETE

The Romans are credited with inventing "modern" concrete as a building material. It was a completely revolutionary material at the time. It was lightweight, extremely strong, dried underwater, and highly pliable when wet. The basic components of concrete haven't changed in several thousand years, and in some ways, Roman concrete is superior to that which is used today.

2 MECHANICAL ASTROLOGICAL CALCULATOR

The earliest known example of a mechanical calculator used in the calculation of astronomical objects is the Antikythera Mechanism. Its gears were used to compute the position of the sun, the moon, and possibly other astrological objects. Its complexity rivals that of clocks produced in the 1700s. The Antikythera Mechanism was produced sometime between 150 and 100 BC.

1 GLASSWARE

The earliest known use of glassware occurred in ancient Mesopotamia. Its use was later copied and refined by several civilizations including, but not limited to, the Romans, Greeks, and Egyptians.

✳✳✳✳✳✳

TOP 10 COMMON HISTORICAL MYTHS

10 ABNER DOUBLEDAY INVENTED BASEBALL

This very common myth of baseball credits Doubleday with inventing the game, supposedly in Elihu Phinney's cow pasture in Cooperstown, New York, in 1839. In 1905, a committee was appointed to investigate the origins of the game; their conclusion was:

> *"The first scheme for playing baseball, according to the best evidence obtainable to date, was devised by Abner Doubleday at Cooperstown, New York, in 1839. [In] the years to come, in the view of the hundreds of thousands of people who are devoted to baseball, and the millions who will be, Abner Doubleday's fame will rest evenly, if not quite as much, upon the fact that he was its inventor … as upon his brilliant and distinguished career as an officer in the Federal Army."*

In fact, this conclusion was based on the testimony of one man, who was of questionable credibility. Jeff Idelson of the Baseball Hall of Fame has said that baseball was not really invented anywhere, but as far as history is concerned, the first written rules of baseball were penned by Alexander Joy Cartwright for the baseball club The Knickerbockers. On June 3, 1953, Congress officially credited Cartwright with inventing the modern game of baseball.

9 THE COLOSSUS OF RHODES

Most ancient and even modern paintings of the now long-gone Ancient Wonder of the World, the Colossus of Rhodes, show him straddling the harbor entrance with ships entering the port beneath his legs. The Colossus was a statue (the tallest in the ancient world) of the Greek God Helios, built between 292 and 280 BC, and standing at a height of 100 feet. Contrary to the popular misconception that the statue's legs were apart, the Colossus actually stood with his legs slightly apart on one side of the entrance to the harbor. This renders virtually all illustrations of the statue, incorrect.

8 WITCHES WERE BURNED IN SALEM

In 1692 and 1693, anti-witch mania hit Salem, Massachusetts, resulting in a series of trials that led to the deaths of twenty accused witches. Over 150 people were tried for the crime of witchery. Contrary to the popular myth that the witches were burned, they were, in fact, hanged to death. Of the twenty, fourteen were women and six were men. All were executed according to this method with the exception of one man who died during judicial torture.

7 LIZZIE BORDEN TOOK AN AXE...

Unfortunately, this myth rears its ugly head quite often, and often no amount of effort is sufficient to disprove it to the true believers. First off, Lizzie—she is famous through the children's poem:

"Lizzie Borden took an axe
And gave her mother forty whacks.
And when she saw what she had done
She gave her father forty-one."

In fact, her father was axed eleven times and her stepmother eighteen or nineteen, but that is not the real myth; the real myth is the belief that Lizzie Borden committed the crime at all. After a mere one hour of jury deliberation, Lizzie was found innocent of the crime. To give further weight to her innocence, shortly before her trial a second axe murder happened in the area. Additionally, Lizzie was found with no blood on her minutes after the crime took place, and no murder weapon was ever found.

6 SALOME WANTED JOHN THE BAPTIST KILLED

The Bible tells the tale of Herod executing John the Baptist and giving his head as a gift to his daughter in reward for her dance at his birthday. Most people mistakenly believe that Salome, the daughter, requested this out of anger for John refused her advances. It was, in fact, Herodias, her mother, who wanted John killed, not Salome—she was merely the messenger.

> "And when the daughter of the same Herodias had come in, and had danced, and pleased Herod, and them that were at table with him, the king said to the damsel: 'Ask of me what thou wilt, and I will give it thee.' And he swore to her: 'Whatsoever thou shalt ask I will give thee, though it be the half of my kingdom.' Who when she was gone out, said to her mother, 'What shall I ask?' But her mother said: 'The head of John the Baptist.' And when she was come in immediately with haste to the king, she asked, saying: 'I will that forthwith thou give me in a dish, the head of John the Baptist.'" (Mark 6:22-25)

This popular myth has been seen in opera, poetry, and painting.

5 EDISON INVENTED THE LIGHTBULB

In fact, Thomas Edison not only did not invent the lightbulb, he did not invent many of the things attributed to him. His shrewd business skills enabled him to steal, improve, and patent many ideas before their original inventors were able to. He was, in addition, a ruthless man who attempted to discredit other inventors in order to gain popularity for his own. Prior to Edison's patent for the electric lightbulb in 1880, electric lights had already been invented. In 1840, British astronomer and chemist, Warren de la Rue, enclosed a platinum coil in a vacuum tube and passed an electric current through it, thus creating the world's first lightbulb—a full forty years before Edison.

4 POPE JOAN

This myth tells us that a young woman dressed as a priest and went to Rome to study. Eventually, she became pope but gave birth to a child while in a papal procession, causing the crowds to kill her by stoning. In fact, there never was a Pope Joan. The myth seems to have originated around the thirteenth century from the writings of Martin of Opava (Martin Polonus), a Polish chronicler, and it generally places Joan in the ninth century papacy. Aside from Catholic literature, even enemies of the Catholic Church at the time (for example, Photius), make no mention at all of a female pope. According to the *Catholic Encyclopedia*:

> *"Between Leo IV and Benedict III, where Martinus Polonus places her, she cannot be inserted, because Leo IV died July 17, 855, and, immediately after his death, Benedict III was elected by the clergy and people of Rome; but owing to the setting up of an antipope, in the person of the deposed Cardinal Anastasius, he was not consecrated until September 29. Coins exist which bear both the image of Benedict III and of Emperor Lothair, who died September 28, 855; therefore Benedict must have been recognized as pope before the last-mentioned date."*

The recent resurgence in the belief in this myth is most likely the result of anti-Catholic and feminist wishful thinking, according to Philip Jenkins, author of *The New Anti-Catholicism*.

3 LADY GODIVA RODE NAKED

Lady Godiva was an Anglo-Saxon noblewoman who is supposed to have ridden through the streets of Coventry naked in order to force her husband, Leofric (968–1057), to remove an unfair tax on his tenants. Both she and her husband were very generous to the poor and religious institutions in their time. In 1043 Leofric founded and endowed a Benedictine monastery at Coventry and it is believed that his wife, Godiva, was the primary instigator of this. It is very possible that the legend has sprung from this particular event. But there is no doubt that her husband was a very generous man with little need for coercion. Interestingly, the legend of the Peeping Tom also arises from this myth as later versions of it describe a man, Tom, who peeped at Lady Godiva while she rode naked, and was struck blind.

2 "LET THEM EAT CAKE"

According to popular myth, Queen Marie Antoinette was heard to say, *"S'ils n'ont plus de pain, qu'ils mangent de la brioche"* ("If they have no bread, let them eat brioche."), referring to the poor. First of all, even if Queen Marie had made this comment, it would have not had the same meaning as it does today. Laws at the time of her reign meant that bakers who ran out of cheap bread had to sell their finer bread (such as brioche) at the lower price, in order to protect people from ruthless bakers who would make insufficient quantities of inexpensive bread in order to make a bigger profit. That aside, the queen did not say these words at all; they were actually written by Jean-Jacques Rousseau in his book *Confessions*, written a number of years before Marie Antoinette became queen. His exact words:

> *"I recalled the make-shift of a great princess who was told that the peasants had no bread and who replied: 'Let them eat brioche.'"*

The misattribution and perpetuation of this myth is most likely a result of anti-royal propaganda following the revolution in which she and her husband were murdered.

1 NERO FIDDLED WHILE ROME BURNED

From July 18 to July 19, 64 AD, the Great Fire of Rome occurred. The popular myth surrounding this event is that Nero played the fiddle while he watched Rome burn, and later benefited from its burning by using cleared land for his new palace.

Suetonius and Cassius Dio said that Nero sang the "Sack of Ilium" in stage costume while the city burned. However, Tacitus's account has Nero in Antium at the time of the fire. Tacitus said that Nero playing his lyre and singing while the city burned was only rumor. In fact, according to Tacitus, upon hearing news of the fire, Nero rushed back to Rome to organize a relief effort, which he paid for from his own funds. After the fire, Nero opened his palaces to provide shelter for the homeless, and arranged for food supplies to be delivered in order to prevent starvation among the survivors. In the wake of the fire, he made a new urban development plan. Houses after the fire were spaced out, built in brick, and faced by porticos on wide roads. Nero also built a new palace complex known as the Domus Aurea in an area cleared by the fire.

Incidentally, the violin (fiddle) would not be invented for a full thousand years after the Great Fire of Rome.

✳✳✳✳✳✳

TOP 10 ANCIENT INVENTIONS

10 THE WHEEL, 5000 BC

When talking about ancient inventions, the wheel is one that always comes to mind, but it is actually relatively young compared to some of the other items on this list. It was most likely invented in Sumer (which is now Iraq) in 5000 BC. It eventually spread across the Indus Valley civilization by 3000 BC. Interestingly, wheels only occur in nature in microscopic form so its invention was not the result of imitating objects from the natural environment.

9 TWISTED ROPE, 17,000 BC

Rope has been used by humans since prehistoric times. It was used in hunting, lifting, and even climbing. The first ropes would have been vines, which were eventually twisted together for increased durability. Fragments of man-made twisted rope were discovered in caves in France dating to 15,000 BC. The ancient Egyptians developed tools for rope making around 4000 BC.

8 MUSICAL INSTRUMENTS, 50,000 BC

The first instruments were flutes made of bone, mammoth tusk to be exact. Fragments of these instruments have been found in caves dating back to 43,000 years BC. More recently, bone flutes dating from 9000 BC were in such good condition that they could be played.

7 THE BOAT, 60,000 BC

Humans began to travel by boat around 60,000 BC and archeological evidence shows that the ancestors of the Australian Aborigines traveled across the Lombok Strait to Australia in 50,000 BC. The ancient Egyptians were making watertight hulls with pitch and nails by 2500 BC.

6 PIGMENTS, 400,000 BC

Pigments have been used since 400,000 BC for body decoration and painting (such as cave painting). Naturally occurring pigments, such as iron oxide and ocher, were the first to be used and there have even been discoveries of equipment for grinding paints from the same period. Eventually, various pigments were traded over long distances making the range of colors available more diverse. The most difficult pigments to produce (blue and purple) were reserved almost exclusively for royalty because of their high cost.

5 SPEARS, 400,000 BC

Because wood does not preserve well, the estimate that man used spears 400,000 years ago is extremely conservative with some anthropologists suggesting that we may have been using them as long as five million years ago. By 250,000 BC, spears were being tipped by stone blades making them far more effective than the fire-hardened tips previously in use.

4 CLOTHING, 500,000–100,000 BC

The earliest clothing used by man was made of fur, leather, and plant life. It was initially used for protection from the elements but was eventually used for decorative purposes also. Interestingly, analyses of human body lice (which require clothing to survive) has been instrumental in dating our use of clothing as the fragile nature of ancient cloth means that no examples survive from our earliest days.

3 HOUSING, 500,000 BC

Primitive man used caves for shelter and even for religious uses, but from 500,000 BC we began to build huts. A fascinating archeological discovery in

Tokyo uncovered a house built with ten posts, forming an irregular pentagon shape, as well as numerous stone tools.

2 FIRE, 1,000,000 BC

Fire is perhaps the most important discovery of man because it dramatically reduced the chances of illness from bad food and allowed our ancient ancestors to clear large areas through controlled fires. This made it possible to begin farming land on a large scale.

1 KNIFE, 2,500,000–1,400,000

The first knives were made by flaking rocks. It is possible that the same technique may have been used to produce knives from other materials, but none have survived. Archeologists discovered the oldest group of stone tools (called olduwan) which date to 1.5 million BC. These were used by Australopithecines and other similar hominids who probably shared the knowledge of manufacture between species.

✳✳✳✳✳✳

TOP 10 INVENTIONS OF THE MIDDLE AGES

10 HEAVY PLOUGH, FIFTH CENTURY AD

While primitive ploughs had been in use since perhaps the late Stone Age, they were usually fragile and ill-suited for heavy soils. Moreover, the only way to adjust the depth of a furrow was for the ploughman to physically lift the plough as it cut. With the introduction of wheels (replacing the runner), the weight of the plough could be increased, and ploughs could be sheathed with metal to increase their strength. Furrows could be cut to uniform depths, with less physical exertion by the operator. The heavy plough thus led to more efficient farming, increased food production, and, in turn, allowed the population of Europe to increase.

9 TIDAL MILLS, SEVENTH CENTURY AD

Tidal mills are driven by the tidal rise and fall of water, and are thus more efficient than mills that rely strictly on the flow of water from streams and rivers. A body of water affected by tides is dammed, and a one-way sluice gate allows for water to enter a millpond with the high tide. As the tide falls, the gate closes, and the stored water is then released at will to work the water wheel. The tidal mill dates back to at least as early as AD 787 in Northern Ireland.

8 HOURGLASS, NINTH CENTURY AD

The hourglass was one of the first portable and reusable methods of determining time. Fairly accurate and highly versatile, hourglasses could be employed in a variety of places, most importantly at sea, where timekeeping was a vital necessity. It's known that Magellan, in his trip around the globe, employed some eighteen hourglasses on each of his ships.

7 BLAST FURNACE, TWELFTH CENTURY AD

The Cistercian monks, known for their skills in metallurgy, are believed to be responsible for transmitting the technological know-how behind the blast furnace, with every monastery possessing a factory and water system to drive the machinery therein. For several centuries they were leading producers of iron in France.

6 LIQUOR, TWELFTH CENTURY AD

While true distillation dates back to Babylon of the fourth millennium BC, it wasn't until the time of the Muslim alchemists in the eighth and ninth centuries that alcohol distillation became truly efficient and allowed for the invention of liquor as we know it today.

5 EYEGLASSES, THIRTEENTH CENTURY

Historians argue whether lenses for eyeglasses were first developed in the West or in China, but in any case, they appear in the thirteenth century and are first remarked upon, in print, by Roger Bacon. They also appear in Italian art of the time, and it was because of a Ghirlandaio painting showing St. Jerome with a pair of eyeglasses that the saint became the patron of opticians. Convex lenses for farsightedness were apparently developed first, while concave lenses (for nearsightedness, or myopia) do not appear in print or art until a portrait done by Raphael in 1517 of Pope Leo X.

4 MECHANICAL CLOCK, THIRTEENTH CENTURY AD

No one is certain when the mechanical clock was first invented, but it's assumed that their earliest uses were in monasteries to call the monks to prayer. The first such clocks known for certain are called "turret clocks," as they were large machines housed in towers. The earliest of these tolled only the hour, and had no hands or dial. A clock from Rouen, France, is still extant and dates from 1389.

3 SPINNING WHEEL, THIRTEENTH CENTURY AD

It's believed that the spinning wheel has its origins in India, though this is uncertain. At any rate, it came to Europe in the Middle Ages and replaced the handheld distaff, which had been in existence perhaps since the late Stone Age.

2 QUARANTINE, FOURTEENTH CENTURY AD

The first quarantine we know of occurred in Venice in the fourteenth century, and was, of course, an attempt to stem the spread of the plague. Ships arriving from the East were held in isolation for a period of time sufficient to indicate whether plague was aboard, and if so, to allow it to dissipate. The period of time designated for this was a *quarantina*, or "forty days." Supposedly, this was settled on as an appropriate period because it was the amount of time that both Christ and Moses had spent alone in the desert.

1 PRINTING PRESS OF GUTENBERG, FIFTEENTH CENTURY AD

While the Chinese had first used movable type and paper, it wasn't until the development of Gutenberg's press that the process became mechanized and allowed for true mass dissemination of the printed word. The press was clearly modeled on the wine and olive presses that had existed in the Near East and the Mediterranean since ancient times.

✳✳✳✳✳✳

TOP 10
HISTORICAL ODDITIES
YOU DON'T KNOW

10 BEFORE THE BOSTON TEA PARTY, THE BRITISH ACTUALLY LOWERED TEA TAXES, NOT RAISED THEM.

9 ABEL TASMAN "DISCOVERED" TASMANIA, NEW ZEALAND, AND FIJI ON HIS FIRST VOYAGE, BUT MANAGED TO COMPLETELY MISS MAINLAND AUSTRALIA!

8 WHEN THE AMERICAN CIVIL WAR STARTED, CONFEDERATE ROBERT E. LEE OWNED NO SLAVES. UNION GENERAL U.S. GRANT DID.

7 KAISER WILHELM II, TSAR NICHOLAS II, AND GEORGE V WERE ALL GRANDCHILDREN OF QUEEN VICTORIA.

6 JOSEF STALIN ONCE STUDIED TO BE A PRIEST.

5 HENRY KISSINGER AND YASSIR ARAFAT WON THE NOBEL PEACE PRIZE. GANDHI NEVER DID.

4 THE CONSTITUTION OF THE CONFEDERATE STATES OF AMERICA BANNED THE SLAVE TRADE.

3 THE "D" IN D-DAY STANDS FOR "DAY," SO IT'S "DAY-DAY."

2 A NEW ORLEANS MAN HIRED A PIRATE TO RESCUE NAPOLEON FROM HIS PRISON ON ST. HELENA.

1 **IN 1839, THE U.S. AND CANADA FOUGHT THE BLOODLESS "WAR OF PORK AND BEANS."**

TOP 10 FASCINATING BUILDINGS NEVER BUILT

10 HOTEL ATTRACTION

Designed in 1908 for New York City

Hotel Attraction was to be the tallest building in New York at the time and was designed by architect Antoni Gaudi. The planned total height was 1181 feet and was probably unrealistic for its time. Little is known about the origins of Hotel Attraction and was unknown until 1956, when a report called "The New World Called Gaudi" was published.

Interesting Fact: The drawings by Gaudi of the Attraction Hotel had actually been proposed as a basis for the rebuilding of the Ground Zero project in Manhattan.

9 THE ILLINOIS

Designed in 1956 for Chicago, Illinois

The Illinois was a proposed mile-high (5280 feet) skyscraper, envisioned by Frank Lloyd Wright. Wright believed that it would have been technically possible to construct such a building even at the time it was proposed. The design included 528 stories, with a gross area of 18.46 million square feet.

Interesting Fact: A number of problems occurred in Wright's design of The Illinois, including space that was needed to service the elevators which would occupy all of the space available on the lower floors, thus defeating the purpose of the building's height.

8 FOURTH GRACE
Designed in 2002 for Liverpool, England

Despite what many believe was the ugliest of all the proposals, architect Will Alsop entered the winning design for this project and named it "The Cloud." The project's name, Fourth Grace, is due to the development being located adjacent to the three historic buildings at the Pier Head site known as "The Three Graces." The project was cancelled in 2004 due to spiraling costs.

Interesting Fact: The Fourth Grace was designed for office space, a 107-room hotel, and 50,000 square feet of community facilities, including a bar, restaurant, and viewing gallery.

7 BEACON OF PROGRESS
Designed around 1891 for Chicago, Illinois

Plans called for a 1500-foot stone tower in Jackson Park, Chicago, on the site of the 1893 Chicago World's Fair. French-born architect and MIT professor Désiré Despradelle came up with the winning design. With more financial backing the structure would have been, by far, the tallest man-made object in the world.

Interesting Fact: The design called for an amphitheater at the base to seat 100,000 people and sweeping piers that would extend into Lake Michigan for regattas.

6 VILLE CONTEMPORAINE
Designed in 1922 for Paris, France

The Ville Contemporaine was to house three million inhabitants and was designed by the French-Swiss architect Le Corbusier. The centerpiece of this plan was the group of sixty-story skyscrapers built on steel frames and encased in huge curtain walls of glass. They housed both offices and apartments of the most wealthy inhabitants. At the very center was a huge transportation center on different levels that would include depots for buses and trains, as well as highway and an airport at the top.

Interesting Fact: For a number of years French officials had been unsuccessful in dealing with the squalor of the growing Parisian slums. Le Corbusier thought this design was an efficient way to house large numbers of people in response to the urban housing crisis.

5 TATLIN'S TOWER
Designed around 1917 for St. Petersburg, Russia

Tatlin's Tower would have dwarfed the Eiffel Tower in Paris. The tower was to be built from industrial materials: iron, glass, and steel. It was envisioned as a towering symbol of modernity. The tower's main form was a twin helix that spiraled up to 1312 feet in height, where visitors would be transported around with the aid of various mechanical devices.

Interesting Fact: At the base of the structure was a rotating cube, designed as a venue for lectures, conferences, and legislative meetings. The cube would complete a rotation in the span of one year. Above that cube would be a smaller pyramid housing executive activities and completing a rotation once a month.

4 SHIMIZU MEGA-CITY PYRAMID
Designed in 2004 for Tokyo, Japan

The Shimizu Mega-City Pyramid was a proposed project for construction of a massive pyramid over Tokyo Bay in Japan. The structure would be twelve times higher than the Great Pyramid at Giza, and would house 750,000 people. It would be the largest man-made structure on Earth. The pyramid structure would be composed of fifty-five smaller pyramids stacked five high. Each of these smaller pyramids would be about the size of the Luxor Hotel in Las Vegas.

Interesting Fact: The reason this project cannot be built is the design of the Mega-City Pyramids relies on the future availability of super-strong lightweight materials that are currently unavailable.

3 ULTIMA TOWER
Designed in 1991 for San Francisco, California

Architect Eugene Tsui originally conceived the idea of the Ultima Tower as part of a study of the compact urban area of San Francisco. The structure would utilize atmospheric energy conversion by converting the difference in atmospheric pressure at the top and bottom of the structure into electrical power. The Ultima Tower is five hundred stories tall (two miles high) and is intended to house one million residents.

Interesting Fact: The structure's shape is modeled after the tallest structure not made by man—African termite nests.

2 PALACE OF SOVIETS
Designed in 1933 for Moscow, Soviet Union

If the Palace of Soviets had been built, it would have become the world's tallest structure. It was to be built on the site of the demolished Cathedral of Christ the Savior. A public international contest to design the Palace attracted 272 concepts from architects all over the world. The contest was won by Boris Iofan, who literally expressed the idea of "Lenin atop the skyscraper" in the clearest form.

Interesting Fact: Construction was actually started on this project in 1937 and was terminated because of the German invasion. In 1942 its steel frame was disassembled for use in fortifications and bridges. Also: The Cathedral was rebuilt in 1995 to 2000.

1 VOLKSHALLE (THE GREAT DOME)
Designed around 1930 for Berlin, Germany

The Volkshalle (People's Hall) was a huge monumental building planned by Adolf Hitler and his architect Albert Speer. It was to be the capital's most important and impressive building in terms of its size and symbolism and the architectural centerpiece of Berlin. Thankfully, the Great Dome was never built due to the breakout of the war.

Interesting Fact: What makes the Volkshalle even more interesting is the illustration plans show a pedestal with the Nazi eagle figure. The eagle along with the pedestal and just the right shadowing gives an illusion in the form of Hitler's face and is believed designed to appear only at a particular time of the year.

✳✳✳✳✳✳

TOP 10 ANCIENT MYSTERIES

10 RONGORONGO
Everyone knows about the giant stone heads (or Moai) of Easter Island. Less well-known, however, is that the Easter Islanders evidently possessed a written language, in the form of a hieroglyphic script called "Rongorongo."

This is itself a curiosity, as any form of written language was apparently unknown to the neighboring oceanic societies. Rongorongo has never been deciphered, in part due to the fact that Europeans who came to colonize the island banned the language, and destroyed most examples of it.

9 LOST CITY OF HELIKE

Helike was a city in the Peloponnesus mentioned by the Greek travel writer Pausanias in the second century AD. According to Pausanias, the city—capital of the Achaean League and a center of worship dedicated to the god Poseidon—had been devastated by a powerful earthquake and tsunami which erased almost all traces of it in a single night. It was not until modern times that clues began to surface as to the precise location of the lost city, and in 2001 archeologists finally found the ruins of it in a lagoon.

8 THE BOG BODIES

Unearthed in and around the wetlands of Northern Europe, the bog bodies are hundreds of mummified corpses—many remarkably preserved—some of which date back as far as two thousand years. Some of the bodies show the clear indications of having suffered torture, and some are apparent victims of strangulation, throat-cutting, and other methods of execution. The supposition made by many archeologists is that the bog people were victims of ritual sacrifice.

7 FALL OF THE MINOANS

Over four thousand years ago, the island of Crete was inhabited by a people who were known as "Minoans," after the legendary king Minos, who was supposed to have ruled the Aegean at that time. The Minoans were contemporaries of the other great ancient civilizations of the Near East: Egypt, Sumer, Babylon, and the Hittites. Tradition says that they ruled a trading empire centered on the islands of the eastern Mediterranean and mainland Greece. They apparently lived in peace and in great security, as none of their cities that have so far been excavated show any signs of fortifications. What they do show, however, is that the Minoans were a highly sophisticated, artistic, and inventive people, clearly responsible for influencing the early Greeks who were their immediate neighbors. We know very little about them, however, because the few examples of Minoan language that have been found have proven undecipherable, and thus the Minoans are cloaked in mystery, and the greatest mystery of all is what brought their society to an end. We know that after about 1500 BC, the archeological record indicates that Crete was in the hands of mainland Greeks and the ancient Minoan styles of art and architecture come to an end. This date, interestingly enough, coincides with the date of a vast volcanic explosion on the island of Thera, which may have sent huge tsumanis crashing into Crete and blanketed the island with ash. It is theorized that Crete is the real "Atlantis" of legend, since so many of the circumstances surrounding it fit the story. But without a written record, we may never know what truly happened.

6 THE CARNAC STONES

The Carnac Stones are examples of ancient monument building that may share much in common with other megalithic sites and stone circles, the most famous of which is Stonehenge. The Carnac Stones however, are some three thousand megaliths, set up in straight lines near the coast of northwest France, covering some seven miles. Neither the purpose of the stone lines, nor the people who erected them, are known. Myth says that they were a legion of Roman soldiers turned to stone; current theories run the gamut from astronomical markers of some kind to a kind of ancient earthquake detector.

5 WHO WAS ROBIN HOOD?

There are various figures mentioned in historical rolls who could have been the basis of the legend of Robin Hood, among them a man known as "Hobbehod" or Robert Hod, of Yorkshire. The search for a "historic" Robin Hood is made all the more difficult by later embellishments to the story, and additions of characters that obscure the time and place where he may have lived. We will probably never know who he really was or if he even actually existed.

4 THE LOST ROMAN LEGION

Legend has it that a number of Roman soldiers escaped the defeat of the Roman general Crassus at the hands of the Parthians. These legionnaires supposedly went eastward, and were said to have founded a town near the Gobi desert. There are reports in ancient Chinese records of an army fighting in the style of a Roman legion, and there have even been DNA tests done on local inhabitants in recent years to see if they were the possible descendants of this lost legion. The tests were inconclusive, indicating a possible European origin for some, but nothing more specific.

3 THE VOYNICH MANUSCRIPT

The so-called Voynich Manuscript (named for the book dealer who acquired it in the early twentieth century) is a document of unknown origin and authorship, written in an unknown alphabet and language. It is believed to date from the Middle Ages. Ever since its discovery various individuals and groups have tried to decipher it with no success, and to this day it remains a complete enigma. The illustrations included within suggest it is some kind of pharmacological text, but even this is uncertain. Theories abound as to the contents, their purpose, and who authored it.

2 THE TARIM MUMMIES

In the 1990s there was a discovery of some highly unusual two-thousand-year-old mummies in the Tarim basin of Western China. The mummies—which were subjected to DNA testing—were Caucasian in appearance, with blonde hair and long noses. The tests indicated that the mummies were indeed of possible European origin, despite being found in China. The mystery, of course, is who these people were and how they got there. Chinese texts dating back to the first millennium BC make mention of Caucasians living in the Far East, but their actual identity remains unknown.

1 DISAPPEARANCE OF THE INDUS VALLEY CIVILIZATION

The Indus Valley Civilization (also known as the Harappans after one of their cities was uncovered in an area of the same name in India) was an advanced culture that coexisted with the great civilizations of Mesopotamia. It's believed that this society stretched from what is today Western India to Afghanistan, but they are largely shrouded in mystery since their language has never been deciphered. Archeological study has unearthed evidence of sophisticated sewage systems in their cities, as well as large, complex baths. To date, however, no one has ever found conclusive evidence as to what brought the Indus Valley Civilization to an end.

✳✳✳✳✳✳

TOP 10 GREAT ANCIENT CHINESE INVENTIONS

10 ROW PLANTING (FEUDAL PERIOD–SIXTH CENTURY BC)
The Chinese started planting crops in rows sometime in the sixth century BC. This technique allows the crops to grow faster and stronger. It facilitates more efficient planting, watering, weeding, and harvesting. There is also documentation that they realized that as the wind travels over rows of plants there is less damage. This obvious development was not instituted in the Western world for another 2200 years. Master Lu wrote in the "Spring and Autumn Annals": "If the crops are grown in rows they will mature rapidly because they will not interfere with each other's growth. The horizontal rows must be well drawn, the vertical rows made with skill, for if the lines are straight the wind will pass gently through." This text was compiled around 240 BC.

9 COMPASS (FEUDAL PERIOD–FOURTH CENTURY BC)
The Chinese developed a lodestone compass to indicate direction sometime in the fourth century BC. These compasses were south pointing and were primarily used on land as divination tools and direct finders. Written in the fourth century BC, in the *Book of the Devil Valley Master*, it is written that "lodestone makes iron come or it attracts it." The spoons were made from lodestone, while the plates were of bronze. Thermoremanence needles were being produced for mariners by the year 1040, with common use recorded by 1119. Thermoremanence technology, still in use today, was "discovered" by William Gilbert in about 1600.

8 THE SEED DRILL (HAN DYNASTY: CIRCA 202 BC–220 AD)
The seed drill is used to plant seeds into the soil at a uniform depth and cover it. Without this tool, seeds are tossed by hand over the ground resulting in waste and inefficient, uneven growth. Chinese farmers were using seed drills as early as the second century BC. The first known European instance was a patent issued to Camillo Torello in 1566, but was not adopted by Europeans into general use until the mid-1800s.

7 IRON PLOWS (HAN DYNASTY: CIRCA 202 BC–220 AD)

One of the major developments of the ancient Chinese agriculture was the use of the iron moldboard plows. Though probably first developed in the fourth century BC and promoted by the central government, they were popular and common by the Han dynasty. (So I am using the more conservative date.) A major invention was the adjustable strut, which, by altering the distance of the blade and the beam, could precisely set the depth of the plow. This technology was not instituted in England and Holland until the seventeenth century, sparking an abundance of food which some experts say was a necessary prerequisite for the industrial revolution.

6 DEEP DRILLING (HAN DYNASTY: CIRCA 202 BC–220 AD)

By the first century BC the Chinese had developed the technology for deep drilling boreholes. Some of these reached depths of 4800 feet. They used technology that would be easily recognizable to a modern engineer and layperson alike. Derricks would rise as much as 180 feet above the borehole. They stacked rocks with center holes (tube or doughnut shaped) from the surface to the deep stone layer as a guide for their drills (similar to today's guide tubes). With hemp ropes and bamboo cables reaching deep into the ground, they employed cast iron drills to reach the natural gas they used as a fuel to evaporate water from brine to produce salt. The natural gas was carried via bamboo pipes to where it was needed. There is also some evidence that the gas was used for light. While I could not find exactly when deep-drilling was first used by the Europeans, I did not find any evidence prior to the early industrial revolution (mid-eighteenth century). In the United States, the first recorded deep drill was in West Virginia in the 1820s.

5 SHIP'S RUDDER (HAN DYNASTY: CIRCA 202 BC–220 AD)

Chinese naval developments occurred far earlier than similar Western technology. The first recorded use of rudder technology in the West was in 1180. Chinese pottery models of sophisticated slung axial rudders (enabling the rudder to be lifted in shallow waters) dating from the first century have been found. Early rudder technology (circa 100 AD) also included the easier to use balanced rudder (where part of the blade was in front of the steering post), first adopted by England in 1843—some 1700 years later. In another naval development, fenestrated rudders were common on Chinese ships by the thirteenth century, which were not introduced to the west until 1901. Fenestration is the adding of holes to the rudder where it does not affect the steering, yet makes the rudder easy to turn. This innovation finally enabled European torpedo boats to use their rudders while traveling at high speed (about 30 knots).

4 HARNESSES FOR HORSES (AGE OF DIVISION: CIRCA 220–581 AD)

Throat harnesses have been used throughout the world to harness horses to carts and sleds. These harnesses press back on the neck of the horse thus limiting the full strength of the animal. In the late feudal period (fourth century BC), there is pictorial evidence (from the Chinese state of Chu) of a horse with a wooden chest yoke. By the late Han dynasty, the yoke was made from softer straps and was used throughout the country. By the fifth century, the horse collar, which allows the horse to push with its shoulders, was developed. This critical invention was introduced into Europe approximately by 970 and became widespread within 200 years. Because of the greater speed of horses over oxen, as well as greater endurance, agricultural output throughout Europe increased significantly.

3 PORCELAIN (SUI DYNASTY: 581–618 AD)

Porcelain is a very specific kind of ceramic produced by the extreme temperatures of a kiln. The materials fuse and form a glass and mineral compound known for its strength, translucence, and beauty. Invented during the Sui dynasty (but possibly earlier) and perfected during the Tang dynasty (618–906), most notably by Tao-Yue (c. 608–c. 676), Chinese porcelain was highly prized throughout the world. The porcelain of Tao-Yue used a "white clay" found on the edge of the Yangtze River, where he lived. By the time of the Sung dynasty (960–1279), the art of porcelain had reached its peak. In 1708 the German physicist Tschirnhausen invented European porcelain, thus ending the Chinese monopoly.

2 TOILET PAPER (SUI DYNASTY: 581–618 AD)

One of the first recorded accounts of using hygienic paper was during the Sui dynasty in 589. In 851 an Arab traveler reported (with some amazement) that the Chinese used paper in place of water to cleanse themselves. By the late 1300s, approximately 720,000 sheets per year were produced in packages of a thousand to ten thousand sheets. In colonial times in America (late 1700s), it was still common to use corncobs or leaves. Commercial toilet paper was not introduced until 1857 and at least one early advertiser noted that their product was "splinter free"—something quite far from today's "ultra-soft." One rather odd piece of trivia I picked up during my research is that the Romans used a sponge tied to the end of a stick, which may have been the origin of the expression "to grab the wrong end of the stick."

1 PRINTING—MOVABLE TYPE (SONG DYNASTY: 960–1279 AD)

Paper having been invented by the Chinese is well known (by Cai Lun, circa 50–121 AD), and is one of the great Chinese inventions. The recipe for this paper still exists and can be followed by today's artisans. In 868 the first printed book, using full-page woodcuts, was produced. About a hundred years later, the innovations of Bi Sheng were described. Using clay-fired characters he made reusable type and developed typesetting techniques. Though used successfully to produce books, his technology was not perfected until 1298. By contrast, Gutenberg's bibles—the first European book printed with movable type—were printed in the 1450s. Interestingly, the Chinese did not start using metal type until the 1490s.

❉❉❉❉❉❉

TOP 10 GOVERNMENTS-IN-EXILE

10 BELARUSIAN NATIONAL REPUBLIC

The BNR was created as a pro-German buffer state against revolutionary Russia in 1918. The BNR was never a real state, as it had no constitution, no military, and no defined territory. When German troops withdrew from Belarus, the region was quickly overrun by the Red Army, and the BNR provisional council went into exile to facilitate an anti-communist movement there. Its government still exists, though it is unrecognized and in exile in Toronto.

9 REPUBLIC OF CABINDA

Cabinda is a region located in west central Africa between Angola and the Democratic Republic of Congo. Cabinda's claims to independence from Angola trace back to its days as a Portuguese protectorate. When Angola achieved independence in the 1960s, the exiled Cabinda government declared independence as well, though it went unrecognized. Its government is currently based in Kinshasa, Democratic Republic of Congo.

8 THE CROWN COUNCIL OF ETHIOPIA

This governing body once acted as a board of advisors for the reigning emperors of Ethiopia. When the monarchy was driven out in 1975, members of the Crown Council (including descendants of Haile Selassie) claimed that the emperorship still existed, and was thus the only legitimate head of state. Its current leader is Prince Ermias Sahle Selassie and it is based in Washington, D.C.

7 PROGRESS PARTY OF EQUATORIAL GUINEA

The PPGE (as it's abbreviated in Spanish) was founded as a pro-market, pro-democratic party in Equatorial Guinea in west Africa, after a lengthy period of repressive military authoritarianism. The volatile political situation in Equatorial Guinea led to party members' harassment and imprisonment. In response, the party declared a "government-in-exile" in Madrid, where it is still located.

6 MONARCHY OF LAO

The monarchy of Lao traces its origins to the consolidated Kingdom of Laos, formed in 1946. In 1975, the monarchy was dissolved by the communist regime and was sent into exile. It remains opposed to the Lao People's Democratic Republic, and its stated goal is "to institute in Laos a true democracy, one which will ensure freedom, justice, peace, and prosperity for all Lao people." Its headquarters is located in the U.S.

5 NCBUG

The NCGUB (National Coalition Government of the Union of Burma) was formed in 1995 at a convention in Bommersvik, Sweden. Among its founding goals were the support of the political initiatives of imprisoned Nobel laureate Daw Aung San Suu Kyi and the establishment of a democratic multi-party union through talks with the ruling military junta led by General Than Shwe. Members were elected to parliament but not allowed by the junta to take office. It is currently based in Rockville, Maryland.

4 REPUBLIC OF SERBIAN KRAJINA

This government was formed during the Yugoslav civil war of the 1990s but was reinstated in 2005. Serbian Krajina was formerly a self-proclaimed Serbian state within Croatia, later overrun by Croatian forces. More recently, former legislators of the RSK again pushed for greater autonomy (though not independence) from the Croatian government. The RSK exiled government is headquartered in Belgrade.

3 CHECHEN REPUBLIC OF ICHKERIA

Chechnya is a breakaway province in the Northern Caucasus and the site of two devastating wars between Chechen separatists and the Russian Federation. When the Russians overran Grozny in 2000, the Chechen government was exiled to various Arab countries, the UK, the U.S., and Poland. In 2007, Ichkerian President Dokka Umarov declared himself the "emir" of a greater Caucasus Emirate, though this claim has been rejected by pro-republican forces and members of the former Chechen government.

2 MONARCHY OF IRAN

The modern Iranian monarchy was established in 1501 and was presided over by the Shahanshah, the equivalent of an emperor. Through much of its history, Iran was ruled by an absolute monarchy. Its last ruling shah, Mohammed Reza Pahlavi, was deposed by the Islamic Revolution of 1979 and sent into exile. Upon his death, the crown passed to his eldest son Reza Pahlavi. He has used his position to try to influence the Iranian electorate to perform acts of civil disobedience and non-participation, though he opposes foreign military action to oust the Islamic regime. He currently lives in Potomac, Maryland.

1 CENTRAL TIBETAN ADMINISTRATION

Tibet is a region under the administration of the People's Republic of China, a situation considered by the Central Tibetan Administration to be an unlawful occupation. The exiled Tibetan government is headed by Tenzin Gyatso, the fourteenth Dalai Lama. The CTA claims jurisdiction over those regions referred to as "Historic Tibet." Among its current functions are the building of schools, health services, economic development, and cultural activities for the international Tibetan community. Its current policy advocates autonomy rather than total independence. The CTA is based in Dharamsala, India, where the Dalai Lama first settled following the Chinese military occupation of Tibet in 1959.

TOP 10 LESSER-USED OR KNOWN FORMS OF GOVERNMENT

10 TOTALITARIANISM—TOTAL RULE

Totalitarianism is when a country is ruled by an ideology that penetrates every nook and cranny of its society. The regime is often headed by a cult of personality type leader. The government builds up control through eliminating and confining anything that acts independently of the state, until it regulates and enforces nearly every aspect of public and private life, giving themselves power through propaganda, control over media, economy, restricting free discussion, mass surveillance, and use of terror tactics. Totalitarianism is really just a concept, but many countries have advocated and built off it; the two best known being Nazi Germany and the Soviet Union. The George Orwell book *1984* deals extensively with the subject.

9 THEOCRACY—RULED BY GOD

Ruled by a god or deity, the state is governed by an individual that is divinely guided, or more often an institutional representative (a church). The local laws and rules are set by a dominant religious leader, on behalf of God. In pure theocracy, the leader is believed to have a direct connection to God, in the manner in which Moses and Muhammad ruled the early Israelites and Muslims. In an ecclesiocracy, on the other hand, the leaders do not claim to be a direct religious link, but instead uphold a prereceived revelation. Other theocracies may hold a secular government to delegate civil law to religious communities. Vatican City (an absolute theocratic monarchy), Saudia Arabia, and Iran are a few notable theocracies.

8 EXILARCHY—RULED BY ETHNIC OR RELIGIOUS DIASPORA

The exilarchy rules a religious or ethnic group, rather than the place the group originates from. The leader only has power through cultural and honorary means, and only rules the groups' followers who are ultimately governed by their host countries. Two examples of an exilarchy are the Reish Galuta, and Dalai Lama's rule over the Tibetan diaspora.

7 MINARCHISM—MINIMAL STATISM

Not far off from anarchism, minarchists believe government should be limited to protecting the basic right of life, liberty, and property. They endorse a Night Watchman State, which is limited to court, police, and military. Minarchists favor small, local, or city-level jurisdictions, rather than a large national government, leaving anyone who doesn't want to work or live under a certain municipality free to be able to move to another jurisdiction easily. Although closely related to market anarchists, minarchism understands that government is inevitable, so instead of fighting it minarchism seeks to limit it.

6 ETHNOCRACY—RULED BY RACE

Ethnocracies are used to make one race, religious group, or language politically dominant, with all other issues being subordinate to their cause. The degree of discrimination will vary from system to system. In Uganda there is an ethnic cleansing of the Indian people, along with an extreme political favoring of the indigenous people. However, ethnocracy can be a full-fledged democracy, with only a lack of representation for a certain group. A few other places experiencing ethnocracy are Pakistan, Israel, and South Africa.

5 KLEPTOCRACY—RULED BY THIEVES

Similar to a plutocracy, the kleptocracy is ruled by a few people of wealth. In this system, however, the rich get richer by embezzling from its citizens. A kleptocracy degrades the people's quality of life, taking money that is often supposed to go to schools, hospitals, roads, and other public services. In 2004, Transparency International released a list of what is believed to be the ten most self-enriched leaders, Indonesian and Philippine presidents ranked as the top two. The U.S. Senate recently coined the term "narcokleptocracy," building off the existing term for kleptocracy to address societies involved in narcotic trades.

4 PLUTOCRACY—RULED BY WEALTHY

Economic inequality at its finest, the plutocracy gives power to the most wealthy. A few of the places known for their plutocracies are ancient Greece, Carthage, Italian merchant republics of Venice and Florence, and Genoa. In recent times there is no true plutocracy, although many countries are criticized for showing similar signs. Corporations raise and donate significant amounts of revenue for politicians and political parties, and use their financial power to influence favorable legislation, similar to a corporatocracy. The plutocracy is classically an oligarchy, so a handful of the wealthiest people control everything. If there is no proper form of control, the plutocracy collapses into a kleptocracy.

3 LOGOCRACY—RULED BY WORDS

A more ironic or parody government, a logocracy is a government ruling through words. Described in Washington Irving's 1807 work, *Salmagundi*, a logocracy is a government that uses tricky wording to control its people. The Soviet Union has been accused of being a logocracy, citing that its language was a "stereotyped jargon consisting of formulas and empty slogans, whose purpose was to prevent people from thinking outside the boundaries of collective thought." George Orwell's *1984* is a good example of a logocracy, and used the Soviet Union's "Neo-language" as the basis for its Newspeak.

2 TECHNOCRACY—GOVERNED BY TECHNICAL DECISION MAKING

Technocracy is a government run by scientists and engineers, placing the most knowledgeable professionals in charge of their specialized area to ensure administrative functions are carried out efficiently. For example, a group of medical professionals would control the health care system; political scientists would control political policy; judges would control the law; with all the groups working together to maximize each one's performance. The officials would be selected through bureaucratic processes to test knowledge and performance, selecting the most qualified. Though never used in a state-wide setting, there is a technocracy movement pushing to make North America one large technocratic-based land mass. The area would use a system of "energy accounting" instead of money and use a non-market economy, hypothetically becoming the most energy and production efficient place in the world.

1 DEMARCHY—RULED BY PEOPLE

A government run by randomly selected citizens is called a "citizen's jury." The system is similar to a democracy without the need for elections. Proposed by Australian philosopher John Burnheim, this style of government has never actually been used. Hypothetically, the random selection will remove the chance of political corruption, as it is unlikely the elected people involved would be part of a "political machine." A demarchy also avoids the issue of having to please anyone for political gain, and is dependent only on the selected person's opinions on what is best for the population.

✻✻✻✻✻✻

TOP 10 MYTHS ABOUT THE VIKINGS

10 ONE NATION

Misconception: The Vikings were a nation.
The Vikings were not one nation but different groups of warriors, explorers, and merchants led by a chieftain. During the Viking Age, Scandinavia was not separated into Denmark, Norway, and Sweden as it is today; instead, each chieftain ruled over a small area. The word "viking" does not refer to any location, but is the Old Norse word for a person participating in an expedition to sea.

9 WILD, DIRTY PEOPLE

Misconception: The Vikings were all dirty, wild-looking people.
In many movies and cartoons, the Vikings are shown as dirty, wild-looking, savage men and women, but in reality, the Vikings were quite vain about their appearance. In fact, combs, tweezers, razors, and "ear spoons" are among some of the most frequent artifacts from Viking Age excavations. These same excavations have also shown that the Vikings made soap.

In England, the Vikings living there even had a reputation for excessive cleanliness because of their custom of bathing once a week (on Saturday). To this day, Saturday is referred to as *laugardagur / laurdag / lørdag / lördag*, or "washing day," in the Scandinavian languages, though the original meaning is lost in modern speech in most cases. However, *laug* does still mean "bath" or "pool" in Icelandic.

8 BIG AND BLOND
Misconception: The Vikings were all big and blond.

The Vikings are often shown as big, bulging guys with long blond hair, but historical records show that the average Viking man was about five-feet seven-inches tall, which was not especially tall for the time. Blond hair was seen as ideal in the Viking culture, and many Nordic men bleached their hair with a special soap. But the Vikings were great at absorbing people, and many people who had been kidnapped as slaves, became part of the Viking population in time. So, in Viking groups, you would probably find Italians, Spaniards, Portuguese, French, and Russians—a very diverse group built around a core of Vikings from a particular region, say, southern Denmark or an Oslo fjord.

7 SKULL CUPS
Misconception: The Vikings drank from skull cups.

The origin of this legend is Ole Worm's "Reuner seu Danica literatura antiquissima" from 1636 in which he writes that Danish warriors drank from the "curved branches of skulls," i.e. horns, which was probably mistranslated in Latin to mean human "skulls." The fact is, however, no skull cups have ever been found in excavations from the Viking Age.

6 CRUDE WEAPONS
Misconception: The Vikings used crude, unsophisticated weapons.

Vikings are often shown with crude, unsophisticated weapons such as clubs and crude axes, but the Vikings were actually skilled weapon smiths. Using a method called pattern welding, the Vikings could make swords that were both extremely sharp and flexible. According to Viking Sagas, one method of testing these weapons was to place the sword hilt first in a cold stream, and float a hair down to it. If it cut the hair, it was considered a good sword.

5 HOMETOWN
Misconception: The Vikings lived only in Scandinavia.

The Vikings did originate from the Scandinavian countries, but over time they started settlements in many places, reaching as far as North Africa, Russia, Constantinople, and even North America. There are different theories about the motives driving the Viking expansion, the most common of which is that the Scandinavian population had outgrown the agricultural potential of their homeland. Another theory is that the old trade routes of Western Europe and Eurasia experienced a decline in profitability when the Roman Empire fell in the fifth century, forcing the Vikings to open new trading routes in order to profit from international trade.

4 HATED BY THEIR PEERS
Misconception: The Vikings were hated everywhere.

One could imagine that the Vikings were hated everywhere because of their raids, but it seems that they were also respected by some. The French King Charles the III, known as Charles the Simple, gave the Vikings the land they had already settled on in France (Normandy), and he even gave his daughter to the Viking chief Rollo. In return, the Vikings protected France against wilder Vikings.

Also in Constantinople, the Vikings were acknowledged for their strength, so much so that the Varangian guard of the Byzantine emperors in the eleventh century was made up entirely of Swedish Vikings.

3 BLOODTHIRSTY
Misconception: The Vikings were unusually bloodthirsty and barbarian.

The Viking raids were indeed very violent, but it was a violent age, and the question is whether non-Viking armies were any less bloodthirsty and barbarian; for instance, Charlemagne, who was the Vikings' contemporary, virtually exterminated the whole people of Avars. At Verden, he ordered the beheading of forty-five hundred Saxons. What really made the Vikings different was the fact that they seemed to take special care to destroy items of religious value (Christian monasteries and holy sites) and kill churchmen, which earned them quite a bit of hatred in a highly religious time. The Vikings probably enjoyed the reputation they had; people were so scared of them that they often fled from their cities instead of defending them when they saw a Viking ship coming near.

2 RAPE AND PILLAGE

Misconception: The Vikings pillaged as their only way of living.

It was actually only a very small percentage of the Vikings that were warriors; the majority were farmers, craftsmen, and traders. For the Vikings who took to the sea, pillaging was one among many other goals of their expeditions. The Vikings settled peacefully in many places such as Iceland and Greenland, and were international merchants of their time; they peacefully traded with almost every country of the then-known world.

1 HELMET STYLE

Misconception: The Vikings wore helmets with horns.

This must be the biggest misconception about Vikings, but the fact remains, there are no records of such helmets having ever existed. All depictions of Viking helmets, dating to the Viking Age, show them with no horns and the only authentic Viking helmet that has ever been found does not have them either. An explanation for the helmet with horns myth is that Christians in contemporary Europe added the detail to make the Vikings look even more barbarian and pagan, with horns like Satan's on their heads. It should be noted that the Norse god Thor wore a helmet with wings on it, which do look somewhat similar to horns.

※※※※※※

CHAPTER FIVE

Literature

TOP 10 BOOKS THAT CHANGED THE WORLD

10 *ATLAS SHRUGGED* BY AYN RAND, 1957

Atlas Shrugged was Rand's last work before she devoted her time exclusively to philosophical writing. This book contains a variety of themes that would later become the core of her philosophy, Objectivism. She considered it to be her magnum opus and is it the most popular of her nonfiction work.

While the book was largely a critical failure, it had enormous popular success. As far as influence in the world, the Objectivist philosophy gave much to the Libertarian movement, which has enjoyed great popularity around the world.

In a three-month online poll of reader selections of the hundred best novels of the twentieth century, administered by publisher Modern Library, *Atlas Shrugged* was voted number one. She has a large following in the celebrity world, including Brad Pitt and Angelina Jolie who have been selected to play the two main characters in a trilogy of films that aims to bring *Atlas Shrugged* to the silver screen in the near future.

9 *THE SECOND SEX* BY SIMONE DE BEAUVOIR, 1949

The Second Sex is the best-known work of Simone de Beauvoir who wrote the book after attempting to write about herself. The first thing she wrote was that she was a woman, but she realized that she needed to define what a woman was, which became the intent of the book. It is a work on the treatment of women throughout history and often regarded as a major feminist work. In it she argues that women throughout history have been defined as the "other" sex, an aberration from the "normal" male sex.

Simone de Beauvoir (a pioneer of the feminist movement) argues that women have historically been considered deviant and abnormal. She submits that even Mary Wollstonecraft considered men to be the ideal toward which women should aspire. Beauvoir says that this attitude has limited women's success by maintaining the perception that they are a deviation from the normal, and are outsiders attempting to emulate "normality." For feminism to move forward, this assumption must be set aside.

8 ON THE ORIGIN OF SPECIES BY CHARLES DARWIN, 1859

This book by Darwin is considered a seminal work in the field of evolutionary biology. It proposes that over time, through natural selection, species evolve. It was a highly controversial book as it contradicted many religious views on biology at the time. Darwin's
book was the culmination of evidence he had accumulated on the voyage of the *Beagle* in the 1830s and expanded through continuing investigations and experiments since his return to England.

The book is readable even for the non-specialist and attracted widespread interest on publication. The book was controversial, and generated much discussion on scientific, philosophical, and religious grounds. The scientific theory of evolution has itself evolved since Darwin first presented it, but natural selection remains the most widely accepted scientific model of how species evolve. The at-times bitter creation-evolution controversy continues to this day.

7 EXPERIMENTAL RESEARCHES IN ELECTRICITY BY MICHAEL FARADAY, 1855

Faraday was an English chemist and physicist whose many experiments with electricity ultimately led to his invention of electromagnetic rotary devices, which formed the foundation of electric motor technology. Although he received little formal education and thus higher mathematics like calculus were always out of his reach, he went on to become one of the most influential scientists in history. It was largely his experiments that led to electricity becoming viable for use in technology.

During his lifetime, Faraday rejected a knighthood and twice refused to become President of the Royal Society. He died at his house at Hampton Court on August 25, 1867. He has a memorial plaque in Westminster Abbey, near Isaac Newton's tomb, but he turned down burial there and is interred in the Sandemanian plot in Highgate Cemetery.

6 THE COMMUNIST MANIFESTO BY KARL MARX AND FRIEDRICH ENGELS, 1848

This tract, written by Communist theorists Karl Marx and Friedrich Engels at the behest of the Communist League, has become one of the most influential political tracts in history. The manifesto suggested a course of action for a proletarian (working-class) revolution to overthrow the bourgeois social order and to eventually bring about a classless and stateless society.

Perhaps the most famous quote from the work reads: "The Communists disdain to conceal their views and aims. They openly declare that their ends can be attained only by the forcible overthrow of all existing social conditions. Let the ruling classes tremble at a communist revolution. The proletarians have nothing to lose but their chains. They have a world to win. Working men of all countries, unite!"

5 *EITHER/OR* BY SØREN KIERKEGAARD, 1843

Either/Or portays two lifeviews, one being consciously hedonistic and one based on ethical duty and responsibility, in two volumes. Each lifeview is written and represented by a fictional pseudonymous author and the prose of the work depends on which lifeview is being discussed. For example, the aesthetic lifeview is written in short essay form, with poetic imagery and allusions, discussing aesthetic topics such as music, seduction, drama, and beauty. The ethical lifeview is written as two long letters, with a more argumentative and restrained prose, discussing moral responsibility, critical reflection, and marriage.

This book, by the father of existentialism, has been highly influential with other existentialists. Despite its great popularity, it was not published in English until 1944. Existentialism is a philosophical movement that claims that individual human beings have full responsibility for creating the meanings of their own lives. It is a reaction against more traditional philosophies, such as rationalism and empiricism.

4 *THE RIGHTS OF MAN* BY THOMAS PAINE, 1791

Paine, an English writer, influenced American democracy, and democracy in general, with his writings. According to Paine, the sole purpose of the government is to protect the irrefutable rights inherent to every human being. Thus, all institutions which do not benefit a nation are illegitimate, including the monarchy (and the nobility) and the military establishment.

When the French Revolution broke out, Paine went to France where, despite his ignorance of the French language, he was promptly elected to the National Convention. His absence from England at this time was fortuitous because the publication of *The Rights of Man* caused such a furor in the country that Paine was put on trial in absentia and convicted for seditious libel against the crown.

3 THE *SUMMA THEOLOGICA* BY ST. THOMAS AQUINAS, 1265–1274

The Summa Theologica is a multi-volume set of books that outline, in the most precise manner, the doctrines and beliefs of Christianity. It was held in such high regard, that second to the Bible, it was the book most used for reference at the Council of Trent (1545–1563). Its influence was felt all across the Christian world as the reforms of the Council of Trent were implemented.

To this day, *The Summa Theologica* is the primary teaching tool used in Roman Catholic seminaries and its author is regarded as a Doctor of the Church (a title reserved for only thirty-three great thinkers in the history of Christianity). It is also worth noting that St. Isidore (popularly considered Patron Saint of the Internet) is also seen as a Doctor of the Church.

2 THE QUR'AN BY VARIOUS AUTHORS, 650–656AD

The Qur'an is the holy book of the Islamic religion. The founder of Islam, Mohammed, told his followers he had been given revelations by the Angel Gabriel. These revelations (spanning twenty-three years) form the basis of the Qur'an. After Mohammed's death in 632, the Qur'an was recorded by word of mouth only; it was not for another twenty years that the various memories of his words were collected and combined.

The Qur'an is considered by Muslims to be the last revealed word of God (after the Old Testament and the New Testament of the Christian Bible). In recent years much debate has occurred over the content of the Qur'an, with its opponents claiming that it advocates war and murder of non-believers. Muslims generally claim that this is not the case and state that opponents of Islam are taking the text out of context.

1 THE BIBLE BY VARIOUS AUTHORS, CIRCA 30–90AD

There can be no doubt that the Bible has done more to change the face of the world than any other book. A mere two hundred years after it was created, it brought about the conversion of the entire Roman Empire from paganism to Christianity. Since then, Christianity has become the largest single religion in the world (with 2.1 billion adherents). The oldest and largest of the Christian groups is the Roman Catholic Church whose membership (1.05 billion) is equal to the size of all other Christian groups combined.

The Bible comprises two books: the Old Testament (taken from the Greek edition used by Christ and the apostles), and the New Testament (written by some of the apostles of Jesus after his death, including St. Paul who did not meet Christ during His lifetime).

The Gutenberg Bible (a copy of the Latin Vulgate) was the first book ever published on the printing press. The Bible is the most purchased book in the world.

❊❊❊❊❊❊

TOP 10 GRUESOME FAIRY TALE ORIGINS

10 THE PIED PIPER

In the tale of the Pied Piper, we have a village overrun with rats. A man arrives dressed in clothes of pied (a patchwork of colors) and offers to rid the town of the vermin. The villagers agree to pay a vast sum of money if the piper can do it, and he does. He plays music on his pipe, which draws all the rats out of the town. When he returns for payment, the villagers won't cough up so the Pied Piper decides to rid the town of children, too! In most modern variants, the piper draws the children to a cave out of the town and when the townsfolk finally agree to pay up, he sends them back. In the darker original, the piper leads the children to a river where they all drown (except a lame boy who couldn't keep up). Some modern scholars say that there are connotations of pedophilia in this fairy tale.

9 LITTLE RED RIDING HOOD

The version of this tale that most of us are familiar with ends with Riding Hood being saved by the woodsman who kills the wicked wolf. But, in fact, the original French version (by Charles Perrault) of the tale was not quite so nice. In this version, the little girl is a well-bred young lady who is given false instructions by the wolf when she asks the way to her grandmothers. Foolishly, Riding Hood takes the advice of the wolf and ends up being eaten. And here the story ends. There is no woodsman, no grandmother, just a fat wolf and a dead Red Riding Hood. The moral to this story is to not take advice from strangers.

8 THE LITTLE MERMAID

The 1989 version of the *Little Mermaid* might be better known as "The Big Whopper!" In the Disney version, the film ends with Ariel, the mermaid, being changed into a human so she can marry Eric. They marry in a wonderful wedding attended by humans and merpeople. But, in the very first version by Hans Christian Andersen, the mermaid sees the prince marry a princess and she despairs. She is offered a knife with which to stab the prince to death, but rather than do that, she jumps into the sea and dies by turning to froth. Hans Christian Andersen modified the ending slightly to make it more pleasant. In his new ending, instead of dying when turned to froth, she becomes a "daughter of the air" waiting to go to heaven so, frankly, she is still dead for all intents and purposes.

7 SNOW WHITE

In the tale of Snow White that we are all familiar with, the queen asks a huntsman to kill her and bring her heart back as proof. Instead, the huntsman can't bring himself to do it and returns with the heart of a boar. Now, fortunately, Disney hasn't done too much damage to this tale, but they did leave out one important original element: in the original tale, the queen actually asks for Snow White's liver and lungs, which are to be served for dinner that night! Also in the original, Snow White wakes up when she is jostled by the prince's horse, as he carries her back to his castle, not from a magical kiss. What the prince wanted to do with a dead girl's body I will leave to your imagination. Oh, in the Grimm version, the tale ends with the queen being forced to dance to death in red-hot iron shoes!

6 SLEEPING BEAUTY

In the original Sleeping Beauty, the lovely princess is put to sleep when she pricks her finger on a spindle. She sleeps for one hundred years when a prince finally arrives, kisses her, and awakens her. They fall in love, marry, and (surprise, surprise) live happily ever after. But alas, the original tale is not so sweet (in fact, you have to read this to believe it). In the original, the young woman is put to sleep because of a prophesy rather than a curse. And it isn't the kiss of a prince that wakes her up: the king seeing her asleep, and rather fancying having a bit, rapes her. After nine months she gives birth to two children (while she is still asleep). One of the children sucks her finger, which removes the piece of flax that was keeping her asleep. She wakes up to find herself raped and the mother of two kids.

5 RUMPELSTILTSKIN

This fairy tale is a little different from the others because rather than sanitizing the original, it was modified by the original author to make it more gruesome. In the original tale, Rumpelstiltskin spins straw into gold for a young girl who faces death unless she is able to perform the feat. In return, he asks for her first-born child. She agrees, but when the day comes to hand over the kid, she can't do it. Rumpelstiltskin tells her that he will let her off the hook if she can guess his name. She overheard him singing his name by a fire and so she guesses it correctly. Rumpelstiltskin, furious, runs away, never to be seen again. But in the updated version, things are a little messier. Rumpelstiltskin is so angry that he drives his right foot deep into the ground. He then grabs his left leg and rips himself in half. Needless to say, this kills him.

4 GOLDILOCKS AND THE THREE BEARS

In this heartwarming tale, we hear of pretty little Goldilocks who finds the house of the three bears. She sneaks inside and eats their food, sits in their chairs, and finally falls asleep on the bed of the littlest bear. When the bears return home they find her asleep—she awakens and escapes out the window in terror. The original tale (which actually only dates to 1837) has two possible variations. In the first, the bears find Goldilocks and rip her apart and eat her. In the second, Goldilocks is actually an old hag who (like the sanitized version) jumps out of a window when the bears wake her up. The story ends by telling us that she either broke her neck in the fall, or was arrested for vagrancy and sent to the "House of Correction."

3 HANSEL AND GRETEL

In the widely known version of Hansel and Gretel, we hear of two little children who become lost in the forest, eventually finding their way to a gingerbread house that belongs to a wicked witch. The children end up enslaved for a time as the witch prepares them for eating. They figure their way out and throw the witch in a fire and escape. In an earlier French version of this tale (called "The Lost Children"), instead of a witch, we have a devil. Now the wicked old devil is tricked by the children, in much the same way as Hansel and Gretel, but he works it out and puts together a sawhorse to put one of the children on to bleed. The children pretend not to know how to get on the sawhorse so the devil's wife demonstrates. While she is lying down the kids slash her throat and escape.

2 THE GIRL WITHOUT HANDS

Frankly, the revised version of this fairy tale is not a great deal better than the original, but there are sufficient differences to include it here. In the new version, a poor man is offered wealth by the devil if he gives him whatever is standing behind his mill. The poor man thinks it is an apple tree and agrees, but it is actually his daughter. The devil tries to take the daughter but can't because she is pure; he threatens to take the father unless the daughter allows her father to chop off her hands. She agrees and the father does the deed. Now that is not particularly nice, but it is slightly worse in some of the earlier variants in which the young girl chops off her own arms in order to make herself ugly to her brother who is trying to rape her. In another variant, the father chops off the daughter's hands because she refuses to let him have sex with her.

1 CINDERELLA

In the modern Cinderella fairy tale, we have the beautiful Cinderella swept off her feet by the prince, and her wicked stepsisters marrying two lords, with everyone living happily ever after. The fairy tale has its origins way back in the first century BC where Strabo's heroine was actually called Rhodopis, not Cinderella. The story was very similar to the modern one with the exception of the glass slippers and pumpkin coach. But, lurking behind the pretty tale is a more sinister variation by the Grimm brothers: in this version, the nasty stepsisters cut off parts of their own feet in order to fit them into the glass slipper, hoping to fool the prince. The prince is alerted to the trickery by two pigeons who peck out the stepsisters' eyes. The stepsisters end up spending the rest of their lives as blind beggars while Cinderella gets to lounge about in luxury at the prince's castle.

✳✳✳✳✳✳

TOP 10 LOST WORKS OF LITERATURE

10 **VARIOUS WORKS BY ARISTOTLE**
Aristotle is probably the most well known—and certainly the most important—name in Western philopshy. While he has left us an immense body of work, fully two-thirds of what he is believed to have written is now lost to us. His views helped to shape medieval thought and, consequently, modern ethics.

9 *CANTERBURY TALES* **BY GEOFFREY CHAUCER**
The *Canterbury Tales* contain a series of tales told by pilgrims on their way to Canterbury Cathedral to visit the shrine of St. Thomas Becket. It is one of the most significant works of Middle English writing (though many of the tales were prefigured in earlier works by other writers). Ultimately, Chaucer planned to write 124 tales, but only 22 were completed or remain intact today.

8 *LOVE'S LABOUR'S WON* **BY WILLIAM SHAKESPEARE**
There is some doubt that *Love's Labour Won* is a lost work; it is perhaps another title for *The Taming of the Shrew*. But because it appears along with *Taming* in a list of published plays from Shakespeare's time, many consider it to be separate. In this case, it is a lost work.

7 *SANDITON* **BY JANE AUSTEN**
Just a small fragment of this last novel of Jane Austen remains today—and it shows that it was likely to be a great hit, bearing the usual signature of Austen: a brilliant wit. It was originally called *The Brothers* after the Parker brothers who appear in the story, but her family renamed it after her death.

6 *THE MAGIC HARP* **BY WOLFGANG VON GOETHE**
The Magic Harp was to be the glorious and more triumphal sequel to *The Magic Flute*—the Goethe work set to music by Mozart. The spectacular effects of the first book were to be upstaged by even more extravagant scenes. Some believe that it would have been as great as *Faust*, but, alas, Goethe abandoned it without completing it.

5 MEMOIRS BY LORD BYRON

A tale as tragic as this, is not often seen. Upon his death, Lord Byron's publisher and friends destroyed his memoirs—thinking them scandalous and damaging to his reputation. The influence of Byron in poetry is significant, and the loss of his memoirs (an insight into his writing) is a tragedy of epic proportions.

4 *THE MYSTERY OF EDWIN DROOD* BY CHARLES DICKENS

The Mystery of Edwin Drood was to be a typical Dickens masterpiece, filled with mystery and colorful characters. Dickens gave Queen Victoria a preview of the work as it progressed and even offered to tell her what the ending was to be. She declined (not wanting to spoil the surprise) and Dicken's died shortly after, leaving the work unfinished. The ending will now never be known.

3 *THE MYSTERIOUS STRANGER* BY MARK TWAIN

After three attempts at writing this book, Twain gave up on it and it remains incomplete. It tells the strange tale of a young Satan (the nephew of the biblical Satan) who lives a sinless live in an Austrian village. The book was also sometimes referred to as *The Chronicle of Young Satan*.

2 WORKS BEFORE 1922 BY ERNEST HEMINGWAY

In 1922, Ernest Hemingway's wife, Hadley, was traveling in Europe and carrying a trunk filled with everything that her husband had written up to that time, including a novel about his experiences in the First World War. Unfortunately, the luggage was stolen and never returned. The possibility always exists that it will one day emerge from the shadows, but until that unlikely time, all of his early work is lost.

1 *DOUBLE EXPOSURE* BY SYLVIA PLATH

In 1963, Sylvia Plath (perhaps the greatest female writer of the twentieth century) committed suicide. She left behind her a journal full of her thoughts and musings prior to her death, as well as a nearly completed novel, *Double Exposure*. Her estranged husband, Ted Hughes, inherited the lot and destroyed much of it. Many people believe that this was because she wrote negatively about him and he did not wish to have the public humiliation. In a strange twist, his mistress committed suicide in the same manner as Plath, some years later.

TOP 10 SHAKESPEARE MISQUOTES

10 FROM: *HAMLET*

Misquote: "To the manor born."

Actual Quote: "but to my mind,—though I am native here and to the manner born,—it is a custom more honour'd in the breach than the observance." (Referring to drunken carousing.)

This misquote, while sounding the same, has a very different meaning. *Hamlet* is actually a reference to being excellent, so good that you appear to have been born with the skill.

9 FROM: *FALSTAFF*

Misquote: "Discretion is the better part of valor."

Actual Quote: "The better part of valor is discretion."

8 FROM: *RICHARD III*

Misquote: "Now is the winter of our discontent."

Actual Quote: "Now is the winter of our discontent / Made glorious summer by this sun of York."

This is less a misquote than a misappropriation; when the second line is excluded from the quote, it means "the winter of our discontent is happening now," but when we add the second line, the true meaning of the quote is "the winter of our discontent has now become a glorious summer"—the opposite of what most people use the quote for.

7 FROM: *ROMEO AND JULIET*

Misquote: "A rose by any other name smells just as sweet."

Actual Quote: "What's in a name? That which we call a rose by any other word would smell as sweet."

6 **FROM:** *HAMLET*
Misquote: "The rest is science."
Actual Quote: "The rest is silence."

5 **FROM:** *HAMLET*
Misquote: "Alas, poor Yorick. I knew him well."
Actual Quote: "Alas, poor Yorick. I knew him, Horatio, a fellow of infinite jest, of most excellent fancy."

4 **FROM:** *HAMLET*
Misquote: "Methinks the lady doth protest too much."
Actual Quote: "The lady doth protest too much, methinks."

This is another of the "same meaning" quotes. This is probably one of the most commonly heard misquotes of Shakespeare.

3 **FROM:** *MACBETH*
Misquote: "Bubble bubble, toil and trouble."
Actual Quote: "Double, double toil and trouble."

It should be noted that a film by Disney used the incorrect quote in this sense: "Bubble, bubble toil and trouble, leave this island on the double." It is possible that this is partly the reason for the misconception today. In fact, the witches are asking for "double" the trouble and toil.

2 **FROM:** *MACBETH*
Misquote: "Lead on, Macduff."
Actual Quote: "Lay on, Macduff, and damned be him who first cries 'Hold! enough!'"

This misquote suggests that Macbeth wants Macduff to begin moving in to fight. The actual quote is more emphatic and shows us that Macbeth wants Macduff to begin fighting immediately.

1 **FROM** *THE LIFE AND DEATH OF KING JOHN*
Misquote: "Gild the lily."
Actual Quote: "To gild refined gold, to paint the lily."

This is one of those odd misquotes in which the meaning remains essentially the same, though clearly Shakespeare's actual quote is stronger due to the doubling up of the point.

TOP 10 MOST DISTURBING NOVELS

10 MISERY BY STEPHEN KING

Anyone who has read this book will appreciate its inclusion here; if for no other reason than the axe scene (in which the protagonist chops off one of the main character's feet with an axe—this is the "hobbling" scene in the movie). That scene aside, the pages upon pages of descriptions of the pain suffered by the bedridden main character, coupled with the psychological torment as he tries to move through the house unnoticed, make this a much-deserved entry.

9 PERFUME BY PATRICK SUSKIND

This gruesome book is set in the eighteenth century in France. In it, a young man, Jean-Baptiste Grenouille, who is born without a scent of his own, murders young women in order to try to distill their scent—making the perfect perfume. The style of the book makes this something of a macabre fairy tale.

8 JUSTINE BY MARQUIS DE SADE

Justine, "the most abominable book ever engendered by the most depraved imagination," according to Napoleon, is so disturbing (even today) that it was banned and a warrant was put out for the arrest of the Marquis de Sade. Every page is filled with some kind of sexual abuse or depravity. It is, of course, the very book from which the term "sadism" has come.

7 AMERICAN PSYCHO BY BRETT EASTON ELLIS

This is one of the only books that I have not finished reading. I was so horrified by a scene early in the book (involving a dog, a bum, and a very sharp knife) that I could not go on. It was my first introduction to truly disturbing writing. Within the pages we read of the most violent acts (described in incredible detail, as is the habit of the author), which will make even the most hardened person cringe. This book will change you.

6 *THE PAINTED BIRD* BY JERZY KOSIŃSKI

The Painted Bird is about a young boy who is sent by his parents to the countryside to escape the tyranny of the Nazis. Unfortunately, his experiences in the country are perhaps far worse than anything he would have suffered at home. His sufferings verge on the hellish.

5 *GEEK LOVE* BY KATHERINE DUNN

Geek Love is about a couple who, in order to improve their freak show's popularity, begin a program of breeding their own freaks using drugs and radiation. The resulting children go on to live extraordinary and incredibly disturbing lives. One child creates a cult in which its members progress by having chunks of their bodies amputated. This is a bizarre and sickening book that will enthrall lovers of the unusual.

4 *WE NEED TO TALK ABOUT KEVIN* BY LIONEL SHRIVER

We Need to Talk About Kevin is about Kevin, a fifteen-year-old mass murderer. It is written from the perspective of the mother who, like her son, is emotionally disturbed. Perhaps most disturbing is the fact that the mother could be any one of the many parents of children who have taken guns to school and slaughtered their peers.

3 *THE WASP FACTORY* BY IAIN BANKS

The Wasp Factory describes in vivid detail the disturbing and violent practices of the narrator, Frank, a seventeen-year-old murderer. In a bizarre twist, Frank considers himself the most sane person alive, despite his need to perform bizarre rituals (which need to be read to be believed).

2 *GLAMORAMA* BY BRETT EASTON ELLIS

I normally restrict lists to one book per author, but I have to break that rule in this case because of the gut-churning violence depicted throughout the entire second half of the novel. There is a poisoning scene, which you will never forget, a scene involving dismemberment (and described in every detail as is always the case with this author), and a plane crash. The book does have many elements of humor (for example, the main character, a male model, thinks that global warming is a type of shampoo), and it is perhaps this humor that makes the book a little easier to stomach, but the fact remains, it is full of vividly described gore and carnage.

1 HAUNTED BY CHUCK PALAHNIUK

Unlike the other items on the list, this is a book of short stories. By the author of *Fight Club*, it pushes the boundaries of good taste and, as is evidenced by one reviewer: "I thought that if I made it through story #1 (eating your way through your own prolapsed rectum) that I could get through anything, but I was wrong."

✳✳✳✳✳✳

TOP 10 MOST CONTROVERSIAL NONFICTION BOOKS

10 THE HOAX OF THE TWENTIETH CENTURY BY ARTHUR R. BUTZ

The Hoax of the Twentieth Century: The Case Against the Presumed Extermination of European Jewry is considered to be the book that started the holocaust denial movement. It claims that the Germans did not try to exterminate the Jews during the Second World War. Many attempts have been made to have the book banned from libraries and other attempts have been made to make it illegal to import into Canada. The book was first published in 1975 and it has enjoyed many republications since that date. Dr. Butz is an associate professor of electrical engineering at Northwestern University and he recently caused controversy by publicly approving Iranian President Mahmoud Ahmadinejad's statements denying the holocaust.

9 THE POPULATION BOMB BY PAUL R. EHRLICH

This 1968 book predicted disaster for man due to population explosion. The book has been included as number 11 in Human Events most harmful books of the nineteenth and twentieth centuries, as well as making the Intercollegiate Studies Institute's "50 Worst Books of the Twentieth Century." The most shocking prediction made in the book was that the world would suffer the death of millions through starvation in the 1970s and 1980s. The author claimed that "radical action" was needed to prevent this from taking place. The radical action? Ehrlich recommended starving entire nations if they refused to implement policies to reduce or suspend population growth.

8 THE HOLY BLOOD AND THE HOLY GRAIL BY MICHAEL BAIGENT, RICHARD LEIGH, AND HENRY LINCOLN

In *The Holy Blood and the Holy Grail*, the authors claim that Jesus had offspring with Mary Magdalene, and that a secret society (the Priory of Sion) was formed that ultimately created the Knights Templar and tried to protect the offspring of Jesus. They also included (as fact) sections of the Protocol of the Elders of Zion (an anti-Semitic tract written in Russia). Unfortunately for them, it turned out that the entire book was based on a hoax by a Frenchman in 1961. This book was widely believed to be factual (by the authors and readers) until the hoax was uncovered. Dan Brown copied the basic ideas from this book for his novel *The Da Vinci Code, which* he still claims is based on fact. Historians and professionals in the field consider *The Holy Blood and the Holy Grail* to be an example of "counterknowledge" (misinformation packaged to look like fact).

7 ICONS OF EVOLUTION: SCIENCE OR MYTH? BY JONATHAN WELLS

Icons of Evolution is often cited by creationists as proof against evolution, and that was the intent of the author (a prominent promoter of intelligent design). Wells attempts to overthrow the idea of evolution by critiquing the manner in which it is taught. The author contends that the ten case studies used to illustrate and teach evolution are flawed.

6 THE SKEPTICAL ENVIRONMENTALIST BY BJØRN LOMBORG

Lomborg, in this highly controversial book, states that various environmental issues (such as global warming, overpopulation, species loss, and water shortages) are not supported by analysis of the appropriate data. Lomborg claims that the excess attention being given to these "insignificant" events is used politically to distract people from real and more important issues facing the world today. When word got out that this book was to be published by Cambridge University Press, efforts were launched by supporters of the theories he disputes to prevent it from being published, or, subsequently banned if it was.

5 ***HITLER'S WILLING EXECUTIONERS* BY DANIEL GOLDHAGEN**
This book posits that ordinary Germans knew about, and supported, Hitler's plans for genocide. One critic says of the book, "[It is] totally wrong about everything. Totally wrong. Exceptionally wrong." Goldhagen claimed that a German "anti-Semitism" had grown up over the centuries—starting from a religious basis and eventually becoming secularized—to a point that the Germans eventually became "eliminationist."

4 ***SILENT SPRING* BY RACHEL CARSON**
This book is credited with helping launch the environmental movement. Unfortunately, it is also credited with the widespread ban of DDT (which was commonly used as a defense against malaria-carrying mosquitos) which some believe is the reason that malaria has become rampant, leading to the deaths of millions. One critic is quoted as saying, "If man were to follow the teachings of Miss Carson, we would return to the Dark Ages, and the insects and diseases and vermin would once again inherit the earth."

3 ***THE BELL CURVE*
BY RICHARD J. HERRNSTEIN AND CHARLES MURRAY**
In this book, the authors contend that intelligence is a better predictor of crime, income, unwed pregnancy, and job performance than parents' socio-economic background. It also made some claims regarding racial difference in intelligence. Consequently, critics said that the book promotes "scientific racism." Many people rallied in support of the book, while many others rallied against it. The authors also recommended policy for the U.S. government completely ending all welfare assistance to poor unwed mothers as they believed it "encourages" low IQ women rather than high IQ women to have children.

2 ***HITLER'S POPE* BY JOHN CORNWELL**
Hitler's Pope is a book written by John Cornwell (an English journalist and an ex-Catholic Seminarian) which claims that Pope Pius XII contributed to the demise of the Jews in the Second World War by bowing down to Hitler. The book caused a huge controversy due to the fact that many Jews had spoken out in defense of Pius XII (during and after the war) and there was little evidence to corroborate the views in the book. Cornwell has since stated that he no longer believes the negative conclusions he came to in his book. Interestingly, Cornwell

has also publicly criticized Richard Dawkins and his book *The God Delusion*, calling it "extremist and dogmatic."

1 THE HOLY BIBLE BY JEWISH AND CHRISTIAN RELIGIOUS FIGURES

It would be wrong not to include the Holy Bible on this list. It is probably the most debated book in existence and has been for a very long time. From controversy over what books to include (and what books to remove in the case of Martin Luther in the sixteenth century), to controversy over what it actually means, the Bible has been a source of constant difficulty for many people. Despite this, it is still one of the most popular sources of moral direction in the world today and it cannot be denied that this book gave more to the growth of the West than any other.

✳✳✳✳✳✳

TOP 10 BOOKS THAT SCREWED UP THE WORLD

10 MALLEUS MALEFICARUM BY HEINRICH KRAMER AND JACOB SPRENGER, 1486

On the list because: It inflamed witch hunts across Europe.

Malleus Maleficarum (The Hammer of Witchcraft) was a manual for witch hunters and judges to catch witches and stamp them out. It came out just prior to the Protestant reformation and it was one of the most popular books among the reformers wanting to smash "evil" out of their countries. Between 1487 and 1520, twenty editions of the *Malleus* were published, and another sixteen editions were published between 1574 and 1669. This book single-handedly launched centuries of witch hunts.

9 COMING OF AGE IN SAMOA BY MARGARET MEAD, 1928

On the list because: It turned out to be a creation of her own sexual confusions and aspirations.

Margaret Mead was a cultural anthropologist who traveled to Samoa to answer the questions on sexuality posed in America in the 1920s (particularly with reference to women). Unfortunately for Mead, the youths she interviewed in Samoa told her wild tales of sexual promiscuity and Mead reported it all as fact. One of the girls later said, "She must have taken it seriously, but I was only joking. As you know, Samoan girls are terrific liars when it comes to joking. But Margaret accepted our trumped-up stories as though they were true." If challenged by Mead, the girls would not have hesitated to tell the truth, but Mead never questioned their stories. Interestingly, Mead was a highly regarded academic and had a large part in the formulation of the 1979 *American Book of Common Prayer* (Church of England).

8 *THE PRINCE* BY NICCOLÒ MACHIAVELLI, 1532
On the list because: It was the inspiration for a long list of tyrannies (Stalin had it on his nightstand).

The Prince is a treatise meant for rulers who had shed all scruples, to a point that they might see evil as potentially more beneficial to society than good. Machiavelli hoped to start a revolution in the hearts of his readers, and he certainly achieved that. He proudly stated things that others before him had only dared to whisper, and he whispered things that had not even been considered. According to Machiavelli, "it is not necessary for a prince to have all the above-mentioned qualities (merciful, faithful, humane, honest, and religious), but it is indeed necessary to appear to have them. Nay, I dare say this, that by having them and always observing them, they are harmful; and by appearing to have them they are useful." Some of the people inspired by this book are Stalin, Hitler, Mussolini, and Napoleon I of France.

7 *MEIN KAMPF* BY ADOLF HITLER, 1925
On the list because: It helped spread Hitler's genocidal anti-Semitism.

In *Mein Kampf*, Hitler outlined his racist plan for a new Germany, which included mass murder of Jews, and a war against France and Russia to make living space for Germans. At the time of publication the book was largely ignored, but once Hitler rose to power that changed. It is believed that over ten million copies were in circulation in 1945. Hitler's book is largely influenced by *The Crowd: A Study of the Popular Mind* by Gustave Le Bon (1895), which suggested propaganda as a means to controlling the irrational behavior of crowds. In addition, Hitler drew on the fabricated *The Protocols of the Elders of Zion* to give support for the need for his anti-Semitic plans. Hitler speaks of "The Jewish Peril" which he believed was a conspiracy by Jews to take over the world. The book outlines the racial worldview in which people are classified by race as superior or inferior. In 2003 the sequel to *Mein Kampf, Zweites Buch*, was published in English for the first time. *Zweites Buch* (Second Book) expands on the original ideas of *Mein Kampf* and outlines further plans for a war with the United States and the British Empire for entire world domination by Germany.

6 THE PIVOT OF CIVILIZATION BY MARGARET SANGER, 1922

On the list because: It preaches eugenics.

Margaret Sanger is the mother of modern contraception and the founder of Planned Parenthood. In her 1922 book, *The Pivot of Civilization*, she outlined her theories of eugenics (control of the human race by selective breeding) and racial purity (three years before Hitler did the same in *Mein Kampf*). The basis of her support of contraception was entirely due to her belief that inferior humans should be killed to enable a superior race to appear over time. Sanger did not just entertain popular ideas of her time, she was the champion of the cause. In her book she says that "the most urgent problem of today is how to limit and discourage the overfertility of the mentally and physically defective." She goes on to say that "possibly drastic and Spartan methods may be forced upon American society if it continues complacently to encourage the chance and chaotic breeding that has resulted from our stupid, cruel sentimentalism." Birth control was, in her mind, "the greatest and most truly eugenic method." Needless to say, Planned Parenthood today has tried very hard to distance themselves from their founder.

5 DEMOCRACY AND EDUCATION BY JOHN DEWEY, 1916

On the list because: It convinced the world that education is not about facts.

In *Democracy and Education*, Dewey disparages schooling that focuses on traditional character development and endowing children with hard knowledge, and encourages the teaching of thinking "skills" instead. His views have had great influence on the direction of American education, particularly in public schools. This book could be considered to be the anti-classical education manifesto. And its consequence? A generation of youth with an inferior education, lacking a foundation in solid facts and knowledge. Dewey was one of the three founders of the philosophical school of Pragmatism, a school of thought that proposes "truth" is made and can change.

4 *BABY AND CHILDCARE* BY BENJAMIN SPOCK, 1946
On the list because: It caused deaths through bad advice.

Regardless of whether you agree with the methodology of Spock, no one can deny that many children probably died of crib death as a result of his advice to put babies to sleep on their stomachs. This advice was extremely influential on healthcare providers, with nearly unanimous support through to the 1990s. Spock believed that babies on their backs can choke on their own vomit, leading to death. Scientists eventually found that Spock's advice actually led to more deaths by suffocation. Estimates of the number of deaths caused by this bad advice are as many as fifty thousand. Spock also advocated a method of child rearing that moved away from discipline-based methods. Previously, experts had told parents that babies needed to learn to sleep on a regular schedule, and that picking them up and holding them whenever they cried would only teach them to cry more and not to sleep through the night. Spock taught the exact opposite.

3 *THE PROTOCOLS OF THE ELDERS OF ZION* BY UNKNOWN
On the list because: It was a propaganda book designed to incite racial hatred.

The Protocols of the Elders of Zion is a booklet that purports to describe a plot by world Jewry and Masonry to take over the world. Despite the fact that the booklet is a hoax, it was spread wide and far and believed by most Europeans to be true. Many people today still consider it factual. It was instrumental to Hitler's anti-Jewish efforts in Germany and was used after the Russian Revolution to perpetrate hatred and violence against Jews. The booklet continues to be published and disseminated in many Middle Eastern states, which are political enemies of Israel.

2 *DARWIN'S BLACK BOX* BY MICHAEL BEHE, 1996
On the list because: It fuels fundamentalist attacks on science.

By arguing against aspects of Darwin's theories, this book has given fuel to the fundamentalists who argue that a literal interpretation of the Book of Genesis describes the only possible manner in which the earth could have been created. Despite much refutation from the scientific community, many fundamentalists still use this as a "source" for proof that evolution is not true. The book itself was not peer reviewed as Behe claimed under oath, and the science community has overwhelming rejected it. It should be noted that Behe himself is not a fundamentalist and does not believe in a literal interpretation of the Bible.

1 THE MANIFESTO OF THE COMMUNIST PARTY BY KARL MARX AND FRIEDRICH ENGELS, 1848

On the list because: It could win the award for the most malicious book ever written.

This book has inspired some of the most brutal regimes in man's history. Regardless of whether there has been a state which is a true Marxist state, this book has inspired so many evil actions that it cannot be left off a list of this nature. Some of the principles found in the manifesto are the abolition of private ownership of land, confiscation of property of emigrants, heavy taxes, and the abolition of inheritance.

❊❊❊❊❊❊

TOP 10 GREAT POSTAPOCALYPTIC SCIENCE FICTION NOVELS

10 LUCIFER'S HAMMER BY LARRY NIVEN AND JERRY POURNELLE

This best-selling 1997 novel details the approach and aftermath of a comet striking Earth with disastrous results. A large number of disparate characters are well drawn and the book essentially focuses on the changes in their lives. In fact, much of the novel takes place before the comet actually strikes. But when the "hammer" falls, civilization as we know it crumbles and the very survival of the characters is certainly in doubt. New social mores are developed through necessity, as humans are put in the catch-22 of having to band together while being able to trust no one. The book is noteworthy for making us actually care about the characters we come to know, even though there are dozens of them.

9 ON THE BEACH BY NEVIL SHUTE

Probably the earliest (1957) postapocalyptic science fiction novel to truly achieve mass distribution. The mechanism of destruction is atomic war. Though widely taught in high schools around the world during the 1960s and '70s, when concerns about the Cold War were as rampant as they were in the '50s, the book is not a treatise on the triumph of the human spirit. In fact, stoic acceptance and even government-sponsored euthanasia figure prominently. But the characters, for the most part, do not wallow in self-pity… they just go about their business. The main story is that of a United States submarine being placed under the command of Australian authorities (the northern latitudes become uninhabitable first). Although it certainly made an impression on millions of young adult readers back in the day and is widely considered a classic, I view it as the weakest science fiction novel on the list.

8 EARTH ABIDES BY GEORGE R. STEWART

Published in 1949, before *On the Beach*, *Earth Abides* posits a global epidemic that makes the Black Death look like last year's winter cold. One gets the feeling that 99.9 percent of the entire human race is wiped out. The novel did win some awards, and has never been truly unavailable, but it never got the "buzz" of *On the Beach*. And, although it can be powerful on first reading, it really doesn't hold up. You see, our protagonist is essentially alone for a god-awful number of pages. He was up in the mountains and got bit by a rattlesnake, almost dying, so he "missed" the huge turmoil that mass death imposed on society. A lot of that part is very interesting, in detailing why and where power either stays on or fails, what happens to critters and plants, that sort of stuff. But it does tend to drag, and when the protagonist finally hooks up with a woman, that part starts to drag as well. It all builds toward what sort of society the progeny of the few survivors will create.

7 A CANTICLE FOR LEIBOWITZ BY WALTER M. MILLER, JR.

This novel won the 1961 Hugo Award and is widely considered an outright classic, even outside the science fiction genre. That said, for anyone who is not Catholic or interested in that religion, it can be an extremely difficult read.

Centuries after your standard nuclear holocaust, we have a monastery in the U.S. dedicated to preserving scientific knowledge until the time comes to rebuild a technology-based civilization. It was founded by one Leibowitz, who had converted from Judaism (this is an extremely religious-themed novel). Anyway, the book's nominal main character comes across a cache of writings and stuff that appears to have belonged to Leibowitz himself. Enter the church for verification. There's a long section on whether Leibowitz will be canonized or not. Then, we have another Renaissance and the rise of a new technological age. All with the usual politics and backstabbing you would expect in such a cycle involving the church, of course. The novel could be considered an allegory of the role of the church from the Dark Ages to the Industrial Revolution.

6 THE POSTMAN BY DAVID BRIN

Huge numbers of people were disappointed with the movie starring Kevin Costner. And no wonder, for the movie failed to emotionally capture the central theme of the novel: that people, faced with a holocaust, will cling to anything that strikes of normalcy. In the movie, Costner's character was presented pretty much as a standard cinematic hero, whereas in the book he is extremely uncomfortable with his "role" and becomes amazed at the trust people place in him just because he is wearing the clothing of a postman. So he "becomes" one, agreeing to try and deliver mail, at first with no real intention of doing so. What makes this book excellent is that the protagonist gradually morphs into a real version of the facade he adopts. This in turn serves as the foreground of humanity in very trying times desperately attempting to rebuild communication and a sense of community. Of course, there are those who opt to go in the other direction and take what they can, and the postman becomes a critical player in that essentially good-vs-evil conflict.

5 ETERNITY ROAD BY JACK MCDEVITT

This is the only "quest" novel on the list. About a thousand years from now, after a huge plague, humanity exists in isolated pockets with essentially Amish-type technology (and a concurrent insular social structure). However, ruins and trashed roads remain—the Roadmakers, as the ancients are called, have plenty of visible reminders of their existence. Many believe that there is a place known as "Haven" where the secrets of their technology remain to be discovered. But as we get started, one previous expedition to find Haven has been wiped out—to all but the very last man. There's a lot of stuff about how esteemed, rare, and valued actual books of the Roadmakers are, but eventually a new group sets out on the path of the one that met with disaster. They have adventures along the way, as you might expect. The book is very craftsman-like in its construction, with believable characters.

4 *THE WILD SHORE* BY KIM STANLEY ROBINSON

We start with nuclear war in the recent past, but this novel is quite different from most such. It is set on the coast of California. A passable existence is being eked out by a small community. Some farm and some run nets for fish. A group of teenagers do their work, but also take jaunts to places they probably should not go. There is a very fascinating depiction of folks from various lifestyles and communities coming together for a combination of trade and carnival. But the crux of the book is that the Japanese are the world's foremost power now, not the U.S.—but they are leaving the state pretty much to its own, as long as rebuilding does not occur. Folks try to rebuild bridges and railroads, but those keep getting hit from the sky. Ultimately, this novel is about relationships. One particularly cantankerous relationship is between our protagonist and his father, a cold, stern man of importance to the community who oversees the fishing operation. This ambitious book represents a truly unique take on the postapocalyptic theme. And then the author went ahead and wrote two more books of two completely different possible futures of Orange County.

3 *I AM LEGEND* BY RICHARD MATHESON

Here we have to talk movies and television as well as books. Taking care of the movies first, the best adaptation of this 1954 novel was 1971's *The Omega Man*. Lesser films were *The Last Man on Earth* (1964) and *I Am Legend* (2007). As for TV, well, chances are that every single *Twilight Zone* episode you ever loved was written either by Rod Serling or Richard Matheson himself, with Matheson getting the nod most often. It would be fair to say that Matheson's foremost work was in his insanely extensive television credits. But he could write for print, as well; his short story "Born of Man and Woman" is twice as freaky as Shirley Jackson's "The Lottery." As far as *I Am Legend* goes, the ending of *The Omega Man* is superior to the ending in the novel… something that is quite rare. Anyway, we have another plague story (biological weapons rather than nature, this time around). Our hero has an experimental vaccine, and injects himself just in time. Well, there are also naturally resistant folks, but who can't stand light as a result, and they form a cult. So every day, the protagonist goes out for supplies and whatnot, but must return before dark for his daily battles with these weird "vampires" who are out to get him. Subplots that actually help (for once!) get woven in, and we end up with a fine example of the absolute mastery that was cranked out continually by Matheson over a long and storied career.

2 *PLANET OF THE APES* BY PIERRE BOULLE

Who doesn't know this classic story? It's as pop culture as it comes. But while the movies maintained many of the core concepts of the novel (time-dilation, division of ape culture into military, judiciary, and science based on race, degradation of humans, etc.), most folks will be surprised that the book is quite different from what we normally think of as the *Planet of the Apes* saga. In fact, an argument could be made that this book does not fit within the title of this list at all! That's all that will be said about that so as not to spoil it. Ultimately, fudging had to occur to include *POTA*, because otherwise the comments would have been overwhelming regarding its absence.

1 *ALAS, BABYLON* BY PAT FRANK

Sadly, this once-popular 1959 novel has been fading into obscurity for a long time. It is without doubt one of the best-imagined depictions of the aftermath of nuclear war for a small community that gets somewhat lucky regarding the fallout pattern. It is set in Florida. The protagonist gets a little bit of warning, due to the fact that his brother works for SAC. Then folks start figuring out what to do. It becomes almost a treatise on surviving once everything we accept as normal fails. Of particular interest is how race relations are treated… the reader must understand that this was written in the late 1950s, right before the civil rights movement, and many of today's readers will come away with Malachai as their favorite character. *Alas, Babylon* must have been quite an eye-opener when it first hit the stands. Depictions such as a little girl figuring out how to catch fish to put fish on the table when they aren't biting due to oppressive heat, and folks realizing that an actual expedition to find salt (of all things!) is critical to survival, combined with superb characterizations, make this one the best of all. An utter classic, and worth putting in your bomb shelter should you ever build one.

✳✳✳✳✳✳

TOP 10 SCIENCE FICTION BOOK SERIES

10 RAMA SERIES BY ARTHUR C. CLARKE AND GENTRY LEE

Rendezvous with Rama (the first in the Rama series) was published in 1972. It is set in the twenty-second century when a thirty-mile long cylindrical object passes through the solar system of Earth. It is revealed to be an alien starship and man decides to intercept it in order to unlock its mysteries. This is a brilliant book and was accordingly given both the Hugo and Nebula awards upon its release. It is considered to be one of the cornerstones of Clarke's total output and is seen as a science fiction classic. Under pressure to produce a sequel, Clarke teamed up with Gentry Lee to write the remainder of the series. Lee did the majority of the work and Clarke merely looked over and edited the writing.

9 DUNE SERIES BY FRANK HERBERT

The Dune universe ("Duniverse") is the political, scientific, and social setting of this six-book series of science fiction meets fantasy books. The first book (*Dune*) was extremely popular and was ultimately adapted into a film by David Lynch. It was also televised as a miniseries in 2000, and in 2003, its first two sequels also appeared as miniseries. The universe is set in the distant future of man and it has a history stretching some sixteen thousand years, covering considerable changes in political, social, and religious structures.

8 HEECHEE SAGA BY FREDERIK POHL

Frederik Pohl's HeeChee are an extremely advanced star-traveling race that explored Earth's solar system millennia ago, disappearing without a trace before man began space exploration. They originated as a plot device to allow Pohl to give a plausible reason for humans to make the effort of colonizing the inhospitable planet Venus. In one book of the series *The Merchants of Venus*, the Heechee are nowhere to be found, but the discovery of tunnels beneath the surface of the planet proves that they were there.

7 THE HITCHHIKER'S GUIDE TO THE GALAXY BY DOUGLAS ADAMS

The Hitchhiker's Guide to the Galaxy is a comedy in science fiction form. It was originally a radio broadcast on BBC Radio 4, later adapted into various other formats. The first series was six self-contained episodes, each ending with the planet Earth being destroyed in a different way. When Adams was writing the first episode, he realized that he needed an alien on the planet to provide context; he settled on making the alien a roving researcher seeking the book *The Hitchhiker's Guide to the Galaxy*.

6 RINGWORLD BY LARRY NIVEN

Ringworld was the 1970 winner of both the Hugo and Nebula awards. It is considered to be one of the classics of science fiction literature and was followed by three sequels. The series is set around the year 2855. Two humans and two aliens explore a mysterious "ringworld"—a large artificial ring-shaped structure surrounding a star. It is set in a very technologically advanced universe, which allows for instant teleportation. The ring has a habitable flat inner surface of an area equal to roughly three million Earth-sized planets.

5 ENDER'S GAME SERIES BY ORSON SCOTT CARD

This series started with a small novel, *Ender's Game*, which was later expanded into a full-sized novel of the same name. It now consists of nine novels, ten short stories, and two yet-to-be published books. The first two novels in the series both won the Hugo and the Nebula awards and are considered to be among the most influential science fiction books of the 1980s. The main character, Andrew "Ender" Wiggin, is a child soldier trained in a battle school to be a future leader of Earth.

4 FUTURE HISTORY SERIES BY ROBERT HEINLEIN

Heinlein's Future History described the future of the human race from the middle of the twentieth to the early twenty-third century. He wrote most of the stories early in his career (between 1939–1941 and 1945–1950). The series primarily defines a core group of stories, but Heinlein scholars now agree that some books not included by Heinlein also belong in the series. Two of the better known books included in the series are *The Man Who Sold the Moon* and *Time Enough for Love*.

3 BARSOOM SERIES BY EDGAR RICE BURROUGHS

Barsoom is a fictional version of the planet Mars invented by Burroughs for his series of stories. In 1911 he began his career as a writer with *A Princess of Mars*. Several sequels followed, developing the planet in much greater detailer. *A Princess of Mars* was probably the first twentieth-century fictional work to feature a constructed language. Its influence can be clearly seen in both the *Star Trek* and *Farscape* franchises. While many of the tales appear to be rather dated today, they were extremely innovative in their time and helped to inspire serious interest in Mars and space exploration.

2 LENSMAN SERIES BY E. E. SMITH

The Lensman series by E. E. Smith introduced many innovative concepts into the science fiction genre. It was also a runner-up for the Hugo All Time Best Series award. The series begins with Triplanetary two billion years before the present day and it is based in a universe with few life-forms. The peaceful Arisian race understands life and life-forces in a way that no other race does, and as a result they create the lens—an object which gives its wearer a variety of special mental capabilities including those needed to enforce the law on alien planets and to bridge the communication gap between different life-forms.

1 FOUNDATION SERIES BY ISAAC ASIMOV

The Foundation Series is an epic series of books written over a span of forty-four years. It contains seven volumes all closely linked (though they can be read separately). The term "Foundation Series" is also sometimes used to include the Robot Series and the Empire Series, all of which are set in the same fictional universe (though in earlier times). Including these other series, there are a total of fifteen novels and dozens of short stories. The Foundation Series won the 1965 All Time Best Series Hugo award. The premise of the series is that a scientist (Hari Seldon) develops a branch of mathematics known as psychohistory, in which the future can be predicted due to mass behavior of humans.

✲✲✲✲✲✲

TOP 10 LITERARY ONE-HIT WONDERS

10 *BLACK BEAUTY* BY ANNA SEWELL

Anna Sewell had a fall at the age of fourteen, which ultimately rendered her lame. As a consequence, she frequently used horse-drawn carriages to get around which led to her great fondness for horses. In later life she became confined to her home and it was during this time that she wrote her one and only book: *Black Beauty*, the tale of a highbred horse who leads a difficult life in London pulling cabs.

9 *GONE WITH THE WIND* BY MARGARET MITCHELL

Pulitzer Prize–winner Margaret Mitchell wrote this book while recovering from a broken ankle. She used dramatic moments from her own life combined with her knowledge of the Civil War to produce one of the great books of the Old South. She did write one other book (*Lost Laysen*), but it was not published until after her death.

8 *THE DEVIL IN THE FLESH* BY RAYMOND RADIGUET

Raymond Radiguet was only fourteen when he involved himself with the modernist set in Paris (Picasso, Juan Gris, and Jean Cocteau, who became his lover). Despite the homosexual relationship with Cocteau, Radiguet also had relationships with women and it was one of these that inspired his great novel *The Devil in the Flesh*.

7 *WUTHERING HEIGHTS* BY EMILY BRONTE

Emily Bronte wrote much poetry, but only one book: *Wuthering Heights*. It is considered to be a classic in English literature and many people consider it to be of greater merit than the works of any of her sisters. She died in 1848 of tuberculosis after refusing medical help.

6 IN SEARCH OF LOST TIME BY MARCEL PROUST

French writer Proust is best known for his extremely long novel *In Search of Lost Time*, which spans thirty-two hundred pages. Proust spent his entire literary career on the novel and, in fact, the last three parts were not completely revised when he died. They were published posthumously.

5 THE BELL JAR BY SYLVIA PLATH

Sylvia Plath is undoubtedly one of the greatest female poets of the twentieth century but she also wrote two novels (one of which was destroyed by Ted Hughes, her husband, after her death). The novel, *The Bell Jar*, is semi-autobiographical and describes the life of a young woman with mental illness. One month after it was published, Plath committed suicide.

4 THE PICTURE OF DORIAN GRAY BY OSCAR WILDE

Oscar Wilde is best known for his witty plays, but he also wrote poetry and one novel: *The Picture of Dorian Gray*. The novel delves into the mind of a young gentleman whose obsession with youth and beauty lead him into a life of debauchery and horror. It was to be the only novel written by one of the greatest minds of English literature in the Victorian era.

3 TO KILL A MOCKINGBIRD BY HARPER LEE

To Kill a Mockingbird won Harper Lee a Pulitzer Prize. The book describes racism and tension in a small town in the South and contains autobiographical elements describing elements of an event that occurred near her home when she was ten years old. Two of the main characters are based on herself and Truman Capote, who was her childhood friend.

2 CATCHER IN THE RYE BY J. D. SALINGER

Catcher in the Rye (1951) is the only novel by J. D. Salinger, in which a young man, Holden Caulfield, suffers teenage angst and rebellion. The book is written in the first person and became a worldwide hit, regularly read in schools. After the publication of the book, Salinger became reclusive and has not written another novel, though he did write a novella entitled *Hapworth 16, 1924*, which was published in the *New Yorker*.

1 *DOCTOR ZHIVAGO* BY BORIS PASTERNAK

Doctor Zhivago is the best-known book of Boris Pasternak, the famed Russian Nobel Prize–winning poet. The book covers the period of the last days of Tsarist Russia to the beginning stages of Communism. The book discusses the plight of a man whose life is torn apart by a changing society.

✳✳✳✳✳✳

TOP 10 GREAT ALCOHOLIC WRITERS

10 DYLAN THOMAS, OCTOBER 27, 1914–NOVEMBER 9, 1953

Dylan Thomas is considered to be one of the most influential poets of the twentieth century. He regularly boasted about his drinking habits, saying, "An alcoholic is someone you don't like, who drinks as much as you do." As a result of his excessive drinking, his health declined, and two days after his thirty-ninth birthday, he slipped into a coma while drinking at the White Horse Tavern in Manhattan and died four hours later.

9 TENNESSEE WILLIAMS, MARCH 26, 1911–FEBRUARY 25, 1983

Thomas Lanier Williams III was a significant writer of the twentieth century. He is best known for his play *Cat on a Hot Tin Roof*, which contains many autobiographical elements of his life such as homosexuality and alcoholism.

8 EDGAR ALLEN POE, JANUARY 19, 1809–OCTOBER 7, 1849

Poet and short story writer Edgar Allen Poe died at the age of forty of an unknown cause, but it is believed it was either alcohol or drug related. He is best known for his horrifying tales and for inventing the detective-fiction genre of literature.

7 TRUMAN CAPOTE, SEPTEMBER 30, 1924–AUGUST 25, 1984

Truman Capote is probably best known for his short novel, *Breakfast at Tiffany's*, and his nonfiction novel, *In Cold Blood*. When Capote was writing he began with a double martini. He was arrested for drunk driving and eventually ended up in rehab. At most he managed to stay dry for three to four months but invariably found his way back to the bottle.

6 **JACK KEROUAC, MARCH 12, 1922–OCTOBER 21, 1969**
Beat Generation writer Jack Kerouac was a heavy drinker for his whole adult life. His drinking habit ultimately led to death from cirrhosis of the liver at the age of forty-seven. He is best remembered for his novel *On the Road*, an autobiographical description of a road trip across America.

5 **WILLIAM FAULKNER, SEPTEMBER 25, 1897–JULY 6, 1962**
William Cuthbert Faulkner was awarded a Nobel Prize in Literature in 1949. Throughout his life he had a serious drinking problem, but unlike many of the other writers on this list, he did not drink while working and even thought that alcohol hindered, rather than helped, his creative energies. It is now believed that he used alcohol to escape the harsh realities of life outside of his literary efforts.

4 **CHARLES BUKOWSKI, AUGUST 16, 1920–MARCH 9, 1994**
At the age of thirteen, Henry Charles Bukowski began drinking—the beginning of a lifetime of alcoholic episodes. His childhood was abusive and it is perhaps that which led Bukowski to the bottle. Despite his alcoholism, he was a prodigious and influential writer who lived to the age of seventy-three.

3 **F. SCOTT FITZGERALD, SEPTEMBER 24, 1896– DECEMBER 21, 1940**
Francis Scott Key Fitzgerald was the leading light of the Jazz Age (a term he coined) literary movement in the United States. He became an alcoholic during his college days and never stopped drinking. The alcohol caused him ill health and he suffered a fatal heart attack in 1940 at the age of forty-four. He is best remembered for his novel *The Great Gatsby*, which describes the life of the eponymous Jazz Age millionaire Jay Gatsby.

2 **JAMES JOYCE, FEBRUARY 2, 1882–JANUARY 13, 1941**
James Augustine Aloysius Joyce is undoubtedly one of the most influential twentieth century Irish writers. He is best known for his novel *Ulysses* and the controversial followup novel, *Finnegans Wake*. He spent the majority of his adult life binge drinking and involving himself in pub brawls.

1 **ERNEST HEMINGWAY, JULY 21, 1899–JULY 2, 1961**
Ernest Miller Hemingway was an alcoholic for the majority of his adult life and this, in combination with mental illness, ultimately led to his death at his own hand in 1961. He is best known for his book *The Old Man and the Sea*. He was considered to be a member of the "Lost Generation," a group of American expatriates living in Paris in the 1920s.

✳✳✳✳✳✳

TOP 10 POLITICALLY INCORRECT CHILDREN'S BOOKS

10 **LITTLE HOUSE ON THE PRAIRIE BY LAURA INGALLS WILDER, 1935**
This book is considered off-limits now because of its treatment of American Indians (the Osage figure prominently in the story). Despite the fact that Laura Ingalls Wilder gives us an important historical look at social perspectives through this book, it is still considered bad. The book is based on decades-old memories of Laura Ingalls Wilder's childhood in the Midwest during the late nineteenth century.

9 **HUCKLEBERRY FINN BY MARK TWAIN, 1884**
Huckleberry Finn is undoubtedly the most challenged book in American history; to this day attempts are made to make the book more "suitable" for a modern audience. Although the Southern society it satirized was already a quarter-century in the past by the time of publication, the book immediately became controversial, and has remained so to this day. CBS Television went so far as to produce a made-for-TV version of *Huck Finn* that included no black cast members, no mention of slavery, and without the critical character Jim.

8 *KIM* BY RUDYARD KIPLING, 1900

Kim is about an Anglo-Irish boy on his travels across the Indian continent. Its depiction of colonial India has caused it to be considered controversial by many people. Kipling is, of course, most famous for his *Jungle Book*.

7 *BABAR THE ELEPHANT* BY JEAN DE BRUNHOFF, 1931

Babar the Elephant is a popular French children's fictional character who first appeared in *L'Histoire de Babar*. Some writers have argued that, although superficially delightful, the stories are politically and morally offensive for their justification of French colonialist ideas.

6 *NODDY AND BIGEARS* BY ENID BLYTON, 1949

Noddy and Bigears are two characters by Enid Blyton who have recently been under scrutiny and even accused of homosexuality for various scenes in the books in which they share a bed. This is entirely ridiculous, but it has meant that modern editions of the books have had those scenes removed, as well as any mention of the naughty golliwogs that live in the woods.

5 *DR. DOLITTLE* BY HUGH LOFTING, 1920

The books have been accused of racism, due to the usage of derogatory terms for and depiction of certain ethnic groups therein, both written and illustrated. Editions in the United States sometimes had alterations made from the 1960s, but the books went out-of-print in the 1970s. In 1986, to mark the centenary of Lofting's birth, new editions were published which had such passages rewritten or removed (sometimes called bowdlerization). Offending illustrations were either removed (and replaced with unpublished Lofting originals) or altered.

4 *LITTLE BLACK SAMBO* BY HELEN BANNERMAN, 1899

Despite this book being about an Indian boy, the illustrations in the original European version portray Sambo using "darky iconography," with black skin, wildly curly hair, and bright red lips. The word "sambo" has a long history as a racial slur against blacks. Because the story itself does not contain any racist ideas, recent publications tell the same story, with new images to replace the originals.

3 *THE THREE GOLLIWOGS* BY ENID BLYTON, 1946

The Three Golliwogs is a book about three friendly golliwogs that discover an abandoned house in the woods and move in. The controversy over this book (and in fact, many of Blyton's books) lies simply in the fact that the Golliwog character is now deemed to be racist. Golliwogs have been depicted as both villains and heroes.

2 *TINTIN AU CONGO* BY HERGÉ, 1930

Tintin in the Congo has often been criticized as having racist and colonialist views, as well as several scenes of violence against animals. Hergé has later claimed that he was only portraying the naïve views of the time. When the story was redrawn in 1946, Hergé removed several references to the fact that the Congo was at that time a Belgian colony.

1 *TEN LITTLE NIGGERS* BY SEPTIMUS WINNER, 1860

I am sure no one needs to be told why this rhyme is now considered to be politically incorrect. It is found in the adult novel *Ten Little Niggers*, which is now called *And Then There Were None*. It is Agatha Christie's best-selling novel. Derived from the original rhyme by Septimus Winner, which was written for his minstrel show, in his original, it was called "Ten Little Injuns."

✻✻✻✻✻✻

TOP 10 COMMON ENGLISH LANGUAGE ERRORS

10 PRACTICE / PRACTISE

In U.S. English, practice is used as either a verb (doing word), or noun (naming word). Hence, a doctor has a practice, and a person practices the violin. In UK English, practice is a noun, and practise is a verb. A doctor has a practice, but his daughter practises the piano.

9 BOUGHT / BROUGHT

Bought relates to buying something. Brought relates to bringing something. For example, I bought a bottle of wine brought over from France. The easy way to remember which is which is that bring starts with *br* and brought also does. Buy and bought start with *b* only. This is one of those difficult ones that a spelling checker won't catch.

8 YOUR / YOU'RE

Your means "belonging to you." You're means "you are." The simplest way to work out the correct one to use is to read your sentence out loud. For example, if you say "you're jeans look nice," expand the apostrophe. The expanded sentence would read, "you are jeans look nice"—obviously nonsensical. Remember, in English, the apostrophe often denotes an abbreviation.

7 ITS / IT'S

As in the case above, the apostrophe denotes an abbreviation: it's = it is. Its means "belongs to it." The confusion arises here because we also use an apostrophe in English to denote possession, except in this case: if you want to say "the cat's bag," you say "its bag," not "it's bag." "It's" always means "it is" or "it has": It's a hot day. It's been fun seeing you.

6 TWO / TO / TOO

With a *w* it means the number two. With one *o*, it refers to direction: "to France." With two *o*'s, it means "also" or refers to quantity, for example, "There is too much money." A good way to remember this one is that too has two *o*'s, more *o*'s than to, therefore, it refers to quantity.

5 DESERT / DESSERT

This is a confusing one because in English an *s* on its own is frequently pronounced like a *z* and two *s*'s are usually pronounced as an *s* (for example: prise, prissy). In this case, desert follows the rule—it means a large stretch of sand. However, dessert is pronounced "de-zurt" with the emphasis on the second syllable—i.e., something we eat as part of our meal. To make matters worse, when a person leaves the army without permission, it is spelled "desert." So, let's sum up:

desert (pronounced dez'-urt): barren expanse of land

desert (pronounced de-zurt'): abandon (or punishment, as in "just deserts")

dessert (pronounced de-zurt'): yum yum!—Remember, two s's because you want second helpings!

4 DRYER / DRIER

If your clothes are wet, put them in a clothes dryer. That will make them drier. A hair dryer also makes hair drier.

3 CHOSE / CHOOSE

This is actually quite an easy one to remember—in English we generally pronounce oo as it is written, such as moo. The same rule applies here: choose is pronounced as it is written (with a z sound for the s) and chose is said like nose. Therefore, if you had to choose to visit Timbuktu, chances are you chose to fly there. Chose is the past tense; choose is the present tense.

2 LOSE / LOOSE

This one is confusing. In this case, contrary to normal rules of English, the single s in loose is pronounced like an s, as in wearing trousers that are too loose. Lose, on the other hand, relates to loss, for example, "I hope we don't lose this game." A good way to remember this is that in the word "lose" you have lost the second o from loose. If you can't remember a rule that simple, you are a loser!

1 LITERALLY

This one is not only often used in error, it is also incredibly annoying when it is used in the wrong way. Literally means "it really happened," therefore, unless you live on a parallel universe with different rules of physics, you cannot say, "he literally flew out the door." Saying someone "flew out the door" is speaking figuratively; you could say, "he figuratively flew out the door" but figuratively is generally implied when you describe something impossible. Literally can only be used in the case of facts, for example, "he literally exploded after swallowing the grenade." If he did, indeed, swallow the grenade and explode, then that last sentence is perfectly correct. It would not be correct to say, "she annoyed him and he literally exploded," unless she is Wonder Woman and her anger can cause people to blow up.

✳✳✳✳✳✳

TOP 10 PROBLEMS IN *THE DA VINCI CODE*

10 DA VINCI'S *THE LAST SUPPER*

The contention that Mary Magdalene is depicted sitting next to Jesus in Leonardo's famous *The Last Supper* is disputed by virtually all art historians. Since there are twelve disciples (including Judas), one would have to be missing for Mary to be present. The figure to the right of Christ, also wearing blue and red, is usually identified as John the Apostle, who was customarily depicted in the Renaissance period as a beardless, often "effeminate" youth with very long hair. The "femininity" of the figure can be attributed to Leonardo's artistic training in a workshop of the Florentine School, which had a long tradition of often depicting young males as sweet, pretty, rather "effeminate" persons.

9 PRIORY OF SION

The portrayal of the Priory of Sion as an ancient organization connected to goddess-worship is incorrect: The actual "Priory of Sion" was founded in 1956 by Pierre Plantard, Andre Bonhomme, and others, not in 1099 as claimed in the book. It was named after a mountain in France, not the biblical Mount Zion. Les Dossiers Secrets was a forgery created by Philippe de Cherisey for Plantard. Plantard, under oath, eventually admitted that the whole thing was fabricated.

8 OPUS DEI

The depiction of Opus Dei as a monastic order which is the pope's "personal prelature" is inaccurate. In fact, there are no monks in Opus Dei, which primarily has lay membership and whose celibate lay members are called "numeraries." Moreover, Opus Dei encourages its lay members to avoid practices that are perceived as fundamentalist to the outside world. Silas, the murderous "Opus Dei monk," uses a cilice and flagellates himself. Some members of Opus Dei do practice voluntary mortification of the flesh, as has been a Christian tradition since at least St. Anthony in the third century and has also been practiced by Mother Teresa, Padre Pio, and slain archbishop Óscar Romero. Critics charge Brown of greatly sensationalizing the practice of such mortifications and exaggerating the extent of their practice. It is impossible to gain the kind of wounds Silas is described as having from a normal cilice.

7 ROSSLYN CHAPEL

The chapel is a major feature in the last part of the novel, though many incorrect assertions were made about the structure. For example, Brown's book states that the chapel was built by the Knights Templar, and contains a six-pointed Star of David worn into the stone floor, although such a star has never been seen. Many sources say that Dan Brown didn't visit the chapel until after the publication of his *Da Vinci Code* book, and most of his material came from previously published material. Another claim is that the name "Rosslyn" is a form of the phrase "Rose line," and that a line starting in France also runs through the chapel. In fact, the name "Rosslyn" comes from two Celtic words: *ros*, meaning promontory or point, and *lyn*, meaning waterfall. As far as the "secret code" that Brown claims exists in the chapel, most recently father-and-son team Thomas and Stuart Mitchell have shown it is actually encoded music.

6 PROBLEMS WITH PARIS

Several claims about the Church of Saint-Sulpice in Paris are disputed. While there is a brass line running north-south through the church, it is not a part of the Paris Meridian, which passes about 110 yards east of it. The line is instead more a gnomon or sundial/calendar, meant to mark the solstice and equinoxes. Further, there is no evidence that there was ever a temple of Isis on the site. The reference to Paris having been founded by the Merovingians (chapter 55) is false; in fact, the city was settled by Gauls by the third century BC. The Romans, who knew it as Lutetia, captured it in 52 BC under Julius Caesar, and left substantial ruins in the city, including an amphitheater and public baths. The Merovingians did not rule in France until the sixth century AD, by which time Paris was at least eight hundred years old. The novel claims that the top of the Centre Pompidou can be seen from the Arc du Carrousel (chapter 3). This is incorrect. The book erroneously places Versailles to the northwest of Paris, when actually it is approximately 15 miles west-south-west of Paris city center.

5 THE VATICAN

In the story, it is repeatedly said that the Vatican was the center of power in the early Catholic Church, including reference to "the Vatican" suppressing Gnostic writings in the fourth century. Until the early Renaissance, the papal palace was in different locations, ranging from the cathedral of St. John Lateran, to Anagni, to Avignon. It was not until the fifteenth century that there was anything like official power in the vicinity of the Vatican Hill in Rome. In the fourth century, the Vatican was little more than a church and cemetery by the side of the road. Also, St. Peter's is referred to as a cathedral; it is technically a church. St. Peter's is the second largest church in the world, and covers 5.7 acres.

4 MARY MAGDALENE
Historians have disputed the claim that Mary Magdalene was of the tribe of Benjamin. There is no mention of this in the Bible or in other ancient sources. The fact that Magdala was located in northern Israel, whereas the tribe of Benjamin resided in the south, weighs against it. Furthermore, Paul was a Benjamite but makes no mention of this supposed heritage. Mary Magdalene is revered as a saint in France; a cave in the Sainte-Baume Mountains of Provence, where she is believed to have lived, is a popular pilgrimage site. It is believed that she died and is buried there.

3 GNOSTICISM
The book claims that the Gnostic Gospels (e.g. the Gospels of Thomas, Philip, Mary Magdalene, and the recently rediscovered Judas) are far older, less corrupted, and more accurate than the four included in the Bible. With the possible exception of Thomas, the other gospels date from the second through the fourth century, while the canonical four are thought by most scholars to date from the first or early second century. In the story, a character claims that the label "heretic" was used only after the Nicene Council (325 AD), in order to persecute Gnostics. In fact, St. Irenaeus used the term "heresy" to label Gnostic teachings in the second century, long before the church had any political power to persecute anyone.

2 GEOGRAPHY
The book's storyline that the "Albino Monk" was arrested in France, imprisoned in Andorra, and escaped to Spain, demonstrates the lack of basic research that would be gleaned from a quick glance at a map or tourist guide. It is improbable that someone arrested along the French coast would be imprisoned in another country (in this case, Andorra, which is a different jurisdiction and several hundred miles away up in the Pyrenean Mountains). After the scene in the Temple Church, London, the heroes of the story take the tube from Temple Station to King's College. In fact, King's College is nearer to the Temple Church than to Temple Station, and any tube journey would have carried them further away from King's College. At the start of chapter 104, (Rosslyn Chapel), Brown

states, "The chapel's geographic coordinates fall precisely on the north-south meridian that runs through Glastonbury." This statement is incorrect: Rosslyn Chapel lies on longitude 3:07:13 west and Glastonbury Tor 2:42:05 west. Brown appears to have confused geographic north with magnetic north.

1 ASSORTED ERRORS

Albinos typically have very poor vision; in fact, many are legally blind. It is, therefore, highly unlikely that the albino Silas could ever become an expert marksman or even drive.

✳✳✳✳✳✳

TOP 10 SLANG WORDS AND PHRASES EXPLAINED

10 IDIOT

Idiot originally comes from the Greek word *idiotes* used to refer to a person who was a private individual, or more specifically, one who was so preoccupied with their own personal life that they would not take part in the democratic process. In the biblical sense, the word referred to an uneducated person. By the fourteenth century, it could also refer to a clown, a layman (non-religious), or an individual. Later, however, the *Oxford English Dictionary* gave it the following definition that has stuck: "A person so deficient in mental or intellectual faculty as to be incapable of ordinary acts of reasoning or rational conduct." When IQ tests arrived, a person scoring less than twenty was regarded to have earned the "idiot's score."

9 MORON

Another Greek word, *moron* meant foolish or stupid. It was first propagated in English by a psychologist, Henry Goddard (1886–1957). In his report to the *Journal of Psycho-asthenics* about his study of the feeble-minded, he argued for the adoption of the word, which he defined as, "One who is lacking an intelligence, one who is deficient in judgment or sense." It was originally used to refer to an adult with a mental age between eight and twelve. The term has not really made its way into high literature.

8 BOB'S YOUR UNCLE

"Bob's your uncle" generally means that something is simple or easy or a "job done." It is most likely that this phrase came about as a result of nepotism (family favoritism). In the late 1800s, Lord Robert Salisbury was prime minister of Great Britain. After his third term, he was succeeded by his nephew, Arthur. Arthur had been made Chief Secretary of Ireland in 1886, which caused some scandal. Suspicions arose that Robert was favoring his nephew Arthur. The term "Bob's your uncle" could be used at the time as a sly reference to this charge of nepotism.

7 THIRD DEGREE

To get the third degree means to be thoroughly questioned. The third degree of something has been regarded as the upper limit (or extreme) even since the time of Shakespeare when he wrote, "For he's in the thirde degree of drinke, he's drown'd," referring to a very drunk man. Therefore, it is a natural progression that when referring to the most extreme type of questioning, it would be referred to as the third degree.

6 SLUT

This unpleasant term is used these days to refer to an immoral woman. But the origin of the term had a far less sinister meaning. It actually meant a woman who did not keep her room tidy, though it is easy to see that this could be a metaphor for immorality of a sexual type. In Thomas Hoccleve's 1402 *Letter to Cupid*, we read, "The foulest slutte of al a toune." This meaning eventually crossed to the word *slattern*, which retains its original meaning of being an untidy woman. In Victorian English, sluts wool referred to the little piles of dust that gather on the floor if it is not swept.

5 WELL HEELED

According to the *Chambers Dictionary*, well heeled means "comfortably supplied with money" and states that it comes from the word *heeled*, meaning provided with a heel. Heeled also used to refer to being armed with a revolver. A person

carrying a set of guns was said to be long-heeled. Despite the *Oxford English Dictionary* saying otherwise, it appears that the origin of the term actually comes from cockfighting. In the early days of cockfighting, the owners would sometimes add spurs to the feet of their birds, putting them at an advantage. If you did not add spurs to the bird it was said to be naked-heeled. The use of the term well-heeled in this context is first seen in print in 1866 in a story by Mark Twain.

4 KICK THE BUCKET

This means "to die." Many people consider the term to have come from a condemned man standing on an upturned bucket, which was then kicked out from under his feet leaving him to hang, but there is no written evidence that this is the case. In fact, it is more likely from a different type of bucket entirely. In butchery, when a pig was slaughtered it would be hung from a piece of timber called the bucket beam. It is mostly likely that in his death throes, the pig's feet would bang against the rail to which they were tied. Therefore, kicking the bucket was a term referring to the last actions of the pig before he finally died.

3 KINKY

Originally this word simply meant something with a bend or twist, probably coming from the Icelandic word meaning to bend your knees. In time the word was adopted by the criminal world to mean something that was illicit; for example, a stolen car may have been referred to as a "kinky car." But then in 1959, Colin MacInnes changed the meaning of the word forever. In his book *Absolute Beginners*, he says, "Suze [...] meets lots of kinky characters [...] and acts as agent for me, getting orders from them for my pornographic photos." From that time on the word was associated with the steamy side of sex.

2 UNDERHAND

Underhand means "surreptitious" or on the sly. The *Chambers Dictionary* also adds "with the hand below the elbow or shoulder," which would suggest doing something on the sly with your hand while distracting the eye. But the actual origin of the term most likely comes from archery. A well-known lover of archery, Roger Ascham (circa 1515–1568) wrote, "Thus the underhande [shaft] must have a small breste, to go cleane awaye oute of the bowe." To shoot underhand was and is a common archery term.

1 COOL

Who hasn't used this word at least once in their life when speaking highly of something? This meaning of the word is relatively new in English, but not as new as you might think. The earliest record found so far is from 1884 in the phrase "Dat's cool!" After that, the next is from 1902 from the lyrics of a song from the Black and White minstrel show: "de way we dress is cooler."

✳✳✳✳✳✳

TOP 10 FASCINATING FICTIONAL LANGUAGES

10 ALIENESE

Alienese is a set of fictional languages that often appear, usually as graffiti, in the background of the show *Futurama*. The first transliterates directly into English, but the second is much more complex; the alphabet is described as one in which "next letter is given by the summation of all previous letters plus the current letter." Fans have spent their time translating these messages and revealing additional, hidden humor on the show.

9 PARSELTONGUE

In the Harry Potter books, Parseltongue is the language of snakes, and can be understood by human Parselmouths, which are very rare. It can be spoken by Salazar Slytherin and his descendants, including Voldemort, who passed the ability on to Harry when he tried to kill him. J. K. Rowling has stated that she named the language after "an old word for someone who has a problem with the mouth." To non-speakers, it sounds like a series of hisses, but Parselmouths hear it in their native language.

8 AKLO

Aklo is a fictional language often associated with the writing of forbidden or occult texts. It was first invented by Arthur Machen in his 1899 short story "The White People," in which two men discussing the nature of evil consult a diary of a young girl, written with Aklo words. It is notable for its widespread use in other fiction; H. P. Lovecraft used it in two stories from his Cthulhu Mythos, "The Dunwich Horror" and "The Haunter of the Dark." Alan Moore used the language in his story "The Courtyard," in which Aklo is not only an alien language, but also a key that opens the human mind. Since it is only used fleetingly and by a wide range of authors, there is no set grammar or vocabulary, and it is unclear just what languages from which it draws its most influences.

7 MANGANI

Mangani is the language of the apes from Edgar Rice Burrough's Tarzan novels, and also the word by which the apes refer to themselves. It is described as being composed of guttural sounds that represent nouns and basic concepts. However, the written lexicon as provided by Burroughs is much more complex, and made of real words similar in pronunciation to many African languages from the area in which the books take place. The recently discovered Bili Ape has been retroactively compared to the Mangani, both in size and habitat.

6 NEWSPEAK

Yes, the language that is the bane of high school seniors everywhere. Invented by George Orwell for his dystopian novel *1984*, Newspeak was designed by fictional totalitarian regime the Party to enforce its rule on people. Closely based on English, its vocabulary constantly shrinks to preclude any words that convey the ideas of freedom, rebellion, or free thought. Its main goal is to remove any ambiguity from language, giving one word total meaning; this is commonly done by making one word, such as "think," both a noun and a verb. Opposite words were replaced by a pre- or suffixed version of a word; for example, "bad" became "ungood." This is thought to have been influenced by Esperanto, which frequently creates new words through a complicated system of adding prefixes and suffixes.

5 NADSAT

Invented by author Anthony Burgess, Nadsat is the idiomatic language spoken by the teenagers in *A Clockwork Orange*. The word itself comes from a transliteration of the Russian word for "teen." It is a vernacular speech, composed by the youth counterculture; it is basically English, with some transliterated words from Russian, patterns from Cockney rhyming slang, the King James Bible, and words invented by Burgess himself. All Nadsat words are concrete, lacking the complexity to discuss a subject such as philosophy. The author intended this to show the shallow nature of the juveniles' minds.

4 SIMLISH

Simlish is the spoken language of the Sims, first heard in SimCopter, but most prominently featured in The Sims, Sims 2, and Sims 3. In order to avoid the cost of recording repetitive dialogue and translating it, the project director had the voice actors improvise a gibberish language. The end result was that players were able to fill in their own dialogue, and imagine the character interactions more realistically than a computer could simulate. Soon, the games had songs sung in Simlish, and many famous recording artists have since rerecorded some of their tracks for various Sims games and expansions. Written Simlish, glimpsed in reading materials and on television, is a combination of the wingdings font and zodiac symbols, but have no grounding in real grammar. All other games made by Sims genre creator Will Wright employ Simlish as a language.

3 ESPERANTO

The only actual language on this list, Esperanto is noteworthy for being one of the most successful constructed languages in history. Esperanto was first detailed by L. L. Zamenhof, in his book *Unua Libro* in 1887, published under the pseudonym Doktoro Esperanto. The word "esperanto" means "one who hopes" in the language. Today, it is estimated that there are between one hundred thousand and two million fluent Esperanto speakers, and between two hundred to two thousand native speakers. Both Google and Wikipedia provide services in Esperanto. It is the language of instruction at the Akademio Internacia de la Sciencoj in San Marino. Its structure is heavily influenced by the Indo-European languages, and its vocabulary is mostly derived from the Romance and, to a lesser extent, the Germanic languages.

2 KLINGONESE

Qapla'! The language of *Star Trek*'s Klingons is today a nearly fully developed language. It was first heard in *Star Trek: The Motion Picture* (1979), and its sound was devised by actor James Doohan (Scotty). Paramount Pictures subsequently hired linguist Marc Okrand to fully flesh out the language, which he deliberately designed to be "alien." The first Klingon dictionary was published in 1985, and other books such as Klingon phrasebooks have supplemented the language. The Shakespeare plays *Much Ado About Nothing* and *Hamlet* have been famously translated into Klingonese, after a famous line in *Star Trek VI: The Undiscovered Country*: "Shakespeare is best read in the original Klingon." It is said that Okrand was heavily influenced by Native American languages, and the tendency of the language to develop long chains of nouns (for example, "gun and sword and spear") comes from Sanskrit. As of 2006, it held the world record for the fictional language spoken by the most people.

1 LANGUAGES OF ARDA

The above term is used to describe the many fictional languages invented by J. R. R. Tolkien for *The Lord of the Rings* and other works taking place in Middle-Earth. This was done out of a desire to give real linguistic depth to names and places that Tolkien felt was lacking in fantasy and science fiction. The two most mature of these languages are Quenya (High-Elvish) and Sindarin. Quenya is comparable to Latin in that it is an old language used contemporarily (in Middle-Earth) as an official language. When written in English, the words contain many accents, which are usually on every vowel (they also employ the dieresis, the two little dots above a letter). These two languages were heavily influenced by Finnish and Welsh, though as they developed further, the influence became less and less apparent. The depth and complexity of these two languages are incredible, as demonstrated by their influence on Middle-Earth culture and other Middle-Earth languages. What is even more amazing is the sheer number of languages Tolkien created for his world, with each race having dozens of offshoots and dialects. His work with the many tongues of Middle-Earth truly exemplified the potential of fictional language, and demonstrates the importance that language plays in creating a society.

✳✳✳✳✳✳

TOP 10 MEMORABLE ALIEN RACES IN SCIENCE FICTION

10 OVERLORDS

Widely included in university science fiction courses everywhere, Arthur C. Clarke's 1953 classic *Childhood's End* depicts yet another conqueror of Earth, but a benign one, in many ways. The Overlords make life better for everyone and end many of our persistent woes, all while sitting aloof in their gigantic starships positioned over major cities. Mankind adapts, as is his nature. But the Overlords will not reveal themselves for fifty years and the reason why incorporates the Jungian concept of racial memory. No spoiler coming, but this inclusion is probably why so many professors love to teach the novel. Anyway, of course there is a secret to why the Overlords are doing what they do. What happens when that is revealed might best be described as "poignant."

9 FITHP

Larry Niven didn't need the money but Jerry Pournelle did. Doesn't really matter, because both guys are science fiction authors whether they're eating Hamburger Helper or filet mignon. Together they are one of the most successful collaborations the field has ever seen. 1985's *Footfall* is an excellent example. People who don't read science fiction were reading Niven/Pournelle novels in college during the '80s while waiting for the next Heinlein to come out. Anyway, anyone who has read the book has to think of the Fithp as elephants. As humans are a culture of individuals, as ants are a colony culture, the Fithp are a herd culture. Excellent treatment of that basic premise, and being herd creatures, they do not understand the concept of diplomatic compromise… you either dominate or you submit. In particular, the internal politics of an intelligent herd engaged in difficult conquest are handled with admirable skill.

8 DRAC

OK. So a guy publishes a novelette and it wins the Nebula—mere months after the guy publicly denounces the awards themselves! Then it wins the Hugo. Along with the John W. Campbell award because, after all, the guy is new. So he's the first person ever to win all three of those awards in one year. Big deal? Sort of. Along came Hollywood and a somewhat underrated film starring Dennis Quaid and Louis Gossett, Jr. (Gossett got a Best Actor nomination, even though the film wasn't really a hit.) Suddenly, Barry B. Longyear is a major player in science fiction as a result of 1979's *Enemy Mine*. Drac and humans are at war. One human fighter pilot and one alien fighter pilot are marooned on a world where existence is difficult, to say the least. They are forced to pool resources just to stay alive. Problem is, the Dracs are hermaphrodites and Jeriba doesn't need a partner to reproduce. Spoiler alert next sentence: An untimely death and our human is forced to raise the alien progeny as his own. Both the book and the movie are essentially the story of one human and one alien interacting, with a beginning and an ending tacked onto either end. If you're in the right frame of mind, you'll cry. You will absolutely know the Drac, especially if you have both seen the movie and read the book. The Drac are included here because they fit the criteria; I own many Longyear books mainly as a result of the sheer pathos in *Enemy Mine* but find the majority of his stuff barely readable.

7 FUZZIES

H. Beam Piper solidified his place in science fiction history with the publication of 1962's *Little Fuzzy*. The adjectives most used in reviews of this book might well be "delightful" and "charming" and one can't blame the reviewers for that. Cute and cuddly, the Fuzzies are. But the novel explores a rather important theme: how do we define sapience? Is this life-form just a critter, over which we can claim dominion, or a thinking creature in its own right, in which case exploitation, and even murder, rears its ugly head? Sequels followed, not always written by the originator—none are as enjoyable as the original.

6 GROACI

It's problematical whether Keith Laumer is best known for his Bolo series of works or what he has done with his James Bond-ish assistant diplomat character, Jame Retief. Probably the latter. Lots of stories and novels over several decades. Regardless, these tongue-in-cheek tales of derring-do and human ingenuity in the face of human diplomatic incompetence have sold quite well for many years. In most of them, there is an insidious plot behind whatever the current weird aliens are doing that is being masterminded by the Groaci. No slouches at the diplomatic bargaining table, the Groaci are, nonetheless, almost incapable of dealing squarely. The books are pun-filled and light-hearted, but the Groaci are badass unless put on a leash. Almost not included on the list, as they are rather a two-dimensional race. Fun, nonetheless.

5 YTHRIANS

Poul Anderson is undoubtedly one of the deans of science fiction; his word count alone contains way too many commas. Many of those words were as a result of cranking out short story after short story for the magazines back in the day. He had sort of a "Future History"—a term associated with Robert A. Heinlein— but Anderson's future history was rather a disjointed one. Many of his stories were set in the backdrop of the so-called Polesotechic League which spanned four thousand years of human interstellar exploration. The League is a thinly veiled (if veiled at all) allegory of nineteenth century robber-baron capitalism. So what about the Ythri? 1978's *The Earth Book of Stormgate* violates a criterion: it's a story collection, not a novel. But Hloch of the Stormgate Choth introduces each story as a scholar/historian. And the interwoven stories themselves, combined with Hloch's notes, definitely give the reader a sense of Ythrian culture. The best way to include that race in this list—and they are worthy of inclusion—is via the *Earth Book* (although Ythrians also appear in other works by Anderson).

4 HROSHII

It is hard to explain these guys without spoiling everything, but I'll try. Well over half of Robert A. Heinlein's 1954 "juvenile" SF novel, *The Star Beast*, has played out before the word "Hroshii" ever appears. But, they're plenty powerful—and disinclined to negotiate. They're looking for someone, and they simply will not take no for an answer. The someone they are looking for has a little trouble taking no for an answer, as well. Not truly disobedient, and with no desire to cause harm, just kind of literal-minded in following instructions and always a little hungry. "Lummox" is so a person and more than that, s/he's a friend!

3 FORHILNOR

Pretty danged human for being essentially giant spiders. Canadian author Robert J. Sawyer, who is probably today's foremost purveyor of "hard" science fiction, introduced us to this race in 2000's *Calculating God*. Even though the events in the novel deal with the Forhilnors coming to Earth and interacting with a human paleontologist, it could be said that the aliens are simply bystanders… Sawyer uses that encounter to tackle really mind-blowing concepts of creation, cosmology, and why life exists at all. Nevertheless, the reader would love to have Hollus as a dinner guest and would be proud to have that [person] as a friend. Satisfies the criterion of knowing what those folks are really like. But as a digression: Take three good friends. One is a fundamentalist assured of his salvation. The second is an agnostic who feels he believes in God but doesn't quite know what that means. The third is an atheist who looks strictly to chemical processes. Remember, they are all good friends. *Calculating God* is the book they should discuss around a campfire.

2 CHTORRANS

If you don't know David Gerrold, you, nonetheless, probably know one thing he did—he wrote the *Star Trek* episode, "The Trouble with Tribbles." His output includes a number of short stories and novels of varying quality. But in 1983 he published *A Matter for Men*, volume one in what became known as "The War Against the Chtorr." Although the "worms" are the most visible face of the Chtorr, what we have here is nothing less than the attempt of an entire biosphere to conquer Earth. Several books resulted, and happily some of the latter ones are just as good as the first. They really have to be read in order, though, as the Chtorran infestation multiplies and human reaction changes accordingly. This comes close to violating a criterion—it would be stretching it to call a Chtorran worm a "person"... even with absolutely zero speciesism. A God, maybe, but not a person.

1 YILANE

Another rather well-known race, and here's hoping someone with a real budget will get around to making a movie of Harry Harrison's 1984 masterpiece *West of Eden*. It spawned a few sequels (with the usual slight lowering of quality) and is a stunning example of meticulous alien-creation. Although, the Yilane aren't truly aliens in one sense of the word... this is an alternate evolution of Earth story. Humans are at the hunter-gatherer stage. The Yilane are four-feet tall, erect, intelligent reptiles descended from dinosaurs. Theirs is a matriarchal society whose technology is based almost exclusively on the manipulation of the biological sciences. They literally grow plants and animals that are modified to perform such diverse functions as microscopes, boats, and living blankets. The Yilane are tropical whereas the humans are temperate. But impending climate changes push the two societies toward one another and conflict erupts. Kerrick, the human protagonist, is uniquely situated; he was captured by the Yilane at an early age and raised among them. This upbringing is the true beauty of the book: it allows the author to show the reader the awesomely rich Yilane culture without having to rely heavily on exposition. As Kerrick learns, so do we. And quite an education it happens to be, as readers end up truly knowing a completely alien culture, without any sacrifice in good storytelling whatsoever. Harrison is rather erratic in the quality of his various works—some are horrible, many are craftsman-like, a handful are quite good—but he undoubtedly triumphed with this one.

✳✳✳✳✳✳

CHAPTER SIX
Miscellaneous

TOP 10 INCREDIBLE SELF-SURGERIES

10 DR. JERRI NIELSEN, BORN 1952
Surgical Procedure: Biopsy

Dr. Jerri Lin Nielsen is a physician with extensive ER experience. In 1998 she was hired to spend a year at the Amundsen-Scott South Pole Station where she would be the only doctor during the winter. In early March 1999, she discovered a lump in her right breast. After consulting U.S. physicians via e-mail and video conference, she performed a biopsy upon herself. The results were inconclusive because the material used on site was too outdated to allow for a precise diagnosis. It was then decided to send a military plane to airdrop supplies and medication for her treatment. Using the new supplies, she performed another biopsy, which allowed for better scans to be sent to the U.S., where it was confirmed the cells were cancerous. With the help of her makeshift medical team, Nielsen then began self-administering chemotherapy. In October a military transport aircraft was sent several weeks ahead of schedule to bring her back home. Once back in the United States, after multiple surgeries, complications, and a mastectomy, Nielsen went into remission.

Interesting Fact: Nielsen became a motivational speaker and wrote a book about her experience. The book, *Ice Bound*, was later adapted into a made-for-TV movie starring Susan Sarandon.

9 AMANDA FEILDING, BORN 1943
Surgical Procedure: Trepanation

Amanda Feilding is a British artist and scientific director. Feilding suffered from a condition that left her feeling exhausted and spent years looking for a reputable surgeon who would perform a technique known as trepanning. This is a procedure where a tiny portion of the skull is drilled into to allow blood to flow more easily around the brain. Eventually she gave up and at age twenty-seven she decided to do the surgery herself. Equipped with a dentist's electric drill operated by a foot pedal, she taped dark glasses to her face to stop the blood running into her eyes. She first made an incision with a scalpel and then drilled, dipping the drill bit in water every so often to cool it down. She lost almost a liter of blood but she was pleased with her surgery. Over the next four hours she noticed herself rising up with a feeling of elation and relaxation. Feilding says, "I went out and had steak for supper, and then I went to a party."

Interesting Fact: Feilding made a short cult art film entitled *Heartbeat in the Brain*, which is shown only to invited audiences. She also ran for British Parliament twice, on the platform "Trepanation for the National Health," with the intention of drawing attention to the fact that its potential benefits should be scientifically investigated.

8 DEBORAH SAMPSON, 1760–1827

Surgical Procedure: Extraction of Musket Ball

Deborah Sampson is actually mentioned in the "Top 10 Men Who Were Really Women" list as a notable omission. In 1782 Deborah Sampson was enlisted in the Fourth Massachusetts Regiment of the Continental Army. Going by the name of Robert Shutleff, she was strong and tall enough to look like a man and it was thought she didn't have to shave because she was a very young man. When her unit was sent to West Point, New York, she was wounded in a battle nearby. She was taken to a hospital to be treated but snuck out so that she would not be discovered to be a woman. She operated on herself and removed one of the musket balls out of her thigh with a penknife and sewing needle. When she recovered from her wound, she went back to her regiment. The next time Sampson was wounded her doctor found out she was a woman and in 1783 he arranged for her to be discharged from the Continental Army.

Interesting Fact: Due to her wounds, Sampson received a military pension. Later, in 1838, Congress passed a special act granting a pension to her heirs.

7 DR. EVAN O'NEILL KANE, 1862–1933

Surgical Procedure: Appendectomy and Inguinal Hernia Repair

Dr. Evan O'Neill Kane was a pioneer in the medical profession and chief surgeon of New York City's Kane Summit Hospital. Kane wanted to prove to the world that general anesthesia was often unnecessary for minor operations. He used himself for a test case and operated on himself removing his own appendix using only local anesthetic. Dr. Kane propped himself up on the operating table with a mirror over his abdomen and three other doctors in the operating room as backup. Kane made the large incision needed to remove the appendix and his assistants sutured him up. (This was before new techniques allowed doctors to make small "Band-Aid"–size incisions for appendix removal.) Then, in 1932, at the age of seventy, Dr. Kane performed an even more complicated surgery on himself to repair an inguinal hernia. Because of the close proximity to the femoral artery, it was a particularly delicate operation, which Kane performed in just under two hours.

6 JOANNES LETHAEUS, BORN CIRCA 1620

Surgical Procedure: Lithotomy (Removal of stones formed inside certain hollow organs such as the bladder and kidneys)

I found this particularly interesting because this self-surgery occurred over 360 years ago. Dr. Nicolaes Tulp was a Dutch surgeon and mayor of Amsterdam. Below is the exact text from his book *Observationes Medicae.* In this case he describes Joannes Lethaeus, a blacksmith who performed lithotomy surgery on himself.

> *"Having decided that no one but himself would cut into his flesh, he sent his wife to the fish market, which she didn't mind doing. Only letting his brother help him, he instructed him to pull aside his scrotum while he grabbed the stone in his left hand and cut bravely in the perineum with a knife he had secretly prepared, and by standing again and again managed to make the wound long enough to allow the stone to pass. To get the stone out was more difficult, and he had to stick two fingers into the wound on either side to remove it with leveraged force, and it finally popped out of hiding with an explosive noise and tearing of the bladder. Now the more courageous than careful operation was completed, and the enemy that had declared war on him was safely on the ground, he sent for a healer who sewed up the two sides of the wound together, and the opening that he had cut himself, and properly bound it up; the flesh of which grew so happily that there no small hope of health was, but the wound was too big, and the bladder too torn, not to have ulcers forming. But this stone weighing 4 ounces and the size of a hen's egg was a wonder how it came out with the help of one hand, without the proper tools, and then from the patient himself, whose greatest help was courage and impatience embedded in a truly impenetrable faith which caused a brave deed as none other."*

Interesting Fact: There is an oil painting by Rembrandt called *The Anatomy Lesson of Dr. Nicolaes Tulp,* showing Dr. Nicolaes Tulp (who wrote the above text) explaining the musculature of the arm to medical professionals, and is housed in the Mauritshuis Museum in The Hague, the Netherlands.

5 SAMPSON PARKER, BORN CIRCA 1960
Surgical Procedure: Amputation of Right Arm

In September 2007, Parker, a farmer from South Carolina, was harvesting corn when some stalks got stuck in a set of rollers that shuck the cut corn. He reached in the still-running machine to pull the stalks out and the rollers grabbed first his glove and then his hand. Parker tried yelling for help, but there was no one near the isolated field in Kershaw County. For more than an hour, he tried to pull his hand free, only to have it pulled ever further into the machinery. He was able to reach an iron bar and jam it into a chain-and-sprocket that drove the rollers, and, with his fingers growing numb he pulled out a small pocketknife and started to cut his own fingers off to free himself. Before he could do that, the sprocket grinding against the rod he'd jammed in threw off sparks and set the ground litter on fire. Parker then knew he had to cut his arm off or die right there. Parker credits the fire with keeping him from passing out from the shock of cutting through his arm. When he got down to the bone, he dropped onto the ground, using the force of his own weight to break the bone and free him from the machine. When he was finally loose he got in his pickup truck and started driving into the middle of the road to force a car to stop. Finally a motorist stopped and a rescue helicopter was called in to take him to a hospital. Parker spent three weeks in a burn center before going home.

Interesting Fact: While he was recuperating, about twenty-five of his neighbors got together to finish harvesting his corn.

4 DR. LEONID ROGOZOV, BORN 1937
Surgical Procedure: Appendectomy

At the age of twenty-seven, Soviet doctor Leonid Rogozov was stationed at the Novolazarevskaya base in the Antarctic. The doctor recognized his own acute appendicitis and worsening condition. Because of the absence of a support aircraft and inclement weather along with the danger of a burst appendix, the doctor decided he would have to perform surgery on himself. With the team's meteorologist holding the retractors, a driver to hold the mirror, and other scientists passing surgical implements, he sat in a reclined position and cut out his own appendix under local anesthetic. During the operation he passed out, but was able to continue and complete the procedure in little less than two hours.

Interesting Fact: Dr. Rogozov wrote a detailed report documenting the unusual event. The doctor made a full recovery and resumed all duties in two weeks.

3 DOUGLAS GOODALE, BORN 1965
Surgical Procedure: Amputation of Right Arm

In 1998, Douglas Goodale, a thirty-five-year-old lobster fisherman from Maine, was hauling lobster pots up from the sea floor. When he reached his first trap and started pulling up his catch, a huge wave hit the boat creating a slack in the rope, which then spooled around the drum. As he reached to turn off the drums motor and untangle the rope, his sleeve got caught in the winch. Within seconds the winch had taken hold of his hand and his arm. Alone and unable to free himself and his body hanging outside the boat, the fisherman's survival instincts took over and used his good arm to pull his body back into the boat. Because of the way his right arm was twisted he had to dislocate the shoulder joint of his injured arm in the process. The only way for Goodale to free himself was to cut off his own arm. Thinking about his wife and two daughters, Goodale grabbed his twine knife and began to saw off his right arm. The cold ocean water and the twisting had cinched up the wounds and helped to reduce blood loss. Goodale then managed to pilot his boat back into the harbor to get medical help.

Interesting Fact: Having only one arm has not kept Goodale from two seasons of lobstering and from completely overhauling his thirty-five-foot wooden boat down to the bare planks. Goodale was also featured in the television show *Extreme Makeover: Home Edition* where a thousand volunteers replaced Goodale's double-wide mobile home with a $500,000 log home.

2 ARON RALSTON, BORN 1975
Surgical Procedure: Amputation of Right Arm

Aron Ralston's experience made international news, so many will be familiar with his story. Ralston is a mountain climber and a mechanical engineer. He left his career in engineering to climb all of Colorado's "fourteeners," or peaks over fourteen thousand feet high. In 2002, while on a canyoneering trip alone in Blue John Canyon, a boulder fell and pinned his right forearm. After five days of unsuccessfully trying to lift or break the boulder, a dehydrated and delirious Ralston prepared to cut off his already dead arm. Using a dull blade, he cut the soft tissue around the break and then used the tool's pliers to tear at the tougher tendons. Finally freed, Ralston was still eight miles from his truck, he had to rappel down a sixty-five-foot cliff, then hike out of the canyon. Eventually he met with other hikers and was given food and water. Ralston was finally transported to St. Mary's Hospital in Grand Junction, Colorado, for surgery.

Interesting Fact: Later Ralston's arm was retrieved by park authorities and removed from under the boulder. It was cremated and given to Ralston. He later returned to the boulder and left the ashes there. Aron Ralston still enjoys mountain climbing with the aid of a prosthetic arm.

1 INES RAMÍREZ, BORN 1960

Surgical Procedure: Caesarean Section

Ines Ramírez lives in rural Rio Talea, Mexico, which has five hundred people and only one phone. In March 2000, the forty-year-old mother of seven was alone in her cabin when her labor started. She assumed her birthing position by sitting up and leaning forward. At midnight, after twelve hours of continual pain and little advancement in labor, rather than experience another fetal death as had occurred with her last pregnancy, Ramírez decided to operate on herself. She drank from either a bottle of rubbing alcohol or three small glasses of hard liquor (different accounts vary). She then grabbed a six-inch knife and began to cut. Ramírez sawed through skin, fat, and muscle and, after operating on herself for an hour, she reached inside her uterus and pulled out her baby boy, who breathed and cried immediately. She says she cut his umbilical cord with a pair of scissors and then passed out. When she regained consciousness she wrapped clothes around her bleeding abdomen and asked her six-year-old son to run for help. Several hours later the village health assistant found Ramírez alert and lying beside her healthy baby. She was then taken to the nearest hospital eight hours away by car and underwent surgery to repair complications resulting from damage to her intestines incurred during her C-section. She was then released from the hospital and ended up making a complete recovery.

Interesting Fact: Ramírez is believed to be the only woman known to have performed a successful caesarean section on herself. Her case was written up in the March 2004 issue of the *International Journal of Obstetrics and Gynecology*.

※※※※※※

TOP 10 HISTORICAL MONSTERS

10 ONI, JAPANESE

The oni is a monster from Japanese tradition. It is normally depicted as a giant creature with sharp claws and horns, much like the Judeo-Christian devil. Onis are generally colored red or blue and often have extra fingers, toes, and eyes. They almost always appear carrying an iron club.

9 OGRE, FRENCH

The ogre is a gigantic man-like monster, often portrayed as a man-eater. Ogres have a long history in literature in which they are usually described as being bearded men with fat bellies and superhuman strength.

8 VAMPIRE, SLAVIC

Vampires have been known to the Western world since the eighteenth century when they were derived from folk tales from Eastern Europe. In the early tales of vampires, they were depicted as bloated, dark-skinned beings without fangs, a stark contrast to the modern idea of pale, blood-starved, fanged creatures.

7 MUMMY, EGYPTIAN

The idea of a mummy being a monster most likely comes from curses associated with the ancient Egyptian dead. Furthermore, the Egyptians believed that the dead continued to live after burial, which may also be a contributing factor. Mummies are popular monsters in modern days and they appear frequently in films, both horror and comedy.

6 WEREWOLF, GERMANIC

Werewolves are either depicted as human-turned-wolf or humans with wolf-like qualities. The concept of a werewolf dates back as far as the ancient Greeks (appearing in the writing of Petronius, for example). There is speculation that the werewolf mythology may have come from a case of mistaken identity where people suffering from the disease porphyria may have been confused for monsters due to their shunning of light and living away from other humans.

5 GOBLIN, ANGLO-SAXON

Goblins are usually depicted as evil or naughty creatures with disfigured bodies. They can range in height from dwarflike to full human height. Different countries have their own version of the goblin and descriptions vary greatly from place to place.

4 GHOUL, MIDDLE EASTERN

Ghouls are from ancient Arabian folklore. They are usually found in graveyards and other places devoid of living humans. They belong to the family of Jinn—evil spirits believed to be the offspring of Satan. They can change form and this ability is often used to lure humans into their lairs where they eat them. They are also depicted as robbing graves to eat the dead.

3 BANSHEE, CELTIC

Banshees are usually ghostly women who can be heard wailing when someone is going to die. They are usually described as dressed in white or gray with long silver hair. When a large number of banshees are seen or heard, it is believed that someone great or holy is going to die.

2 GORGON, GREEK

The gorgon is a female monster with snakes for hair. They are sometimes shown with gold wings and claws. When a human looks at the face of a gorgon, they are turned to stone. Medusa is probably the most famous of the gorgons and she was regarded in Greek mythology as the Queen of Gorgons.

1 ZOMBIE, LATIN AMERICAN

Zombies in modern folklore are humans who have been restored to life after death. In entertainment they are a supernatural "undead," but they are also sometimes depicted in literature as having been brought back to life through scientific means. Zombies have become extremely popular characters in modern horror movies.

�֎✖✖✖✖✖

TOP 10 ACCIDENTAL DISCOVERIES

10 VIAGRA

Millions of men around the world owe a salute to the hard-working stiffs in the Welsh village of Merthyr Tydfil where, in 1992, testing of this new angina drug produced firm evidence of its unexpected sex-enhancing power. This discovery would be much higher on the list if it weren't for the fact that it is the cause of 90 percent of the spam I receive every day!

9 CHOCOLATE CHIP COOKIES

According to Nestle, Mrs. Wakefield (owner of the Toll House Inn) was making chocolate cookies but ran out of regular baker's chocolate, so she substituted it with broken pieces of semi-sweet chocolate, thinking it would melt and mix into the batter. It clearly did not, and the chocolate chip cookie was born. Wakefield sold the recipe to Nestle in exchange for a lifetime supply of chocolate chips (instead of patenting it and making billions!). Every bag of Nestle chocolate chips in North America has a variation of her original recipe printed on the back (margarine is now included both as a variant on butter and for those people who want to pretend it is healthy).

8 POPSICLES

The Popsicle was invented by an eleven-year-old, who then kept it secret for eighteen years. The inventor was Frank Epperson who, in 1905, left a mixture of powdered soda and water with a stir stick in it out on the porch. That night, temperatures in San Francisco, where he lived, reached a record low. When he woke the next morning, he discovered that it had frozen to the stir stick, creating a fruit-flavored ice treat that he humbly named the Epsicle. Eighteen years later, he patented it and called it the Popsicle.

7 ARTIFICIAL SWEETENER

Like many artificial sweeteners, the sweetness of cyclamate was discovered by accident. Michael Sveda was working in the lab on the synthesis of anti-fever medication. He put his cigarette down on the lab bench and when he put it back in his mouth he discovered the sweet taste of cyclamate. Cancer-inducing aspartame was discovered in 1965 by James M. Schlatter, a chemist working for G. D. Searle & Company. Schlatter had synthesized aspartame in the course of producing an anti-ulcer drug candidate. He discovered its sweet taste serendipitously when he licked his finger, which had accidentally become contaminated with aspartame. Saccharin (the oldest artificial sweetener) was first produced in 1878 by Constantin Fahlberg, a chemist working on coal tar derivatives in Ira Remsen's laboratory at the Johns Hopkins University, and it was he who, accidentally, discovered its intensely sweet nature.

6 BRANDY

Initially wine was distilled as a preservation method and as a way to make it easier for merchants to transport. It was also thought that wine was originally distilled to lessen the tax that was assessed by volume. The intent was to add the water removed by distillation back to the brandy shortly before consumption. It was discovered that after having been stored in wooden casks, the resulting product had improved over the original distilled spirit. No one is sure who it was that discovered the delightful taste of this distilled liquor, but he was clearly guided in its discovery by God for the betterment of man.

5 TEFLON

Teflon was invented accidentally by Roy Plunkett of Kinetic Chemicals in 1938. Plunkett was attempting to make a new CFC refrigerant, the perfluorethylene polymerized (say that three times fast!) in a pressurized storage container. In this original chemical reaction, iron from the inside of the container acted as a catalyst. In 1954, French engineer Marc Grégoire created the first pan coated with Teflon nonstick resin under the brand name of Tefal after his wife urged him to try the material that he'd been using on fishing tackle on her cooking pans. Teflon is inert to virtually all chemicals and is considered the most slippery material in existence—second only to the political wrangling of ex-President George Bush.

4 MICROWAVE

Percy LeBaron Spencer of the Raytheon Company was walking past a radar tube and noticed that the chocolate bar in his pocket melted. Realizing that he might be on to a hot new product, he placed a small bowl of popcorn in front of the tube and it quickly popped all over the room. Tens of millions of lazy cooks now have him to thank for their dull food!

3 POTATO CHIPS

The first potato chip was invented by George Crum (half American Indian, half African American) at Moon's Lake House near Saratoga Springs, New York, on August 24, 1853. He was fed up with the constant complaints of a customer who kept sending his potatoes back to the kitchen because they were too thick and soggy. Crum decided to slice the potatoes so thin that they couldn't be eaten with a fork. Against Crum's expectation, the customer was ecstatic about the new chips. They became a regular item on the lodge's menu under the name "Saratoga Chips" and a large contributing factor of the Western world's obesity problems.

2 LSD

LSD was first created by Albert Hofmann in 1938 as part of a study into the usefulness of ergot in medicine. Five years after the first discovery, Hofmann became dizzy and had to stop work. He went home and experienced what is now known to be the first LSD trip. In his own words, Hofmann experienced an "intoxicated-like condition" along with an overactive imagination. He described seeing "fantastic pictures, extraordinary shapes with intense, kaleidoscopic play of colors." After two hours he returned to normal and the rest is history.

1 PENICILLIN

In 1928, Scottish scientist Sir Alexander Fleming was studying Staphylococcus, the bacteria that causes food poisoning. He turned up at work one day and discovered a blue-green mold that seemed to be inhibiting growth of the bacteria. He grew a pure culture of the mold and discovered that it was a Penicillium mold. After further experiments, Fleming was convinced that penicillin could not last long enough in the human body to kill pathogenic bacteria, and stopped studying it after 1931, but restarted some clinical trials in 1934 and continued to try to get someone to purify it until 1940. The development of penicillin for use as a medicine is attributed to the Australian Nobel Laureate Howard Walter Florey; he shared the Nobel Prize with Fleming and Ernst Boris Chain.

✳✳✳✳✳✳

TOP 10 THINGS THAT ARE SURPRISINGLY GOOD FOR YOU

10 ICE CREAM

Ice cream is a low GI (glycemic-index) food. This means that it is a slow sugar release food that keeps you satisfied for a longer period of time than a high GI food. For that reason, you are less likely to binge after eating ice cream. Seventy-five grams of Ben and Jerry's Cookies and Cream ice cream contains only 114 calories, while a slice of cheesecake has 511 calories. Furthermore, ice cream is made of milk, which contains many essential nutrients and vitamins. One cup of milk contains up to 30 percent of a person's daily recommended intake. Other nutrients in ice cream are biotin, iodine, potassium, selenium, and vitamins A, B12, D, and K. Studies show a possible link between milk consumption and a lowered risk of arterial hypertension, coronary heart disease, and colorectal cancer.

Interesting Fact: In the fifth century BC, the ancient Greeks sold snow cones made with fruit and honey in the markets of Athens.

9 DIRT

Throw away the rubber globes! Dirt is back in vogue! Remember the days when kids played in dirt, food was served with bare hands, and straws didn't come in individual wrappers? It turns out that they were healthier days than our modern sterile ones! Early childhood exposure to bacteria, viruses, and parasites has been found to give a massive boost to our immune systems, making us less likely to get sick when we do come in contact with various bugs. Research has found that children with a dog in the home are less likely to suffer allergies, and regular social interaction can reduce the risk of leukemia by up to 30 percent. Those are statistics not to ignore—so throw away the antibacterial cleaners and get dirty!

Interesting Fact: There are as many as ten times more bacterial cells in the human body than human cells! The vast majority of these are harmless.

8 STRESS

Stress is universally considered a bad thing, in some cases people have successfully won lawsuits against companies for work-related stress. But, what most people don't know is that a little stress goes a long way to making us healthier. In short doses, stress can help boost the body's immune system. In the first stage of stress (the "alarm" stage, often known as the "fight or flight" response), the body produces cortisol—a stress-fighting hormone which has many benefits to the body. Stress can give a feeling of fulfillment; when this is the case it is called "eustress" as opposed to "distress."

Interesting Fact: The term "stress" and the mental properties of it were not known before the 1950s. Until that time it referred simply to hardship or coercion.

7 CAFFEINE

Not only is coffee tasty, it is a mild stimulant with many medical uses. Caffeine contains a muscle relaxant that is very beneficial to people with bronchial problems; it can alleviate the symptoms of asthma. Additionally, caffeine releases
certain fatty acids into the bloodstream that become a useful source of fuel for muscles. It even seems that the only serious side effect to too much caffeine is a small amount of body-weight loss—a danger if you are anorexic. Caffeine should be avoided by people with fecal incontinence as it loosens the anal and sphincter muscles.

Interesting Fact: Caffeine can be toxic to animals, in particular dogs, horses, and parrots. It also has a much more significant effect on spiders than humans.

6 RED WINE

Red wine contains a group of chemicals called polyphenols (once called Vitamin P), which have been found to be very beneficial for health. They reduce the risk of heart disease and cancer. Wine has also been found to be an effective antibacterial agent against strains of Streptococcus (found most often in the human mouth), by helping to reduce infections. Some wine varieties have extra health benefits; Cabernet Sauvignon appears to reduce the risk of Alzheimer's disease. In addition to the benefits already listed, wine is chock-full of antioxidants, which play a huge role in the health of the human body. The wines found to have the greatest benefits are found in the South of France and the Sardinia region of Italy.

Interesting Fact: Wine originated in the regions of Israel, Georgia, and Iran around 6000 BC.

5 CHOCOLATE

As a result of recent research into chocolate and health, it appears to be something of a panacea (cure-all), and coupled with the great taste and mood-enhancing properties, it might be seen as a wonder drug! Cocoa, or dark chocolate, improves the overall health of the circulatory system, stimulates the brain, prevents coughs and diarrhea, and may even be an anti-cancer agent. Like coffee, chocolate is toxic to many animals. A BBC study indicates that melting chocolate in your mouth increases brain activity and the heart rate more intensely than passionate kissing, with the effect lasting four times longer after the activity ends. Eating regular small quantities of chocolate reduces cholesterol and the chances of a heart attack. Sign me up for some of that medication!

Interesting Fact: Chocolate has been used as a drink since at least 1100–1400 BC.

4 CANNABIS

Cannabis is said to be beneficial for over 250 conditions. For this reason it is legal by prescription in a number of Western countries. Cannabis is believed to help with arthritis, asthma, depression, glaucoma, and pain. It is also reported to be a good treatment for constipation. Cannabis is also useful in dealing with the side effects of treatments for cancer, AIDS, and hepatitis. Cannabis has been used medicinally for over three thousand years! Strangely, the cultivation and use of cannabis is outlawed in most countries.

Interesting Fact: Evidence of the use of cannabis as a non-medicinal drug exists as charred seeds found in Romania dating back to the third millennium BC.

3 BEER

The moderate consumption of beer has been associated with the lowered risk of heart disease, stroke, and mental decline. In addition, brewers yeast (used in the production of beer) contains many nutrients that are carried through to the final drink: magnesium, selenium, potassium, phosphorus, biotin, and B vitamins. For this reason, beer is sometimes referred to as "liquid bread." In 2005, a Japanese study found that low-alcohol beer may contain strong anti-cancer properties. Contrary to popular belief, a "beer belly" or "beer gut" is not produced by the beer, but rather overeating and lack of exercise.

Interesting Fact: Beer is one of the oldest beverages, dating back to the sixth millennium BC.

2 SMOKING

Often referred to as "smoker's paradoxes," there are a number of therapeutic uses of nicotine or smoking. For example, smokers are less likely to need surgery to provide extra blood to their heart after an angioplasty, the risk of ulcerative colitis is reduced, and it even interferes with the development of Kaposi's sarcoma (a type of cancer of the lymphatic endothelium). Perhaps most surprising are the connections to smoking and a reduction in allergic asthma. There is also a large body of evidence to suggest that smokers have a dramatically reduced risk of developing Alzheimer's disease and Parkinson's disease. Nicotine is currently being investigated as a treatment for ADHD, and schizophrenia.

Interesting Fact: Tobacco smoking has been a practice of humans since at least 5000 BC.

1 PORNOGRAPHY

Amid the loud angry cries against pornography, a few serious scientific studies have been performed on the subject. It seems that men and women who view pornography have improved sex lives, better sexual knowledge, and an overall better quality of life. Surprisingly, one study found the more that pornography is viewed, the greater the improvements. In an extensive study performed in Australia, the majority of married respondents stated that they believed that pornography has had a positive effect on their marriage. While clearly not always linked to pornography, studies have found that men who had fewer orgasms were twice as likely to die of any cause as those having two or more orgasms a week.

Interesting Fact: Pornography (and the anti-pornography movement) as it is understood today is a concept of the Victorian era (nineteenth century) that was extremely moralistic. Sexual imagery was not taboo before that time.

✳✳✳✳✳✳

TOP 10 WORST PRODUCTS EVER

10 DISPOSABLE EATING IMPLEMENTS

It is becoming more and more common these days for people to use throwaway cups, plates, and cutlery instead of glass, china, and metal. Not only is this a ridiculous waste of money (for the sake of saving a few minutes of dish-washing time), it places a burden on our natural environment. I am not an environmentalist, but even I can't see any benefit to using disposable eating equipment. There is no reason that children shouldn't use glass like everyone else; they did in the old days and it didn't kill them. Do yourself a favor, save some money and buy a real dinner set.

9 DISPOSABLE RAZORS

The razor companies have it made—they have a virtual monopoly on the shaving market and people have become so reliant on them that they no longer know how to shave without a throwaway razor. These razors use cheap blades, which go blunt quickly and can't be reused. Prior to these razors becoming so popular, men would use a straight razor, which could be sharpened as needed on a razor strop. The initial price of the razor and strop needed to be paid once in most men's lifetimes. You can still buy straight razors (or, as they are affectionately known, cutthroat razors) and it is well worth the investment.

8 DIET PRODUCTS

There are two main types of diet products: the first are strong medications that can be very dangerous, and the others are powders, herbal pills, and drinks. At the worst end of the scale we have drinks that solidify in the stomach so you feel full without eating (anorexia anyone?), and at the safer end of the scale are protein drinks used as meal substitutes. The fact is that all of these products are bad because they perpetuate the myth that you need to "diet" to lose weight. The only diet that truly works is moderation—eat less. It saves you money and makes you feel better.

7 COUGH MIXTURES

When you get a cold or flu, there is virtually nothing you can do except keep warm and eat well. Cough medicines are marketed to people who are suffering and want respite, but it doesn't come in a bottle. Instead of buying incredibly expensive mixtures (which do little or nothing to help), mix together a little beaten egg white, honey, and vinegar and take it by the spoonful—it is cheap and just as effective at clearing phlegm. If you have flu ache, take Tylenol (or paracetamol) and lie down for the afternoon. The flu will run its course naturally and you won't be out of pocket.

6 SELF-HELP BOOKS

Self-help books don't help. They are merely marketing gimmicks to get people to part with their hard-earned money. When was the last time you met a person who had become a property tycoon after reading *Rich Dad Poor Dad*? When was the last time you saw someone beat depression after reading a self-help book? This huge market now has books for virtually everything you could need, and ultimately the only person being helped is the author who is slowly getting rich. If you really feel that you need advice on life, try searching the Internet for examples from real people who really found a way out of their problems.

5 SLEEPING PILLS FOR CHILDREN

Takeda Pharmaceuticals is a company that produces sleeping tablets for prepubescent and pubescent children. They used loopholes in the U.S. marketing laws to advertise their products without mentioning the fact that they had not been fully tested on children and without listing any of the potential side effects. While that is bad enough, it is even worse that there are people who would consider buying these for their children. In most cases, a child who is not sleeping well can have their insomnia cured by more vigorous activity during the day. You don't get side effects from turning off the television and computer.

4 MICROWAVE OVENS

Microwaves have played a large part in the removal of decent cooking from so many of our homes and have helped the chemical-laden "ready meal" market to blossom. In some supermarkets it is nearly impossible to find raw ingredients for cooking as the precooked, premade meals now take up so much room. In most cases, there is nothing you can do in a microwave that can't be done better on a regular stove and oven, and in many cases it can take as little time! Furthermore, oven cooking won't give you food that is soggy, limp, and colorless—a microwave will. Every time, guaranteed.

3 AB MACHINES

Infomercials have been pumping out a variety of ab-building machines for the last ten years. The fact is, these machines are used once or twice and then end up in the garage or a cupboard never to be used again. The machines do nothing that the human body can't already do, and if you are earnest about building up good abs, you would be far better off doing regular sit-ups and getting a gym membership. It will probably cost the same price and won't clutter up your home!

2 SUGARED CEREALS

It was a true genius that came up with the idea of taking something healthy and coating it with loads of sugar to appeal to children. Unfortunately, this concept has now become so popular that many children will refuse to eat any cereal that is not sugary. All around the world governments are whining about fat children and trying to find a solution by banning all manner of things and trying to promote healthy living, but no one seems to be concerned about the fact that the majority of children start their day with a huge sugar rush followed by a crash and carbohydrate cravings.

1 BOTTLED WATER

Bottled water is an utter waste of money and resources. To illustrate just how ridiculous a concept it is, I will demonstrate with Dasani Bottled Water. This product was created by Coca-Cola and was marketed as superior bottled water. First of all, bottled water is a ridiculous concept in the Western world where we all have easy access to tap water, which is drinkable in most areas. Coca-Cola wanted to be part of the ridiculous fad so they entered the bottled water market, but they simply filled their bottles with tap water! When the product was released in the UK it was a disaster. They used the slogan "bottled spunk" which may seem innocuous to the Americans who came up with the idea, but, unfortunately, in the UK "spunk" is a slang word for sperm. Just when you think it couldn't get any worse, scientific testing of the bottled water showed traces of bromate—a carcinogen. Coca-Cola had to withdraw half a million bottles of the water and they pulled the product from the UK market.

✳✳✳✳✳✳

TOP 10 AMERICAN ICONS THAT ARE NOT AMERICAN

10 **FIRESTONE, JAPAN**
The Firestone Tire and Rubber Company was created in 1900 to provide tires for wagons and buggies. As the automobile became popular, the company began to make tires for this new mode of transport. In 1988, Bridgestone bought the company out. Bridgestone is now ranked as the number-one company in the global tire market. The company is based in Tokyo and was founded in 1931.

9 **DIAL SOAP, GERMANY**
In 2004, Henkel (a German consumer products company) bought out the Dial Corporation, at the time the U.S. leading manufacturer of household cleaning products. Henkel also owns Sellotape and Persil.

8 **SHELL, NETHERLANDS**
Shell Oil is owned by the Royal Dutch Shell Company—one of the largest oil companies in the world. The U.S. branch of the company employs twenty-two thousand people. The company is a 50/50 partnership with Saudi Aramco, a Saudi Arabian government-owned business. The Royal Dutch Shell Company originated in Holland and Britain.

7 **CHURCH'S CHICKEN, BAHRAIN**
Church's Chicken is a chain of fast-food fried chicken restaurants. It was founded in 1952 in San Antonio and has sixteen hundred locations around the world. In 2004 the company was bought out by Arcapita, an Islamic venture capital firm. Because the company is strictly Islamic, all pork products were removed from the menu. Arcapita also owns Caribou Coffee.

6 TOLL HOUSE COOKIES, SWITZERLAND

Toll House Cookies were created in the 1930s by Ruth Graves Wakefield. Because they were so popular, Nestle approached her for the recipe, which she handed over in exchange for a lifetime supply of chocolate. Nestle is a Swiss company and they now own the rights to the recipe and cookies made with it.

5 HOLIDAY INN, UNITED KINGDOM

Holiday Inn was founded in Memphis in 1952 by Kemmons Wilson, who wanted to provide cheap accommodation to families traveling within the U.S. Holiday Inn is now owned by a British company, InterContinental Hotels Group, which is a conglomeration of various hotel brands.

4 THE CHRYSLER BUILDING, UNITED ARAB EMIRATES

The iconic Chrysler Building in New York City is owned by the Abu Dhabi Investment Council, which manages the oil reserves of the United Arab Emirates (worth one trillion dollars). The building appears frequently in movies and literature as it clearly sets the scene in New York. The Abu Dhabi Investment company paid over eight hundred million dollars for its share of the building.

3 TRADER JOE'S, GERMANY

Trader Joe's was created in 1958 by Joe Coloumbe to sell exotic foods, filling a gap in the supermarket industry at the time. The original California store is still open today. The chain was sold to the family trust of Theo Albrecht, a German billionaire who owns the German supermarket chain Aldi.

2 7-ELEVEN, JAPAN

7-Eleven is the largest chain store in the world. It is located in eighteen countries. The company is now owned by Seven and I Holdings Co. (the fifth largest retailer in the world), which also owns Denny's and White Hen Pantry.

1 BUDWEISER, BELGIUM

Budweiser (or "Bud") is one of the most popular beers in the U.S. It is made with a mixture of barley and rice and is produced all across the States. In 2008, Belgian company InBev bought the majority of the company's stock, making it the world's largest beer manufacturing company.

✳✳✳✳✳✳

TOP 10 INCREDIBLE REAL LIFE CASTAWAY STORIES

10 JOHN F. KENNEDY AND CREW, 1917–1963
Survived: Six days on Plum Pudding and Olasana Islands.

In 1943, John F. Kennedy was the twenty-six-year-old skipper of PT-109. As the PT-109 was prowling the waters late at night, a Japanese destroyer suddenly emerged and cut Kennedy's craft in half in an instant. Two of his twelve-member crew were killed instantly and two others badly injured. The survivors clung to the drifting bow for hours. At daybreak, they embarked on a three-and-a-half-mile swim to the tiny deserted Plum Pudding Island. They placed their lantern and non-swimmers on one of the timbers used as a gun mount, and began kicking together to propel it. Braving the danger of sharks and crocodiles they reached their destination in five hours. After two days on the small island without food and water, Kennedy realized they needed to swim to a larger island, Olasana, if they were to survive. Kennedy and his men were found and rescued by scouts after surviving six days on coconuts.

Interesting Fact: The island where Kennedy's crew washed ashore has become a minor attraction and has been renamed Kennedy Island.

9 LEENDERT HASENBOSCH, CIRCA 1695–1725
Survived: About six months on the Ascension Islands.

Leendert Hasenbosch was a Dutch soldier who went aboard a VOC-ship as the bookkeeper. After the ship made a stop at Cape Town in 1725, he was sentenced for sodomy and set ashore on Ascension Island. He was given a tent and the amount of water for about a month, some seeds, a Bible, clothing, and writing materials. Hasenbosch survived by eating sea turtles and seabirds, as well as drinking his own urine. It is believed he probably died in a terrible condition after about six months.

Interesting Fact: Leendert Hasenbosch wrote a diary that was found by British mariners in 1726, and brought back to Britain. The diary was rewritten and published a number of times.

8 MARGUERITE DE LA ROCQUE, CIRCA 1523–?

Survived: Two years on Isle of Demons.

In 1542 French explorer Jacques Cartier led a voyage to Newfoundland accompanied by nineteen-year-old Marguerite de La Rocque. During the journey, Marguerite became the lover of a young man. Displeased with her actions, Marguerite's uncle, Lieutenant General and pirate Jean-François Roberval, marooned her on the "Isle of Demons" (now called Harrington Island) near the Saint Paul River. Also marooned were Marguerite's lover and her maidservant. Marguerite gave birth to a child while on the island but the baby died (probably due to insufficient milk), as did the young man and the maidservant. Marguerite survived by hunting wild animals and lived in a cave for two years until she was rescued by Basque fishermen.

Interesting Fact: Returning to France after her rescue, Marguerite achieved some celebrity when her story was recorded by the Queen of Navarre in 1558.

7 CAPTAIN CHARLES BARNARD AND PARTY, 1781–1840

Survived: Eighteen months on Eagle Island (part of the Falkland Islands).

In 1812, the British ship *Isabella* was shipwrecked off Eagle Island. Most of the crew were rescued by the American sealer *Nanina*, commanded by Captain Charles Barnard. However, realizing that they would require more provisions for the extra passengers, Barnard and four others went out to retrieve more food. During their absence the *Nanina* was taken over by the British crew. Barnard and his men were left on Eagle Island, by the very men they had saved. Barnard and his party were finally rescued in November 1814.

Interesting Fact: The evening of the rescue, Barnard dined with the *Isabella* survivors and finding that the British party was unaware of the War of 1812 informed the survivors that technically they were at war with each other. (Maybe he shouldn't have mentioned that.) Barnard later wrote a narrative, *Marooned*, detailing his experience.

6 ADA BLACKJACK, 1898–1983

Survived: Two years on Wrangel Island.

In the fall of 1921 a team of five people were left on Wrangel Island, north of Siberia. Arctic explorer Vilhjalmur Stefansson planned the expedition with the intention of claiming the island for Canada or Britain. A twenty-three-year-old Eskimo woman, Ada Blackjack, was hired as a cook and seamstress and was paid fifty dollars a month. Ada needed the money for her son who was suffering from tuberculosis. The plan was to stay one year on the island and bring six months' worth of supplies. This would be enough to sustain them for a year while they lived off the land itself. The men were unable find enough food and began to starve, so in January 1923, three of the men made a desperate attempt to seek help. Ada was left to care for the fourth man who was sick with scurvy. The three men were never heard from again and the man she was caring for eventually died. Ada, somehow, learned how to survive until she was rescued in August 1923 by a former colleague of Stefansson's. Ada used the money she earned to take her son to Seattle to cure his tuberculosis.

Interesting Fact: Except for the salary that Ada made on the trip and a few hundred dollars for furs that she trapped while on Wrangel Island, she did not benefit from the subsequent publication of several very popular books and articles concerning her survival story.

5 ALEXANDER SELKIRK, 1676–1721

Survived: Four years and four months on Más a Tierra Island.

Alexander Selkirk was a Scottish sailor and a skillful navigator, which led to his appointment as a Sailing Master on the *Cinque Ports*. The captain of the ship was a tyrant and after a few sea battles with the Spanish, Selkirk feared the ship would sink. So in an attempt to save his own life, he demanded to be put ashore on the next island they encountered. In September 1704, Selkirk was dropped off on the uninhabited island of Más a Tierra, over four hundred miles off the west coast of Chile. He took with him some clothing, a musket, some tools, a Bible, and tobacco. At first Selkirk simply read his Bible awaiting rescue, but it soon became apparent that the rescue wasn't imminent. He resigned himself to a long stay and began to make island life habitable with only rats, goats, and cats for company. Finally, in February 1709, two British privateers dropped anchor offshore and Alexander Selkirk was rescued. In 1713 Selkirk published an account of his adventures that many believe were fictionalized six years later by Daniel Defoe in his now famous novel *Robinson Crusoe*.

Interesting Fact: In 1966 Más a Tierra Island was officially renamed Robinson Crusoe Island. At the same time, the most western island of the Juan Fernández Islands was renamed Alejandro Selkirk Island.

4 ERNEST SHACKLETON, 1874–1922

Survived: 105 days on Elephant Island.

Ernest Shackleton was an Anglo-Irish explorer who launched the Imperial Trans-Antarctic Expedition in 1914. During the expedition, the ship *Endurance* became trapped in ice and for ten months drifted until the pressure of the ice crushed and sank it. Shackleton and his men were stranded on ice floes where they camped for five months. The men sailed three small lifeboats to Elephant Island, which was uninhabited and provided no hope for rescue. Shackleton and five others set out to take the crew's rescue into their own hands. In a twenty-two-foot lifeboat, they survived a seventeen-day, eight-hundred-mile journey through the world's worst seas to South Georgia Island, where a whaling station was located. The six men landed on an uninhabited part of the island so their last hope was to cross twenty-six miles of mountains and glaciers (considered impassable) to reach the whaling station on the other side. Shackleton and two others made the trek and arrived safely in August 1916 (twenty-one months after the initial departure of the *Endurance*). With the help of the Chilean government and its navy, Shackleton returned to rescue the men on Elephant Island. Not one of the twenty-eight-man crew was lost.

Interesting Fact: It would be more than forty years before the first crossing of Antarctica was achieved by the Commonwealth Trans-Antarctic Expedition between 1955–58.

3 JOHN ADAMS AND THE *BOUNTY* MUTINEERS, 1768–1829

Survived: On the Pitcairn Islands.

After the famous mutiny in 1789 and several months of landing and sailing around the eastern islands of Fiji, the *Bounty* mutineers decided to settle on the uninhabited Pitcairn Islands to elude the Royal Navy. To prevent the ship's detection and anyone's possible escape, the ship was burned to the water. Nine crewmen, along with six Tahitian men and eleven women, one with a baby, had found a home. The Tahitians were treated poorly, which led them to revolt and kill some of the mutineers. By 1794, crewmen Young, Adams, Quintal, and McCoy were left for a household of ten women and their children. McCoy, who had once worked in a distillery, discovered how to brew a potent spirit from the roots of the ti plant. By 1799, Quintal had been killed by Young and Adams in self-defense and McCoy had drowned himself. Adams and Young turned to the Scriptures using the ship's Bible as their guide for a new and peaceful society. As a result, Adams and Young converted to Christianity and taught the children to read and write using the Bible. Then, in 1800, Young died of asthma, leaving John Adams as the sole male survivor of the party that landed just ten years earlier.

Interesting Fact: Later, in 1808, the ship *Topaz* arrived at Pitcairn Island and found Adams ruling over a peaceful community of ten Tahitian women (including his wife) and several children. The Royal Navy granted him clemency in 1825, and he died four years later.

Also: The main settlement and capital of Pitcairn, Adamstown, is named for John Adams.

2 JAN PELGROM AND WOUTER LOOS, CIRCA 1611–?

Survived: (Unknown) on the Australia mainland.

In 1629, a Dutch East India ship, *Batavia*, with 316 people on board, was wrecked off the coast of Western Australia. Most of the people on board made it safely to the nearby Abrolhos islands. A fanatic named Jeronimus Cornelius led a mutiny and with thirty-six men under his command began systematically murdering, raping, and torturing men, women, and children. Before help arrived, 125 people had been murdered and their bodies dumped in mass graves. Cornelius and other mutineers had their hands cut off after they signed a confession and then were hanged. Two of the youngest of the mutineers, Wouter Loos and Jan Pelgrom, avoided execution when they were sentenced to be marooned on the Australian mainland. They were given some provisions and put ashore near the mouth of the Murchison River and told to explore the land and try and make contact with Aborigines. They were instructed to keep watch for a vessel to take them off after two years. They were never seen again, and might be considered as Australia's first known European residents.

Interesting Fact: Later European exploration recorded Aborigines with blue eyes, suggesting at least one of the men survived.

Also: The mass graves were later excavated and became a morbid tourist attraction. The story is frequently taught in schools and has even been made into an opera.

1 JUANA MARIA, THE LONE WOMAN OF SAN NICOLAS, ?–1853

Survived: 18 years on San Nicolas Island.

In 1835, Russian sea otter hunters clashed with Indian people living on remote San Nicolas Island. The bloody conflict drastically reduced the native population. Missionaries requested that these Indians be moved to the mainland for their own safety. When a ship was sent to pick them up high winds forced it to depart early leaving Juana Maria behind. In 1853, a party headed by sea otter hunter George Nidever found the Indian woman alive and well. Clad in a dress of cormorant skins sewn together, she lived in a shelter made from whale bones. She willingly went with her rescuers, bringing along only a few possessions. Nidever brought her home to live with him and his wife in Santa Barbara, California. No one, including the local Chumash Indians, could understand her language. The new living conditions altered her diet and affected the woman's health. She contracted dysentery and died after she had been on the mainland for only seven weeks. The Lone Woman was baptized conditionally with the Christian name Juana Maria (her Indian name is unknown). She is buried at Mission Santa Barbara where a plaque remains in her memory.

Interesting Fact: Juana Maria's life story was turned into a book, *Island of the Blue Dolphins*.

✳✳✳✳✳✳

TOP 10 FAILED APOCALYPTIC PREDICTIONS

10 MONTANUS

Montanus was an early "heretic" in Christianity who predicted that the end of times were upon the world. Joined with two "prophetesses," Montanus claimed to be the embodiment of the Holy Spirit and began to preach a third testament. Montanus's beliefs became fairly widespread and caused a great deal of confusion and dissent within the early Christian church. Tertullian, the Christian writer, rejected mainstream Christianity and converted to montanism. Montanus was eventually condemned at the Council of Ephesus in 431 AD.

Interesting Fact: Montanus taught that Turkey would become the "New Jerusalem" and that all of Christianity would settle there before the final judgment.

9 CHARLES WESLEY

Charles Wesley, one of the founders of the Methodist Church, believed that the world was going to end in 1794. This view concurred with that of the Shakers, who also predicted that year as the end. Despite his error, Charles's brother John also later made a prediction of the end times; John predicted that 1836 would be the year that the Great Beast would come to Earth, marking the beginning of the end.

Interesting Fact: Despite being a founding member of Methodism, Charles Wesley begged an Anglican minister to bury him in an Anglican graveyard, stating, "Sir, whatever the world may say of me, I have lived, and I die, a member of the Church of England."

8 JEHOVAH'S WITNESS PREDICTIONS

The Jehovah's Witness religion has made a number of predictions about the end of the world. The first was 1914; they based their prediction on prophecies from the Book of Daniel. After the end did not come, they changed the meaning of the prediction and stated that it was the date that Jesus would begin to rule invisibly (yes, invisibly). Some other years that the group have predicted the end of the world to come are: 1914, 1915, 1918, 1920, 1925, 1941, 1975, and 1994. One member of the cult actually built a house for the Jewish prophets to live in when they returned to Earth as part of the end times.

Interesting Fact: Charles Taze Russell, founder of the cult, sold "Miracle Wheat" at extremely inflated prices, which promised wheat of miraculous proportions.

7 THE GREAT DISAPPOINTMENT

Between the years of 1831 and 1841, William Miller (a Baptist minister), predicted the return of Jesus and the end of the world based on prophecies in the Book of Daniel (Daniel 8:14). "My principles in brief, are, that Jesus Christ will come again to this earth, cleanse, purify, and take possession of the same, with all the saints, sometime between March 21, 1843, and March 21, 1844." The day came and went and the Millerites kept their faith. After further discussion, the date of the end of the world was changed to April 18th. Again the day came and went. Again the date was changed—this time to October 22, 1844. Miller continued to wait for the end until his death in 1849.

Interesting Fact: The Millerite religious movement eventually became the Seventh-Day Adventist Church. They believe that the prediction was correct, but that it referred to an event in Heaven, not on Earth. They continue to believe that to this day. Members of the Bahá'í Faith also believe the prediction; they think it referred to the coming of a forerunner of their own religion, the Bab.

6 JOANNA SOUTHCOTT

Joanna Southcott was a self-proclaimed English mystic born in 1750. She was originally a Methodist, but she became convinced that she had supernatural powers and declared herself the woman spoken of in Apocalypse, in the King James Version, Revelation 12:1-6: "And there appeared a great wonder in heaven; a woman clothed with the sun, and the moon under her feet, and upon her head a crown of twelve stars." Joanna predicted that she would give birth to the Messiah, hailing the end of the world, on October 19, 1814. The world didn't end on that date, but two months later it did end for Joanna, who died. Her followers kept her body for some time in the hopes that she would raise herself from the dead. They finally handed her over to authorities when she began to decay.

Interesting Fact: Joanna left behind a sealed box which she claims contained a series of prophesies. The box is not to be opened until twenty-four Anglican Bishops gather together for that purpose. Will the secret of Joanna's box ever be revealed?

5 1910 HALLEY'S COMET

Even though Halley's Comet had been visible many times before without any reported deaths, the passing of the comet on May 18, 1910, was thought to be a deathly threat to people because of poisonous gas coming from its tail. It is not only religious misapprehension that can cause apocalyptic panic. This may have been the first time science caused this grave fear.

Interesting Fact: Mark Twain was born in 1835. Halley's Comet had made an appearance that same year. He has been quoted as having said he would "go out with comet." Mark Twain died in April of 1910.

4 PLANETARY CONJUNCTION

Respected meteorologist Albert Porta predicted that on December 17, 1919, a conjunction of six planets would "cause a magnetic current that would pierce the sun, cause great explosions of flaming gas, and eventually engulf the Earth." This prediction led to some mob violence and a few suicides. It also caused Albert to lose his job as a "respected" meteorologist and he ended up working for a local paper writing the weather column.

Interesting Fact: The study of meteorology dates back to ancient times with the first book on the subject being written by Aristotle in 350 BC. The book was called *Meteorology*.

3 THE JUPITER EFFECT

The Jupiter Effect came out in 1974 and was written by two astrophysicists, John Gribben and Stephen Plagemann. It was about all nine planets aligning on March 10, 1982, to create a gravitational pull that would cause a huge increase in sunspots, solar, flares, and/or earthquakes. Many credophiles took this as a prediction. Although author Gribben even came out and said it was a theoretical "what if" festival without much of any real substance behind it, people believed it was going to happen and would not be deterred.

Interesting Fact: While the effect did not cause major catastrophe, there was some influence by the planets, with high tide calculated at 0.002 inches higher than normal.

2 HALE-BOPP COMET

The comet Hale-Bopp was visible to the naked eye for a record eighteen months. Amateur astronomer Chuck Shramek "observed" a companion object following the comet. He then called the Art Bell radio show to report his findings. This led many to believe a variety of "end of the world" theories. The Internet helped spread the word even faster. The Heaven's Gate cult felt this was their signal to commit mass suicide in March of 1997. The cult believed the companion object was a spaceship coming to pick them up only to be reached by leaving their earthly vessels behind.

1 YEAR 2K

Nostradamus, arguably the best-known seer of all time, predicted July of 1999 to be the chosen date of Armageddon. A "great King of Terror" was to descend from the sky. When that didn't come true the doomsayers began spreading rumors that the *Cassini* space probe was going to crash on Earth. The *Cassini* probe was filled with radioactive fuel. If this was spilled in a crash it would fulfill the prediction in Revelation 8:11: "And the name of the star is called Wormwood: and the third part of the waters became wormwood; and many men died of the waters, because they were made bitter." And, of course, no one can forget the years leading up to 2000 in which doomsayers the world over predicted catastrophe for man due to the Y2K bug.

Interesting Fact: Nostradamus was, by profession, an apothecary, which, in modern terms, is a pharmacist.

✳✳✳✳✳✳

TOP 10 CODES YOU AREN'T MEANT TO KNOW

10 TEN CODES

The ten codes are a list of codes used by law enforcement officers. They are available on the Internet, which would make them seem inappropriate for this list, but a large number of police departments have tried to have them made illegal for distribution, so they deserve a mention. The codes were developed initially in 1937 and were expanded in 1974. The California police use a variety of extra codes, which predated the ten codes. For example, a "187" (one-eighty-seven) means homicide. In the ten codes' system, a "10-31" means that a crime is in progress, a "10-27-1" means homicide (the 10 is usually not said when it is a three-number sequence), and a "10-00" (ten-double-zero) means officer down, all patrols respond.

9 PROFESSIONAL CODES

In computer support, a variety of codes can be used when referring to a customer. One of these codes, PEBKAC (Problem Exists Between Keyboard And Chair), has become fairly well known on the Internet, but there are a variety of others that are lesser known. One of these is used when reporting a fault which has been fixed: "The fault was a PICNIC" (problem in chair—not in computer), or "ID 10 T Error." ID 10 T is, of course, IDIOT. Let us hope that you never see this noted down on your file when a serviceman is fixing your computer.

8 TIME CHECK

"Time check" (usually taking a similar form to "Time check: the time is 12:00") can be a code in stores for a bomb alert. It alerts the staff to follow the bomb procedure, which can be to either try to locate any suspicious packages or prepare to get the hell out. If you hear a "time check" in a store, it is probably a good idea to start moving toward the exit. Surprisingly, and shockingly, the majority of stores that use this code actually expect their staff to search for the bomb, certainly an aspect of the job that the majority of teenage checkout operators weren't expecting when they signed up, I am sure.

7 CODE 10

A "code 10" in hospitals can refer to a mass casualty or serious threat (such as a bomb alert), but the majority of people experiencing a "code 10" will do so for another far more common reason: a "code 10 authorization" is made by a merchant when he needs to call a credit card company to enquire about your card. This means that he is suspicious of you or your card and doesn't want you to know it while he gets it checked out. When the credit card company hears that they have a "code 10," they will ask a series of yes/no questions to the merchant in order to find out what the situation is. This will often result in the merchant keeping your card if they believe it is safe to do so. This type of call often results in a call to law enforcement.

6 DOCTOR BROWN

"Doctor Brown" is a code word often used in hospitals to alert security staff to a threat to personnel. If a nurse or doctor is in danger from a violent patient or non-staff member, they can page "Doctor Brown" to their location and the security staff will rush to their aid. In some hospitals, "code silver" is used to refer to a person with a weapon, and "code gray" can mean a violent person without a weapon. Hospitals have a huge array of various codes to describe all manner of situations. They often differ from hospital to hospital and they are usually not internationally recognized.

5 CODE OSCAR

On a ship, a "code oscar" means someone has gone overboard. If the ship has to maneuver erratically to handle the situation, it must also send out blasts on the signal so that other ships nearby are aware of the fact that it is about to change its course. It should be noted that ships don't have an internationally standardized set of PA signals and they can differ from place to place, but this is a fairly commonly used one. Oh, and a "code delta" can mean that there is a biological hazard, though who knows what that might be on a passenger ship. And, finally, "code alpha" often means medical emergency.

4 CODE BRAVO

"Code bravo" is the code phrase for a general security alert at airports. Unlike most of the codes on this list, the code is meant to cause alarm, but not through knowing what it means: when this alert is raised, all of the security agents will begin to yell "code bravo" in order to frighten the passengers—this is supposed to make it easier for the agents to locate the source of the problem without interference from the general public. For those of you who travel on ships from time to time, you may like to know that "code bravo" means "fire" and it is the most serious alert on a ship; if the ship burns, you either get off or burn with it. Ships also often use sound signals, such as seven short and one long, meaning "man the lifeboats."

3 INSPECTOR SANDS

"Inspector Sands" (or sometimes "Mr. Sands") is a code for fire in the United Kingdom. Obviously it would not be appropriate for the service staff of a store to announce a fire publicly, so this code is used to alert the appropriate staff to the danger without upsetting customers. The wording differs from place to place, and in the Underground network a recorded "Inspector Sands" warning is automatically triggered by smoke detectors. In some shops you will hear the code used in a phrase such as "Will Inspector Sands please report to the men's changing room," if the fire is in the men's changing room. It was played on a continuous loop through the Underground during the July 7, 2005 bombings, and has been incorrectly described as a code word for a bomb; the frequently used code for a bomb in the Underground is "Mr. Gravel," for example, "Mr. Gravel is in the foyer." "Mr. Sands" (or sometimes "Mr. Johnson") is also used in theaters in the case of fire.

2 WAL-MART

Wal-Mart gets its own item on this list because they have a large number of codes that are store-specific. Some of their codes should not worry you; for example, a "code 10" or a "code 20" just means that there has been a dry spill or a wet spill; the biggest danger this poses to you is that you might slip over. A "code 300" calls for security and a "code orange" means there has been a chemical spill. But here are the ones you really need to worry about: "code red" means there is a fire in the building—get the hell out if you hear this. Worse still, a "code blue" means there is a bomb in the building. Exit swiftly but don't run, in case they think you planted it. A "code green" means there is a hostage situation and a "code white" means there is an accident. The one you are most likely to hear is a "code c," which is simply a call for customer service (usually meaning that more cashiers are needed). And finally, the most famous Wal-Mart code… well, it's so famous it needs its own item:

1 CODE ADAM

"Code Adam" was invented by Wal-Mart but it is now an internationally recognized alert and means, "missing child." The code was first coined in 1994 in memory of Adam Walsh, a six-year-old, who went missing in a Sears department store in Florida in 1981. Adam was later found murdered. The person making the announcement will state, "We have a code Adam," followed by a description of the missing child. As soon as the alert is heard, security staff will begin to monitor the doors and other exits. If the child is not found within ten minutes, the police are alerted and a store search begins. Also, if the child is found in the first ten minutes in the company of an unknown adult, the police must be called and the person detained if it is safe to do so. In 2003, Congress passed legislation making a "Code Adam" program compulsory in all federal office buildings. A similar alert is called an AMBER alert, a backronym for "America's Missing: Broadcasting Emergency Response" but initially named for Amber Hagerman, a nine-year-old girl who was abducted and murdered.

✳✳✳✳✳✳

TOP 10
BADASS SWORDS

10 THE SWORD OF OMENS
Wielded by: Lion-O of *The ThunderCats*

Kicking off the list at number ten we have the Sword of Omens. Any child of the '80s should remember this cartoon series. More mighty than anyone else of his age, young Lion-O was only twelve years old when he and his Thunderian teammates sought refuge on Third Earth while their home planet of Thunderia was being destroyed.

Upon arrival, Lion-O and his allies fought against the tyrannical Mumm-Ra and his hordes of evil fiends who sought to not only destroy The ThunderCats, but also obtain great power from The Eye of Thundera, the jewel inlayed within the hilt of the Sword of Omens, which is the source of The ThunderCats' own power.

9 THE BRIDE'S HATTORI HANZO SWORD
Wielded by: The Bride in *Kill Bill* Vols. 1 & 2

This particular sword is artistically used by one of the most ass-kicking females to grace the silver screen within the past several years. After being betrayed and nearly beaten to death by her would-be cohorts, The Deadly Viper Assassination Squad, and then having a bullet put through her head by Bill himself, The Bride is left inside of a chapel to die.

Why not? After all, who could possibly survive a point-blank gunshot to the head? The Bride, that's who!

She very slowly recovers and eventually seeks the guidance of a couple of highly secretive and skilled individuals, one of whom is the infamous Sonny Chiba, whose character is the long since retired Japanese sword-crafting legend Hattori Hanzo. One month is spent crafting her *katana*. After Hattori's long and arduous task is completed, The Bride is both justifiably relentless and unstoppable in seeking vengeance against those who wronged her.

8 CONAN'S ATLANTEAN SWORD
Wielded by: Conan in *Conan the Barbarian*

As a young boy Conan witnessed his entire village get pillaged and destroyed by the evil warlord Thulsa Doom. After his mother and father are murdered, Conan, being one of the few survivors of Doom's pillage, is sold into slavery. During this time he grows in both age and strength, eventually being put in the rings of the gladiators to fight for the entertainment of others. He is a formidable opponent and wins fight after fight until his slave owner decides to send him out east to hone his skills as a fighter by learning to fight with a sword. Then one day he is simply set free.

During his journey away from slavery he stumbles upon an old tomb deep within the side of a mountain. Buried there is an Atlantean king sitting on a throne with his royal garments adorning him and a mighty sword at his side. Conan takes the sword and decides to find the warlords who destroyed his village and murdered his family.

7 EXCALIBUR
Wielded by: King Arthur in *Excalibur*

Not only is this sword very well known in the movie arena, it is also included in countless pieces of classic literature. Given to King Arthur by The Lady of the Lake, Excalibur is the true sword of swords and can only be obtained by the true of heart. In many versions of the story the sword is imbued with magical powers that aid King Arthur in his battles.

A lot of confusion between Excalibur and the Sword in the Stone has arisen through time. From the information I have gathered, the two stories mention separate swords, though there is still some debate about that. Regardless of how you came to know the famous name of Excalibur, you must admit that it is a fine piece of legendary weaponry. So the next time you are walking near a lake look for The Lady. She just might have something to give to you.

6 THE HESSIAN
Wielded by: The Headless Horseman in *Sleepy Hollow*

The classic 1820 story of *The Legend of Sleepy Hollow* by Washington Irving was again adapted to film in 1999. As the story goes, Ichabod Crane is sent to Sleepy Hollow to investigate and put a stop to the Headless Horseman who has been terrorizing the town. Riding upon a black horse, The Headless Horseman stalks his seemingly random victims at night and uses an ominous looking double-edged sword to remove the heads of those unfortunate souls. The motives behind the murders are eventually unraveled as Crane's investigation continues. The real twist for me is that Christopher Walken is the Headless Horseman.

5 THE BEASTMASTER SWORD
Wielded by: Dar in *The Beastmaster*

This movie is one of my personal favorites, and the sword Dar uses is equally impressive. There is an evil priest, Maax, who learns of a prophecy concerning the birth of a child who will eventually kill him years later. Maax is determined to put a stop to this at once and sends one of his evil minions out to find this unborn child, brand it with a sign of their evil deity, and sacrifice it. As fate would have it, the baby is saved by a man who lives in the village of Emur. This is where Dar grows to be a strong young man.

Eventually, Dar realizes that by being branded with the sign, he was given the ability to psychically communicate with animals, and this power will come in handy after his entire village and all of its inhabitants are slaughtered by the wicked Jun Horde. It seems that Maax has been looking for Dar all these years and his search has led him to the village of Emur.

Dar survives the attack and, as the last living member of the Emurite clan, he seeks vengeance and uses his adoptive father's mighty sword along with his psychic power to fulfill his destiny and make the prophecy a reality.

4 STING
Wielded by: Frodo Baggins in The Lord of the Rings Trilogy

Sting is the perfect sword for someone who is as small as a hobbit. In the hands of a normal-sized human it would simply be an elaborate elfish dagger. Not so for the hobbit. Sting is the perfect short sword for Frodo, and it also has magical properties and can detect the presence of orcs by glowing blue at the blade. Exceptionally sharp, the sword is engraved with the Sindarian phrase, "*Maegnas aen estar nin dagnir in yngyl im*," which means "Maegnas is my name and I am the spider's bane."

It came into hobbit hands when Frodo's adoptive uncle, Bilbo Baggins, stole Sting from a band of orcs and used it to fight with. The name Sting was given to the sword after Bilbo's encounter with a bunch of huge arachnids. Bilbo used it many times over the years until Frodo required a weapon for himself as he set out on the quest to destroy The Ring of Sauron.

3 HE-MAN'S POWER SWORD
Wielded by: He-Man in *He-Man and The Masters of The Universe*

I grew up watching this cartoon series as a child so I had to throw this one on here. Looking back I now realize all of the sexual innuendoes within the series.

As the regular, average Prince Adam, no one really cares about him, but when he takes the power sword out, points it in the air, and shouts "By the power of Grayskull...I have the power!" he is magically transformed into He-Man, the most powerful man in the universe, capable of any feat. No one ever figures out that they are one in the same person, despite looking identical.

Although his sword is mighty and magical, he rarely uses it. Instead, he uses his immeasurable strength and wit to overcome his foes and constantly defeat Skeletor. If you are a die-hard He-Man fan to this day, then read below.

2 INIGO MONTOYA'S RAPIER
Wielded by: Inigo Montoya in *The Princess Bride*

Inigo is a straight-shooting Spaniard and the child of a sword-craftsman. While learning the craft, Inigo's father was approached by a unique man of nobility, who requested a very custom and equally costly rapier—a jeweled rapier that would befit a six-fingered man.

After the extensive completion of this sword, the six-fingered man refused to pay the agreed amount for the rapier and, subsequently, murders young Inigo's father right in front of him. The six-fingered man left Inigo alive, but not before he gave him two scars, one across each cheek.

Romantic and steadfast, Inigo, in his life-quest to avenge his father's tragic and unwarranted death, eventually tracks down the six-fingered man and slays him with the very same rapier.

1 THE SWORD OF WILLIAM WALLACE
Wielded by: William Wallace in *Braveheart*

The character of William Wallace was magnificently portrayed by Mel Gibson in this epic film. I remember watching the movie for the first time and my jaw dropped when I saw that massive sword strapped to his back as he rode his horse around his fellow countrymen in preparation for battle. Although the film is a classic, a lot of the actual facts about the real life of William Wallace have been lost.

It is known that Wallace was a fighter against the oppressive English rule during the 1200s, but the huge sword used in the movie by Gibson was most likely never actually used by the real William Wallace. The real William Wallace's sword is on display in Stirling, Scotland, at The National Wallace Monument, and it looks nothing like what is seen in the movie. That doesn't stop this huge two-handed sword from being an awesome weapon though!

✳✳✳✳✳✳

TOP 10 COMMON MISCONCEPTIONS

10 NAPOLEON WAS UNUSUALLY SHORT

Much of the reason for the rumors that Napoleon was a short man (and thus had to compensate by invading countries and becoming ruler of Europe) comes from the confusion between old French feet and Imperial (British) feet. Measured shortly after his death in 1821, Napoleon was recorded at five-feet, two-inches in French feet, which corresponds to five-feet, six-and-a-half inches in Imperial feet. This makes him slightly taller than the average Frenchman of the nineteenth century. Napoleon's nickname of "*le petit caporal*" has also perpetuated the rumor, with non-francophones interpreting "*petit*" to refer to his height, when it was actually a term of affection referring to his camaraderie with ordinary soldiers.

9 DANISH PASTRIES COME FROM DENMARK

Arguably the world's most misleadingly named food, Danish pastries actually originated in Austria and were inspired by Turkish baklava. Their name comes from Danish chef L. C. Klitteng who popularized them in Western Europe and the United States in the early twentieth century, including baking them for the wedding of President Woodrow Wilson in 1915. In Denmark and much of Scandinavia, Danish pastries are called "Viennese Bread."

During the Islamic cartoon controversy of 2006, Danish pastries were renamed "Roses of the Prophet Muhammad" in Iran due to their association with the offending country.

8 METEORITES ARE HOT WHEN THEY HIT EARTH

We've all seen the cartoons where a meteor falls to Earth (at which point it becomes a meteorite) with a red-hot tinge and smoke blowing off it in all directions. In truth, small meteorites are cold when they hit Earth; in fact, many are found with frost on them. A meteorite has been in the near-absolute zero

312 THE ULTIMATE BOOK OF TOP 10 LISTS

temperature of space for billions of years, so the interior of it is very cold. A meteor's great speed is enough to melt its outside layer, but any molten material will be quickly blown off, and the interior of the meteor does not have time to heat up because rocks are poor conductors of heat. Also, atmospheric drag can slow small meteors to terminal velocity by the time they hit the ground, giving them time to cool down.

7 WATER SPINS IN DIFFERENT DIRECTIONS

Toilet water does *not* spin in a given direction due to being in a particular hemisphere of Earth. That phenomenon only occurs in weather patterns of hundreds of miles in size, like hurricanes, due to the rotation of Earth. So there.

6 BATS ARE BLIND

A common misconception perpetuated by its use in metaphors and similes (see also number five), bats actually have fairly normal eyesight, although they are very photosensitive and often dazzled by excessive light. However, bats do often use echolocation in situations where their eyesight fails them, such as times of darkness.

5 CHAMELEONS CHANGE COLOR TO MATCH THEIR SURROUNDINGS

An interesting and fun idea, sure, but simply not true. While chameleons can be perceived to change their color to match their background, a chameleon's color change is actually the expression of the physical and physiological condition of the lizard. Chameleons are already naturally camouflaged to match their surroundings and change their colors depending on their mood and sometimes as a sign of communication. A chameleon that is frightened, for example, will turn black.

4 A DUCK'S QUACK DOESN'T ECHO

Sounds ludicrous, right? Well, this rumor somehow worked up a cult following on the Internet, where people protested its factuality with an almost religious fervor. It got to the point that a respected scientist actually decided to take valuable time out of his day, when he could be curing cancer or something else unimportant, to test this theory. Trevor Cox, of the University of Salford, England, confirmed what all us logical people knew all along: a duck's quack *does* echo.

He placed a duck in a reverberation chamber and tested its quack. Sure enough, he concluded that a duck's quack does echo, though the sound that comes back is very soft due to the fading nature of the actual quack. Hooray for science.

3 HITLER WAS AN ATHEIST

"We were convinced that the people need and require this faith. We have, therefore, undertaken the fight against the atheistic movement, and that not merely with a few theoretical declarations: we have stamped it out."

—Adolf Hitler, Berlin, 1933

Christianity—a religion of peace and tolerance that preaches moral values and love for one's enemies. Well, clearly, from a historical perspective, this has certainly not always been the case, although it's not so much the religion's fault as the people who attempt to follow it. With over a billion worldwide adherents, is it really probable that everyone who considers themself a Christian is pious, holy, and a moral human being?

One of the most damning criticisms of Hitler and of atheism in general is that Hitler, as an atheist, had no morals and thus could kill freely without care or feeling. Well, Hitler was certainly not an atheist; he was born a Roman Catholic, although how religious he actually was is debatable. It is clear though that Hitler was an evil man and that his religion was irrelevant to his malevolent personality.

In *Mein Kampf*, Hitler wrote fondly of his experiences in church festivals, and as leader of the Nazi party, he made many references to the glory of Christianity in his speeches. Including making references to Jesus' death at the hand of the Jews in an attempt to rile up anti-Semitic sentiment in his mostly religious audiences. He adopted many aspects of Catholic hierarchy, liturgy, and symbolism, though he was very critical of Catholicism in private. In fact, Hitler favored Protestantism, due to its being open to interpretation. He also ridiculed occultism and neo-Paganism that were relatively popular in Germany at the time.

Strangely enough, Hitler greatly admired the Muslim faith and tradition saying, "the Mohammedan religion too would have been much more compatible to us than Christianity. Why did it have to be Christianity with its meekness and flabbiness?"

2 HUMANS EVOLVED FROM MONKEYS

One of the most common misconceptions about Darwin's theory of evolution by natural selection is that Darwin claimed we evolved from chimpanzees. Darwin never actually said this, nor will any respectable biologist. This myth was actually spread by religious zealots during the nineteenth century, in order to try and discredit Darwin and promote anti-evolutionism among the religious. Humans and chimpanzees are actually cousins (we share about 94 percent of our DNA with them) and both evolved from a common ancestor, thought to be Sahelanthropus tchadensis, around seven million years ago.

1 THE NORTH POLE IS NORTH AND THE SOUTH POLE IS SOUTH

Actually, in terms of physics, the North Pole (while geographically in the north) is actually a south magnetic pole, and the South Pole (geographically in the south) is a north magnetic pole. When your compass is pointing north, it is actually pointing to the south pole of Earth's magnetic field. About 780,000 years ago, this would not have been the case, as the magnetic poles of the Earth were reversed (this is called a geomagnetic reversal). Oh—and just to complicate things further, the poles drift around randomly—they are not in fixed spots. This is most likely due to movements in the molten nickel-iron alloy in the Earth's core.

✳✳✳✳✳✳

TOP 10 MISCONCEPTIONS ABOUT COMMON SAYINGS

10 SCOT FREE

Common Saying: "To get off scot free."

Many people think this saying refers to Scottish people being tight with money, hence something being free, but in fact the word "scot" is an old Norse word which means "payment," specifically a payment made to a landlord or sheriff. So this phrase, while meaning what most people think it means, has no connection to the Scottish people; it just means to get off without having to pay.

9 FIT AS A FIDDLE
Common Saying: "As fit as a fiddle."
This is another phrase where a single word has confused people: "fit" in the context of this saying does not mean "healthy," which is a nineteenth-century definition. Its original meaning was "suitable," and it is still used in that context in the sentence, "fit for a king." "As fit as a fiddle" means "as appropriate as can be," not "in excellent health." The first use of the phrase, incidentally, was in the sixteenth century and was originally "as right as a fiddle."

8 ANOTHER THING COMING
Common Saying: "If you think that, you have another thing coming."
This is a complete aberration of the original phrase because of the sound of English. The correct phrase is "if you think that, you have another think coming," in other words, "what you think is wrong, so think again." Because the "k" in "think" often ends up silent when saying, "think coming," people have changed the phrase over time. Of course, "another thing coming" makes no sense at all. To illustrate how global this error is, when you search the Internet for "another thing coming" it returns 139,000 results; when you search "another think coming" it returns a mere 39,000 results.

7 EAT HUMBLE PIE
Common Saying: "Eat humble pie."
This phrase means, "to be humble in apologizing for something." I was slightly reluctant to put it on the list because it actually does mean what people think it means, but there is still a misconception here; people think that this phrase means to eat a pie made of humbleness but it actually means to eat a pie made with umble. "Umble" is an old English word for offal, the bits of the animal seldom eaten today (sadly). It was a pie that was normally eaten by the poor as the finer cuts of meat were left for the rich only. "To eat a humble pie" is an example of metanalysis (words being broken down into parts or meanings that differ from the original) as it sounds just like "to eat an umble pie." Another example of this in English is "an apron," which used to be "a napron."

6 RULE OF THUMB

Common Saying: "Rule of thumb."

People commonly think that this saying is a reference to a law allowing a man to beat his wife as long as he uses a rod no thicker than his thumb. It is, of course, completely untrue. There is no record of any judge in Britain ever making a ruling like this, or any lawmaker passing a law. The phrase actually refers to doing something by estimates rather than using an exact measure.

5 ON TENDER HOOKS

Common Saying: "On tender hooks."

This phrase is very commonly misspelled. First off, what exactly is a tender hook? It doesn't seem logical, does it? Well, that is because it isn't. The phrase is actually "on tenterhooks." A tenter was a medieval tool used for making cloth—the tenterhooks were small hooks to which the fabric would be stretched in the manufacturing process. To be "on tenterhooks" means to be left hanging or to be in a state of suspense.

4 TAKE A RAINCHECK

Common Saying: "I'll take a raincheck."

This phrase is usually meant to mean, "I won't do it now but I will later." This is the commonly accepted meaning (and has been for a long time) so it is now considered to be correct. It is included here merely out of interest because its original meaning was slightly different. Initially, a raincheck was offered to people who had tickets to a baseball game that was rained out; they would be offered a "raincheck," which was a ticket for a game at a later date to make up for the missed game. This eventually found its way into shopping jargon in general where a raincheck was an offer to sell an out-of-stock good when it arrived back in stock. The meaning has eventually broadened to a point that it is not an offer any longer but a response.

3 FREE REIGN

Common Saying: "To give someone free reign."

This is a spelling error that leads to a misunderstanding, though the meanings remain the same fundamentally. Many people presume this phrase to mean that a person given free reign has the "royal" power to do anything they want. In fact, the correct phrase is "free rein" and it comes from the days before cars when horses were used as our main mode of transport. When navigating a steep or winding path, one would relax the reins so that the horse could pick the safest path, as he was more likely to do a better job than the rider.

2 WRECK HAVOC
Common Saying: "To wreck havoc."

Havoc means chaos, and to wreck something is to put it into a state of chaos. So why would you make chaos out of chaos? You wouldn't. What you might do is wreak havoc though, because "to wreak" means "to cause to happen." The two words are pronounced differently: "wreck" sounds like "rek" while "wreak" sounds like "reek." It is a small, but common, error.

1 BEG THE QUESTION
Common Saying: "To beg the question."

"To beg the question" does not mean, "to raise the question." Originally the phrase was "to begge the question" and it appeared in English around the 1580s. It is a reference to a question (or phrase) that implies the truth of the thing it is trying to prove. Confusing? Okay, here is an example: "Why does England have fewer trees per acre than any other country in Europe?" This is a "begged question"—the person asking is implying that England has fewer trees, when, in fact, it may not. Another example is, "He must be telling the truth because he never lies." Decartes was begging the question when he said, "I think, therefore I am." Oh, and for those of you who are used to using the term in the wrong way, consider using "prompt the question" as a correct alternative.

✳✳✳✳✳✳

TOP 10 CHILD PRODIGIES

10 FRÉDÉRIC CHOPIN, COMPOSITION, MARCH 1, 1810–OCTOBER 17, 1849

Chopin, now most famous for his virtuosic piano music, was also a child prodigy in his own time. In his homeland of Poland, he gained the reputation as a "second Mozart," having already composed two polonaises by the age of seven. "Little

Chopin" became a popular attraction in the salons of the Polish aristocracy and went on to become the greatest Polish composer of the nineteenth century and one of the greatest international composers of piano music.

9 CARL FRIEDRICH GAUSS, MATHEMATICS, APRIL 30, 1777–FEBRUARY 23, 1855

Gauss made his first astonishing mathematical breakthroughs while still a teenager. His greatest work (*Disquisitiones Arithmeticae*) was completed by the age of twenty-one and published at twenty-four. Gauss is generally regarded as the greatest mathematician since antiquity and he has had an immense influence on modern math and science.

8 LOPE DE VEGA, LITERATURE, NOVEMBER 25, 1562–AUGUST 27, 1635

Lope de Vega was a Spanish playwright and poet, regarded as second only to Cervantes. In his lifetime he completed thousands of plays (though only 425 remain). By the age of five, Lope was reading Spanish and Latin, and by the age of ten, he was translating Latin poetry into Spanish. His first play was completed by twelve. He shaped the path of Spanish poetry.

7 YEHUDI MENUHIN, VIOLIN, APRIL 22, 1916–MARCH 12, 1999

Yehudi Menuhin was such a talented child that he performed his first solo violin performance with the San Francisco Symphony at the age of seven. During the Second World War, he performed regularly for Allied troops and he was the first Jewish musician to return to Germany after the war to perform. He left behind him a great treasure trove of recordings made during his youth.

6 JOHN VON NEUMANN, MATHEMATICS, DECEMBER 28, 1903–FEBRUARY 8, 1957

John von Neumann was an Austria-Hungary–born mathematician who made significant contributions to quantum physics, statistics, and numerous mathematical fields. He received his Ph.D. in experimental physics and chemistry at the age of twenty-three. He is reputed to have been able to divide two eight-digit numbers in his head at the age of six.

5 JEAN-FRANÇOIS CHAMPOLLION, LINGUISTICS, DECEMBER 23, 1790–MARCH 4, 1832

Champollion is most famous for unlocking the key to understanding ancient Egyptian hieroglyphics, but even as a child he had an astonishing talent for linguistics. By sixteen he had mastered a dozen languages, and by twenty he was able to speak Latin, Greek, Hebrew, Sanskrit, Chinese, and numerous other languages. At thirty-two, he was able to use the Rosetta Stone to translate ancient Egyptian for the first time.

4 MARIA GAETANA AGNESI, MATHEMATICS, MAY 16, 1718–JANUARY 9, 1799

Maria Gaetana Agnesi was a linguist, mathematician, and philospher. By the age of five, she could speak French and Italian, and by thirteen she could speak Greek, Hebrew, Spanish, German, and Latin. She was referred to as the "walking polyglot," and at the age of nine, she delivered a one-hour-long speech in Latin at an academic conference on women's right to be educated.

3 BLAISE PASCAL, MATHEMATICS, JUNE 19, 1623–AUGUST 19, 1662

Blaise Pascal was a child prodigy who received his education entirely at the hands of his father. He was a brilliant mathematician and made many contributions to the field of applied science. He is considered to have influenced the development of two new sciences: social science and modern economics.

2 PABLO PICASSO, PAINTING, OCTOBER 25, 1881–APRIL 8, 1973

Picasso is undoubtedly the most famous artist of the twentieth century for his invention of the school of cubism. From the age of thirteen his career as a significant artist began in earnest, though he painted a considerable amount of mature serious work prior to that. He is regarded, by some, as the greatest painter in the history of Spain.

1 WOLFGANG AMADEUS MOZART, COMPOSITION, JANUARY 27, 1756–DECEMBER 5, 1791

Wolfgang Amadeus Mozart is undoubtedly the greatest composer in the history of classical music. He left behind an enormous quantity of music for all manner of instruments and voices, and contributed enormously to the shape of music to come. By the age of five, he was already a brilliant pianist and had composed two works. His music is as much loved today as when it was first written.

TOP 10 PARANORMAL ABILITIES

10 PSYCHOKINESIS

Psychokinesis (mind over matter) is the ability to move or change objects using only the power of the mind. The desire (undoubtedly resulting from the desire to sit on your butt all day) to obtain this ability has spawned a huge market in books designed to teach you how. Most scientists consider it to be impossible, and believe that those who demonstrate the ability are doing so through the use of fraud.

9 EXTRASENSORY PERCEPTION

ESP is the ability to gather information without using the other five senses (hence it being referred to as the sixth sense). While many tests exist to "prove" that some people have the ability, the law of averages means the majority of people should be able to "pass" the tests 20 percent of the time by mere randomness. However, these tests are still frequently touted as proof for the existence of ESP.

8 TELEPATHY

Telepathy is the ability to communicate with others via the mind alone. This is a form of ESP and there do appear to be some legitimate cases—most often in moments of crisis involving close family members. There have also been claims by some people to be able to telepathically communicate with (and understand) animals.

7 CLAIRVOYANCE

Clairvoyance is the gathering of information allegedly passed on by people in the spirit world. Clairvoyants often claim to be able to see the dead with whom they are communicating. Some people say that they can hear but not see the dead—this is called clairaudience. Various institutions exist which claim to teach people to develop this ability.

6 PYROKINESIS

Pyrokinesis is the ability to light or stop fires with only the power of the mind. It was prominently featured in the book *Firestarter* by Stephen King, in which a young girl has this ability but is unable to control it. There is no scientific evidence at all that suggests this ability exists.

5 PSYCHOMETRY

Psychometry is the ability to "read" information from objects. This is the ability often seen on television programs in which the psychic will hold a watch or wallet from a person in the audience and try to describe the person and aspects of their life. This is the ability featured in Stephen King's book *The Dead Zone*.

4 PRECOGNITION

Precognition is the ability to see an event before it happens. The most famous psychic who claimed to have this ability was Jeane Dixon, who allegedly predicted the death of President John F. Kennedy; however, she admitted later that she saw Nixon as the assassinated president, not Kennedy. Her abilities were so highly regarded that President Nixon ordered preparations for a terrorist attack that she predicted. Needless to say, the attack did not occur.

3 BILOCATION

Bilocation is the ability to appear in more than one place at the same time. Through history there have been many saints who allegedly had the ability, including St. Pio of Pietrelcina in modern days. The occultist Aleister Crowley was believed to have this ability, though he denied being aware of it. This is sometimes used to explain mysterious tales of people appearing to loved ones just prior to death.

2 POSTCOGNITION

Postcognition is the ability to see an event in the past. From time to time people offer to help the police solve a crime by "seeing" into the past to find the perpetrator. There are claims that this has been successful in many cases, but there appears to be no documentary evidence that it is anything other than lucky guessing or hoaxing.

1 ASTRAL PROJECTION

Astral projection is the ability to separate your "soul" from your body and transmit it over potentially vast distances. The concept has existed since ancient times, though there is no evidence at all that the ability exists in reality and no tests on the subject have returned anything more than circumstantial evidence.

※※※※※※

TOP 10 CONSPIRACY THEORIES

10 9/11 WAS PLANNED BY THE U.S. GOVERNMENT

While many conspiracy theories exist around 9/11, probably the most common is that the Bush administration organized it in order to provide an excuse to wage international war on foreign nations that were not in support of the administration. Some people even claim that it was meant to give the government the powers to implement a police state. This is such a common conspiracy theory that the phrase "9/11 was an inside job" has become something of an Internet phenomenon.

9 UFO RECOVERED AT ROSWELL

In July 1947, materials were recovered from Roswell, New Mexico, which sparked rumors about an alien crash-landing. To this day speculation about the event is rife with some people even claiming that alien bodies were recovered from the crash scene. When questioned, the military states the materials recovered were part of a secret research balloon.

8 JOHN F. KENNEDY'S ASSASSINATION

Despite the fact that the Warren Commission (the group who conducted the investigation into the assassination of John F. Kennedy) stated that Lee Harvey Oswald acted alone as the killer, conspiracy theories abound even today. There is speculation that there were others who helped in the killing and even parties such as the Federal Reserve and CIA are implicated.

7 GLOBAL WARMING IS A FRAUD

While many scientists assert that global warming is a real event caused by humans, a large number of people claim it is part of a conspiracy to allow the larger governments of the world to exert control over the smaller via pacts like the Kyoto Protocol. Scientists have come forward to say that they have been denied funding because they don't accept the global warming theorists, giving fuel to the fire of this conspiracy theory.

6 PRINCESS DIANA WAS MURDERED BY THE ROYAL FAMILY

The scandal surrounding the relationship of Princess Diana (the mother of the future head of the Church of England) and Dodi Fayed (a Muslim) led many to believe that the couple was killed in order to prevent a marriage from occurring, thereby preventing a future scandal in the church. Some suggest that the royal family organized the deaths, while others speculate that it was British intelligence, the CIA, the Israeli Secret Service, and even the Freemasons.

5 JEWISH WORLD DOMINATION

The idea of Jewish world domination largely comes from the anti-Jewish sentiment of Russia in the early twentieth century when a pamphlet entitled *The Protocols of the Elders of Zion* was published. The pamphlet lists a series of steps to be taken by the Jews to bring about world domination. It was later found to be a hoax, but that did not stop the Nazis using it to their advantage during the Second World War. It is still referred to frequently in nations such as Iran to support the anti-Jewish sentiment there.

4 APOLLO MOON LANDING HOAX

As crazy as it seems, there is a large body of people who believe that the *Apollo* moon landing was a hoax perpetrated by NASA in order to not be beaten to it by the Soviets. Its occurrence at the height of the Cold War may appear to give credence to the theory, but virtually every piece of evidence put forward to prove the hoax has been debunked, by scientists and photographic experts.

3 PEARL HARBOR WAS ALLOWED TO HAPPEN

This conspiracy theory asserts that President Roosevelt not only knew in advance that Pearl Harbor was going to be attacked, but that he provoked it in order to make an excuse to enter the war (which Congress was vehemently opposed to at the time). Conspiracy theorists claim the Soviet Union and government of Britain warned the U.S. of the impending attack.

2 THE THIRD SECRET OF FATIMA

The third secret of Fatima is the last of three messages allegedly given to three young children in Fatima in 1917 by the Virgin Mary. The third message was kept secret from all but the pope and a few other clergy members. The church finally revealed the secret in June 2000. Experts on Fatima immediately spoke out, saying that the secret was not authentic, as it did not match descriptions given by the young children of what it contained. The most vocal proponent of this theory is Father Nicholas Gruner who has been suspended from his priestly duties because of it.

1 THE PHILADELPHIA EXPERIMENT

The Philadelphia Experiment is allegedly a military experiment that occurred in 1943. The aim of the experiment was to make a ship invisible to observers. The conspiracy theorists claim that the experiment was a success. The U.S. Navy denies that it occurred but that has not stopped the speculation. It is postulated that the Navy destroyer escort USS *Eldridge* was the ship involved and that the experiment was conducted by Dr. Franklin Reno.

❋❋❋❋❋❋

TOP 10 SECRET SOCIETIES

10 SKULL AND BONES

The Order of Skull and Bones, a Yale University society, was originally known as the Brotherhood of Death. It is one of the oldest student secret societies in the United States. It was founded in 1832 and membership is open to an elite few. The society uses Masonic-inspired rituals to this day. Members meet every Thursday and Sunday of each week in a building they call the "Tomb."

According to Judy Schiff, Chief Archivist at the Yale University Library, the names of the members were not kept secret until the 1970s, but the rituals always have been. Both of the Bush presidents were members of the society while studying at Yale, and a number of other members have gone on to great fame and fortune.

The society is surrounded by conspiracy theories, the most popular of which is probably the idea that the CIA was built on members from the group. The CIA released a statement in 2007 (coinciding with the popularity of the film *The Good Shepherd*) in which it denied that the group was an incubator for the CIA.

9 FREEMASONS

The Grand Masonic Lodge was created in 1717 when four small groups of lodges joined together. Membership levels were initially first and second degree, but in the 1750s this was expanded to create the third degree, which caused a split in the group. When a person reaches the third degree, they are called a Master Mason.

Masons conduct their regular meetings in a ritualized style. This includes many references to architectural symbols such as the compass and square. They refer to God as "The Great Architect of the Universe." The three degrees of Masonry are: 1: Entered Apprentice, a basic member of the group; 2: Fellow Craft, an intermediate degree in which you are meant to develop further knowledge of Masonry; and 3: Master Mason, a degree necessary for participating in most Masonic activities. Some rites (such as the Scottish Rite) list up to thirty-three degrees of membership.

Masons use signs and handshakes to gain admission to their meetings, as well as to identify themselves to other people who may be Masons. The signs and handshakes often differ from one jurisdiction to another and are often changed or updated. This protects the group from people finding out how to gain admission under false pretenses. Masons also wear stylized clothing based upon the clothing worn by stone-masons from the Middle Ages. The most well-known of these is the apron.

In order to become a Mason, you must generally be recommended by a current Mason. In some cases you must be recommended three times before you can join. You have to be at least eighteen years old and of sound mind. Many religions frown upon membership of the Masons, and the Roman Catholic Church forbids Catholics to join under pain of excommunication.

8 ROSICRUCIANS

The Rosicrucian Order is generally believed to have been the idea of a group of German Protestants in the 1600s when a series of three documents were published: Fama Fraternitatis Rosae Crucis, Confessio Fraternitatis, and The Chymical Wedding of Christian Rosenkreutz anno 1459. The documents were so widely read and influential that the historian Frances Yeats refers to the seventeenth century as the "Rosicrucian Enlightenment." The first document tells the story of a mysterious alchemist, Christian Rosenkreutz, who traveled to various parts of the world gathering secret knowledge. The second document tells of a secret brotherhood of alchemists preparing to change the political and intellectual face of Europe. The third document describes the invitation of Christian Rosenkreutz to attend and assist at the "chemical" wedding of a king and queen in a castle of Miracles.

Current members of the Rosicrucian Order claim that its origins are far more ancient than these documents. The authors of the documents seemed to strongly favor Lutheranism and include condemnations of the Catholic Church. Rosicrucianism probably had an influence on Masonry and, in fact, the eighteenth degree of Scottish Rite Masonry is called the Knight of the Rose Croix (red cross).

There are a large number of Rosicrucian groups today, each claiming to be closely tied to the original. Of the two main divisions, one is a mix of Christianity with Rosicrucian principles, and the other is semi-Masonic. The Masonic type tends to also have degrees of membership.

7 ORDO TEMPLIS ORIENTIS

The OTO (Order of the Temples of the East) is an organization that was originally modeled on Masonry, but, under the leadership of the self-styled "Great Beast" Aleister Crowley, it took on the principles of his religious system called Thelema. Thelema is based around a single law: "Do what thou wilt shall be the whole of the law, love is the law, love under the will" (1904). Membership is based upon degrees of initiation and highly stylized rituals are used. The OTO currently claims over three thousand members worldwide.

Crowley created a "Mass" for the OTO, which is called the Gnostic Mass. Of the "Mass," Crowley wrote:

"I resolved that my Ritual should celebrate the sublimity of the operation of universal forces without introducing disputable metaphysical theories. I would neither make nor imply any statement about nature which would not be endorsed by the most materialistic man of science. On the surface this may sound difficult; but in practice I found it perfectly simple to combine the most rigidly rational conceptions of phenomena with the most exalted and enthusiastic celebration of their sublimity."

The ritual is very stylized and uses virgin priestesses, children, and priests. Many ancient Egyptian gods are invoked, as is the devil, and, at one point, the priestess performs a naked ritual.

6 HERMETIC ORDER OF THE GOLDEN DAWN

The Hermetic Order of the Golden Dawn was created by Dr. William Robert Woodman, William Wynn Westcott, and Samuel Liddell MacGregor Mathers. All three were Freemasons and members of Societas Rosicruciana in Anglia, an organization with ties to Masonry. It is considered by many to be a forerunner of the Ordo Templi Orientis and a majority of modern occult groups.

The belief system of the Golden Dawn is largely taken from Christian mysticism, Qabalah, Hermeticism, the religion of ancient Egypt, Freemasonry, Alchemy, Theosophy, Magic, and Renaissance writings. William Yeats and Aleister Crowley are two of the more famous members of the group.

The fundamental documents of the order are known as the Cipher Documents. These were translated into English using a cipher attributed to Johannes Trithemius. The documents are a series of sixty folios containing magic rituals. The basic structure of many of these rituals appears to originate with Rosicrucianism. There is a great deal of controversy surrounding the origins of these documents.

5 THE KNIGHTS TEMPLAR

The Knights Templar (full name The United Religious, Military, and Masonic Orders of the Temple and of St. John of Jerusalem, Palestine, Rhodes, and Malta) is a modern offshoot of Masonry and does not have a direct tie to the original Knights Templar, a religious military group formed in the twelfth century. Members of the Masonic Knights Templar do not claim a direct connection to the medieval group, but merely a borrowing of ideas and symbols.

In order to become a member of this group, you must already be a Christian Master Mason. This organization is a distinct one, and is not just a higher degree of Masonry. Despite Freemasonry's general disclaimer that no one Masonic organization claims a direct heritage to the medieval Knights Templar, certain degrees and orders are obviously patterned after the medieval Order.

These are best described as "commemorative orders" or degrees. Nevertheless, in spite of the fraternity's official disclaimers, some Masons, non-Masons, and even anti-Masons insist that certain Masonic rites or degrees originally had direct Templar influence.

4 THE ILLUMINATI

A movement of freethinkers that were the most radical offshoot of the Enlightenment and whose followers were given the name Illuminati (but who called themselves "Perfectibilists") was founded on May 1, 1776, in Ingolstadt (Upper Bavaria), by Jesuit-taught Adam Weishaupt. This group is now known as the Bavarian Illuminati. While it was not legally allowed to operate, many influential intellectuals and progressive politicians counted themselves as members. Even though there were some known Freemasons in the membership, it was not considered to be endorsed by Masonry. The fact that the Illuminati did not require a belief in a supreme being made them particularly popular among atheists. This, and the fact that most members were humanists, is the reason for the widespread belief that the Illuminati want to overthrow organized religion.

Internal panic over the succession of a new leader and government attempts to outlaw the group saw to it collapsing entirely in the late 1700s. Despite this, conspiracy theorists, such as David Icke and Was Penre, have argued that the Bavarian Illuminati survived, possibly to this day, though very little reliable evidence can be found to support the idea that Weishaupt's group survived into the nineteenth century. It has even been suggested that the Skull and Bones club is an American branch of the Illuminati.

Many people believe that the Illuminati is still operating and managing the main actions of the governments of the world. It is believed that they wish to create a One World Government based on humanist and atheist principles.

3 THE BILDERBERG GROUP

This group is slightly different from the others in that it does not have an official membership. It is the name given to a group of highly influential people who meet every year in secrecy (and usually with strong military and government-sponsored security). The topics discussed are kept secret. The structure of the meetings is that of a conference, usually held in five-star hotels around the world. Attendance at the meeting is strictly by invitation only. The first meeting took place in 1954 at the Hotel Bilderberg in the Netherlands.

The original meeting was initiated by several people. Polish emigre and political adviser Joseph Retinger, concerned about the growth of anti-Americanism in Western Europe, proposed an international conference at which leaders from European countries and the United States would be brought together with the aim of promoting understanding between the two.

Although the agenda and list of participants are openly available to the public, it is not clear that such details are disclosed by the group itself. Also, the contents of the meetings are kept secret and attendees pledge not to divulge what was discussed. The group's stated justification for secrecy is that it enables people to speak freely without the need to carefully consider how every word might be interpreted by the mass media.

Needless to say, this group is constantly surrounded by controversy and conspiracy theories.

2 THE PRIORY OF SION

After the publication of *The Da Vinci Code* by Dan Brown, a great deal of interest in the Priory of Sion was created. Unfortunately for those hoping to find and join the Priory, it is, in fact, fictional. It was a hoax created in 1956 by a pretender to the French throne, Pierre Plantard. Letters in existence dating from the 1960s written by Plantard, de Cherisey, and de Sède to each other confirm that the three were engaging in an out-and-out confidence trick, describing schemes on how to combat criticisms of their various allegations and how they would make up new allegations to try to keep the whole thing going. Despite this, many people still continue to believe that the Priory exists and functions to this day.

The authors of the well-known *The Holy Blood and the Holy Grail*, misled by the hoax, stated:

> "1. The Priory of Sion has a long history starting in AD 1099, and had illustrious Grand Masters including Isaac Newton and Leonardo da Vinci.
>
> 2. The order protects certain royal claimants because they believe them to be the literal descendants of Jesus and his alleged wife Mary Magdalene or, at the very least, of king David.
>
> 3. The Priory seeks the founding of a 'Holy European Empire' that would become the next hyperpower and usher in a new world order of peace and prosperity."

1 OPUS DEI

Opus Dei is an organization of the Catholic Church that emphasizes the Catholic belief that everyone is called to holiness and that ordinary life is a path to sanctity. The celibate numeraries and numerary assistants live in special centers, while associates are celibate members living in their private homes. The order was founded in Spain in 1928 by Roman Catholic priest Josemaría Escrivá with the approval of Pope Pius XII.

When Dan Brown's *The Da Vinci Code* was published, it claimed that Opus Dei was a secret organization within the church whose aim was to defeat the Priory of Sion and those who seek to uncover the "truth" about Christianity and the alleged royal bloodline of Christ. Outside of the book, there has been a great deal of controversy over Opus Dei because of the strictness of its religious structure.

The Catholic Church forbids secret societies and membership in them, and Opus Dei investigators have frequently debunked claims that this organization is acting in secrecy to further a sinister agenda.

✳✳✳✳✳✳

TOP 10 WORST URBAN JOBS

10 POLICE OFFICER

Unless you are patrolling Mayberry, you are risking your life every day you start your shift. Most cities have budget constraints that prevent an adequate number of police on the street in the first place. They are often undertrained and outgunned in the most dangerous situations. Every traffic stop, domestic dispute call, or drug-house bust could be the last. Although the benefits are great, the pay is only adequate, and many officers moonlight doing private security or work as bodyguards. Moving through the ranks and becoming a detective or some other non-street-level position is usually the best option for a long career.

9 FIREMAN

Arson for profit. Old, abandoned buildings full of homeless people. These are a couple of reasons that big-city firemen have to risk their lives every day. They have to go in, save lives, and put out a fire before it spreads to surrounding buildings. In times of riots (like Detroit and Watts in the 1960s and LA after the Rodney King verdict), they have actually been the victims of attack from angry mobs. It is a demanding job, not for those weak in mind or body.

8 EXTERMINATOR

If a roach- or rat-infested house is your idea of fun, then this job is for you. For the rest of us, the prospect of going into a stranger's house that is overrun by disease-spreading vermin is a nightmare job. This is such an awful job it even inspired a Stephen King short story!

7 CONVENIENCE STORE WORKER

A job where your life could be lost over a few dollars in the register. Some stores are mom-and-pop businesses that are family run. Others are large twenty-hour conglomerate stores that offer a chance for people to work hours suitable to their lifestyles. Despite closed circuit cameras and even an occasional gun hidden under the counter, many employees are shot even before a demand of money is made.

6 PROSTITUTE

The world's oldest profession is alive and well on city streets all across the planet. Besides the risk of being raped, assaulted, or even killed, there is always the real chance of catching an STD or AIDS. Since it's illegal in most states, prostitutes also run the risk of being arrested and jailed.

5 FACTORY WORKER

The five dollars a day that Henry Ford offered people to work in his Detroit factories almost a hundred years ago was life changing to some families. Many laborers and skilled tradesmen jumped at the chance to double their income. Although conditions are safer nowadays and the pay is much more, thanks to unions and collective bargaining agreements, the typical factory job is still dirty, hard, and tedious.

4 OFFICE WORKER

A long commute to spend an even longer day in a cube. You work just hard enough to keep from getting fired and get paid just enough to keep from quitting. (That's a quote from Les Brown, the motivational speaker). Most people spend a lot of time surfing the 'net, exchanging humorous e-mails, or updating their resume. It's a wonder any business gets done at all!

3 CAB DRIVER

Most drivers have to put in long hours behind the wheel to make a living. You have to deal with traffic jams and passengers that don't tip. Sometimes passengers are actually out to rob you of the few dollars you have made and will kill you in a heartbeat. This is why some cabbies will not pick up certain fares, which of course leads to more controversy.

2 DRUG DEALER

Crack, weed, meth, etc. They're available on any street corner for a few dollars a hit. In neighborhoods where drug use is rampant and jobs are scarce, many people choose this fast money option to make some cash to pay the bills. Whether it is the low-level, street-corner dealer or someone in a "middle management" capacity, the risks are high (prison, rival gangs) and pay is surprisingly low.

1 TELEMARKETER

They call at dinnertime, in the middle of your favorite movie, or right when you finally get the baby to sleep. They are prescripted, auto-call–generated denizens of call centers trying to sell us magazines, insurance or to get us to change our long distance service. The truth is most of those people calling us are hard-working young people that really are paying their way through college or older people in between "real jobs" trying to keep up with their mortgage payments. They are practically tied to the phone by a headset and breaks and lunches are also tightly monitored.

※※※※※

TOP 10 COMMON MISCONCEPTIONS ABOUT BRITAIN

10 BRITISH NATION

Misconception: Britain is a country.

While "Britain" or "Great Britain" does refer to the general area, neither of them refers to a country. Britain is a general term for Wales, Scotland, and England collectively, while the British Isles also includes Ireland (Northern and the Republic). England is most often incorrectly named in this way, and English people are often referred to as "British." Northern Ireland is part of the "United Kingdom of Great Britain and Northern Ireland," which differentiates between the part of Ireland that is governed by England (hence the suspension of the Northern Ireland government in 1972 and the Northern Ireland Assembly in 2002) from the Republic of Ireland, which is a self-governing nation.

While calling an English person British is technically correct, it is quite unspecific in the same way that calling a Canadian person "North American" would be, only Britain is not a continent.

9 WARM BEER

Misconception: British people drink beer warm or at room temperature.

I myself have heard this said a number of times but I have yet to discover where it comes from. Walking into a British bar and ordering a beer any way but cold would raise eyebrows just like everywhere else.

In fact, the most popular lager beers in Britain tend to be of the "extra cold" variety, and this applies to most bitter beers and ales too! Nobody likes a warm beer, the British included.

Having said that, most Americans like their beer super cold, so an English beer may appear to be warm in comparison, but it is still cold. Chilling beer too much can damage its flavor.

8 THE BOOK OF BRITISH SMILES

Misconception: British people have bad teeth.

This one is commonly referred to in comedy shows poking fun at Britain, but is believed by many to be hard fact.

While a percentage, just like any other country, will suffer from dental problems, the standard of oral hygiene is generally very high. In fact, the shortage of available NHS (National Health Service) dentists is a constant issue in England. Just like anywhere else in the world, a person with bad teeth is considered the slightly gross exception, not the rule in Britain.

7 GOD SAVE THE QUEEN

Misconception: "God Save The Queen" is the National Anthem of England.

That's right, I said England, not Britain. GSTQ is the national anthem of Britain, but not England itself. Despite this, even English people will insist that the song is their national anthem. This is not the case. Wales has its own national anthem, as do Scotland and Northern Ireland. What sets England apart is not that its national anthem is applied to the whole of Britain too, but that it in fact does not even have an official national anthem at all!

So what happens when (for example) England plays against Scotland in a game of football? We can't both use GSTQ for the opening. This isn't a problem for Scotland, who can bring out their own anthem, but England's choice will vary. Common stand-ins for when GSTQ cannot be used (for whatever reason) are "Land of Hope and Glory," "I Vow to Thee My Country," or "Jerusalem," all of which are popular contenders for becoming the official anthem. Sadly, none of them are official, and neither is GSTQ, which is only official for Britain itself.

6 ABSOLUTE POWER

Misconception: The Queen is the ruler of Britain.

Did I hear you say, "But she *is* the ruler of England!"? Sorry, you're still wrong. The monarchy has not had political power in Britain for a long time. Each British country has its own parliament and is ruled politically by their own prime minister.

While the monarchy does technically rule Britain, it does not have any power outside of ceremony. The Queen does not have power in Britain any more than she does in Canada and other commonwealth countries. All of these countries are technically "ruled" by a Queen, but she does not have power in any of them.

The British monarchy exists today mainly for ceremonial and tourist reasons.

5 HOW NOW BROWN COW
Misconception: British people speak the "Queen's English."

Or to use the more common term, British people talk "posh." Look at any representation of Britain from a foreign country and you will see British people speaking in a manner that is considered just as ridiculous to most of Britain. We all know what that sounds like, if not, take a look at Fry's Holophonor tutor in *Futurama*. Know what I mean? Then read on.

This may come from the way in which English is generally written in Britain. It is always taught that you should write "properly" and use correct language in formal writing so that it is easier to understand when read. Despite this, British people rarely speak the way they write.

In reality, Britain has a wide variety of accents, some even bordering on dialects, the majority of which do not sound remotely like how British speech is presented in foreign media. To see some examples of this, I suggest watching some British television or British cinema. (*Not* the news! Newsreaders are told to use Queen's English so they can be understood by all; this is even called "BBC English.")

Good examples are *Trainspotting* (Scottish accent), *28 Days Later* (modern London and Manchester accents), and *Sweeney Todd* (Old London accent).

People who speak the way British people are commonly presented sound just as snooty and posh to British people.

4 FREE HEALTHCARE
Misconception: Britain has free universal healthcare.

Ahhh… The good ol' NHS (National Health Service)! Sadly, as is commonly unknown to people outside of Britain, the NHS is not free, nor will it cover any illness or injury. The NHS is paid for through taxes and donations and will only provide certain approved services or treatments.

While it is true that emergency treatment is almost always free of charge, treatment for long-term illness or injury is almost always charged. Certain drugs will be provided for certain illnesses, but if your illness or the drugs and treatment you require is not on the "approved" list, you will not get it from the NHS. This is always a controversial issue in Britain.

The NHS is also not available to non-British residents except in the case of emergency. Even then the emergency must have taken place within Britain.

3 SCOTTISH MONEY

Misconception: Scottish money is legal tender in the rest of Britain.
If you have ever attempted to use Scottish pounds sterling in England, Wales, or Northern Ireland, you will know that many places will not accept it.

Scottish pounds sterling are not legal tender in all of Britain, and shops outside of Scotland are not legally obliged to accept it. Banks outside of Scotland will accept it, but legally it is down to the manager's discretion whether or not to accept it in any other location. What is the difference between Scottish pounds sterling and the pounds sterling used in the rest of Britain? Actually nothing. Aside from how it looks.

So why do many places outside of Scotland refuse to accept it? The most common reasons are that either they are not commonly seen and so are not recognized, or, due to the idea that its design and the fact that most people outside of Scotland rarely see it makes it easy to forge.

It may be frustrating if you come from Scotland for a trip around Britain, but there really is nothing to say that shopkeepers have to accept Scottish money, no matter how much you insist.

2 RAIN, RAIN EVERYWHERE

Misconception: It always rains in Britain.
When people think of Britain, we all tend to immediately think of bad weather. We see rain clouds, storms, and bitter wind. General misery. However, compared with many other parts of the world, Britain enjoys comparatively pleasant weather!

During the winter the average temperature can become bitterly cold (32–42 degrees Farenheit), but the average summer temperature ranges between 59–73 degrees, often higher. Britain ranks a comfortable forty-sixth in a chart of worldwide average rainfall, falling well behind such countries as New Zealand (twenty-ninth) and even the U.S. (twenty-fifth).

Why does Britain have a reputation for bad weather? Most likely because winters tend to be longer than summers in Britain, most artwork of Britain depicts the weather based on expectation, and we all like to dwell on a period of bad weather, even if the weather is generally good.

1 BRITISH TEA

Misconception: British people drink excessive amounts of tea.

There are many ways of looking at which regions drink the most tea, but whichever way you look at it, Britain is not the biggest tea-drinking region by a long way. Taking population into account, Britain ranks somewhere around third worldwide, falling well behind Turkey and India. Depending on your source, China still sits above Britain in the tea-drinking league tables even when considering population.

Where does this notion come from? Well, it is true that Britain does drink a lot of tea, but it is far from the top. Britain actually drinks almost as much coffee as it does tea. This misconception may actually stem from a linguistic difference between Britain and other English-speaking regions. In most places, the evening meal is referred to as "dinner" or "supper." This is correct terminology in Britain too, but an evening meal is very often referred to as "tea." So when a British person invites you round for tea, they are inviting you for a meal, not to just sit and drink tea, which is how some people imagine the situation. This is also true of the commonwealth nations, where "come for tea" usually means "come for the main evening meal."

A British person will almost never invite you over solely to drink tea, although if you stop by it will commonly be offered. Tea is most often drunk after a meal at dessert, or after strenuous activity as an alternative to coffee.

✳✳✳✳✳✳

TOP 10 ULTIMATE RIVALRIES

10 SPY VS. SPY

Spy vs. Spy is a silent comic strip created by Antonio Prohias and published in *Mad* magazine from 1961 to this day. In the strip, two spies, known only as White and Black, are constantly in a battle of deception to steal the other side's secret plans while at the same time setting up intricate traps to kill each other. Just when it seems that one of them will be falling into a lethal death trap the other one laid out, the trap is ingeniously backfired by the first, and the other spy is comically killed while the first spy escapes with a mischievous smile and doing the "v" sign with both hands. In a few occasions, a third female spy, known as Lady in Grey, is involved, and always ends up besting both Black and White, mostly due to them being helplessly in love with her.

Prohias, whose name appears in every strip in Morse code, and who fled from Cuba just before Castro took over the free press, considered himself a spy of sorts, and drew the cartoon as a satire of the Cold War and a criticism of its pointlessness. By 1990, health complications impeded his work on the strip, and other editors of *Mad* took over the task. Prohias passed away on February 24, 1998. *Spy vs. Spy* is possibly the longest running feature in *Mad* magazine, and the hilarious battles of wit between Black and White are still ongoing in the pages of the satirical magazine.

9 PEPSI VS. COKE

The two biggest cola brands in the world, Coca-Cola and Pepsi, have almost always been in direct competition, as they have both risen to global fame and have come to be hugely popular in all corners of the world. The immense popularity of both carbonated beverages has led to many a battle for the preference of the public in what has come to be known as the Cola Wars. What began as a struggle to strive in the American soft drink market, within a century, became a global battle for cola domination in almost every nation of the world. During most part of the twentieth century, both beverages rose to fame almost shoulder to shoulder, with no apparent winner.

But the "conflict" escalated when Pepsi unveiled its "Pepsi Challenge," where people were given a taste test of two unlabeled cola cans, and most of them turned out to prefer the can containing Pepsi. As a response, Coca-Cola concocted a new formula for their beverage and released it as the "New Coke." This new Coke was quite unpopular among the public, and Coca-Cola quickly returned to its old formula, calling it "Coca-Cola Classic." After this, both companies have undertaken fierce advertising campaigns aimed mostly at a teenage audience, trying to one-up their rival in the global cola market through catchy slogans, different flavors and spinoffs, and celebrity spokespersons. Although Coca-Cola dominates the market overall, Pepsi still possesses several bastions of popularity around the world, and is hot on the heels of its rival in this hundred-year-plus conflict.

8 *STAR WARS* VS. *STAR TREK*

If you want the ultimate conflict within the almighty geek populace, spanning several decades of shaping and reshaping pop culture as we know it and bringing war to space and cyberspace alike, yet with no apparent winner to be found, then you need to look no further than the "*Star Wars* vs. *Star Trek*" debate. Each of these powerful franchises has defined the genre of science fiction across the media industry through TV shows, major feature films, spin-off books, video games, conventions, and toys. As a result, seemingly endless battalions of die-hard fans of each franchise have taken it upon themselves to defend their obsessions by lashing out against their sci-fi counterparts at conventions and Internet chat rooms.

Although both franchises have several similarities which roughly unite them within the science fiction genre, such as laying out an entire galaxy teeming with alien species ready to battle each other in outer space with cool spaceships and other futuristic technologies, they can also be considered completely different and opposing when it comes to thematic undertones and philosophies, among many other things that fans are able to rant incessantly about. No matter how many words are posted in message boards about the subject, no matter how many fan-fiction crossover stories may be written, this battle for the supremacy of sci-fi may never see a true resolution.

7 MICROSOFT VS. APPLE

The impact of the advent of computers onto the modern world is undeniable. On the forefront of this revolution were two particular businesses that started small, but dreamed big, and became the most important computer corporations in the world. By the early '80s, Apple Computer, founded by Steve Jobs and Steve Wozniak, was already enjoying success from its innovative series of "Apple" computers, while Microsoft, founded by Bill Gates and Paul Allen, was just releasing its first operating system (or OS). But after getting a contract with IBM, Microsoft released its DOS series of operating systems and experienced a rise in the industry as it began to dominate the market through DOS and several software products aimed for businesses. Apple acknowledged the presence of Microsoft, and in 1984 launched a major advertising campaign for its new Macintosh computer. The success of the Macintosh was limited, while Microsoft, on the other hand, kept on the rise with its several forays into the computing market and especially its new Windows series. By 1993 Microsoft already dominated the market while the Apple industry started to struggle. During the '90s, Apple was in such a slump that it had to cut deals with both IBM and Microsoft to release joint products in an attempt to recover. Microsoft and its Windows OS series became synonymous with personal computers, while Apple became the less popular alternative.

By the turn of the new millennium, Apple experienced a revival of its brand through the introduction of the iMac and other products sharing a new, fresh, streamlined style of computers. But it wasn't until the release of the iPod that Apple was back again on top of the world. The huge success of the iPod popularized the new Apple style, and the iMac computers would rise in popularity as a result. Nowadays, Apple's "fresh" and "young" style has come to directly antagonize the more "traditional" style of Microsoft, as depicted by the "Mac vs. PC" series of ads. Although Microsoft still dominates the PC industry, Apple has an undeniable influence over modern electronics through the iPod and its more recent iPhone, which have once again made Apple a worthy contender against the Microsoft empire.

6 CATS VS. DOGS

Although they are not predator and prey, dogs and cats could, nevertheless, be considered the most famous "natural enemies" on the planet. Since the dawn of civilization, both canines and felines have held a place of privilege within the cities and homes of mankind; and as such, they have inevitably come to face each other in an ultimate battle for man's fondness.

This rivalry becomes more intense when we consider that they have seemingly opposing traits (even if this is true mostly as a stereotype): one is sly and cunning, while the other is brawny and brash; one acts like a loner who demands man's attentions, and the other glows with friendliness toward its master. Whatever your predilection, dogs and cats will continue to resent each other as long as there are human homes to contest and back alleys to claim.

5 NATURE VS. NURTURE

What makes us who we are? Is it a lifetime of nurturing and experiences, or were we predestined by our genes to become who we are today? Is our behavior defined by biological imperatives, or do we have some say in what we eventually become in life? How important are my genes in defining my life as opposed to the way I was raised? All these questions seek to find a solution to the "nature vs. nurture" debate. Some think that genetics and biology are quite irrelevant when it comes to defining your personality, and we are basically a blank slate ("tabula rasa") ready to be shaped into whatever kind of individual our parents and society wants us to be. Yet others emphasize the importance of heredity and genetics in defining people, since it is through those traits inherited from our parents that we become predisposed to certain behaviors and characteristics. Genes could be the primary trigger which define our propensity to be intelligent, to be fat, to smoke, to be an athlete, to be bitter, to like rock music or classical music, etc.; in short, since the moment we are born, we would be predestined to be who we are.

But, the environment may also play an important role when it comes to those genes actually "expressing" themselves in our lives; so even if genes have an important role in defining our personality, so would the way we are raised and our experiences in life. Genetics and behavioral sciences have come to make the subject very complex and fill it with even more questions about the nature of humanity.

4 BOYS VS. GIRLS

This evident and very significant rivalry could be presented as stemming from the most basic dichotomy in nature, where the biological need for harmony between the male and the female for the purpose of survival contrasts with the usually radical differences between the genders. It could also be presented as an undeniable element in the history of human life, where women have needed to struggle through the ages against the social and cultural injustices of a seemingly male-dominated culture.

I prefer to present this conflict in terms of how kids have defined their reasons for enmity and bitter war against each other: girls have cooties, and boys are gross. Simple, huh?

3 WEST VS. EAST

The rivalry between the so-called Eastern and Western cultures is a very complex and extensive subject, spanning many centuries of history, and deeply defining human civilization up until modern times. Throughout the ages, this conflict has taken many shades and names, with religious and political struggles occurring. Defining the East and the West in itself is difficult, since it is not at all a purely geographical condition. But there's no denying that several major wars and events in world history have happened directly from the opposition between the two. Arguably, religion and political ideologies are the two most important traits used to define this opposition, but these characteristics become evident only by observing the societies that have been established within each; or, in other words, the way human beings have embraced and expressed their lives as a product of living in those cultures of the world.

This rivalry is quite evident in modern times, where the current major global wars taking place can be considered a struggle between the cultures of the East and the West. But, at the same time, thankfully, an important process of global integration and diffusion of information is taking place, through the use of modern communications, as well as an increased interest for foreign cultures all over the world. Hopefully, this process will bring forth a much-needed understanding of other cultures which are not our own and help us appreciate the differences between our cultures so we can perceive, through those very differences, what we all have in common as human beings.

2 REASON VS. EMOTION

One of the most relevant conflicts that defines the very nature of our humanity is the constant struggle between our reason and our emotions. Many philosophical works have been written through the centuries trying to discern how these two aspects of our mind come into play to define human thinking. Yet, as of today, we still know very little about the way our mind works. If reason is the logical use of our mental faculties, something that is arguably exclusive to humans, then it is thanks to this aspect that we have developed as a superior species and have erected our grand civilization throughout time. But it would be foolish to limit human thinking and acting as only out of rationalization, because emotions constantly play a big part in the way we act. So, if emotion is a more primordial aspect of our minds, then how could we claim to be rational beings? What if you're driven by your emotions? What if you're too cold and rational about life? How could we find a true understanding of our minds without falling to the whims of one aspect or the other?

This antagonism is actually deeper than it seems, because it is thanks to this conflict that we have come to wonder about more mystifying aspects of life. What is love? Is it a completely emotional and biological process, or does something else, such as reason, come into play when we decide to be with someone for the rest of our lives? Is religion an emotional urge of some sort, or is it derived from our reasoning of something that may exist beyond us? What are the limits of the power of the mind as it perceives and shapes reality? What is "real"? Does the soul exist? What is God? Are we really able to answer these questions when we know so little about how our very minds work? Scientists, philosophers, priests, and even you and I are looking for answers to these questions, and as long as they remain unanswered, our reason and our emotion will keep on struggling in order to find the answers.

1 GOOD VS. EVIL

The ultimate rivalry is as old as time itself, and has been known by many names throughout the ages: yin vs. yang, light vs. darkness, creation vs. destruction, order vs. chaos, God vs. the Devil… Since antiquity, human beings have been involved in this eternal battle. In just about every story ever written you'll find this struggle between good and evil, whether literally or symbolically.

The presence of good and evil in humanity is not at all straightforward. Ethics and morality have been used to try to define what is inherently good and evil. Many philosophers have tried to explain the nature of evil and the nature of good. All religions explain the reasons and justifications for good and evil acts in their own ways. There are daily acts of goodness as well as daily acts of wickedness throughout the world. Although it seems like the most basic of rivalries, it is, in fact, the most important conflict that humanity has ever seen. Shouldn't all of us be concerned about knowing if what we are doing is for our own benefit only, or is actually helping others' lives as well? Shouldn't we place the welfare of others before our own? Shouldn't we all make certain that our actions are bringing either good or bad to the world? Despite all the confusion, it should be imperative for everyone to understand whether what they are doing with their lives is selfish and harmful to others, or if what they do every day is making the world a better place for everyone on it.

✳✳✳✳✳✳

TOP 10 FASCINATING SKYDIVING MYTHS

10 RIPCORDS

Myth: Skydivers pull ripcords.

Actually, ripcords pretty much went out with the round chute back in the early 1980s. Skydivers using modern-day "rigs" (the entire contraption of harness, container, and canopies) throw out a pilot chute, which is tucked into a pocket on the bottom of the container, just above your butt. The pilot chute is a small parachute attached to a "bridle," which is attached to the main chute. As the pilot chute is deployed, it catches the wind and pulls the closing pin, which releases the packed main chute, pulling it from the container, so it will inflate … we hope.

There are some drop zones that still use ripcord gear when teaching their students. Once they're properly trained, however, they graduate to the common bottom-of-container design. A reserve deployment does use a ripcord to activate the chute, but this is an entirely different design and we hope we never have to pull that handle.

9 FREEFALL CHATTER

Myth: You can talk or yell to each other during freefall.

Despite what you've seen in movies like *Point Break* and *Cutaway*, you cannot hear another skydiver during freefall. Perhaps if you were to yell into his ear, you may hear a little but you certainly can't have any type of conversation. The wind traveling past your ears at well over 100 mph pretty much makes you deaf to all sounds. Additionally, it would be very hard to fight during freefall as well.

8 CHUTE DEPLOYMENT

Myth: When you deploy your chute, you go back up.

This is a common fallacy. One thing a skydiver cannot do is go back up. What you're seeing when a skydiver deploys and goes up is an optical illusion. You're actually seeing the videographer, who is shooting the skydiver, falling away from the one deploying, who is obviously slowing down.

7 UNCONSCIOUS DROP

Myth: If you're ever knocked unconscious in freefall, you're dead.

Another common fallacy; it's understandable how this could be perceived, however. Think about it … if you're ever knocked out by a midair collision with a fellow skydiver, who's going to deploy your chute? Well, most skydivers jump with a device known as an Automatic Activation Device (AAD). It's a small, air-pressure and speed-sensitive unit that will cut the closing loop of your reserve chute so that it deploys automatically. They are usually set so that if you drop below 750 feet above ground level at over 78 mph, it goes off. If you are unconscious, your landing will likely be rough and you may injure yourself or perhaps still die, but landing without any chute at all would be far worse. Some skydivers choose to jump without one, because they are mechanical devices that can fail and possibly misfire, although they rarely do. The odds of it working when needed far outweigh the odds of it malfunctioning and deploying your reserve when you don't want it to.

6 FALL SPEED

Myth: Everyone falls at the same speed.

Despite what some people think, everyone falls at a different rate and the speeds will vary depending on weight (heavier people fall faster), body position, and clothing (baggy jumpsuits slow you down, tight-fitting suits go faster). The average terminal velocity in the belly-down position is around 120 mph. Some of the more advanced freeflying positions like "Head Down" or "Sit Fly" can push a jumper to over 200 mph! Essentially, the less amount of surface area to the wind, the faster you go. It takes a lot of work to contort the body in an arch (to speed up) and cup (to slow down) in order to catch up and stay with a group.

5 CHUTE PACKING

Myth: A skydiver always packs their own chute.

A good skydiver learns to pack their own chutes early on in his or her skydiving career and continues to do so. However, there is no legal obligation to pack your own chute. There are trained packers who work at drop zones and will pack your chute for you. Generally the cost is around five to seven dollars per pack. Many skydivers, however, choose to stick to packing their own chutes because they know how they like it packed (there are small variations for smoother openings) and, ultimately, who are you going to trust with your life? Yourself or some kid working the summer for six bucks a pack? If you choose to use the packer, be sure to tip them well!

4 DEPLOYMENT ALTITUDE

Myth: You can deploy your chute at any altitude.

I had an argument with a friend who was reading about military HALO operations, (High Altitude, Low Opening) and insisted that these military skydivers would freefall all the way down to between 100 and 50 feet then deploy their chute and land safely; this, of course, is simply not possible. Freefall speeds can be anywhere from 100 to 160 mph depending on varying scenarios; that's over 170 feet per second! A good main parachute needs about 600 to 800 feet to open for two reasons. First, it needs to inflate. The cells are closed end and a great deal of air needs to fill the cells before the chute is operational. Second, it needs to open fairly slowly to keep from injuring or even killing the skydiver. A hard-opening chute can kill a person when they go from 120 mph to 18 mph in only two or three seconds. Hard openings are usually a result of packing error. Fatal hard openings are extremely rare but a "normal" hard opening can make you see stars and give you bruises! Minimum opening altitudes (as regulated by the USPA and CSPA) are 2500 feet for A-licensed skydivers and 2200 feet for B, C, and D. Reserve chutes are designed to open much faster due to their necessity to do so quickly.

3 OXYGEN MASKS

Myth: You need to wear oxygen masks at very high altitudes.

Only on the plane. Hypoxia can set in quickly at 18,000 feet, so it's necessary for planes to supply it when climbing to that altitude and beyond. The most common high-altitude jumps are between 10,500 and 14,000 feet. Some larger drop zones with larger planes will offer special "extra-high" jumps of 22,000 feet. This of course costs "extra-cash." Some fancier planes offer masks, but more often it consists of a small hose coming out of the ceiling of the plane and you simply put it in your mouth up until you jump. Once you're out, you're only at that altitude for a short time, so extra oxygen on the jump itself isn't necessary.

2 ALTITUDE DANGERS

Myth: The higher the altitude, the more dangerous the jump.

Actually it's the opposite. Skydivers want as much altitude as possible. It allows for extra freefall time, but also it gives extra time to correct a correctable problem that may arise. It takes about 1480 feet to reach terminal velocity (around 120 mph). Whether it's a 1500-foot fall or 15,000-foot fall, having a bad chute or no chute at all, the outcome is not going to be good. Ultimately, there is no "safer" altitude for a high-speed impact. And considering the 600 to 800 feet it takes for a chute to open, I'll stay above 3000 feet when I jump—anything lower would just be crazy!

1 TERMINAL VELOCITY

Myth: It's possible to survive a terminal-velocity impact.

Everyone has heard the story: A skydiver jumped from 15,000 feet, his chute didn't open, and he landed in a muddy field and only broke his leg, or his back, or only ended up in a wheelchair, but he survived! There's always something wrong with the story, however. Many times it's completely made up. But in almost all these cases, there was "something" out, meaning there was a tangled mess of a chute (malfunction) or both chutes (double malfunction—extremely rare!) trailing behind the jumper. This can slow the descent down considerably. An impact into soft ground or trees at 45 mph is certainly survivable. You won't enjoy it, but you have a better chance of making it.

✳✳✳✳✳✳

TOP 10 TOYS PARENTS DREAD

10 KIDS' KARAOKE MACHINES

Nothing hits the spot more than a seven-year-old screeching out half the words to a Britney Spears number, perhaps only the exception of four seven-year-olds trying to do the same thing "in harmony." House parties have never been so much fun, especially when you can close the patio doors behind you, and walk several hundred miles in the opposite direction.

9 BANGERS

A small firework that is illegal in most parts of the world. Popular in the 1950s and '60s, the banger was the staple implement of torture for many boys who wished to make a huge impact on society. Generally, the banger was used to inflict fear, trauma, and, as a best-case scenario, a severe cardiac arrest on victims of a sensitive disposition.

8 PLAY MAKEUP

By looping the words "Get that off your face!" onto a tape, it is technically possible to save over two hundred hours' worth of mental and vocal stress caused as a result of abusing these substances. As the phrase "won't be seen dead wearing that!" doesn't appear to affect the young, many displays of tragically disheveling art can often be seen on the faces of the innocent.

7 PAINT

Many parents have learned to patiently applaud the appalling efforts of their offspring when it comes to painted art, much of which finds its way to the sides of fridges everywhere. Paint runs, as fast as it can, into clothing, rugs, doors, and pets, and scientific experts have calculated that a single sheet of blank paper typically needs to be surrounded by eight square miles of yesterday's newspapers to save the carpet receiving the traditional Sunday afternoon makeover.

6 STICKERS

Aside from the sheer volume of children's magazines, which pile up under the beds of preteens, by far the worst side effect of this type of behavior is often the infamy of the included stickers. Many wardrobes have suffered in recent years under the sheer weight of stickers festooned over their exteriors. Nothing escapes the tyranny of the sticker, and, to date, no blend of biohazardous toxic chemicals have proven effective at removing their blight on humanity.

5 NURSERY RHYME PLAYERS

When Moms and Dads are busy, they may inadvertently place their faith in musical toys to satisfy the hungry minds of their immediate descendants. Unfortunately, this is counterproductive, and leads to a condition doctors have known for years as "losing one's mind." If taking out frustrations on inanimate objects is your kind of heaven, please send in your address and you will receive your just deserts.

4 VOICE "LEARNERS"

Learning the alphabet or the numbers using an annoying female voice has been around for centuries, but if your mother-in-law is busy, try to avoid using one of these machines at all costs. Listen as an endless series of discordant jingles, similes, and phonics are played repeatedly by the delicate touch of a child's whole hand over all the buttons.

3 MUSICAL INSTRUMENTS

Used successfully by the CIA since the turn of the twentieth century, nothing works more effectively and damagingly on human levels of tolerance than a twelve-year-old playing the violin, a four-year-old playing a miniature drum kit, or a nine-year-old blowing into a recorder (or flute). Scientists in Russia have termed parental exposure to this kind of treatment "neurological meltdown" or "cranium critical mass," and victims have often resorted to quite drastic feats of human strength in order to ensure these kinds of instruments are never capable of playing "music" ever again.

2 PLAY-DOH

What can you do with Play-Doh that you can't do with plasticine or real dough? Experts were baffled for weeks when given this question during the late twentieth century. That was until one man dejectedly pushed the material into a salt shaker and it "looked a bit like hair." Since then, millions of children of all ages have sat this same simple test, all of whom failed to come up with anything at all. The legend of Play-Doh was born.

1 LEGO

Where is the best place to find Lego? In the vacuum cleaner, of course! This was the winning entry of many in this competition; runners-up include on the stairs, between the cracks in the patio, in the bathtub, and, of course, in beds. There are several ways in which Lego has taken the crown of "the most annoying toy." First of all, because Lego is so easy to consume, many "consumers" have found their Lego products have made it all the way down the toilet and into the sea, where they continue to annoy ocean life in the same way. Secondly, because Lego is so small, adult fingers can often lose their ability to manipulate the material, similar to trying to pick up a coin using a bunch of bananas. Many triumphs of model engineering have been crushed underfoot, under car tires, under bottoms, and between fingers, sometimes sending lethal Lego shrapnel in all directions at once. Avoid.

✳✳✳✳✳✳

TOP 10 MOST EXPENSIVE TOYS

10 BARBIE

How about the Diamond Barbie co-designed by De Beers? It comes with a gown sporting 160 diamonds as well as white gold miniature jewelry to give the world's most expensive Barbie doll the world's most expensive look. The one-of-a-kind fortieth anniversary Barbie created in 1999 comes with a full-figured price tag of about $85,000. 1959 Barbie number-one in mint condition runs about $8000. Do you take a check?

9 MATCHBOX CAR

Maybe you would like one of the original Matchbox cars? Well, in that case, it's a boxy sea-green sedan, the 1966 Opel Diplomat. A rare few are being offered for sale, but at $9000, they're beyond most people's budgets. If only you'd bought one years ago when they first hit the market. The price back then: forty-eight cents.

8 TOY GUN

Would you like the 6-mm mini-gun for AirSoft? Sorry. If you were lucky enough to get one while in production, congratulations. Nothing came close to the power of these things in a Gatling-type air-gun. Like a school of piranhas, the steel 6-mm BBs could chew little bits of inch-thick reinforced glass until there was nothing left. And with the three-thousand-round magazine, this mini-gun blows the Japanese guns right off the playing field. Used, in good condition, with accessories, these M134 guns have sold for over $9000.

7 TOY SEWING MACHINE

Perhaps one of your children is into darning? Well, this particularly unusual toy sewing machine adorned with a clown was auctioned in London, England. The bidding went quickly to 6000 pounds and then was down to two strong bidders, neither wanting to give up on the chance of having this toy sewing machine. The last two bidders were an English industrial sewing machine dealer and a German millionaire. Finally, when the Englishman bid a whopping $13,600, the German quietly did not bid. The holes can stay in my clothes, thanks.

6 TEDDY BEAR

Your children love stuffed bears much like so many around the world, so why not "splurge" and get them one of these: to celebrate the 125th anniversary of the teddy bear a German company created a limited edition of 125 bears of which the mouth is made of solid gold and the eyes of sapphires and diamonds. The highest price ever paid for a single one of these teddy bears was $193,000.

5 TOY SOLDIER

So you have a few boys who just love to wage war with their military action figures. Here we have the most expensive toy soldier in the world. It was the creation of Don Levine and was the 1963 G.I. Joe prototype. Levine sold the prototype to Baltimore businessman Stephen A. Geppi on August 7, 2003, during an auction performed by Heritage Comics Auctions of Dallas, Texas. The prototype was purchased for $200,000. When Levine created his toy soldier, he created it on his ping-pong table. The soldier measured eleven-and-a-half inches tall and had twenty-one movable parts. Not only did this G.I. Joe have movable parts, he also wore a hand-stitched sergeant's uniform. Now is that a toy to die for?

4 OFF-ROADER

If you have a kid between the ages of seven and fifteen and want to give them a gift that will make them the instant envy of the neighborhood, then you must check out the off-roader. However, if you do not have a limitless bank account, you may have to get a loan just to purchase it. The cost of a junior off-roader is $40,000. This beauty comes complete with all-weather fiberglass body with a protective frame, dual hydraulic disk brakes, rack and pinion steering, manual emergency brake, full front and rear suspension, front and rear suspension, three-speed transmission, radio and CD player with speakers on the side doors. Oh, and it is also very comfortable with adjustable, upholstered leather seats. They can ride in style at a blistering thirty mph.

3 PEZ DISPENSER
How many times have you gotten one of the thousands of Pez dispenser varieties in your stocking on Christmas? Well, if you love them as many collectors do, then the 1982 World's Fair Astronaut B Pez dispenser is for you. It was on the auction block on eBay and is one of only two to have been created. This one has a white helmet and green stem. It is believed to have been a prototype to the World's Fair board. The Pez dispenser was never put into production and was received from former Pez employees as stated by the auction. The winning bid for the world's most expensive Pez dispenser: $32,205.

2 HAND-HELD VIDEO GAME
Now that the most popular video game system, the Nintendo Wii, is next to impossible to locate, why not find one for your child in the hand-held variety. The world's most expensive Gameboy is made of 18-karat gold, with a display screen surrounded by diamonds. Available through Swiss Supply and created by Aspreys of London, this little toy will set you back a playful $25,000. They will, however, toss in a case, the cables, and a few games for you. Thank goodness, that makes it all worthwhile.

1 *STAR WARS* MOVIE PROP
Forget figures this holiday, your little *Star Wars* fan wants collectible movie memorabilia! So, in that case, get this: the Darth Vader fighting helmet from *The Empire Strikes Back*. It's only a mere $115,000, and was used extensively throughout the climactic fight sequences in the film. It was specially created to allow Bob Anderson, the Olympic fencing champion who took over the role of Darth Vader for the fight sequences, clearer vision. Great, now your child can see so much better while battling the Jedi.

CHAPTER SEVEN
Movies

TOP 10 FILM MISQUOTES

10 WHITE HEAT
Misquote: "Top of the world, Ma!"

In fact, before the tank explodes, James Cagney, in white heat, actually says, "Made it, Ma. Top of the world!"

9 DRACULA
Misquote: "I want to suck your blood!"

This quote, usually attributed to Bela Lugosi, who played Dracula in 1931, was never actually spoken by him. However, it was used for humor in Tim Burton's 1994 *Ed Wood*.

8 FRANKENSTEIN
Misquote: "He's alive!"

The actual phrase used is, "It's alive." This is true of both the original 1931 film and the comedy version in 1974 starring Gene Wilder.

7 BLONDE CRAZY
Misquote: "You dirty rat!"

Attributed to James Cagney, he never said this line in a movie. The closest he ever came to saying this phrase was, "Mmm, that dirty, double-crossin' rat," in the 1931 *Blonde Crazy*.

6 TARZAN
Misquote: "Me Tarzan, you Jane!"

As believable as it seems, this line was not spoken in the 1932 film *Tarzan, the Ape Man*. Here is what was actually said:

> Jane: (*pointing to herself*) Jane.
> Tarzan: (*he points at her*) Jane.
> Jane: And you? (*she points at him*) You?
> Tarzan: (*stabbing himself proudly in the chest*) Tarzan, Tarzan.
> Jane: (*emphasizing his correct response*) Tarzan.

Tarzan: (*poking back and forth each time*) Jane. Tarzan. Jane. Tarzan…
Ah, such eloquence!

5 SHE DONE HIM WRONG
Misquote: "Come up and see me sometime."

Close but not close enough. What Mae West actually said in *She Done Him Wrong* (1933) was, "Why don't you come up sometime 'n' see me?"

4 LIVES OF A BENGAL LANCER
Misquote: "We have ways of making you talk."

This is allegedly from the 1935 film *Lives of a Bengal Lancer*. The actual statement was, "We have ways of making men talk."

3 SNOW WHITE AND THE SEVEN DWARFS
Misquote: "Mirror, mirror on the wall, who is the fairest of them all?"

This is an incorrect quotation. In Disney's animated film *Snow White and the Seven Dwarfs* (1937), the wicked Queen asked: "Magic mirror on the wall, who is the fairest one of all?"

2 STAR WARS
Misquote: "Luke, I am your father."

Commonly believed to have been said by Darth Vader, this quote did not actually occur at all. The actual quote was, "No, I am your father," and it was not even delivered on camera, it was dubbed in later. What was originally said on camera was "Obi-Wan killed your father."

1 CASABLANCA
Misquote: "Play it again, Sam."

This is often believed to have been said by Bogart in *Casablanca*. In fact, the closest Bogart came to the phrase was this: "You played it for her, you can play it for me… If she can stand it, I can. Play it!" Interestingly, Ingrid Bergman's character comes closest when she says, "Play it, Sam."

✳✳✳✳✳✳

TOP 10
JAMES BOND MOVIES

10 LICENSE TO KILL, 1989

After Bond's American friends are attacked by Franz Sanchez (Robert Davi), a drug lord seeking revenge for a drug bust, Bond (Timothy Dalton) wants payback and quits MI6. Bond becomes a rogue agent and, with the assistance of Pam Bouvier (Carey Lowell), tracks down Sanchez to South America to assassinate him.

This movie has unjustly received bad criticism. This film is dark and humorless, unlike other Bond films, but Timothy Dalton managed to perfectly convey what Ian Fleming originally intended to do with the character: portray a cold-blooded professional killer.

9 TOMORROW NEVER DIES, 1997

When a British warship is mysteriously destroyed in Chinese waters, the world is on the brink of World War III, until 007 (Pierce Brosnan) zeros in on the true criminal mastermind of the attack. Bond's do-or-die mission takes him to Elliot Carver (Jonathan Pryce), a dominant industrialist who easily manipulates world events. After soliciting help from Carver's sexy wife, Paris (Teri Hatcher), Bond joins forces with a stunning yet lethal Chinese agent, Wai Lin (Michelle Yeoh), in a series of chases, vicious confrontations, and magnificent escapes as they race to stop Carver's plan of global pandemonium.

8 FOR YOUR EYES ONLY, 1981

A British spy ship accidentally sinks with a secret weapons system onboard. James Bond (Roger Moore) and the Russians are both out to salvage the device in the depths of the Atlantic Ocean. To assist Bond in his quest, which takes him to locales like Italy and Greece, Bond teams up with Melina Havelock (Carole Bouquet), whose parents were assassinated by a spy working for the Soviets.

After the silliness of *Moonraker* (1979), it's nice to see Roger Moore being serious for once. He makes this film one of the most realistic films in the series. The gadgets are all believable and the action sequences are somewhat sane.

7 *THUNDERBALL*, 1965

In a bold scheme, an evil organization called SPECTRE hijacks a NATO plane and seizes two atomic warheads, each capable of killing millions of people. As the world is held hostage by the threat of a total apocalypse, James Bond (Sean Connery) jumps into action, racing against the clock as the evidence leads him to the tropical nation of Nassau. There he meets Emilio Largo (Adolfo Celi), a distinguished agent of SPECTRE, and the beautiful Domino (Claudine Auger), whom Bond is immediately attracted to. The confrontation builds to an epic battle on the ocean floor, as Bond and his allies fight to avert the catastrophe. His mission leads him from a perilous jetpack flight to a terrifying clash with Largo's killer sharks. Interestingly, this film is not without controversy among Bond aficionados as to whether or not Bond maneuvers Fiona Volpe into the path of a SPECTRE gunman's bullet. This film was remade in 1983 as an unofficial Bond film; the remake also featured Sean Connery as Bond.

6 *THE SPY WHO LOVED ME*, 1977

A NATO submarine and a Soviet submarine vanish in the middle of the ocean, and a crazed megalomaniac living under the sea has the technology to track the two submerged vessels. After some initial squabbling, Bond (Roger Moore) must join forces with KGB agent Anya Amasova (Barbara Bach). Traveling from Egypt to the Alps, they will have to face the frightening Jaws (Richard Kiel).

You can really feel Roger Moore coming into his own in his third Bond outing. There's just the right balance of political conflicts and over-the-top action to make this a truly great 007 film.

5 *GOLDENEYE*, 1995

James Bond (Pierce Brosnan) is out to stop a criminal organization from stealing codes to a Russian electromagnetic pulse weapon known as "Goldeneye." With the help of computer programmer Natalya Siminova (Izabella Scorupco), he must stop assassin Xenia Onatopp (Famke Janssen) and her boss, who is Bond's former colleague.

In this film, Brosnan proves he has the necessary charisma to be an exceptional 007. The movie includes some good acting with some amazing action scenes.

4 GOLDFINGER, 1964

The Bank of England has discovered that someone is stockpiling enormous amounts of gold, and James Bond (Sean Connery) is sent to investigate. Gold dealer Auric Goldfinger (Gert Frobe) becomes the prime suspect. With the help of Oddjob (Harold Sakata) and Pussy Galore (Honor Blackman), Goldfinger plans on raiding Fort Knox.

Many consider this to be one of the best Bond movies, and it's a classic in its own right. Although it contains one of the greatest villains in movie history, the plot is very unbelievable and the film seems lacking at parts.

3 CASINO ROYALE, 2006

James Bond's first "007" mission leads him to Le Chiffre (Mads Mikkelsen), banker to most of the world's terrorists. In order to stop him, and bring down the terrorist network, Bond (Daniel Craig) must beat Le Chiffre in a high-stakes poker game at Casino Royale. Bond is primarily irritated when a beautiful British Treasury official, Vesper Lynd (Eva Green), is assigned to watch over the government's money during the game. But, as Bond and Vesper survive a series of lethal attacks by Le Chiffre and his henchmen, an attraction develops between them that might later endanger the mission.

This Bond, like the one in the novels, gets angry, makes mistakes, is tough, loves women, is gifted at killing, and yet doesn't like it. The producers got it right when they brought Bond back without the gadgets and the infallibility of Brosnan.

2 FROM RUSSIA WITH LOVE, 1963

The leader of SPECTRE wants revenge against James Bond (Sean Connery) for killing Dr. No. Bond is lured to Istanbul, where he thinks a Russian operative has a cipher machine for him. Along with Tatiana Romanov (Daniela Bianchi), 007 has to avoid the assassins while trying to steal the cipher machine.

This second movie in the series is slow-paced but very realistic. This film marks the first appearance of Q and his famed gadgets, which will be prominent in the series. The plot is easy to follow and always fun to watch.

1 DR. NO, 1962

Bond (Sean Connery) is sent to Jamaica to find out the mystery behind a fellow secret agent's murder. He discovers that the death is linked to an energy wave that is able to interfere with U.S. missile launches. With the gorgeous Honey

Ryder (Ursula Andress), he soon discovers that a madman known as Dr. No has plans for world domination.

Sean Connery's portrayal of the role launched his career into stardom. He's very callous and tough in the film, but never without humor. This film was extremely successful, and even though the title sequence and gadgets hadn't made an appearance yet, it should still be recognized as the movie that started it all.

✳✳✳✳✳✳

TOP 10 GREAT MOVIES THAT WERE NEVER FINISHED

10 UNCLE TOM'S FAIRY TALES, 1968

Uncle Tom's Fairy Tales was to be the first film starring Richard Pryor. The movie was about a white man who goes on trial for having raped a black woman. At the time of the making of this film, Richard Pryor's wife complained that he was paying more attention to the film than he was to her. The film was eventually canceled and his wife shredded the negative. No copies of the film were known to have survived, however, in 2005, scenes from the film appeared in a retrospective as Pryor was being honored by the Directors Guild of America. There is still a lawsuit pending to this day between Pryor's ex-wife and his daughter over this film and who should own it.

9 WHO KILLED BAMBI, 1978

Russ Meyer was set to direct this film, which was to be the first featuring the Sex Pistols. The movie was intended as a pseudo-punk version of *A Hard Day's Night*. Just a day-and-a-half worth of shooting were completed as the filming stopped when the executives at 20th Century Fox read the script. The producers and decision-makers were so shocked that they pulled all funding.

The footage that exists shows Sting (the leader of a pop group called The Blow-Waves) assaulting drummer Paul Cook as he stops to ask for directions.

8 *KALEIDOSCOPE*, 1971

This film was to be a groundbreaking experimental film directed by Alfred Hitchcock. If it had been completed it would probably have been Hitchcock's darkest film. Even Hitchcock himself worried that some scenes might be too frightening for the audience. *Kaleidoscope* was the story of a bodybuilder who was a serial rapist and killer. David Hemmings and Michael Caine had been suggested as leads in the film. In the script there are several murders, including an attempt on the life of a policewoman. Hitchcock planned to experiment with innovative filming techniques such as hand-held filming and natural light. He also wanted to tell the entire story from the perspective of the killer. Unfortunately, MCA studios stopped the project because they thought the protagonist was too repulsive. All that remains now is an hour-long tape of silent footage. Some of these ideas would be recycled into Hitchcock's 1972 movie *Frenzy*.

7 *THE WORKS*, 1978

This film was to be the first entirely 3D computer animated film. The film was about a villainous giant ant-like creature. The original meaning of the word "robot" in many Slavic languages inspired the name. The story was set somewhere in the future when a last World War had led to an advanced computer network, which now controlled the world. The main problem for this film was the fact that technology could not cope with a full feature-length CGI movie. The film was worked on from 1978 until 1986. In the end it became clear the movie would never be finished so the project was abandoned. However, it is said that all the technology and software that was created for this project made the effort worthwhile.

6 *DUS*, 1997

Dus was to be a Bollywood action film directed by Mukul S. Anand. The storyline was about terrorism and shows an anti-terrorist intelligence officer who is sent on a mission to find an Afghan terrorist. Shooting of the film began in Utah, which was to have depicted scenes of Kashmir, the major setting of the film. Forty percent of the shooting had been completed before director Anand suddenly died. The film was abandoned, never to be completed or released. The music soundtrack of the film was released while the film was still in production.

5 THE MAN WHO KILLED DON QUIXOTE, 2000

Terry Gilliam directed this feature film. The shooting stopped within a week due to an injury to star Jean Rochefort who was playing Quixote. The movie was set to have been one of the biggest European films ever made, with a budget of thirty-two million. The entire movie would have been filmed in Spain and throughout Europe. The character Toby was to be played by Johnny Depp, and Vanessa Paradis would have been his love interest. When Rochefort (an able horseman) attempted to ride, it was obvious that he was in pain and required assistance dismounting and walking. It was discovered after he flew to his doctor in Paris that he had a double herniated disc. When it became apparent that he would not be able to return, Gilliam decided to scrap the project. There may be some plans to restart the production in 2009 with hopes that Michael Palin will play Quixote alongside Johnny Depp.

4 THE DAY THE CLOWN CRIED, 1972

The Day the Clown Cried was a film directed by, and starring, Jerry Lewis. The movie is about a depressed, formerly great German circus clown named Helmut Dorque during the beginning of the Holocaust. Dorque is eventually fired from the circus and is arrested at a bar by the Gestapo for mocking the Fuhrer. Dorque is then imprisoned in a Nazi camp for political prisoners. Lewis reportedly lost forty pounds for the concentration camp scenes. Unfortunately, the producers were not fronted with sufficient finances, causing Lewis to begin paying for the production costs with his own money. Lewis reportedly has the only known videocassette copy of the film, which he keeps locked away in his office. The location of the original film negative is unknown. Lewis refuses to discuss the film at all in interviews to this day.

3 DARK BLOOD, 1993

Dark Blood is about a character named Boy (played by River Phoenix). Boy is a hermit who lives on a nuclear testing site waiting for the end of the world while making dolls that he believes have magical powers. He meets a couple in the Arizona desert due to their car breaking down and holds them prisoner because he desires the woman and wants to create a better world with her. Dark Blood was never completed due to the death of River Phoenix in 1993. The crew was eleven days shy of completing production. Because the film had to be abandoned, Phoenix's mother was sued due to loss of expenses. The unfinished film is owned entirely by George Sluizer who wrote the script. He has hinted that he might use it as footage in a documentary about River's life.

2 THE OTHER SIDE OF THE WIND, 1972

Anyone who is a film buff would know that an Orson Welles film would have to be somewhere on this list. This Welles film was to star John Huston, Peter Bogdanovich, and Dennis Hopper. Some believe that because this film was filled with so much sex and violence it was an attempt to revive Welles's career. Apparently 96 percent of the film was complete, but financial problems prevented it from being finished. Showtime cable network had guaranteed the money to complete the film, but a lawsuit by Welles's daughter caused Showtime to withdraw its funding. In April 2007, Bogdanovich said in a press report that a deal was made to complete the movie. His goal was to release the film in 2008, but Bogdanovich recently said there is still over a year's worth of work to be done.

1 SOMETHING'S GOT TO GIVE, 1962

Something's Got to Give is arguably the most famous unfinished film in Hollywood history. This was to be a light comedy and a remake of the movie *My Favorite Wife*. The film starred Marilyn Monroe, Dean Martin, and Cyd Charisse and was directed by George Cukor. Monroe had recently undergone gallbladder surgery and had dropped over twenty-five pounds, reaching the lowest weight of her adult life. On the first day of production, Monroe called the producer to let him know that she had a severe sinus infection, and would not be on the set that morning. Similar delays continued on an almost daily basis and the film quickly turned into a costly disaster. Because of the delays, Monroe was fired and the film cancelled and shelved. Marilyn Monroe spiraled further into decline and died later that year in 1962.

※※※※※※

TOP 10 ERRORS IN SCIENCE FICTION MOVIES

10 **SIMPLICITY**
This is less a crime of commission than one of omission. Space is full of wonders we cannot even begin to understand, yet most science fiction films are based in a very simplistic environment and do not even begin to investigate the wonderful possibilities that science fiction offers us. We don't see interplanetary tunnels, aliens on planets around pulsars, creatures living on dead suns, alien life-forms that inhabit the edges of supermassive black holes, or so many of the other thought-provoking scenarios. Let's spice up our science fiction movies!

9 **SIMPLISTIC PLANETS**
This is particularly evident in the *Star Wars* movies. Whenever a planet is introduced in a science fiction film, it has one equal ecological system across the entire planet, for example, it might be entirely covered in snow or entirely covered in sand. If people are living on these planets, they must be providing water and other important things needed for survival. This, in turn, would suggest that the planet ought to have a well-developed, complex ecosystem that varies from region to region, for example, ice at the poles and arid land at the center (this is just an example of course).

8 **ALIEN / HUMAN BREEDING**
This is often seen in *Star Trek*, for example Spock—he was half human and half Vulcan. It is not even possible for human/ape crossbreeds to occur due to genetic differences so it is inconceivable that a human and an alien might be able to crossbreed. There are, of course, additional problems: how do you perform the cross-breeding if the alien does not have sexual organs or the means to extract the necessary seeds of life?

7 ALIEN / HUMAN COMMUNICATION

If aliens did exist, it would be extremely unlikely that we could communicate with them in a very short amount of time. In addition to the regular problems in translating an entirely unknown language, we would also have to consider a society that probably involves concepts we do not understand at all. Imagine an alien race trying to understand God if they have never had a notion of religion in their society. Of course, none of this matters if the aliens communicate with their minds or non-audible means; it would be impossible for us to communicate at all with a race that has no concept of sight and sound.

6 INSTANT COMMUNICATIONS

Even if we did use light particles/waves to transmit radio data, the vast distances in space would make instant radio communication impossible. A rare exception to this flaw is in the movie *Contact*; as the camera draws away from the earth we hear the radio emanations getting progressively older until you finally reach silence. This trick is very effectively used to show just how massive space is.

5 HUMANOID ALIENS

This is endemic on the various *Star Trek* series, where creatures from entirely different sectors of the universe look just like humans except for the occasional bulging ridge on their foreheads, for example. Humans evolved on Earth in order to meet very specific criteria for survival; the presumption that this is true of all other planets is ridiculous.

4 EXPLOSIONS IN SPACE

Unfortunately, virtually every science fiction movie makes this error—in fact, in the vacuum of outer space, there can be no flames (as flames need oxygen) and, of course, no boom. An exception to this is the film *2001*, in which Bowman re-enters the *Discovery* by blowing out an airlock.

3 SUPERLUMINAL TRAVEL

According to Einstein's special theory of relativity, as an object approaches the speed of light, the energy required to propel it, is immense. By the time you reach the speed of light, infinite energy is needed; this renders faster-than-light travel impossible for man.

2 EARTH GRAVITY

It doesn't matter what film you watch, almost all of them have Earth-like gravity, no matter where it is set. This is ridiculous, of course, unless you are on a planet, which matches Earth in every way with regards to our level of gravity. One film, which does not fall for this error, is, again, *2001*. The clever devices used in the film to show us how humans would live in a non-gravity environment really make this one of the best films in its genre.

1 SOUND IN SPACE

Sound requires air to travel. Without air (as we find in the vacuum of space), there is no sound. Many films completely ignore this and give us ear-piercing sound effects during battles. The greatest exception to this error is, yet again, the movie *2001*—all outer space activity takes place in silence, with the occasional addition of the "Blue Danube."

✳✳✳✳✳✳

TOP 10 MOST ANNOYING SIDEKICKS IN MOVIES

10 BENJAMIN BUFORD "BUBBA" BLUE, *FORREST GUMP*

I included Bubba on this list for only a couple of reasons. I recognize that Bubba from *Forrest Gump* is a pretty popular character from a very popular movie. But I feel that his speech impediment, his uninspiring speeches, and his lead in the endless "shrimp" scene warrant his inclusion in a list of annoying movie characters. Most of the scenes involving Bubba are usually dominated by Tom Hanks's Forrest Gump character anyway, leaving the viewer wondering why we really needed another slow, confused Southerner with a speech impediment.

9 CHEWBACCA, STAR WARS SERIES

Another very popular character and a wonderful sidekick to Han Solo, but I decided to include him on the list simply because of the noise. Noise, noise, noise. Every scene involving Chewbacca is like trying to watch a movie that has been put through a woodchipper. Most of the *Star Wars* series is shot with great sound quality, due to Lucas's genius work starting up the THX franchise. But even in quiet scenes aboard the *Millennium Falcon* while the cast is deep in hyperspace, Chewie's *"Nyraghgg nyaghhh nanyyyyyy"* slices into the audio with reckless abandon, clogging up an otherwise peaceful scene.

8 GOLLUM, LORD OF THE RINGS TRILOGY

No matter what you think about the Lord of the Rings franchise, you can't argue that most scenes involving Gollum require a certain amount of intestinal fortitude. He is ugly. He is repulsive. He repeats the same phrases over and over again. He eats raw fish. Most scenes that involve Gollum make you wish you were back in the Shire.

7 DAVID LEVINSON, *INDEPENDENCE DAY*

Of all the characters on this list, Jeff Goldblum's portrayal of pseudo-sidekick David Levinson in *Independence Day* is the least obvious. In a way, Levinson is sort of a sneaky annoyance. While Will Smith is busy fighting aliens and saving the world from annihilation, Levinson is trying to figure out how to get back together with his wife. While Bill Pullman is busy organizing the countries of the world, uniting them in liberty and leadership, Levinson is worrying about science and trying to deal with his grumpy old dad. Then, by the end, somehow he finds himself on a secret mission to blow up the mothership, and as they are flying through space, I swear you can see a look on his face that says, "Did I leave the oven on?" Plus, his "drunk" scene is absolutely not believable. He downs a liter of vodka in a fit of depression, then the next minute he is discussing physics with the U.S. Department of Defense. Please, just get off the screen and let Will Smith kick some ass.

6 STIFLER, AMERICAN PIE SERIES

The only thing more annoying than Stifler himself is an impersonation of Stifler, which is something that occurred in frat houses nationwide soon after *American Pie* was released. I am not trying to say that *American Pie* is a good movie (trust me, it isn't), but did we really need a cocky mama's boy to fluff up the scenes and make them even funnier? I actually enjoyed most scenes that involve Eugene Levy, but then inevitably Stifler would appear and force me to remember that I was watching a terrible teenage comedy about sex. Not really a sidekick, but annoying nonetheless.

5 PINTEL AND RAGETTI, PIRATES OF THE CARIBBEAN SERIES

This duo takes a position in this list because the characters simply bring nothing to the table and serve as a good reminder that big movie studios think you (the audience) are stupid. What's not to like about two goofy pirates, especially when one of them keeps losing an eyeball? Everything. They are not funny and they always interrupt any scene involving Johnny Depp, who brings enough comedy to this adventure movie.

4 WILLIE SCOTT, *INDIANA JONES AND THE TEMPLE OF DOOM*

Any movie tends to lose a little bit of watch-ability when there is one single character who does nothing but scream the entire movie. Yes, the entire movie. She is screaming, complaining, whining, crying, and yelling for the whole flippin' movie, and the whole time she thinks that she is a beautiful singer and the object of Indiana's affection. Most scenes involving Willie Scott and Indiana Jones are somewhat uncomfortable because you are just waiting for her to start screaming again. She is a horrible sidekick, too, because she simply has no interest in participating in the adventure. I have seen this movie several times and I have yet to figure out why she is even there.

3 RUBY RHOD, *THE FIFTH ELEMENT*

If you've seen this movie, you know exactly why he (or she?) is on this list. This androgynous brand of annoyance brings new meaning to the term; loud voice, whiny tone, horrible costume, persistent commentary, and amazing ability to make everyone in the audience wish they had stayed at home. A complete distraction in what is at least a decent movie. The only other person capable of truly bringing this character to life would have been Gilbert Gottfried, but I think Chris Tucker did a pretty good job.

2 RILEY POOLE, NATIONAL TREASURE SERIES

Any character that can actually make me wish to see *more* of Nicolas Cage deserves to be included in a list of annoying movie sidekicks. Enter Riley Poole, fledgling sidekick to Nicolas Cage's character Ben Gates. The worst part about

Mr. Poole? The lines. Yes, yes, I know, it's a Disney movie. But these one-liners are horrible. I remember actually wanting Nicolas Cage to start talking, just so I could get a break from Poole's incessant humor. I think the idea behind Riley Poole is to make the audience constantly think, "Oh that Riley, he just can't do *anything* right, can he?" which is okay if we are watching a Tom and Jerry cartoon. But for a full-length, ninety-minute action/adventure movie? It is downright criminal.

1 JAR JAR BINKS, STAR WARS SERIES

I mean, is there really any other option? In the most anticipated prequel of the '90s (and arguably, of all time) the character of Jar Jar Binks took center stage in the Star Wars universe and proceeded to halt all the momentum George Lucas had created in the late 1970s. With his computer-generated baby mumbling, awkward human-alien interactions, and helpless efforts to help the Jedi, Jar Jar made audiences worldwide stare aghast at the screen at probably the most disastrous "comic relief" sidekick in film history. In defense of Jar Jar, George Lucas has said, "there is a small group of fans that do not like comic sidekicks. They want the films to be tough like *The Terminator*, and they get very upset and opinionated about anything that has anything to do with being childlike," clearly showing his intention of making the Jar Jar Binks character purely kid-friendly and nonsensical. Honestly, George, I would have rather seen Elmo or Big Bird tagging along with the Jedi. Jar Jar Binks was a walking catastrophe.

✳✳✳✳✳✳

TOP 10 MOVIE SEQUELS YOU HAVE NEVER HEARD OF

10 THE STING II, 1983

Universal tried to repeat the success they had with the 1973 classic starring Paul Newman and Robert Redford. They failed. By replacing the original's two huge stars—the reason *The Sting* was so great—with Jackie Gleason and

Mac Davis, the filmmakers basically acknowledged they were making a second-rate sequel. The film failed, and *The Sting II* was banished to the forgotten film vault in the sky.

9 *RETURN TO OZ*, 1985

The Wiz it ain't. Disney's sequel to the classic *The Wizard of Oz* came forty-six years after the 1939 original, earning this sequel a place in the record books. Unfortunately, that is about all this is known for, as it was a commercial and critical failure. Director Walter Murch reportedly wanted only scant references to the original film, with the intention of remaining faithful to the L. Frank Baum novels; for instance, the Tin Man, Scarecrow, and Cowardly Lion are only briefly in the film. But why do that when the whole point of this sequel was to capitalize on the success of the original?

8 *THE LAST DAYS OF PATTON*, 1986

George C. Scott reprised his role as the no-nonsense General George S. Patton in this CBS TV movie. Like the original, this movie is based on a book by Ladislas Farago. The setting this time is after World War II, when General Patton is dying after a car accident. With his wife (Eva Marie Saint) at his bedside, the general reminisces about his good ol' pre-WWII days. Ron Berglas plays young Patton. Why such a classic war film like 1970's *Patton* would get a simple TV-movie sequel is beyond me, especially if they were able to convince George C. Scott to reprise his role. The movie ranked ninth in the ratings for the night, but one wonders if audiences weren't keen on seeing such a bombastic man go out with a whimper instead of a bang.

7 *RETURN FROM THE RIVER KWAI*, 1989

Nick Tate, Timothy Bottoms, Edward Fox, and George Takei all star in this war epic follow-up to the 1957 classic *The Bridge on the River Kwai*. It's based on a 1979 book by Joan and Clay Blair, which, in turn, is based on a true story. The plot concerns the workers of the previous bridge who, after it is blown up, are shipped to Japan. Along the way, there is much war-related action.

6 *A DANGEROUS MAN: LAWRENCE AFTER ARABIA*, 1990

One year after the original was re-released to theaters, an unofficial TV sequel was produced with Ralph Fiennes in the titular role. Shown on PBS's "Great Performances" in 1992, the movie dealt with Lawrence at the 1919 Paris

Peace Conference following World War I. The *New York Times* called Fiennes's peformance more authentic than Peter O'Toole's, as in this movie it portrayed him as a complicated, ambivalent, and dark man, rather than a flamboyant, swashbuckling hero. Steven Spielberg reportedly saw Fiennes's performance in this and asked him to sign up as a Nazi in *Schindler's List*.

5 *HAPPILY EVER AFTER*, 1993

Filmation, an animation studio known for *Star Trek: The Animated Series* and *Fat Albert*, came up with the brilliant idea in the 1980s to produce sequels to classic Disney films. Their first one was *Happily Ever After*, a "sequel" to the 1937 *Snow White and the Seven Dwarfs*, picking up where the first left off. Snow White meets the Seven Dwarfelles, cousins of the Dwarves, and they team up to destroy the evil Lord Malice. Despite a big-name cast (Ed Asner, Carol Channing, Zsa Zsa Gabor, and Malcolm McDowell), the film was received poorly by just about everyone. Filmation did produce one other Disney "sequel," *Pinocchio and the Emperor of the Night*, which had a great title but nothing else going for it.

4 *IT RUNS IN THE FAMILY*, 1994

A Christmas Story is a beloved Christmas classic. Its sequel more than a decade later is not. Kieran Culkin takes over as Ralphie, whose quest deals not with obtaining a Red Ryder BB gun, but some kind of top (a dice) to pit against some bully's top. WTF? Tedde Moore returns as Ralphie's teacher, and Jean Shepherd narrates, but the rest of the original cast is kaput. MGM later retitled this *My Summer Story*; you probably don't want this on your Christmas list.

3 *SCARLETT*, 1994

Alexandra Ripley's 1991 novel of the same name, a sequel to *Gone With the Wind*, was turned into a TV miniseries in 1994. Joanna Whalley played Scarlett O'Hara and Timothy Dalton took over as the dashing and suave Rhett Butler. Not taking "I don't give a damn" for an answer, Scarlett attempts to win back Rhett's heart, traveling to Ireland in the process. This eight-hour miniseries, aired on CBS during the November sweeps, garnered substantial ratings, but ones less than hoped for by the network. The era of the epic miniseries was over. Still, it's probably worth enough to take a look, if you can find it on video—after all, Sean Bean is in it playing the evil Lord Fenton.

2 SAHARA, 2005

One of those "technically-a-sequel" films. The 1980 film *Raise the Titanic* featured Richard Jordan as Dirk Pitt, a role sent to Matthew McConaughey in *Sahara*. Both are based on Clive Cussler's novels of the treasure-hunting Dirk Pitt, and both had tremendous budgets (and consequently were tremendous failures). *Raise the Titanic's* producer lamented that it would've been cheaper to "lower the Atlantic." Some reference to the first film can be found during the opening credits, when a clipping in Dirk Pitt's office references a "raising the Titanic."

1 THE QUEEN, 2006

Okay, you've heard of *The Queen*, but did you know that it is essentially a sequel to the 2003 TV movie *The Deal*? Both movies feature Michael Sheen as Tony Blair, and both were written by Peter Morgan and directed by Stephen Frears. *The Deal* is based on a  supposed meeting between Tony Blair and current PM Gordon Brown, with Blair telling Brown to step aside and allow him to run as Labour Party leader while allowing Brown sway over domestic policy.

✳✳✳✳✳✳

TOP 10 BEST NUCLEAR WAR MOVIES

10 BY DAWN'S EARLY LIGHT, 1990

What would happen if the president and much of the government were gone and an unstable man in the chain of succession decided that the only response to a mistaken nuclear attack was to win WWIII?

9 FAIL SAFE, 1964 AND 2000 VERSIONS

An American bomber squadron receives mistaken orders to bomb the Soviet Union, and all "fail-safe" methods to turn them back aren't successful. George Clooney directed and starred in a terrific live broadcast version of the original movie.

8 ON THE BEACH, 1959 VERSION

Although the science is more suspect, I like the original Gregory Peck version better than the updated Armand Assante version. In both, nuclear war has devastated the Northern Hemisphere, and the fallout cloud is heading to a doomed Australia. An American nuclear submarine tries to find survivors.

7 TRINITY AND BEYOND, 1995

This documentary, narrated by William Shatner, traces the development of nuclear weapons from the very first in 1945 through the first Chinese test in 1964. Most of the major test explosions are shown.

6 TESTAMENT, 1983

A Californian small-town family survives a nuclear exchange, only to experience the decay of everything that once was. Their desperate attempts to return things to normal of course fail miserably.

5 WHITE LIGHT/BLACK RAIN: THE DESTRUCTION OF HIROSHIMA AND NAGASAKI, 2007

This HBO documentary features interviews with survivors of the attacks as well as a few Americans who were in/with the bomber crews. Would that in another sixty years we won't be making another documentary with survivors from another nuclear attack!

4 BBC HISTORY OF WORLD WAR II—HIROSHIMA, 2005

This BBC documentary uses computer-generated images and more to recreate the attack. Very hard to watch. Even Malcolm McDowell's notation is chilling.

3 THE DAY AFTER, 1983

Though not as strong as the previous films (and definitely weaker than the next two), *The Day After* is high on this list because of its impact. The horror portrayed is tame compared to things that make their way on TV and in the theaters today, but this film remains an important cultural milestone.

2 HADASHI NO GEN, 1983

This superb Japanese animated film follows a family in 1945 Hiroshima. The tension of the buildup to the bombing on August 6, 1945, is chilling and incredibly done. The attack itself is slowed down to show gruesome details as only anime can do. Horrifyingly unforgettable.

1 **THREADS, 1984**
This is the bleakest and most depressing movie ever made (outside of, perhaps, *Grave of the Fireflies*). The BBC made this TV movie that depicts Sheffield, England, just before, during, and well after the nuclear war. There is absolutely no hope or happiness in this movie whatsoever. All is destruction, death, and terrible decline of what remains.

✳✳✳✳✳✳

TOP 10 MOVIES ABOUT ITALIANS THAT DON'T INVOLVE THE MAFIA

10 **KISS ME GUIDO, 1997**
A gay man is looking for a roommate. A pizza maker from Brooklyn is ready to move out and spots the ad, looking for a GWM (Gay White Male). He thinks it means "guy with money." It's an odd couple–type comedy, with broad stereotypical characters, but it's pretty darn funny.

9 **I LOVE YOU TO DEATH, 1990**
Husband and wife, Joey (Kevin Kline doing his best Italian guy) and Rosalie (the perfect Tracy Ullman doing her best Italian-American), own a pizza parlor. She is convinced that he works all of the time for them until she finds out he has been fooling around for years. Being Catholic, divorce is out of the question, so she and her mother and her best friend decide to kill him… over and over and over again. This is dark and funny as hell.

8 *MAC*, 1992

Written and directed by the great John Turturro, this tale of three brothers who are left the family's construction business after the death of their father is a real joy. It's honest, well written and acted, and true to the whole "family first" attitude of most Italians.

7 *TRUE LOVE*, 1989

A hilarious look at wedding planning, Italian-American style. A young couple from Brooklyn get engaged and the families go nuts with the wedding plans, leaving the two of them dazed and confused. The best bit is when the caterer asks if they want the mashed potatoes to match the color of the bridesmaids' dresses.

6 *MY COUSIN VINNY*, 1992

It's country bumpkins vs. a couple of Brooklyn Italians. This is a funny movie, punctuated by Marisa Tomei's over-the-top Italian princess character. (Some say she shouldn't have gotten the Oscar. Screw them.) And who can forget Fred Gwynne as the judge leaning over to Joe Pesci asking him if he just said "youts"?

5 *BIG NIGHT*, 1996

Can a movie make you hungry? This one can. Stanley Tucci (who also directed the film) and Tony Shaloub are Italian immigrant brothers who own a small restaurant. Shaloub is the chef who absolutely will not compromise, even when a big, cheesy faux Italian place opens down the block. The big party at the end is a gourmet's delight… a must-see.

4 *FATSO*, 1980

Dom DeLuise is a guy who's struggled with his weight his whole life, and finally finds a woman who may turn him around. This funny little film was directed by and starred Anne Bancroft (a great Italian actress herself, and wife of Mel Brooks). It captures the essence of Italian families, one minute yelling, the next hugging. And there's lots of eating too.

3 *MARTY*, 1955

Another film about a "fat, ugly man." This flick from the '50s earned several Oscars, including best actor for Ernest Borgnine, who is just great. It takes place over two days in the life of a guy who just can't meet the right girl. When he does, everyone tells him to dump her. Especially his mom and his friend, Ang. Famous for the lines: "What do you wanna do tonight, Marty?" "I dunno, what do you wanna do?"

2 MOONSTRUCK, 1987

One of my favorite movies of all time. Cher's Oscar-winning role as the woman who is there for everyone else and finally decides to take a chance for herself. Everyone in this movie is absolutely perfect. Olympia Dukakis is wonderful as the matriarch. Danny Aiello as the fiance who heads to Italy for his dying mother ("When I told her we were getting married, she got up and starting cooking for everyone. It was a miracle!"). And even Nicolas Cage is great: "I lost my hand! I lost my girl!" Love it!

1 ROCKY, 1976

Yo! The underdog from South Philly makes good. Despite all the lousy sequels, the original remains a true classic. Stallone, who wrote the script, owned this character. You go through an entire range of emotions with him, and care about him. Now, some people would say there is some undertone of mob activity, with Rocky being a thumb-breaker for the local bookie, but let's let that one slide, aiight? Yo!

✳✳✳✳✳✳

TOP 10 GREATEST FILM SOUNDTRACKS

10 BOOGIE NIGHTS

Capturing the nostalgia of the late '70s and the debauchery of the early '80s, PT Anderson's soundtrack sounds like a great concoction mixed simply to get you drunk off of his already Olympian film. Both volumes contain music that, when seen in the film, contain the tonal equivalent of an epiphany.

9 THIS IS SPINAL TAP

The legend of Spinal Tap was due largely to the insanely uproarious subject matter of their wonderfully realized parodies of nearly every genre in music, defining an unforgettable era and making us laugh about it all the way. The soundtrack by which all parody soundtracks are to be measured.

8 VELVET GOLDMINE

Since David Bowie would not allow the filmmakers the rights to use his music in the story of his life, they were forced to write songs that not only mimicked the Thin White Duke but to do it nearly flawlessly. The result was a classic amalgam of Lou Reed, T.Rex, Iggy Pop, and other contributors who were able to capture the essence of 1970s England without losing the aura that makes them enjoyable in our own time.

7 ALMOST FAMOUS

The ultimate '70s rock mixtape, Led Zeppelin mingles with Elton John and Iggy Pop on this masterwork courtesy of Cameron Crowe, who knows a thing or two about rock and roll. The addition of David Bowie and the incendiary Stillwater keep the flow going until the end. All killer, no filler.

6 RUSHMORE

By combining nostalgic favorites such as the Who and the Kinks with the beautiful score of Mark Mothersbough, Wes Anderson was able to create a compilation of finely tuned tracks that remains as memorable now as at its original release.

5 AMERICAN BEAUTY

Once again, music with a message that only keeps you aware of the power of the film as a whole. From Bob Dylan to the choral Beatles finale to the marvelous score, each song carries its own weight, switching from rocking to lighthearted to contemplative without skipping a beat.

4 BARRY LYNDON

Though not as seminal as *2001: A Space Odyssey*, the *Barry Lyndon* score remains one of the most beautiful additions to modern romanticism, and even won the Oscar for Best Adapted Score for its efforts. Stanley Kubrick took the most interesting movements of the era, substituted a few others, and came up with an inspirational and breathtaking conglomeration that stays with the listener long after the movie reaches its climax.

3 ***THE BIG LEBOWSKI***
The Coens show their love for the Rolling Stones and express their faux-disdain for country rock in this marvelous ode to the bright side of darkness. A wicked set of tunes that never go out of style.

2 ***AMERICAN GRAFFITI***
The ultimate '60s soundtrack. Everything you ever wanted to know that was great about the era can be found in this music, swinging its hips from soul to blues to rockabilly and beyond. Nowhere else is Buddy Holly, the Platters, and Bill Haley in such perfect harmony.

1 ***2001: A SPACE ODYSSEY***
Best heard while viewing the film, this is a feast of cerebral waltzes and monumental epics that increases in sentiment with each passing year. The immortal "Also Sprach Zarathustra" became the anthem of classical soundtracks since its appearance in this film, and that hasn't changed since.

✳✳✳✳✳✳

TOP 10 KIDS' MOVIES ADULTS WILL LOVE

10 *WALL·E*
The first of several Pixar films on this list. This is an amazing film with themes that soar over the heads of little ones. It's almost Chaplinesque in style, and has already been compared to Chaplin's classic *Modern Times*. Extremely intelligent, funny, and touching, with a message worth heeding. Great music, too. What other kid's movie would feature Louis Armstrong's version of "La Vie en Rose"?

9 WALLACE & GROMIT: CURSE OF THE WERE-RABBIT

Absolutely sublime and hilarious. This smart Brit stop-motion feature stars the great clay duo made famous in several shorts and adds a crew of memorable characters. The transformation scene itself is worth the price of admission. And look for the funny little winks throughout, like a jar of "Middle-Aged Spread" or the cleverly placed box with the label "May contain nuts." Bang, zoom, right over kids' heads and into the laps of adults.

8 THE IRON GIANT

This little-seen gem was written and directed by Brad Bird, the genius who later joined Pixar and created *The Incredibles* and *Ratatouille* (see later on list). It's traditional cell animation, with some CG enhancements, but that's not what makes this a classic. The story is kind of a nod to *E.T.* (extraterrestrial stranded on Earth, befriends young boy), but it's told with such unique wit and heart, you can't help but love it for its own outstanding merits. And the retro '50s style and be-bop soundtrack are right on spot.

7 THE MUPPET MOVIE

The original was completely original. It didn't have to resort to making Kermit a character other than himself. The genius hand of Jim Henson is all over this, and the hilarious cameos, like Steve Martin, Carl Reiner, and Big Bird, are great. It's fun, funny and a real classic for kids and adults.

6 RATATOUILLE

Another great Pixar entry from the mind of Brad Bird. These guys are master storytellers, and never resort to winks about pop culture or smarmy asides to make their films connect with audiences. This is a beautiful film, Paris is perfectly rendered, and the food is mouth-watering, even if it is prepared by a rat. Only Pixar could do that. Very little ones might get bored, but for the 'tweens and adults with heart, this is a must-see/must-own.

5 WHO FRAMED ROGER RABBIT?

A fun Disney film, one that Disney seems to have forgotten. Robert Zemekis created an incredibly fun world where toons coexist with humans. The opening cartoon is a hoot, especially for anyone that loves the mayhem of classic Tex Avery cartoons. Kids will think Roger is hilarious, and adults will love the double entendres and Jessica's assets. Patty-cake anyone?

4 DARBY O'GILL AND THE LITTLE PEOPLE

Connery before Bond. Live action Disney at its finest. Sure, *Mary Poppins* was great and *The Absent-Minded Professor* is a classic, but this one is just a real joy. Never silly, always full of whimsy. Kids will love the bouncy fun, adults get to relive childhood. And the effects are pretty darn good for the time.

3 THE SPONGEBOB SQUAREPANTS MOVIE

If you don't love Spongebob, take your pulse, because you're probably dead. He's one of the best cartoon characters to be created since Bugs Bunny. Continually funny and outlandish. And Patrick is the perfect idiot to accompany him. This is an incredibly hilarious movie for everyone. I dare you not to sing the "Goofy Goober" song after it's over.

2 THE INCREDIBLES

It's a superhero movie. It's a dysfunctional family movie. It's a midlife crisis movie. It's all these things and it's an absolute joy. Mr. Incredible's desire to regain his glory is so heartfelt that every guy in the theater will think of their own past success with a tear. Every character is perfectly realized. It's funny and thrilling but with a really big heart in the middle of it. Kudos to Brad Bird and Pixar again. Watch for the winks to the Incredibles' sex life…

1 THE NIGHTMARE BEFORE CHRISTMAS

One of the most memorable and wonderful family films ever. Christmas, Halloween, Tim Burton, how can it miss? The soundtrack from Danny Elfman is amazing, with witty, beautiful tunes and lyrics. Jack is perfectly realized as the "town hero" who seeks more in his life (or death, as it may be), a place we all find ourselves time to time. Sally is lovelorn and pines for Jack to not only love her, but to just notice her. Incredibly animated by Henry Selick, based on Tim Burton's original story, NBX has become a cult classic that Disney often sweeps under the carpet in place of pushing their more mainstream offerings. Too bad. This one is a true masterpiece.

✳✳✳✳✳✳

TOP 10 MODERN BLACK-AND-WHITE MOVIES

10 *NIGHT OF THE LIVING DEAD*, 1968, GEORGE ROMERO

This indie film was produced on a budget of $114,000 and has made over forty million worldwide. The film had a great influence on Vietnam-era U.S. because of its subtle critiques of society. The special effects were all done on the cheap, for example, all of the blood was chocolate syrup, and mortician's wax was used to create the zombie effects. The black-and-white guerrilla-style filming has been described as giving the unflinching authority of a wartime newsreel.

9 *LA HAINE*, 1995, MATHIEU KASSOVITZ

La Haine is a brilliant film about three young men in Paris—an Arab, a Jew, and an Afro-Frenchman. The three friends are struggling during times of racial unrest and the film centers around the consequences of a policeman shooting an Arab during race riots. I have to confess that this is my all-time favorite French film, so be sure to watch it. The black-and-white adds to the feeling of authenticity in the riot scenes and might even be considered a commentary on the racial aspects of the film (no color signifies the hope that we will live in a world free of color discrimination).

8 *ED WOOD*, 1994, TIM BURTON

Ed Wood is a cult movie based on the life of the cross-dressing film director of the same name. When Tim Burton announced that he wanted to film entirely in black and white, Columbia Pictures refused, saying that it would make the film impossible to sell in foreign markets and on video. Burton refused to change his mind and eventually ended up making the film for Disney, where he had complete control. The film only made about six million dollars, but it was highly acclaimed by critics.

7 *YOUNG FRANKENSTEIN*, 1974, MEL BROOKS

Young Frankenstein is a comedy starring Gene Wilder. The film parodies Mary Shelley's *Frankenstein*; in fact, many of the props were the same as those used in the 1930 film of the same tale. To further enhance the atmosphere of the film, Brooks decided to film it entirely in black and white, an unusual choice for its time. The film also used 1930's-style scene transitions such as fades to black, wipes and iris outs.

6 *MANHATTAN*, 1979, WOODY ALLEN

Manhattan is a comedy directed by and starring Woody Allen. The film won the BAFTA award for best film. Woody Allen decided to film in black and white because that was how he remembered Manhattan from his childhood, through picture postcards and books. Allen said, "In *Manhattan* I really think that we succeeded in showing the city. When you see it there on that big screen it's really decadent." When the movie was released to video, Allen demanded that it be released in the same aspect ratio as the big screen, which was highly unusual at the time.

5 *SIN CITY*, 2005, FRANK MILLER, ROBERT RODRIGUEZ

Sin City, the film, was based on the graphic novel of the same name by Frank Miller. This film is one of the few fully digital, live-action motion pictures. This technique also means that the whole film was initially shot in full color, and was converted back to high-quality black-and-white. Colorization was added later to each scene and the whole thing was treated for heightened contrast to give more separation to the blacks and whites (as is often seen in the film noir tradition).

4 *THE ELEPHANT MAN*, 1980, DAVID LYNCH

The Elephant Man is a biopic based loosely around the life of Joseph Merrick (a sufferer of proteus syndrome, not elephantiasis as is commonly thought). The film was a surprise hit and received eight Academy Award nominations. The black-and-white film style gives an authentically historical feeling to this film set in the Victorian era. The film was produced by Mel Brooks, who played down his involvement so as not to have people think it might be a comedy.

3 *DR. STRANGELOVE*, 1964, STANLEY KUBRICK

Dr. Strangelove or: How I Learned to Stop Worrying and Love the Bomb is a film based on the Cold War thriller book *Red Alert* by Peter George. The film satirizes the doctrine of mutual assured destruction. The film is made entirely in black and white which some say helps put an unadorned face on the issues being dealt with. This is, beyond a doubt, one of Kubrick's greatest movies.

2 *SCHINDLER'S LIST*, 1993, STEVEN SPIELBERG

Schindler's List is based on the life of Oskar Schindler, a German businessman who saved the lives of over a thousand Jews during the Second World War. The decision to film in black and white was made to give a timeless feel to the film and was based on German Expressionism and Italian neorealism. The black-and-white filming caused difficulties for the set designers who were used to working in color; they had to darken the sets and costumes in order to prevent the actors from blending in. The color red was added to one girl's coat in order to symbolize the blood on the hands of the Allied forces who did nothing to help the Jews at the time.

1 *RAGING BULL*, 1980, MARTIN SCORSESE

Raging Bull is based on the life story of temperamental boxer Jake LaMotta (played by Robert De Niro). Initially the film received mixed reactions, but it is now considered to be one of the greatest films ever made—along with *Taxi Driver*—also starring De Niro and directed by Scorsese. Scorsese and the cinematographer (Michael Chapman) decided to film entirely in black and white in order to add period authenticity—the film was set in the 1940s and both men remembered boxing from the period in black-and-white photographs. The final decision to go black-and-white was made to help differentiate the film from other boxing movies being released around the same time (such as *Rocky*).

✳✳✳✳✳✳

TOP 10 MOVIE SHOOTOUTS

10 *THE BOONDOCK SAINTS*

The creators of this bloody cult favorite set out to create a unique gunfight sequence in an otherwise well-worn genre. The violence is taken out of the usual urban context and set in an eerily familiar suburban neighborhood. And how many gunfights involve a cigar-chewing, scripture-spouting Billy Connolly (yes, that Billy Connolly) as a grizzled hitman?

9 DICK TRACY

This flamboyant homage to the detective serials of the '40s concludes with a fitting rat-tat-tat. As Warren Beatty and crew ready to take down a gangland nightclub, Al Pacino's band of miscreants (complete with names like Flat-Top, Itchy, and Pruneface) burst through the garage doors in their period cars, tommy-guns blazing. Sure it's over the top, but it's supposed to be!

8 THE KILLER

Pick any segment of this Hong Kong classic and you're likely to see some crazy gunplay. It was here that the iconic John Woo, double-.45 look was born. And way back in 1989 it was still cool! It also paved the way for Yun-Fat Chow's career in Western films, though he hasn't yet been able to top this one.

7 TOMBSTONE

In 1993 there were two separate Wyatt Earp westerns, but this is far and away the superior film. The shootout is a must for any respectable western, and many iconic gunfights have risen from this genre. What makes the OK Corral battle in this film unique among them is the proximity of the combatants— eyeball to eyeball in an enclosed space with little cover. It's a confused and vicious sequence, and is likely very accurate.

6 ROAD TO PERDITION

A group of Prohibition-era thugs stand on a city street in the pouring rain. Suddenly, one drops dead, then another. We see the flickering of machine-gun fire in a dark alley, and the surviving mobsters return fire. There is no sound in this scene, but we know it's surely deafening. Then, when mob boss Paul Newman's bodyguards are all dead, Tom Hanks emerges from the shadows. It's a scene with almost no dialogue; with these two masters, who needs it?

5 THE UNTOUCHABLES

The signature shootout of this DePalma gangster flick is a tribute to the famous Odessa Steps sequence from Eisenstein's *Battleship Potemkin*. As the action unfolds in slow motion, a baby carriage careens wildly down the steps, miraculously avoiding all those pesky bullets. And stick around for the bridge shootout between Al Capone's rumrunners and the Canadian Mounties.

4 OPEN RANGE

The tone for the showdown in this 2003 western is set when a surprisingly badass Kevin Costner struts up to a gunman and asks, "Are you the one who killed our friend?" Those of you who have seen it know what happens next. This is a gritty, exhausting sequence that feels like a genuine Wild West shootout rather than a Hollywood reproduction. No western film collection is complete without this one.

3 THE PROFESSIONAL

How many SWAT teams do you really need to take out a lonely immigrant and a little girl? Apparently, a hell of a lot. A cramped New York apartment may not seem like the ideal place for a massive shootout, but it's disturbingly fun to watch as hitman Leon dispatches wave after wave of armored cops. And it's especially gratifying to see that mean Gary Oldman get what's coming to him.

2 HEAT

Fortunately, in the case of shootouts, life rarely imitates art. Not so in the case of this hyper-frenetic gunfight in the streets of Los Angeles, which seemingly inspired an attempted bank robbery by heavily armed thugs soon after the film's release. This battle does not exhibit the fancy camera work of other heist films, or the redundant slow motion of a John Woo film. It's shockingly real. In fact, it's probably the most realistic shootout ever filmed, a fact made all the more unsettling by its real-world counterpart.

1 SCARFACE

If you look at Al Pacino's portrayal of Tony Montana, you know that it can only end this way. Unlike Michael Corleone (or even Carlito Brigante), Montana exhibits an unfettered recklessness that is the cause of both his rise to power and his meteoric fall. As his Miami mansion is besieged by his rival's private army, blood-drunk Montana takes a hit from a mountain of cocaine before making his last stand—you know the line. Sit back and enjoy. The world is yours.

✳✳✳✳✳✳

TOP 10 DEPICTIONS OF SATAN IN MOVIES

10 **ELIZABETH HURLEY, *BEDAZZLED***
Silly movie, *wonderful* devil! You've got to love female Satans. She offers Brendan Fraser's character wishes so that he can land the girl of his dreams. But this is Satan we're dealing with; she traps and tricks him, as we would expect nothing less from the Prince or Princess of lies.

9 **ALAN CUMMING, *GOD, THE DEVIL, AND BOB***
Alan Cumming voiced the Devil in the short-lived series *God, The Devil and Bob*. The Devil is trying to persuade God to destroy the world, and is constantly trying to thwart Bob in his attempts to save it. He is a margarita drinker and drives a purple Dodge Charger described by Bob as the "coolest car [he's] ever seen." Despite appearances, the Devil is needy and codependent, often reduced to tears when God ignores or forgets about him.

8 **DAN CASTELLANETA, *FUTURAMA***
Dan Castellaneta voiced the horrifying Robot Devil in *Futurama*. The Robot Devil lives in Robot Hell, which is hidden beneath the "Inferno" ride at the amusement park Reckless Ted's Funland in New Jersey. His function is to torment robots that have committed various sins, though it seems this right only applies to those who practice Robotology.

7 **TREY PARKER, *SOUTH PARK***
Trey Parker voices one of the most misunderstood Satans in popular culture. He presides over Hell and is constantly at war with God, but far from being merciless and innately evil as Satan is often portrayed in other media, he is depicted in South Park as a soft-hearted, misunderstood anti-hero capable of compassion and genuine emotional attachment.

6 **VIGGO MORTENSEN, *THE PROPHECY***
Creepy! Before he was snogging Liv Tyler in *Lord of the Rings*, Viggo played a very awesome Lucifer in *The Prophecy*. Mortensen's Satan is savage and just plain vicious. Take this

quote: "Humans… and how I love you talking monkeys for this… know more about war and treachery of the spirit than any angel." Well worth the rental.

5 TIM CURRY, *LEGEND*

Every '80s child remembers being freaked and enchanted by Curry's awesome Devil. Visually stunning and far before its time, The Lord of Darkness stole every scene he was in. Tim's presence and voice make for an unforgettable devil that all Gen X and Yers will remember well into their old age.

4 PETER STORMARE, *CONSTANTINE*

Swedish actor Peter Stormare's Devil is perfect, dressed in white and virtually dripping with evil. So angered that Constantine is about to slip through his fingers, he pulls Constantine's cancer from his lungs, forcing him to live his lonely life rather than be taken into heaven. Truly, a Satan for the ages.

3 AL PACINO, *THE DEVIL'S ADVOCATE*

This Satan was not your usual scaly demon. He was rich, calm, suave, and greedy with a lusty charm that Satan always brings to movies. Kevin Lomax, played by a more-wooden-than-usual Keanu Reeves, takes a job at a powerful law firm where his boss, John Milton (get it?) is really the devil. Pacino was the perfect choice for playing this character.

2 HARVEY STEPHENS, *THE OMEN*

There can be no doubt that young Harvey Stephens's portrayal of Satan as a child is one of the most chilling around. He doesn't have to do much—just look on as things go to "hell" around him. The most disturbing scene in this movie is when the nurse jumps and hangs herself, declaring "this is all for you Damien!" The follow-up movie was also quite good but lacked some of the chilling atmosphere of this original.

1 ROSALINDA CELENTANO, *THE PASSION OF THE CHRIST*

Love or hate this movie, you've got to admit that Rosalinda's androgynous Satan was among the creepiest. She taunts and follows Jesus like a snake. I loved her depiction because it is unlike any other I had ever seen. Instead of being an anti-Christ, the devil is depicted here as a perversion of the Holy Family, with Satan mimicking Mary and carrying a foul child in mockery of the baby Jesus. Extremely scary stuff.

✳✳✳✳✳✳

TOP 10 AMAZING FILM SWORDFIGHTS

10 PIRATES OF THE CARRIBBEAN, JOHNNY DEPP VS. ORLANDO BLOOM

The Pirates series may have overstayed its welcome, but the first entry gave us some of the most inspired and thrilling action sequences in recent memory. Like any respectable blood-and-thunder epic, it comes with some mighty fancy swordplay. The high-flying acrobatics of Depp and Bloom strike just the right balance of adventure and comedy. Interestingly, if Depp had played Jack Sparrow as a classic hero instead of a rum-addled fop, it probably wouldn't be worth mentioning.

9 ADVENTURES OF DON JUAN, ERROL FLYNN VS. ROBERT DOUGLAS

Errol Flynn was no stranger to the adventure genre, and he had more than his share of swordfighting. One instance that is often overlooked is his turn as womanizing, international man-of-mystery Don Juan in 1948. In the midst of a palace coup, Flynn's Don Juan slogs it out with Douglas's scheming Duke de Lorca. It is every bit as grandiose as Robin Hood, and the atmosphere of dimly lit corridors and long shadows adds an impressively artistic look to the film.

8 CROUCHING TIGER, HIDDEN DRAGON, ZIYI ZHANG VS. YUN-FAT CHOW

Hong Kong films had been using the technique dubbed "wire-fu" for years. But this film was the first major release in the West to use it, and the result was spectacular. Combat was no longer restricted by physics; here we see warriors fly through the air, run up vertical walls, and even balance themselves on flimsy tree branches. The confrontation between Jen Yu and Li Mu Bai in the pine forest is imaginative and beautiful, casting white-clad opponents against a palette of jade greens as they battle among the treetops.

7 THE SEVEN SAMURAI, TOSHIRO MIFUNE, ET AL, VS. NASTY BANDITS

Although not a swordfight in the strictest sense, the final battle in this Kurosawa masterpiece is certainly one of the best action sequences of all time. We see the quiet discipline of the vastly outnumbered samurai as they draw their sabers, ready for the coming onslaught of their enemies. The samurai dispatch many of them, even as they arrive on horseback. A swordfight against mounted cavalry. Does it get any cooler than that?

6 RETURN OF THE JEDI, MARK HAMILL VS. UM... DARTH VADER

It is not the most frenetic light-saber duel in the Star Wars saga. It is certainly not the most elaborately choreographed. But this ultimate confrontation between father and son is by far the most dramatic in the series. As Luke unleashes his fury on Vader, nearly killing him, the eerie vocal score swells to convey the magnitude of this apocalyptic moment. Flashes of red and green light illuminate an otherwise pitch-black scene as sabers clash. And it gives us a nice break from the Ewok scenes.

5 THE PRINCESS BRIDE, MANDY PATINKIN VS. CHRISTOPHER GUEST

I must say, I am generally not drawn to films that have the words "princess" or "bride" in the title. However, this is a film that just gets better every time I see it. Rarely has there been a more enjoyable mixture of adventure, comedy, romance, and intrigue. Who could forget the climactic duel between Spanish wanderer Inigo and the sleazy, six-fingered Count Rugen? The conclusion of this fight alone is reason enough to watch the film.

4 THE MARK OF ZORRO, TYRONE POWER VS. BASIL RATHBONE

Many swordfights of Hollywood's Golden Age were epic in scale, spanning entire castles and involving armies of extras. But in this early adventure of the masked Mexican aristocrat, the swordplay occurs entirely within the confines of one room. Zorro crosses rapiers with the magnificently slimy Captain Pasquale in a fast and furious (and likely very dangerous) battle of skill. Oh, and it was done without the use of stunt doubles or special effects.

3 KILL BILL VOL. 1, UMA THURMAN VS. THE CRAZY 88

There was so much blood spilled in Tarantino's living anime that it had to be filmed in black and white for ratings purposes. No worries, in a way it actually adds to the scene. The sheer level of carnage here, morbid, yet strangely beautiful, transcends reality and enters the realm of cartoon. Not only does it pay homage to the flamboyant kung-fu movies of the '70s, it leaves us with imagery that becomes iconic in its own right.

2 ROB ROY, LIAM NEESON VS. TIM ROTH

One aspect of an activity as physically demanding as swordfighting that is rarely addressed in film is the exhaustion that must accompany it. Rob Roy and his opponent, the deceptively effete Cunningham, do not effortlessly fly about the room with balletic dexterity. It is a hard, brutal, draining match whose outcome seems inevitable, until old Rob does something completely unexpected. Of all the swordfights ever depicted on screen, this feels the most realistic.

1 RAIDERS OF THE LOST ARK, HARRISON FORD VS. SCIMITAR GUY

Is it possible that the coolest swordfight in film history never actually takes place? Rumor has it that Ford was suffering from gastroenteritis and wasn't up to an elaborately staged duel with an apparently badass swordsman in the streets of Cairo. The result: one of the most memorable sequences of all time. While the black-clad swordsman gives us the requisite display of skill, Indy pulls out his revolver and shoots him on the spot, to the amazement of the crowd. It is a defining moment for this iconic character who, although he probably could win such a match, would much rather take the easy way out and get on with his day.

✳✳✳✳✳✳

TOP 10 BADASS JAMES BOND VILLAINS

10 AURIC GOLDFINGER, *GOLDFINGER*
Gerte Frobbe was overweight, balding, and didn't even speak English. Yet he remains the single most quoted Bond baddie (you know what I'm talking about). But he did give us a valuable lesson in the dangers of cabin depressurization.
Talks the Talk: "No, Mr. Bond. I expect you to die!"

9 RED GRANT, *FROM RUSSIA WITH LOVE*
Years before he got eaten by that shark, Robert Shaw was kicking some Connery ass as this ruthless SPECTRE heavyweight. The train brawl is still among the most brutal in Bond history.
Talks the Talk: "The first one won't kill you. Not the second. Not even the third. Not until you crawl over here and kiss my foot!"

8 ERNST BLOFELD, *YOU ONLY LIVE TWICE*
The quintessential Bond baddie, complete with shaved head, Kim Jong-il tunic, and white fluffy cat. Met a rather unceremonious end at the bottom of a smokestack.
Walks the Walk: Feeding insubordinate minions to ravenous pirhanas. Mmmmmmmmmm.

7 ROSA KLEBB, *FROM RUSSIA WITH LOVE*
Who could forget the pint-sized KGB pitbull that proved that not all Bond girls have to be easy on the eyes?
Walks the Walk: Dispatching an underling with her famous poison-tipped clogs.

6 FRANCISCO SCARAMANGA, *THE MAN WITH THE GOLDEN GUN*
Innuendo aside (and man this movie's full of it), Christopher "Dracula" Lee's icy cool hitman was almost too much for Roger Moore. Almost.
Walks the Walk: Pleasuring his girlfriend with his signature gold pistol. Paging Dr. Freud…

5 ALEC TREVELYAN, *GOLDENEYE*

This former 006 has all of Bond's suave resourcefulness and none of the scruples. Plus he had a cool underwater fortress and a badass scar on his eye, two essentials for any self-respecting supervillain.

Talks the Talk: "I gave you three minutes, Bond. The same three minutes you gave me."

4 JAWS, *MOONRAKER*

Okay, so he's just a henchman. But, unlike the others, he has staying power. Oh, and he's also a seven-foot-tall, metal-mouthed gorilla.

Walks the Walk: Killing a shark with those trademark pearly-whites. A friggin' shark.

3 FRANZ SANCHEZ, *LICENSE TO KILL*

Ah, the ubiquitous drug lord, the signature supervillain of the '80s. Robert Davi brought a cool menace to an otherwise ho-hum entry.

Talks the Talk: "What did he promise you, his heart? Give her his heart!"

2 MAX ZORIN, *A VIEW TO A KILL*

Definitely one of the weakest of the series, but hey, any film that involves Christopher Walken maniacally swinging an axe high above the Golden Gate Bridge can't be all bad.

Walks the Walk: Gleefully machine-gunning dozens of helpless flood victims.

1 LE CHIFFRE, *CASINO ROYALE*

Maybe not the most physically intimidating baddie on the list, but Mads Mikkelsen's creepy asthmatic proved a nasty foil.

Walks the Walk: Handing new Bond an old school beat-down at the business end of a knotted rope. Ouch.

✳✳✳✳✳✳

TOP 10 BLATANT EXAMPLES OF PRODUCT PLACEMENT IN MOVIES

10 **TACO BELL, *DEMOLITION MAN***
One entire scene revolves around Sandra Bullock's character explaining to Sylvester Stallone's unfrozen cop from the '90s that Taco Bell won the franchise wars and "now all restaurants are Taco Bells." They then proceed to a fancy, sit-down place where no Mexican food is present at all. It has nothing to do with the plot of the movie and any restaurant name could have been used. I guess Taco Bell was the highest bidder.

9 **APPLE COMPUTER, *MISSION:IMPOSSIBLE* AND *INDEPENDENCE DAY***
In the mid-'90s, Apple Computer (now Apple, Inc.) was facing a crisis. Very few people were buying their computers and Apple needed to get in the public eye in a positive way. So in 1996, they put their computers on the silver screen in not one but two blockbuster movies. In *M:I*, Tom Cruise uses a PowerBook to communicate with the bad guy (and girl) and ultimately save the day (and his reputation). In *ID*, Jeff Goldblum uses a PowerBook to plant a deadly computer virus in the attacking aliens' mothership. I even remember an Apple commercial that tied in with *Mission:Impossible*.

8 **MERCEDES BENZ, *THE LOST WORLD: JURASSIC PARK***
The vehicles that Jeff Goldblum and team use while exploring Site B were new Mercedes Benz SUVs. Steven Spielberg took great care to frame a shot that showed the famous Benz logo up close. Again, a commercial by Mercedes was shown on television to capitalize on this movie placement.

7 **DODGE, *TWISTER***
Like number 8, this is another vehicle placement. What makes it so bad is that Dodge, I think, hurt itself. The good guys all have old beat-up clunkers, except for Bill Paxton's character, who drives a brand-new Dodge Ram pickup. But the bad guys, led by Carey Elwes's character, all drive black Dodge minivans.

Of course, one of them gets impaled by a tornado thrown pole and then gets tossed around and eventually blown up by said tornado.

6 FEDEX, *CAST AWAY*
In the DVD commentary, the director, Robert Zemeckis, said they needed a "real" company to be in this movie for authenticity. But I, for one, can't look at a FedEx shipping box without thinking about two things: that weird angel drawing and "Wilson! Wiiilllsooonn!"

5 MELLO YELLO, *DAYS OF THUNDER*
This represents a legitimate practice when advertisers sponsor a NASCAR racing team and plaster their logo all over the car and driver. However, after seeing this movie, every time I see a Mello Yello, I think about Tom Cruise and that black car driving through the wreckage.

4 THE MIAMI DOLPHINS, *ACE VENTURA: PET DETECTIVE*
I mention this one because the National Football League is extremely particular about the fictional use of any of its franchises or logos in movies and television. Most movies that concern a professional football team use a fictional one. It's surprising then that the Miami Dolphins were in this movie at all.

3 SUBWAY, *HAPPY GILMORE*
Like number 5, this represents a legitimate practice: a professional athlete doing product endorsements. But like number 10, this one could have gone to any product. Subway just happened to win the bidding war. This one is also noticeable because in subsequent airings on cable and network television, the Subway T-shirt that Adam Sandler wears in parts of the movie has its logo blurred out.

2 PEPSI, *BACK TO THE FUTURE*
The cola wars were going on hot and heavy in 1985 when the first installment of *Back to the Future* premiered. Pepsi was winning and in order to capitalize on that momentum they were featured heavily in this movie. There's even a scene where Michael J. Fox's character of Marty McFly goes into the 1955 cafe and orders a Pepsi Free, Pepsi's diet drink. The soda jerk tells him if he wants a Pepsi he's gonna have to pay for it. In Part 2, Marty travels to 2015.

Doc Brown tells him to go to the Cafe 80s and order a Pepsi. He gives him a fifty-dollar bill to pay for it.

1 REESE'S PIECES, *E.T.: THE EXTRA-TERRESTRIAL*

This is the one that really started it all. Although product placement had been around before 1981, this movie put the practice into overdrive. No one will ever forget E.T. croaking out the words "Reese's Pieces" as he happily munches his way down the trail that Elliot has left for him. Interestingly, Spielberg wanted to originally use M&Ms, but couldn't secure the rights. Hershey's, who owns Reese's, stepped up and the rest is history.

✖✖✖✖✖✖

TOP 10 MYSTERY OR SUSPENSE MOVIES YOU MUST SEE

10 *THE LAST OF SHEILA*, 1973

This crossword puzzle of a movie is one of the most remarkable murder mysteries ever made. The entire movie plays like a game; indeed, it's all about a game being played by a group of bite-you-in-the-back friends who have subjected themselves to a week's vacation aboard the yacht of a sadistic egotist (James Coburn) who derives enjoyment from humiliating his guests. While they play their amateur detective game, trying to uncover each other's assigned "secrets," one of the group, it seems, is playing for real—because it looks as though their host is trying to blame one of them for the hit-and-run killing of his wife a year before.

If you enjoy board games, puzzles, and thinking fast on your feet, this movie will keep you interested—and guessing—right up to the final minutes. Sole liability: '70s fashion styles throughout. Offset by a fantastic cast: James Mason, Raquel Welch, Dyan Cannon, Coburn, Richard Benjamin, Joan Hackett.

9 *FUNERAL IN BERLIN*, 1966

Second in the series of films in which Michael Caine plays Harry Palmer, Len Deighton's ordinary-guy-as-unwilling-spy (the previous film, *The Ipcress File*, is a must-see as well). Palmer, former army sergeant, is caught in some unnamed crime, and given a choice—work for British intelligence or go to the stockade. This film sends Palmer to Berlin to oversee the defection of a cynical Russian general ("Americans? Bah!" the general says to Palmer's suspicions about why he doesn't offer himself to the Americans instead, since they have more money to offer him. "They're revolutionaries gone decadent. They're Russians in blue jeans.") In the process, Palmer meets up with an untrustworthy old German friend and a beautiful Israeli operative, and gets framed for murder. Is the Russian up to something, or is he on the level? And what do the Israelis have to do with it?

One of the best and most realistic spy movies of the '60s (this isn't some flashy, gadget-laden James Bond flick), with humor, tension, and a riveting dark side.

8 *SCREAM OF FEAR*, UK TITLE: *TASTE OF FEAR*, 1961

In the 1950s and '60s, Britain's Hammer Films was known for their lush, Technicolor horror movies—latter day (and gorier) takes on the classic old Universal Studios monster movies. Beginning with remakes of *Dracula* and *Frankenstein*, Hammer went on to revive mummies and wolfmen, zombies and phantoms, and stretched out Christopher Lee's indestructible Dracula and Peter Cushing's morally challenged Frankenstein into multi-film series.

For a time Hammer also delved into psychological thrillers, and *Scream of Fear* is perhaps the best of these. The film begins with a pretty girl being fished out of a Swiss lake, the victim of a drowning. We learn she was the friend and care companion to beautiful (and morose) Susan Strasberg, who has been confined to a wheelchair after a riding accident. Mourning the loss, Strasberg makes the journey to see her estranged father for the first time in ten years at his hilltop Riviera estate. Met at the airport by a handsome and sympathetic chauffeur, she learns that her father has unexpectedly gone away on business, due to return in a few days' time. The chauffeur hints at something mysterious going on, and Strasberg begins to suspect her new stepmother of plotting her father's murder along with the local doctor (played by Christopher Lee). Her suspicions turn to paranoia—and perhaps madness—when she begins seeing her father's corpse in the house—only to discover it gone when she comes back with help. Is her father really dead? And if he is—who killed him? Or is she simply losing her mind?

This film made a lasting impression on me when I was a kid—I saw it once—and only once—on a Saturday afternoon on local television, and it gave me nightmares. Thirty-plus-years years later I had forgotten most of the plot, but still remembered a scene where the chauffeur dives to the bottom of a weed-choked pool and finds the old man's corpse hidden there, staring out emptily with wild, open eyes. Years later I sought help on the Internet from a fellow classic horror-movie buff, who quickly identified what film this memory came from, and within a week I had my own copy from eBay. The thrill of seeing this riveting picture again after all those years made me damn grateful for the 'net and how it makes the rediscovery of old gems possible.

I can't recommend this film enough. Not a great work of art, just a tense, chilling, and edgy psycho-thriller with a hint of ghost story and an unexpected twist at the end.

7 THE MASK OF DIMITRIOS, 1944

Really a classic that any old movie buff will have heard of and seen—but since we're in a post-literate age, it seems like almost all old films are candidates for rediscovery—especially when there's no longer much incentive for young people to check out old movies on TV anymore, with hundreds of cable channels making it easy to avoid the challenge of giving old cinema a chance. Things were different thirty-five years ago when all we had were a mere handful of local TV stations that were network affiliates of the Big Three—NBC, CBS, and ABC—as well as PBS...and nothing else. If you wanted to watch TV, sometimes you *had* to sit down and try to get into an old movie—especially since that was all that was on during many afternoons.

Anyway, this great film, told partly in flashback, presents Peter Lorre as a crime novelist who by chance meets a Turkish police detective who for years has been chasing a murderer, spy, and terrorist named Dimitrios, whose dead body recently washed ashore in Turkey. Lorre is taken to see Dimitrios's body, and is told some of the story of how this petty criminal became one of the most wanted men in the Near East. Lorre becomes fascinated with this character, and decides to start writing a book about Dimitrios. This takes him on a trip around Europe, from Greece to Switzerland to Paris, interviewing various people who had encounters—and even had their lives ruined—by the unscrupulous and dangerous Dimitrios. Along the way he finds himself partnered with a mysterious man (Sydney Greenstreet) who turns out to be one of Dimitrios's former criminal colleagues, betrayed to the police by Dimitrios years before. After speaking with

Lorre, Greenstreet finds reason to believe that the slippery Dimitrios is actually still alive, and involves Lorre in a scheme to blackmail the slippery master criminal and spy.

6 NIGHTMARE, 1964

Another tense Hammer psycho-thriller, *Nightmare* is the story of a schoolgirl who, years before, had witnessed her insane mother stab her father to death. Emotionally fragile and obsessed by this horribly traumatic incident, the girl begins having terrible nightmares which eventually cause her to be sent home from boarding school accompanied by a sympathetic teacher. Once there she enters into the care of her guardian, the old family servants, and a hired nurse—but despite the presence of these familiar and caring faces, the girl's nightmares worsen, and she begins seeing a spectral woman wandering the house at night. Believing she's going mad like her mother, her hold on reality plummets… until a tragedy occurs. But even then we learn there's more to the story than mere madness.

Twisting, creepy, and reeking with betrayal, this is a neatly disturbing little thriller worthy of the Hammer name.

5 THE TAKING OF PELHAM ONE TWO THREE, 1974

There was something about the 1970s and realistic, gritty crime dramas. They just went together. *The French Connection* films, *The Godfather* films, *Serpico*, *Dog Day Afternoon*… even *The Yakuza*… and then there's *The Taking of Pelham One Two Three*. While in the same league as these other great films, what makes *Pelham* different is that it takes itself just a shade less seriously—at least at times. It even stars Walter Matthau as a transit police officer, and of all people, Jerry Stiller as a cop. It shouldn't be a surprise, then, that there's the occasional light moment to relieve the tension.

But this is no comedy—not by a long shot. It's an extremely tense and even violent thriller with moments of shock and terror. A group of ruthless and highly organized men (led by the quintessential Quint of *Jaws*, tough guy Robert Shaw) hijack a New York City subway car and threaten to kill the passengers one by one unless a ransom is paid. Working frantically against the hijackers' deadline, Matthau and his detectives are stymied at every turn by Shaw, who seems to anticipate every move they make.

4 KLUTE, 1971

Creepy and ambiguous, *Klute* is the film that made Jane Fonda a serious actress (prior to this she'd starred mostly in light comedies and, of course, had played the title space-vixen in the sci-fi/soft-core cult flick, *Barbarella*) and even managed to redeem her reputation (slightly) from the harm done it by her pro-Vietcong antics a couple years earlier.

Hired by a company CEO to investigate the disappearance of a fellow executive, private detective John Klute (Donald Sutherland) soon discovers that the missing man may have had something to do with the brutal torture-murder of a hooker. Klute traces the man's movements (and prior patronage) to a group of prostitutes working for pimp Roy Scheider. One of the hookers in particular seems to have information about the killer—Bree Daniels (Fonda)—and seems, also, to be next on his list.

In between moments of truly chilling tension, the film delves into the personal life of Fonda's character, who's trying to get out of the call-girl life (her therapy sessions serve as a centerpoint) and her ambiguity toward strait-laced and protective Klute, whom she is both attracted to and disdainful of. All the while the killer is getting closer, clearly stalking Fonda.

3 THE SEVENTH VICTIM, 1943

In the 1940s, RKO Pictures, one of the major Hollywood studios, had fallen on hard times due to their bankrolling of Orson Welles's extravagant (if artistically brilliant) *Citizen Kane* and *The Magnificent Ambersons*. Neither film had recouped its cost at the box office, putting RKO in jeopardy. The studio needed to get back to making cheap but profitable movies. Noting the huge success rival Universal Studios was having with the horror genre, RKO decided they wanted a piece of the fright action. But what producer could outdo Universal at its own game for a fraction of the cost?

Enter Selznick Studios chief script editor Val Lewton. Lewton, who had worked on *Gone with the Wind* as well as a number of other Selznick properties, had grown tired of playing second banana to David O. Selznick's Hollywood mogul. Lewton wanted a chance to play the mogul himself, and RKO gave him the ideal opportunity.

Or so he thought. Lewton *was* given full power to produce some low-budget "B" horror pictures, but also found himself saddled with the cheesy titles that RKO had dumped on him. (It was common practice in those days for a studio to hand a producer a title, or at most a title and concept, and he then had to come up with a story to go with it.) Lewton proved his genius, however, by taking low-grade concepts and titles *Cat People* and *I Walked with a Zombie* and turning them into minor moody masterpieces of suspense and horror.

The Seventh Victim was another of Lewton's highly successful and brilliant "B" films. The story of devil worshippers in New York City who have marked an errant member for death, the film moves from noir-ish mystery to darkly sad exploration of futility. What makes the film such a delight to watch are the memorable bits of tense imagery (a threatening hand touching the heroine's hand from around a dark alleyway corner; an empty apartment with a single chair positioned directly under a noose; a murder occurring off-camera, down a dark hallway) and the moody, tragically-tinged performance of Jean Brooks as the beautiful, depressed victim of the Satanists, being driven hard to take her own life to pay the price for betraying the group.

2 ODDS AGAINST TOMORROW, 1959

Seemy film noir with the great Robert Ryan as a racist bank robber, enlisted by criminal old-timer Ed Begley for one last big heist—though it involves Ryan having to partner with inside man Harry Belafonte to make the job happen. Of course, part of the tension comes from the electric hostility going on between Ryan and Belafonte, but underscoring this is the need for Begley to pull off a final, successful robbery. The team works carefully to make sure every aspect of the job comes off right—timing it to the minute—but of course something goes wrong.

Ryan's performance takes this film to a higher level (Belafonte is also excellent) and it becomes impossible not to identify, a little, with this unsavory character—or to not get caught up in the tension and danger of the crime the group is trying to pull off. One of the best scenes: Ryan beats the crap out of a young and cocky Wayne Rogers in a bar.

1 THE MOON SPINNERS, 1964

Okay, bear with me on this one. This is the lightweight entry, and one for the kids—but enjoyable for adults too, if they put a little effort into it. Plus, I only had nine titles and needed a tenth. Still, this is an enjoyable little romance/mystery worth seeing at least once. It *is* a little suspenseful (sometimes)… and *is* a thriller (of sorts)… if a fluffy one. And yes, it's a Disney film.

Now, ordinarily I detest Disney, but this one's from back in the day (1960s) when Disney produced some decent (if ultimately forgettable and yes—totally lightweight) live action films. Best, by far, in this category was Disney's excellent version of *Treasure Island*, while the worst was… well, take your pick. *That Darn Cat*, maybe? *The Apple Dumpling Gang*?

But *The Moon Spinners* is closer to the *Treasure Island* end of the scale, if not quite in the same (relatively) rarified air. Disney contract player Hayley Mills, on vacation in Greece, meets up with a mysterious young man who turns out to be the former employee of a London banking house who is chasing a group of international jewel thieves in hopes of clearing his name (they framed him). Okay, sounds hokey right? And it is. But it's also fun, and richly photographed, and you can't beat the Greek location for timeless beauty. It even stars Eli Wallach as the villain.

✳✳✳✳✳✳

TOP 10 BADASS DRUGGIES IN MOVIES

10 TERRY CREWE, *WHITE CHICKS*
No matter how hard they try, agents Marcus and Kevin Copeland (Marlon and Shawn Wayans) have fallen fast to the bottom of the FBI ladder. Eventually, they go undercover as two Hilton-esque bimbos and hilarity ensues. Though not chock-full of drug references, the blown-out scene featuring bodybuilder Latrelle (Terry Crewe) on the dance floor is nuts. After doping a drink to give to one of the undercover Wayans, he inadvertently drinks it himself.

9 JASON SCHWARTZMAN AND JOHN LEGUIZAMO, *SPUN*
For a speed freak, time is a relative and obscure concept. The movie really starts when Ross (Jason Schwartzman) arrives at Spider Mike's (John Leguizamo) shack, looking to score and in dire need enough to risk Mike's paranoid and tumultuous temper. Spider Mike's companions at the bungalow that day are: Cookie (Mena Suvari), Frisbee (Patrick Fugit), and Nikki (Brittany Murphy), a vapid and annoying Vegas stripper, whose boyfriend, The Cook (Mickey Rourke), makes up the local speed supply in his motel room lab. Seduced by Nikki and her guarantee of a limitless supply of drugs, Ross agrees to become a taxi-service

for The Cook. Over the next few days, Ross careens between the hysterical and the loony as he makes his nosedive into the carnivorous world of meth junkies.

8 SEAN PENN, *FAST TIMES AT RIDGEMONT HIGH*

The epicenter of this future-star–riddled film is Jennifer Jason Leigh as Stacy Hamilton. She is a young, virgin high school student who, as the film begins, is asking for "relationship" advice from her friend, the sexually promiscuous Linda Barrett (Phoebe Cates, who has perhaps the finest topless pool-exit scene in cinematic history). While meandering away frequently from the main characters, the film spends time with baked surfer dude Jeff Spicoli (Sean Penn) and his ongoing feud with his teacher Mr. Hand (Ray Walston).

7 MATT DILLON AND KELLY LYNCH, *DRUGSTORE COWBOY*

The word "drug" in the title pretty much sums it up. Matt Dillon plays the leader of a group of dope-fiends who roam around the country stealing from pharmacies in order to feed their habits. When one of the young druggies dies of an overdose, it prompts Dillon to try to go straight, a trial made all the more difficult by the fact that his wife wants to stay high and by the further corrupting presence of an ex-priest, played by *Naked Lunch* author William Burroughs. *Drugstore Cowboy* was director Gus Van Sant's breakthrough picture.

6 MARLON WAYANS, *SCARY MOVIE*

Basically created to mock the horror genre of the previous years, most namely *Scream* and *I Know What You Did Last Summer*, *Scary Movie* was created by those *In Living Color* family members, the Wayans Brothers. Marlon Wayans shares a tender, puff-puff moment with the masked Munch character from *Scream*.

5 ELLEN BURSTYN, *REQUIEM FOR A DREAM*

Perhaps the coolest druggie, who is in it for more than money or just getting high, Ellen Burstyn's diet-pill-popping character has quite the whacked out moment with a none-too-friendly refrigerator. This is an astonishing film with an incredible cast. You absolutely must see this movie.

4 JOHNNY DEPP AND BENICIO DEL TORO, *FEAR AND LOATHING IN LAS VEGAS*

Based on Gonzo author Hunter S. Thompson's road book, Johnny Depp fully embodies the marble-mouthed pill-popper to a T. Journalist Raoul Duke and his lawyer Dr. Gonzo drive from LA to Las Vegas on a drug binge. They sort of cover some news stories, including a convention on drug abuse, but also sink deeper into a frightening psychedelic otherworld.

3 JOHNNY DEPP, *BLOW*

A grown-up George Jung (Johnny Depp) moves to Southern California with his friend "Tuna" (Ethan Suplee) and they get a beachside apartment and make friends with all the locals. They do not want to get real jobs so Tuna comes up with the idea of selling pot. George's new girlfriend, Barbara Buckley (Franka Potente), gets them in the game to do just that by introducing them to her friend/entrepreneur Derek Foreal (Paul Reubens), who is the top dealer in the area. With Derek's help, George and Tuna make a lot of money selling to all the people in the area. George becomes one of the most famous cocaine dealers in the world, even meeting Pablo Escobar at one point, and spends far too much time doped out of his mind.

2 AL PACINO, *SCARFACE*

"Say hello to my little friend!" Al Pacino stars as Tony Montana, an exiled Cuban criminal who goes to work for Miami drug lord Robert Loggia. Montana rises to the top of Florida's crime syndicate, eventually horning in on Loggia's cokehead mistress (Michelle Pfeiffer) in the process. Howard Hawks's mystery-novel "whodunnit" approach in depicting the storyline's many murders is dispensed with in the 1983 *Scarface*; instead, we are inundated with blood by the bucketful, especially in the now-infamous buzzsaw scene. And in case it did not register, Montana does entirely too much coke.

1 CHRIS TUCKER, *FRIDAY*

Ice Cube and Chris Tucker as perhaps the world's finest slackers spend Friday doing absolutely nothing constructive once finding out that Craig (Cube) no longer has a job. Smokey (Tucker) spends the bulk of the film nicely toasted and, for my admission price, acting like the absolute perfect pothead. Just watching him work on a joint and teaching Craig how to "Puff-Puff Give, Puff-Puff Give, you're messin' up the flow!" is priceless. The hallucination scene and

Smokey's nervous ticks really make you understand just how much potentially laced dope this dude has done.

✳✳✳✳✳✳

TOP 10 FILMS ABOUT ALCOHOLICS

10 *BAD SANTA*
This movie often gets a bad rap, but I consider it to be pretty solid. Though it's a comedy, the film doesn't really make light of the main character's alcoholic state. In the film the main character, Willie T. Stokes, is a bitter, lonely alcoholic. Willie works the holiday seasons as a mall Santa along with his dwarf friend, Marcus, who works as Santa's elf. Every Christmas Eve, the two of them disable the security alarm after the mall closes and rob the mall safe; afterward, Marcus returns to living with his wife, while Willie goes to Miami and spends all his money on booze. The Christmas season that year begins like any other but outside forces make sure it doesn't end the same. The portrayal of the hopeless alcoholic lifestyle in this film gives you a really bad taste in your mouth. Though it's embellished a fair amount, the aesthetic effect of the "alcoholism" scenes give you a dirty feeling that can be true to what "rock-bottom" looks like.

9 *STRANGE BREW*
When I was researching for this list I kept running into this movie and people really seem to love it. Here is a synopsis of the premise the movie begins with: two unemployed brothers, Bob and Doug McKenzie, are in a bind when they give away their father's beer money and then run out of beer. The brothers place a mouse in a beer bottle in an attempt to get free Elsinore beer from the local beer store, but are told by the no-nonsense clerk—under threat of being shoved into a bottle themselves—to take up the matter at the Elsinore brewery instead. After presenting the evidence to management at Elsinore brewery, the brothers are given jobs on the line inspecting the bottles for mice. They take this opportunity to drink lots of free beer off the line; later, they surprise their

parents with a van full of Elsinore products. Then; along with some ridiculously cheesy plot twists, hilarity ensues.

8 DAYS OF WINE AND ROSES

This is a classic cautionary tale. *Days of Wine and Roses* is the quintessential piece of cinema for warning people of the dangers of alcoholism. It's often loaned from person to person in Alcoholics Anonymous meetings all over, and is suggested viewing in many other programs designed for recovering alcoholics. The film centers on Joe Clay, who meets and falls in love with Kirsten Arnesen, a bright, non-drinking secretary. They marry, conceive a child, and make a home for themselves. It's then that Joe introduces Kirsten to social drinking and its pleasures. Reluctant at first, after her first few Brandy Alexanders, she admits that having a drink "made me feel good." Joe slowly goes from the "two-martini lunch" to alcoholism and in due time both succumb to the pleasures and pain of alcohol addiction. The movie is old-fashioned and can feel preachy, but its draw is in its honesty and genuine nature. It's a good example of how the motives of Hollywood filmmaking have changed over the years—it was produced with talented actors, talented filmmakers, and a solid budget for its time, and still has a positive moral motive. It's a good film and shows the downward spiral that alcoholism can be.

7 ARTHUR

I wouldn't say this film contains the most honest portrayal of an alcoholic, but this list isn't necessarily based on realism. In the movie the late Dudley Moore (a real-life alcoholic) plays Arthur, a thirty-year-old alcoholic who will inherit 750 million dollars if he complies with his family's demands and marries the woman of their choosing. Arthur falls in love with Linda, a tie-stealing waitress from Queens and has to choose between true love and his inheritance. His father and fellow millionaire Burt Johnson plot to have him marry Burt's daughter, Susan. If he doesn't, he loses the three-quarter-billion family fortune. But Arthur gets a push in the right direction from his Gentleman's Gentleman, Hobson. The movie is genuinely funny and heartfelt, despite the fact it can make light of alcoholism.

6 LEAVING LAS VEGAS

This is film based on a semi-autobiographical novel of the same name and written by an alcoholic writer. It's easy to imagine why the best of these stories of alcoholism come straight from the source. *Leaving Las Vegas* begins with an introduction to Ben Sanderson, a late-stage alcoholic who has hit rock bottom. Trashing all personal and professional ties to his LA existence, he sets off for the lights of Vegas on a mission: to drink himself to death. There he meets Sera, a beautiful, seen-it-all hooker. Drama and romance ensue. Tragically John O'Brien, the author of the novel, committed suicide just before the film was to be made. The often over-the-top Nicolas Cage does a fantastically believable job playing the drunken Ben Sanderson, and like many other films dealing with alcoholics, his performance makes the movie.

5 UNDER THE VOLCANO

Under the Volcano isn't necessarily an amazing film, but Albert Finney's subtle and scrupulous portrayal of alcoholic Geoffrey Firmin is unmatched in its ironically graceful stupor and is in itself amazing. Against a background of war breaking out in Europe and the Mexican fiesta Day of Death, we are taken through one day in the life of the lead character Firmin, a British consul living in alcoholic disrepair and obscurity in a small southern Mexican town in 1939. The consul's self-destructive behavior is a source of perplexity and sadness to his nomadic, idealistic half-brother, Hugh, and his ex-wife, Yvonne, who has returned with hopes of healing Geoffrey and their broken marriage. It is based on the 1947 novel of the same name, which is a semi-autobiographical account of author Malcolm Lowry's life.

4 WHO'S AFRAID OF VIRGINIA WOOLF?

At the time of its release, *Who's Afraid of Virginia Woolf?* was considered very controversial and progressive for a big Hollywood production because of its brassiness and vulgar language. In the film an associate professor of history has turned to alcohol to deal with his mean and vituperative wife. Early on, an acquainted couple are invited over for drinks, and over the course of the evening, the polished veneer of the hosts tarnishes grotesquely. The repartees of the history professor's consummately sophisticated wife degenerate into increasingly violent verbal abuse of both her husband and her guests, leading to the physical and emotional crumbling of the professor's apathetic façade. Soon the guests begin mirroring their hosts in mutual antagonism, giving voice to buried resentments and alcohol-fueled revelations. Though the film's age has made it seem a bit preachy, its construction and acting is more than enough for it to retain its greatness. It feels like an honest portrayal of alcoholism's consequences.

3 FACTOTUM

Factotum is a film based on (the late) Charles Bukowski's novel of the same name. In the film, the main character Hank Chinaski (based on Bukowski himself, a real-life alcoholic) is working toward becoming a writer, and follows his own advice: "If you're going to try, go all the way." The film follows Chinaski's various jobs and relationships with women. The only things consistent in his life seem to be his drinking and his writing. He has a more lasting relationship with one woman, Jan, who is also a broke alcoholic. As the film unravels it seems it will be impossible for Chinaski to stop ending up where he started, or make any reasonable progress at all. No bother to him, of course, he knows what kind of life he's living and never seems to consider any other option. This is probably my favorite film on the list because there aren't any tricks or fireworks; it's simply about a man who is an alcoholic, one that knows he'll never live any other way and deals with it accordingly.

2 HOUSE OF SAND AND FOG

House of Sand and Fog doesn't revolve solely around alcoholism, but the obliviously selfish nature of the main character is a common, and damaging, aspect of alcoholism. In the film, Kathy Nicolo is a recovering drug addict and current alcoholic living in a small house near the coast in Northern California. She and her brother inherited the house from their father. Abandoned by her husband and trapped by a malaise that has left her depressed and unresponsive to her surroundings, she ignores a number of notices threatening her with eviction for an alleged nonpayment of business taxes. She only becomes aware of her precarious situation when the police forcibly remove her and her belongings from the house and put it up for auction. The movie unfurls as she quarrels with her old house's new residents while attempting to regain ownership of her home. This is one of my favorite plot-oriented films, and as Kathy, Jennifer Connelly delivers one of the finest performances I've ever seen.

1 BARFLY

The praise for *Barfly* seems so universal I felt as though it had to be number one. This is the second film on the list based on a Bukowski novel, centered on his alter ego Henry Chinaski (or Hank Chinaski in *Factotum*). The film focuses on the alcoholic life of Chinaski, who writes poetry and short stories, which he submits to literary magazines. Drinking and fighting are how he spends his nights. Chinaski is officially "discovered" when one of his submissions is published. The publisher, Tully Sorenson, immediately takes a fascinated interest with the proudly adamant alcoholic author and his lifestyle, which results in an altercation in the end of the film with another woman, Wanda, an alcoholic who has been living with Chinaski. *Barfly* is a high-caliber film with a top-notch job by Mickey Rourke in the lead. You can actually empathize with Chinaski, which is quite an incredible feat, considering how perplexing his lifestyle can seem to a non-alcoholic. That reason alone could justify its position at number one, but it has much more to offer besides that; I think it's a pretty easy number one.

✳✳✳✳✳✳

TOP 10 FILM PORTRAYALS OF TWENTIETH-CENTURY LEADERS

10 BRIAN KEITH AS TEDDY ROOSEVELT, *THE WIND AND THE LION*

Those looking for a thorough history lesson on North African geopolitics in this Milius sand-and-saber epic will be sorely disappointed. But it's an enjoyable and completely watchable adventure flick, with Sean Connery starring as the Berber king and Brian Keith as the embodiment of America as a rising imperial power. His Roosevelt is at once admirable and despicable, affable yet flamboyantly arrogant, complete with TR's trademark broad grin.

9 JOHN LONE AS EMPEROR PU YI, *THE LAST EMPEROR*

Pu Yi is one of the twentieth century's most tragic figures. He was born the sovereign of a vast and ancient empire, only to witness it collapse entirely within his lifetime. Hong Kong actor Lone, in a ridiculously underappreciated performance, portrays Pu Yi as a man desperately clinging to an outmoded sense of tradition. In the end, as an old man visiting the Forbidden City as a tourist, he bequeaths the reins of power to the new Maoist generation before silently passing into history.

8 LYNN COHEN AS GOLDA MEIR, *MUNICH*

"Every civilization finds it necessary to negotiate compromises with its own values." At its core, this account of the Israeli punitive operation against those believed responsible for the 1972 Olympics massacre asks where justice ends and revenge begins. Based on outward impression, Cohen's grandmotherly Meir hardly seems the type that would bless a secret mission of retribution. Then again, vengeance has a way of hardening even the softest heart.

7 ANTHONY HOPKINS AS RICHARD NIXON, *NIXON*

The British Hopkins might not have seemed an obvious choice to play the often-maligned U.S. president in Oliver Stone's biopic. However, he plays Nixon as an extremely complicated man beset by feelings of inadequacy, not only from his political superiors (yes, superiors) but also from his mother, whose ghostly presence haunts Nixon at every turn. As his administration unravels amid a torrent of scandal and addiction, he resigns in an effort to avert what could have been a second civil war. In doing so, he reclaims not only his own destiny, but also a measure of nobility.

6 ALBERT FINNEY AS WINSTON CHURCHILL, *THE GATHERING STORM*

Could it be that Winston Churchill might have found his doppelganger in Albert Finney? It's hard to watch this made-for-cable docudrama and not think so. He begins as an outsider, marginalized for his supposedly alarmist warnings about the rise of Nazism. He is singularly dedicated to his political career, leading to bouts of depression and tension with his wife. Finney shatters the stone layers of Churchill the character to bring us Churchill the man, complete with weakness and imperfection, as well as nerve and dignity.

5 BRUNO GANZ AS ADOLF HITLER, *DER UNTERGANG*

There is simply no way to sympathize with Adolf Hitler, and any attempt to do so through film (or any other means) is abominable. Ganz never sets out to create a sympathetic Hitler here. Instead, he gives us the living cadaver of a sick and twisted spirit who deceived millions into following him into perdition. Hitler and his regime are stripped of their mystique and invincibility—gone are the earth-trembling parades, the fluttering banners, and the hollow promises of empire. Utterly demystified and abandoned, Ganz's Hitler awaits his coming ignominious death, but not before unleashing his madness, one last time, on those most loyal to him.

4 HELEN MIRREN AS QUEEN ELIZABETH II, *THE QUEEN*

Helen Mirren may be the most talented actress of her generation, and with good reason: no one else has two Queen Elizabeths on her resume. Here, her portrayal of Elizabeth II is much like Pu Yi, holding fast to a tradition that fewer and fewer understand. Nobility is no longer a birthright, a fact that apparently everyone but the royal family now accepts. In the wake of Princess Diana's death, the queen must finally capitulate to the realities of a changed world or risk destroying the monarchy forever. Kudos also to actor Michael Sheen as Tony Blair.

3 FORREST WHITAKER AS IDI AMIN, *THE LAST KING OF SCOTLAND*

The thing that makes Amin the stuff of nightmares is not just his monstrous brutality, but the fact that we are so drawn to him. When we first meet Whitaker's Amin here, we understand how he seduced the masses of Uganda into following him. He's jovial, amiable, even fun. However, when the opposition nearly assassinates him, we get a glimpse of his savagery, but not before our protagonist has become entangled in his web. As Amin sinks deeper in paranoia and violent mood swings, his true nature is revealed—a cruel, capricious child who charms the media as a quaint curiosity, while his death squads carry out mass murder on a rarely surpassed scale.

2 GEORGE C. SCOTT AS GENERAL PATTON, *PATTON*

Patton tells the tale of General George S. Patton, famous tank commander of World War II. The film begins with Patton's career in North Africa and progresses through the invasion of Germany and the fall of the Third Reich. Side plots also speak of Patton's numerous faults, such his temper and habit toward insubordination, which would, eventually, lead to his being relieved as Occupation Commander of Germany. While Patton was not a political leader, like the others on this list, there is no doubt that he was a great military leader and the film itself is so good that it was selected for preservation in the United

States National Film Registry by the Library of Congress as being "culturally, historically, or aesthetically significant."

1 BEN KINGSLEY AS MAHATMA GANDHI, *GANDHI*

Simply one of the greatest performances of all time. Kingsley portrays the Mahatma from his early days in South Africa through India's independence and postcolonial troubles and finally his assassination following the India-Pakistan partition. We feel the weight of the world that rests upon Gandhi's shoulders as he strives to change society through nonviolence, a philosophy contrary to man's inherently barbarous nature. This film does not set out to tell the life story of Gandhi, impossible for a reasonable time frame. Rather, we focus on his humility, piety, and impossible serenity in the face of fanaticism and suffering. If you see only one more film for the rest of your life, let it be this one.

❉❉❉❉❉❉

TOP 10 COOLEST SANTAS

10 BILL GOLDBERG (*SANTA'S SLAY*)

Bill Goldberg plays the devil's son, who lost a wager with an angel and was forced to spend a thousand years playing Santa, but now the wager of that time has run out, and Mr. Santa isn't so joyful anymore. He makes up for lost time and starts to kill people. And really, how incredibly cool does WWE wrestler Goldberg look as the holiday elf? Bad ass.

9 PAUL GIAMATTI (*FRED CLAUS*)

As Nick Claus, later on the eponymous Santa, Paul Giamatti really embodies and looks like the jolly old fat man. Sure, it's all suit and makeup, but in the facial expressions and mannerisms lie the real persona. Though I still see him as a masturbating wino in *Sideways*, Giamatti really pulls it off.

8 RICHARD ATTENBOROUGH (*MIRACLE ON 34TH STREET*)

Six-year-old Susan has doubts about childhood's most enduring miracle—Santa Claus. Her mother told her the "secret" about Santa a long time ago, so Susan doesn't expect to receive the most important gifts on her Christmas list. But after meeting a special department store Santa (who is convinced he's the real thing), Susan is given the most precious gift of all—something to believe in. Sure, it's a remake, and for the most part those really suck, but just look at the guy! Now *that* is a Santa!

7 TIM ALLEN (*THE SANTA CLAUS*)

Scott Calvin (Allen) reads *The Night Before Christmas*...then receives an unexpected visitor on his roof. When he's startled by Scott's calling out and falls, the Santa impersonator disappears, leaving only an eight-reindeer sleigh and a suit with instructions to put it on if he's involved in an accident. Scott does, and is transported around the town dropping gifts through chimneys until he's taken to the North Pole and informed by a group who claim they're elves that he is now Santa. For actually being a relatively thin fellow, Allen looks surprisingly convincing as Father Christmas.

6 JACK BLACK (*SATURDAY NIGHT LIVE*)

In a hilarious Debbie Downer sketch, Rachel Dratch, in her most sob-storied, rotten-lived best, portrays Downer on Christmas morning. Jack Black as Santa (wonderfully done, by the way) attempts to get past Debbie's neuroses by asking repeatedly what she really wants for Christmas only to be blocked at every corner by her constant hypochondriacal issues.

5 ED ASNER (*ELF*)

Though Will Farrell steals the movie as Buddy, the elf, Ed Asner does a fine job as the portly man in red and arrives only at the end in a ruined sleigh to explain to Buddy that the Christmas spirit is going to need to be refurbished in the city in order for him to fly again. He looks really cool as Santa, too, especially considering he's kind of a grumpy ass.

4 SANTA (*RUDOLPH THE RED-NOSED REINDEER*)

At first, Santa is a skinny jerk who croons madly about being the King of Jingle-Ling to Rudolph's family just moments after telling Donder that his son is a shiny-nosed freak. He let the father deer know, in no uncertain terms, that he is a failure of a father for producing such an abomination of an offspring. Well, as it goes, old Saint Nick eats his shitty words as he requires Rudolph's assistance to guide his fogged-in sleigh. Take that, fatty!

3 THE GRINCH (*HOW THE GRINCH STOLE CHRISTMAS*)

When the Grinch, annual loather of the poor little Whos down in Who-ville, decides to finally take matter into his own hands by raping the town of its Christmas celebration, he chooses to do so dressed as "Santy Claus." By slicing up a curtain and attaching some white fluff, the Grinch looks really nothing like Santa to the human eye, but to Cindy Lou Who, he apparently does. Nice suit though.

2 BILLY BOB THORNTON (*BAD SANTA*)

As the most obnoxious of all mall Santas, Billy Bob, with his lanky and bony build, really looks nothing like the Jolly Fat Man. He's drunk, rude, mouthy, and a thief, but he is as cool as it comes when it comes to what matters: women and good old-fashioned holiday cheer.

1 SANTA (COCA-COLA)

This is it: the one and only. The popularity of the Santa Claus as we know him comes from an ad campaign from the Coca-Cola Corporation in which the well-established Victorian English image of Father Christmas was spread worldwide.

CHAPTER EIGHT
Music

TOP 10 BIZARRE MUSICAL INSTRUMENTS

10 AEOLIAN HARP

Named after the ancient Greek god of the wind, Aeolus, Aeolian harps were very popular during the Romantic Era. "Played" by the wind, the instrument is essentially a wooden box with strings strung on the top of it. When wind passes over, the strings vibrate into a sound-hole in the box, and whatever pitch the strings are tuned to echoes out. As well as being household instruments, some can be found built into monumental metal sound sculptures on tops of buildings and hills.

9 ONDES MARTENOT

Invented by and named after Maurice Martenot in 1928, the Ondes Martenot is an early electronic instrument similar in sound to the theremin. Incorporating a keyboard and slide, the instrument uses the addition of filter banks and switchable loudspeakers to expand its sonic capabilities. Using thermionic valves to produce oscillating frequencies, it is especially known for its ability to make an eerie wavering note. A popular instrument with composers, Olivier Messiaen was a notable user.

8 THEREMIN

One of the first fully electrical musical instruments, and uniquely designed to be the first instrument to be played without being touched, the theremin was invented by Russian inventor Léon Theremin in 1919. Using two radio frequency oscillators and two metal antennas, the theremin detects where the player's hand is, affecting volume and pitch. The signals are then amplified and sent to a loudspeaker.

7 GLASS ARMONICA

Known as many things, such as the glass harmonica, glass armonica, "hydrocrystlaophone," or simply the armonica (derived from the Italian word for harmony, *armonia*). This instrument consists of glass bowls, goblets, or wine glasses filled with water. When the player runs wet fingers over the top of the cups, the friction produces a ringing tone consistent to the size of the goblet. A mechanical version where the bowls are placed in a horizontal row along a spindle was invented in 1761 by Benjamin Franklin.

6 GRAVIKORD

Invented by Robert Grawi in 1986, the gravikord is an electric double harp modeled after the twenty-one-string West African *kora*. Made of stainless-steel tubing and using twenty-four nylon strings, it also has no resonating gourd or skin. Another feature that makes it different than the *kora* is the use of synthetic material for the bridge, using a very different design. While having a much greater pitch and range than the *kora*, the playing technique is similar: the player uses his thumb and index finger from each hand to pluck the strings. Still, the hands are placed in a much more ergonomic and natural position than its West African counterpart.

5 KAISATSUKO

The *kaisatsuko* is a fiddle-like instrument invented in Tokyo, Japan, by Yuichi Onoue. Unlike most fiddle instruments, the *kaisatsuko* does not use a bow to vibrate its two strings. Rather, it uses a hand crank that spins a nylon wheel, bowing the strings and producing a sustained drone sound. The technique of using a rotating wheel to bow the strings is also used on the hurdy-gurdy, invented before the eleventh century.

4 MUSICAL SAW

Also called a "singing saw," the musical saw is the use of a regular handsaw as a musical instrument. There are many positions the saw can be held at, the most common being sitting down or standing, with the saw handle held between the legs. When the blade is bent into an S-shape, a bow pulled across a "sweet spot" in the center will produce a droning note. The ethereal tone made by the instrument can be compared to a theremin or a woman's clear voice. Alfred Schnittke has used the singing saw in many of his works.

3 BAZANTAR

The bazantar is a five-string acoustic bass, equipped with an additional twenty-nine sympathetic, and four drone strings underneath the top five original bass strings. Spanning over five melodic octave ranges, the sympathetic section holds four more octaves. Combining the large melody range of the bass, drone, and sympathetic sections creates a truly rich landscape of resonance.

2 CIMBALOM

Found mainly in the music of Hungary, Romania, Moldova, Ukraine, Greece, and Iran, the cimbalom is known by many names and spelling variations, including cimbalom (most commonly used), cymbalum, cymbalom, tambal, tsymbaly, tsimbl, santouri, or santur. The instrument is a type of hammered dulcimer, with strings pulled across a sounding board and either struck with a mallet or plucked to produce sound. The instrument wasn't well known outside of Eastern Europe until composer Zoltán Kodály used it extensively in his orchestral suite, *Háry János*. Igor Stravinsky was another enthusiast, and included it in his ballet *Renard*. A more recent use is in the film *The Lord of The Rings: The Two Towers* to highlight Gollum's sneakiness.

1 STALACPIPE ORGAN

Deep inside the Luray Caverns in Virginia's Shenandoah Valley is housed the Great Stalacpipe Organ. The stalacpipe organ is the world's largest musical instrument. Stalactites covering three-and-a-half acres of the surrounding caverns were chosen and shaped to produce a symphonic tone, similar to that of a pipe organ, when tapped with rubber mallets. A custom-made keyboard panel controls the mallets, with each key hitting a specific stalactite shaped for that note.

❋❋❋❋❋❋

TOP 10 LITTLE-KNOWN BUT INFLUENTIAL MUSICIANS

10 RICHIE HAVENS, BORN JANUARY 21, 1941

Havens is a folk singer/guitarist best known for his performance at the original Woodstock. He is also known for his unusual method of using open

D tuning and fretting all strings, which creates an intense rhythmic style. Also heard on some song recordings is a unique drumming sound, which is actually his foot tapping. He had moderate fame when he reached the Billboard charts in the '70s but until then had maintained a fairly local success within his Greenwich Village scene. He rarely wrote his own songs, but is known for the distinctive interpretations of songs uniquely his.

9 IAN CURTIS, JULY 15, 1956–MAY 18, 1980

Vocalist and genius lyricist of Joy Division, Curtis committed suicide in 1980. The suicide was thought to be related to a combination of anxiety over an upcoming North American tour the band was embarking on as well as his severe epilepsy. His onstage seizures were often mistaken for an erratic style of dance, which resulted in Curtis having to be carried off stage at some performances. His legacy has grown and continues to grow worldwide since his death.

8 VINI REILLY, BORN AUGUST 1953

Reilly is a guitarist, singer, and Durutti Column post-punk pioneer. He worked with Morrissey on his groundbreaking first album, *Viva Hate* (1988). He also worked with John Cooper Clarke, Pauline Murray, Anne Clark, The Wake, Richard Jobson, Quando Quango, and more. He has been very influential in the musical movement now known as "chill-out electronica."

7 GRAM PARSONS, NOVEMBER 5, 1946–SEPTEMBER 19, 1973

Parsons was rated eighty-seventh on the *Rolling Stones* list of "Greatest Artists of All Time." He was a pioneer of the '70s rock movement in such bands as International Submarine Band, The Byrds, and The Flying Burrito Brothers. He was best known for his "anticipation" recordings of the rock country movement of the '70s. He had a self-described style of "Cosmic American Music." He died of a drug overdose.

6 JEFF BUCKLEY, NOVEMBER 17, 1966–MAY 29, 1997

Raised as Scotty Moorhead, Buckley was an acclaimed singer, songwriter, and guitarist. Known for his ethereal singing voice, he was considered one of the most promising artists of his generation, especially after the release of his critically acclaimed 1994 debut album *Grace*. At the height of his popularity Buckley drowned during an evening swim in 1997. There was speculation of suicide as he had taken prescription drugs for his bipolar disorder before the swim. His work and style continue to be highly regarded by critics and fellow musicians.

5 ANTON NEWCOMBE, BORN AUGUST 29, 1967

Newcombe is a multi-instrumental musician and founder of the moderately successful band Brian Jonestown Massacre. Unfortunately, his heroin addiction fueled his paranoid tendencies and erratic behavior both on and off stage. He would sometimes berate his band mates and destroy instruments in fits of rage. He proclaims to be versed with eighty or so instruments including guitar, sitar, upright bass, bagpipes, mandolin, lute, piano, organ, accordion, drums, and more. The band went their separate ways after Newcombe failed to produce a highly anticipated and hyped album that he obsessed over, so much so that he insisted they build a studio in his home so he could record at his leisure. He has since toured with a bevy of bands and claims to be sober as of 1999.

4 DOCK BOGGS, FEBRUARY 7, 1898–FEBRUARY 7, 1971

Boggs was a singer, songwriter, and banjo master who played in the style of old-time mountain music and blues. He developed a three-finger method of picking on the banjo, which allowed for single-note runs, much like guitarists. He recorded in 1927 with Brunswick music but didn't record again until Mike Seeger rediscovered him in the 1960s.

3 TOWNES VAN ZANDT, MARCH 7, 1944–JANUARY 1, 1997

Townes was a musician's musician in his time, though a virtual unknown until after his death. He was a country folk-rock performer and poet with a style often referred to as "outlaw country." Being a heavy drinker, he lived a reclusive life during the '70s in a cabin in Tennessee making music. He died on New Year's Day, 1997, due to complications from heart surgery. He has left a legacy of music that to this day is held sacred and performed by a bevy of musicians such as Lyle Lovett, Emmylou Harris, My Morning Jacket, and even the Meat Puppets.

2 MOONDOG: LOUIS THOMAS HARDIN, MAY 26, 1916– SEPTEMBER 8, 1999

Blind, and homeless by choice, Hardin was a composer who invented several instruments. He was also known as a poet and cosmologist. Eccentric at best, he went so far as to wear clothing that only he made and interpreted to be in the likeness of the Norse God Thor. It wasn't until his later years that he began to be recognized as a musical genius and innovator. He was known for twenty years of the thirty that he lived in New York as the "The Viking of 6th Ave."

1 DANIEL JOHNSTON, BORN JANUARY 22, 1961

The bizarre and heartbreaking story of Daniel Johnston is one recently made popular by the documentary *The Devil and Daniel Johnston*, which is about his music and art, as well as his fight with mental illness. His songs poignantly display childlike wonder and hope, infused with darker themes. He had never recorded inside a studio until recent coercing because of his growing popularity and until then his method had been to simply record into a boombox. Nirvana front man Kurt Cobain was sometimes seen wearing a T-shirt with the cover of a Daniel Johnston tape, the words "Hi, how are you?" and a quirky drawing. Johnston still produces art and music and is often called "genius" and "brilliant."

✳✳✳✳✳✳

TOP 10 CHILD SINGERS

10 CHARLOTTE CHURCH

First appearing on the television show *This Morning*, Charlotte Church was only eleven years and sang "Pie Jesu" over the phone. The next year she performed again on ITV's *Big, Big Talent Show*. After the televised debuts, she went on to play concerts at Cardiff Arms Park, Royal Albert Hall, and scored an opening spot for Shirley Bassey during her Antwerp show.

9 TANYA TUCKER

Releasing her first hit at only thirteen years old, Tanya Tucker had even been able to stun people with her voice as a child. Her abilities even captured the attention of country music star Mel Tillis, who invited her to perform onstage. After moving to Las Vegas, Nevada, Tucker began performing regularly, and recorded a demo that her father sent around. Eventually, the demo tape made its way to Nashville, Tennessee (the country music capital of the U.S.), where it got attention from songwriter Dolores Fuller, who sent it to A&R head Billy Sherrill. Sherrill quickly signed up the young singer in 1972 after hearing her voice. Tanya is one of the rare child stars in music to keep a successful career well past her teen years, making hits into the '80s and '90s.

8 GAYLA PEEVEY

Born in 1943, Gayla Peevey was only ten years old and living in Oklahoma City when she recorded her most famous song, "I Want a Hippopotamus for Christmas" (Columbia, 1953). The Oklahoma City Zoo capitalized on the song's popularity in 1953, using it to energize a fundraising campaign to "buy a hippo for Gayla." The zoo had never owned its own hippopotamus, but raised three thousand dollars and bought a baby hippo named Matilda. The animal was flown to Oklahoma City and presented to the zoo by Peevey herself.

7 JIMMY BOYD

Jiimy Boyd first started singing professionally at seven years old after a local radio station heard him sing and he was invited to sing regularly for them, paying fifty dollars a show. After getting a cataract surgery in Los Angeles, Boyd auditioned for the *Al Jarvis Talent Show* on KLAC-TV. He was such a hit that they had him perform on the show the same night. He was a major hit, and the station received over twenty thousand calls from viewers. He was instantly invited to be a regular on Al Jarvis's five-hour show block, and made several appearances with Frank Sinatra on his KLAC-TV show. By the time he was twelve, he signed to Columbia Records and recorded the famous song, "I Saw Mommy Kissing Santa Claus."

6 LULU

Lulu was born in Glasgow, Scotland, where she was taken under the wing of Marion Massey. Her first hit, "Shout!" delivered in a mature raucous voice, shot her to fame at only fifteen years old. After several more British hits, she dropped her backup band, The Luvvers, to continue her career solo. Her song, "To Sir, With Love," was an instant hit in the United States and shot to number one.

5 FRANKIE LYMON

Frankie Lymon, an African-American rock-and-roll/rhythm-and-blues singer, was born in 1942. Frankie was the soprano lead singer of an early rock and roll group called The Teenagers. The Teenagers were a huge influence on R&B and rock, most notably The Jackson 5, Michael Jackson, and The Beach Boys. Frankie Lymon rose to fame with The Teenagers song "Why Do Fools Fall in Love," and after five more songs that landed on the Top 10 Singles charts, Lymon went solo. His new venture wasn't as successful as The Teenagers, and he soon fell into a heroin addiction that killed him at age twenty-five.

4 HELEN SHAPIRO
The youngest female chart topper in the UK, Helen Shapiro's mature voice made her a household name overnight. Her first four singles all made it to the top three of the UK singles chart, the songs "You Don't Know" and "Walkin' Back to Happiness" becoming number-one hits. Before the age of sixteen, she was voted Britain's Top Female Singer, and The Beatle's first national tour was with her as the opening act in 1956. Her fame eventually waned, and she became a Christian Messianic believer. She devoted her later career to gospel and has since retired to concentrate on gospel outreach events.

3 STEVIE WONDER
Blind from birth, Stevie Wonder learned how to play piano, harmonica, drums, and bass by the age of ten. Discovered in 1961, at age eleven, he was heard singing on a street corner by a relative of Ronnie White. Ronnie White took him into Motown Records where he was quickly signed and given the name "Little Stevie Wonder." After a couple less-than-successful releases, he finally caught public eye with the number-one chart-topper "Fingertips (Pt. 2)," a live recording of a Motor Town Revue performance. Soon he lost the "Little" in his name, and became the prominent figure he is today.

2 JUDY GARLAND
Garland is best known for her role in 1939 as Dorothy Gale in MGM classic film *The Wizard of Oz*. She was only sixteen at the time, and has been associated with the song "Over the Rainbow," voted number-one movie song of all time in the American Film Institute's 100 Years 100 Songs list, ever since. After her prized role, she became MGM's most bankable star, starring in many more "backyard musicals" and shows. She died at forty-seven due to a drug overdose, an addiction she fought since her first rise to fame.

1 MICHAEL JACKSON
The "King of Pop" made his debut at eleven years old, the youngest of The Jackson 5. They hit stardom when their first four singles, "I Want You Back," "ABC," "The Love You Save," and "I'll Be There," all charted at number one, the

first time anyone had ever put out four number-ones in a row. During his time in The Jackson 5, he was promoted as being nine instead of eleven, in order to make him look cuter and media friendly. While still with his family band, he began releasing solo material under Motown in 1972. With four studio CDs, also came three more successful singles: "Got to Be There," "Ben," and the remake of Bobby Day's "Rockin' Robin." He quickly became a musical phenomenon, with numerous awards and world records.

✳✳✳✳✳✳

TOP 10 INFLUENTIAL ALBUMS THAT BOMBED

10 THE KINKS—*THE VILLAGE GREEN PRESERVATION SOCIETY*

In 1968, a year after the fabled summer of love, one of the biggest and best bands in England released this concept album. Based around a series of nostalgic events and characters, its sales were disastrous.

9 VELVET UNDERGROUND—*THE VELVET UNDERGROUND*

Though the Velvet Underground famously sold few albums in their time, their first two efforts did creep into the top 200 of the American charts. This, their third album and their first without John Cale, did not even make it that far. It is a surprise because in comparison, *The Velvet Underground* is their most accessible, and, "Murder Mystery" aside, with none of their previous avante garde posturing.

8 MILES DAVIS—*KIND OF BLUE*

Though this album has sold three million copies, it has taken fifty years to do so. To put this figure into perspective, the Michael Jackson album *Thriller* has sold twenty-seven million copies in half that time.

7 NICK DRAKE—*FIVE LEAVES LEFT*

One of the best folk albums of all time, this was the legendary Nick Drake's first record. None of his albums really sold, but now critics consider all three as modern-day classics and Nick Drake as the Kurt Cobain of folk.

6 WIRE—*PINK FLAG*

This album contains twenty-three punk-pop songs, yet its total running time is less than thirty minutes. REM covered the excellent "Strange" on their album *Document*, but *Pink Flag* is full of great pop songs.

5 MY BLOODY VALENTINE—*ISN'T ANYTHING*

My Bloody Valentine has come to the forefront of popular culture recently, making a number of appearances on the *Lost in Translation* soundtrack. *Isn't Anything* is their first album and one of the best British indie albums ever. Kevin Shields was a forerunner of postmodern rock.

4 ROBERT JOHNSON—*KING OF THE DELTA BLUES SINGERS*

Keith Richards was probably the only person who bought this record when it came out in 1961. He played it to Mick Jagger and Brian Jones and they went on to form the Rolling Stones, together popularizing rhythm and blues and paving the way for the British blues movement in the '60s. Robert Johnson's *King of the Delta Blues Singers* is where it all started.

3 RICHARD AND LINDA THOMPSON—*I WANT TO SEE THE BRIGHT LIGHTS TONIGHT*

You would have thought, after his success with the Fairport Convention, that Richard Thompson's name alone could sell a few albums. Unfortunately, his first solo record, *Henry the Human Fly*, was panned by the critics, which certainly didn't help the sales of this second effort. However, its angry lyrics ("Every handshake is just another man to beat") and Linda Thompson's haunting vocals have contributed to its status as the thinking man's album of the '70s.

2 IGGY POP AND THE STOOGES—*FUNHOUSE*

We would see the influence of this album seven years after its release with the explosion of punk. Recorded live in the studio, *Funhouse* sounds more raw and angry than anything the Sex Pistols ever recorded.

1 PIXIES—*SURFER ROSA*

The famous track on *Surfer Rosa* is "Where Is My Mind," played over the end credits of the film *Fight Club*. It is an unconventional track, but still relatively commercial; it is surprising this album did not sell more. In the UK, it did not even chart. The Pixies of course went on to become one of America's most influential indie bands.

❋❋❋❋❋❋

TOP 10 GREATEST FICTIONAL BANDS

10 SCRANTONICITY—*THE OFFICE*

Notable Members: Kevin Malone
Style: Cover Band
Essential Listening: "Roxanne," "You Were Meant for Me"

Originally a Steve Miller tribute band known as "Jokers and Tokers," Scrantonicity now plays covers of The Police (though they have been known to cover other artists at live shows). The band has recently gone through a huge upheaval as Kevin Malone, the band's lead vocalist and drummer, left the group. He has gone on to form a new band, Scrantonicity II. Immediately, the two bands began an intense rivalry that continues to this day.

9 DR. FÜNKE'S BAND—*ARRESTED DEVELOPMENT*

Notable Members: Tobias Fünke, Lindsay Fünke, Maeby Fünke
Style: Folk
Essential Listening: "Teamocil"

"Dr. Funke's 100% Natural Good Time Family Band Solution" was a 1990s folk trio consisting of the family of Tobias and Lindsay Fünke and their daughter, Maeby. The group was underwritten by the Natural Life Food Company, a division of Chem-Grow, an Allen Crayne acquisition, which was part of the Squimm Group. As a result, the group's songs tended to focus upon the various drugs the company offered. Nevertheless, the band gained a very small but very devoted following. The band eventually split up due to growing tensions within the family. A reunion show at a Los Angeles wellness convention ended with Lindsay and Maeby storming offstage, leaving Tobias to finish the show with the help of an eager fan.

8 AUTOBAHN—*THE BIG LEBOWSKI*
Notable Members: Uli Kunkel
Style: Electronica
Essential Listening: "Hit and Run," "Faking It"
German techno-pop pioneers Autobahn released only one album, *Nagelbett*, in the late seventies. They are perhaps the best example of a band being "ahead of its time." Though they are now recognized as great innovators in the world of techno, their album was almost universally disparaged, by both critics and audiences alike. Utterly demoralized, the band dissolved. All of its members fell on hard times, with band leader Uli Kunkel even resorting to the adult film industry before disappearing from the public eye completely.

7 THE BE-SHARPS—*THE SIMPSONS*
Notable Members: Homer Simpson, Barney Gumble, W. Seymour Skinner, Apu de Beaumarchais
Style: Barbershop Quartet
Essential Listening: "Baby On Board," "Number 8"
A barbershop quartet hailing from Springfield, The Be-Sharps experienced a meteoric rise to fame following the release of their first album, *Meet the Be-Sharps*, which featured the unlikely hit "Baby on Board." Success, however, was fleeting. By the time of their sophomore effort "Bigger Than Jesus," the band was divided by creative differences, which led to the group splitting up. In recent years, they reunited only once for a concert atop Moe's Tavern, though reunion tour rumors continue to abound.

6 JESSE AND THE RIPPERS—*FULL HOUSE*
Notable Members: Jesse Katsopolis
Style: Rock
Essential Listening: "Forever"
Jesse and the Rippers came roaring out of the San Francisco rock scene when they recorded a cover of the classic Beach Boys tune "Forever." The song became a surprise hit with both fans and the Beach Boys themselves. In fact,

three of the Beach Boys even appeared as the band's backup singers in the official video. The band split shortly after their first tour. The breakup was primarily due to lead vocalist and guitarist Jesse Katsopolis's unwillingness to put the band ahead of his family. (He was helping raise his dead sister's three daughters in addition to his own twin sons.) Since then the members have gone on to various other projects, most notably Katsopolis's new band, Hot Daddy and the Monkey Puppets.

5 THE BEETS—*DOUG*

Notable Members: Monroe Yoder, Wendy Nespott, Chap Lippman, Flounder
Style: Pop Rock
Essential Listening: "Killer Tofu," "I Need Mo' Allowance"
After their first single "I Sneezed on My Face" dropped in the mid-'90s, The Beets were an unstoppable force in pop music releasing such modern pop classics as "Where's My Sock?" and "You Gotta Shout Your Lungs Out." Hit after hit resulted in a huge fan base and a declaration of "Beet Mania" by the press. Eventually, the band members decided to go their separate ways but not before releasing their masterful final album, *Let It Beet*. Each of The Beets has now gone on to a solo career, leaving fans only dreaming of a reunion.

4 DRIVESHAFT—*LOST*

Notable Members: Charlie Pace, Liam Pace
Style: Pop Rock
Essential Listening: "You All (Everybody)"
DriveShaft exploded onto the modern music scene in 1999 with their infectious single "You All (Everybody)." That single rose all the way to number one in both the UK and the U.S. Following the monumental success of their first album, the band experienced a great deal of difficulty in recording a follow-up. When it was finally released, *Oil Change* found little popularity with critics or the public. The group disbanded shortly after. Charlie Pace, the band's bassist and main songwriter, expressed interest in reforming the group in the fall of 2004. Sadly, Pace was among those who died on September 22, 2004, in the crash of Oceanic Flight 815. His death, however, sparked renewed interest for the band. Now, Charlie Pace is widely appreciated as songwriter by the critics and fans who once wrote him off as a one-hit wonder.

3 DISASTER AREA— RESTAURANT AT THE END OF THE UNIVERSE

Notable Members: Hotblack Desiato
Style: Loud
Essential Listening: "Only the End of the World Again"
The band Disaster Area is commonly cited as being the loudest band in the universe, and in fact the loudest sound of any kind, anywhere. Their legendary live shows are generally considered to be best when experienced at a safe distance of thirty-seven miles away in a well-built concrete bunker. Their most recent shows have featured a segment in which an actual spaceship is crashed into the nearest sun. This stunt resulted in the planet of Kakrafoon being transformed from a harsh desert planet into a tropical paradise. A spokesman for the band commented that it was "a good gig." The band is currently touring in spite of the fact that photon-ajuitar player Hotblack Desiato is currently spending a year dead for tax purposes.

2 STILLWATER—ALMOST FAMOUS

Notable Members: Jeff Bebe, Russell Hammond
Style: Classic Rock
Essential Listening: "Fever Dog," "Love Comes and Goes"
Hailing from Troy, Michigan, Stillwater is still known as one of the wild and raucous bands of the 1970s, both onstage and off. After stints opening for such legends as Black Sabbath and the Allman Brothers Band, the group embarked on its now notorious Almost Famous Tour in support of their second album, *Farrington Road.* Sex, drugs, and every other rock and roll excess permeated the tour which culminated in a *Rolling Stone* cover. The tour also caused tension between the band's core members, Jeff Bebe and Russell Hammond, resulting in the band dissolving after only one more album.

1 SPINAL TAP—THIS IS SPINAL TAP

Notable Members: Derek St. Hubbins, Nigel Tufnel, Derek Smalls
Style: Heavy Metal
Essential Listening: "Sex Farm," "Lick My Love Pump," "Big Bottom"
In the history of rock and roll, there has never been a career more unlikely than that of Spinal Tap. Dubbed "England's Loudest Band," the group has gained far-reaching popularity unrivaled by its musical contemporaries. This is undoubtedly due to the Marty DeBergi documentary *This Is Spinal Tap,* which chronicled the

group's 1982 tour that was plagued by band infighting and poor ticket sales. Following the film's release, the band's fan base greatly expanded and the group went on to become one of the most beloved in the history of rock. They reunited for a show at Wembley Stadium in London as a part of Live Earth where they unveiled a new song, "Warmer Than Hell."

✳✳✳✳✳✳

TOP 10 INFLUENTIAL BEATLES SONGS

10 "ABBEY ROAD"
Influenced: EMI

It's slightly odd starting with the Beatles' last album, but it's also a slightly odd influence; Abbey Road Studios is named after the *Abbey Road* album, not the other way around. When the Beatles recorded there, it was the EMI London Recording Studio. The name was changed (and a zebra crossing logo

developed) after the album was released, with Abbey Road suddenly becoming the most famous recording studio in the world. Staff members became celebrities when people found out they worked there.

9 "STRAWBERRY FIELDS FOREVER"
Influenced: Jeff Lynne and ELO

The first song to be recorded after the Beatles stopped touring and approached with the attitude that they were going to get it right—there was to be no compromise. The final recording is actually two different versions of the song edited together, thanks to heroic efforts by George Martin. Lennon was still dissatisfied, but he didn't like most of his recordings.

The influence of this song was actually seen a few years later. In 1971, Jeff Lynne formed the Electric Light Orchestra with the intention of picking up from "Strawberry Fields Forever," mixing traditional rock band instruments with classical instruments.

8 "I WANNA BE YOUR MAN"
Influenced: Mick Jagger and Keith Richards

As Paul has openly admitted, this was not one of their better songs. It was given to Ringo as his contribution to *With the Beatles*. However, its biggest influence was when Mick Jagger told Lennon and McCartney they needed a follow-up to their first hit single. At that time, the Rolling Stones were a cover band; they didn't write their own material. Legend has it that John and Paul disappeared for fifteen minutes and returned with "I Wanna Be Your Man." It made Jagger and Keith Richards realize that writing their own songs was possible.

7 "RUBBER SOUL"
Influenced: Brian Wilson

Brian Wilson was "knocked out" by the Beatles album *Rubber Soul*; as he put it, each track "was a gas." As a response he produced *Pet Sounds*. It was as a response to *Pet Sounds* that the Beatles produced *Sgt. Pepper*. Paul McCartney has acknowledged that there was a definite feeling of competition between the Beatles and the Beach Boys.

George Martin recalled that when they listened to *Pet Sounds*, the Beatles asked, "Can we do something as good as this?" Martin replied, "No. We can do better."

6 "I WANNA HOLD YOUR HAND"
Influenced: The Beatles and the U.S.

"I Wanna Hold Your Hand" changed the life of the Beatles; it was their first number-one in America. As George Martin has pointed out, they had tremendous difficulties getting records released in the U.S. EMI actually owned Columbia Records, and Columbia still wouldn't release Beatle singles—the early singles were released on tiny labels (Swann comes to mind) in the U.S. It was partly the successful sales of these singles that forced Columbia to release Beatle singles. "I Wanna Hold Your Hand" was a huge hit in the U.S. just as the Beatles arrived for their first tour. Their timing, as ever, was perfect.

5 "TWIST AND SHOUT"
Influenced: EMI Staff at Abbey Road

This was a performance that amazed EMI staff. People working on the Beatles session have memories of playing the tape to staff members the next day and saying, "Wait until you hear this!" Within EMI, it was realized that something special was happening. George Harrison recalled attitudes changing toward the band between their first visits to Abbey Road (to record their first singles) and after they'd had a hit and recorded "Twist and Shout."

"Twist and Shout" was recorded at the end of a single day in which the entire first album was recorded. EMI would only give them a day's studio time; it was winter and the band had colds, Lennon's was particularly bad. What makes "Twist and Shout" all the more remarkable is that it was recorded in one take and as a "live" recording; there was no overdubbing possible in those days.

George Martin did record a second take, but Lennon's voice had gone so it was the first take that was used.

4 "TOMORROW NEVER KNOWS"

Influenced: Pop musicians everywhere

"Tomorrow Never Knows" was the first Beatles track to use artificial double tracking (ADT). In fact, it was almost certainly the first track anywhere to deliberately use the effect. Double-tracked vocals (where the singer sings the same part twice) became popular when four-track recording arrived, quite late at Abbey Road Studios, around 1964. Lennon, in particular, didn't like singing the same thing twice—it was obviously important that exactly the same words and phrasing were used, making such sessions tedious and tiring.

With this in mind, Ken Townsend, EMI engineer, "had an idea" driving home after such a session. The singer would sing the part once, and then a copy made and played alongside the original with a slight, varying delay—the effect was double-tracked vocals without having to sing the part twice. Lennon loved the effect, but not being in the least bit technical he had no chance of understanding the technique involved. George Martin gave him a pseudoscientific explanation ("There's feedback on the sploshing flange") and after that, Lennon started calling the effect "Ken's Flanger" and said in interview, "Every track on *Sgt. Pepper* had flanging, it's great!"

To this day, the effect is called "flanging"; some people claim that it is named after pressing the flange wheel on a reel-to-reel tape deck, but if you tried that on a professional tape deck, you'd lose a finger!

3 "PLEASE, PLEASE ME"

Influenced: George Martin and Dick James

After recording "Please, Please Me," Martin was able to tell the Beatles, "Congratulations, Gentlemen, you have recorded your first number one." A big moment not only for the Beatles, but also for George Martin himself.

George Martin was known as a producer of comedy and novelty records. His highest-placed record before "Please, Please Me" was "Love Me Do," but that only reached number seventeen. Before that his only "hit" had been the *Robin Hood* theme tune, sung by Dick James. So, when "Please, Please Me" was being recorded, Martin was the most junior producer in EMI (he was the youngest, and Parlophone, Martin's label, was the smallest). A year later, he was one of the most famous producers in the world.

The aforementioned Dick James became a music publisher when baldness ended his singing career. He had given a song ("How Do You Do It?") to George Martin for the Beatles, which the Beatles hated. The Beatles offered up "Please, Please Me" instead. George Martin, to his credit, let them record their own song. Dick James recalled getting a phone call from Martin that started, "You know that song the Beatles *were* going to release?"

There is a happy ending for Dick James. He offered to publish "Please, Please Me" and became the Beatles song publisher, forming Northern Songs especially for the band.

2 "RAUNCHY"

Influenced: George Harrison and more or less everyone

"Raunchy" was never released by the Beatles, but it was George Harrison's audition piece, which got him into the Beatles and performed for John at Paul's prompting to John on top of a Liverpool bus. According to Paul, George's guitar work was "perfect." George was three years younger than John; you can imagine John's attitude (being nearly eighteen) to a fourteen-year-old wanting to join the band. George must have been pretty good!

1 "TWENTY FLIGHT ROCK"

Influenced: John, Paul, George, and Ringo and pretty much everyone since

Never recorded by the Beatles, this was the song that Paul played to John when they first met at a garden fête where John was performing with his band, the Quarrymen. John was so impressed he asked Paul to join the band the next day. He delayed because he was trying to reconcile strengthening the band with the weakening of his own position as band leader and the fact that Paul was two years his junior. Finally, he decided that the improvement to the band was most important.

In fairness, the surviving members of the Quarrymen can't remember what Paul sang; John couldn't remember, as he was somewhat drunk at the time (despite being four years under age). However, if the story is true, Paul performing "Twenty Flight Rock" might be the most influential performance in pop history.

✳✳✳✳✳✳

TOP 10 MOST INFLUENTIAL METAL BANDS

10 NAPALM DEATH
Napalm Death is the creator of grindcore. On top of that they influenced all sorts of death and doom metal bands around their time. They have had great members in their band, some of whom found success over the years in bands like Cathedral and Carcass.

9 DEATH
Death was one of the original death metal bands. Late guitarist Chuck Schuldiner was often considered the "Father of Death Metal." It is no surprise that they paved the way for bands like Cannibal Corpse and Napalm Death.

8 SLAYER
Slayer is one of the big four that founded thrash metal along with Metallica, Anthrax, and Megadeth. Other bands even created the genre speed metal around Slayer. With insane riffs and songs like "Raining Blood," "Seasons in the Abyss," "Angel of Death," and "Black Magic," it is obvious why they are on the list.

7 MANOWAR

Manowar is power metal, often singing about fantasy and looking the part of the warriors they claim to be. You can see lyrical similarities with current power metal bands such as Blind Guardian, Hammerfall, and Dragonforce.

6 CELTIC FROST

Celtic Frost is an incredibly influential gothic metal band. It is hard to say that they aren't influential considering all of the covers of their songs that bands have done. They helped create that gloomy sound that metal has become so accustomed to.

5 VENOM

Another founder of death/black metal. They directly influenced Slayer and bands of that ilk. They were not afraid to depict Satan in their music and that helped contribute to their fame. Although not a widely known band, their sound and depictions of religion are seen throughout metal today.

4 MOTORHEAD

"Ace of Spades," "Overkill," and "Bomber." Need I say more? Lemmy's gritty vocals and wild bass playing were unheard of at the time. It is very hard to say that Motorhead did not impact the world of metal.

3 IRON MAIDEN

The NWOBHM (New Wave of British Heavy Metal) has by far the greatest impact and was the start of metal. Iron Maiden helped lead the pack with wailing vocals, catchy and memorable songs and also helped lead the way for power metal with its lyrical content. Still going strong today, any band looking for influence cannot cancel out Iron Maiden.

2 JUDAS PRIEST

Another band out of the NWOBHM, they started with two guitarists in the band and high-pitched vocals. Songs like "Painkiller," "You've Got Another Thing Comin'," and "Breaking the Law" have become timeless classics. Judas Priest is arguably one of the best bands to ever sport metal as their genre.

1 BLACK SABBATH

As soon as you read the topic I'm sure you knew that this would be the number one. The very first metal band, it's only fair to give them the top spot.

They started everything. You hear a riff or sound a guitar makes, it evolved from Black Sabbath. Thrash sounds are apparent in "Symptom of the Universe" and epic tones are present in "Iron Man" and "War Pigs." The lyrical ideals of "Geezer Butler" were amazing and opened the eyes of the people.

✖✖✖✖✖✖

TOP 10 CLASSICAL ONE-HIT WONDERS

10 CAUCASIAN SKETCHES, MIKHAIL IPPOLITOV-IVANOV

Caucasian Sketches is an orchestral suite written in 1894 by Russian composer Mikhail Ippolitov-Ivanov. It is the most often performed of his compositions and can be heard frequently on classical radio stations. The final movement, entitled "The Procession of the Sardar," is often heard by itself, and is a favorite of "Pops" concerts. The suite is an excellent example of Ippolitov-Ivanov's debt to his composition teacher Rimsky-Korsakov, as well as to the influence of folksong, in this case the music of Georgia.

9 "THE FLOWER DUET," LÉO DELIBES

This is probably best known for its use as the theme music for British Airways advertisements. The "Flower Duet" is taken from Delibes's opera *Lakmé*. The subject of the opera was suggested as a vehicle for the American soprano Marie van Zandt. Delibes wrote the score during 1881–82. Like many other French operas of the late nineteenth century, *Lakmé* captures the ambience of the Orient that was in vogue during the latter part of the nineteenth century; Bizet's *The Pearl Fishers* and Massenet's Le *Roi de Lahore* being two other examples.

8 CAVALLERIA RUSTICANA, PIETRO MASCAGNI

Cavalleria Rusticana is an opera in one act by Pietro Mascagni to an Italian libretto by Giovanni Targioni-Tozzetti and Guido Menasci, adapted from a Sicilian short story written by Giovanni Verga. Considered one of the classic verismo operas, it premiered on May 17, 1890, at the Teatro Costanzi in Rome.

Since 1893, it has often been performed in a so-called Cav/Pag double-bill with *Pagliacci* by Ruggero Leoncavallo.

7 *MEDITATION FROM THAIS*, JULES MASSENET

Massenet was a French composer. He is best known for his operas, which were very popular in the late nineteenth and early twentieth centuries; they afterward fell into oblivion for the most part, but have undergone periodic revivals since the mid-1970s. The opera *Thais* is based on the novel of the same name by Anatole France. It was first performed at the Opéra in Paris on March 16, 1894, starring the American soprano Sybil Sanderson, for whom Massenet had written the title role. In 1907, the role served as Mary Garden's American debut in New York.

6 "THE PRINCE OF DENMARK'S MARCH," JEREMIAH CLARKE

This voluntary commonly, though wrongly, known as the "Trumpet Voluntary," is a work by Jeremiah Clarke, composed around 1699. For many years, the piece was incorrectly attributed to the better-known composer Henry Purcell. The piece is actually taken from the semi-opera *The Island Princess*, a joint musical production of Clarke and Daniel Purcell (Henry Purcell's younger brother). The march was originally written in honor of George, Prince of Denmark, the consort of Queen Anne of Great Britain. It is very popular as wedding music (it was played during the wedding of Princess Diana and Prince Charles in St. Paul's Cathedral) and was often broadcast by the BBC during World War II, especially when broadcasting to occupied Denmark. Clarke was born in London in 1674 and killed himself with a gun in 1707.

5 "MINUET" FROM *STRING QUINTET IN E*, LUIGI BOCCHERINI

Boccherini was a classical-era composer and cellist from Italy, whose music retained a courtly and galante style while he matured somewhat apart from the major European musical centers. Boccherini is mostly known for one particular minuet from his *String Quintet in E*, Op. 13, No. 5.

4 "RONDEAU," JEAN-JOSEPH MOURET

Mouret was a French composer whose dramatic works made him one of the leading exponents of Baroque music in his country. Even though most of his works are no longer performed, Mouret's name survives today thanks to the popularity of the "Fanfare-Rondeau" from his first *Suite de Symphonies*, which has been adopted as the signature tune of the PBS program *Masterpiece Theatre*. Mouret died in an asylum.

3 "ADAGIO IN G MINOR," TOMASO ALBINONI

"Adagio in G Minor for Strings and Organ" is a piece composed by Remo Giazotto while supposedly based on a fragment from "Sonata in G Minor" by Tomaso Giovanni Albinoni, which was found among the ruins of the old Saxon State Library, Dresden, after it was firebombed by the Allies during World War II. The adagio was first published in 1958. This has appeared in many movies and television shows.

2 "ADAGIO FOR STRINGS," SAMUEL BARBER

While this adagio is his most famous work, Barber put out a large amount of extremely beautiful vocal music. Barber's "Adagio for Strings" originated as part of his *String Quartet No. 1*, Op. 11, composed in 1936. In the original it follows a violently contrasting first movement, and is succeeded by a brief reprise of this music. Barber's own arrangement for string orchestra was given its first performance by Arturo Toscanini with the NBC Symphony Orchestra on November 5, 1938, in New York.

1 "CANON IN D," JOHANN PACHELBEL

The very well known "Canon in D" was written in or around 1680, during the Baroque period, as a piece of chamber music for three violins and basso continuo, but has since been arranged for a wide variety of ensembles. The canon was originally paired with a gigue in the same key, although this composition is rarely performed or recorded today.

✳✳✳✳✳✳

TOP 10 INFLUENTIAL ARTISTS IN ELECTRONIC MUSIC

10 APHEX TWIN

Richard David James, aka Aphex Twin, is an electronic musician who has been described as "the most inventive and influential figure in contemporary electronic music." His unique production style and arrangment popularized a then-small genre of music (gabba). In 1992 *Rolling Stone* magazine wrote of the album, "Aphex Twin expanded way beyond the ambient music of Brian Eno by fusing lush soundscapes with oceanic beats and bass lines." He has been credited for composing the most interesting music ever created with a keyboard and a computer. Aphex's "alternative" sound is at the forefront of today's multi-genre, iPod-listening culture.

9 THE PRODIGY

The Prodigy is an electronic music group formed by Liam Howlett in 1990 in Braintree, Essex, England. They have sold over sixteen million records worldwide, unequaled in dance-music history. Their music consists of various styles ranging from rave, hardcore, industrial, and breakbeat in the early 1990s, to alternative rock and big beat with punk vocal elements in later times. The Prodigy first emerged on the underground rave scene in the early 1990s, and has since achieved immense popularity and worldwide renown. The Prodigy's success is a tribute to their sound, bringing in listeners who did not "enjoy" electronic music until they heard them.

8 DAFT PUNK

Daft Punk is an electronic music duo consisting of French musicians Guy-Manuel de Homem-Christo and Thomas Bangalter. The duo is considered one of the most successful electronic music collaborations of all time, both in album sales and critical acclaim. Daft Punk reached significant popularity in the late 1990's house movement in France, and is also credited with producing songs considered essential in the French house scene. With their iconic appearance they have molded and shaped an imaginative career and worked with massive artists, such as Kanye West, and even stepped into directing and writing films to branch out their creative stem.

7 PETE TONG

Peter "Pete" Tong is an English DJ who works for BBC Radio 1. He is known worldwide by fans as the groundbreaking voice of electronic music for hosting programs such as "Essential Mix" and "Essential Selection" on the world's largest radio station. Pete is a household-name superstar, a club-filling DJ who consistently has his finger on the electronic music button. Tong has the ability to create or deflate an artist and has no intention of changing his position in the electronic music scene.

6 FRANKIE KNUCKLES

Frankie Knuckles is a DJ, record producer, and remix artist. He played an important role in developing house music (an electronic, disco-influenced dance music) as a Chicago DJ in the 1980s and helped to popularize house music in the 1990s with his work as a producer and remixer. In 2005, Knuckles was inducted into the Dance Music Hall of Fame for his achievements as a DJ. As his productions and remixes were becoming more popular, he was also breaking new ground. When Junior Vasquez took a sabbatical from Manhattan's The Sound Factory, he took over and launched a successful run as resident DJ until Vasquez made his return, at which point Knuckles became the resident DJ at The Sound Factory Bar. Knuckles remained part of the underground scene. In 1992, *Billboard*'s Larry Flick commented, "He's probably the best dance music producer we have in America. He understands the groove, but he understands songs, and the whole picture." Knuckles won the 1997 Grammy Award for Remixer of the Year, Non-Classical.

5 KING TUBBY

King Tubby (born Osbourne Ruddock) was a Jamaican electronics and sound engineer, known primarily for his influence on the development of dub music in the 1960s and 1970s. Tubby's innovative studio work, which saw him elevate the role of the mixing engineer to a creative fame previously only reserved for composers and musicians, would prove to be highly influential across many genres of popular music. He is often cited as the inventor of the concept of the remix, and so may be seen as a direct antecedent of much dance and electronic music production.

4 AFRIKA BAMBAATAA

Afrika Bambaataa (aka Kevin Donovan) is a DJ from the South Bronx, who was instrumental in the early development of hip-hop throughout the 1980s. Afrika Bambaataa is one of the three main originators of breakbeat deejaying, and is respectfully known as the "Grandfather" and "Godfather" and the Amen Ra of Universal Hip-Hop Culture as well as The Father of the Electro Funk Sound. Through his co-opting of the street gang the Black Spades into the music and culture-oriented Universal Zulu Nation, he is responsible for spreading rap and hip-hop culture throughout the world and helping create a multi-million-dollar-giant of a music genre. Many artists owe a lot to Afrika Bambaataa and his peers.

3 KRAFTWERK

Kraftwerk is a German musical group influential in the evolution of modern electronic music. The signature Kraftwerk sound combines driving, repetitive rhythms with catchy melodies, mainly following a Western classical style of harmony with a minimalistic one. They were the first group to strictly use electronic instrumentation only in their production. The group's simplified lyrics are at times sung through a vocoder or generated by computer-speech software. In the early to late 1970s and the early 1980s, Kraftwerk's distinctive sound was revolutionary for its time, and has had a lasting impact across many genres of modern popular music. One of the first major recording artists to claim a direct influence from Kraftwerk's music was David Bowie. Part of this can be heard in a series of albums that start with *Station to Station* and continue with the Berlin Trilogy—*Low, Heroes,* and *Lodger.* Iggy Pop's association with Bowie during this period would result in the classic albums *Lust for Life* and *The Idiot.* Kraftwerk's members were mutual fans of both artists, name-dropping them in the lyrics of its 1977 single, "Trans-Europe Express." Afrika Bambaataa's *Planet Rock* (1982) was a major defining hit for hip-hop and the birth of electro music, which contains elements of "Trans-Europe Express" and "Numbers." Legal action was pursued against Bambaataa, and Kraftwerk won for Bambaataa's blatant use of these particular sounds and melodies without giving proper credit to the group. Since the lawsuit, proper credit is now given on the song's writing credits. Numerous artists have continued to sample and pilfer various elements from Kraftwerk's catalogue.

2 DAVID MANCUSO

David Mancuso is arguably the single most influential individual in the development of the dance music DJ. He is the creator of the famous "by invitation only" parties in New York City which have come to be known as "The Loft." The first such party was held in 1970 and was called "Love Saves the Day." Prior to that, he was playing records for his friends on a semi-regular basis as early as 1966, and these parties became so popular that by 1971 he and Steve Abramowitz, who worked the door, decided to do this on a weekly basis. His parties have the freewheeling feel and intimacy found in the classic rent party or house party. Mancuso is a pioneer in that he carefully thought out and refined his concept of "private party," as distinct from the more overtly commercial business model of the nightclub. This change of direction in club promotion goes hand in hand with the world of electronic music.

1 FRANCIS GRASSO

Francis Grasso was one of the many unsung heroes in the DJ world! He was the first DJ to perfect how to slip-cue a record and release it on beat in order to create a nonstop mix of music in the nightclub scene. Yes, radio DJs had used this technique previously, but not to create a continuous mix of music; furthermore, Francis started paying attention to the energy and feeling of each song and began putting the songs together into sets that corresponded with the energy he was getting from the dancers on the floor. The more they gave off, the more he gave back. More importantly, he was the first DJ to segue (or overlay) two records together in order to maintain a consistent flow of energy throughout the night while matching the beats of the music. Though these things seem simple by today's standards, in the late '60s and early '70s these techniques, along with his progressive and innovative programming style, were quite revolutionary and provided the basis for the rest who followed.

✳✳✳✳✳✳

TOP 10 UNCOMMON ORCHESTRAL INSTRUMENTS

10 ORGAN

The pipe organ is one of the world's oldest wind instruments, with examples found as far back as the third century BC in ancient Greece. The organs back then would have looked a lot different than the ones we are used to seeing, with water power supplying the air pressure required to push air through the pipes. Modern pipe organs are a lot more complicated than this, with multiple keyboards (including one played by the feet) and rows of stops.

9 BARITONE/EUPHONIUM

I've lumped these two instruments together because a baritone is, to the casual observer, essentially a small euphonium. The euphonium is best known for being the "small tuba" in a wind or marching band, though it's range is a lot higher than a tuba. It is very rare to see a baritone or euphonium in an orchestra, as they are usually found in big bands or marching bands.

8 SAXOPHONE

The saxophone, apart from maybe one other, is probably the most well known of all the instruments on this list. It is a single-reed instrument, similar to the clarinet. It is best known as a jazz instrument, although it has surfaced in some pop songs, most notably in the famous solo in Gerry Rafferty's "Baker Street." The saxophone has only appeared in orchestras relatively recently, only starting to appear in late romantic and early twentieth century music. The saxophone  has been popularized in recent years thanks to the character Lisa Simpson, whose "sax-a-ma-phone" has brought the instrument to even more people.

7 PIANO

Well, what is there to say about the piano? Apart from maybe the guitar, it is probably the most well known instrument in the world. The piano is mainly used as an accompaniment to soloists, though there are many thousands of pieces written for solo piano. In an orchestral environment, pianos are mostly used as solo instruments, in concertos and other similar pieces.

6 CELESTA

The celesta is a keyboard instrument, similar to a piano, but instead of having hammers hitting strings, the hammers in it hit metal tubes suspended over wooden resonators. It was invented in the late 1880s in Paris. The first major user of the celesta was Tchaikovsky, who most famously used it in the "Dance of the Sugarplum Fairies," from the ballet *The Nutcracker*.

5 HARP

The harp has been one of the most common instruments in history, with use of the different styles found all over the world. The most basic harp would have simply been a bow used for hunting, played by plucking the string. The type of harp most used in modern classical music is the pedal harp, which can have up to forty-seven strings spanning six-and-a-half octaves and is an impressive six-feet high. Pedal harps usually have seven pedals, one for each natural note of the scale, and these can be put into one of three positions. The first position, with the pedal up, flattens the note by a semitone. The second position, in the middle, keeps the note at its natural tone, and the third position sharpens the note by a semitone.

4 COR ANGLAIS

The cor anglais is probably the most common of these "unusual" instruments, usually being played by an oboist. It is longer than an oboe, pitched a fifth lower, and has a pear-shaped bell at the end. Unlike the oboe, which has a reed set straight into the instrument, the cor anglais has a bent crook to attach the reed onto. The name literally means "English horn," though the cor anglais is neither English nor a horn.

3 ALTO FLUTE

The alto flute is, in basic terms, a long flute. Much like the piccolo, it is used to augment the flute section and add a deeper tone. Unlike the piccolo, however, which is pitched an octave higher, the alto flute is pitched a fourth below a normal flute. There are two designs for an alto flute. The first, favored by smaller players, has the neck bending back on itself, so the fingers are closer to the player, and so easier to reach. The second, and more common, design is simply a longer flute.

2 BASS CLARINET

The bass clarinet is a much longer version of the standard B-flat clarinet, with a curved mouthpiece and bell more resembling a long saxophone. It is pitched an octave lower than a B-flat clarinet, and has a much deeper tone. The bass clarinet was invented in the late 1700s, with different forebearers of the instrument we know now being created in Germany and France. The bass clarinet as we know it now was finalized by Adolph Sax in 1838, who, in the following decade, invented another instrument on this list (see if you can guess which one!).

1 CONTRABASSOON

The contrabassoon is almost twice as long as a standard bassoon, which comes to almost sixteen feet of tubes! It is pitched a whole octave lower than a standard bassoon, which, to put it in context, is a semitone higher than the lowest note on the piano. It is usually supported by a spike at the bottom, similar to a contrabass or cello, rather than a seat strap or sling. It takes a hell of a lot more breath to play than a bassoon, and the lowest note can make the room you're in shake!

CHAPTER NINE
Nature

TOP 10 WEIRD AND WONDERFUL ODDITIES OF NATURE

10 MIRACLE MICE

Weird Fact: A mouse can fit through a hole the size of a ballpoint pen. During the summer months, mice will generally live outside and remain content there. But as soon as the weather begins to cool, they seek the warmth of our homes. Because of their soft skulls and gnawing ability, a hole the size of a ballpoint pen (a quarter-inch) is large enough for them to enter. Once inside, they will constantly gnaw at virtually anything, including concrete, lead, and plastic to keep their ever-growing teeth at a convenient length. Contrary to popular belief, mice don't generally like cheese but will eat it on occasion. Mice can jump up to eighteen inches, swim, and travel vertically or upside-down. To mouse-proof your house, check all small openings with a ballpoint pen; if it fits the hole, it will let mice in.

9 SQUARE EYES

Weird Fact: Unlike most creatures, goats have rectangular pupils.
We all imagine pupils to be round, as they are the type we see most often (on humans), but goats (and most animals with hooves) have horizontal slits that are nearly rectangular when dilated. This gives goats vision covering 320–340 degrees; this means they can see virtually all around them without having to move (humans have vision covering 160–210 degrees). Consequently, animals with rectangular eyes can see better at night due to having larger pupils that can be closed more tightly during the day to restrict light. Interestingly, octopuses also have rectangular pupils.

8 BLIND HORSES

Weird Fact: Horses can't see directly in front of themselves.
A horse has considerably wide vision (and the largest eyes of any land mammal), being able to see a total field of up to 350 degrees. Horses have two blind spots: the first is directly in front of them and the other is directly behind their

head. As far as seeing details, horses are red-colorblind and have vision of 20/33 (compared to a perfect human vision of 20/20).

7 SICK RATS
Weird Fact: Rats can't vomit.

Rats can't vomit or burp because of a limiting wall between their two stomachs and their inability to control the diaphragm muscles needed for the action. Neither rabbits nor guinea pigs can vomit either. This makes rats particularly susceptible to poisoning (hence its popularity in controlling rat infestations). Because of this inability, rats will nibble at food to see if it makes them feel sick (they can't vomit, but they can feel like they sure as hell want to!). If they don't feel nausea, they will scarf it down.

6 GORILLA GORILLA GORILLA
Weird Fact: The scientific name for a gorilla is "Gorilla gorilla gorilla."

First off, let us just be clear: this is the scientific name for a particular type of gorilla—the Western Lowland Gorilla (this is the type you are most likely to see in a zoo and the most common). For some reason the poor gorillas got stuck with the weird names; if you aren't a Gorilla gorilla gorilla, you are a Gorilla gorilla diehli, Gorilla beringei beringei, or Gorilla beringei graueri.

5 KILLER SWANS
Weird Fact: A swan can break a man's arm.

Next time you are feeding the beautiful swans and want to give one a nice pat on the back—don't do it! Swans are very protective of their young and will use their incredibly powerful wings to fend off dogs (and sometimes humans). They have a wingspan of around nine feet. In 2001, a young man in Ireland had his leg broken by a swan when he was trying to provoke it. The following year another person had their arm broken.

4 FRAGILE SPIDER
Weird Fact: If you drop a tarantula, it will shatter.

First of all, unless you are allergic to tarantula venom, they are harmless to humans (though they pack a painful bite). Some tarantulas can also shoot the "hairs" off their legs, which can pierce human skin and cause great discomfort. Now, back to the weird fact. Tarantulas have an exoskeleton (that means its skeleton is on the outside) like crayfish and crabs. They shed their exoskeleton regularly, normally by lying on their back. (When they are shedding their skeleton, it is a good idea to keep away as they will attack due to their vulnerable state.) Because the exoskeleton is very fragile, if a tarantula is dropped from a low height, it will shatter and die.

3 SCARY SPICE
Weird Fact: Nutmeg is poisonous.

Nutmeg is a hallucinogenic drug regularly used to flavor such lovely things as tarts and fruitcakes. It is also a poison that will kill you while you suffer a variety of extremely revolting (and one or two not-so-revolting) side effects on the way. Ingesting two grams of nutmeg will give you similar feelings to having taken amphetamines (the not-so-revolting side effect) but will also cause nausea, fever, and headaches. Ingesting seven-and-a-half grams will cause convulsions, and eating ten grams will cause hallucinations. Eating a whole nutmeg can lead to "nutmeg psychosis," which includes feelings of impending doom, confusion, and agitation. There have been two recorded cases of death by nutmeg (in 1908 and in 2001).

2 SHAKING LEAVES
Weird Fact: The telegraph plant is capable of rapid movement even in the absence of wind.

The telegraph plant is a tropical plant usually found in Asia and also in the South Pacific. The plant has the amazing ability to shake its leaves (which rotate on their axis and jerk up and down). There are a few other plants with rapid movement abilities (such as the Venus flytrap) but this is the most bizarre and least known. It should be noted that when we refer to "rapid" in relation to plants it is not super-fast but is definitely visible with the naked eye.

1 BURNING ISSUE
Weird Fact: The bombardier beetle shoots boiling liquid as a defense mechanism.

The incredibly complex bombardier beetle has an amazing and unique ability: when threatened, it rapidly shoots boiling hot chemicals from its abdomen up to seventy times. The liquid is a combination of hydrogen peroxide and hydroquinones that join together inside the beetle causing a chemical reaction. The liquid is fatal to small insects and creatures and can be very painful to humans.

TOP 10 WORST THINGS IN NATURE

10 HONEY BADGER, MOST VICIOUS ANIMAL

The honey badger is usually found in Africa and Western and Southern Asia. For a number of years the *Guinness Book of Records* has named it the "most fearless creature." This animal (which looks deceptively cute) will attack virtually anything and it is smart enough to know its opponents' weak spots. For example, when confronted by a human male, it will attack the testicles. This is also one of the few animals that uses tools, for example, making use of logs as ladders. The honey badger loves honey and will dive right into a beehive with no regard to its own safety, which, unfortunately, often leads to its death. Honey badgers can kill crocodiles, and are very efficient snake killers. It takes only fifteen minutes for the animal to eat a five-foot snake. The ferocity of these creatures is well known in nature and not even a leopard or lion will attempt to kill one.

9 MOSQUITO, WORST INSECT

There is no doubt that the mosquito has to be the worst insect in the world. Just as summer starts, the mosquitoes come out in force ready to feast upon the pasty white legs of humans that have been locked inside for winter. At night as you lie in bed you can hear them buzzing but you can't see them and then the next morning a huge welt appears on the tip of your nose because the mosquito chowed down on it. Oh, and it also happens to be the most deadly insect in the world because it spreads malaria; in fact, it is believed that half the human population that has died throughout history died because of the female mosquito bite.

8 FATAL FAMILIAL INSOMNIA, WORST DISEASE SYMPTOMS

Fatal familial insomnia is a terrible disease found in only 50 families around the world. The disease prevents you from sleeping and no medication available can help you. When the disease begins, you generally have from seven to thirty-six months of sleepless nights until you finally die. Wikipedia describes the stages of the disease thus:

"1. The patient suffers increasing insomnia, resulting in panic attacks, paranoia, and phobias. This stage lasts for about four months.

2. Hallucinations and panic attacks become noticeable, continuing for about five months.

3. Complete inability to sleep is followed by rapid loss of weight. This lasts for about three months.

4. Dementia, where the patient becomes unresponsive or mute over the course of six months. This is the final progression of the disease, and the patient will subsequently die."

7 BULLET ANT, MOST PAINFUL BITE

The bullet ant is ranked as having the most painful sting in the world, often likened to the pain of being shot, described as, "waves of burning, throbbing, all-consuming pain that continues unabated for up to twenty-four hours." The ant is found in Nicaragua south to Paraguay and, like other ants, they live in large colonies usually situated at the base of trees. The ants are used in an initiation rite for boys in the Satere-Mawe tribe of Brazil. Boys are made to wear a glove with hundreds of these ants attached and suffer the stings for ten minutes and they must perform this ritual multiple times. The boys' arms are usually paralyzed temporarily from the poison and their bodies can shake for days.

6 SALVINIA MOLESTA, MOST INTRUSIVE WEED

Also known as kariba weed, the salvinia molesta plant is an aquatic fern from Brazil. It floats on top of water and doubles in size every few days. This usually results in lakes that become completely covered by a mat of the plant up to twenty-four inches high. The intrusive weed prevents sunlight from entering the water, which, in turn, prevents animal and plant life from surviving. To make matters worse, you can't kill the plant. If you break it into small pieces, each piece will spawn a new plant. In the U.S. attempts have been made to remove it using cranes, but all it takes is one tiny piece to restart the whole growing process. It is now found around the world and causes havoc everywhere it goes.

5 CORPSE FLOWER, SMELLIEST PLANT

The corpse flower thrives in the grasslands bordering rain forests in Sumatra (though it is now found around the world in display gardens). It grows a single enormous flower that produces a smell remarkably similar to a rotting corpse (hence its name). The flower grows to over ten feet wide and its coloring is designed to mimic the look of rotting meat to help entice the carrion-eating insects that pollinate it. The tip of the corpse flower is nearly the same temperature as the human body, which probably helps to spread the stink, and adds to the illusion that it is really rotten flesh.

4 BRAZILIAN WANDERING SPIDER, WORST SPIDER

It is huge. It has one of the most painful bites in the spider world. It is the most deadly spider; forget the funnel web spider, this thing is dangerous. It has the highest human kill rate in the world. To make things even worse, a bite from this spider causes an erection that lasts for hours. No, this is not a subtle ad for Viagra; it really is a side effect of a wandering-spider bite. Emergency room staff are able to immediately recognize a person suffering from a bite. Needless to say, the venom is being studied for possible medical uses for people suffering erectile dysfunction.

3 CANDIRU, NASTIEST FISH

The candiru is a small parasitic catfish found mostly in the Amazon River where it is the most feared fish, even more so than piranhas. The fish can grow to a maximum length of around six inches. Candiru feed on the blood of their host creatures by swimming into the gills and using razor sharp spines on its head to attach itself. It then chews its way through the host until it reaches a major artery and drinks blood until it is satiated. The fish finds its prey by sniffing the water and this is where it starts to get nasty: the smell of human urine appeals to candirus and they can find their way to a human penis or vagina under the water and enter it. When this happens, the fish attaches itself (causing great pain to the poor human) and it can generally only be removed through surgery. This is a very unpleasant situation to be in, so be warned: don't pee in the Amazon River.

2 MAN, MOST DAMAGING TO ITS ENVIRONMENT

First of all, we need to get one thing clear, I am not a "greenie" or an "environmentalist," but even a hard-hearted non-recycler like me can see how much damage man causes to nature. We pollute our waterways and air, we tear down whole forests, we flatten mountains, and we bury nuclear waste beneath the earth. Nature has every reason to hate us and perhaps that is in part the reason for the many plagues and pandemics that have struck our kind since time immemorial.

1 BOTULINUM TOXIN, DEADLIEST THING EVER

Botulinum toxin is produced by the bacterium clostridium botulinum and it is, beyond a doubt, the deadliest known protein. If the clostridium botulinum spores find their way to food or wounds, they will begin to release the toxin, which leads to poisoning if eaten. It is so deadly that a mere two pounds of the stuff is enough to kill the entire human population. It is so deadly that it is potentially useful as a biological weapon. This is the kind of thing we obviously want to keep right away from, right? Well, no. Millions of people have this deadly protein injected into their face every year; it is present in minute quantities in Botox used to "treat" wrinkles.

✳✳✳✳✳✳

TOP 10 MOST DISGUSTING PARASITES

10 BEDBUGS

Some of you may not know that bedbugs are actually more than just part of a cute little goodnight rhyme that your parents said to you before you went to sleep. They are as real as the other nine entries, and while bedbugs are not the worst or deadliest on this list, they certainly present their share of difficulties.

The bedbug is like a small tick that typically lives in and around the area of the mattress. They feed mostly during the night, although they have been known to feed during any hour of the day. Due to their small size, the bedbug can hide in mattresses, mattress seams, baseboards, headboards, screw holes, carpets, cracks in walls, bedroom clutter, practically anywhere in or around the bedroom. Bedbugs have been known to nest and walk as far as a hundred feet in order to feed on their host.

9 LICE

The human louse is an epidemic affecting both children and adults, though children seem to be more susceptible to infestation. African Americans are less likely to get lice because of the characteristics of their hair. Other hair types seem to be more ideal and suitable to the louse.

There are many different types of lice. The most commonly known is the head louse, though there is also the body louse and the pubic louse. These aforementioned lice species are the only ones that are solely reliant upon humans for blood. Other species exist, but are limited to other animals.

8 LEECHES

A common misconception surrounding leeches is they are completely reliant on blood from animals and humans. Blood-seeking leeches are only one type of leech. Some species of leeches feed on invertebrates and do not live in the water, but on the moist earthen floor and, under more dry circumstances, underground. Leeches are segmented worms closely related to the common earthworm.

The sanguivorous, or blood-sucking, leech is most often found in still or slowly moving water, but can also be found on land. The usual method of attachment to a host is by waiting on the ground or at the bottom of the floor of a body of water. The leech will use the sucker part of its mouth and the jawed leech will use its many-toothed jaw to create an incision on the host. Afterward the leech will secrete mucuslike substances in order to remain attached to the host. The leech then relaxes its body after using anti-coagulants and a histamine to prevent clotting of blood and also to prevent the blood from turning indigestible. This is the amazing attribute of leeches that aids in using them for medicinal purposes.

7 TICKS

Ticks are classified as arachnids and there are many, many different varieties both hard and soft. The most commonly known are the black-legged tick, the lone star tick, the deer tick, and the dog tick. The tick is capable of carrying diseases as well. The most well known are Rocky Mountain spotted fever and lyme disease.

Ticks are usually found in areas with heavy underbrush and high weeds and grass as well as areas commonly traversed by deer and horses. The tick will wait in this type of environment as its host walks by and will grab a hold and work its way toward a suitable area of the body, most often where an abundance of hair is present. On humans this is usually the scalp, but on other mammals this could be anywhere. This allows the tick to remain virtually undetected for several weeks as it gorges on the blood of the host.

6 FLEAS

The flea is another common parasite. These things easily reproduce and can become a very big problem in only a short amount of time. Have you ever heard of the Black Plague? You can thank the flea for that.

Fleas are very versatile. Their bodies are flattened laterally to allow them to move easily on their host and also avoid being crushed. Their ability to jump is also a marvel. They have been known to jump over a hundred times their body length. The fleas that typically bite humans are often cat fleas.

5 MOSQUITOES

These pesky flying insects are not only a nuisance but also a deadly health threat. They can carry many different types of parasites and diseases that cause conditions such as West Nile virus, malaria, and yellow fever, and also can inject a parasite which causes elephantiasis. Mosquitoes are responsible for millions of deaths due to their ability to carry disease from host to host.

The mosquito needs blood in order to reproduce. Thus, it is the female of the species that is responsible for biting mammals. Interestingly enough, both the male and female mosquitoes regularly feed on nectar from flowers and fruits. However, the female requires the necessary proteins from blood to reproduce.

4 MITES

Mites are a very common type of organism. There are many classifications of mites including, but not limited to, dust mites, fowl mites, dog mites, deer mites, chigger mites, and scabies mites just to name a few. There are even mites living on you right now called hair follicle mites that are feeding on the oily secretions from your hair and scalp, but don't worry. These mites are a normal part of the living process for us humans, and those of us with good hygiene will never even notice that they exist since they are microscopic and completely harmless. Most of the time mites do not pose any type of threat or problem for humans, but the mites will feed on the blood of humans if its usual host is unavailable.

The most common mites that cause problems for humans are scabies. These microscopic parasites can cause extreme itching and red lesions on infected areas as they live their lives in and on the skin. Oftentimes the infection is diagnosed as parasitic dermatitis and can be easily treated with prescription topical ointments.

3 HUMAN BOTFLIES

"Botfly" is a rather broad term given to any species of fly whose larvae live as parasites within the body of mammals. This can include anything from horses to sheep and deer and, as the title indicates, humans.

The human botfly maggot is contracted by mosquitoes and is most often found in Central and South America. The fly will capture the mosquito and lay several eggs on its body. Eventually, the mosquito will find a human and, during feeding, the eggs will fall onto the person and hatch. The botfly maggot will then chew its way into the host's body. There it remains for approximately five to six weeks until it becomes engorged with flesh, all the while carving a hole in its hungering wake. At this stage, if left undetected, the maggot will pop its way out of the small hole that it has eaten inside of the host and fall to the ground where they pupate into an adult botfly in about twenty days' time. Thus, the life cycle begins all over again.

2 TAPEWORMS

Tapeworms are similar to hookworms. They are intestinal parasites that can be transmitted through soil and fecal matter, but most often are ingested by humans through undercooked meats that have not been adequately cooked to kill the tapeworm eggs. The tapeworms set up shop in the muscles of the host animal after being ingested through the feeding of grass or contaminated vegetables. The animal is eventually slaughtered and becomes food for us as humans.

The human host will ingest the tapeworm egg and as digestion of the food occurs the egg will eventually hatch and grow from a larva to an adult while feeding on blood and nutrients via the intestinal wall. The adults, being hermaphrodites, can then produce more eggs, which will be released from the body through the stool. The eggs can linger around the toilet bowl or can even be flushed down the commode where they can infest the soil through sewage and irrigation water, thus, beginning the cycle all over again.

1 HOOKWORMS

The hookworm is transmitted through fecal matter. The eggs will hatch within about a week and grow into larvae that can live for close to a month within the soil of the earth or the feces that bore them. Upon contact with humans, usually through the foot, the worm will work its way through the host's veins, into the heart and eventually the lungs. After entering the lungs they are sometimes expelled through mucus during a cough or simply swallowed by themselves. This gives the worm a one-way ticket into the small intestine.

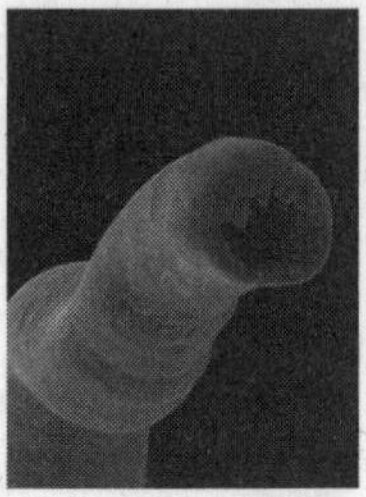

After setting up residence in the intestine the worm will attach itself to the intestinal wall and begin feeding on the host's blood. If left undetected and untreated the hookworm can reproduce resulting in a serious intestinal infestation. This can lead to anemia, extreme abdominal pain, diarrhea, constipation, fatigue, and even a bizarre hunger for inedible things like dirt and mud. The life cycle of the worm begins anew when the host releases more eggs through bowel movements.

******

TOP 10 EXTINCT CREATURES THAT AREN'T EXTINCT

10 NEW HOLLAND MOUSE

The New Holland mouse is a rodent first described in 1843. It vanished from view after that and was presumed extinct until it was rediscovered in 1967. It is found only in Australia. The mouse is currently listed as endangered, and a number of the populations are now considered extinct, some due to the Ash Wednesday Wildfires in 1983.

9 TERROR SKINK

The terror skink (Phoboscincus bocourti) was long thought extinct until a specimen was discovered in 2003 in New Caledonia. The skink measures around twenty inches and has long, sharp curved teeth, unusual for a skink, as they are normally omnivores. The only other known example of the skink was also discovered in New Caledonia in 1876.

8 GIANT PALOUSE EARTHWORM

The giant Palouse earthworm, from North America, was considered to be extinct in the 1980s but recently it has resurfaced. Little is known about the worm, but what is known is very strange. It can grow up to three feet in length and when handled, gives off a smell like lilies. The creature is believed to be able to spit in defense. It is albino in color.

7 TAKAHE

The takahe is a flightless bird native to the South Island of New Zealand. It was thought to be extinct after the last four specimens were taken in 1898. After an extensive search for the bird, it was rediscovered near Lake Te Anau in 1948. The bird is currently endangered. Takahes have an unusual eating habit, in which they pluck grass with their beak, grasp it in one claw, and eat only the softest parts at the bottom of the leaf. They then throw away the rest.

6 MOUNTAIN PYGMY POSSUM

The mountain pygmy possum was first described as a Pleistocene fossil in 1896. It was rediscovered alive in 1966 in a ski-hut on Mount Hotham, Australia. The possum is mouse-sized and is found in dense alpine rocks and boulders. The female possums live at the top of the mountain while the males live lower down. In order to mate, the males travel up to the females. Because they need to cross a road, their survival was in danger, so the Australian government built them a "tunnel of love" beneath the road.

5 GRACILIDRIS

Gracilidris is a genus of nocturnal ants that were only known through the fossil record; in fact, the only known fossil existing of this ant is a specimen in amber. The ants were discovered alive and were described in 2006, but to this day very little is known about them. The ants live in small colonies and nest in soil.

4 BERMUDA PETREL

The Bermuda petrel, a nocturnal ground-nesting seabird, was thought extinct for 330 years. It is the national bird of Bermuda and was rediscovered in 1951 when eighteen pairs were found. It was believed extinct after the English settled Bermuda and introduced cats, rats, and dogs. The bird has an eerie call that caused Spanish sailors to believe the isles were haunted by devils. For that reason, they never settled there.

3 LAOTIAN ROCK RAT

The Laotian rock rat (also known as the rat squirrel) was first described in 2005, by a scientist who put it into its own family of creatures (Laonastidae). One year later, the classification was disputed by others, who believe the rock rat is actually a member of the extinct family Diatomyidae, which vanished in the late Miocene period. The animals are like large dark rats with tails like a squirrel. Surprisingly, the first specimens were found on sale as meat at a market in Laos.

2 LA PALMA GIANT LIZARD

The La Palma giant lizard was thought extinct from 1500. It lived in La Palma in the Canary Islands and it is believed that the introduction of cats caused its final downfall. In 2007 it was rediscovered in its original location despite the belief that the only lizards left in the Canary Islands were on Gran Canaria. An interesting sidenote is that the islands are named after dogs, not canaries; the name comes from the Latin *Insula Canaria*, which means "Island of the Dogs." Canary birds are actually named after the islands.

1 THE COELACANTH

This entry is number one because it is the coolest. The coelacanth was thought to be extinct since the end of the Cretaceous period. In 1938 it was rediscovered in various African nations, making it a Lazarus Taxon—one of a group of organisms that disappears from the fossil record only to come back to life later. Coelacanths first appear in the fossil record 410 million years ago. They normally live near the bottom of the ocean floor but have, on some occasions, been caught closer to the surface. They have been known to grow past fifteen feet long, but there isn't a single attack record on a human as the fish live so deep.

✳✳✳✳✳✳

TOP 10 PSYCHOACTIVE SUBSTANCES USED IN RELIGIOUS CEREMONIES

10 "HEAVENLY BLUE" MORNING GLORY—IPOMOEA TRICOLOR
Active Constituents: Ergoline alkaloids

This plant has been used for hallucinogenic reasons since the days of the Aztecs. It was used as part of the sacraments of the Zapotecs, often in combination with other natural drugs. As well as hallucinations, the seeds from this plant cause a dramatically increased awareness of colors.

9 FLY AGARIC MUSHROOMS—AMANITA MUSCARIA
Active Constituents: Ibotenic acid

This is the very well known red toadstool with white spots found all over the world. While it is seldom used in modern times for achieving a high, it was (and still is) used by the people of Western Siberia, where shamans took it to achieve a trance state. These mushrooms can cause nausea and twitching and often cause mild amnesia, but their hallucinogenic properties are what draw the shamans to them.

8 JIMSON WEED, OR HELL'S BELLS—DATURA STRAMONIUM
Active Constituents: Atropine, hyoscyamine, and scopolamine

Jimson weed was used in sacred ceremonies by the Native Americans. Hindu holy men combine it with cannabis and smoke it in order to meditate on God and holiness. The effects can last for days and people who have experienced it describe a trance-like state. A person under the influence can appear to be awake, but they are disconnected from reality.

7 WORMWOOD—ARTEMISIA ABSINTHIUM
Active Constituents: Thujone
Wormwood has been associated with religion since the ancient Greeks attributed it to the moon goddess Artemis. While it was used in religious rituals, it is most famous for being the prime ingredient of the popular nineteenth-century drink absinthe. Modern absinthe is made without wormwood, so any "high" effects from drinking it are a result of the high alcohol content only.

6 KAVA—PIPER METHYSTICUM
Active Constituents: Kavalactones
Kava has been used by Pacific Islanders for hundreds of years; it is often used to obtain inspiration and it is still drunk to this day at social gatherings. The effects are slightly numbing and it causes sociable behavior, relaxtion, and euphoria.

5 SALVIA, OR DIVINER'S SAGE—SALVIA DIVINORUM
Active Constituents: Diterpenoid known as "Salvinorin A"
Most people will have sampled salvia, which is consumed in the West in the form of the herb sage. Salvia can be chewed, drunk, or smoked, and it causes a wide range of effects, such as uncontrollable laughter, and a sense of calmness. The Mazatec Indians used it primarily to bring about shamanic visions. They usually mixed it with water to create a special tea.

4 MAGIC MUSHROOMS—PSILOCYBIN MUSHROOMS
Active Constituents: Psilocybin and psilocin
Magic mushrooms have been in use since earliest recorded history. There are even ancient cave paintings showing humanoids with mushroom heads. Southern American cultures built temples to mushroom gods and magic mushrooms were used in religious ceremonies by the Aztecs. They create a feeling of inward orientation and cause visions. The effects can be exhilarating or disturbing.

3 PEYOTE—LOPHOPHORA WILLIAMSII
Active Constituents: Phenethylamine alkaloids, principally Mescaline
Peyote has been used by Native American tribes (such as the Huichol in Northern Mexico) so extensively that there is even a peyote religion. It is typically taken as

a tea and the effects last for up to twelve hours. It creates a state of introspection and can also be accompanied by visions and unusual sounds.

2 AYAHUASCA, OR YAGE
Active Constituents: Beta-carboline harmala alkaloids, MAOIs, and DMT (dimethyltryptamine)

Ayahuasca means "vine of the souls" in reference to the medicinal and religious uses of the plant. Consumption of a tea made from yage can cause hallucinations, which were used to set the mood for shamanic rituals in the Amazon basin among South American tribes. Unfortunately, a very common side effect is vomiting immediately after consumption, which was believed to help with purifying the shaman.

1 CANNABIS
Active Constituents: THC (tetrahydrocannabinol)

Cannabis is probably the most commonly used modern drug on this list, though it is seldom (if at all) used for religious purposes these days except by the Rastafari movement. Some historians believe that it was used by the Jews for religious reasons, and also by Sufi Muslims. These days it is normally smoked, but in the past it was also consumed (less common today) in a variety of ways. Cannabis produces a feeling of euphoria and can also lead to feelings of paranoia and anxiety.

✳✳✳✳✳✳

TOP 10 BIZARRE ANIMAL MATING RITUALS

10 RED-SIDED GARTER SNAKES
The small red-sided garter snake is a venomous snake found mostly in Canada and the northwestern United States. In order to mate, thousands of the snakes get together and have an orgy. One female can have hundreds of

males vying for her. When this happens, it is called a "nesting ball" and they can grow to over two feet high, sometimes killing the female.

Interesting Fact: Some male garter snakes are able to release the same scent that females release, causing them to be mounted by hundreds of other snakes. Scientists believe this may be for warmth and protection.

9 OCTOPUSES

Octopuses (or octopodes if you prefer) have an incredibly unique way of mating. At the end of one of the male arms is something akin to a penis (usually the third right arm). He inserts this into the female octopus and then breaks it off from his body. At that point a transfer of sperm occurs and the female becomes pregnant. The male usually dies within three months of copulation. The female dies once her eggs have hatched.

Interesting Fact: Octopuses are capable of altering their color. They can blend in with their surroundings to avoid predators. Oh, and did you know that the correct plural for octopus is "octopuses" or "octopodes"? Contrary to popular belief, "octopi" is a false plural that makes no sense in the original Latin, which people believe they are using. For the technically minded, "octopodes" is a third declension noun (which is the common declension for Greek loan words in Latin); "octopi" would be a second declension noun.

8 WHIPTAIL LIZARDS

The whiptail lizard is a fascinating creature. There are no male whiptail lizards—they are all female. They use a method of reproduction called parthenogenesis in which the offspring is a perfect clone of its mother. During mating, one female will mount the other, behaving like a male. This simulated sex helps increase fertility.

Interesting Fact: In the lab, through genetic manipulation, scientists have been able to artificially create true male whiptail lizards.

7 ANGLERFISH

Anglerfish males are born without a digestive system, so they need to find a female very quickly. Once a female is found, the male will bite her side and attach himself to it. The poor male then wastes away and dies, leaving the female with a permanent supply of his sperm for future fertilization of her eggs.

Interesting Fact: The anglerfish is a culinary speciality in certain Asian countries. In Japan, each fish sells for as much as $150.

6 BEDBUGS
Bedbugs are awful creatures, and their mating methods are equally revolting. The male doesn't bother trying to find the female's sex organs; instead he simply stabs any part of her body with his sharp penis and inserts his sperm. Curiously, these creatures seem to not be particularly discriminating, as there have been males found with the same stab marks on their bodies. This type of sex is called traumatic insemination.

Interesting Fact: Bedbugs are generally active only at dawn, with a peak attack period about an hour before dawn.

5 GIANT PANDAS
Giant pandas in captivity tend to dislike mating, causing serious problems at zoos trying to increase their endangered population. In 1998, however, a bright spark at a zoo came up with a great idea: show the pandas "panda porn." The consequence of this porn was that the zoo population doubled!

Interesting Fact: Two of President Theodore Roosevelt's sons were the first Westerners to shoot a giant panda for sport.

4 PERCULA CLOWNFISH
The main fish in *Finding Nemo* made the percula clownfish famous. But what the film doesn't discuss (perhaps for obvious reasons) is the fact that clownfish don't really have a gender. All clownfish are both potentially male and female. In a group of clownfish, the largest acts as the female and the second-largest acts as the male. If the female dies, the male becomes the female and a new fish becomes the male.

Interesting Fact: Clownfish and damselfish are the only fish that can avoid the venomous stings of an anemone.

3 GIRAFFES
The sex life of a giraffe is a fascinating one. They tend to live in packs, with the younger males hanging out together and the older males living on the outskirts of the community. The males take turns impregnating the females of

the pack. In order to determine whether a female is ready for sex, the male will give her butt a few jabs until she pees in his mouth; he can then determine (by the taste) whether to bother getting it on with her.

Interesting Fact: Giraffes have extremely long tongues, often up to eighteen inches.

2 PORCUPINES

How do porcupines have sex? Very gently. Okay—joking aside, this is another rather revolting sex tale. The male will stand on his hindlegs and pee on the female. If she is interested in him, she will expose her stomach (lacking quills) to him. If she is not interested, she will scream (truly) and shake the urine off.

Interesting Fact: Porcupine meat is valued as a food for humans in parts of Africa, Italy, and Vietnam.

1 THE SPOTTED HYENAS

In the spotted hyena family, the female really does wear the pants. The female spotted hyena has a fake penis (it is actually a very large clitoris). She uses this pseudo-penis to give birth, to have sex, and to urinate. When it is copulation time, the enlarged clitoris stretches to allow the male to get in on the action. During sex, because of this unusual clitoris, the female dominates the act.

Interesting Fact: Hyenas, unlike other canids, do not raise their leg when urinating.

✻✻✻✻✻✻

TOP 10 ANIMALS YOU DIDN'T KNOW WERE VENOMOUS

10 CUTTLEFISH

The cuttlefish is closely related to the squid and octopus. It has ten arms covered with tiny suckers and at the base is their beak. This beak injects a fast-acting venom not harmful to humans. The venom works by attacking the victim's nervous system.

9 HOODED PITOHUI
A songbird from New Guinea. Its skin and feathers contain a very powerful poison called homobatrachotoxin. This is the same poison found in the South American dart frogs, although it is severely less toxic than the frogs' and a whole bird would have to be eaten for any real harm to occur. The poison is transferred easily to humans by merely touching or handling the bird.

8 DUCK-BILLED PLATYPUS
The male platypus has a spur located on the heel behind each leg. Their venom is not known to be deadly to humans. The venom is produced only by mature males and is most potent during mating season, leading some researchers to believe it is used primarily against competing males.

7 GILA MONSTER
The Gila monster is one of only two known venomous lizards; it can be found in southwest U.S. and Mexico. The Gila monster's venomous bite is different than most animals in that most of its teeth have grooves that conduct the flow of the poison. Also, rather than an injecting bite, the venom flows from these grooves and is injected through chewing. They are rarely fatal to humans.

6 CENTIPEDE
The centipede is very common in the U.S. Its body is made up of up to 150 segments with a pair of legs for each segment. The head has long antennae and a pair of large clawlike structures. These claws carry the venom glands. While centipedes are for the most part not fatal to humans, some of the large or giant species can be very dangerous to children.

5 MILLIPEDE
Closely related to the centipede, some millipedes emit poisonous liquid secretions or hydrogen cyanide gas through microscopic pores on their bodies. Some of these substances are caustic and can burn the exoskeleton of ants and other insect predators, and the skin and eyes of larger predators.

4 CONE SNAIL

The cone snail's harpoon is a modification of the radula, an organ in molluscs that acts as both tongue and teeth. The harpoon is hollow and barbed, and is attached to the tip of the radula inside the snail's throat. When the snail detects a prey animal nearby, it turns its mouth —a long flexible tube called a proboscis—toward the prey. The harpoon is loaded with venom and, still attached to the radula, is fired from the proboscis into the prey by a powerful muscular contraction. The venom paralyzes small fish almost instantly. The snail then retracts the radula, drawing the subdued prey into the mouth. The cone snail's bite is similar to a bee sting, but the larger species are responsible for thirty known cases of human death.

3 SLOW LORIS

The slow loris is one of the few mammals that is venomous. In addition, it is the only mammal both venomous and poisonous at the same time. Slow lorises produce a toxin on the inside of its elbows, which it smears on its young to prevent them from being eaten. In addition it will lick these patches to put the poison in its mouth, giving it a venomous bite used for self-defense.

2 KOMODO DRAGON

While they do not technically produce venom, their diet consists of pretty much anything dead and that creates a special mixture of deadly bacteria buildup in their mouths. Their saliva contains more than fifty types of bacteria and seven are highly septic and four have no known specific antidote. However, if treated with powerful antibiotics, it proves nonfatal to humans.

1 CORAL

There are many types of coral and a few of these have toxic chemicals that are not fully researched yet. The most deadly coral is the palythoa. It can kill a rabbit with only a twenty-five-nanogram injection. To kill a human would only take four micrograms. Palytoxin is considered one of the most toxic organic poisons. Symptoms of palythoa poisoning include chest pains, difficulty breathing, racing pulse, and low blood pressure. Death occurs within minutes, and there is no treatment.

✳✳✳✳✳✳

TOP 10 INCREDIBLE EARTH EXTREMES

10 ANIMAL SURVIVING IN THE HOTTEST EXTREME (878 DEGREES)—SHRIMP

At a thermal vent 1.9 miles below the surface in the equatorial Atlantic, census researchers found shrimp on the edge of fluids billowing from Earth's core at this unprecedented marine recording. This is a temperature that would melt lead easily. Although the species resembles those around other vents, scientists want to study how, surrounded by near-freezing 35.6°F water, their chemistry allows them to withstand heat bursts that approach the boiling point, up to 176°F. Precooked for your convenience!

9 FARTHEST MIGRATORY BIRD—SHEARWATER—44,000 MILES

Tracking tagged sooty shearwaters by satellite, scientists mapped the small bird's 44,000-mile search for food in a giant figure eight over the Pacific Ocean, from New Zealand via Polynesia to feeding grounds in Japan, Alaska, and California and then back! Making the longest-ever electronically recorded migration in only two hundred days, the bird averaged a surprising 217 miles daily. In some cases, a breeding pair made the entire journey together.

8 THE LOWEST POINT ON DRY LAND—1378 FEET BELOW SEA LEVEL

The Dead Sea is a salt lake between the West Bank and Israel to the west, and Jordan to the east. Its shores are the lowest point on Earth on dry land. At 1,083 feet, the Dead Sea is the deepest hypersaline (saltiest) lake in the world. It is also the world's second saltiest "body of water," after Lake Asal in Djibouti.

7 DEEPEST EARTH DEPRESSION—8325 FEET

The lowest point on Earth is located in the icy basin of the Bentley Subglacial Trench. This is not considered dry land but rather below sea level as it is the world's lowest elevation not under seawater. It is not accessible because it is buried under the thickest ice yet discovered.

6 THE MOST DESOLATE PLACE ON EARTH—371 FEET BELOW SEA LEVEL / 145°F

The Danakil depression is an area along the Great Rift where Earth's crust has stretched and thinned and the land has sunk over time to 371 feet below sea level, one of the lowest points on Earth's surface. Here Earth's crust is thin enough that new land surface is constantly being created by new lava that oozes upward. Water also seeps down, to be ejected again as steam. Volcanic cones are common sights, as are deep cracks in the earth. Hundreds of small earthquakes convulse the area every year.

5 GREATEST VERTICAL DROP—4100 FEET

Mount Thor is a mountain in Auyuittuq National Park, on Baffin Island, Nunavut, Canada. The mountain features Earth's greatest purely vertical drop at an angle of 105 degrees. The location is popular with climbers due to this feature, despite its remoteness. It is also mentioned in the Led Zeppelin song "No Quarter."

4 TALLEST TREE NEST—MARBLED MURRELET—150 FEET

The marbled murrelet is a small seabird from the North Pacific. Its habit of nesting in trees was not known until a tree-climber found a chick in 1974 about 135 feet up. The marbled murrelet, together with the closely related long-billed murrelet and Kittlitz's murrelet, have been recently considered endangered. Their decline and association with forests have made them a flagship species in the forest preservation movement.

3 HIGHEST RAINFALL TOTAL IN ONE MINUTE—1.5 IN

Guadeloupe is an archipelago located in the eastern Caribbean Sea with a land area of 629 square miles. It is an overseas department of France. On November 26, 1970, it received the record for the most rainfall in one minute.

2 EARTH'S MOST VENOMOUS ANIMAL—TAIPAN SNAKE

Taipans are the largest, fastest, most venomous snakes on Earth; they are Thoroughbreds of the snake world. Taipan-snake venom contains potent presynaptic neurotoxins (toxins in venom that cause paralysis or muscle weakness) and also postsynaptic neurotoxins, which are less potent but more rapid acting than the presynaptic neurotoxins. This snake's venom also contains potent procoagulants (toxins in venom that interfere with blood clotting, causing consumption of the clotting protein, fibrinogen; this causes defibrination, with non-clottable blood, putting victims at risk of major bleeding). Taipan-snake pro-coagulants are among the most powerful snake-venom procoagulants known.

1 ANTARCTICA—COLDEST, WINDIEST, HIGHEST ELEVATED CONTINENT, LARGEST DESERT OVER ALL

Let us talk about world records: Antarctica is the land of extremes. It is the coldest, windiest, and highest elevated continent anywhere on Earth. With an average elevation about 7544 feet above sea level, it is the highest continent. Even though it is covered in ice, it receives nearly the least amount of rainfall, getting just slightly more than the Sahara Desert, making it the largest desert on Earth. Most people have the misconception that a desert is a hot, dry, sandy, lifeless place, but the true definition of a desert is any geographical location that receives almost no rainfall.

✳✳✳✳✳✳

TOP 10 MOST DEADLY INSECTS

10 HEMIPTERA—KISSING BUGS

The hemiptera classification is wide and varied including all of the so-called true bugs. Most have distinctive "sucking" mouthparts that resemble tubes. Most, in fact, feed on plant sap in one form or another, but a few, such as the kissing bug, feed on blood of larger animals. The bug can transmit Chagas disease, which can cause malformation of the intestine and heart disease.

9 GIANT JAPANESE OR ASIAN HORNETS

This massive hornet can achieve lengths of three inches full grown and has been known, in numbers of only twenty or thirty, to decimate an entire hive of honeybees. The sting can be lethal not just by allergic reactions but also due to its many toxins. Here are four interesting things about its sting: 1) it has a higher concentration of the pain-causing chemical called acetylcholine than any other stinging insect; 2) enzyme in its venom can dissolve human tissue; 3) containing at least eight distinctly different chemicals, the venom itself produces one such that actually attracts others of its kind to the victim; and 4) like all other hornets, it can sting repeatedly.

8 SIAFU (AFRICAN ANTS)

Twenty million ants strong, one single colony can ravage the African countryside obliterating everything in their path. When food shortages present themselves, the colony as a whole will march through whatever happens to be in its path in order to acquire sustenance. Though not difficult to avoid, the very young or elderly can find themselves victims of asphyxiation and twenty to fifty die each year as well as thousands of dollars in foodstuffs is damaged yearly.

7 WASPS

Including the yellow jackets and hornets within the class, wasps vary in that they are relatively social, generally terrestrial, and almost every subspecies has a specific parasite or pest that it preys upon exclusively. Though wasps do not necessarily seek out humans to sting (unless territories are being threatened), it is the oft-allergic sting that does the most damage. Many people go into anaphylactic shock and die because of a single wasp sting.

6 LOCUSTS

Though not known for killing humans directly, this sub family of the grasshopper is a relentless plant-consuming machine. In the Bible, locusts are the eighth of the Plagues of Egypt, wreaking havoc on farmland and crops. Locusts strip to bare earth thousands of acres of cropland every year and in very little time since each swarm can consist of several thousand insects. As a result, they can indirectly contribute to starvation.

5 FIRE ANTS

Typically nesting in sand or soil, fire ants build rather large mounds and tend to feed on plant life and occasionally crickets and smaller insects. When bothered, however, the fire ant sting is a venomous prick that feels like it's burning with fire, hence the name, and swells up into a painful pustule. A few small stings can be quickly treated and cured, but when the ants swarm, which they are often wont to do, that's when the trouble starts. One hundred fifty deaths per day as well as millions of dollars in crop damage yearly make these ants fearsome indeed.

4 TSETSE FLIES

Another carrier of the deadly sleeping sickness, the Tsetse fly feeds on the blood of vertebrates. They spread the disease, trypanosomiases, in humans by biting their victims and passing it through their mouth parts. Living in Africa, Tsetse flies kill more than a quarter-million victims per year.

3 BEES

Thanks largely to the introduction of the Africanized honey bee, the death toll from bee stings has sharply upturned over the past fifteen years. Normal solitary bees are not known to sting humans for the sheer need to do so, and, even so, they die once the deed is done. However, many people the world over are seriously allergic to bee stings and can experience anaphylactic shock, causing death. But, unlike those standard bees, Africanized bees, or killer bees, will attack with the slightest provocation in large numbers, swarming over the victims. The death toll per year is in the thousands.

2 FLEAS

In addition to spreading the annoying little bites you receive as one of the lovely perks of owning a pet, fleas are directly responsible for the spread of the bubonic plague from their rat hosts to humans carrying the bacteria Yersinia pestsis. Feeding on the blood of warm-blooded vertebrates, fleas can infest an animal or area rather quickly. If bitten, the wound swells into a pustule and can cause allergic reactions. But, thanks to the spread of the plague killing millions, the flea can be a terrible pest.

1 ANOPHELES MOSQUITOES

Mosquitoes are a terrible irritant and, because they feed on blood, can drive a person mad just by being outside in the right conditions. Eggs get laid and grow in stagnant areas of water and millions can hatch from one spot. But, the worst aspect of the mosquito is that it's a carrier for blood-borne diseases, specifically malaria. Still numbering in the hundreds of million cases per year, malaria is responsible for more deaths than every other insect-carried disease combined.

✳✳✳✳✳✳

TOP 10 AMAZING ANIMAL FACTS

10 CYANIDE BUGS

Amazing Fact: Some millipedes (Apheloria virginiensis) are able to secrete cyanide.

Laboratory study of these millipedes (that are slow-moving and feed on plants) shows they are able to release clouds of hydrogen cyanide gas through small vents in their body. This is most likely to occur when being handled, or attacked by other creatures such as ants. It is essential to wash one's hands after touching one of these millipedes. This large creature is found in North America and is also known as the Kentucky flat millipede.

9 UNLIKELY MATES

Amazing Fact: Red ants and large blue butterflies work together.

After feeding, large blue caterpillars seek the nests of red ants and hibernate for three weeks. During their time there they rub their heads against the walls of their cocoons in order to conceal their presence by sounding like other ants. They will also amazingly adopt the ant's smell and sounds. Once they are ready to leave, the red ants escort them from the nest and encircle them, protecting them from other predators until their wings are dry enough to protect themselves.

8 FERRET SEX

Amazing Fact: If a female ferret goes into heat but can't get any sex, she will die.

Because of estrogen toxicity, a female ferret that goes into heat must have sex or she will die. Without the help of a male, the female is unable to go off heat, causing the toxic buildup of estrogen, ultimately causing the bone marrow to stop producing red blood cells.

7 DOLPHIN SEX

Amazing Fact: Dolphins, like humans, have sex for pleasure.

Dolphin copulation happens belly to belly, and though many species engage in lengthy foreplay, the actual act is usually brief, but may be repeated several times within a short timespan. Dolphins are known to have sex for reasons other than reproduction, sometimes also engaging in acts of a homosexual nature. Various dolphin species have been known to engage in sexual behavior with other dolphin species, resulting in various hybrid dolphin species. Sexual encounters may be violent, with male dolphins sometimes showing aggressive behavior toward both females and other male dolphins. Occasionally, dolphins will also show sexual behavior toward other animals, including humans.

6 HUMMINGBIRD FEET
Amazing Fact: Hummingbirds don't walk.

There is a popular misconception that hummingbirds don't have feet. It is, of course, wrong. But while they do have feet, they don't use them to walk because they are so poorly developed, due to the fact that they spend most of their time in flight and seldom need to walk. Hummingbirds also have an incredibly fast metabolism, which means they are always just a few hours away from starvation.

5 PISTOL SHRIMP
Amazing Fact: The pistol shrimp makes such a loud noise with its claws it can kill other fish.

The snap of the pistol shrimp's claw is so loud it competes with animals such as the sperm whale for the title of loudest creature of the sea. When it snaps its claws together, it creates a vapor bubble with pressure sufficient to kill nearby small fish; these are then eaten. Incredibly, when the bubble bursts it produces temperatures of up to 8,540°F, close to the temperature of the surface of the sun. This is not visible to the naked eye because of its low intensity.

4 NATURE'S CHASTITY BELT
Amazing Fact: The males of some species (including bees, baboons, rats, squirrels, scorpions, mice, and spiders) create a "mating plug" after sex that prevents other males from having sex with the same female.

The mating plug is a gelatinous compound inserted in the female's vagina after copulation. When it hardens, it prevents other males from having sex with the female. This is useful in the case of beehives, where there may be thousands of males wanting to have sex with the queen. When a drone in the beehive has had sex with the queen, his entire genitalia detachs to form the plug, which also means that he dies shortly after. Future drones that wish to mate with the queen must forcibly remove the plug.

3 FROG HEARING
Amazing Fact: Some frogs hear with their lungs.
Panamanian golden frogs don't have outside ears; their lungs pick up sound waves and direct them to their eardrums. Interestingly, many fish hear in this same manner, which supports the link between frogs and their evolutionary ancestors. Due to internal air pressure controlled by the frog, it is able to largely ignore its own voice, which is incredibly loud.

2 OCTOPUS EATING
Amazing Fact: Octopuses eat with their hands like humans.
With the suckers on its arms, an octopus seizes prey and pulls it up to its mouth, where a poisonous salivary secretion is immediately released from its beak. The secretion paralyzes the prey and begins the digestion process. Fortunately for the octopus, if it loses an arm, another one grows to replace it. Another interesting fact about octopuses is that one of the legs of the male is used for copulation and it is broken from the body in the act of sex.

1 PIG'S ORGASM
Amazing Fact: A pig's orgasm lasts thirty minutes.
Before you start pining to be a pig, remember, after the orgasm the pig eventually ends up on our dinner table! But that aside, it is true that a pig can have an orgasm that lasts up to thirty minutes.

✖✖✖✖✖✖

TOP 10 FASCINATING FACTS ABOUT SPIDERS

10 SPIDERS ARE YUMMY
Tarantula spiders are a delicacy in several parts of the world, eaten by the indigenous Piaroa tribes of Venezuela and also in Cambodia. Remember,

though, the hairs of the tarantula are an irritant and must be removed first (for those wanting to try the recipe). A news article quoted a Cambodian local as saying "They taste a bit like crickets, only much better."

9 SPIDERS ARE GREEN
Well, not the spiders themselves, of course. However, in a relatively new development, certain spider venom is being investigated as an eco-friendly insecticide. In synthetic or natural form it can, potentially, target crop-destroying insects with little or no effect on non-target species (e.g. birds, humans, other mammals, etc.) An additional benefit is that many scientists believe that the target insects may not become naturally resistant.

8 SPIDERS ARE CHEMISTS
Spider silk is amazing and humanity can benefit from studying, and perhaps synthesizing, its properties. Pound-for-pound this protein fiber (or silk) is stronger than steel. It is reputed to be as strong as the aramide filaments (e.g. Kevlar). It is also extremely ductile and can flex and stretch up to 30 percent (or in some cases 50 percent) of its length. As a fiber for protective clothing it may prove invaluable. Spider silk is also very light-weight. Twenty-five thousand miles—the circumference of Earth—of a single fiber would weigh about sixteen ounces.

7 SPIDERS ARE GREAT GARDENERS
Spiders love to eat insects. In fact, in absolute terms, spiders eat more insects than birds and are better at pest control (they chow down on the little insects that are too small for birds and young insects that haven't bred yet). In spite of having eight eyes (though some have different amounts), they do not see very well and will rarely attack without provocation. Jumping spiders, on the other hand, have a better visual acuity than almost anything else its size. Human eyes are only about five times better than a jumping spider. On the plus side (for people) is that though they can jump twenty to sixty times their body length, they prefer to jump at their insect prey.

6 SPIDERS ARE COWARDS
Most spiders are skittish creatures, and really do not like to bother people. If a spider is on you, it probably just wants off you as much as you want it off. A flick is probably better than a squash.

5 SPIDERS BRING GOOD LUCK

Spiders are, naturally, good luck symbols for weavers and spinners, and, by extension, those in the fabric and garment industry. The word "spider" is derived from "spin." According to some sources, spiders also bring good luck in money matters. As a spider attracts and traps prey, so a spider amulet should attract and hold wealth. In the tradition of the Pueblo Indians (Southwestern North America), the creation goddess was called Spider Woman. Also known as Creation Thinker Woman, she spins life and all creation out of her thoughts as a spider spins from her body substance. She is a powerful and loved goddess.

4 SPIDERS ARE VENOMOUS HUNTERS

Of all the approximately forty thousand species of spiders, only one (so far) has been found to be a non-predator. All the others are hunters. Less than fifty are known to have venom harmful to humans. There are two main classifications of spider venom: necrotic, which attacks the soft tissue around the bite, and neurotoxic, which attacks the nervous system of the victim. For the spider bite to be harmful or fatal to humans several factors must all be taken into account: a) the size of the fangs (properly, the chelicerae)—they must be large enough to break the skin; b) the venom compound—it must be toxic to human physiology; and c) the quantity of venom used. Because a spider can control the amount of venom used, and they do not see us as "food," almost all bites are defensive, so most spider bites are dry or contain a reduced amount of toxin. The aggressive Brazilian wandering spider is a notable exception.

3 SOME SPIDERS ARE SOCIAL

Almost all spiders are solitary hunters. However, a few species are social and form colonies. And whereas most of these colonies are only between five hundred and a thousand individuals, an anelosimus eximius colony can be the home of more than twenty thousand spiders. It is a good thing that these are scarce (the forests of northwestern South America). A single nest was reported to be over twenty-five feet in length, six to eight feet wide, and four to five feet high—perhaps the home to fifty thousand spiders.

2 SPIDERS LOVE US

Well, that's not entirely true. The truth is that they like our environment. Unlike many other poisonous creatures that live on this planet, spiders can live very well in the same habitat as humans. In the world there are various poisonous snakes, two species of poisonous lizards (Gila monster and beaded lizard), two species of poisonous birds (hooded pitohui and ifrita), and many species of amphibians, fish, and jellyfish—and, for the most part, few of them tend to come into our homes, walk on our ceilings, or sleep in our beds. In the U.S., the black widow and the brown recluse can be found in homes. In Australia, the redback can be found just about everywhere, and especially loves dense, urban areas. The Sydney funnel-web spider can be particularly nasty. They like water and often fall into swimming pools. They survive in the water for quite a bit, and will bite when fished out. They are not known for their gratitude. There is an anti-venom, thankfully, so there have been no reported deaths since 1980.

1 SPIDERS ARE SCARY

Arachnophobia is officially known as DSM-IV –TR: 300.29 Specific Phobia (subtype animal, specifically spider). The Diagnostic and Statistical Manual of Mental Disorders, fourth edition (copyright 2000 American Psychiatric Association) is the authoritative source of these things. This list, by the way, is not intended to be diagnostic or to provide medical advice. Arachnophobia is defined as: a) marked and persistent fear that is excessive or unreasonable, cued by the presence or anticipation of a specific object or situation; b) exposure to the phobic stimulus almost invariably provokes an immediate anxiety response; c) the person recognizes that the fear is excessive or unreasonable; d) the phobic situation(s) is avoided or else is endured with intense anxiety or distress; e) the avoidance, anxious anticipation, or distress in the feared situation(s) interferes significantly with the person's normal routine; f) in individuals under the age of eighteen years, the duration is at least six months; and g) the anxiety, panic attacks, or phobic avoidance associated with the specific object or situation not better accounted for by another mental disorder.

✳✳✳✳✳✳

TOP 10 COMMON MYTHS ABOUT CANNABIS

10 FAT STORAGE

Myth: Cannabis's active ingredient, THC, gets stored in body fat and its effects can last days or even weeks.

Fact: It is true that cannabis (like many other drugs) enters the body's fat stores, and it is for this reason it can be detected long after use, but that is the only part of this myth that is true. The fact is, the psychoactive aspects of the stored cannabis are used up quickly and while the residue of the drug remains, it no longer has any effect on the person. Furthermore, the presence of THC in body fat is not harmful to the fat, the brain, or any other part of the body.

9 MEMORY LOSS

Myth: Cannabis use causes memory loss and a general reduction in logic and intelligence.

Fact: This is another myth that has elements of truth to it, no doubt the reason it is believed by so many. Laboratory tests have shown that cannabis diminishes the short-term memory, but only when a person is intoxicated with it. A person who has taken cannabis will be able to remember things learned before they took it but may have trouble learning new information during intoxication. There is no scientific evidence whatsoever to suggest this can become a long-term or permanent problem when sober.

8 SCIENTIFIC PROOF

Myth: Cannabis has been scientifically proven to be harmful.

Fact: Let us start with a quote: "The smoking of cannabis, even long term, is not harmful to health." This quote comes from the peer-reviewed British medical journal *The Lancet* (founded in 1823). There is certainly no scientific consensus on cannabis use, and certainly no scientific proof that casual use is dangerous to health.

7 LOSS OF MOTIVATION

Myth: Cannabis use causes apathy and a lack of motivation.

Fact: In fact, studies done on test subjects in which they were given a high dose of cannabis regularly over a period of days or weeks found that there was no loss in motivation or ability to perform. Of course, abuse of any intoxicating substance over long periods will reduce a person's ability to function normally, but cannabis is no better or worse. Furthermore, studies indicate that cannabis users tend to have higher paid jobs than non-users.

6 CRIME STATISTICS

Myth: Cannabis causes crime.

Fact: Some people believe that cannabis use leads to violence and aggression, which, in turn, leads to crime. But the facts just don't stack up. Serious research into this area has found that cannabis users are often less likely to commit crimes because of its effect in reducing aggression. Having said that, because of the number of nations that have outlawed cannabis, most users in the world are technically classified as criminals merely for possessing the drug.

5 BRAINDEAD

Myth: Cannabis kills brain cells.

Fact: Cannabis does not cause any profound changes in a person's mental ability. It is true that after taking the drug some people can experience panic, paranoia, and fright, yet these effects pass and certainly don't become permanent. It is possible for a person to consume so much of the drug that they suffer from toxic psychosis, but again, this is not unique to cannabis and is very rare.

4 GATEWAY TO OTHER DRUGS

Myth: Cannabis is a gateway drug—in other words, it leads to abuse of more potent drugs.

Fact: For most people, cannabis is a terminus drug, not a gateway drug. Users of high-strength drugs such as heroin or LSD are also statistically more likely to have used cannabis in the past, but this is just toying with statistics; when comparing the number of cannabis users with hard-drug users, the numbers are extremely small, suggesting there is no link at all.

3 MODERN POTENCY

Myth: Cannabis is more potent now than in the past.

Fact: The reason that this myth has come about is that samples taken by drug enforcement agencies are used to test for potency but they are a tiny sample of the cannabis on the market. The vast majority of cannabis taken today is the same potency as it has been for decades. In fact, even if the potency were greatly higher, it would make little difference to the user as cannabis of varying potency produces very similar effects. Furthermore, there is statistical data on cannabis potency dating back to the 1980s which is more reliable than present methods of detection, and that shows little or no increase.

2 LUNG DAMAGE

Myth: Cannabis is more damaging to the lungs than cigarettes.

Fact: First of all, people who smoke cannabis but not cigarettes tend to smoke far less frequently, thereby limiting their exposure to the dangers in the smoke. Furthermore, smokers of cannabis are not inhaling the many additives that go into commercial cigarettes to make them burn down faster or to stay alight. There has even been some evidence that marijuana smoke does not have the same effect on the bronchial tubes as cigarette smoke, so even heavy use may not lead to emphysema.

1 ADDICTION

Myth: Cannabis is highly addictive.

Fact: Less than one percent of Americans smoke cannabis more than once per day. Of the heavy users, a tiny minority develop what appears to be a dependence and rely on the assistance of drug rehabilitation services to stop smoking but there is nothing in cannabis which causes physical dependence, and the most likely explanation for those who need assistance is that they are having difficulty breaking the habit, not the "addiction."

✳✳✳✳✳✳

TOP 10 AMAZING AND UNUSUAL WEATHER PHENOMENA

10 COLORED MOONS
Due to different atmospheric issues, the moon will occasionally appear tinged with a color, such as blue, orange, or red. Excess smoke, dust, and eclipses can cause the moon to change color.

9 ST. ELMO'S FIRE
This weather phenomenon is luminous plasma that appears like fire on objects, such as the masts of ships or lightning rods, in an area that is electrically charged during a thunderstorm. This occurrence was named the after St. Elmo, the patron saint of sailors.

8 SUN PILLARS
Sun pillars occur when the setting sun reflects off high, icy clouds at different layers. It creates a pillar of light that reaches high into the sky. It is also possible to see moon pillars.

7 NON-AQUEOUS RAIN
Rare and yet real, cases exist of rains of animals instead of water. This has occurred occasionally throughout history, from the Biblical times through recent history. Meteorologists are still unsure of the cause.

6 VIRGA
Virga is when ice crystals in clouds fall but evaporate before hitting the ground. They appear as trails from clouds reaching for the surface, sometimes giving the cloud a jellyfish-like appearance.

5 KATABATIC WINDS
These are winds that carry dense air from a higher elevation to a lower elevation due to gravity. They are known locally as the Santa Ana (southern California), the Mistral (Mediterranean), the Bora (the Adriatic Sea), Oroshi

(Japan), Pitaraq (Greenland), and the Williwaw (Tierra del Fuego). The Williwaw and winds traveling over the Antarctic are particularly hazardous, blowing over a hundred knots at times.

4 FIRE RAINBOW

A fire rainbow is an extremely rare phenomenon that occurs only when the sun is high allowing its light to pass through high-altitude cirrus clouds with a high content of ice crystals.

3 GREEN RAY

Also known as the green flash. This occurs very briefly before total sunset and after sunrise. It appears as a green flash above the sun that lasts very briefly, generally only a few moments. It is caused by refraction of light in the atmosphere.

2 BALL LIGHTNING

This is a very rare phenomenon that involves ball-shaped lightning that moves much slower than normal lightning. It has been reported to be as large as eight feet in diameter and can cause great damage. There are reports of ball lightning destroying whole buildings.

1 SPRITES, JETS, AND ELVES

All refer to phenomena that occur in the upper atmosphere in the regions around thunderstorms. They appear as cones, glows, and discharges. They were only discovered last century, because of their placement and their very brief lifespan (they last less than a second).

✳✳✳✳✳

TOP 10 OFFENSIVE ODORS IN NATURE

10 BAD FISH

Fresh seafood should be odorless or smell a bit like fresh sea air or a hint of brininess. Fish that has gone bad, however, has an odor so undeniably offensive that other smells equally as putrid have come to be compared to it, such as certain overtly pungent body scents. Bad fish raises the gorge of nearly everyone unaccustomed to it.

9 SEWER GAS

The smell of a stagnant sewer is unmistakable in its odoriferous and cloying funk. The mixture of waste material from a hundred or more different people and their flushed and discarded flotsam backing up under an open-air sewage grate is cause for gagging and watering eyes. Knowing quite well what oddities human beings will dispose of via toilet is disgusting enough, but add that to the potent combination already at hand, and you have yourself a revolting scent.

8 ROTTEN FOOD

Imagine: a long-forgotten container in the back of the refrigerator, an old fridge full of food without power, an overturned semi on the freeway spilling its contents of store-ready chicken. All of these represent the most foul scent of spoiled food. We have all had the displeasure of the assault of some far-too-old food item spurting its putrid stench into the air.

7 SKUNK

A skunk's defense mechanism to ward off predators is its ability to fire off scent glands located around, but not in, the anus, near the base of the tail. Smelling surprisingly like rotten cabbage or, to some people, very bad marijuana, skunk spray is a potent and rather adhesive mess. Fortunately, it can be effectively removed with a tomato juice bath. A skunk's smell can be tracked for a great distance, even when the animal has retreated into hiding.

6 DECAYING / GANGRENOUS / BURNT FLESH

Have you ever accidentally singed your fingers when cooking or forgetting to extinguish a match? Then you will already know the acrid scent of burnt flesh in its most minor form. Take that smell and multiply it ten-fold and you'll understand the true meaning of what many firefighters and rescue workers smell after a blaze. Similarly, an equally repugnant smell is that of rotting or gangrenous flesh, both caused by bacterial infection. In addition, bedsores are known to release smells similar to that of rotten flesh.

5 STAGNANT WATER

From ponds to puddles, bacteria-laden water takes on a repugnant stink that can be detected from quite a distance. Not only are these bodies of water a breeding ground for mosquitoes, they are also extremely harmful to both animals and humans.

4 THE HUMAN MOUTH

Inside your mouth reside billions of bacteria feeding off the sugars and starches that cling to your teeth and the back of your tongue. Without proper dental hygiene, and especially in those suffering from halitosis, bad breath becomes a most foreboding olfactory hazard and can lead to ostracism and shame.

3 FOOT / BODY ODOR

B.O.: It's always pungent, always repulsive, and always embarrassing. Who wants to be the one to tell a coworker that he needs a shower and some deodorant? Though not necessarily caused by infrequent bathing, bromhidrosis, or body odor, is the smell of bacteria growing on the body. These bacteria multiply considerably in the presence of sweat, but sweat itself is almost totally odorless. Body odor is associated with the hair, feet, groin (upper medial thigh), anus, skin, armpits, genitals, and pubic hair.

2 HYDROGEN SULFIDE

This is the chemical compound with the formula H_2S. This colorless, toxic, and flammable gas is responsible for the foul odor of rotten eggs. It often results from the bacterial breakdown of organic matter in the absence of oxygen, as is found in swamps and sewers. It also occurs in volcanic gases, natural gas, and some well waters. The odor of H_2S is commonly misattributed to elemental sulfur, which is, in fact, odorless.

1 CORPSE

Some of the strongest constitutions around are those of morgue attendants, members of the police force, emergency technicians, "corpse divers," CSI field agents, and anyone else who repeatedly comes in contact with bloated, rotten, and mishandled corpses. The odor is formed from the release of gases by bacteria. Nearly all of the people who have had to describe such horrific odors have stated that the two most recognizable smells of a corpse are ozone and meat.

❋❋❋❋❋❋

TOP 10 AMAZING BIG CATS

10 BOBCAT

The bobcat is a North American member of the big cat family. As a predator, it inhabits wooded areas, desert edges, semi-desert edges, and swampland environments. The bobcat's diet consists of rabbits, hares, deer, small rodents, and even insects. Similar to many other big cats, the bobcat is a solitary hunter. Each bobcat will use a single method to mark its territory. Although bobcats are hunted by humans, for both sport and fur, their population is under no immediate threat at this time. However, continuous hunting of bobcats could jeopardize their population. Bobcats will travel for the last three hours of sunlight and three hours after sunrise. They are also very skilled at adapting to a new environment. This is a very important skill for the animal because humans have a tendency to invade their habitat. The grayish brown coat, black-tipped ears, and whiskered face resemble many species of lynx. The bobcat may be considered a "big cat" but in relation to other big cats, it is very small in size. In fact, it is only about twice as large as a domesticated cat.

9 OCELOT

The ocelot is famous for looking extremely similar to a domestic cat. Its fur may resemble that of a clouded leopard or jaguar. Regrettably, this amazing coat has made them a valuable hunting target. Ocelots often hunt for lizards, amphibians, deer, rodents, and frogs. Ocelots are mostly found in South America, Central America, and Mexico. Ocelots were considered endangered during the 1980s but have since been removed from the endangered species list. They are rarely seen together and enjoy resting in dense foliage. They are exceedingly territorial and will sometimes fight to the death at the invasion of land. Since ocelots are nocturnal, they have the best night vision of the big cats.

8 CARACAL CAT

The caracal cat is also known as the Persian or African Lynx. It is closely related to the African golden cat. They are best known for their extraordinary climbing and jumping skills. The caracal is distributed over Africa and Western Asia and will usually hunt alone at night. They have an amazing ability to snatch birds out of the sky, but their diet also consists of antelope, gazelle, rodents, and the occasional ostrich. When a caracal catches its prey, it will shear the meat off the skin so they won't have to eat the fur of the animal. If food is scarce, it will eat bird feathers and even rotten meat. A sighting of a caracal cat is extremely rare because they are also very skilled at hiding from humans.

7 JAGUARUNDI

The jaguarundi is found in Mexico and Central and South America. It is said to resemble an otter because the coat is a solid color (except for the spots they have at birth) and it has rounded ears. There has been no desire for this animal's fur, but the jaguarundi is suffering due to the loss of habitat. Many Spanish-speaking countries call the jaguarundi *leoncillo*, which means "little lion." Unlike many big cats, this cat hunts during the day. They usually eat rabbits, hares, birds, and sometimes fruit. Most jaguarundis live in low brush places near running water.

6 MARBLED CAT

Almost matching the size of a domesticated cat, the marbled cat is one of the smallest of the big cats. The cat's eighteen-inch tail will sometimes be used as a balance when hunting. The marbled cat's range stretches from parts of India to Southeast Asia. Their diet consists of squirrels, reptiles, and birds. Unfortunately, this cat is rarely studied because they are extremely difficult to spot. Their population is said to be under ten thousand because of their shrinking forest habitat. Scientists have discovered that the marbled cat is closely related to Asiatic golden cats.

5 JAGUAR

The jaguar is the third largest big cat in the world. It is the national animal of Brazil. Jaguars closely resemble leopards but are much larger. It is also one of the few big cats that enjoys swimming. They are solitary predators and are known to regulate the populations of prey species. The powerful bite of the jaguar allows them to break through shell and hard reptile skin. Sadly, their numbers are dropping quickly and are nearly threatened because they are often killed by humans. Jaguars' short, stocky limbs make them skilled in climbing, crawling, and swimming.

4 SNOW LEOPARD

The snow leopard lives in the mountain ranges of Central Asia, Afghanistan, and many other parts of the world. Its lifespan is usually about fifteen to eighteen years. It is about the size of a regular leopard but has a long tail used for balance in rugged terrain. They may live in caves in mountainous regions. There are estimated to be about five thousand snow leopards left, making them an endangered species. The snow leopard will occasionally kill prey three times its size. Their diet consists of ibexes, boars, and deer. A snow leopard will not fight hard for its territory.

3 LION

Lions usually inhabit savanna and grasslands and will sometimes be found in forests. A group of lions is called a pride and consists of females, lion cubs, and a few male lions. The female lions usually do the hunting in groups (males will rarely ever hunt). The lion is known as a vulnerable species with a population decline of 30–50 percent. A male lion is recognized by its mane. The lion is the second largest feline in the entire world. The color of their coat is usually a light yellow. Lion cubs are born with spots on their bodies but they disappear as they mature. The diet of a lion includes wildebeest, impalas, zebras, and buffalo.

2 CHEETAH

Many people classify the cheetah as the world's fastest land animal with the ability to reach speeds of seventy miles per hour. The round, black spots on the cheetah help them to camouflage when hunting. The head of the cheetah is said to be small compared to other big cats. They will eat mostly mammals including gazelles, wildebeests, and zebras. When a cheetah sprints for its prey, its body temperature becomes so high that it would become fatal if kept at that level for a long period of time. Cheetahs are on the World Conservation Union list of vulnerable species. There are said to be about 12,400 cheetahs left in the wild.

1 TIGER

Tigers are usually found in southern and eastern Asia. Like many big cats, they are territorial and solitary. The dark, vertical stripes that overlay the reddish orange color are one of the most noticeable characteristics of the tiger. They are featured in many forms of ancient mythology. Tigers living in the wild will usually prey on animals such as buffalo, boar, deer, and sometimes leopards and pythons. In the wild, tigers can leap up to sixteen feet. They always live close to water because they enjoy bathing. Unfortunately, the tiger is one of the big five game animals of Asia.

CHAPTER TEN
People

TOP 10 PEOPLE
WHO SAVED JEWS
DURING WORLD WAR II

10 IRENA SENDLER

Irena Sendler was a Polish Catholic social worker. During World War II, she was a member of the Polish Underground and the Żegota Polish anti-Holocaust resistance in Warsaw. She helped save twenty-five hundred Jewish children from the Warsaw Ghetto by providing them with false documents and sheltering them in individual and group children's homes outside the ghetto. As an employee of the Social Welfare Department, she had a special permit to enter the Warsaw Ghetto to check for signs of typhus, something the Nazis feared would spread beyond the ghetto. During these visits, she wore a Star of David as a sign of solidarity with the Jewish people and so as not to call attention to herself. She cooperated with the Children's Section of the Municipal Administration, linked with the RGO (Central Welfare Council), a Polish relief organization tolerated under German supervision. She organized the smuggling of Jewish children from the ghetto, carrying them out in boxes, suitcases, and trolleys. Under the pretext of conducting inspections of sanitary conditions during a typhoid outbreak, Sendler visited the ghetto and smuggled out babies and small children in ambulances and trams, sometimes disguising them as packages. Despite being tortured and imprisoned by the Nazis, Sendler continued to do all she could to help Jewish children in Warsaw. In 1965 she was made "Righteous Among the Nations," and she died in 2008.

9 HUGH O'FLAHERTY

Hugh O'Flaherty was an Irish Catholic priest who saved about four thousand Allied soldiers and Jews in Rome during World War II. O'Flaherty used his status as a priest and his protection by the Vatican to conceal the escapees—Allied soldiers and Jews—in apartments, farms, and convents. Despite the Nazis desperately wanting to stop his actions, his protection by the Vatican prevented them officially arresting him. He survived an assassination attempt and, along with the Catholic Church, saved the majority of Jews in Rome. He died in 1963.

8 GIORGIO PERLASCA

Giorgio Perlasca was an Italian who helped save thousands of Hungarian Jews from the Holocaust by issuing them fake passports to travel to neutral countries. Despite fighting alongside Franco in the Spanish Civil War, Perlasca became disillusioned with fascism and escaped from Italy to the Spanish embassy in Budapest in 1944, where he became a Spanish citizen on account of his war experience. While there he worked with Spanish diplomat Angel Sanz Briz in creating fake passports to smuggle Jews out of the country. When Sanz Briz was removed from his post, Perlasca pretended to be his substitute so that he could continue printing false passports. He also personally sheltered thousands of Hungarian Jews while they were waiting for their passports. It is estimated he saved over five thousand Jews from the Holocaust. After the war, he returned to Italy where he lived in obscurity until he was contacted in 1987 by a group of Hungarian Jews he had rescued, and his remarkable story became public. He died in 1992.

7 CHIUNE SUGIHARA

Chiune Sugihara was a Japanese diplomat, serving as Vice Consul for the Japanese Empire in Lithuania. Soon after the occupation of Lithuania by the Soviet Union, he helped an estimated six thousand Jews leave the country by issuing transit visas to Jewish refugees so that they could travel to Japan. Most of the Jews who escaped were refugees from Poland or residents of Lithuania. From July 31 to August 28, 1940, Sugihara began to grant visas on his own initiative. Many times he ignored the requirements and arranged the Jews with a ten-day visa to transit through Japan, in direct violation of his orders. Given his inferior post and the culture of the Japanese Foreign Service bureaucracy, this was an extraordinary act of disobedience. He spoke to Soviet officials who agreed to let the Jews travel through the country via the Trans-Siberian railway at five times the standard ticket price. Sugihara continued to handwrite visas (reportedly spending eighteen to twenty hours a day on them, producing a normal month's worth of visas each day) until September fourth, when he had to leave his post before the consulate was closed. By that time he had granted thousands of visas to Jews, many of them heads of household who could take their families with them. According to witnesses, he was still writing visas while in transit from the hotel and after boarding the train, throwing visas into the crowd of desperate refugees out the train's window even as the train pulled out. Sugihara returned to Japan where he lived in obscurity until he was made "Righteous Among the Nations" by Israel in 1985. He died the following year.

6 GEORG FERDINAND DUCKWITZ

Georg Ferdinand Duckwitz was a German member of the Nazi party who worked as a special envoy to Nazi-occupied Denmark. Although Danish Jews were initially treated quite favorably by the Nazis, by 1943 it was planned that they would be rounded up and deported to concentration camps. Risking his career, Duckwitz made a secret visit to neutral Sweden where he convinced Prime Minister Per Albin Hansson to allow Danish Jewish refugees to escape to Sweden. He then went to Denmark and notified Danish politician Hans Hedtoft about the deportation. Hedtoft warned senior rabbis in the country, and in the following two months, over six thousand Jews were ferried secretly to Sweden in boats. After his actions, Duckwitz returned to his duties as a Nazi official, refusing to reveal what he had done in case of losing his job or worse. After the war, he continued working as West Germany's ambassador to Denmark. He died in 1973. Due to his actions, it is estimated that around 99 percent of Denmark's Jews survived the Holocaust.

5 FRANK FOLEY

Frank Foley was a British secret service agent estimated to have saved ten thousand Jews from the Holocaust. In his role as passport control officer he helped thousands of Jews escape from Nazi Germany. At the 1961 trial of former ranking Nazi Adolf Eichmann, he was described as a "Scarlet Pimpernel" for the way he risked his own life to save Jews threatened with death by the Nazis. Despite having no diplomatic immunity and being liable to arrest at any time, Foley would bend the rules when stamping passports and issuing visas, to allow Jews to escape "legally" to Britain or Palestine, which was then controlled by the British. Sometimes he went further, going into internment camps to get Jews out, hiding them in his home, and helping them get forged passports. He died in 1958.

4 ARISTIDES DE SOUSA MENDES

Aristides de Sousa Mendes was a Portuguese diplomat who ignored and defied the orders of his own government for the safety of war refugees fleeing from invading German military forces in the early years of World War II. Between June 16 and June 23, 1940, he frantically issued Portuguese visas free of charge to over thirty thousand refugees seeking to escape the Nazi terror, twelve thousand of whom were Jews. De Sousa Mendes worked in the Portuguese consulate in Bordeaux, France, despite explicit orders not to give visas to "foreigners of indefinite or contested nationality; the stateless; or Jews expelled from their countries of origin." De Sousa Mendes sporadically began printing Portuguese visas illegally as early as 1939, but between June 16 and June 22, 1940, when Portugal's status was expected to change from "neutral" to "non-belligerent," which would make Portugal more allied to Nazi Germany, de Sousa Mendes and his friend, the Rabbi Chaim Kruger, began frantically issuing visas to refugees waiting in line. De Sousa Mendes travelled to the border town of Irun on June 23, where he personally raised the gate to allow disputed passages into Spain to occur. It was at this point that Ambassador Teotónio Pereira arrived at Irun, declared de Sousa Mendes mentally incompetent and invalidated all further visas. An Associated Press story the next day reported that some ten thousand persons attempting to cross over into Spain were excluded because authorities no longer granted recognition to their visas. As de Sousa Mendes continued the flow of visas, Dictator Salazar sent a telegram on June 24 recalling him to Portugal, an order he received upon returning to Bordeaux on June 26 but followed only slowly, not arriving in Portugal until July 8. Along the way he issued Portuguese passports to refugees now trapped in occupied France, saving them by preventing their deportation to concentration camps. After the war, de Sousa Mendes lived in destitute poverty, dying in 1954.

3 DIMITAR PESHEV

Dimitar Peshev was the Deputy Speaker of the National Assembly of Bulgaria and Minister of Justice during World War II. He rebelled against the pro-Nazi cabinet and prevented the deportation of Bulgaria's forty-eight thousand Jews. Bulgaria was a strong supporter of the Holocaust, rounding up thousands of Jews in occupied Thrace and Macedonia to be deported to death camps. However, when it came to its own Jewish citizens, the government faced strong opposition from Peshev and the Bulgarian Orthodox Church. Although Peshev had been involved in various anti-Semitic legislations passed in Bulgaria during the early years of the war, the decision by the government to deport Bulgaria's Jews on March 8, 1943, was too much for Peshev. After being informed of the deportation, Peshev tried several times to see Prime Minister Bogdan Filov but the prime minister refused. Next, he went to see Interior Minister Petur Gabrovski insisting that he cancel the deportations. After much persuasion, Gabrovski finally called the governor of Kyustendil and instructed him to stop preparations for the Jewish deportations. By 5:30 p.m. on March 9, the order had been cancelled. After the war, Peshev was charged with anti-Semitism and anti-communism by the Soviet courts, and sentenced to death. However, after outcry from the Jewish community, his sentence was commuted to fifteen years imprisonment, though he was released after just one year. His deeds went unrecognized after the war, as he lived in poverty in Bulgaria. It was not until 1973 that he was awarded the title of "Righteous Among the Nations." He died the same year.

2 RAOUL WALLENBERG

Raoul Wallenberg was a Swedish humanitarian who worked in Budapest, Hungary, during World War II to rescue Jews from the Holocaust. Between July and December of 1944 he issued fake passports and housed several thousand Jews, saving an estimated hundred thousand people from the Nazis. On July 9, 1944, Wallenberg travelled to Budapest as the First Secretary to the Swedish legation in Budapest. Together with fellow Swedish diplomat Per Anger he issued "protective passports," which identified the bearers as Swedish subjects awaiting repatriation and prevented their deportation. Although not legally valid, these documents looked official and were generally accepted by German and Hungarian authorities, who sometimes were also bribed.

Wallenberg rented thirty-two buildings in Budapest, and declared them to be extraterritorial, protected by diplomatic immunity. He put up signs such as "The Swedish Library" and "The Swedish Research Institute" on their doors and hung oversize Swedish flags on the front of the buildings to bolster the deception. The buildings eventually housed almost ten thousand people.

Wallenberg started sleeping in a different house each night, to avoid being captured or killed by Arrow Cross Party members or by Adolf Eichmann. Two days before the Russians occupied Budapest, Wallenberg negotiated with both Eichmann and General Gerhard Schmidthuber, the commander of the German army in Hungary. Wallenberg bribed Arrow Cross Party member Pál Szalai to deliver a note in which Wallenberg persuaded them to cancel a final effort to organize a death march of the remaining Jews in Budapest by threatening to have them prosecuted for war crimes once the war was over.

People saved by Wallenberg include biochemist Lars Ernster, who was housed in the Swedish embassy, and Tom Lantos, the only Holocaust survivor to serve in the United States House of Representatives, who lived in one of the Swedish protective houses.

After the war, Wallenberg was captured and imprisoned by the Soviets, and died in prison in 1947, though the date and circumstances of his death remain disputed.

1 POPE PIUS XII (EUGENIO PACELLI)

Contrary to popular belief and much calumny, Pope Pius XII was a vigorous defender of the Jews during World War II and did as much as was possible to help them. He was so outspoken on the matter that the fascist press referred to the Vatican paper as "a mouthpiece of the Jews." After the war, the Chief Rabbi of Rome converted to Catholicism because he was so inspired by the humanitarian behavior of the Pope.

Once the possibility of getting Jews out of Germany passed, the Pope ordered German bishops to give false baptismal certificates to any Jews who requested them:

> "[T]he Pope sent out the order that religious buildings were to give refuge to Jews, even at the price of great personal sacrifice on the part of their occupants; he released monasteries and convents from the cloister rule forbidding entry into these religious houses to all but a few specified outsiders, so that they could be used as hiding places. Thousands of Jews—the figures run from 4,000 to 7,000—were hidden, fed, clothed, and bedded in the 180 known places of refuge in Vatican City, churches and basilicas, church administrative buildings, and parish houses. Unknown numbers of Jews were sheltered in Castel Gandolfo, the site of the Pope's summer residence, private homes, hospitals, and nursing institutions; and the Pope took personal responsibility for the care of the children of Jews deported from Italy." (Joseph Lichten, "A Question of Moral Judgement: Pius XII and the Jews")

TOP 10 INFLUENTIAL PEOPLE WHO NEVER LIVED

10 SANTA CLAUS

What child has not been frightened into behaving thanks to the ever-present youthful fear of Santa not providing come Christmas? Almost all Western children were told by their parents that Santa would leave them nothing if they misbehaved. I speak from experience when I say that it was one of the most effective methods of stopping tantrums! Funnily enough, though, the fear always dissipates on Christmas Eve when you just know that Santa will be coming, even if you did slip up a few times.

9 BARBIE

As Barbie has progressed from a pretty young woman to whom all girls could aspire to be like to something often verging on the likeness of a harlot, one can wonder whether it was Barbie influencing children, or children influencing Barbie. There are certainly many similarities. Barbie has depicted almost every possible female lifestyle choice and there can be no doubt she has been at the start of the path many women have taken in life.

8 ROBIN HOOD

This could potentially lead to a debate about whether Hood existed or not, but I am of the opinion that he did not. I am sure we have all heard someone justifying theft because the victim is wealthy, and where did this justification come from? Not just the principles of redistribution of wealth that many of us live under in Western society (read envy taxes) but the fact that, to this day, we are all raised believing Robin Hood was a hero, when, in fact, he was a thief. Stealing is almost always wrong, and just because Robin Hood gave the proceeds of his crimes to poor people, it is not a valid justification. As for the previously mentioned taxes, there is every reason for us to believe that the majority of people accept these taxes because of their prior belief in the false morality of the Robin Hood story.

7 COWBOYS

This is one for the boys obviously! All boys played "Cowboys and Indians." The cowboy was a great hero with a shining gun who represented the morality of Western ideals: manliness, defense of justice, protection of women and children. No doubt many now cringe at the lack of political correctness involved in the game and stereotype, but kids aren't politically correct (thank God) and certainly won't be hindered because of it. The influence of the cowboy movie genre is indisputably an immense one. Oh, and for those who say "but cowboys are real!" yes, but this is about the concept—not about a specific person—just as we might say Santa existed as St. Nicholas; the concept is bigger than any one person.

6 THE MARLBORO MAN

How many men who smoke are smoking cigarettes with filters? I would say all of them. Before the Marlboro Man campaign began, "real men" didn't smoke cigarettes with filters—they were for women. The aim of the Marlboro Man campaign was primarily to get men smoking filtered Marlboro cigarettes. The influence of the campaign is abundantly clear today and is considered to be one of the best in all history. According to Wikipedia, it transformed a feminine campaign, with the slogan "Mild as May," into one that was masculine in a matter of months.

5 ROSIE THE RIVETER

And now another for the girls! Rosie the Riveter may not be a familiar name, but her picture certainly is. Rosie the Riveter told women that they can do anything—and they did! Rosie managed to motivate an entire generation of working-age women to get out of the home and into factories to help the war effort. This is probably one of the most influential events of World War II. Once the floodgates of women working were opened, they would never be closed again. All women working in traditional male jobs have Rosie to thank.

4 DAEDALUS AND ICARUS

In a short twenty-four hours, you can fly from one side of the planet to another. This (one of man's greatest achievements) may never have happened if it had not been for the mythological characters Daedalus and Icarus. The story tells of Daedalus building mechanical wings for his son Icarus, and ever since the tale was told, man has lusted after the ability to take to the sky and fly. This eventually came true and the entire planet is a changed place as a consequence of it.

3 THE LITTLE ENGINE THAT COULD

The moral of this children's tale is that self-belief, optimism, and hard work result in achievement—of even the most difficult tasks. The book first appeared in 1906 in a slightly different version than today and has been regarded as a metaphor for the "American Dream." The popularity of this book may also be a contributing factor to the huge number of self-help and "positive thinking" seminars and books we see today.

2 BIG BROTHER

A relatively modern addition to this list, Big Brother has been an influence in so many social protests that he has to be included here. His name comes up every time a government passes a restrictive law or a law that seems to remove aspects of our eternal freedoms. Everyone recognizes his face, everyone knows what he stands for, and everyone is terrified of the potential for our own lives to be governed by our own version of the fictional character. Big Brother was created by George Orwell for his novel *1984*.

1 ROMEO AND JULIET

Not only can Romeo and Juliet be blamed for much of our ideas of the "perfect relationship," they can also be blamed for a high percentage of divorces. Couples going into marriage seek the ideal of a relationship based entirely on passion and romance, and when that romance dims (as so often is the case), they feel cheated and believe the marriage has failed. In reality, passionate romance is not required for a healthy marriage, while respect, love, and charity are. Romeo and Juliet have much to answer for!

❋❋❋❋❋

TOP 10 LUCKY SUICIDE SURVIVORS

10 CONNIE MERCURE, NEW YORK CITY

Location: Verrazano-Narrows Bridge (Estimated over 30 suicides)

In 1995 after a failed relationship, twenty-nine-year-old Connie Mercure from Brooklyn jumped over two hundred feet into the Lower New York Bay. Rescuers immediately pulled her from the chilly waters. Mercure survived with a broken leg, extensive internal bleeding, and hypothermia.

9 MATTHEW SICOLI, NEW YORK CITY

Location: Throgs Neck Bridge (Estimated over 40 suicides)

In 2001, twenty-six-year-old Matthew Sicoli, after a fight with his girlfriend and with job woes, walked on the pedestrian lane toward the center of the Throgs Neck Bridge. Authorities spotted Sicoli kneeling and then watched in horror as he hopped over a railing and disappeared. Police quickly mounted a rescue effort and saved Sicoli in less than ten minutes. Matthew survived the 140-foot leap and suffered only bruises to his ribs, stomach, and face. It is estimated he went into the East River hitting the water at 64 mph. Sicoli's fifty-one-year-old mother committed suicide by jumping off the Whitestone Bridge just five years earlier.

8 HANNS JONES, TAMPA BAY, FLORIDA

Location: Sunshine Skyway Bridge (Over 120 suicides)

In May of 2001, thirty-five-year-old artist and inventor Hanns Jones was despondent over business pressures. After heavy drinking and a horrible fight with his wife, Jones drove his pickup to the Sunshine Skyway Bridge to end his life. Right after Jones jumped he said he knew it was a big mistake. Jones described the jump as "You just accelerate and accelerate so fast and then it stops, but when you stop you don't feel like you hit water, you feel like you hit concrete." The force of the impact ripped Jones's clothes off. Despite multiple rib fractures, internal bleeding, and a collapsed lung, he was able to swim to the rocks near one of the pylons. He was sitting there naked when rescuers arrived, and then spent weeks in the hospital recovering. Jones says he's fine and happy today, and he often wonders why he survived when so many others didn't.

7 DID BÉLIZAIRE, QUEBEC, CANADA
Location: Jacques Cartier Bridge (Over 140 suicides)

Did Bélizaire was addicted to gambling, which started when he was seventeen years old. In 2003 at the age of thirty-six, he had another losing night playing the video lottery terminals at the nearby Casino de Montréal. Bélizaire found himself deep in a hole and called his girlfriend on his cell phone, asked for her blessing, and ended the call without telling her what he was about to do. Bélizaire then jumped off the Jacques Cartier Bridge into the St. Lawrence River. Bélizaire survived the jump and was unable to force himself to drown because his survival instincts took over. The jump cost Bélizaire the use of his legs and he is now a paraplegic. Bélizaire is quoted as saying, "Once I was a strapping six-foot-seven basketball and football player and now I'm three-feet three-inches in a wheelchair." Bélizaire takes every opportunity he can to tell young people his story and sound the alarm against compulsive gambling.

6 "MICHELLE," BROOKLYN, NEW YORK
Location: Brooklyn Bridge (Estimated suicides in the hundreds)

In June of 2008, a thirty-four-year-old woman identified as "Michelle" decided to end her life by jumping off the pedestrian walkway of the Brooklyn Bridge. After her ten-story leap into the East River, several witnesses called 911 and the woman was quickly plucked from the chilly waters. Paramedics were amazed that she came out of it with no broken bones and hardly a scratch. She was rushed to Bellevue Hospital, where she was admitted for having water in her lungs.

5 ANGELA SCHUMANN, NEAR KINGSTON, ENGLAND
Location: Humber Bridge (Over 200 suicides)

Twenty-eight-year-old Angela Schumann was going through a custody battle with her ex-husband over their daughter. She wrote several letters, including one that said, "I can be with my daughter all the time. I can be free and far away where no Julio [her husband] of this world can reach us and separate us. And I can be with my daughter on her birthday." In the fall of 2005 Angela jumped off Humber Bridge (three days prior to her daughter's second birthday) holding onto her daughter all the way down. The little girl was taken to Hull Royal Infirmary where she was found to be hypothermic, but five days later was able to go home. Angela Schumann spent almost two months in hospital for treatment of lower body fractures. In the hospital, Schumann was found to have faded writing on her stomach saying, "Cause of death Julio." The mother and daughter are two of only five to have ever survived a fall from Humber Bridge.

4 JOHN DITTMANN, SEATTLE, WASHINGTON
Location: Aurora Bridge (Over 220 suicides)

John Dittmann felt suicidal, blaming it on a daily regimen of taking tranquilizers to treat mental illness and drinking alcohol to offset the pills. Dittmann often would stare at the Aurora Bridge from his Wallingford halfway house and in 1979 at the age of twenty-two he decided to end his life with a leap off the bridge. After jumping, Dittmann had a change of heart and decided he didn't want to die. He then frantically threw his arms back and fought to keep his body from pitching forward and tried to keep his feet extended as he plunged 174 feet. He hit Lake Union at 70 mph with a crack and struggled to swim meekly to shore. Dittmann fractured his back and injured his lungs, but survived. The Seattle man is one of about thirty people who have survived a leap from the landmark bridge.

3 SARAH HENLEY, NORTH SOMERSET, ENGLAND
Location: Clifton Bridge (Over 500 suicides)

This miraculous escape from death happened over 120 years ago. Twenty-two-year-old Sarah Henley received a letter from her fiancé breaking up their engagement. In a state of despair she rushed to end her life by jumping off the Clifton Suspension Bridge. That particular morning there was a slight wind blowing and Sarah's skirt was inflated (acting like a parachute), which considerably slowed down her descent and prevented her from falling straight into the water. Sarah lived a full life and died in 1948. Her incredible luck gave her an extra sixty-two years of life. Sarah Henley's jump has become legend and is recorded in the official history of the Suspension Bridge.

2 MARTIN HINCHCLIFFE, EAST SUSSEX, ENGLAND
Location: Beachy Head (Over 500 known suicides)

In June of 1995, fifteen-year-old Martin Hinchcliffe had a fight with his girlfriend's parents. After writing a note to his mother saying he would kill himself he walked to Sugar Lump cliff on Beachy Head and jumped. Thirty-five feet into his fall he was caught by some extending rocks and was completely hidden from view in a deep crevasse. After spending seventy-two hours holding onto the cliffs, his cries were finally heard by a man walking on the beach below. Coastguard, police, and firefighters went to the scene and were able to rescue Hinchcliffe, who had suffered a broken leg and several cracked ribs. Hinchcliffe said he sucked on rocks during the seventy-two hours to avoid dehydration.

1 KEVIN HINES, SAN FRANCISCO, CALIFORNIA

Location: Golden Gate Bridge (Over 1500 suicides)

At the age of nineteen Kevin Hines's battle with bipolar disorder became so intense that he finally decided to end his life. In 2000 he attended his first class at school, and then took a bus to the Golden Gate Bridge, crying all the way. Hines picked his spot and stood there for forty minutes. No one approached him to ask what was wrong, and when a tourist came up and asked whether he could take her photo, Hines thought that was clear proof that no one cared. He took the picture, and then jumped. Instantly he realized he had made a mistake and thought to himself "God save me." As he was falling Hines came up with a plan to save his life, and threw his head back and tried to hit feet first. Hines was hurtled forty feet underwater but miraculously survived. Hines endured arduous physical rehabilitation after his near-death experience but said dealing with his bipolar disorder had been far more difficult. He now lives by a strict schedule, and has found a combination of drugs and therapy that allows him to regulate his manic highs and depressions. Currently, Hines works with several mental health groups and suicide prevention hot lines.

✳✳✳✳✳✳

TOP 10 MOST SUCCESSFUL MILITARY COMMANDERS

10 GEORGY KONSTANTINOVICH ZHUKOV, 1896–1974

The First World War came as something of a relief to Georgy Zhukov. As a furrier's apprentice his life was nothing but hardship, sleeping on the same factory floor where he toiled twelve hours a day; proper food and a warm bunk were well appreciated. Although Zhukov's childhood was rife with poverty, he was luckier than most peasants of the day and was able to attend the village school and received a rudimentary education.

Zhukov was conscripted into the Red Army in 1915, serving first in the 106th Reserve Calvary and then in the Dragoon Novgorod Regiment. His courage and discipline while under fire was noted; he was awarded the Cross of St. George twice and was promoted to the rank of non-commissioned officer for bravery. He joined the Bolshevik Party after the October Revolution and his peasant background allowed him to survive Stalin's Great Purge of the Red Army. Commanding the First Soviet Mongolian Army Group, Zhukov was able to win a decisive victory over Japan in the undeclared war of 1938 to 1939, mobile armored-tank divisions and Zhukov's brilliant tactics swaying the outcome in his favor. He was awarded the title "Hero of the Soviet Union," but unfortunately this was largely overlooked in the West these same tactics were used to disastrous effect by the German Army.

9 ATTILA THE HUN, 405–453

Called Flagellum Dei or The Scourge of God by the Romans, Attila the Hun ruled the Hun Empire as King and General from AD 433 to 453. A fierce and ruthless warrior, Attila expanded Hun territory from the steppes of Central Asia into modern Germany, and from the River Danube to the Baltic Sea.

Succeeding his uncle King Roas, Attila, with his brother Bleda (killed in a hunting accident in 445), inherited the Scythian Hordes, a loose and disorganized group of tribes prone to infighting. Considered the epitome of barbarism and bloodletting in the West, he was a good administrator and a fair leader to his own people. He succeeded in unifying the tribes into the most formidable and feared army that Asia had ever seen. A brilliant tactician, he took advantage of terror tactics; those that resisted Hun rule were slaughtered and made example of. Heads displayed on posts surrounding conquered cities ensured their next target got the message. Those that weren't attacked paid heavily for their safety; the Eastern Roman Empire was attacked twice when they refused to pay up, and the Western Roman Empire once when they refused to pay three times the usual fee. He was defeated only once—at the Battle of the Catalaunian Plains—by the combined forces of the Romans and the Visigoths in what is now France. After this loss he successfully invaded Italy, with Rome only being saved from pillage by a combination of disease, food shortages, and Papal intervention. The empire of the Huns died with Attila.

8 WILLIAM THE CONQUEROR, 1028–1087

William the Conqueror was the Duke of Normandy from 1035 and the King of England from late 1066 until his death. The illegitimate and only son of Robert I, Duke of Normandy, he inherited the title at the very young age of seven. Surviving intrigue and the death of three guardians at the hands of rival Norman noblemen, William managed to consolidate his power and find favor with the king of France. Knighted by King Henry I at the age of fifteen, by age nineteen he had secured Normandy and quelled all rebellion.

Upon the death of the childless King Edward the Confessor, William, with a tenuous claim to the throne and the blessing of Pope Alexander II, invaded England in what would become known as the Norman Conquest. Its most famous and decisive battle, the Battle of Hastings, was followed by the March to London and William claiming the crown. The last successful invasion of England had far reaching effects; land was parceled out in smaller lots to Norman aristocracy, replacing the larger holdings of the British, in effect strengthening the monarchy; French replaced English as the language of the ruling class; the courts were given more power and centralized government was established by reinforcing the shire system. England was now a European society, no longer a Scandinavian one.

7 ADOLF HITLER, 1889–1945

Although he was consumed by madness and paranoia by the end of WWII, in its beginning years Hitler was extremely bold and successful. Within three years, Germany and the Axis powers had conquered most of Europe, large parts of Africa, East and Southeast Asia, and large parts of the Pacific Ocean.

The German strategies of WWII were all either designed or approved by Hitler himself. Blitzkrieg, or lightning attack with little warning, and air raids followed by tanks followed by infantry gave Germany victory after victory. A period of stalemate or peace after these victories gave the German war machine time to rearm. These early victories strengthened Hitler's hold on the German people, effectively stifling any remaining opposition to his policies. Had Hitler's assault on Moscow not been delayed into the fall rainy season and had he not diverted the majority of his tank regiment, the outcome may have been very different. German forces, spread too thin, combined with successful attacks on supply routes preventing rearming, assured the final outcome of WWII.

6 GENGHIS KHAN, 1162–1227

Genghis Khan was the founder of the Mongol Empire, the largest contiguous empire in history. Named Temüjin at birth and rumored to have been born clutching a blood clot in his hand, Genghis Khan was destined to lead. His military strategies stressed the need for good intelligence and an understanding of his enemies' needs. He adapted foreign techniques when appropriate, like siege warfare from the Chinese, for example. He had an extensive spy network and employed a supply-point route-messenger system. The Yam route—relay stations to supply food, shelter, and spare horses for the Mongol armies' messengers—was expanded extensively during his reign. By 1206 Temüjin had managed to consolidate all the Mongol tribes under his rule. At a Kurultai or council of chiefs he was confirmed as "Khan" and took the name Genghis Khan.

After uniting the tribes, Genghis Khan began the series of conquests known collectively as the Mongol Invasions. The western Xia Dynasty was the first to fall followed in quick succession by the Jin Dynasty, the Khanate, Caucasus, Khawarezid Empire—by the time of his death, Genghis Khan ruled most of central Asia. His descendents expanded Mongol rule to eventually include most of Eurasia—all of China, Korea, the Caucasus, and substantial portions of eastern Europe and the Middle East.

5 HANNIBAL, 248–183/182 BC

Hannibal's leading of the Carthaginian army across the Alps stands as one of the most amazing military feats in ancient military history. After subjugating all of Spain in violation of treaty, Rome declared war on Carthage beginning the Second Punic War. Rather than wait to be attacked, Hannibal decided to take the war directly to Rome. Although losing many of the fifty thousand men and forty elephants that accompanied him through the Alps, Hannibal's better-trained and disciplined army defeated the unprepared Romans.

Hannibal was Carthage's greatest general. For fifteen years he led a successful campaign far from home by surviving off the land, the spoils of war, and tactical wits. He shared the hardships and dangers with his men, his leadership skills unquestioned, and his tactics and strategies copied by his enemies. Taking poison rather than be captured, Hannibal died after stating, "Let us release the Romans from their long anxiety, since they think it too long to wait for the death of an old man."

4 NAPOLEON BONAPARTE, 1769–1821

Napoleon Bonaparte was a masterful soldier, an unequaled grand tactician, and a superb administrator. Portrayed as a power hungry conqueror, Napoleon himself disagreed, arguing that he was building a federation of free peoples of Europe united under a liberal government. The fact that he intended to do this by taking power into his own hands wasn't mentioned, nor was the fact that France itself was a police state with a vast network of secret police and spies.

Crowning himself Emperor of the French in 1804, Napoleon successfully used the armies of the French Empire against every major European power of the time. Forming extensive alliances and appointing family and friends to rule countries as client states, Napoleon dominated continental Europe. Russia proved insurmountable, resulting in decimation of the French armies and Napoleon's eventual fall. While considered a tyrant by his opponents, he is also remembered for the establishment of the Napoleonic code, which laid the administrative and judicial foundations for much of western Europe.

3 JULIUS CAESAR, 100–44 BC

Julius Caesar was a politician and general of the late Roman republic who greatly extended the Roman Empire before seizing power and making himself dictator of Rome and paving the way for the imperial system.

Julius Caesar joined the Roman Army in 81 BC and was the first Roman army commander to invade England, which he did in 55 BC and again in 54 BC. Appointed consul to Gaul, Caesar was very successful, adding the whole of modern France and Belgium to the empire and securing Rome from Gallic invasions. After his successes in Gaul, Caesar returned to Italy, famously crossing the Rubicon River without disbanding his army. In the ensuing civil war, Julius Caesar defeated the republican forces and made himself consul and dictator. After instituting needed reform Caesar declared himself dictator for life, an act that enraged the fiercely republican senate. Led by Cassius and Brutus, Caesar was assassinated on the Ides of March, 44 BC. This sparked the final round of civil wars that ended the republic and brought about the elevation of Caesar's great nephew and designated heir, Octavian, as Augustus, the first emperor.

2 ALEXANDER THE GREAT, 356–323 BC

Alexander III of Macedon, better known as Alexander the Great, single-handedly changed the nature of the ancient world.

Taught discipline and the ways of war by Leonidis and mathematics and philosophy by Aristotle, Alexander was a brave and formidable leader by the time he inherited the Kingdom of Macedonia from his father Phillip II. After reasserting Macedonian power in Greece, Alexander set out to conquer the Persian Empire. Leading his troops to victory in Asia Minor, Syria, and Egypt without defeat his greatest victory was yet to come. The Battle of Gaugamela, in northern Iraq, installed Alexander, already overlord of Asia Minor and Pharaoh of Egypt, as King of Persia at the age of twenty-five.

As king, Alexander led his army a further eleven thousand miles, founding over seventy cities and creating an empire that stretched across three continents and covered around two million square miles. The entire area from Greece in the west, north to the Danube, south into Egypt, and as far to the east as the Indian Punjab, was linked together in a vast international network of trade and commerce. His legacy and conquests lived on long after him—the Hellenistic period—centuries of Greek settlement featuring a combination of Greek, Middle Eastern, and Indian culture.

1 CYRUS THE GREAT, CIRCA 600–530 BC

The first Achaemenid Emperor, Cyrus founded the Persian Empire by uniting the two original Iranian tribes, the Medes and the Persians. A great military leader, attributing his own success to "Diversity in counsel, unity in command," Cyrus expanded his kingdom from Turkey, Palestine, and Armenia in the west to Kazakhstan, Kyrgyzstan, and the Indus River in the east—the largest empire the world had ever seen. A new era of empire building began with Cyrus: the era of the superstate, an empire comprised of many different races, religions, and languages, ruled under a single administration and a central government.

Cyrus is remembered not only as a great military leader, but also as a great statesman and liberator. Called "Lord's anointed" by the Jews and the "Lawgiver" by the conquered Hellenes, Cyrus showed respect toward religious beliefs and cultural traditions of other races. Proclaiming he "would not reign over the people if they did not wish it," his policies of conquest, mercifulness, and assimilation allowed his empire to thrive for more than two hundred years after his death.

✳✳✳✳✳✳

TOP 10 MEN WHO WERE REALLY WOMEN

10 BRANDON TEENA

Teena Brandon was born in 1972 in Lincoln, Nebraska. As a child she was regarded as a tomboy and everyone called her Brandon. After being sexually abused by a male relative, she moved to Richardson County, Nebraska, and began to live entirely as a male. She became friends with two ex-convicts, John Lotter and Marvin "Tom" Nissen. She also began dating a woman, Lana Tisdel. None of her friends knew she was female. Brandon was jailed for forging checks and his girlfriend, Lana, bailed him out. Because Brandon was in the women's section of the prison, Lana discovered his true sex. According to Lana she stopped "dating" Brandon at this time. When Brandon's arrest was published in the paper under her proper name, Lotter and Nissen discovered the truth. They raped Brandon and beat her. Brandon went to the police but a large number of administrative errors resulted in her case not being investigated. Eventually Lotter and Nissen would go on to shoot Brandon and two others who were hiding her. Lotter was sentenced to death and Nissen to life imprisonment. The story of Brandon Teena became the subject of the Academy Award–winning film *Boys Don't Cry*.

9 JAMES GRAY

James Gray was born Hannah Snell in 1723 in Worcester, England. As a child she played "soldiers" but was otherwise seen as a normal young girl. In 1744 she married James Summs and two years later gave birth to a daughter. Within a year her daughter had died and her husband had deserted her. She borrowed a man's suit from her brother-in-law, James Gray, whose name she assumed. She began to travel, trying to find her husband whom she later discovered had been executed for murder. She traveled to Portsmouth and joined the Royal Marines. She was sent into battle twice, during which time she was wounded eleven times in the legs and once in the groin. It is not known how she concealed her sex when her groin wound was treated. In 1750 her unit returned to England and she revealed her true sex to her shipmates. She told her story to the papers and petitioned for a military pension, which was, surprisingly, granted. Her military service was officially recognized and she eventually opened a pub called The Female Warrior. She eventually remarried and had two children. Hannah died in 1792.

8 PETTER HAGBERG

Brita Nilsdotter was born in 1756 in Finnerödja, Sweden. In 1785 she married Anders Peter Hagberg who was a soldier of the guard. Shortly after the marriage he was called away to participate in the Russo-Swedish War (1788–1790). At a loss without her husband, Brita dressed herself as a man and enlisted in the army to find him. She participated in the Battle of Svensksund and the Battle of Vyborg Bay as a marine. During her time there her commanding officer called out the name "Hagberg" and both she and her husband stepped forward—she found him at last. The two kept her sex a secret. Later, at the battle of Björkö Sund, Brita was wounded and ordered below deck to have her wounds taken care of. She went unwillingly and her sex was revealed. After the war she was given a pension (unheard of at the time) and was granted a license to trade (also unheard of for a married woman). She was awarded a medal of bravery and given a military funeral.

7 ALBERT CASHIER

Albert Cashier was born Jennie Irene Hodgers in 1843. In 1862, Hodgers disguised herself as a man and enlisted in the 95th Illinois Infantry Regiment under the name Albert Cashier. The regiment was under Ulysses S. Grant and fought in over forty battles. Cashier managed to remain undetected as the other soldiers thought she was just small and preferred to be alone. Cashier was captured in battle but managed to escape back to Union lines after overpowering a guard. She fought with the regiment through the war until 1865. After the war, Cashier continued to live as a male, convincing everyone around her. For forty years Cashier worked as a church janitor, cemetery worker, and street lamplighter, voted as a man, and claimed a veteran's pension. In 1910, she was hit by a car and broke her leg. A doctor discovered her secret but agreed to keep quiet. In 1911, Cashier moved to a soldier's retirement home. After her mind began to deteriorate, attendants gave her a bath and discovered her true sex. She was forced to wear a dress from that time on. Cashier died in 1915 and was buried in her military garb. Her tombstone carried the words, "Albert D. J. Cashier, Co. G, 95 Ill. Inf." When she was finally traced back to Jennie Hodgers, a second tombstone was erected with both names on it.

6 MARINUS

Marinus was born Marina in the sixth century. Her father wanted to join a monastery (Monastery of Qannoubine, in the Holy Valley, Lebanon) so he took his daughter—disguised as a boy—with him. Both were admitted and became monks. After living in the monastery for a number of years, it became necessary for both father and daughter to travel. While staying at an inn, the innkeeper's wayward daughter was attracted to Brother Marinus and tried to seduce her. When Marinus refused the advances, the innkeeper's daughter claimed that "he" had seduced her and she was pregnant. Marinus refused to debunk the claims by showing that she was, in fact, female, and she was kicked out of the monastery. She lived outside the monastery walls begging. To make matters worse, Marinus was forced to take custody of the child and raise him. She remained there, raising the child, performing harsh penances, and undertaking menial jobs. It was not until her death that her sex was finally revealed. Marinus is revered as a saint in the Roman Catholic and Orthodox churches. She is known as Saint Marina the Monk.

5 DENIS SMITH

Denis Smith (born Dorothy Lawrence) was an English reporter who disguised herself as a man to go undercover during World War I. Dorothy, nineteen, was living in Paris and wanted to be a war reporter—something that was impossible due to her sex and the difficulty that even males were having at the time getting to the front lines as journalists. She persuaded two young English soldiers to give her a uniform; she had her hair cut short in a military style, and colored her skin with diluted furniture polish to give it a bronzed look. With forged identity papers as Private Denis Smith of the 1st Bn, Leicestershire Regiment, she cycled to the Somme and the front lines. A friend found her work as a sapper with the British Expeditionary Force, laying mines under constant fire. He also found her an abandoned cottage to sleep in at night. After ten days, she became worried that if her sex were discovered, the men who had helped her would be in danger. She presented herself to the company chiefs and was placed under arrest. She was interrogated as a spy and declared a prisoner of war. The military were concerned that if her story got out, other women would try to enter the army in disguise. Dorothy was compelled to sign an affidavit that she would not tell her story. When she returned to London she was unable to work due to the affidavit. When the war ended she wrote her story but the war office censored it and it would not come out until many years later. In 1925,

Dorothy was institutionalized as insane and she died at Colney Hatch Lunatic Asylum in 1964.

4 MALINDA BLALOCK

Malinda Blalock was a female soldier during the American Civil War who fought bravely on both sides. When the war started, rather than be separated from her husband Keith, she decided to disguise herself as a man and join the army too. She was officially registered on March 20, 1862, as "Samuel 'Sammy' Blalock"—claiming to be the older brother of her husband. Her registration papers are one of the few surviving records of female soldiers in the Civil War. Malinda was a good soldier and her identity was never revealed. One of the army surgeons said of her, "She drilled and did the duties of a soldier as any other member of the Company, and was very adept at learning the manual and drill." Eventually the couple deserted from the army.

3 JAMES BARRY

James Barry (born c. 1792–1795) was a military surgeon in the British Army, and by the end of his career was Inspector General in charge of military hospitals. He served in South Africa and India. Among his accomplishments was the first successful cesarean section in Africa by a British surgeon, in which both the mother and child survived the operation. James Barry was born Margaret Ann Bulkley and is, therefore, the first female Briton to become a qualified medical doctor. It is believed that Bulkley took on the role of a man in order to achieve her dreams of working in medicine—a dream that could not be fulfilled if she remained a woman. Letters reveal that there may have been a conspiracy by Barry's mother and uncles to get him into medical school. He died from dysentery July 25, 1865, and apparently the charwoman who took care of the body, Sophia Bishop, was the first to discover his female body, and revealed the truth after the funeral. Afterward many people claimed to "have known it all along." The British Army sealed his records for a hundred years.

2 CHEVALIER D'EON

Charles-Geneviève-Louis-Auguste-André-Timothée d'Éon de Beaumont (try saying that three times fast!) was born in 1728 in France. D'Eon was born a female but lived the first half of her life as a man. D'Eon's autobiography states that she was raised as a boy because her father could only inherit money from his in-laws if he had a son. As was usual for the day, because her family were nobles without a title, they styled themselves as "Chevalier," meaning "Knight." In 1756, d'Eon joined the spy service of King Louis XV and traveled on a secret mission to Russia to meet the Empress Elizabeth. In 1761, d'Éon returned to France. The next year she became a captain of dragoons under the Marshal de Broglie and fought in the later stages of the Seven Years' War. She was wounded and received the Order of Saint-Louis. She was eventually granted a pension and lived in political exile in London. As part of her negotiation with the crown of King Louis XVI, she was told she could return to France but would have to live as a woman—an offer she accepted because the king offered to pay for her new clothes. She lived out the rest of her life as a woman.

1 BILLY TIPTON

Billy Tipton (born Dorothy Lucille Tipton in 1914) was a jazz pianist and saxophonist. In 1933, she began her career as a musician in various small Oklahoma bars. As time passed Tipton began to associate with her father's name, Billy, and eventually she began to present as male by breast-binding and packing. At first Tipton appeared male only in performances, but by 1940 she was living entirely as a male. She ultimately gained great success as a musician and went on to record a series of very popular albums. Tipton had a number of lesbian relationships during which she was able to keep her sex concealed. She eventually had a long-term relationship with a woman—concealing her sex the whole time—and they adopted three sons. She was described as "a good father who loved to go on scouting camps." In 1989, at the age of seventy-four, Tipton died. It was not until then that the coroner revealed to her family and friends that she was, in fact, a woman.

✳✳✳✳✳✳

TOP 10 SOLE SURVIVORS OF A PLANE CRASH

10 FIRST LIEUTENANT MARTIN FARKAŠ

Date of Crash: January 19, 2006

Aircraft Type: Antonov An-24

Operator: Slovak Air Force

Crash Site: Hejce, Hungary

Passengers and Crew: 43

Fatalities: 42

Cause of Crash: Pilot Error

This airplane was carrying Slovak peacekeepers. The aircraft crashed in snowy and forested terrain on Borsó Hill at an elevation of 2300 feet near the Hungarian village of Hejce and the town of Telkibánya. The plane hit the tops of trees before catching fire and crashing. The bodies and wreckage were scattered over a large area. Michaela Farkasova, the wife of the only survivor, reported that she received a cell phone call from her husband who told her that his plane had crashed in a forest. He asked her to alert rescue services. Shortly after the phone call Farkaš was found. According to rescuers, his survival was pure luck as he was found in the aircraft's lavatory, which received little damage. Farkaš suffered minor brain swelling and lung injuries after the crash. He was put into a medically induced coma, and was soon reported to be in stable condition. Further investigations indicated that the pilot descended too early in the dark toward the lights of Košice.

9 JAMES POLEHINKE

Date of Crash: August 27, 2006

Aircraft Type: Bombardier Canadair Regional Jet (CRJ) CRJ-100ER

Operator: Comair (d.b.a. Delta Connection)

Crash Site: Blue Grass Airport, Lexington, Kentucky

Passengers and Crew: 50

Fatalities: 49

Cause of Crash: Pilot Error

This aircraft was assigned the airport's runway 22 for the takeoff, but used runway 26 instead. Runway 26 was too short for a safe takeoff, causing the aircraft to overrun at the end of the runway before it could become airborne, killing all forty-seven passengers and two of the three crew. The flight's first officer James Polehinke was the only survivor and suffered serious injuries, including multiple broken bones, a collapsed lung, and severe bleeding. Doctors later determined that Polehinke had suffered brain damage and had no memory of the crash or the events leading up to it. Polehinke was flying the plane when it crashed, but it was the flight's captain, Jeffrey Clay, who taxied the aircraft onto the wrong runway.

8 FOYE KENNETH ROBERTS

Date of Crash: June 14, 1943
Aircraft Type: B-17C Flying Fortress
Operator: U.S. Army
Crash Site: Bakers Creek near Mackay, Queensland, Australia
Passengers and Crew: 41
Fatalities: 40
Cause of Crash: Unknown

For reasons of military security and morale, this incident was hushed-up by U.S. Army and Australian civil authorities for many years. The plane carried forty-one American servicemen returning from ten days of leave. The aircraft took off into ground fog and leveled off at an altitude of about three hundred feet. In a matter of minutes the plane had caught fire in the air, and as it dived into the trees one of its wings came away leaving a great opening in the fuselage through which most of the passengers were emptied into the bush before the final impact. The only survivor was Foye Kenneth Roberts. Roberts suffered head injuries that were not diagnosed at the time of the crash and lost his speech for many years after undergoing lifesaving brain surgery. Roberts did not recall anything of the actual crash. In February 2004, Foye Kenneth Roberts passed away. Another fact that is remarkable is that still to this day this crash rates as the worst aviation disaster in Australian history.

7 NESTOR MATA

Date of Crash: March 17, 1957
Aircraft Type: C-47 Skytrain

Operator: Philippine Air Force

Crash Site: 22 miles northwest of Cebu City, Philippines

Passengers and Crew: 26

Fatalities: 25

Cause of Crash: Metal Fatigue

This crash killed the seventh president of the Philippines, Ramon Magsaysay, as well as many high-ranking military officials. A reporter for the *Philippine Herald*, Nestor Mata, was the sole survivor of the accident. The aircraft took off from Lahug Airport for Nichols Field; eyewitnesses on the ground observed that the airplane had not gained enough altitude as it approached the mountain ranges in Balamban. Mata was sitting in the second seat next to the president's compartment when the crash occurred and remembers there was a blinding flash for a moment, then he fell unconscious. When he regained consciousness he found himself on the side of a steep cliff among trees and bushes. As he was in agonizing pain, he began shouting, "Mr. President! Mr. President!" When some farmers found him they had to return to the village to get a hammock on which they loaded and carried him for eighteen hours through rugged terrain. As soon as Mata reached the Southern Island Hospital in Cebu he was treated for severe shock and pain from second- and third-degree burns. Mata did not lose consciousness in the hospital and was able to dictate to a nurse a press dispatch to his paper. It began "President Magsaysay is dead."

6 ERIKA DELGADO

Date of Crash: January 13, 1995

Aircraft Type: DC-9

Operator: Intercontinental Airlines

Crash Site: Maria La Baja, 500 miles northwest of Bogota

Passengers and Crew: 52

Fatalities: 51

Cause of Crash: Unknown

This airliner exploded in midair as the pilot attempted an emergency landing near a swamp. Instead the plane hit a grassy field, exploded, and then toppled into a lagoon. A farmer said he heard cries for help and found a nine-year-old girl, Erika Delgado, on a mound of seaweed, which had broken her fall. She was the only survivor. She was traveling with her parents and a younger brother from Bogota to the Caribbean resort city of Cartagena. The rescuers said she told them her mother had shoved her out of the plane as it broke up and burst into flames. She was taken to the hospital in shock and with a broken arm. Erika later recalled that someone approached but ignored her cries for help and actually ripped a gold necklace from her neck and ran away. Witnesses say scavengers also looted the bodies of other passengers. Erika issued a plea for the return of the necklace, which she says was her only memento of her father.

5 GEORGE LAMSON, JR.

Date of Crash: January 21, 1985
Aircraft Type: Lockheed Electra 188
Operator: Galaxy Airlines
Crash Site: Reno, Nevada
Passengers and Crew: 71
Fatalities: 70
Cause of Crash: Pilot/Ground Crew Error

After a weekend of skiing, seventeen-year-old George Lamson had taken a seat next to his father in the front row of the airplane's cabin, directly behind the bulkhead. The plane began an ill-advised right turn, and as it began to shudder the right wing dipped. Lamson pulled his knees to his chest just as the plane hit the ground. The force of the crash ripped Lamson's seat from the fuselage and he was catapulted out of the plane, landing upright in the middle of the highway and still strapped in his seatbelt. He unbuckled and dashed toward a field at the far edge of the pavement as the plane exploded. Three people survived the crash initially, including Lamson's father, but both others died a few days later of severe burns and head injuries. It was later determined that the probable cause of this accident was the captain's and the copilot's failure to control and monitor the flight path and airspeed of the aircraft. This is what caused the unexpected vibration shortly after takeoff. Lamson was recently contacted by the press and is a now a father himself. He asked the reporter not to reveal anything more of his work or whereabouts and remains a very private person.

4 MOHAMMED EL-FATEH OSMAN

Date of Crash: July 8, 2003
Aircraft Type: Boeing 737
Operator: Sudan Airways
Crash Site: Port Sudan
Passengers and Crew: 116

Fatalities: 115

Cause of Crash: Unknown

About ten minutes after takeoff, heading from Port Sudan on the northeastern coast to the capital, the pilot radioed the control tower about a problem in one engine. The pilot killed that engine and told the tower he was returning to the airport. Ten minutes later the Sudanese airliner plunged into a hillside while attempting an emergency landing, killing 116 people and leaving only three-year-old Mohammed el-Fateh Osman amid a scene of charred corpses as the only survivor. The boy was found injured and lying on a fallen tree by a nomad. The boy's mother was among the victims. Mohammed lost part of a lower leg and was treated for severe burns. The bodies were buried in a mass grave after performing the Muslim prayer because the conditions of the bodies would not allow transporting and delivering them to the relatives. The country blamed the United States for the crash, saying that sanctions had restricted vital aircraft parts. The U.S. denied that claim, stating there was no ban on equipment required for aviation safety.

3 VESNA VULOVIĆ

Date of Crash: January 26, 1972

Aircraft Type: McDonnell-Douglas DC-9

Operator: Jugoslovenski Aero Transport

Crash Site: Hinterhermsdorf, East Germany

Passengers and Crew: 28

Fatalities: 27

Cause of Crash: Bombing

This is close to the top of the list because of the overall circumstances and the unbelievable survival story of Vesna Vulović. Vesna was a flight attendant onboard when a bomb went off at the altitude of 33,000 feet. This terrorist act was attributed to Croatian Ustashe terrorists. The explosion tore the jet into several pieces in midair. The wreckage fell through the sky for three minutes before striking a frozen mountainside. A German man, upon arriving at the crash, found Vesna lying half outside of the plane, with another crew member's body on top of her, and a serving cart pinned against her body. The man was a medic in the Second World War, and did what he could for her until further help arrived. Vesna's injuries included "a fractured skull, two broken legs, and three broken vertebrae, which left her temporarily paralyzed from the waist down." She regained the use of her legs after surgery and continued working for JAT at a desk job. It was discovered later her schedule had been mixed up with that of another flight attendant named Vesna, and she was subsequently placed on the wrong flight. Vesna still holds the Guinness World Record for the highest fall survived without a parachute, at 33,330 feet. She is considered a national heroine throughout the former Yugoslavia.

2 CECELIA CICHAN

Date of Crash: August 16, 1987
Aircraft Type: McDonnell Douglas MD-82
Operator: Northwest Airlines
Crash Site: Romulus, Michigan (western Detroit)
Passengers and Crew: 155
Fatalities Onboard: 154 (2 on the ground were also killed)
Cause of Crash: Pilot Error
After taking off from Metro Airport, during the initial climb the plane rolled about 35 degrees in each direction. The left wing struck a light pole about a half-mile from the end of the runway, struck other light poles and the roof of a car rental building, and then the ground. Cecelia Cichan was located by rescue workers in her seat several feet away from her mother's body along with Cecelia's father, and her six-year-old brother. Her survival was considered unexplainable and miraculous by many including airline crash investigators. The National Transportation Safety Board determined that the probable cause of the accident was the flight crew's failure to use the taxi checklist to ensure the flaps and slats were extended for takeoff. Cecelia is now married and earned a psychology degree from the University of Alabama. Although she has made no public statements nor attended annual memorial services regarding the tragic crash, she corresponds with some of the crash victims' loved ones.

1 JULIANE KOEPCKE

Date of Crash: December 24, 1971
Aircraft Type: Lockheed Electra L-188A
Operator: LANSA
Crash Site: Puerto Inca, Peru
Passengers and Crew: 92
Fatalities: 91
Cause of Crash: Human Error and Structural Failure, Possibly Struck by Lightning

On Christmas Eve, 1971, the Peruvian airliner had taken off from the Jorge Chavez International Airport in Lima on a flight to Pucallpa, Peru. About a half hour after takeoff and at about 21,000 feet, the aircraft entered a thunderstorm and heavy turbulence and was possibly struck by lightning. The pilots had difficulty controlling the aircraft and it soon went into a dive. The crew attempted to level out the plane, but the fire and turbulent forces on the wings caused the right wing and most of the left wing to separate from the aircraft. The aircraft came crashing down in a mountainous region of the Amazon. Miraculously, a German teenager, Juliane Koepcke, seventeen, who was traveling with her mother, survived the crash and was still strapped in her seat. After searching for her mother in vain, Koepcke wandered through the jungle for nine days looking for help. On the ninth day, she found a canoe and shelter. Soon after, local lumbermen returned and found her. The men took her on the final seven-hour journey via canoe down the river to a lumber station where she was airlifted to a hospital. Koepcke is now a successful biologist in Germany.

✳✳✳✳✳✳

TOP 10 NOTABLE PEOPLE WHO DROWNED

10 ROBERT MAXWELL
Profession: British Media Mogul
Date of Birth: June 10, 1923
Date of Drowning: November 5, 1991
Age at Death: 68

Maxwell is presumed to have fallen overboard from his luxury yacht while cruising off the Canary Islands. His body was found floating in the Atlantic Ocean. The official verdict was accidental drowning. It came to light in early 2006 that, before his death, Maxwell was being investigated for possible war crimes in Germany in 1945. This led to renewed speculation that his death was a suicide.

Maxwell's death triggered a flood of revelations about his business dealings and activities. It was discovered that, without prior authorization, he had used hundreds of millions of pounds from his companies' pension funds to finance his corporate debt and lavish lifestyle. Thousands of Maxwell's employees lost their pensions.

9 JOE FLYNN
Profession: Actor
Date of Birth: November 8, 1924
Date of Drowning: July 19, 1974
Age at Death: 49

Anyone who watches *McHale's Navy* will know who Joe Flynn is. He also appeared in a bunch of Disney films. This is another drowning under odd circumstances. Shortly after completing voiceover work for the Disney animated feature *The Rescuers* (1977), the forty-nine-year-old Flynn was discovered by family members in the swimming pool of his Beverly Hills home. Apparently, he had gone into the pool with a cast on his broken leg. His body was found at the pool's bottom, held down by the weight of the cast. Some celebrity friends including Merv Griffith expressed concern about the unusual circumstances surrounding Flynn's death, though authorities found no evidence of foul play. Many believe Flynn suffered a heart attack while swimming.

8 JEFF BUCKLEY
Profession: Singer/Songwriter and Guitarist, Son of Singer/Songwriter Tim Buckley
Date of Birth: November 17, 1966
Date of Drowning: May 29, 1997
Age at Death: 30

On the day he was scheduled to reunite with his band members to resume work on an album, Buckley spontaneously decided to take a swim, fully clothed, in the Mississippi River; he was caught in the wake of a passing boat and disappeared. Despite a determined rescue effort that night, Buckley remained missing. On June 4, his body was discovered. An album was released posthumously in 1998 under the title *Sketches for My Sweetheart the Drunk*. His life and music were celebrated in May and June 2007, the tenth anniversary of Jeff Buckley's death. There were tributes in Australia, Belgium, Canada, United Kingdom, Iceland, Ireland, Macedonia, France, and the U.S.

7 ART PORTER

Profession: Jazz Saxophonist, Son of Legendary Jazz Musician Art Porter, Sr.

Date of Birth: August 3, 1961

Date of Drowning: November 23, 1996

Age at Death: 35

Porter traveled to Thailand to appear at the Thailand International Jazz Festival. After the festival he went boating on the Kratha Taek reservoir. Tragically, the boat Porter was traveling on overturned, and Porter, along with several others, drowned. Porter was survived by his wife and two sons. In 1998, the album *For Art's Sake* was posthumously released in his honor.

6 JESSICA SAVITCH

Profession: News Correspondent and Anchorwoman

Date of Birth: February 1, 1947

Date of Drowning: October 23, 1983

Age at Death: 36

Jessica Savitch was a very skilled reporter and anchorwoman with a great future ahead of her. Savitch had dinner with Martin Fischbein, vice-president of the *New York Post*, in New Hope, Pennsylvania. After the meal, they began to drive home (around 7:15 p.m.). Fischbein was behind the wheel and Savitch was in the backseat with her dog, Chewy. Apparently Fischbein missed posted warning signs in a heavy rainfall, and he drove out of the wrong exit from the restaurant and up the towpath of the Pennsylvania Canal on the side of the Delaware River. The car veered over the edge into the shallow water of the canal. The car landed upside down, and sank into deep mud that sealed the doors shut. Savitch and Fischbein were trapped inside as water poured in. When the car was discovered, Fischbein's body was still strapped behind the wheel, with Savitch and her dog in the rear. After the subsequent autopsies, the coroner ruled that both Savitch and Fischbein had died from asphyxiation (by drowning). He noted that Fischbein was apparently knocked unconscious in the wreck but Savitch had struggled to escape. There was no finding that drugs or alcohol had played any part in the crash.

5 JOSEF MENGELE
Profession: Nazi Camp Doctor at Auschwitz
Date of Birth: March 16, 1911
Date of Drowning: February 7, 1979
Age at Death: 67

If there were a list of people you would most like to drown, Mengele would be on it. He is on this list because he really did drown, but most would say not soon enough. While swimming in the sea, Mengele accidentally drowned, possibly from a stroke, in Bertioga, Brazil, where he was in hiding and going by the name of Wolfgang Gerhard.

4 JOHN JACOB ASTOR IV
Profession: Businessman, Inventor, Writer
Date of Birth: July 13, 1864
Date of Drowning: April 15, 1912
Age at Death: 49

This is obviously the most famous of circumstances on this list surrounding a notable person drowning. John Jacob Astor IV was the wealthiest passenger onboard the *Titanic* and came from one of the richest families in the U.S. After the accident, Astor left his suite to investigate; he quickly returned and reported to his wife, who was pregnant at the time, that the ship had struck ice. He reassured her that the damage did not appear serious. Even as the boats were loaded Astor appeared unbothered; he ridiculed the idea of trading the solid decks of the *Titanic* for a small lifeboat. He changed his mind by 1:45 a.m. when Second Officer Charles Lightoller arrived on A deck to finish loading Lifeboat 4. Astor helped his wife to climb onto the lifeboat and then asked if he might join her, as she was in "a delicate condition." Lightoller told him that no men could enter until all the women and children had been loaded. Astor's body was recovered on Monday, April 22, by the cable ship *McKay-Bennett*. Reports say his body was covered in soot and blood, thus it is assumed he was struck by the first funnel when it collapsed as the *Titanic* made its final plunge.

3 BRIAN JONES
Profession: Musician, One-Time Rolling Stone
Date of Birth: February 28, 1942
Date of Drowning: July 3, 1969
Age at Death: 27

This is another drowning under suspicious circumstances. At around midnight, Jones was discovered motionless at the bottom of his swimming pool at his home in Hartfield, Sussex, England. His girlfriend, Anna Wohlin, said he was alive when they took him out of the pool, insisting he still had a pulse. However, when the doctors arrived, it was too late and he was pronounced dead. The coroner's report noted his liver and heart were heavily enlarged by drug and alcohol abuse. Some felt it was suicide, blaming Jagger and Richards for his mental state. His girlfriend, Wohlin, claimed in 1999 that Jones had been murdered by a builder who had been renovating the house the couple shared. The builder, Frank Thorogood, allegedly confessed to the murder on his deathbed to the Rolling Stones's driver, Tom Keylock; however, there were no other witnesses.

2 DENNIS WILSON
Profession: Musician, Drummer for the Beach Boys
Date of Birth: December 4, 1944
Date of Drowning: December 28, 1983
Age at Death: 39

Wilson was on a friend's yacht and after several drinks announced he was going for a swim. His friends thought he was nuts, because the water was so cold, yet he dove in and decided to swim near the spot where his old yacht used to be docked. He emerged from the water holding a picture of his ex-wife that he threw from his yacht years before. Wilson dove in again for more treasures but this time he didn't resurface. Wilson was known for practical jokes so his friends thought he was playing around. They even checked the local bars to see if Wilson was hiding there. It took four divers working in the dark with a pole probing the ocean floor forty-five minutes to find Wilson's body in thirteen feet of water.

1 NATALIE WOOD
Profession: Actress
Date of Birth: July 20, 1938
Date of Drowning: November 29, 1981
Age at Death: 43

If you ask people if they can name a well-known person who drowned, Natalie Wood's name would probably come up first nine out of ten times. She would also be at the top or near the top of any most beautiful women in Hollywood list. The circumstances concerning her drowning are still puzzling to this day. After Thanksgiving, she and her husband Robert Wagner, and Christopher Walken, whom she was working with on a film, went to Catalina Island for the weekend. Apparently Wood tried to either leave the yacht or secure a dinghy from banging against the hull when she accidentally slipped and fell overboard. Later it was discovered a witness nearby heard calls for help at around midnight. She said the cries lasted for about fifteen minutes and were answered by someone else who said, "Take it easy. We'll be over to get you." "It was laid back," the witness recalled. "There was no urgency or immediacy." An investigation by Los Angeles County coroner Thomas Noguchi resulted in an official verdict of accidental drowning. Noguchi concluded Wood had drunk several glasses of wine and was intoxicated when she died. There were marks and bruises on her body that could have been received as a result of her fall.

✳✳✳✳✳✳

TOP 10 AMAZING PEOPLE WHO CHEATED DEATH

10 ISIDRO MEJIA

He's nail-free today, but in 2004, Mejia was doing construction work on the roof of a house when he fell. The fall didn't kill him, but the six three-and-a-half-inch nails that accidentally shot into his neck and skull certainly should have. He survived because the nails barely missed his brain stem and spinal cord.

9 RICHARD BLASS

In 1968, the first Mafia attempt against this Canadian gangster took place. Two hired gunmen entered a bar where he was enjoying some drinks. Although he was shot at multiple times, Blass was able to escape unscathed. Two weeks later, Blass was tracked by the Mafia to a motel named Le Manoir de Plaisance in a Montreal suburb. The motel was set on fire and three people died, but Blass escaped the blaze. Police investigation indicated arson as the fire's cause. In

October, Blass was injured by shots to the head and back after being ambushed with his partner inside a garage. The two were able to save their lives by driving through the garage door. Blass required hospitalization for his wounds. In January 1969, a bungled bank robbery and a shot cop put Blass in jail. Within the first year of serving four consecutive terms of ten years in jail, Blass managed to escape. He was caught, thrown back in the slammer, and escaped a second time. With a spurt of freedom, and blood in his eyes, he set out and killed two coconspirators in a bar that had testified against him. Everyone else in the bar was locked in and the place was set on fire. Three days later, Blass's death finally came when he was shot twenty-three times. During his life Blass was given the nickname "The Cat" because of his luck in evading death.

8 AHAD ISRAFIL

"I try to appreciate things a lot more. You never know what moment you won't be there." In 1987, an accidental discharge of a gun blew half of fourteen-year-old Israfil's brains away, yet he survived and later graduated with honors. Doctors were able to fill the hole with a silicone block, and "the flap of skin was pulled over and hair grew back, giving him a fairly normal appearance." Cranioplast was used to put the "icing on the cake" (*Dayton Daily News*).

7 VESNA VULOVIC

It was twenty-six days into 1972 when twenty-two-year-old flight attendant Vesna Vulovic found herself at 33,000 feet in the air and quickly descending to the earth without a parachute. JAT Flight JU 367 had been cruising over Srbska-Kamenice (now the Czech Republic) when an explosion occurred (the terrorist group, Croatian National Movement, was named as responsible for the deaths of all but one) and, as astonishing as it sounds, Vulovic survived with a "fractured skull, two broken legs, and three broken vertebrae, which left her temporarily paralyzed from the waist down. She regained the use of her legs after surgery and continues to fly sporadically." She holds the Guiness World Record for the highest freefall.

6 LUDGER SYLBARIS

On the day before the Pelee eruption in May 1902, Sylbaris was locked in a single cell with stone walls that was partially underground and ventilated only through a narrow grating in the door which faced away from Pelee. His prison was the most sheltered building in the city, and this saved his life. On the day of the eruption, it grew very dark. Hot air mixed with fine ashes entered his cell through the door grating, despite his efforts in urinating on his clothing and stuffing it in the door. The heat lasted only a short moment, enough to cause deep burns on his hands, arms, legs, and back, but his clothes did not ignite, and he avoided breathing the searing-hot air. Superheated steam and volcanic gases and dust, with temperatures reaching over 1000°C, flattened the buildings in the city and the entire population burned or suffocated to death. Sylbaris was said to be the only survivor, but in fact there was one other man and possibly two children.

5 SHANNON MALLOY

Shannon Malloy was in a car crash that caused her to be internally decapitated; her spine was separated from her skull and all connecting ligaments and tendons were cut loose. Despite this, she managed to survive. Shannon had to endure several surgeries, one "fusing her skull to her spinal cord; she suffered nerve damage that made her eyes constantly cross and limited her speech ability. Her pelvis and ankle were severely broken, but could not be repaired until swelling in the brain and spinal cord reduced" (Associated Content).

4 ROY C. SULLIVAN

The chances of being struck by lightning are very slim, the chances of being struck by lightning twice (on different days) is seemingly impossible; so what are the odds of being struck by lightning seven times? For our world-record holder, Roy Sullivan, the events happened as follows:

1942—Sullivan was hit for the first time when he was in a lookout tower. The lightning bolt struck him in a leg and he lost a nail on his big toe.

1969—The second bolt hit him in his truck when he was driving on a mountain road. It knocked him unconscious and burned his eyebrows.

1970—The third strike burned his left shoulder while in his front yard.

1972—The next hit happened in a ranger station. The strike set his hair on fire. After that, he began to carry a pitcher of water with him.

1973—A lightning bolt hit Sullivan on the head, blasted him out of his car, and again set his hair on fire.

1974—Sullivan was struck the sixth time while in a campground, injuring his ankle.

1977—The seventh and final lightning bolt hit him when he was fishing. Sullivan was hospitalized for burns in his chest and stomach.

His "lightning hats" are on display in New York's and South Carolina's Guinness World Exhibit Hall.

3 ANN HODGES

In Sylacauga, Alabama, in 1954, Hodges was napping on her living room couch when a grapefruit-sized meteoroid crashed through her roof and ricocheted off her large wooden console radio, before it struck her on the arm and hip. She was badly bruised but able to walk. The Air Force arrived and took the meteorite from her. Ann's husband, Eugene, hired a lawyer to get it back. Then the landlord claimed it, wanting to sell it in order to cover the damage done to the roof. By the time the meteorite was returned to Ann and Eugene (over a year later) public attention had diminished and they were unable to find a buyer willing to pay much for the eight-and-a-half-pound alien chondrite rock. Against her husband's wishes, Ann donated it to the Alabama Museum of Natural History, where it can be seen today.

2 BEN CARPENTER

When crossing the street in Paw Paw, Michigan, Ben Carpenter, twenty-one and wheelchair-bound, was "picked up" accidentally by a truck. He was pushed by the semi for four miles at 50 mph, after the arms of his wheelchair got stuck in the grill. The story goes that the driver had stopped at a red light, and couldn't see Carpenter crossing in front of him. The light changed and Carpenter ended up having the ride of a lifetime. "What I learned is that I never would want to be a Hollywood celebrity," he said after all the fuss being made by TV and newspapers. "I don't know how they do it with the TV cameras and people taking their picture all the time. I went through it, and it was OK for a while, but a couple days was enough" (*Kalamazoo Gazette*).

1 PHINEAS GAGE

On September 13, 1848, Gage (a railway worker) was packing a hole with gunpowder, adding a fuse and sand, and then packing the charge down with a large tamping iron. The gunpowder ignited and the iron bar shot through his left cheekbone, exited out the top of his head, and was later recovered some thirty yards from the site of the accident. Within minutes he was up and walking. A few days later, he had fungus of the brain. After a couple of weeks, eight fluid ounces of pus from an abscess under his scalp were released. Damage to Gage's frontal cortex had resulted in a complete loss of social inhibitions, which often led to inappropriate behavior. He was no longer the same Gage that his friends and family knew. Today his skull and the iron bar that shot through it are on display at Boston's Warren Anatomical Museum.

✳✳✳✳✳✳

TOP 10 PEOPLE RUMORED TO BE ALIVE AFTER DEATH

10 TUPAC SHAKUR, 1971–1996

Tupac was a rapper who was killed in a drive-by shooting. The murder remains unsolved, inspiring many theories over who was responsible. In addition, many fans insisted Tupac was still alive. The rumors were partly fueled by Tupac's release of eight albums in the decade after his death. In a strange coincidence, the first of those albums included the song "Blasphemy" on which Tupac raps, "Brother's getting shot and coming back resurrected."

9 ANDY KAUFMAN, 1949–1984

The offbeat comedian, best known for playing Latka on the TV series *Taxi*, died from lung cancer at the age of thirty-five. Partly because he had kept his illness a secret almost until the day he died, many fans thought the death announcement had been staged as an elaborate prank. Kaufman's frequent collaborator, fellow comedian Bob Zmuda, admitted that he and Kaufman had discussed faking his death and he seemed "obsessed with the idea." However, in a 1999 interview Zmuda declared, "Andy Kaufman is dead. He's not in some truckstop with Elvis." Just in case, Kaufman's friends held a "Welcome Home Andy" party on the twentieth anniversary of his death. The guest of honor failed to appear.

8 ELVIS PRESLEY, 1935–1977

There have been thousands of sightings of "The King" since his death. At the funeral, Elvis's father Vernon allegedly acknowledged that the corpse in the coffin did not look like his son. He said that Elvis was "upstairs," adding, "We had to show the people something." Presley was also said to have been fascinated with *The Passover Plot* by Hugh Schoenfield, who speculated that Jesus' resurrection was faked with a drug that temporarily made him appear dead. Presley, no stranger to prescription drugs, may have had the knowledge to pull off a similar scheme.

7 JIM MORRISON, 1943–1971

In March 1971, Jim Morrison, lead singer of the Doors, moved to Paris to write poetry. On Friday, July 2, Morrison left his apartment, telling his girlfriend, Pamela Courson, that he was going to see a movie. On Monday, Courson called Elektra Records representative Bill Siddons and told him to come to Paris. When he arrived, Siddons found Courson, a sealed coffin, and a death certificate saying that Morrison had died from a heart attack. Exactly what had happened that weekend remained a mystery. Despite the claim on the death certificate, rumors suggested that an overdose of drugs or alcohol had killed Morrison. Unconfirmed reports that the singer had been spotted boarding a plane that weekend fueled speculation that he was still alive. Even Doors keyboardist Ray Manzarek said in a 1973 interview, "I don't know to this day how the man died and in fact I don't even know if he's dead. Nobody ever saw Jim Morrison's body . . . it was a sealed coffin. So who knows, who knows how Jim died."

6 ADOLF HITLER, 1889–1945

Hitler and his bride of one day, Eva Braun, committed suicide in the bunker under the Reich Chancellery on April 30, 1945. The next day, German radio announced that the führer had died leading his troops in battle. The Soviet news service Tass picked up the report but added, "by spreading the news of Hitler's death, the German fascists apparently wish to give Hitler the means of leaving the stage and going underground." During the Potsdam Conference in July, Joseph Stalin insisted that Hitler had escaped to either Spain or Argentina. In fact, by this time the Russians possessed the remains of Hitler and Braun, having recovered them from the bomb crater they had been buried in. When Soviet autopsy reports on the pair were released in 1968, they showed the bodies had been positively identified as Hitler and Braun from dental records. Despite this evidence, alleged sightings of Hitler continued.

5 GRAND DUCHESS ANASTASIA, 1901–1918

The youngest daughter of Nicholas II, the last tsar of Russia, was shot with the rest of the royal family by a Communist firing squad. Over the years, several women declared themselves to be Anastasia. The most famous was Anna Anderson, who began making her claims after being rescued from a Berlin canal in 1920. She later lost a lawsuit in which she sought to be recognized as a Romanov heir, married Jack Manahan, and settled in Virginia, where she died in 1984. A decade after her death, DNA testing established that Anna Anderson Manahan was not related to the Romanovs but instead came from a Polish family, the Schanzowskis, as her detractors had long claimed.

4 JESSE JAMES, 1847–1882

In 1948, a hundred-year-old Oklahoma man named J. Frank Dalton announced he was Jesse James, who officially had been killed by Robert Ford sixty-six years earlier. Dalton convinced both writer Robert Ruark and Rudy Turilli, an acknowledged expert on James, of his claims. The man allegedly killed in James's stead was another outlaw, Charlie Bigelow. Reportedly, when James's mother was first shown the body of the man Ford had shot, she blurted out, "No, gentlemen, that is not my son." However, in 1995, the body buried in Jesse James's grave was exhumed for DNA testing. The results confirmed it was the famed outlaw.

3 ALEXANDER I, 1777–1825

Toward the end of his reign, the Russian tsar expressed to his family and close friends a desire to give up his throne. During an inspection tour of the Crimea in the winter of 1825, Alexander died suddenly of either malaria or pneumonia. He was buried in a closed casket. The hazy circumstances of his death fed rumors that Alexander had faked his death and secretly abdicated. Feodor Kuzmich, a wandering holy man who died in Siberia in 1864, was rumored to have been the former emperor. Further enhancing the mystery around the tsar, in 1925 the Soviets opened Alexander's tomb and did not find a body.

2 LOUIS XVII, 1785–1795

The *dauphin*, who was heir to the throne of France, died in prison of tuberculosis during the French Revolution. Even before the death was announced, rumors circulated that royalist sympathizers had freed him and replaced him with a double. Madame Simon, the wife of the jailer, asserted that

Louis had been smuggled out of prison in a basket of dirty laundry and replaced by a child with rickets. Eventually, over a hundred royal pretenders claimed his identity, a situation Mark Twain satirized in the duke and "dolphin" sections of *Huckleberry Finn*.

1 JESUS CHRIST

Obviously, this is a complicated item, as many people (over one billion in fact) believe that Jesus rose from the dead. But we are not talking about the resurrection aspect of Christ—we are talking about what happened later. According to Christianity, Jesus ascended into heaven after his resurrection and was henceforth gone from the world. But some people believe that he continued to live for a longer period of time and, believe it or not, went to America and taught the people there a new gospel. It is, of course, the Mormons who believe this. There are even some people who believe that Jesus married Mary Magdalene, lived a long life, and had many children.

❋❋❋❋❋❋

TOP 10 FAMOUS NATIVE AMERICANS

10 PONTIAC, 1720–1769

Known in his Ottawa tongue as Obwandiyag, Chief Pontiac is most well known for his defense of the Great Lakes region from British troops. In 1763, Pontiac and three hundred of his followers attempted to take Fort Detroit by surprise. Eventually the revolt rose to nine-hundred-plus natives and they eventually took the fort at the Battle of Bloody Run. Following the incident, Pontiac became increasingly ostracized, and in 1769 he was assassinated by a Peoria Indian in Illinois. Though he was historically a prominent figure, there is still debate about whether he actually was a leader in the revolt.

9 CRAZY HORSE, 1840–1877

With a name in his Lakota tribe, Thasuka Witko, that literally means "His-Horse-Is-Crazy," this Native American was actually born with the name Cha-O-Ha, meaning in Lakotan, "In the Wilderness," and he was often called Curly due to his hair. In the Great Sioux War of 1876, Crazy Horse led a combined group of nearly fifteen hundred Lakota and Cheyenne in a surprise attack against General George Crook's force of a thousand Englishmen and three hundred Crow and Shoshone warriors. The battle, though not substantial in terms of lives lost, nearly prevented Crook from joining up with General Custer, ensuring Custer's subsequent defeat at the Battle of Little Bighorn. Crazy Horse went on to oppose the U.S. Government in their various decisions on how to handle Indian affairs.

8 SACAJAWEA, 1788–1812

Sacajawea is most well known for accompanying Meriwether Lewis and William Clark during their Corps of Discovery of the western United States in 1806. She was born in a Shoshone tribe as Agaidika, or "Salmon Eater" in 1788. In February of 1805, just after meeting Lewis and Clark, Lewis assisted in the birth of her son, Jean Baptiste Charbonneau. Her face now appears on the dollar coin.

7 WILL ROGERS, 1879–1935

Born William Peen Adair Rogers, a Cherokee-Cowboy, "Will" became best known as an actor, vaudevillian, philanthropist, social commentator, comedian, and presidential candidate. Known as Oklahoma's favorite son, Rogers was born to a well-respected Native American territory family and learned to ride horses and use a lasso/lariat so well that he was listed in the *Guinness World Records* for throwing three ropes at once—one around the neck of a horse, another around the rider, and a third around all four legs of the horse. He ultimately traveled around the world several times, made seventy-one films (fifty silent and twenty-one "talkies"), wrote more than four thousand nationally syndicated newspaper columns, and became a world-famous figure. He died in a plane crash in 1935.

6 GERONIMO, 1829–1909

Geronimo (meaning "one who yawns" in Chiricahua; often spelled Goyathlay or Goyahkla in English) was a prominent Native American leader of the Chiricahua Apache who defended his people against the encroachment of the U.S. on their tribal lands for over twenty-five years. While Geronimo said he was never actually a chief, he was rather a military leader. As a Chiricahua Apache, this meant he was also a spiritual leader. He consistently urged raids and war upon many Mexican and later U.S. groups. Geronimo eventually went on to marry six wives, an Apache tradition. He staged what was to be the last great Native American uprising, and eventually moved to a reservation and often appeared at fairs and schools.

5 TECUMSEH, 1768–1813

A Shawnee leader whose name means "Panther in the Sky," Tecumseh became well known for taking disparate tribes folk and maintaining hold on the land that was rightfully theirs. In 1805, a religious native rebirth led by Tenskwatawa emerged. Tenskwatawa urged natives to reject the ways of the English and to stop handing over land to the U.S. Opposing Tenskwatawa was the Shawnee leader, Black Hoof, who was working to maintain a peaceful relationship with the U.S. By 1808, tensions built and compelled Tenskwatawa and Tecumseh to move further northwest and establish the village of Prophetstown near Battle Ground, Indiana. He died in the War of 1812.

4 BLACK HAWK, 1767–1838

Though not a traditional tribe chief, even after inheriting a very important medicine bundle, Black Hawk would become well known as a war chief. In his tribe's, Sauk's, tongue, his name, Makataimeshekiakiak, means, "Be a large black hawk." During the War of 1812, Black Hawk, so name-shortened by the English, became a fierce and powerful opponent. First fighting on the side of the British, Black Hawk eventually led a band of Sauk and Fox against settlers in Illinois and Wisconsin, eventually dying in Iowa. His legend is kept alive by many claiming to be directly related, like Jim Thorpe. This is, however, myth.

3 SEQUOIAH, 1767–1843

Though the exact location of Sequoiah's birth and death are unknown due to historically inaccurate writings, he is well known through translation and spoken accounts of having grown up with his mother in Tuskegee, Tennessee. Sequoiah (S-si-quo-ya in Cherokee), known as George Guess, Guest, or Gist, was a silversmith who invented the Cherokee writing system.

2 SITTING BULL, 1831–1890

Sitting Bull (or Tatanka Iyotake in Sioux, first named Slon-he, or, literally, slow) was a Hunkpapa Lakota medicine man and holy man. He is famous in both American and Native American history mostly for his major victory at the Battle of Little Bighorn against Custer, where his "premonition" of defeating the enemy became reality. Even today, his name is synonymous with Native

American culture, and he is considered to be one of the most famous Native Americans ever.

1 POCAHONTAS, 1595–1617

Having taken many liberties with her overall appearance, Disney created the image many of us believe to be what Pocahontas may have looked like. This is far from accurate. Though the film's history is similarly flawed, it does hold some truths. Pocahontas was a Native American woman who married an Englishman called John Rolfe and became a celebrity in London in the last year of her life. She was a daughter of Wahunsunacock (also known as Chief or Emperor Powhatan), who presided over an area comprised of almost all of the neighboring tribes in Virginia (called Tenakomakah then). Her formal names were Matoaka and Amonute; "Pocahontas" was a childhood nickname referring to her frolicsome nature. In her last days she went by Rebecca Rolfe, choosing to live an English life by abandoning her Native American heritage.

✳✳✳✳✳✳

TOP 10 AMAZING TRUE LIFE GIANTS

10 BERNARD COYNE, 8 FEET 2 INCHES

Coyne was born in 1897 in Iowa. His 1918 World War I draft card listed his height as eight feet. His *Guinness World Records*'s entry states he was refused entry to the war due to his height. At the time of his death it was possible he had reached the height of eight feet four inches. He died in 1921 of hardening of the liver and a glandular condition. He is buried in his place of birth in a specially made extra-large coffin.

9 VÄINÖ MYLLYRINNE, 8 FEET 3 INCHES

Myllyrinne was born in Finland in 1909. At one point he was officially the world's tallest man. At the age of twenty-one, he was seven feet three-and-a-half inches tall, and weighed 434 pounds. He experienced another growth spurt after that, which took him to his final height of eight feet three inches. He is considered to be the tallest soldier in history as he was in the Finnish army. He died in 1963.

8 EDOUARD BEAUPRÉ, 8 FEET 3 INCHES

Edouard Beaupré, born in 1881, was a circus sideshow freak, a strongman, and a star in the Barnum and Bailey circus. He was the eldest of twenty children and was born in Canada. While he was of normal height during his first few years of life, by the age of nine he was six feet tall. His death certificate showed him as being eight feet three inches and still growing. As a strongman, his featured stunt was crouching down and lifting a horse to his shoulders. He reportedly lifted horses as heavy as nine hundred pounds. He died in 1904 of tuberculosis.

7 ELLA EWING, 8 FEET 4 INCHES

Ella Ewing was born in Missouri in 1872. She is known as the "Missouri giant." She grew normally until the age of seven, at which time she began to grow rapidly. Her maximum height is disputed and, due to the lack of records, she is not listed in *Guinness World Records*. She toured as a sideshow freak until she died of tuberculosis in 1913.

6 AL TOMAINI, 8 FEET 4 INCHES

Al Tomaini was a giant who claimed a height of eight feet four inches (though *Guinness World Records* stated that he was seven feet four inches). Weighing 356 pounds and wearing size 27 shoes, Al spent most of his life as a circus giant. He was working with a circus at the Great Lakes Exposition in Chicago, in 1936, when he met his future wife, Jeanie. Jeanie was born without legs and was only two feet six inches tall. After retiring from the circus life, he and Jeanie settled in the circus community of Giant's Camp, Gibsonton, Florida.

5 LEONID STADNYK, 8 FEET 5 INCHES

Leonid Stadnyk was born in 1971 in Ukraine. He is a registered veterinary surgeon and lives with his mother. He is currently the world's tallest human, noted in the *Guinness World Records*. According to *Pravda*, Stadnyk's health is slowly failing and he needs to hold onto limbs of trees and lean on structures to walk about. A group of Ukrainian business people donated a satellite dish and a computer to Stadnyk and now he has Internet access.

4 JOHN F. CARROLL, 8 FEET 7 INCHES

John Carroll was born in Buffalo, New York, in 1932 and was known as the "Buffalo giant." Despite a large number of medical treatments, he grew at a very rapid rate. He grew seven inches in a matter of a few months. He died in 1969, and while his height was not recorded at the time, it is believed that he was very close to nine feet.

3 JOHN ROGAN, 8 FEET 9 INCHES

John Rogan was born in 1868 and he grew normally until the age of thirteen. His height was not officially recorded until his death, at which point he was eight feet nine inches tall. Due to illness, he weighed only 175 pounds. He is the tallest African American ever. He died in 1905 due to complications from his illness.

2 JOHAN AASON, 8 FEET 9.25 INCHES

Aason was born in America, the son of a Norwegian mother. He beats John Rogan to the second spot on this list by a mere quarter of an inch. Interestingly, his mother was also a giant, at seven feet two inches. According to his death certificate from Mendocino State Hospital, at the time of death he was nine feet two inches; if this is true, then he is the tallest recorded human, beating our number-one-spot holder by three inches. He is buried in Montana.

1 ROBERT WADLOW, 8 FEET 11.1 INCHES

Robert Wadlow is the tallest man in history whose height is verified by indisputable evidence. He is often referred to as the "Alton giant" because he came from Alton, Illinois. At the time of his death he weighed 440 pounds and was still growing. He was born in 1918, the oldest of five children. He died at the age of twenty-two from an infection caused by a blister on his ankle, which he got while making a professional appearance at the National Forest Festival. His coffin weighed half a ton and required twelve pallbearers to carry. He was buried in a vault of solid concrete as his family had fears that his body would be interfered with by curiosity seekers.

※※※※※※

TOP 10 EXTRAORDINARY TWINS

10 PSYCHIC TWINS, LINDA AND TERRY JAMISON (BORN 1955)

Linda and Terry Jamison are twins who claim to have predicted the September 11th attacks two years ahead of time. On November 2, 1999, they claimed through an automatic writing process that there would be a terrorist attack on the federal government and the World Trade Center in 2001. The actual quote is, "We are seeing various terrorist attacks on federal government and also the New York Trade Center, the World Trade Center." The twins did not specify the time or indicate who would be responsible. The Jamison twins also predicted that John F. Kennedy, Jr. would die by plane crash. However, it has been pointed out that the Jamison twins are frequently incorrect. In December 2003, they incorrectly predicted that Saddam Hussein would be killed by U.S. troops and that Pope John Paul II would die in June 2004.

9 OLDEST MOTHER TO GIVE BIRTH TO TWINS, OMKARI PANWAR (BORN 1938; TWINS BORN 2008)

Seventy-year-old Omkari Panwar and her husband, seventy-seven, from India already have two adult daughters and five grandchildren. Male children are especially important among India's Hindus. Only a male heir can carry out funeral rites, and female infanticide remains a chronic problem. Their male child will also be able to work the family's land. To pay for the IVF treatment vital to producing a male heir to the family's smallholdings, they sold their buffaloes, mortgaged their land, spent their life savings, and took out a credit card loan. Mrs. Panwar gave birth to twins, a boy and girl, by emergency Caesarean section. The twins were born a month premature and weighed two pounds each but are healthy according to doctors.

8 BLACK AND WHITE TWINS, ALICIA AND JASMIN SINGERL (BORN 2006)

Alicia and Jasmin were born to a mother of Jamaican-English descent and a father of German descent. Alicia's eyes are brown and her hair is dark. Jasmin's eyes are blue and her hair is white. Genetic expert's explanation for this very unusual occurrence is the mother has a mixture of genes that determines skin color. When egg cells are formed in the mother, a random selection of genes will be allocated to each egg. The set of chromosomes in each egg cell is unique. In most cases a mixed-race woman's eggs will be a mixture of genes for both black and white skin. In very rare cases the eggs may contain genes for predominantly one skin color. In this case, the mother released two such eggs—one with predominantly dark pigmentation genes and one with predominantly fair genes.

7 TELEPATHY TWINS, RICHARD AND DAMIEN POWLES

The idea of a special connection between identical twins is often myth and legend, and little research has been done in this field. The book *Twin Telepathy* claims an overwhelming body of evidence indicating there is indeed a special connection. One of the experiments involved eight-year-old Richard Powles, who was put in a soundproof room in front of a bucket filled with ice-cold water. On command, Richard plunged his arm into the ice-cold water, giving a gasp as he did so. In another room, well out of sight or earshot, his identical twin brother Damien was wired up to a polygraph. A polygraph expert monitored his respiration, abdominal muscles, pulse, and galvanic skin response (sweat on the hands). All Damien had to do was sit quietly and "tune in" to his brother's feelings. At the exact moment of Richard's sharp intake of breath caused by the freezing water, there was a sudden blip on the line monitoring Damien's respiration rate. In another experiment, Richard was asked to open a cardboard box; in it was a huge rubber snake that jumped out at him. This, too, was instantly picked up by his twin as the pulse line on the chart clearly indicated. The book also concludes there are three especially telepathy-prone groups—mothers and newborn babies, dogs and their owners, and identical twins. Of these, it is the twins who pick up the signal at full strength most often, provided they are in the right states of mind.

6 SEPARATED AT BIRTH TWINS, TAMARA RABI AND ADRIANA SCOTT (BORN 1983)

Tamara and Adriana were born in Guadalajara, Mexico, and were separated at birth and raised by different adoptive parents. Tamara was adopted by a Jewish couple who lived close to Central Park in Manhattan. Adriana was adopted by a Roman Catholic family and grew up near Long Island, just twenty miles away from where Tamara lived. Neither knew she had a twin sister. Tamara's adoptive mother also did not know, but Adriana's adoptive mother knew but kept it a secret from her daughter. When the twins were twenty years old, they were constantly getting confused by the other sister's friends. Eventually, mutual friends put two and two together and arranged for them to meet. Despite different upbringings, Tamara and Adriana discovered they had led very similar lives. The twins' adoptive fathers both died of cancer; Adriana plays the clarinet and Tamara plays the sax; and they both love listening to R&B and hip-hop. They also both wanted to be vets when they grew up. The reunited twins and their widowed moms have now formed a close bond.

5 SILENT TWINS, JUNE AND JENNIFER GIBBONS (BORN 1963)

June and Jennifer grew up in Britain. The twin sisters were inseparable, and had speech impediments that made it very hard for them to mix in with other children. The Gibbons also were the only black children in their school, and faced racism. Their language eventually became unintelligible to outsiders, and they spoke to no one except each other and their little sister. They would complete each other's sentences and could communicate with no more than facial expressions. In their early teens they were given two diaries as Christmas gifts. This inspired them to send away for a mail-order course in creative writing, and each wrote several novels that were published. It is theorized that because they were so desperate for recognition, fame, and publicity for their books, the girls committed a number of petty crimes, including arson. June and Jennifer were committed to a mental health hospital where they remained for fourteen years. Because of the medications given to them in the hospital, they lost most of their interest in creative writing. The girls apparently had an agreement that if one died, the other must begin to speak and live a normal life. During their stay in the hospital, they began to believe that it was necessary for one twin to die. Jennifer eventually agreed to be the sacrifice. Within hours after their release at the age of thirty, Jennifer died of sudden inflammation of the heart. To this day, Jennifer's death remains a mystery. After losing her twin, June was able to speak with other people and contemplates resuming her writing career.

4 BORN TWO MONTHS APART TWINS, CATALIN AND VALENTIN TESCU (BORN 2004 AND 2005)

Catalin and Valentin are Romanian are twins with different years of birth. Catalin was born in December, two months premature. The doctors were able to wait and deliver the second son, Valentin, two months later in February. Romanian doctors attributed the time lag in the births to a rare congenital condition that gave the twins' mother two uteruses due to a congenital malformation that occurred when she was herself an embryo in her mother's womb. Approximately one in every fifty thousand women has a double uterus, but the hospital believes this was the first case where a woman had become pregnant at the same time in both wombs and given birth nearly two months apart. The two brothers were both healthy when they were released from the hospital on the same day.

3 HALF-BROTHER TWINS, TUEN AND KOEN STUART (BORN 1993)

Wilma and Willem Stuart, a Dutch couple, had been unsuccessfully trying to conceive for years and decided to try IVF. They soon learned they would be parents of twins. When the two boys were born, Koen had blue eyes, dark hair, and pink skin, while Tuen had dark eyes, dark hair, and brown skin. A DNA test revealed that Koen was the Stuarts' child but Tuen was not Willem's. The report of the investigation has not been made public, but speculation is that a piece of lab equipment called a pipette, like a large eyedropper, had been used twice, causing another man's sperm to be mixed with Willem's. The hospital called it a "deeply regrettable mistake." The Stuarts remembered there was a black couple in the waiting room the same day during the IVF process. The hospital located the man and confirmed he was Tuen's biological father. Although he was under no obligation to meet his son he never knew he had, he did when Tuen was eighteen months old. The biological father only looked at him from a distance and didn't try to claim him. The father was comfortable that the Stuarts loved the child, and let them continue raising him.

2 CONJOINED TWINS, ABIGAIL AND BRITTANY HENSEL (BORN 1990)

Many know and have followed the story of the Hensel twins. They are now nineteen and recently graduated from high school. Only four known sets of conjoined twins who share an undivided torso and two legs have ever survived into adulthood. By coordinating their efforts, they have been able to enjoy many hobbies and sports, including volleyball, kickball, swimming, basketball, and cycling. Three years ago the girls passed their driver's test and had to test twice because each girl received a driver's license. They also play the piano and are avid computer users. Abigail and Brittany expect to date, get married, and have children. They hope that by providing some information about themselves they will be able to lead fairly typical lives.

1 EXPERIMENTAL TWINS, ELYSE SCHEIN AND PAULA BERNSTEIN (BORN 1969)

Elyse and Paula were born to a woman with schizophrenia and were put up for adoption. Child psychologist Dr. Viola Bernard, a consultant to the adoption agency, believed twins should be separated to improve their psychological development, so Elyse and Paula were sent to different families. Elyse knew she had been adopted, but neither one knew they were twins. When Elyse turned thirty-three, she decided to contact the New York State Adoption Information Registry to look for her birth mother and later discovered she had a twin. About six months later the twins were reunited. What makes this story even more incredible is that Elyse Schein and Paula Bernstein were part of a secret nature-versus-nurture study by Dr. Neubauer and his colleague Dr. Viola Bernard. Neubauer was a noted child psychiatrist and studied five sets of twins and one set of triplets, all deliberately separated at birth. The adoptive families would travel separately to the center once a month for twelve years for IQ tests and speech analysis. Researchers would also visit their homes and film the children playing. The adoptive parents were told they were part of a child development study but were kept in the dark about the twin/triplet aspect. The set of triplets and two other sets of twins in the study have also been reunited, but it is not known if the remaining two sets of twins have. The controversial study has not been published, but will be in 2066, when most of the participants will likely be dead.

CHAPTER ELEVEN

Religion

TOP 10 BIZARRE BIBLICAL TALES

10 A LESSON FOR THOSE WHO DARE MOCK MALE PATTERN BALDNESS

Found in: 4 Kings 2:23-24

One of the more inspirational passages in the Bible tells the story of Elijah, a wise man, yet one cursed with male pattern baldness. One day he is minding his own business, making the long walk to Bethel, when he is attacked by a roving band of children who tease him with names like "bald head." But Elijah is having none of this. He turns around and curses them in the name of the Lord, and instantly two female bears emerge from a nearby wood and maul all forty-two children to death.

The moral of this story? Don't make fun of bald people. Frankly, why this story isn't included along with the Ten Commandments is anybody's guess, but it would serve as an excellent lesson for children who think baldness is something to be made fun of.

9 EGLON'S IGNOBLE DEATH

Found in: Judges 3:21-25

Ehud is the Bible's sneakiest assassin (and also the only left-handed person mentioned in the Holy Book). He is on a mission to deliver a "message from God" to smarmy King Eglon. Ehud waltzes in to meet the gluttonous king, pulls out a sword, and stabs Eglon in the stomach. At first he can't get it in, but he pushes harder and eventually reaches his intestine. Eglon is so overweight, we learn, that his fat actually covers the hilt of the sword, pushing it further into his stomach until it's not even visible. It's at this point that Eglon loses control of his bowels and begins to defecate mercilessly all over his chamber. The king's attendants eventually come back but do not enter Eglon's bedchamber, assuming he is relieving himself. After waiting "to the point of embarrassment," his attendants burst in to find their king dead on the floor, covered in his own fecal matter. Meanwhile, Ehud has escaped to the town of Seriah.

The moral of this story? Who cares, but it's damn cool.

8 ONAN—CAUTIOUS, YET FOOLISH
Found in: Genesis 38:8-10

A story so eponymous, it gave way to its own neologism—onanism, an archaic term for masturbation. Basically, God kills Er. Why? We don't really find out. However, in a stroke of good luck, Er's father, Judah, has given him the right, nay the duty, to have sex with his dead brother's wife. Onan is a bit apprehensive at first, but agrees to go through with this bizarre scheme to create a "true heir" to Er. He begins to have sex with the girl, but at the last minute decides to pull out and spill "his seed upon the ground." God is so irked he decides to kill Onan too, and thus nobody gets an heir. This story is the basis for the Christian condemnation of masturbation and birth control.

The moral of this story? In the words of Monty Python, "Every sperm is sacred..."

7 A VERY DISTURBING TALE
Found in: Judges 19:22-30

Within the Bible, occasionally there are stories so horrible that one wonders what their purpose is. Not only is this story utterly bizarre, it is absolutely disgusting. A man and his concubine are wandering the streets when they decide to seek shelter for the night, and find a man kind enough to let them stay. That night, however, a group of men turns up at the door and demands to see the guest so that they may have sex with him. The owner is unwilling to let his male lodger be raped, and so he offers up his virgin daughter instead. However, this is still not good enough for the men, so the owner offers them his guest's concubine and the men accept. The men brutally rape the woman and leave her on the doorstep where she bleeds to death. If that is not enough, when she is found by her husband, he chops her up into twelve pieces which he sends to each of the twelve tribes of Israel.

The moral of this story? Hopefully none.

6 A NOVEL WAY TO SHOW YOUR LOVE
Found in: 1 Kings 18:25-27

Before Byron, before Casanova, there was David. Young and in love, David desperately wants to marry Saul's daughter, Michal, and offers Saul anything he wants to let him marry her. What could Saul possibly want? Money? A vow of love? No. Saul wants foreskins. One hundred, to be exact. Why? Who cares. If you want my daughter, you're going to have to find a hundred foreskins by tomorrow. David finds this odd, but then again this girl is hot, so he goes out and kills two hundred men and collects their foreskins. It's only then he remembers that he only needs a hundred. Oops. Oh well, maybe if he hands over twice as many foreskins, Saul will be doubly as impressed. Indeed, he is, and duly hands over his daughter to David.

The moral of this story? Never be ashamed to do crazy things for love.

5 LIKE SLICING SALAMI
Found in: Exodus 4:24-26

Continuing the Bible's fascination with all things foreskin, we get the bizarre story of God trying to kill Moses because his son isn't circumcised. God is about to obliterate Moses when his wife Zipporah takes out a flint and quickly cuts the foreskin of his son (ouch), throwing the bloody skin fragment at Moses' feet. "You are a bloody husband to me!" squeals Zipporah, flint in one hand, child in other. God, clearly freaked out by this woman, backs off and Moses is saved.

The moral of this story? Never turn down a woman for being a psycho. Someday she may save your life.

4 JESUS AND THE FIG TREE
Found in: Matthew 21:19; Mark 11:13-14

So, Jesus is walking from Bethany and he's feeling a bit peckish. He encounters a fig tree, but, unfortunately, it is barren, as it's the off-season for figs. Annoyed, Jesus demands the fig tree bear him fruit; however, the fig tree doesn't respond (it's a tree), so Jesus, in an act of uncharacteristic rashness, curses the fig tree to death. This story is bizarre for many reasons, but mainly for how little it means to the Jesus story and how Jesus seems to react so harshly. Okay, so he's hungry, and we all get a little cranky when we're hungry, but come on, the fig tree had done nothing wrong. This just seems like abuse of powers.

The moral of this story? I honestly can't think of one. This story seems so unimportant and purposeless yet both Mark and Matthew mention it so it must have some importance. Perhaps it is: don't disobey Jesus, even if you're an inanimate tree.

3 EVEN GOD IS PROUD OF HIS BACKSIDE
Found in: Exodus 33:23

It's a big day for Moses. He's finally going to meet God face-to-face and is giddy with anticipation. Soon the time comes and Moses positions himself on a rock ready to see the divine creator himself. But God backs out at the last minute, claiming that no man can see his face and live. However, he has a solution. He will let Moses have a peek at his backside: "And I will take away mine hand, and thou shalt see my back parts: but my face shall not be seen." Moses must be heartbroken. He was hoping to see God's face, not his bottom! Imagine explaining that to the wife: "Oh honey, did you see God's face?" "Umm not quite...I got a great look at his ass though!" Moses most likely slept alone that night.

The moral of this story? God works in mysterious (and slightly gay) ways.

2 BALAAM AND HIS TALKING DONKEY
Found in: Numbers 22:28-30

Balaam is just minding his own business, spanking his ass (donkey) when suddenly he hears a voice. It's his donkey asking why he is spanking him. Balaam doesn't seem the least bit miffed that his donkey has starting talking in the same language as him and says, "Because thou hast mocked me." The donkey then gets philosophical and explains the nature of their relationship and how his feelings have been hurt. Eventually, they make peace. Oh yeah, did I mention it was a talking donkey?

The moral of this story? Don't beat animals. If they could talk, they would probably tell you how upset they were.

1 JACOB AND THE CASE OF THE MAGICAL GENETICS
Found in: Genesis 30:37-39

And the most bizarre tale in the Bible goes to...this head-scratcher from Genesis, with its utterly bemusing explanation of the genetic code. Basically, Laban is taking all of Jacob's beloved striped and spotted cattle. Jacob is left with boring, old, plain-colored cattle, which he doesn't seem to like at all. So Jacob concocts a cunning plan: he gets some sticks and begins painting stripes on them. He then plants them next to his cattle. What Jacob thinks is that if he gets his cattle to look at the striped sticks while copulating, then they will give birth to striped young. Now, we'd all expect this idiotic plan to fail and Jacob to learn a lesson about something or other, but no, it actually works. The cattle give birth to striped young, and Jacob is happy. What on earth is going on here? Anyone with the most basic understanding of genetics knows this is bunk. The odd thing is that this story seems to have no purpose and moral—it's just there. How many scientists with painted sticks attempted to repeat this process before Mendel came along and said, "I'm pretty sure that's not how it's supposed to happen fellas, why don't we try this instead?"

The moral of this story? Your guess is as good as mine.

✳✳✳✳✳✳

TOP 10 ASTONISHING MIRACLES

10 MARIAN APPARITION IN ZEITOUN, 1968–1970

Marian apparitions are actually quite common in the history of the Catholic Church, with the most famous being the apparition of Mary to St. Bernadette at Lourdes in France. The Zeitoun apparition occurred in Cairo and, unlike many of the other cases, the image of Mary was witnessed by millions of people over two years and was photographed. The Coptic Orthodox Church issued a statement that the apparitions were real, but the Catholic Church has not yet made an official declaration.

9 INCORRUPTIBLE CORPSES

An incorruptible corpse is the body of a person after death that does not decompose. In all approved cases, the bodies have undergone no embalming or other postmortem procedures. The Catholic Church considers it to be a sign of sanctity and it counts toward the miracles required for canonization as a saint. In most cases, the body is normally flexible, as if alive, and frequently exudes a scent of flowers, called the Odor of Sanctity. Incorrupt bodies are usually put on display in churches for pilgrims to see.

8 THERESE NEUMANN, 1896–1962

Therese Neumann was a German Catholic woman who had stigmata (the wounds of Christ). In 1926 on the first Friday of Lent, the first wound appeared above her heart. By November of that same year she had nine wounds on her head, back, and hands. From 1922 through 1962, Therese consumed no food other than Holy Communion and from 1926 she drank no liquids at all (including water). She suffered no ill effects from this rigorous lifestyle. Formal proceedings for her beatification (the first step to canonization) began in 2005.

7 STATUE IN AKITA, 1973–1975

In 1973, Sister Agnes Katsuko Sasagawa had visions of the Virgin Mary. A cross-shaped wound appeared on her hand causing her great pain. In July of that year, while praying in the chapel, the statue of Mary began to speak to her. That same day, a number of other sisters noticed blood flowing from the statue's hand—it continued to flow for two months. Two years later the statue began to weep human tears and scientific testing verified this. It continued to weep for six years and eight months. Additionally, Sister Agnes was completely cured of total deafness. In June 1988, Cardinal Ratzinger (now Pope Benedict XVI) judged the Akita events and messages as reliable and worthy of belief.

6 LOURDES, 1858

The apparitions at Lourdes and the miracles that continued afterward are probably the most famous miracles of modern times. On February 11, 1858, a young girl (Bernadette Soubirous) had an apparition of the Virgin Mary in a cave near her village. The apparition appeared seventeen more times that year. During one of the visitations, Bernadette was directed by Mary to dig near a rock. She complied and from the hole sprung the well that is now the source of the water in the grotto to which millions of pilgrims flock every year. The Lourdes Medical Bureau has declared sixty-eight cases of inexplicable cures have occurred there since.

5 JOSEPH OF CUPERTINO, 1603–1663

St. Joseph of Cupertino, an Italian saint, was reputed to be dimwitted. In 1630, during a procession in honor of Saint Francis, Joseph suddenly levitated in front of the crowd. This was to be the first of so many levitation episodes that he became known as the Flying Saint. His most famous case of levitation occurred when meeting Pope Urban VIII; he bent down to kiss the Pope's feet and rose into the air. Thousands witnessed his levitation during his last Mass in 1663. A movie entitled *The Reluctant Saint* was made about his life.

4 TILMA OF JUAN DIEGO, 1474–1548

Saint Juan Diego Cuauhtlatoatzin had an apparition of the Virgin Mary in Guadalupe, Mexico, in 1531. The consequences of this apparition and the events that followed had a profound effect on the spread of the Catholic faith in Mexico. The apparition told him to gather flowers at the top of a hill. The apparition arranged the flowers in his cloak and told him to open it for the bishop only. Upon doing so, an icon of the apparition had been impressed on the cloth. The original cloak with the icon is on display in Guadalupe today and is one of the most visited pilgrimage sites in the world.

3 PADRE PIO (ST. PIO OF PIETRELCINA), 1887–1968

Padre Pio was born Francesco Forgione and was a Capuchin Priest. He was made famous by the stigmata that he bore for the majority of his life as a priest. In addition to stigmata, other miracles surrounding his life involve healing, bilocation, levitation, prophesy, and complete abstinence from food. In 2008, fifty years after his death, his coffin was opened revealing he was incorrupt. He was canonized a saint in 2002 and his body is now on display in San Giovanni Rotondo.

2 THE MIRACLE OF LANCIANO, 700 AD

In 700 AD in Lanciano, Italy, a monk was saying Mass in a small church. During the words of consecration, the bread physically transformed into flesh and the wine, blood. The flesh and blood remain to this day, and scientific tests performed in the 1970s verified that it is human and of blood type AB, curiously the same blood type found on the Shroud of Turin. The flesh is a human heart, complete in its essential structure.

1 THE MIRACLE OF THE SUN, 1917

The Miracle of the Sun is a miraculous event witnessed by a hundred thousand people on October 13, 1917, in Fatima, Portugal. The number of witnesses present was due to the fact that three children who had seen apparitions of Mary told people the date it would occur. Skeptics, scientists, and believers all turned out for the miracle and weren't disappointed. The sun spun in the sky and made rapid movements toward the earth. The wet ground was dried by the event as were the clothes of the people present, who had been drenched by a downpour while waiting. The skeptics present all changed their minds on the event and stated that it was, indeed, a miracle. Photographs were also taken of the miracle.

✳✳✳✳✳✳

TOP 10 SELF-APPOINTED MESSIAHS

10 RAM BAHADUR BOMJON

Ram Bahadur Bomjon, also known as Palden Dorje (his official Buddhist name), is from Ratanapuri village, Bara district, Nepal, and has drawn thousands of visitors and media attention for spending months in meditation. Nicknamed the Buddha Boy, he began his meditation on May 16, 2005, disappeared from his hometown on March 11, 2006, and reappeared elsewhere in Nepal on December 26, 2006, only to leave again on March 8, 2007. On March 26, 2007, inspectors from the Area Police Post Nijgadh in Ratanpuri found Bomjon meditating inside a bunker-like seven-foot square ditch.

9 FATHER DIVINE

George Baker, also known as Father Divine, was an African American spiritual leader from about 1907 until his death. His full self-given name was Reverend Major Jealous Divine, and he was also known as "the Messenger" and George Baker early in his life. He founded the International Peace Mission movement and claimed to be God. Some contemporary critics also claimed he was a charlatan, and some suppose him to be one of the first modern cult leaders. However, Father Divine made numerous contributions toward his followers' economic independence and racial equality.

8 BAHA'U'LLAH

Baha'u'llah was born Shiite, adopting Babism later in life. He claimed to be the promised one of all religions, and founded the Baha'i Faith. Baha'u'llah declared that he was the "Promised One" of all religions, fulfilling the messianic prophecies found in world religions. He stated that his claims to being several messiahs converging into one person were the symbolic, rather than literal, fulfillment of the messianic and eschatological prophecies found in the literature of the major religions.

7 JOSE LUIS DE JESUS MIRANDA

Jose Luis de Jesus Miranda was a Puerto Rican preacher who has claimed to be "the Man Jesus Christ," who is indwelled with the same spirit that dwelled in Jesus. He is the founder and leader of Creciendo en Gracia (Growing In Grace International Ministry, Inc.), a movement that teaches the "doctrine of Grace" and is based in Miami, Florida. He claims to be both Jesus Christ returned and the Antichrist, and exhibits a "666" tattoo on his forearm. He has referred to himself as "The Man Christ Jesus." Creciendo en Gracia has been described as a cult, by cult expert Rick Ross and Freedom of Mind's Steven Hassan.

6 MARSHALL APPLEWHITE

Applewhite posted a famous Usenet message declaiming, "I, Jesus Son of God acknowledge on this date of September 25/26, 1995..." This was two years before he and his Heaven's Gate cult committed suicide to rendezvous with a spaceship hiding behind the comet Hale-Bopp.

5 YISRAYL "BUFFALO BILL" HAWKINS

Nuclear war was to begin on Thursday, June 12, 2008, or sooner, according to the prediction of self-proclaimed prophet Yisrayl "Buffalo Bill" Hawkins, the founder of a religious sect in Abilene, Texas. "It could be turned loose before then," Hawkins told *20/20*. "You're going to see this very soon, really soon," he said. Hundreds of truck trailers were loaded with food and water on the group's forty-four-acre compound in preparation for the coming war.

4 SUN MYUNG MOON

Sun Myung Moon is the founder of the Unification Church ("Moonies"). Moon claims he is the Second Coming of Christ, the "Savior," "returning Lord," and "True Parent." He teaches that all people should become perfect like Jesus and like himself and that as such he "appears in the world as the substantial body of God Himself." He is well known for holding Blessing ceremonies, which are often called "mass weddings."

3 DAVID KORESH (VERNON WAYNE HOWELL)

David Koresh was the leader of a Branch Davidian religious sect and believed himself to be the final prophet. A 1993 raid by the U.S. Bureau of Alcohol, Tobacco, Firearms, and Explosives and the subsequent siege by the FBI ended with the burning of the Branch Davidian ranch. Koresh, fifty-three adults, and twenty-one children died in the fire.

2 JIM JONES

Jim Jones claimed to be the reincarnation of Jesus, Akhenaten, Buddha, Lenin, and Father Divine. He performed supposed miracle healings to attract new converts. Members of Jones's church called him "Father" and believed their movement was the solution to the problems of society; many did not distinguish Jones from the movement. He was the founder of the Peoples Temple, which became synonymous with group suicide after the November 18, 1978, death of over nine hundred people from cyanide poisoning in their isolated agricultural intentional community called Jonestown. Nine other people at a nearby airstrip and in Georgetown died in the mass suicide as well.

1 L. RON HUBBARD

L. Ron Hubbard was the founder of the Church of Scientology, and in his 1955 poem "Hymn of Asia" he declared himself to be "Metteya" (Maitreya), the forthcoming world spiritual teacher and leader. In his book's preface, his editors indicated that Hubbard possessed specific physical characteristics said to be outlined in unnamed Sanskrit sources as properties of Maitreya.

✳✳✳✳✳✳

TOP 10 MISCONCEPTIONS ABOUT THE BIBLE

10 DEVILISH SERPENT

The serpent that convinced Eve to take the fruit from the tree of Knowledge and Evil is not referred to as Satan in Genesis. He is known only as the serpent "more subtle than any of the beasts of the earth." Additionally, the term "Lucifer," used in reference to Satan, comes from the Vulgate translation of Isaiah 14:12; at no point in the Bible is Satan directly referred to by the name Lucifer. [Genesis 3]

9 NOAH'S ARK

We all know that the "animals went in two by two"... right? Wrong! In fact, all clean animals went in in groups of seven, and unclean animals in groups of two. According to Jewish dietary law, there are far more clean animals than unclean, so the majority of creatures entering the ark went in as groups of seven. [Genesis 7:2-3]

8 THE TEN COMMANDMENTS

Considering the importance of the Ten Commandments to so many people, you would think they would have a clear idea of how they are defined, but most people do not. The Bible does not list a consistent set of Ten Commandments at all. In Exodus, the list includes fourteen or fifteen "statements." Though the Bible does refer to a set of "ten" rules, it does not mention them in the same sections as the list commonly known as the Ten Commandments. Various Christian sects have divided the list of commandments up differently. The Catholic Church combines the first three statements into one commandment, and the Protestants combine the final two into one statement. To add to the confusion, there is also another set of Ten Commandments called the Ritual Decalogue, which includes laws such as, "Do not cook a kid in its mother's milk." [Exodus 20]

7 THE IMMACULATE CONCEPTION

The Immaculate Conception is not a reference to Jesus being born without sin, but to his mother Mary. Most Christians believe that all people are conceived with original sin (the sin inherited from Adam and Eve) but that Jesus was not. Additionally, the Catholic Church teaches that Mary was also conceived without sin and this is where the term "Immaculate Conception" has come from. [Luke 1:28]

The Immaculate Conception is the conception of Mary, the mother of Jesus, without any stain of original sin in her mother's womb: the dogma thus says that, from the first moment of her existence, she was preserved by God from the lack of sanctifying grace that afflicts mankind and that she was instead filled with divine grace.

6 THE THREE KINGS

No doubt most of us have heard the Christmas carol "We Three Kings of Orient Are," but in fact, the three "kings" are never referred to as kings in the Bible. Additionally, they are not referred to as a group of three. The only reference to the number three is the number of gifts they carried. [Matthew 2:7-11]

5 MARY MAGDALENE'S CAREER

Nowhere in the Bible does it say that Mary Magdalene was a prostitute. In fact, she is barely mentioned at all. Aside from her presence at the resurrection, the only other thing the Bible does say is that she was possessed by seven demons. [Luke 8:2]

4 THE PRODIGAL SON

Contrary to popular belief, "prodigal" means "characterized by a profuse or wasteful expenditure." It is not a reference to leaving or returning. [Luke 15:11-32]

3 EMPEROR CONSTANTINE AND THE BIBLE

The Emperor Constantine did not define the canon of the New Testament at the first Council of Nicaea in 325 AD; in fact, the Council did not even make mention of the Biblical canon. It was already defined by common use by the early second century in the form in which it is still found in Catholic Bibles. Another little known fact is the Emperor Constantine had no voting power at the Council; he was there merely as an observer. [Canons of the Council of Nicaea]

2 ADAM AND EVE'S FRUIT

Contrary to popular belief, Adam and Eve did not eat an apple in the book of Genesis. The fruit is not actually named at all; it is referred to only as the fruit of "the tree of Knowledge of Good and Evil." The reason this misconception has come about is most likely due to the fact that in Middle English, the word "apple" was used to refer to all fruit and nuts (except berries). Over the centuries, this word has stuck in reference to the Genesis fruit. [Genesis 2:17]

1 CHANGING TEXT

Some people believe that over the centuries, the Bible text has been altered to suit the ideologies of the editors. In fact, there are only a very small number of textual alterations that modern philologists and critics consider intentional changes; most are simply errors in spelling or copying. Bart D. Ehrman, a New Testament textual critic, says:

> "It would be a mistake . . . to assume that the only changes being made were by copyists with a personal stake in the wording of the text. In fact, most of the changes found in our early Christian manuscripts have nothing to do with theology or ideology. Far and away the [sic] most changes are the result of mistakes, pure and simple—slips of the pen, accidental omissions, inadvertent additions, misspelled words, blunders of one sort or another."

Aside from the removal of a number of books in the sixteenth century by Martin Luther, the text of the books that comprise the full canon of the Bible is essentially the same now as it was in the second century.

✳✳✳✳✳✳

TOP 10 UNUSUAL PATRON SAINTS

10 SAINT GERTRUDE OF NIVELLES, PATRON SAINT OF THE FEAR OF MICE (SURIPHOBIA)

Saint Gertrude was the younger daughter of Blessed Pepin I of Landen and Blessed Ida of Nivelles; she was the sister of Saint Begga. She became devoted to religious life from an early age, and turned down a noble marriage to pursue the religious life. On the death of Pepin in 639, and on the advice of Saint Amand of Maastricht, Ida built a double monastery at Nivelles where both she and her daughter retired. Gertrude became abbess about age twenty. She was known for her hospitality to pilgrims and aid to Irish missionary monks. She gave land to Saint Foillan, on which he built the monastery of Fosses, and helped Saint Ultan in his evangelization. In 656, Gertrude resigned her office in favor of her niece, Saint Wilfetrudis, and spent the rest of her days studying Scripture and doing penance. She is normally depicted with mice running up her staff or dress.

9 SAINT SCHOLASTICA, PATRON SAINT OF CONVULSIVE CHILDREN

St. Scholastica, sister of St. Benedict, consecrated her life to God from her earliest youth. After her brother went to Monte Cassino, where he established his famous monastery, she took up her abode in the neighborhood at Plombariola, where she founded and governed a monastery of nuns, about five miles from that of St. Benedict, who, it appears, also directed his sister and her nuns. She died about the year 543, and St. Benedict followed her soon after. Her feast day is February tenth.

8 SAINT HUBERT OF LIEGE, PATRON SAINT OF MAD DOGS

Saint Hubert was the grandson of Charibert, King of Toulouse, and the eldest son of Bertrand, Duke of Aquitaine. Hubert was passionately devoted to hunting. While hunting a stag on a Good Friday morning, he received a vision of a crucifix between its antlers. When his wife died soon after this incident, Hubert renounced all his worldly positions, titles, and wealth, handed his patrimony, and the care of his son, to his brother, and studied for the priesthood. He was highly revered in the Middle Ages; there were several military orders named in his honor. His association with the hunt led to his patronage of furriers and trappers and against rabies and bad behavior in dogs, primarily hunting dogs.

7 SAINT MONICA, PATRON SAINT OF ALCOHOLICS

Saint Monica was the mother of Saint Augustine of Hippo, whose writings about her are the primary source of our information. A Christian from birth, she was given in marriage to a bad-tempered pagan named Patricius. She prayed constantly for the conversion of her husband (who converted on his deathbed), and of her son (who converted after a wild life). She was the spiritual student of Saint Ambrose of Milan and was, herself, a reformed alcoholic, hence her patronage of alcoholics.

6 SAINT DOMINIC SAVIO, PATRON SAINT OF JUVENILE DELINQUENTS

St. Dominic Savio was one of ten children of a blacksmith and seamstress. He was a protege of Saint John Bosco and an altar boy at age five. At twelve he entered the Oratory School preparatory to becoming a priest. He was well liked and pious, but his health forced him to give up his dream of the priesthood. He died at age fifteen and his dying words were, "What beautiful things I see!"

5 SAINT ISIDORE OF SEVILLE, PATRON SAINT OF THE INTERNET

St. Isidore was the Archbishop of Seville around 601, succeeding his brother to the position. He was a teacher, founder, and reformer. He was a prolific writer whose works include a dictionary, an encyclopedia, a history of Goths, and a history of the world beginning with creation. He completed the Mozarabic liturgy, which is still in use in Toledo, Spain, and presided at the Second Council of Seville, and the Fourth Council of Toledo. He also introduced the works of Aristotle to Spain. He was proclaimed Doctor of the Church by Pope Benedict XIV in 1722, and became the leading candidate for patron of computer users and the Internet in 1999.

4 SAINT BRENDAN THE NAVIGATOR, PATRON SAINT OF WHALES

St. Brendan was the brother of Saint Briga. He was educated by Saint Ita of Killeedy and Saint Erc of Kerry and was a friend of Saint Columba, Saint Brendan of Birr, Saint Brigid, and Saint Enda of Arran. He was ordained in 512 and built monastic cells at Ardfert, Shankeel, Aleth, Plouaret, Inchquin Island, and Annaghdown in Ireland. The legend which led to his patronage of whales is as follows: Brendan and his brothers figure in Brendan's Voyage, a tale of monks traveling the high seas of the Atlantic, evangelizing to the islands, possibly reaching the Americas in the sixth century. At one point they stop on a small island, celebrate Easter Mass, light a fire, and then learn the island is an enormous whale!

3 SAINT RENE GOUPIL, PATRON SAINT OF ANESTHESIOLOGISTS

St. Rene Goupil studied medicine, and in 1639 offered to work as a medic for the Jesuit missionaries in America. He acted as missionary to the Hurons, working as a *donné*, a layman who worked without pay. He worked in a hospital in Quebec, Canada, in 1640 and was an assistant to Saint Isaac Jogues on his missionary travels. He was captured and tortured by Iroquois, enemies of the Huron, for making the sign of the cross over a child's head. While they were in captivity, Father Isaac received Goupil into the Jesuits as a religious brother. He is the first North American martyr and his death by tomahawk in the head led to his patronage of people who work with or receive anesthesia.

2 SAINT POLYCARP, PATRON SAINT AGAINST DYSENTERY

Saint Polycarp was an associate of, converted by, and disciple of Saint John the Apostle. He was also a friend of Saint Ignatius of Antioch. He fought against Gnosticism and became the Bishop of Smyrna (modern Izmir, Turkey). He was a revered Christian leader during the first half of the second century. The Asia Minor churches recognized Polycarp's leadership and chose him to be representative to Pope Anicetus on the question of the date of the Easter celebration. Only one of the many letters written by Polycarp has survived, the one he wrote to the Church of Philippi, Macedonia. At eighty-six, Polycarp was to be burned alive in a stadium in Smyrna; the flames did not harm him, so he was killed by a dagger and his body was burned. The "Acts" of Polycarp's martyrdom are the earliest preserved reliable account of a Christian martyr's death.

1 SAINT FIACRE, PATRON SAINT OF SEXUALLY TRANSMITTED DISEASE

Saint Fiacre was raised in an Irish monastery, which, in the seventh century, were great repositories of learning, including the use of healing herbs, a skill studied by Fiacre. His knowledge and holiness caused followers to flock to him, which destroyed the holy isolation he sought. Fleeing to France, he established a hermitage in a cave near a spring, and was given land for his hermitage by Saint Faro of Meaux, who was bishop at the time. Saint Fiacre is also the patron saint of gardeners and taxi drivers.

❋❋❋❋❋❋

TOP 10 UNUSUAL MORMON BELIEFS

10 TITHING
While tithes are not uncommon among religions, rarely are they mandatory. LDS (Latter-Day Saints) theology states that in order to make it to the highest kingdom of heaven, you must pay a full and honest tithe.

9 PLEASURE IN LIFE
This is one of the most famous pieces of LDS doctrine. It's also the cause of many myths about Mormons. Basically, it means no coffee, drugs, or tobacco.

8 SPIRITS
This one is very unique to the LDS faith. Basically, everyone on Earth now was a spirit in the pre-existence. When we die, our spirits are separated from our bodies and if we were good they go to "spirit paradise." If we were bad they go to "spirit prison." The spirit world exists as a place for spirits to go while awaiting the second coming.

7 MODERN REVELATION
Almost everyone who knows anything about the Mormon religion knows they have a prophet. What many don't know is that anything the prophet says in an official capacity is considered official canon.

6 JESUS VISITED THE AMERICAS
The Book of Mormon is a book of LDS scripture that takes place during the same time as the Bible and takes place on the American continent. It follows the stories of two tribes who descended from the family of Lehi. After Jesus' resurrection LDS people believe he visited the peoples of the Americas.

5 THE NATURE OF GOD
While most religions believe in God, the LDS religion believes in God, Jesus, and the Holy Spirit as completely separate beings. They also believe that God, Jesus, and resurrected beings have bodies of "flesh and bone."

4 PRIESTHOOD

In the LDS religion any worthy male can be given the priesthood and specific duties. Black people were not allowed to have the priesthood until 1978. Females are not allowed to have the priesthood.

3 MULTIPLE HEAVENS

In LDS doctrine there are three heavens: the Celestial Kingdom, Terrestrial Kingdom, and Telestial Kingdom. The Celestial is the highest, where God and the ones who followed his law reside. The Terrestrial is the middle, where people who followed the Law of Moses reside. The Telestial is the lowest, where the ones who followed carnal law reside.

2 FORGIVENESS

In LDS theology you can be forgiven for any sin, save two. First, denying the Holy Spirit, and second, murder. Also, God is infinitely forgiving, until the second coming. After that, you end up where you end up, no matter what. There are no second chances. Period.

1 MULTIPLE WORLDS AND MULTIPLE GODS

This deserves some explanation. Mormons believe that God created multiple worlds and each world has people living on it. They also believe that multiple Gods exist but each has their own universe. We are only subject to our God and if we obtain the highest level of heaven we can become gods ourselves.

✳✳✳✳✳✳

TOP 10 UNIQUE ASPECTS OF CATHOLICISM

10 THE SCAPULAR

The scapular is a type of necklace worn by many Catholics. It is worn across the scapular bones (hence its name) and it consists of two pieces of wool connected by string. One piece of wool rests on the back while the other piece rests on the chest. When a Catholic wishes to wear the scapular, a priest says a set of special prayers and blesses the scapular. This only occurs the first time a person wears one.

For wearing the scapular, Catholics believe that Mary, the mother of Jesus, will ensure they do not die a horrible death (for example by fire or drowning) and that they will have access to a priest for confession and the last rites before they die. As a condition for wearing the scapular and receiving these benefits, the Catholic must say certain prayers every day.

The brown scapular, known as the Scapular of Our Lady of Mount Carmel, is the most commonly worn scapular, though others do exist. When the scapular is worn out it is either buried or burned and a new one is worn in its place.

9 THE CILICE

A cilice is an item worn on the body to inflict pain or discomfort for the sake of penance (remorse for your past actions). Originally a cilice was an undergarment made of rough hair (such as a hairshirt) or cloth. In recent times it has been seen as more discreet to wear a chain with spikes on it. Contrary to popular belief, the cilice does not break the skin—it merely causes discomfort. It is usually worn around the thigh.

In recent years the cilice has gained a great deal of publicity due to the book *The Da Vinci Code*, in which it is worn by the main antagonist of the story, though in the story it is exaggeratedly described as causing wounds. Wearing the cilice has always been an optional practice for Catholics. Some famous people in the past to have worn them are Saint Thomas More and Saint Patrick.

8 THE FLAGRUM

The flagrum is a type of scourge with small hard objects attached to the length of its cords. It is traditionally used to whip oneself (self-flagellation) and is most commonly found in conservative religious orders. The flagrum is held in one hand and thrown over the shoulder in order to cause the cords to strike the flesh. The purpose of self-flagellation is voluntary penance and mortification of the flesh (a safeguard against committing further sins).

The most famous saint to use the flagrum is probably Saint John Vianney, who would give his parishioners very light penances in confession and then flog himself in privacy for their benefit (it is believed by Catholics that acts of penance can be offered for the sins of other living people or the souls of the dead). When

Saint John Vianney died, the walls of his bedroom had spatterings of blood on them from his extreme use of the flagrum.

Most Catholics who practice this form of discipline will not admit it publicly as it would be seen as a lack of humility that could lead to the sin of pride.

7 CONFRATERNITIES OF THE CORD

The third (and final) of the penance-related objects, the Confraternities of the Cord are groups who wear a knotted cord around their waist as a form of penance and in order to help prevent future sins. The cord can be worn loosely in remembrance of the saint for whom the cord is named, or it can be worn tight enough to cause pain, as has been the case with numerous saints in history.

St. Joseph, St. Francis, St. Thomas, St. Augustine, St. Nicholas, and St. Monica all have Confraternities of the Cord named after them. The *Catholic Encylopedia* says, "In the early Church virgins wore a cincture as a sign and emblem of purity, and hence it has always been considered a symbol of chastity as well as of mortification and humility. The wearing of a cord or cincture in honor of a saint is of very ancient origin, and we find the first mention of it in the life of St. Monica."

The various confraternities differ in the number of knots on the cord.

6 RELIC

Relics are objects related to saints. There are three categories of relics:

First Class: The physical remains of a saint or anything relating to Jesus (such as the cross on which he was crucified).

Second Class: An item worn by or owned by a saint.

Third Class: Anything that has touched a first- or second-class relic of a saint.

In order to prevent abuses, Catholic Church law (canon law) forbids the sale of relics (Can. 1190 §1). Catholics venerate relics in the same way as they venerate images, statues, and saints. This is often confused for idol worship, but veneration is actually the act of giving respect, rather than the act of worshipping, which is forbidden. By canon law there must be a relic in the altar stone of any altar in a Catholic Church upon which Mass is to be offered.

5 INDULGENCES

Catholics believe that when a person sins, they have two punishments to suffer: eternal (Hell) and temporal (punishment by suffering on Earth or in

Purgatory). Indulgences are special actions that a person can perform in order to reduce or remove the temporal punishment they are owed. The idea behind it is that certain acts of holiness can take the place of punishment. Indulgences must be declared by the Pope.

There are two types of indulgence: plenary (removes all temporal punishment) and partial (removes some punishment). A partial indulgence can be for a specific number of days or years. Some indulgences only apply to the souls in Purgatory but any personal indulgences can also be offered for those souls, rather than your own. An example of an indulence is "an indulgence, applicable only to the Souls in Purgatory, is granted to the faithful, who devoutly visit a cemetery and pray, even if only mentally, for the departed. The indulgence is plenary each day from the 1st to the 8th of November; on other days of the year it is partial" (from the Enchiridion of Indulgences).

During the Middle Ages, a number of bishops and priests, seeking to make money, told people that they could pay for indulgences. This abuse partly contributed to the sparking off of the Protestant Reformation. While the Catholic Church tried to suppress this behavior, it took a great deal of time for the traffic in indulgences to stop completely.

It is quite common for the Pope to announce new indulgences from time to time to mark special occasions, such as the Jubilee in which Pope John Paul II granted a plenary indulgence.

4 THE REAL PRESENCE

The "Real Presence" is used to describe the bread and wine in a Catholic Mass. Catholics believe that after the words of consecration have been spoken by the priest, the bread (host) and wine change their substance to become the body and blood of Jesus. It is considered by Catholics, therefore, to be appropriate to worship and adore the changed objects, which is often seen as idol worship by non-Catholics as they do not believe the change of substance has occurred.

Because of this belief, Catholics have a special ceremony called Benediction, in which a consecrated host is placed in an ornate case called a monstrance and the people are blessed with it and kneel and pray before it.

An interesting side note is that it is believed that the modern term "hocus pocus" comes from an aberration of the words used by a priest at the moment of the consecration, in which he says, "*Hoc est enim corpus Meum*," meaning "for this is My body."

3 EXORCISM

Exorcism is the practice of evicting demons or other evil spiritual entities from a person or place believed to have been possessed (taken control of). Solemn exorcisms, according to the canon law of the church, can only be exercised by an ordained priest (or higher prelate), with the express permission of the local bishop, and only after a careful medical examination to exclude the possibility of mental illness.

During the ritual of exorcism, the priest commands the devils within the body of the afflicted to leave and uses a number of blessings with Holy Water and oils. Of interesting note, the Catholic Church gave permission for a priest to appear in the film *The Exorcist* on the grounds that is was true to the methods used by the church to determine whether an exorcism is warranted.

2 PAPAL INFALLIBILITY

Roman Catholics believe that, under certain circumstances, the Pope is infallible (that is, he cannot make a mistake). The Catholic Church defines three conditions under which the Pope is infallible: 1) the Pope must be making a decree on matters of faith or morals; 2) the declaration must be binding on the whole church; and 3) the Pope must be speaking with the full authority of the Papacy, and not in a personal capacity.

This means that when the Pope is speaking on matters of science, he can make errors (as we have seen in the past with issues such as heliocentricity). However, when he is teaching a matter of religion and the other two conditions above are met, Catholics consider the decree is equal to the Word of God. It cannot contradict any previous declarations and must be believed by all Catholics. Catholics believe that if a person denies any of these solemn decrees, they are committing a mortal sin—the type of sin that sends a person to hell. Here is an example of an infallible decree from the Council of Trent (under Pope Pius V):

> "If anyone denies that in the sacrament of the most Holy Eucharist are contained truly, really and substantially the body and blood together with the soul and divinity of our Lord Jesus Christ, and consequently the whole Christ, but says that He is in it only as in a sign, or figure or force, let him be anathema."

The last section of the final sentence, "let him be anathema," is a standard phrase that normally appears at the end of an infallible statement and means "let him be cursed."

1 STIGMATA

Stigmata is when a person has unexplained wounds on their body that coincide with the traditional wounds that Christ had. In some cases the wounds can appear in only one or two of the areas, but there have been instances of it occurring in all five places that Christ was wounded. The wounds can cause considerable pain, which has been known to worsen on certain religious feast days. There have been occasional cases of falsified stigmata in the past and some people claim that even those not proven to be falsified are somehow part of a hoax. It is also alleged that Saint Pio was able to bilocate (appear in two places at once) and to read the sins on a person's soul.

✳✳✳✳✳✳

TOP 10
STRANGE LEGENDS
AND IMAGES OF SAINTS

10 SAINT DYMPHNA

St. Dymphna's story is truly sad, but one that parallels many popular folk legends. Dymphna was a virgin daughter of a pagan king. She secretly baptized into Christianity. After her mother died, her father became insane with grief and declared that he would only marry another woman as beautiful as his wife. Eventually he noticed that Dymphna, his own daughter, shared his wife's beauty. He determined to marry her, but the girl fled from him in horror, accompanied by a trusted priest. They sought sanctuary elsewhere but were found by her father's men. The priest was promptly killed, and her father once again proposed to her. She refused to marry him, and he himself struck off her head. Dymphna is depicted as a beautiful, virginal, young girl. She is often holding a holy Bible and white flowers. She is the patroness of incest victims and the mentally disturbed.

9 SIMON ZELOTES

Simon Zelotes (or Simon the Zealot) was one of the twelve disciples. He had previously been a violent man but was converted by Jesus. Not much is known of his life after Jesus' death, but he is believed to have traveled widely preaching the gospel. Legend has it that he was martyred in Mesopotamia by being hung upside down and sawed to death, longitudinally. He is often depicted holding the saw that was the instrument of his martyrdom.

8 SAINT APOLLONIA

St. Apollonia was an old deaconess who fell victim to the persecutions of Christians in Alexandria. As Christians fled the city, Apollonia was seized by a mob. They beat her and knocked all her teeth out. They then lit a huge fire to burn her if she did not renounce Christianity. Begging for time as though she would comply with their demands, instead she jumped into the flames herself and died without renouncing her faith. She is the patroness of dentists, and is depicted holding pincers containing her tooth or with a gold tooth on a necklace.

7 SAINT MARGARET OF ANTIOCH

St. Margaret of Antioch was a popular saint in the Middle Ages. Legend states she was the daughter of a pagan priest, but decided to convert to Christianity. This angered her father as well as a suitor whose advances she rejected. They had her reported to the authorities as a Christian, and she was jailed. In jail she met the devil in the form of a dragon who proceeded to swallow her whole. The cross she carried, however, irritated the dragon's belly, and she was able to tear her way out using the cross and emerge whole from the dragon. Several attempts were then made to execute her by drowning and fire, all of which failed, leading many who witnessed her tortures to be converted. She was finally beheaded. She is often depicted emerging from the dragon's belly, cross in hand. Appropriately, she is the patroness of childbirth.

6 SAINT BARTHOLOMEW

St. Bartholomew is one of the apostles of Christ. After Christ's death he traveled the world as far as India, evangelizing and preaching the gospel. He fell afoul with the pagans in Armenia where he was martyred. Legend states he was flayed alive (removing the skin from the body while keeping it as intact as possible), and then crucified upside down on a cross. He is the saint invoked by those who deal with skins and leather and is depicted in art as a man holding his flayed skin.

5 SAINT ROCH

St. Roch was born of nobility but soon renounced his life of wealth and privilege and traveled the country effecting many healings of plague victims. When he too contracted the plague, he retreated to a secret hut in the woods. He was there befriended by a dog, who brought him sustenance and licked the sores on his leg until he was healed. When he eventually returned to civilization, many who had previously known him were dead. He was imprisoned, and with his dog  continued to minister to suffering prisoners until his death. He is the patron saint of dogs and is invoked against diseased body parts. He is depicted lifting one hem of his robe to reveal his leg sores, while his faithful dog licks them.

4 SAINT AGATHA OF SICILY

As a beautiful woman St. Agatha attracted the attentions of a powerful judge named Quintianus. When she refused his advances he had her sent to a brothel. She prayed and after thirty days remained still untouched. Quintianus then ordered she be chained, whipped, stretched on a rack, and burned. During these tortures her breasts were cut off. Legend states St. Peter miraculously healed her wound that night. The enraged Quintianus then had her rolled on hot coals and glass until she finally expired. She is the patron saint of breast cancer sufferers. She is depicted carrying her breasts on a plate. On her saint day, February fifth, in Sicily, little marzipan confections resembling breasts are still eaten today.

3 SAINT LUCY

St. Lucy as a young girl decided to devote her life to Christ and refused to marry the groom selected by her mother. Though her mother eventually accepted her decision, her jilted suitor was not so generous and reported her as a Christian to the authorities. Trying unsuccessfully to force her into prostitution, the soldiers found her body strangely heavy and immovable. Thus as punishment, she was tortured by having her eyes gouged out, and then killed. Legend states that God restored her sight before she died. She is represented in iconography as a young martyr holding her eyes on a plate, and is the patron saint of eye problems and blindness.

2 SAINT DENIS

St. Denis had an exceptional youth, testifying and converting pagans to Christianity. He eventually became bishop of Paris. His many conversions, however, ultimately enraged the pagan priests, who decided to execute him by beheading. Legend states that after his head was chopped off, St. Denis picked it up and walked several miles with it tucked under his arm, preaching all the way. He is represented as a headless body holding its decapitated head in its hands.

1 SAINT CHRISTOPHER

St. Christopher belonged to a tribe in North Africa known as the Marmaritae. That area of the world was then largely unknown and considered inhabited by all sorts of strange creatures, including dog-headed men. Some conflicting legends surround Christopher. In one, he is a dog-head captured by the Romans and forced to serve them. He becomes a Christian convert and thus a unique figure among his kind. Another legend has St. Christopher carrying an infant across a river, only to find him growing unbelievably heavy as they progress. The child then reveals himself to be the Christ child and his heaviness is due to the weight of the world on his shoulders. Still other legends exist about St. Christopher where he is actually being granted the face of a dog by God, to ward off unwanted female attention. He is often depicted as a richly robed dog-headed man—a cynocephalus.

CHAPTER TWELVE
Science

TOP 10 FASCINATING "FACTS" THAT ARE WRONG

10 "PEENUTS"

False Fact: A scientific study on peanuts in bars found traces of over one hundred unique specimens of urine.

After rigorous searching for more information, it turns out that no scientific study (or non-scientific study for that matter) has ever been conducted into peanuts at bars. However, there was a study on ice cubes in UK bars in 2003, which discovered that 44 percent of ice cubes tested contained coliform bacteria, bacteria from human poop. Even more shockingly, 5 percent were infected with the potentially deadly E. Coli bacteria. So, next time you are in London, pass on the ice and enjoy some peanuts instead.

9 ELEVATOR FREEFALL

False Fact: Elevators have killed or can kill when their cables snap.

There is a small element of truth to this "fact," but we will get to that soon. Elevators usually have a minimum of four operating cables, as well as a built-in braking system and a backup braking system in the shaft, which forces a wedge into the shaft to prevent too rapid a drop. If the cables were all to snap (and elevator cables are strong), the car's braking system would detect the freefall and automatically apply. If that also fails, the shaft's braking system takes over. There has been one recorded account of a complete elevator freefall, caused by an airplane crash into the Empire State Building in 1945. The crash caused the cables in the elevator to be weakened, ultimately leading to them breaking. The person riding the lift, Betty Lou Oliver, survived the seventy-five-floor freefall because of air pressure beneath the car.

8 FOLDING PAPER

False Fact: You can't fold a piece of paper in half more than seven times.

This is one we all hear regularly and we believe because it was true when we tried it. But, in 2002 a high school student, Britney Gallivan, proved it wrong by folding a piece of thin gold leaf more than seven times with the use of tweezers.

To further prove that it could be done, she bought a giant roll of toilet paper from the Internet, and she and her family took it to the local mall where they attempted to fold it more than seven times. Seven hours of folding later, they had it folded into twelve folds.

7 JUMPING ELEPHANTS

False Fact: Elephants are the only mammals that can't jump.

First of all, it is true that adult elephants can't jump—if by jumping we mean the state of having no feet on the ground at the same time after propelling oneself from a stationary position. But, contrary to the popular myth it is the only mammal that cannot, it is joined by a few others: the sloth is unable to jump, which suits its lazy lifestyle rather well and rhinoceroses and hippopotamuses also cannot jump, though unlike elephants, when they run it is possible for them to have all four feet off the ground.

6 OLD DOGS

False Fact: One dog year is equal to seven human years.

This bogus fact is usually worked out so that a dog life is equal to a human life in total years, but the numbers just don't add up. The average human life expectancy is seventy-eight, while the average dog life expectancy (in false dog years) would equal around ninety years. Furthermore, different dog breeds have dramatically different life expectancies, ranging from a short six years to thirteen or more years (in general, the smaller the dog, the longer its life expectancy). Dogs have a very short "childhood" and a very long middle age, making the comparison completely invalid.

5 OFFER TO BUY

False Fact: If someone wrongly advertises goods for the wrong price, they have to sell it to you at that price.

This is a very popular misconception and people argue about it in stores. But the reality is a little more bland. A store price is an "invitation to bargain" not an "invitation to buy." This is true in the United States, United Kingdom, Commonwealth nations, and probably the rest of the Western world. If a shop makes a mistake, they can simply continue to sell the goods at the normal price.

Attempts to defraud by advertising lower prices are caught in other consumer laws. However, it should be noted that if an electronic transaction is completed you may be eligible to keep the goods if a mistake is made.

4 SPACE DUST

False Fact: NASA invented the DustBuster.

First of all, how do you vacuum in a vacuum? You don't, so why would NASA need a vacuum cleaner for its space missions? It didn't, but what it did need was a small battery powered drill, so they teamed up with Black and Decker to come up with the perfect device. Once the device had been realized, Black and Decker was left with great technology from which they eventually developed the DustBuster and other useful home devices.

3 POLAR BEARS

False Fact: Polar bears are left-handed.

Where this myth came from is now lost in the dark recesses of history. The spread of this myth is quite extraordinary with more Google results announcing it as gospel than not. But in reality, scientists who have spent their working lives studying polar bears have found that they are actually ambidextrous (they use both hands equally well). It is possible that the myth was started when people observed the bears working well with their left hands, but they neglected to notice they also worked well with their right.

2 MCDONALD'S WARS

False Fact: No two countries with McDonald's franchises have ever gone to war.

This theory was proposed by Thomas Friedman and became massively popular all around the world. It was used to show that countries loving democracy (those most likely to have a McDonald's franchise) have lived peacefully together due to the merits of that political system (this is also called the Democratic Peace Theory and the Golden Arches Theory of Conflict Resolution). Friedman proposed this theory in his book *The Lexus and the Olive Tree*. So, is it true? No. Georgia and Russia were recently at war with each other and both have McDonald's. Furthermore, Israel and Lebanon also defy the theory for their conflict in 2006, and right after Friedman's book was published, NATO bombed Serbia, again disproving the idea.

1 THE GREAT WALL

False Fact: The Great Wall of China is the only man-made structure visible from space.

Well, this is wrong on many levels. While you are still close enough to Earth to actually see the Great Wall, you can also see road networks and other large objects created by man. There is, in fact, no distance from Earth in which you can only see the Great Wall. By the time you get a few thousand miles away, you can see nothing man-made. Astronaut Alan Bean said, "The only thing you can see from the moon is a beautiful sphere, mostly white (clouds), some blue (ocean), patches of yellow (deserts), and every once in a while some green vegetation. No man-made object is visible on this scale. In fact, when first leaving Earth's orbit and only a few thousand miles away, no manmade object is visible at that point either."

✳✳✳✳✳✳

TOP 10 COMMON MEDICAL MYTHS

10 SUGAR HYPERACTIVITY

Myth: Sugar makes kids hyperactive.

Dr. Vreeman and Dr. Carroll, both pediatricians at the Riley Hospital for Children, recently said, "In at least 12 double-blinded, randomized, controlled trials, scientists have examined how children react to diets containing different levels of sugar. None of these studies, not even studies looking specifically at children with attention deficit-hyperactivity disorder, could detect any differences in behavior between the children who had sugar and those who did not." This includes artificial and natural sources of sugar. Interestingly, in the study, parents who were told their children had been given sugar when they hadn't, noted that the child was more hyperactive. So it seems it is all in the parent's mind.

9 BODY HEAT

Myth: You lose most of your body heat through your head.

A military study many years ago tested the loss of temperature in soldiers when exposed to very cold temperatures. They found rapid heat loss in the head, and so the idea that we lose heat through our heads was born. But what they didn't tell you was that the soldiers were fully clothed except for their heads. This obviously skews the statistics considerably. The fact is, completely naked, you lose approximately 10 percent of your body heat through the head; the other 90 percent is lost via the other parts of your body.

8 WATER CONSUMPTION

Myth: You should drink at least eight glasses of water a day.

The origins of this myth is most likely due to the fact that a 1945 government agency said the human body needed around eight glasses of fluid a day. This included the fluid from all of the foods we eat and drinks like tea and coffee. Somehow over time "fluid" turned to "water" and the modern water myth arose. This also lead to silly slogans like "if you are thirsty it is too late," a concept that would seem to have been invented by water bottlers who have something to gain from excess water consumption in the population in general. So, in reality, if you are thirsty, drink some water. If you are not, don't.

7 GUMMED UP

Myth: Chewing gum takes seven years to pass through your system.

We have all been told at least once in our life by a concerned adult not to swallow gum as it will take seven years to leave our bodies. This is right up there with the whole "fruit seed growing a tree in your stomach" silliness, but while most adults realize the tree story is a myth, they don't realize that the gum one is too. It is true that gum is not digestible in the human body, but it simply passes whole through your system. It doesn't stick to your insides; it just continues along with any food you have eaten and pops out the other end. This myth may have partly arisen from the fact that swallowing gum was once viewed as lower class and ignorant.

6 ARTHRITIC KNUCKLES

Myth: Cracking your knuckles will cause arthritis in later life.

The cracking sound in the knuckles is caused by bones moving apart and forming a gas bubble; the sound is the bubble bursting. It is quite common to hear someone warning a knuckle-cracker they will get arthritis, but the worst that can happen to a compulsive cracker is that their finger joints may weaken over time. Arthritis is caused by a variety of things (such as crystal formations in the case of gout), but knuckle-cracking isn't one of them.

5 BABY TEETH
Myth: Teething causes a fever.

Scientific studies have been done in the area of teething, which show no correlation at all between fever and teething. If your baby is suffering from a new tooth and they also have a fever, it is advisable to check for other causes of the fever. The same is true of diarrhea, which is also often blamed on teething in infants. It is always better to be safe than sorry when dealing with the health of children.

4 CANCER TREATMENT
Myth: Cancer treatment is painful and pointless; furthermore, cancer is incurable.

While this may have been almost true thirty years ago, medical advances have meant that modern cancer treatments are far more effective and cause less suffering for the patient. A few decades ago, 90 percent of children with leukemia died; today 80 percent survive. Many people think cancer is incurable as there isn't a "one drug fixes all" cure, but there are many people who are completely cured of cancer. Various drugs exist to treat different types of cancer, and many of them are extremely effective and well worth trying if you do get the disease.

3 BACK PAIN
Myth: Back pain should be treated with bed rest.

The opposite is actually true in this case. Bed rest can prevent the lower back from fully recovering, or, at the very least, delay the recovery significantly. Patients who continue to engage in ordinary activities recover faster and usually have fewer problems with recurring pain and other back troubles. Interestingly, many studies have shown that this is not just true of back problems but also many other medical problems. Thirty-nine independent studies found bed rest to be more harmful than good in a broad range of illnesses.

2 TURKEY SLEEP

Myth: Eating turkey makes you sleepy because it contains tryptophan.

This is one of the most common myths on this list and it pops up every year around Thanksgiving. But actually, chicken and ground beef contain almost identical quantities of tryptophan as turkey does. Other foods such as cheese and pork contain significantly more of the chemical than turkey. So why do people think turkey makes them sleepy? It is most likely due to turkey appearing at very large meals often eaten during the day rather than the evening. The heavy meal slows blood flow, which can cause drowsiness, and the timing can have a huge psychological impact. In other words, you are imagining it.

1 MIDNIGHT SNACKS

Myth: Eating at night makes you fat.

Secret snackers rejoice! This is a complete myth. It doesn't matter what time of day you eat as long as you eat only the total calories that you burn each day, you will not gain weight. If you eat fewer calories than you burn, you will lose weight, and if you eat more calories, you will gain. It is as simple as that. Having said that, the routine of three meals a day at the same time each day can have other benefits in life (routine is good and it helps humans work more effectively), but snacks at night are no worse than snacks in the morning or afternoon.

❋❋❋❋❋❋

TOP 10 SCIENTISTS KILLED OR INJURED BY THEIR EXPERIMENTS

10 KARL SCHEELE—DIED FROM TASTING HIS DISCOVERIES

Scheele was a brilliant pharmaceutical chemist who discovered many chemical elements: the most notable of which were oxygen (though Joseph Priestley published his findings first), molybdenum, tungsten, manganese, and chlorine. He also discovered a process very similar to pasteurization. Scheele had the habit of taste testing his discoveries and, fortunately, managed to survive his taste-test of hydrogen cyanide. But, alas, his luck was to run out: he died of symptoms strongly resembling mercury poisoning.

9 JEAN-FRANCOIS DE ROZIER—FIRST VICTIM OF AN AIR CRASH

Jean-Francois was a teacher of physics and chemistry. In 1783 he witnessed the world's first balloon flight, which created in him a passion for flight. After assisting in the untethered flight of a sheep, a chicken, and a duck, he took the first manned free flight in a balloon. He traveled at an altitude of three thousand feet using a hot air balloon. Not stopping there, De Rozier planned a crossing of the English Channel from France to England. Unfortunately, it was his last flight; after reaching fifteen hundred feet in a combined hot air and gas balloon, the balloon deflated, causing him to fall to his death. His fiancée died eight days later, possibly from suicide.

8 SIR DAVID BREWSTER—NEARLY BLINDED

Sir David was a Scottish inventor, scientist, and writer. His field of interest was optics and light polarization, a field requiring excellent vision. Unfortunately for Sir David, he performed a chemical experiment in 1831 that nearly blinded him. While his vision did return, he was plagued with eye troubles until his death. Brewster is well known for having been the inventor of the kaleidoscope, a toy that has brought joy to millions of children over the years.

7 ELIZABETH ASCHEIM—KILLED BY X-RAYS

Elizabeth Fleischman Ascheim married her doctor, Dr. Woolf, shortly after her mother died. Because of his medical position, Woolf was very interested in the new discovery of Wilhelm Conrad Röntgen—x-rays. His new wife became equally interested and she gave up her job as a bookkeeper to undertake studies in electrical science. Eventually she bought an x-ray machine, which she put in her husband's office; this was the first x-ray lab in San Francisco. She and her husband spent some years experimenting with the machine, using themselves as subjects. Unfortunately they did not realize the consequences of their lack of protection, and Elizabeth died of an extremely widespread and violent cancer.

6 ALEXANDER BOGDANOV—KILLED HIMSELF WITH BLOOD

Bogdanov was a Russian physician, philosopher, economist, science fiction writer, and revolutionary. In 1924, he began experiments with blood transfusion, most likely in a search for eternal youth. After eleven transfusions (which he performed on himself), he declared he had suspended his balding, and improved his eyesight. Unfortunately for Bogdanov, the science of transfusion was a young one and he was not one to test the health of the blood he was using or the donor. In 1928, Bogdanov took a transfusion of blood infected with malaria and tuberculosis and consequently died shortly after.

5 ROBERT BUNSEN—BLINDED HIMSELF IN ONE EYE

Robert Bunsen is probably best known for having given his name to the Bunsen burner, which he helped to popularize. He started out his scientific career in organic chemistry but nearly died twice of arsenic poisoning. Shortly after his near-death experiences, he lost the sight in his right eye after an explosion of cacodyl cyanide. These being excellent reasons to change fields, he moved into inorganic chemistry and went on to develop the field of spectroscopy.

4 SIR HUMPHREY DAVY—A CATALOG OF DISASTERS

Sir Humphrey Davy, the brilliant British chemist and inventor, got a very bumpy start to his science career. As a young apprentice he was fired from his job at an apothecary because he caused too many explosions! When he eventually took up the field of chemistry, he had a habit of inhaling the various gases he was dealing with. Fortunately, this bad habit led to his discovery of the anesthetic properties of nitrous oxide. But, unfortunately, this same habit led to him nearly killing himself on many occasions. The frequent poisonings left him an invalid for the remaining two decades of his life. During this time he also permanently damaged his eyes in a nitrogen trichloride explosion.

3 MICHAEL FARADAY—SUFFERED CHRONIC POISONING

Thanks to the injury to Sir Humphrey Davy's eyes, Faraday became his apprentice. He went on to improve on Davy's methods of electrolysis and to make important discoveries in the field of electromagnetics. Unfortunately for him, some of Davy's misfortune rubbed off and Faraday also suffered damage to his eyes in a nitrogen chloride explosion. He spent the remainder of his life suffering chronic chemical poisoning.

2 MARIE CURIE—DIED OF RADIATION EXPOSURE

In 1898, Curie and her husband, Pierre, discovered radium. She spent the remainder of her life performing radiation research and studying radiation therapy. Her constant exposure to radiation led to her contracting leukemia and she died in 1934. Curie is the first and only person to receive two Nobel Prizes in science in two different fields: chemistry and physics. She was also the first female professor at the University of Paris.

1 GALILEO GALILEI—BLINDED HIMSELF

Galileo's work on the refinement of the telescope opened up the dark recesses of the universe for future generations, but it also ruined his eyesight. He was fascinated with the sun and spent many hours staring at it, leading to extreme damage to his retinas. This was the most likely cause of his near-blindness in the last four years of his life. Because of his life's work, he is sometimes referred to as the "father of modern physics."

✳✳✳✳✳✳

TOP 10 SCIENTISTS WHO COMMITTED SUICIDE

10 VIKTOR MEYER

Viktor Meyer was a German chemist and significant contributor to both organic and inorganic chemistry. Born in Berlin in 1848, he is best known for inventing an apparatus to measure vapor densities, the Viktor Meyer apparatus, and for discovering thiophene. A hugely gifted chemist, Meyer was a workaholic whose taxing lifestyle took tolls on his nervous system. After a series of mental breakdowns, he killed himself by taking cyanide in 1897 at the age of forty-nine.

9 DAVID KELLY

David Christopher Kelly was an employee of the United Kingdom Ministry of Defence (MoD), an expert in biological warfare and a former United Nations weapons inspector in Iraq. His doubts about the veracity of the WMD dossier compiled by the Blair Government caused a political scandal, and he was forced to attend a Parliamentary committee hearing about the remarks. A modest man,

David Kelly was savagely grilled by the Committee, and spoke in a voice so soft that the air conditioning had to be turned off so that his words could be heard. On July 17, 2003, Kelly went on his daily walk through the Oxfordshire country, and, according to the official report, swallowed up to twenty-nine painkillers and slashed his wrist. However, many figures, including MPs and paramedics, continue to raise doubts over the exact cause of Kelly's death, with some going so far as to say it was murder.

8 LUDWIG BOLTZMANN

Ludwig Eduard Boltzmann was an Austrian physicist famous for his founding contributions in the fields of statistical mechanics and statistical thermodynamics. He was one of the most important advocates for atomic theory when that scientific model was still highly controversial. Born in Vienna, February 20, 1844, Boltzmann attended the University of Vienna, gaining a Ph.D. degree at age twenty-two and becoming Professor of Mathematical Physics at the University of Graz at age twenty-five. In 1893, he achieved his goal of becoming Professor of Theoretical Physics at the University of Vienna, succeeding his old mentor, Joseph Stefan. Most likely suffering from bipolar disorder, Boltzmann took his own life while on holiday with his family. He is buried in Vienna with a tombstone that reads $S = k * logW$.

7 VALERI LEGASOV

Valeri Alekseevich Legasov was a prominent Soviet scientist in the field of inorganic chemistry and a member of the Academy of Sciences of the USSR. He is most famous for his work as the chief of the investigation committee of the Chernobyl disaster on April 26, 1986.

After the Chernobyl disaster, Legasov became a key member of the government commission formed to investigate the causes of the catastrophe and to plan the liquidation of its consequences. In August 1986, he presented the report of the Soviet delegation at the special meeting of International Atomic Energy Agency in Vienna. His report struck the Western colleagues with the depth of analysis and full honesty in discussing the extent and consequences of the tragedy.

Legasov's open and firm stance, however, caused a lot of trouble for him at home: the Soviet government was very uncomfortable with the frankness and rigor of his position. As a result, when in 1986–1987 his name was twice entered into the list for those to be awarded the title of Hero of Socialist Labor in recognition for his work, both times it was rejected: the second time his name was crossed out by Gorbachev himself. Having exposed himself to the radiation on the ground of Chernobyl, Legasov's health began to rapidly deteriorate, which coupled with his depression over his lack of recognition, led him to take his own life on April 27, 1988. On September 20, 1996, Russian President Boris Yeltsin conferred to Legasov the honorary title of "Hero of the Russian Federation" (posthumously) for his "courage and heroism" shown in the course of the liquidation of the after effects of Chernobyl disaster.

6 HANS BERGER

Hans Berger, born in Neuses, Germany, in 1873, is best known as the first person to record electroencephalograms (EEGs) from human subjects and is the discoverer of the rhythmic alpha brain waves. Berger studied medicine, neurology, psychiatry, and psychology at the University of Jena. He concentrated on neurology, and following the pioneering work done by British scientist Richard Caton on animals, successfully recorded the first EEG from a human in 1924. This allowed him to discover the alpha wave and described, for the first time, the effect epilepsy had on the brain. Disturbed by the rise of Nazism and the effects of the Second World War, Berger hanged himself on June 1, 1941.

5 EDWIN ARMSTRONG

Edwin Armstrong, born December 18, 1890, was an electrical engineer who invented FM radio. He first began work on the idea of FM radio at university, and patented his idea in 1914. However, numerous patent disputes and a blocking attempt by the Radio Corporation of America, who thought it would destroy AM radio, halted its advancement. Determined that FM radio would never succeed, Armstrong jumped from the thirteenth floor of his apartment in 1954. He was sixty-three at the time.

4 NICOLAS LEBLANC

Nicolas Leblanc was a French chemist and surgeon famous for being the first person to manufacture soda from common salt. Born in 1742, Leblanc developed an interest in medicine at a young age and enrolled in the Paris College of Surgeons in 1759. In 1780, he became private physician to the household of Louis Philip II, Duke of Orleans. In 1775, the French Academy of Sciences offered a prize for a process whereby soda ash could be produced from salt. The French Academy wanted to promote the production of much-needed sodium carbonate from inexpensive sodium chloride. By 1791, Nicolas Leblanc had succeeded in producing sodium carbonate from salt by a two-step process. The prize was awarded to Nicolas Leblanc for a process that used sea salt and sulphuric acid as the raw materials. Later, a plant of his own was in operation producing 320 tons of soda ash per year.

Two years later the plant was confiscated by the French revolutionary government, which refused to pay him the prize money he had earned ten years earlier. In 1802, Napoleon returned the plant (but not the prize money) to him, but by then Leblanc was so broke he could not afford to run it. He killed himself in 1806.

3 GEORGE EASTMAN

George Eastman, born in Waterville, New York, in 1854, founded the Eastman Kodak Company and invented roll film, helping to bring photography to the mainstream and planting the seeds for the invention of motion picture film in 1888. In 1874, Eastman became intrigued with photography but was frustrated by the awkward method that required coating a glass plate with a liquid emulsion that had to be used before it dried. In 1884, he patented a photographic medium that replaced fragile glass plates with a photo-emulsion coated on paper rolls. The invention of roll film greatly speeded up the process of recording multiple images. On September 4, 1888, Eastman registered the trademark Kodak. In 1932, Eastman committed suicide, leaving a note that read, "My work is done. Why wait?" He is buried in Rochester, New York.

2 WALLACE CAROTHERS

Wallace Hume Carothers was a chemist credited with the invention of nylon. Carothers was a group leader in DuPont's Experimental Station laboratory, near Wilmington, Delaware, where most polymer research was done. In addition to first developing nylon, he also helped lay the groundwork for neoprene. After receiving his Ph.D., he taught at several universities before he was hired by the DuPont Company to work on fundamental research. After his monumental discovery, Carothers suffered depression stemming from "inventor's block," which coupled with the sudden death of his sister caused him to take his own life by poisoning in 1937. He was forty-one at the time.

1 ALAN TURING

Alan Turing was an English scientist, mathematician, logician, cryptographer, and arguably the greatest British scientist of the twentieth century. Often considered to be the father of modern computer science, Turing provided an influential formalization of the concept of the algorithm and computation with the Turing machine. With the Turing test, he made a significant and characteristically provocative contribution to the debate regarding artificial intelligence: whether it will ever be possible to say a machine is conscious and can think. He later worked at the National Physical Laboratory, creating one of the first designs for a stored-program computer, although it was never actually built. In 1948 he moved to the University of Manchester to work on the Manchester Mark I, then emerging as one of the world's earliest true computers. During the Second World War, Turing worked at Bletchley Park, Britain's code-breaking center, and was for a time head of Hut 8, the section responsible for German naval cryptanalysis. He was largely responsible for the breaking of the German Enigma code. In 1952, he was convicted of "Acts of Gross Indecency," after admitting a sexual relationship with another man. He was given a choice between eighteen months prison time (which, considering his crime, was not exactly wise), or chemical castration, which included side effects such as breast enlargement. He chose the latter. On June 8, 1954, unable to endure the humiliation and pain of his punishment, Turing took his own life by eating an apple laced with cyanide. Despite this, it would take another thirteen years for homosexuality to be decriminalized in Britain.

❋❋❋❋❋❋

TOP 10 DEBUNKED SCIENTIFIC BELIEFS OF THE PAST

10 RAIN FOLLOWS THE PLOW

"Rain follows the plow" is the name given to a climatology concept now completely debunked. The theory said human settlement caused a permanent increase in rainfall, thus enabling man to move to areas previously considered arid. It is this nineteenth-century theory that brought about the settlement of the Great Plains (previously known as the Great American Desert) and parts of South Australia. The theory was eventually refuted by climatologists, and in the settled areas of South Australia, drought brought an end to the attempted settlements.

9 WORLD ICE THEORY

This strange theory has a relatively normal name, but rest assured, the concept is far from it. Hans Hörbiger, an Austrian engineer and inventor, received a vision in 1894 that told him ice was the substance of all basic substances and had created the ice moons, ice planets, and a "global ether." He said, "I knew that Newton had been wrong and that the sun's gravitational pull ceases to exist at three times the distance of Neptune." Unbelievably, this theory got a great deal of support. One of the strongest supporters of the concept was Houston Stewart Chamberlain (British-born posthumous son-in-law of composer Richard Wagner), who went on to become one of the leading theorists behind the development of the Nazi Party in Germany.

8 ALCHEMY

Alchemy has its roots (in the Western world) in ancient Egypt where it combined with metallurgy in a form of early science. The Egyptian alchemists discovered the formulas for making mortar, glass, and cosmetics. From Egypt it eventually spread to the rest of the ancient world and led to modern alchemy in which men would try to turn metals into gold, to conjure up genies, and perform all manner of bizarre not-so-science-like activities. While it has contributed in some ways to modern science, the discipline of true science caused the death of alchemy, which could not stand up to the rigorous testing of its pseudoscience.

7 CALIFORNIA ISLAND

From the sixteenth century, European experts in geography were convinced California was an island separate from the North American mainland. Maps of the time show a large island on the left of the land mass and California continued to appear this way even into the eighteenth century. There was at the time also a rumor that California was an earthly paradise like the Garden of Eden or Atlantis. A romance novel by Garci Rodríguez de Montalvo, *Las Sergas de Esplandián*, from 1510 describes it as, "Know, that on the right hand of the Indies there is an island called California very close to the side of the Terrestrial Paradise; and it is peopled by black women, without any man among them, for they live in the manner of Amazons. The matter was finally put to rest indisputably by the 1774–1776 expeditions of Juan Bautista de Anza. Interestingly, it is likely that within twenty-five-million years, Baja California and part of Southern California really will separate from North America due to tectonic plate movement.

6 GEOCENTRICITY

Geocentricity is the concept that states Earth is the center of the universe and that all other objects move around it. The view was universally embraced in ancient Greece and very similar ideas were held in ancient China. The idea was supported by the fact that the sun, stars, and planets appear

to revolve around Earth, and the physical perception that the Earth is stable and not moving. This was combined with the belief that the Earth was a sphere; belief in a flat Earth was well gone by the third century BC. The geocentric model was eventually displaced with the work of Copernicus, Galileo, and Kepler in the sixteenth century.

5 THE FOUR HUMORS

In classical antiquity right up to modern times, it was believed the body contained four humors: blood, yellow bile, black bile, and phlegm. It was believed that the right balance of these four humors made a person healthy but an excess or decrease in any one of these would cause illness. Because of this belief, treatments of sickness would include bloodletting, purges, and emetics. Occasionally a mixture of herbs would be used to restore the balance. The humors were also applied to foods; for example, wine was choleric (yellow bile). This classification still exists today to some extent, as we refer to some foods as "hot" and others as "dry." The concept of humors was not replaced until 1858 when Rudolf Virchow published theories of cellular pathology.

4 VITALISM

Vitalism states that the functions of living things are controlled by a "vital force" and not biophysical means. Vitalism has a long history in medical philosophies, has ties to the four humors, and is sometimes referred to as a "life spark" and even as the soul. In the Eastern traditions it is essentially the same thing as "qi" or "chi," which is heavily tied into Asian medicinal methods. The concept is (as can be expected) completely rejected by most mainstream scientists. In 1967, Francis Crick, the co-discoverer of the structure of DNA, stated, "And so to those of you who may be vitalists I would make this prophecy: what everyone believed yesterday, and you believe today, only cranks will believe tomorrow."

3 MATERNAL IMPRESSION

Maternal impression is an old belief that a mother's thoughts while pregnant can impart special characteristics on the child in her womb. For many years this idea was used to explain congenital disorders and birth defects. Maternal impression was used to explain the disorder suffered by the Elephant Man: it was suggested his mother was frightened by an elephant while she was pregnant with him, thereby imprinting the memory of an elephant on her child. Depression was also explained in this manner. If a mother had moments of strong sadness during pregnancy, it was believed her child would ultimately suffer from depression in later life. Genetic theory caused the almost complete eradication of this belief in the twentieth century.

2 PHLOGISTON

The theory of phlogiston dates to 1667 when Johann Joachim Becher (a German physicist) suggested there was a fifth element, phlogiston, which was contained within objects that could burn, to go with the four classical elements (earth, water, air, fire). It was believed that when an object burned, it released its phlogiston (an element without taste, mass, odor, or color) and left behind a powdery substance called calx (what we now know to be oxide). Objects that burned in air were considered to be rich in phlogiston, and the fact that a fire burned out when oxygen was removed was seen as proof that oxygen could only absorb a limited amount of the substance. This theory also led to the idea that the human need to breathe had a sole function—to remove phlogiston from the body. The entire concept was superseded by Antoine-Laurent Lavoisier's discovery that combustion could only occur with the help of a gas such as oxygen.

1 SPONTANEOUS GENERATION

Before microscopes and theories of cells and germs, man had other ideas about the creation of living things. He bizarrely believed that life arose from inanimate matter (for example, maggots come spontaneously from rotting meat). Proponents of this view (virtually everyone) used the Bible as a source of evidence, due to the fact that God made man from dust. However, the view did exist before Christianity and Aristotle said, in no uncertain terms, that some animals grow spontaneously and not from other animals of their kind. Earlier believers had to come up with some pretty strange ideas to make their theory work: Anaximander (a Greek philosopher who taught Pythagoras) believed that at some point in man's history, humans had been born from the soil spontaneously in adult form, otherwise they could never have survived. Before we laugh too hard at the ancients, we should note that many scientists right up to the nineteenth century believed this, and some even wrote recipe books for making animals. One such recipe (to make a scorpion) calls for basil placed between two bricks and left in sunlight. The theory was not finally put to rest until 1859, when Louis Pasteur proved it wrong once and for all.

✳✳✳✳✳✳

TOP 10 COMMON DREAMS AND THEIR MEANINGS

10 CAR TROUBLES

In these types of dreams you are usually in or near a car or some other type of vehicle that is out of control or has other problems that seem insurmountable. For example, the brakes may have failed, you may have lost control of the steering, or you might be heading over a cliff or crashing. You can either be the driver or the passenger. This is a very common type of nightmare and it occurs for all people, not just those who can drive. This dream usually means that you are feeling powerless over something in your life or that you are heading for a crash (metaphorically speaking).

9 FAULTY MACHINERY

In the faulty machinery dream you are trying to operate mechanical equipment that either fails to work or fails to work in the way that you expect it to. The vast majority of these dreams involve a telephone and trouble dialing, losing a connection, or dialing a wrong number. It can involve a lost Internet connection or something manual like a jammed or broken machine. This dream often means that you feel you are losing touch with reality or that a part of your body or mind is not functioning as it should. It can also occur when you are feeling anxious about making a connection with another person in real life.

8 LOST OR TRAPPED

Dreaming about being lost is very common and will usually occur when you are having conflict in deciding how to react in a situation in real life. In the dream you are trying to find your way out of an area, such as a forest, city streets, a large building, or other maze-like structures. Another way this dream plays out involves you being trapped, buried alive, caught in a web, or unable to move for some other reason. This is often accompanied by a feeling of terror. This dream usually means that you are trapped in real life and unable to make the right choice.

7 MISSED A BOAT OR PLANE

In this type of dream you are rushing to catch a bus, train, plane, or other type of public transportation, but you miss it, usually by a fraction of a second. Rather than feeling fear in this dream, you usually feel frustration. This dream can also occur in a different form, in which you arrive late for an important performance or sporting event that you are supposed to participate in, only to find that the event has already begun. This dream usually means that you feel that you have missed out on an important opportunity in your real life. It will often occur when you are struggling over an important decision.

6 FAILING A TEST

This dream usually manifests itself in people who have been out of school for a long time. In the dream you are prevented from passing a test in a variety of different possible scenarios. In one scenario you find that you are unable to make it to the test on time, often through being unable to find the test room. In other versions you are unprepared, either through lack of study or you are missing equipment. This dream usually means that you are feeling tested in some way in your real life. You may feel that you are unprepared for something or playing the wrong part in life.

5 ILL OR DYING

In this dream, you (or a loved one) are ill, injured, or dying. It is a moderately common dream and, not surprisingly, occurs often at the onset of an illness. Aside from becoming ill, this dream can mean that you are emotionally hurt or are afraid of becoming hurt. The dream may also be warning you of an upcoming physical risk to yourself or a loved one. When it is someone else in the dream that dies, it can mean that you feel that part of yourself (that you see represented by that person) is dead. It may also mean that you wish the person would go away, or that you fear losing them.

4 BEING CHASED

Dreaming of being chased can be a truly horrifying experience. Most often the chaser is a monster or some person that is frightening, and occasionally it may be an animal. You may be surprised to know that this is the most commonly experienced nightmare theme. The meaning of these dreams is that someone or something (possibly something as obscure as an emotion) is making you feel threatened. One way to determine the root of the threat is to ask yourself who or what in your real life most closely resembles the "creature" or circumstance in your dream. It is also worth noting that sometimes this dream is a replay of an actual event in your life.

3 BAD OR MISSING TEETH

Teeth dreams are fairly common and they usually involve the discovery of extremely decayed or missing teeth in your own mouth. Sometimes you will dream that you open your mouth and your teeth begin to fall out. The majority of people today have reasonable teeth so it is not surprising that we feel so emotionally disturbed by these dreams. So, what does it mean when we dream about missing teeth? At the most basic level it means that we are afraid of being found unattractive. At a deeper level, it can signify a fear of embarrassment or a loss of power in real life.

2 DREAM NUDITY

In this type of dream you are in a state of undress, partial undress, or inappropriate dress (for example wearing pajamas to work). Occasionally you are the witness of another person who is naked while you are clothed. This is accompanied often by feelings of embarrassment and shame but occasionally with feelings of pride or freedom. The meaning of this dream is that you are feeling exposed, awkward, or vulnerable, or you are afraid that you have revealed too much of yourself (such as a secret or a very personal feeling) in a real life situation. An interesting fact about this type of dream is that it occurs much more frequently in people who are involved in a wedding ceremony in real life.

1 FALLING OR SINKING

We have all had falling dreams—they are so common, in fact, that myths have arisen about them; the most common myth is, of course, that you will die if you hit the ground in the dream. I can assure you, having hit the ground in more than one falling dream, that this is not true at all. In the falling dream we are usually falling through the air and frightened. Occasionally we may be sinking in water (and in danger of drowning). Typically a person having this dream is feeling insecure or lacking in support in their waking life. These dreams often occur when you are overwhelmed in life and feel ready to give up. If you have this dream you should evaluate your current situation and try to locate the problem that is overwhelming you. Deal with it and this dream should go away.

✳✳✳✳✳✳

TOP 10 SIGNS OF EVOLUTION IN MODERN MAN

10 GOOSE BUMPS—CUTIS ANSERINA

Humans get goose bumps when they are cold, frightened, angry, or in awe. Many other creatures get goose bumps for the same reason; for example, this is why a cat or dog's hair stands on end and the cause behind a porcupine's quills raising. In cold situations, the rising hair traps air between the hairs and skin, creating insulation and warmth. In response to fear, goose bumps make an animal appear larger, hopefully scaring away the enemy. Humans no longer benefit from goose bumps and they are simply left over from our past when we were not clothed and needed to scare our own natural enemies. Natural selection removed the thick hair but left behind the mechanism for controlling it.

9 JACOBSON'S ORGAN—VOMERONASAL ORGAN

Jacobson's organ is a fascinating part of animal anatomy and it tells us a lot about our own sexual history. The organ is in the nose and it is a special "smell" organ that detects pheromones (the chemicals that trigger sexual desire, alarm, or information about food trails). It allows some animals to track others for sex and to know of potential dangers. Humans are born with the Jacobson's organ, but in early development its abilities dwindle to a point that it is useless. Once upon a time, humans would have used this organ to locate mates when communication was not possible. Single's evenings, chat rooms, and bars have now taken its place in the process of human mate seeking.

8 JUNK DNA—L-GULONOLACTONE OXIDASE

While many of the hangovers from our "devolved" past are visible or physical, this is not true for all. Humans have structures in their genetic makeup that were once used to produce enzymes to process vitamin C (it is called L-gulonolactone  oxidase). Most other animals have this functioning DNA but at some point in our history, a mutation disabled the gene while leaving behind its remnants as junk DNA. This particular junk DNA indicates a common ancestry with other species on earth, so it is particularly interesting.

7 EXTRA EAR MUSCLES—AURICULARES MUSCLES

Also known as the extrinsic ear muscles, the auriculares muscles are used by animals to swivel and manipulate their ears (independently of their heads) in order to focus their hearing on particular sounds. Humans still have the muscles that we would once have used for the very same reason but our muscles are now so feeble that all they can do is give our ears a little wiggle. The use of these muscles in cats is very visible (as they can nearly turn their ears completely backward), particularly when they are stalking a bird and need to make the smallest movements possible so as to not frighten its future meal.

6 PLANTARIS MUSCLE

The plantaris muscle is used by animals in gripping and manipulating objects with their feet and is something you see with apes who seem to be able to use their feet as well as their hands. Humans have this muscle as well, but it is now so underdeveloped that it is often taken out by doctors when they need tissue for reconstruction in other parts of the body. The muscle is so unimportant to the human body that 9 percent of humans are now born without it.

5 WISDOM TEETH

Early humans ate a lot of plants, and they needed to eat them quickly enough that they could eat a sufficient amount in one day to get all of the nutrients they needed. For this reason, we had an extra set of molars to make the mouth more productive. This was particularly essential as the body lacked the ability to sufficiently digest cellulose. As evolution made its selections, our diets changed, our jaws grew appropriately smaller, and our third molars became unnecessary. Some human populations have now all but completely stopped growing wisdom teeth, while others have an almost 100 percent likelihood of developing them.

4 THIRD EYELID

If you watch a cat blink, you will see a white membrane cross its eye that is called its third eyelid. It is quite a rare thing in mammals, but common in birds, reptiles, and fish. Humans have a remnant (but non-working) third eyelid. It has become quite small in humans, but some populations have more visible portions than others. There is only one known species of primate that still has a functioning third eyelid, and that is the Calabar angwantibo (closely related to lorises) that lives in West Africa.

3 DARWIN'S POINT—PLICA SEMILUNARIS

Darwin's point is found in the majority of mammals, and humans are no exception. It is most likely used to help focus sounds in animals, but it no longer has a function in humans. Only 10.4 percent of the human population still has this visible leftover mark of our past, but it is possible that a much larger number of people carry the gene that produces it as it does not always cause the ear tubercle to appear. The point is a small thick nodule at the junction of the upper and middle sections of the ear.

2 COCCYX

The coccyx is the remnant of what was once a human tail. Over time we lost the need for a tail (as tree swinging was replaced by hanging out at the local water hole grunting Neanderthal gossip), but we did not lose the need for the coccyx: it now functions as a support structure for various muscles and a support for a person when he sits down and leans back. The coccyx also supports the position of the anus.

1 APPENDIX

The appendix has no known use in modern humans and is often removed when it becomes infected. While its original use is still speculated on, most scientists agree with Darwin's suggestion that it once helped to process the cellulose found in the leaf-rich diet that we once had. Over the course of evolution, as our diet has changed, the appendix became less useful. What is particularly interesting is that many evolutionary theorists believe that natural selection (while removing all of the abilities of the appendix) selects larger appendices because they are less likely to become inflamed and diseased. So unlike the little toe, which may eventually vanish and is equally useless, the appendix is likely to stay with us for a long time, just hanging around doing nothing.

❋❋❋❋❋❋

TOP 10 OLD WIVES' TALES DEBUNKED

10 FEED A FEVER, STARVE A COLD

In fact, both colds and fevers cause dehydration, so liquids are essential when suffering from either. In addition, missing out on food when you are sick is never a good idea as food provides the body with the sustenance it needs to get healthy. So, you should feed a fever and feed a cold. This, of course, does not mean to overeat—it means to eat healthy balanced meals.

9 EATING BEFORE SWIMMING

There is an old wives' tale that says if you eat within an hour of swimming you will get a cramp. The Red Cross says that eating directly prior to swimming does not increase risk of cramps at all. They do, however, recommend at least waiting for digestion to begin if you have eaten a particularly fatty meal. They also recommend that you not eat gum or food while you are swimming.

8 CHOCOLATE CAUSES ACNE

There is actually not an iota of evidence to support this tale: no food type (not just chocolate) can cause acne or bad skin. Needless to say, eating too much chocolate or sugary food is unhealthy for the body, but it will not cause skin problems. Acne is actually caused by changes in the lower layers of the skin surrounding hair follicles.

7 CARROTS IMPROVE YOUR VISION

It is possible that this tale came about due to Allied propaganda during the Second World War when rumors were spread that British airmen had excellent night vision due to eating carrots. The myth was spread to stop the Germans from discovering that the British were using radar. While carrots contain vitamin A, which is good for healthy eyes, eating lots of them will do nothing to improve your vision.

6 CATCHING A COLD

There are a huge number of myths about how to catch a cold, but, in fact, there is only one way to catch a cold virus—by direct contact with the virus itself. You can stand outside on a cold night with wet hair and your chances of getting a cold do not increase at all. The reason that colds seem to spread more in winter is not from the cold itself but from the fact that people tend to live more often indoors and this increases your chances of coming into contact with a sufferer. It is also worth mentioning that if you get a cold in your nose, you cannot stop it from spreading to your chest if the virus is programmed to attack you there. Most cold medicines are completely pointless and do nothing to help except alleviate the pain through the inclusion of painkillers.

5 TV AND EYESIGHT

My parents constantly told me off for sitting too close to the television when I was a kid and that my eyesight would deteriorate from doing so. The same was also said of reading in dim light. In fact, neither of these things do any damage to the eyes. It should be noted, however, that spending too much time in front of the TV is not good for children (regardless of how close they sit) as research has shown that children who spend ten hours or more in front of the television each week are more likely to become overweight, aggressive, and slower in school.

4 MASTURBATION CAUSES BLINDNESS

The tale states that masturbation will cause blindness (in France it is said it will cause deafness). This is not true (at least not completely), and the idea has probably been spread in order to prevent children from masturbating for religious reasons. Curiously, sperm contains quite a lot of zinc, and a serious zinc deficiency can cause a decline in vision. However, it is nearly impossible to cause a zinc deficiency through masturbating.

3 KNUCKLES AND ARTHRITIS

While it is true that constant knuckle-cracking can reduce the strength of your grip and cause swelling, it does not lead to arthritis. There are many causes of arthritis (such as trauma, infection of a joint, or old age), but knuckle-cracking is not one of them.

2 SPICY FOOD AND ULCERS

If a person suffers from an ulcer, spicy food can often aggravate it; however, ulcers are not caused by spicy food at all—if they were, ulcers would be pandemic in many Eastern nations. An ulcer is usually caused by overuse of medications like aspirin and anti-inflammatories.

1 TOADS AND WARTS

It is almost certain that this strange old wives' tale has come about because of the appearance of wart-like growths on many toads. In fact, these growths are not human compatible at all. Warts are caused by viruses and are almost always exclusive to a particular genus of creature. Humans cannot catch warts from other animals, and animals cannot catch human warts. The most common human wart virus is called the human papillomavirus.

✳✳✳✳✳✳

TOP 10 STRANGE PHENOMENA OF THE MIND

10 L'ESPRIT DE L'ESCALIER

L'esprit de l'escalier ("stairway wit," pronounced *less-pree disc alley eh*) is the sense of thinking of a clever comeback when it is too late. The phrase can be used to describe a riposte to an insult, or any witty, clever remark that comes to mind too late to be useful—when one is on the "stairway" leaving the scene. The German word *treppenwitz* is used to express the same idea. The closest phrase in English to describe this situation is "being wise after the event." The phenomenon is usually accompanied by a feeling of regret at having not thought of the riposte when it was most needed or suitable.

9 DÉJÀ VU

Déjà vu (pronounced *day-ja voo*) is the experience of being certain that you have experienced or seen a new situation previously. You feel as though the event has already happened or is repeating itself. The experience is usually accompanied by a strong sense of familiarity and a sense of eeriness, strangeness, or weirdness. The "previous" experience is usually attributed to a dream, but sometimes there is a firm sense that it has truly occurred in the past.

8 DÉJÀ VÉCU

Déjà vécu (pronounced *day-ja vay-koo*) is what most people are experiencing when they think they are experiencing déjà vu. Déjà vu is the sense of having seen something before, whereas *déjà vécu* is the experience of having seen an event before, but in great detail, such as recognizing smells and sounds. This is also usually accompanied by a very strong feeling of knowing what is going to come next. In my own experience of this, I have not only known what was going to come next but have been able to tell those around me what is going to come next, and I am right. This is a very eerie and unexplainable sensation.

7 DÉJÀ VISITÉ

Déjà visité (pronounced *day-ja visee-tay*) is a less common experience and involves an uncanny knowledge of a new place. For example, you may know your way around a new town or a landscape despite having never been there, and knowing that it is impossible for you to have this knowledge. *Déjà visité* is about spatial and geographical relationships, while *déjà vécu* is about temporal occurrences. Nathaniel Hawthorne wrote about an experience of this in his book *Our Old Home* in which he visited a ruined castle and had a full knowledge of its layout. He was later able to trace the experience to a poem he had read many years earlier by Alexander Pope in which the castle was accurately described.

6 DÉJÀ SENTI

Déjà senti (pronounced *day-ja son-tee*) is the phenomenon of having "already felt" something. This is exclusively a mental phenomenon and seldom remains in your memory afterward. In the words of a person having experienced it, "What is occupying the attention is what has occupied it before, and indeed has been familiar, but has been forgotten for a time, and now is recovered with a slight sense of satisfaction as if it had been sought for. The recollection is always started by another person's voice, or by my own verbalized thought, or by what I am reading and mentally verbalize; and I think that during the abnormal state I generally verbalize some such phrase of simple recognition as 'Oh yes—I see,' or 'Of course—I remember,' etc., but a minute or two later I can recollect neither the words nor the verbalized thought which gave rise to the recollection. I only find strongly that they resemble what I have felt before under similar abnormal conditions."

You could think of it as the feeling of having just spoken, but realizing that you, in fact, didn't utter a word.

5 JAMAIS VU

Jamais vu (meaning "never seen," pronounced *jah-may-voo*) describes a familiar situation that is not recognized. It is often considered to be the opposite of déjà vu and involves a sense of eeriness. The observer does not recognize the situation despite knowing rationally that they have been there before. It is commonly explained as when a person momentarily doesn't recognize a person, word, or place that they know. Chris Moulin, of Leeds University, asked 92 volunteers to write out "door" thirty times in sixty seconds. He reported that 68 percent of his guinea pigs showed symptoms of *jamais vu*, such as beginning to doubt that "door" was a real word. This has led him to believe that *jamais vu* may be a symptom of brain fatigue.

4 PRESQUE VU

Presque vu (meaning "almost seen," pronounced *press-ki voo*) is very similar to the "tip of the tongue" sensation; it is the strong feeling that you are about to experience an epiphany, though the epiphany seldom comes. The sensation of *presque vu* can be very disorienting and distracting.

3 CAPGRAS DELUSION

Capgras delusion is the phenomenon in which a person believes a close friend or family member has been replaced by an identical-looking impostor. This could be tied in to the old belief that babies were stolen and replaced by changelings in medieval folklore as well as the modern idea of aliens taking over the bodies of people on earth to live among us for reasons unknown. This delusion is most common in people with schizophrenia, but it can occur in other disorders.

2 FREGOLI DELUSION

Fregoli delusion is a rare brain phenomenon in which a person holds the belief that different people are, in fact, the same person in a variety of disguises. It is often associated with paranoia and the belief that the person in disguise is trying to persecute them. The condition is named after the Italian actor Leopoldo Fregoli who was renowned for his ability to make quick changes of appearance during his stage act. It was first reported in 1927 in the case study of a twenty-seven-year-old woman who believed she was being persecuted by two actors whom she often went to see at the theater. She believed that these people "pursued her closely, taking the form of people she knows or meets."

1 PROSOPAGNOSIA

Prosopagnosia is a phenomenon in which a person is unable to recognize faces of people or objects that they should know. People experiencing this disorder are usually able to use their other senses to recognize people, such as a person's perfume, the shape or style of their hair, the sound of their voice, or even their gait. A classic case of this disorder was presented in the 1998 book by Oliver Sacks (and later opera by Michael Nyman) called *The Man Who Mistook His Wife for a Hat*.

TOP 10 MISCONCEPTIONS ABOUT EVOLUTION

10 NATURAL SELECTION GIVES ORGANISMS WHAT THEY "NEED"

Natural selection has no "intelligence"—it cannot tell what a species needs. If a population has genetic variants more suited to their environment, they will reproduce more in the next generation and the population will evolve. If a genetic variant is not present, the population will most likely die, or it will survive with little evolutionary change.

9 EVOLUTION IS "JUST" A THEORY

Scientifically speaking, a theory is a well-substantiated idea that explains aspects of the natural world. Unfortunately, other definitions of theory (such as a "guess" or a "hunch") cause a great deal of confusion in the non-scientific world when dealing with the sciences. They are, in fact, two very different concepts.

8 EVOLUTION IS A THEORY IN CRISIS

There is no debate in science as to whether or not evolution occurred; there is, however, debate over how it happened. The minutiae of the process are vigorously debated which can cause anti-evolutionists to believe that the theory is in crisis. Evolution is sound science and is treated as such by scientists worldwide.

7 GAPS IN THE FOSSIL RECORD DISPROVE EVOLUTION

Actually, many transitional fossils do exist; for example, there are fossils of transitional organisms between modern birds and their dinosaur ancestors, as well as whales and their land mammal ancestors. There are many transitional forms that have not been preserved, but that is simply because some organisms do not fossilize well or exist in conditions that do not allow for the process of fossilization. Science predicts that there will be gaps in the record for many evolutionary changes. This does not disprove the theory.

6 EVOLUTIONARY THEORY IS INCOMPLETE
Evolutionary science is a work in progress. Science is constantly making new discoveries with regard to it and explanations are always adjusted if necessary. Evolutionary theory is like all of the other sciences in this respect. Science is always trying to improve our knowledge. At present, evolution is the only well-supported explanation for all of life's diversity.

5 THE THEORY IS FLAWED
Science is an extremely competitive field; if any flaws were discovered in evolutionary theory, they would be quickly corrected. All of the alleged flaws that creationists put forth have been investigated carefully by scientists and simply do not hold water. They are usually based on misunderstandings of the theory or misrepresentation of the evidence.

4 EVOLUTION IS NOT SCIENCE BECAUSE IT IS NOT OBSERVABLE
Evolution is observable and testable. The confusion here is that people think science is limited to experiments in laboratories by white-coated technicians. In fact, a large amount of scientific information is gathered from the real world. Astronomers obviously cannot physically touch the objects they study (for example, stars and galaxies) yet a great deal of knowledge can be gained through multiple lines of study. This is true also of evolution. It is also true that there are many mechanisms of evolution that can be, and are, studied through direct experimentation as with other sciences.

3 MOST BIOLOGISTS HAVE REJECTED DARWINISM
Scientists do not reject Darwin's theories; instead, they have modified them over time as more knowledge has been discovered. Darwin considered that evolution proceeds at a deliberate, slow pace, but, in fact, it has now been discovered that it can proceed at a rapid pace under some circumstances. There has not been, so far, a credible challenge to the basic principles of Darwin's theory. Scientists have improved and expanded on Darwin's original theory of natural selection so it has not been rejected, it has only been added to.

2 EVOLUTION LEADS TO IMMORAL BEHAVIOR

All animal species have a set of behaviors that they share with other members of their species. Slugs act like slugs, dogs act like dogs, and humans act like humans. It is preposterous to presume that a child will begin to behave like another creature when they discover that they are related to them. It is nonsensical to link evolution to immoral or inappropriate behavior.

1 EVOLUTION SUPPORTS "MIGHT MAKES RIGHT"

In the nineteenth and early twentieth centuries, a philosophy called "Social Darwinism" sprung up from misguided attempts to apply biological evolution to society. This philosophy said that society should allow the weak to fail and die, and that not only is this an ideal situation, but a morally right one. This enabled prejudices to be rationalized and ideas such as the poor deserved their situation due to being less fit were very popular. This was a misappropriation of science. Social Darwinism has, thankfully, been repudiated. Biological evolution has not.

�֎✖✖✖✖✖

TOP 10 AMAZING FACTS ABOUT DREAMS

10 BLIND PEOPLE DREAM

People who become blind after birth can see images in their dreams. People who are born blind do not see any images, but have dreams equally vivid involving their other senses of sound, smell, touch, and emotion. It is hard for a seeing person to imagine, but the body's need for sleep is so strong that it is able to handle virtually all physical situations to make it happen.

9 YOU FORGET 90 PERCENT OF YOUR DREAMS

Within five minutes of waking, half of your dream is forgotten. Within ten, 90 percent is gone. The famous poet, Samuel Taylor Coleridge, woke one morning having had a fantastic dream (likely opium induced); he put pen to paper and began to describe his "vision in a dream" in what has become one of English's most famous poems, "Kubla Khan." Partway through, fifty-four lines in fact, he was interrupted by a "person from Porlock." Coleridge returned to his poem but could not remember the rest of his dream. The poem was never completed.

> *"In Xanadu did Kubla Khan*
> *A stately pleasure-dome decree:*
> *Where Alph, the sacred river, ran*
> *Through caverns measureless to man*
> *Down to a sunless sea.*
> *[...]"*

Curiously, Robert Louis Stevenson came up with the story of Doctor Jekyll and Mr. Hyde while he was dreaming. Mary Shelley's Frankenstein was also the brainchild of a dream.

8 EVERYBODY DREAMS

Every human being dreams (except in cases of extreme psychological disorder) but men and women have different dreams and different physical reactions. Men tend to dream more about other men, while women tend to dream equally about men and women. In addition, both men and women experience sexually related physical reactions to their dreams regardless of whether the dream is sexual in nature; males experience erections and females experience increased vaginal blood flow.

7 DREAMS PREVENT PSYCHOSIS

In a recent sleep study, students who were awakened at the beginning of each dream, but still allowed their eight hours of sleep, all experienced difficulty in concentration, irritability, hallucinations, and signs of psychosis after only three days. When finally allowed their REM sleep the students' brains made up for lost time by greatly increasing the percentage of sleep spent in the REM stage.

6 WE ONLY DREAM OF WHAT WE KNOW

Our dreams are frequently full of strangers who play out certain parts. Your mind is not inventing those faces because they are real faces of real people that you have seen during your life but may not know or remember. The evil killer in your latest dream may be the guy who pumped gas into your dad's car when you were just a little kid. We have all seen hundreds of thousands of faces throughout our lives, so we have an endless supply of characters for our brain to utilize during our dreams.

5 NOT EVERYONE DREAMS IN COLOR

A full 12 percent of sighted people dream exclusively in black and white while the remaining number dream in full color. People also tend to have common themes in dreams, which are situations relating to school, being chased, running slowly or in place, sexual experiences, falling, arriving too late, a person now alive being dead, teeth falling out, flying, failing an examination, or a car accident. It is unknown whether the impact of a dream relating to violence or death is more emotionally charged for a person who dreams in color than one who dreams in black and white.

4 DREAMS ARE NOT ABOUT WHAT THEY ARE ABOUT

If you dream about some particular subject, it is not often that the dream is about that. Dreams speak in a deeply symbolic language. The unconscious mind tries to compare your dream to something else, which is similar. It is like writing a poem and saying that a group of ants were like machines that never stop. But you would never compare something to itself, for example, "That beautiful sunset was like a beautiful sunset." So whatever symbol your dream picks up on, it is most unlikely to be a symbol for itself.

3 QUITTERS HAVE MORE VIVID DREAMS

People who have smoked cigarettes for a long time who stop have reported much more vivid dreams than they would normally experience. Additionally, according to the *Journal of Abnormal Psychology*:

> "Among 293 smokers abstinent for between 1 and 4 weeks, 33 percent reported having at least 1 dream about smoking. In most dreams, subjects caught themselves smoking and felt strong negative emotions, such as panic and guilt. Dreams about smoking were the result of tobacco withdrawal, as 97 percent of subjects did not have them while smoking, and their occurrence was significantly related to the duration of abstinence. They were rated as more vivid than the usual dreams and were as common as most major tobacco withdrawal symptoms."

2 EXTERNAL STIMULI INVADE OUR DREAMS

This is called "dream incorporation" and it is the experience that most of us have had where a sound from reality is heard in our dream and incorporated in some way. A similar (though less external) example would be when you are physically thirsty and your mind incorporates that feeling into your dream. It is like repeatedly drinking a large glass of water in a dream that is satisfying, only to find the thirst returning shortly after. This thirst … drink … thirst … loop often recurs until you wake up and have a real drink.

1 PARALYZED WHILE YOU SLEEP

While you sleep, glands in your body release hormones that help you sleep, and neurons send signals to the spinal cord telling it to relax and finally enter a state of paralysis. This occurs during the deep stage of sleep.

✳✳✳✳✳✳

TOP 10 COOL FACTS ABOUT SPACE

10 LIGHTWEIGHT

Fact: If you put Saturn in water it would float.

The density of Saturn is so low that if you were to put it in a giant glass of water it would float. The actual density of Saturn is 0.687 g/cm3 while the density of water is 0.998 g/cm3. At the equator Saturn has a radius of 60,268 ± 4 km, which means you would need an extremely large glass of water to test this out.

9 CONSTANTLY MOVING

Fact: We are moving through space at the rate of 530 km per second.

Our galaxy, the Milky Way, is spinning at a rate of 225 kilometers per second. In addition, the galaxy is traveling through space at the rate of 305 kilometers per second. This means that we are traveling at a total speed of 530 kilometers (330 miles) per second. So in one minute you are about nineteen thousand kilometers away from where you were. Scientists do not all agree on the speed with which the Milky Way is traveling, with estimates ranging from 130–1,000 km/s. It should be said that Einstein's theory of relativity, the velocity of any object through space is not meaningful.

8 FAREWELL OLD FRIEND!
Fact: The moon is drifting away from Earth.

Every year the moon moves about 3.8 cm further away from Earth, which is caused by tidal effects. Consequently, the Earth is slowing in rotation by about 0.002 seconds per day per century. Scientists do not know how the moon was created, but the generally accepted theory suggests that a large Mars-sized object hit the Earth causing the moon to splinter off.

7 ANCIENT LIGHT
Fact: The light hitting the earth right now is thirty thousand years old.

The energy in the sunlight we see today started out in the core of the sun thirty thousand years ago—it spent most of this time passing through the dense atoms that make the sun and just eight minutes to reach us once it has left the sun! The temperature at the core of the sun is 13,600,000 kelvins. All of the energy produced by fusion in the core must travel through many successive layers to the solar photosphere before it escapes into space as sunlight or kinetic energy of particles.

6 SOLAR DIET
Fact: The sun loses up to a billion kilograms a second due to solar winds.

Solar winds eject huge amounts of particles from the surface of the sun; in fact, it ejects up to a billion kilograms a second! Also, did you know that one pinhead of the sun's energy is enough to kill a person at a distance of 160 kilometers?

5 THE BIG DIPPER IS NOT A CONSTELLATION
Fact: The Big Dipper is not a constellation; it is an asterism.

Many people consider the Big Dipper to be a constellation but, in fact, it is an asterism. An asterism is a pattern of stars in the sky that is not one of the official eighty-eight constellations; they are also composed of stars not physically related to each other and can be vast distances apart. An asterism can be composed of stars from one or more constellations; in the case of the Big Dipper, it is composed entirely of the seven brightest stars in the Ursa Major (Great Bear) constellation.

4 GEORGE'S STAR

Fact: Uranus was originally called George's Star.

When Sir William Herschel discovered Uranus in 1781, he was given the honor of naming it. He chose to name it Georgium Sidus (George's Star) after his new patron, King George III (Mad King George). This is what he said:

> *"In the fabulous ages of ancient times the appellations of Mercury, Venus, Mars, Jupiter, and Saturn were given to the planets, as being the names of their principal heroes and divinities. In the present more philosophical era it would hardly be allowable to have recourse to the same method and call it Juno, Pallas, Apollo, or Minerva, for a name to our new heavenly body. The first consideration of any particular event, or remarkable incident, seems to be its chronology: if in any future age it should be asked, when this last-found planet was discovered? It would be a very satisfactory answer to say, 'In the reign of King George the Third.'"*

Uranus was also the first planet to be discovered with the use of a telescope.

3 EXTRA MOONS

Fact: Earth has at least four moons.

Okay, that is not actually true, but it is very close. In 1986, Duncan Waldron discovered an asteroid (5 km across) that is in an elliptic orbit around the sun with a period of revolution virtually identical to that of Earth. For this reason the planetoid and Earth appear to be following each other. The periodic planetoid is named Cruithne (pronounced *krin-ye*) after an ancient group of Scottish people (also known as the Picts). Because of its unusual relationship with Earth, it is sometimes referred to as Earth's second moon. Cruithne is fainter than Pluto and would require at least a twelve-and-a-half-inch reflecting telescope to attempt to be seen. Since its discovery, at least three other similar asteroids have been discovered. These types of objects are also found in similar relationships to other planets in our solar system.

2 SUNSPOT MUSIC

Fact: Sunspot activity may be the primary reason for the beautiful sound of Stradivarius violins.

Antonio Stradivari is considered to be the greatest violin maker ever. He lived in Italy during the seventeenth and early eighteenth centuries. Scientists have been unable to work out what it is about his violins that makes them so incredible, but they do know that the timber used to make them is a very important contributing factor. From the 1500s to the 1800s, the earth underwent a little ice age mostly due to increased volcanic activity and decreased solar activity (this is called the Maunder Minimum). As a result of this cooling, the types of trees that Stradivari used for his violins were particularly hard (due to slow growth). Hard timber is especially good when making violins. It is very probable that had Stradivari lived in a different age, his violins would not be prized as they are today.

1 COLD WELDING

Fact: If two pieces of metal touch in space, they become permanently stuck together.

This may sound unbelievable, but it is true. Two pieces of metal without any coating on them will form into one piece in the vacuum of space. This doesn't happen on Earth because the atmosphere puts a layer of oxidized material between the surfaces. This might seem like it would be a big problem on the space station but as most tools used there have come from Earth, they are already coated with material. In fact, the only evidence of this seen so far has been in experiments designed to provoke the reaction. This process is called cold welding.

✳✳✳✳✳✳

TOP 10 RIDICULOUSLY COMMON SCIENCE MYTHS

10 EVOLUTIONARY IMPROVEMENTS

Myth: Evolution causes something to go from "lower" to "higher."

While it is a fact that natural selection weeds out unhealthy genes from the gene pool, there are many cases where an imperfect organism has survived. Some examples of this are fungi, sharks, crayfish, and mosses; these have all remained essentially the same over a great period of time. These organisms are all sufficiently adapted to their environments to survive without improvement. Other taxa have changed a lot, but not necessarily for the better. Some creatures have had their environments changed and their adaptations may not be as well suited to their new situations. Fitness is linked to their environment, not to progress.

9 HUMANS POP IN SPACE
Myth: When exposed to the vacuum of space, the human body pops.
This myth is the result of science fiction movies that use it to add excitement or drama to the plot. In fact, a human can survive for fifteen to thirty seconds in outer space as long as they breathe out before the exposure (this prevents the lungs from bursting and sending air into the bloodstream). After fifteen or so seconds, the lack of oxygen causes unconsciousness, which eventually leads to death by asphyxiation.

8 BRIGHTEST STAR
Myth: Polaris is the brightest star in the northern hemisphere night sky.
Sirius is actually brighter with a magnitude of −1.47 compared to Polaris's 1.97 (the lower the number the brighter the star). The importance of Polaris is that its position in the sky marks north, and for that reason it is also called the "North Star." Polaris is the brightest star in the constellation Ursa Minor and, interestingly, is only the current North Star, as pole stars change over time because stars exhibit a slow continuous drift with respect to Earth's axis.

7 FIVE-SECOND RULE
Myth: Food that drops on the floor is safe to eat if you pick it up within five seconds.
This is utter bunk, which should be obvious to most readers. If there are germs on the floor and the food lands on them, they will immediately stick to the food. Having said that, eating germs and dirt is not always a bad thing as it helps us to develop a robust immune system. I prefer to have a "how-tasty-is-it" rule: if it is something really tasty, it can sit there for ten minutes for all I care, and I will still eat it.

6 DARK SIDE OF THE MOON
Myth: There is a dark side of the moon.
Actually every part of the moon is illuminated at some time by the sun (except some of the deepest craters). This misconception has come about because there

is a side of the moon never visible to the earth. This is due to the fact Earth's gravitational pull on the moon is so immense that it can only show one face to us. The technical term for this is tidal locking.

5 BRAIN CELLS

Myth: Brain cells can't regenerate; if you kill a brain cell, it is never replaced.

The reason for this myth being so common is that it was believed and taught by the science community for a very long time. But in 1998, scientists at the Salk Institute in La Jolla, California, discovered that brain cells in mature humans can regenerate. It had previously been long believed that complex brains would be severely disrupted by new cell growth, but the study found that the memory and learning center of the brain can create new cells, giving hope for an eventual cure for illnesses like Alzheimer's.

4 PENNIES FROM HEAVEN

Myth: A penny dropped from a very high building can kill a pedestrian below.

This myth is so common it has even become a bit of a cliché in movies. The idea is that if you drop a penny from the top of a tall building (such as the Empire State Building), it will pick up enough speed to kill a person on the ground if it lands on them. But the fact is, the aerodynamics of a penny are not sufficient to make it dangerous. What would happen in reality is that the person who gets hit would feel a sting, but they would certainly survive the impact.

3 FRICTION HEAT

Myth: Meteors are heated by friction when entering the atmosphere.

When a meteoroid enters the atmosphere of the earth (becoming a meteor), it is actually the speed compressing the air in front of the object that causes it to heat up. It is the pressure on the air that generates a heat intense enough to make the rock so hot that is glows brilliantly for our viewing pleasure (if we are lucky enough to be looking in the sky at the right time). We should also dispel the myth about meteors being hot when they hit the earth, becoming meteorites. Meteorites are almost always cold when they hit, and, in fact, they are often found covered in frost because they are so cold from their journey through space that the entry heat is not sufficient to do more than burn off the outer layers.

2 LIGHTNING

Myth: Lightning never strikes the same place twice.

Next time you see lightning strike and you consider running to the spot to protect yourself from the next bolt, remember this item! Lightning does strike the same place twice, in fact, it is very common. Lightning obviously favors certain areas such as high trees or buildings. In a large field, the tallest object is likely to be struck multiple times until the lightning moves sufficiently far away to find a new target. The Empire State Building gets struck around twenty-five times a year.

1 GRAVITY IN SPACE

Myth: There is no gravity in space.

In fact, there is gravity in space—a lot of it. The reason that astronauts appear to be weightless is because they are orbiting the earth and are falling toward it, but moving sufficiently sideways to miss it. So they are basically always falling but never landing. Gravity exists in virtually all areas of space. When a shuttle reaches orbit height (around 250 miles above the earth), gravity is reduced by only 10 percent.

✳✳✳✳✳✳

TOP 10 RECENT SCIENTIFICALLY SOLVED MYSTERIES

10 EPIDAURUS THEATER ACOUSTICS

The ancient theater of Epidaurus near Athens, Greece, was constructed in the late fourth century BC and is one of the best preserved ancient theaters. Even in ancient times, the theater was considered to have great acoustics. The actors can be perfectly heard by all fifteen thousand spectators without amplification. To demonstrate the theater's great acoustics, tour guides have their groups scattered in the stands and then show them how faint sounds can be heard at center-stage. How this sound quality was achieved has been the source of academic and amateur speculation for many years. One of the theories suggested that prevailing winds were carrying the sounds. It turns out that that answer is in the seats. In 2007 researchers at the Georgia Institute of Technology have discovered that the limestone material of the seats provide a filtering effect suppressing low frequencies of voices, thus minimizing background crowd noise so the seats act as natural acoustic traps. It is still unknown whether the acoustic properties are the result of an accident or the product of advanced design.

9 CRYSTAL SKULLS

Most people are familiar with crystal skulls from the film *Indiana Jones and the Kingdom of the Crystal Skull*. However, there are actually many serious crystal skull collectors that claim they are pre-Columbian and were made during the Aztec or Maya civilizations and exhibit paranormal phenomena. In 2008 a team of British and American researchers using electron microscopy and x-ray crystallography examined skulls from the British Museum and the Smithsonian. A detailed analysis of the skull's surface revealed minute rotary scratch marks around the eye sockets, teeth, and cranium. This was clear evidence that the skull was cut and polished with a wheeled instrument, and the Aztecs never used the wheel. The researchers concluded that the skulls were cut from a piece of Brazilian rock crystal in Europe. They were then probably sold to collectors as relics from the ancient Aztec civilization. Many museums now have removed the skulls from display because of their questionable origins.

8 NEW ENGLAND'S DARK DAY

On May 19, 1780, an unusual darkening of the day sky was observed over the New England states and parts of Canada. Since communication of the day was very primitive, some people in New England applied religious interpretations to the event. Even today New England's "Dark Day" is still regarded by many as a supernatural event. Different explanations were discussed from volcanic eruptions to celestial cataclysms. In 2008, nearly 230 years later, University of Missouri researchers combined written accounts and tree ring records from fire-damaged trees to determine that the dark day was caused by massive wildfires burning in Canada. During a fire the heat goes through the bark, killing the living tissue; then a couple of years later the bark falls off, revealing the wood and an injury to the tree. The researchers studied tree rings from the Algonquin Highlands of southern Ontario and many other locations. They found evidence that a major fire had burned in that time period that would have affected atmospheric conditions hundreds of miles away. Large smoke columns were created and carried into the upper atmosphere accounting for New England's dark day.

7 FACE ON MARS

The Cydonian region on Mars attracted a great deal of attention because one of the hills in that region looked remarkably man-made. The region was first imaged in detail by the *Viking 1* orbiter that was launched in 1975. Several images were taken by the *Viking* including one taken in 1976 showing one of the Cydonian mesas had the appearance of a face. Scientists dismissed the face as a trick of light and shadow but then a second image also showed the face at a different sun-angle. This caught the attention of organizations interested in extraterrestrial intelligence and some talk show hosts who believed the face was a long-lost Martian civilization. Most scientists still held the belief that the face was just a consequence of viewing conditions. In 2003, when the European space agency launched *Mars Express*, it was able to combine data from a high-resolution stereo camera and create a 3D representation of the "Face on Mars." The most recent image would silence even the most faithful believers. The image shows a remnant massif thought to have formed from landslides and an early form of debris apron formation but no face in sight.

6 THE BARRELEYE FISH

The fascinating aspect of the barreleye fish are its tubular eyes, which are excellent at collecting light at depths up to eight thousand feet. The puzzling part is that the eyes appear to be fixed in place directly above its head. This had baffled physiologists for decades because it would be almost impossible for the fish to look for food. Recently, scientists, using a remotely operated vehicle, studied the fish at depths ranging from two thousand feet. They discovered that the tubular eyes exist behind a transparent fluid-filled dome and the eyes can rotate within a transparent shield that covers the fish's head. This allows the fish to peer up at potential prey or focus forward to see what it is eating. The barreleye fish was first discovered in 1939, but the transparent nature of the fish wasn't known because when the fish was caught in nets at a different depth of water, the see-through part is destroyed.

5 SOLVING CHECKERS

Checkers has been around for more than four hundred years and has been enjoyed by millions of players. Since 1989 computers have worked around the clock to try and decipher the game's 500 billion billion possible moves. In 1992, a computer was narrowly defeated by world champion Marion Tinsley, widely regarded as the best human checkers player ever. Finally, in 2007, a computer program called Chinook, developed by researchers at the University of Alberta, could now play a perfect game of checkers. Using between two hundred desktop computers at the peak of the project, Chinook can recognize every possible move made in a checkers game and determine the correct countermove. If neither player makes a mistake the game will end in a draw.

4 THE UNKNOWN *TITANIC* CHILD

Days after the *Titanic* sank the body of a baby boy was found and recovered from the North Atlantic. After the child could not be identified, he was buried in Nova Scotia with a tombstone reading simply "The Unknown Child." In 2001, researchers at Lakeland University in Ontario were granted permission to exhume the body. By consulting the passenger lists they had narrowed down the possible identity to one of four children: Gosta Paulson, Eino Panula, Eugene Rice, and Sidney Goodwin. Initial tests concluded that the body was Eino Panula. However, in 2007 this was shown to be not true. More advanced DNA testing was carried out on a tooth from the body and when compared to the DNA of a surviving Goodwin relative it proved an indisputable match. It confirmed that "the unknown child" was Sidney Goodwin. Sidney was the youngest of six children born to Fred and Augusta Goodwin from Fulham, England. The family was immigrating to Niagara Falls, New York. (All were onboard.) Neither Sidney's parents 'nor his siblings' bodies were ever recovered.

3 ANCIENT TABLET DECIPHERED

A circular clay tablet was discovered 150 years ago at Nineveh, the capital of ancient Assyria, in what is now Iraq. The tablet shows drawings of constellations and pictogram-based text known as cuneiform, which was used by the Sumerians, the earliest known civilization in the world. For decades scientists have failed to decipher the tablet. In 2008 two scientists, Alan Bond and Mark Hempsell from Bristol University, finally cracked the cuneiform code. By using a computer program that can reconstruct the night sky thousands of years ago, the two scientists were able to establish the tablet was a night notebook of Sumerian astronomers and refers to the events in the sky before dawn on June 29, 3123 BC (Julian calendar).

2 SHARK'S VIRGIN BIRTH

In 2001 a hammerhead shark was born at the Henry Doorly Zoo in Nebraska with three potential mothers in the same tank. All had been in captivity for at least three years. The birth of the shark baffled scientists for years. Some scientists thought one of them might have mated before being captured and stored the sperm for fertilization. Some scientists believed that sharks might be able to reproduce asexually through a rare method known as parthenogenesis (a direct development without the need of a sperm). Many were skeptical, but in late 2007 scientists confirmed this through DNA testing. After they determined which of the three females was the mother, they subtracted the mother's contribution from the offspring and in this particular case after the DNA was subtracted there was nothing left. The researchers were forced to conclude that the pup had no father, making this the first documented case of asexual reproduction of a shark.

1 FLIGHT OF THE BUMBLEBEE

This is at the number-one spot because it inspired the list. As I was growing up I used to hear that when you take into consideration a bee's wingspan along with the bee's weight ratio it is aerodynamically impossible for them to fly. I also used to hear the only reason a bee can fly is because it thinks it can. I always thought that was a really cool explanation even though I knew it was probably not true. Scientists had many theories but were not able to explain exactly how the un-aerodynamic bee was able to fly. Finally, in 2005, with the assistance of high-speed cinematography and mechanical models of the bee's wings, scientists were able to put this perplexing mystery to rest. As it turns out the bee flaps its wings an amazing 230 times per second, much faster than smaller insects. Their analysis revealed sufficient lift was generated by the unconventional combination of short, choppy wing strokes, a rapid rotation of the wing as it flops over and reverses direction, along with a very fast wing-beat frequency.

✳✳✳✳✳✳

TOP 10 LOUDEST NOISES

10 ROCK CONCERT/SPEAKERS

A 400,000-watt rock concert or a similar set of speakers mounted in a vehicle can reach ear-splitting decibel levels. Is it any reason most promoters recommend you wear ear protection to stave off the 135–145 decibel sound waves?

9 FIREWORKS

Though not typically heard up close, fireworks are still explosions and are very loud. The sound heard from the sky is pretty loud, though not damaging, but at the bursting point the decibel levels reach a staggering 145–150. Even tests are performed under strict sound-proofing to avoid any ear injury.

8 GUNFIRE

Gunfire, for anyone unfortunate enough to be standing near it, can be quite damaging to the ears, registering at a quite loud 145–155 decibels. This is the very reason why you should always wear ear protection when on a firing range.

7 NHRA DRAGSTERS

Sitting next to a dragster as it fires up its engines and screams down the raceway can be more than just loud; it can be damaging to your entire body. At the 155–160 decibel range, not only will it severely or permanently damage your hearing, it also vibrates your vision and makes it temporarily difficult to swallow. That's why no one stands next to them.

6 SPACE SHUTTLE LAUNCH

When the rockets fire, it is wise and, in fact, fully enforced, that you stand at least a half-mile away lest you get inundated by 165–170 decibels of painful sound. Unlike many other loud noises, the shuttle rocket sound is constant as it creates the thrust necessary to lift it from the ground.

5 THE BLUE WHALE

Blue whales mostly emit very loud, highly structured, repetitive low-frequency rumbling sounds that can travel for many miles underwater. These songs may be used for communicating with other blue whales, especially in order to attract and find mates. The call of the blue whale reaches levels up to 188 decibels. This extraordinarily loud whistle can be heard for hundreds of miles underwater. The whale is the loudest and largest animal on Earth.

4 KRAKATOA VOLCANO

The 1883 Krakatoa eruption ejected more than six cubic miles of rock, ash, and pumice and generated the loudest sound historically reported at 180 decibels. The cataclysmic explosion was distinctly heard as far away as Perth, Australia, approximately 1930 miles, and the island of Rodrigues near Mauritius, approximately 3000 miles.

3 ONE-TON TNT BOMB

Standing as close as 250 feet away from the impact, the resulting explosion from a one-ton bomb creates a decibel count of 210. Without sufficient hearing protection, not to mention a complete sound-resistant bunker surrounding you, you could die from the intense vibrations that would literally shake you apart, unless, of course, you were under the bomb.

2 5.0 RICHTER EARTHQUAKE

A sufficient enough quake to rend the ground in two and destroy buildings, whole rock, and human life reaches a decibel level of 235. If you are caught in the epicenter and are unlucky enough to not be above the ground in a plane or helicopter, the intense noise and vibrations could kill you long before death by any falling object.

1 TUNGUSKA METEOR

The Tunguska event was a massive explosion that occurred near the Podkamennaya (Under Rock) Tunguska River in what is now Krasnoyarsk Krai of Russia at 7:40 a.m. on June 30, 1908. The explosion was most likely caused by the air burst of a large meteoroid or comet fragment at an altitude of three to six miles above Earth's surface. It was measured with the similar impact of a thousand-megaton bomb with a decibel rating 300–315. This is often considered to be the loudest single event in history.

✳✳✳✳✳✳

TOP 10 PEOPLE IMMORTALIZED IN PRODUCTS

10 LÁZLÓ BÍRÓ, 1899–1985
Product: Biro or Ballpoint Pen

Quick-drying newspaper ink gave Hungarian-born Bíró his primary inspiration for the ubiquitous pen that bears his name. He was working in journalism at the time. On discovering the ink would not function in an ordinary fountain pen, he co-opted his brother Georg, a chemist, and between them they developed the now-famous ball-and-socket tip. The invention was patented in 1938. During the Second World War they took up residence in Argentina and filed a second patent in 1943. The design was used effectively in high-altitude combat aircraft at the time and took off commercially in the years immediately after peace was declared. Ballpoint pens have evolved to become reliable, clean, disposable, and amazingly cheap.

9 ROBERT WILHELM EBERHARDT BUNSEN, 1811–1899
Product: Bunsen Burner

All who have willingly or under duress studied chemistry during their school years will be instantly aware of the piece of fundamental lab apparatus known as a Bunsen burner. For the benefit of those who escaped "stinks," it consists of a round metal base with a vertical open-topped hollow tube connected by a rubber hose to a gas supply. The metal tube has an adjustable air inlet and the gas flow is also adjustable. When the gas is turned on and lit at the top of the tube, it provides a variable flame, which can be brought to considerable heat as required for chemical experiments. Well, here's the guy to blame for it, although you might prefer to hold the Englishman Michael Faraday responsible. He produced the prototype on which Bunsen based his design. Bunsen is also acclaimed for various other achievements in chemistry.

8 RUDOLF CHRISTIAN KARL DIESEL, 1858–1913
Product: Diesel Engine

Nobody is going to deny the mainstream importance of this particular French-born inventor and mechanical engineer of German origin and subsequent German residence, or deny they have ever heard of him. After a glittering career in the refrigeration industry was blighted by patent problems, Diesel turned his attention to the production of a more efficient motor than the steam engine and existing combustion engine. His excellent academic trajectory had left him with a keen knowledge of thermodynamics, from which, in 1892, emerged his first compression-ignition engine. A man from Yorkshire, England, Herbert Akroyd Stuart, is in fact considered to have invented the compression-ignition engine before Diesel. Apparently he even filed his patent two years earlier. So, all together now everybody, "the Stuart engine." Diesel disappeared at sea while on his way by steamship to a company meeting in London. Considering the triumph of his system over steam, he might perhaps be said finally to have poured his oil on troubled waters (or was it Stuart's revenge?). As a curiously modern tailpiece for those becoming more concerned with biofuels in this day and age, Diesel's original motors ran on … peanut oil! Nothing new under the sun.

7 GEORGE WASHINGTON GALE FERRIS, JR., 1859–1896
Product: Ferris Wheel or Observation Wheel

The name Ferris wheel is given to a large, slowly rotating upright wheel of open metal structure with passenger seats or observation gondolas suspended at regular intervals around it. Modest-sized examples are found at local traveling or fixed fairgrounds, larger ones have been created as showpieces for national or international exhibitions. The largest, such as the
London Eye, form permanent fixtures on the urban landscape, and carry large numbers of visitors to considerable heights, from where sweeping vistas can be appreciated. As with so many widespread inventions, earlier precursors existed at a local level, the first recorded examples being constructed of wood and perhaps carrying eight or so passengers. These existed in the Ottoman Empire at least from the seventeenth century onward. Ferris, a railway and bridge engineer, invented and gave his name to his metal wheel (and to all others subsequently) for the 1893 World's Columbian Exposition. The original was 260 feet high and had a capacity of 2160 passengers in thirty-six cars. It was powered by two steam engines and ran until 1906.

Given his full name, what a wonder it didn't get called the Washington wheel! As it was, Ferris claimed that the Exhibition organizers had cheated him and the investors out of most of the profits. Like other inventors, he was driven to waste time, money, and energy in the courts attempting to claim what was rightfully his by contract. As a rule, successful inventors tend to live to a ripe old age. Ferris was one of the unfortunate exceptions. Typhoid fever claimed him early, at thirty-seven, a mere three years after his fame was sealed.

6 DR. JOSEPH-IGNACE GUILLOTIN, 1738–1814
Product: Guillotine

What a terrible object to be immortalized by. Guillotin, a French medic and politician, did not actually invent the gadget. Unlikely as it might seem, too, the impulse that induced it was humanitarian. Up until then, a principle object of capital punishment had often been to inflict the maximum pain by breaking the sentenced person's body as slowly and agonizingly as possible before merciful release by the ending of life. At least once, this so incensed onlookers that they overcame the executioner and released the prisoner. With need for reform in the air, Guillotin proposed a system that would behead instantly and painlessly. Ironically, he was, in fact, opposed to capital punishment and hoped this would lead eventually to its abolition. Happily, he passed away naturally and did not fall victim to his eponymous death machine.

5 W. H. "BOSS" HOOVER, 1908
Product: Vacuum Cleaner

One of the bigger surprises while researching for this list was how little information is readily available for the person whose name is most associated with the vacuum cleaner. In fact, we know no personal details at all. The main reason is clear. He was little more than an early corporate figure who began manufacturing someone else's particular design in 1908 once the invention was already well established. It would make about as much sense to call a computer "a Gates." Hoover was American, yet it is the British who turned "the hoover" into an eponymous generic word. It's rather as if Brits said "hovercraft" while Americans referred to the same machine as a "cockerell" (after its English inventor). For the records, the vacuum cleaner was invented (as a manual machine) in 1868. The actual Hoover prototype with its unique rotating brush was the design of one James Murray Spangler. In fact, this is a classic case of Stigler's Law of Eponymy, of which numerous examples abound: "No discovery is named after its original discoverer."

4 JOHN LOUDON MCADAM, 1756–1836

Product: Macadam road surface, tar Macadam or tarmac

Our present high-speed freeways and interstates can trace their origin back to the aristocratic second son of the Scottish Baron of Waterhead, a sometime resident of the United States. His was one of the first serious advances in major national highway engineering since the excellent initial advances by the Romans. He became involved in this branch of civil engineering due to being an estate owner and turnpike trustee. McAdam's three essential innovations were to create a solid, compacted, well-drained foundation of rock and gravel; to raise the road surface above the surrounding ground level; and to incorporate a camber for surface drainage. The major later development was the addition of a sealed, tarred surface. As with so many important inventors or innovators, he scarcely benefited personally from his system, which was rapidly and widely adopted throughout Western civilization. One might even perhaps aptly consider that he was steamrollered politically.

3 JOHN MONTAGU, 4TH EARL OF SANDWICH, 1718–1792

Product: Sandwich

The placing of a filling between bread had a long and partly accidental history before it was identified and named. The earliest known example was consumed during the ancient Hebrews' Passover feasts, when unleavened bread similar to Indian chapatis or Mexican tortillas would have been used. The noble Earl himself held various high diplomatic and military posts as was typical for English aristocrats of the time. Various explanations are offered as to how he became associated with this early convenience food. One possibility is that being such a busy man, he preferred to take his meals in that cleaner form at his desk. Another suggestion has it that the dry bread on both sides kept his fingers clean during long gambling sessions of cards without him having to leave the table and wash them at intervals. The bread-based type has in turn led to a few culinary variations, such as the sponge sandwich. Philological spinoffs include the sandwich course and being sandwiched between people in a crowd.

2 HENRY SHRAPNEL, 1761–1842

Product: Shrapnel Shell

Henry Shrapnel. So well known are the shards of shells called shrapnel that his family surely acquired its name from them. Not at all. Shrapnel, an active-service English army officer, was the inventor. His original design, a spherical cannon shell, exploded in midair, showering the enemy with lethal metal. It was the birth of a concept which ultimately led to the infamous cluster-bomb. The system became used early on to counter the deployment of aircraft in wartime. Allied pilots of WWI called it "Archie." German shell-smoke was black, Allied white. Shrapnel himself was one of the luckier inventors. He received a princely annual award of over $125,000 (today's equivalent) for life from a grateful British Government.

1 LUIGI GALVANI, 1737–1798
Product: Galvanized Iron

Italy enters the list with the scientist Galvani. A famous experiment with frogs' legs led him to make the first connection between electricity and the movement of animate life. Thanks to a genial technical dispute with the better-known scientist Volta about the essence and origin of organic electricity, he received from Volta the compliment of a direct current of electricity produced by chemical action being called "galvanism." The dispute also led to Volta producing the first battery, and, of course, Volta also reaped his share of eponymous fame. "Galvanism" became an outmoded term, but was modified to the words "galvanization" and "galvanized." These have become a permanent part of our vocabulary for metal plated by electrical process. They have also bequeathed us the figurative phrase "galvanized into action"!

✱✱✱✱✱✱

TOP 10 PROGRAMS THAT CHANGED THE FACE OF COMPUTING

10 THE WORLD WIDE WEB
On November 12, 1990, Sir Tim Berners-Lee wrote a document outlining the basics of what we now know as the world wide web. Within the same year he created the first web server and web browser (which he called WorldWideWeb) on a NeXT computer (NeXT was Steve Jobs's company when he

left Apple; it was this operating system that Apple based its OS X on after Jobs returned there). No one would have guessed the impact the web would have on the world. It is probably the most revolutionary concept in modern history.

The world wide web eventually grew to such an extent that it is now the leading source of news and entertainment for many people. It has already forced traditional enterprises like print media and recording/film media to completely change (or consider changing) their whole business models.

9 PHOTOSHOP

Photoshop, created by Adobe, was an original program developed by brothers John and Thomas Knoll. There are few products that become so ubiquitous as to become a verb; now we Photoshop images. Photoshop is by far the most widely used image-manipulating program with no serious commercial competition available to this day. Adobe has gone on to become the world leader in media software.

8 VISICALC

Visicalc was the first successful spreadsheet program, written for the Apple II (an early computer by Apple Inc.). Successful operating systems are built upon key programs and Visicalc is the prime example. Visicalc was the first computer program that did things that were impossible with a pencil and paper system and made thousands of people realize that they needed a computer. So great was the success of the program, people would go into a computer store and ask for "a Visicalc," meaning an Apple II.

7 WORDSTAR

Visicalc did it with numbers; Wordstar did it with words. Wordstar did things that, at the time, made jaws drop—it could count the words in a document, and when the document was printed on a daisywheel printer, it printed one line forward and the next line backward because it was faster that way.

Suddenly, small companies could send out printed letters, unless companies could afford to employ full-time typists, letters were often handwritten at that time. Writers switched in droves; author Jerry Pournelle said that after seeing Wordstar, he realized that within a few years no one would write with a typewriter again. A side effect was that books became much longer!

6 CP/M

CP/M was something of an accidental invention. The legend is that Gary Kidall was working at Naval Research labs on an operating system and wanted to continue work at home on his own home-built computer.

Unfortunately, the machine at work was different than the one at home, so the solution was to separate out the machine-dependent parts of the operating system (the disk controller and serial input/output) into a small subsection (the BIOS), the bulk of the operating system being left unchanged.

This concept made it relatively simple to "port" (the process of adapting software so that an executable program can be created for a computing environment that is different from the one for which it was originally designed) CP/M to different computers, as long as the computer was 8080 (or Z80) based. Having a single operating system made it possible for applications such as Wordstar to flourish.

5 EMACS

In the early days of small computers, programs were written using text editors, often Wordstar, and then the program files were processed through compilers and linkers to produce a finished program. EMACS was (indeed, still is) an editing system for the UNIX operating system and provided the first programming environment—the compiler and linker were still there, but the process was hidden. Essentially, the programmer always worked in EMACS; the program was edited, a single keypress would compile and link it.

EMACS can be configured to "know" about the format of different languages, keywords are shown in different colors, function parameters are shown automatically—it's changed how programmers program. Virtually all programming languages provide an environment now. But it started with EMACS and it is one of two main contenders in the traditional editor wars, the other being vi.

4 UNIX

UNIX shows the advantage of giving bright guys some time and money. Ken Thompson was the bright guy and he, essentially, developed the first version of UNIX (then called Unics) to make a game run faster.

UNIX had the advantage of CP/M that it could fairly easily be ported to different machines, but it wasn't particularly dependent on the hardware. CP/M needed a 8080/Z80 processor, while UNIX can generally be run on anything from a phone to a supercomputer. This is because UNIX was essentially written in a high-level language. UNIX (and its modern derivative, Linux) is a programmer's dream—it doesn't get in the way too much, has powerful editors and good compilers, is very adaptable, and probably most importantly, has a worldwide community of fans and users.

Apple's Mac OS X is based on UNIX (BSD to be exact), and most developments in modern computing (virtual desktops, virtual memory spring to mind) start on UNIX.

3 C PROGRAMMING LANGUAGE

C is the language of UNIX and was written by Dennis Ritchie in 1972. Pretty much the whole of UNIX and applications that run on UNIX are written in C, or C-derived languages (C# or C++). C is a small language and, therefore, easily learned and easily ported to different operating systems. C compilers are usually written in C.

Some of the key features of C are extendability, close coupling with the hardware, fairly strong variable typing and function pointers. These don't mean much unless you're a programmer! But, essentially, they stop the language getting in the way of what the programmer is trying to achieve.

The influence of C has spread with the influence of UNIX; most applications throughout Windows/Linux/Mac OS are written in C, C++, or C#. C has also influenced other computer languages; Visual Basic now looks very like C.

2 SMALLTALK

Another programming language, Smalltalk, was the first successful object-orientated language. Before Smalltalk, languages dealt largely with strings and numbers. Smalltalk allowed the programmer to describe all kinds of things—shapes, sounds, video—as objects. Imagine writing a drawing program before objects; if you want to draw a circle on the screen, you use a function for drawing circles. If you want to draw a square, you use a different function to draw a square. And so on for all the shapes. With object-orientated languages, you can use a single function to draw a shape, and tell it to be a square, circle, and so on. It made application writing much easier. Smalltalk isn't used much nowadays; C++, C#, and Visual Basic are far more common, but they are all object orientated.

A side effect of object orientation is that the executable applications became much bigger; it was with the introduction of objects, particularly C++, that applications started being delivered on multiple CDs.

1 XEROX ALTO OPERATING SYSTEM

The single most influential operating system, bar none. Are you using a graphical user interface (i.e., Windows, Mac OS X) and a mouse? Are you connected to a network? Are you used to WYSIWYG editing (like MS Word)? Do you print to a laser printer? Is your computer doing more than one thing at once? All of these things originated at the Xerox PARC research facility under Alan Kay around 1973. Think about that year —1973, ten years before the Apple Lisa was released. As you can see from the list of features of Xerox Alto, it more or less defined modern computing.

So why aren't we all using Xerox Alto, instead of Windows/Mac OS? In 1979, Xerox, in exchange for Apple stock, allowed some Apple engineers, including Steve Jobs, to visit Xerox PARC and look at the Alto workstation. There is a lesson here; if you invent a sensational, high-tech product, don't invite competitors to come and have a good look at it.

✳✳✳✳✳✳

TOP 10 WEAPONS THAT COULD HAVE LOST THE ALLIES THE WAR

10 "THE BOMB"

It's a matter of minor debate concerning how far along the Germans were in developing an atomic bomb before Allied bombers wiped out the efforts for good. But make no mistake; they were trying to build one. Could you imagine Hitler having atomic bombs? America, of course, developed the atomic bomb first—initially to be used against Germany. This is number ten rather than number one because everything else on this list actually existed, either as prototypes or as operational weapons.

9 THE FOCKE ACHGELIS FA 223 HELICOPTER

The "Dragon" helicopter was invented some time before the war, but the Germans were the first ones to actually put a whirlybird into production. The Fa 223 was the latest in Focke's helicopter designs and was a good aircraft. And, for once, interference from Nazi bigwigs actually only played a minor part in production and deployment. Twenty examples were built by the winter of 1942 to 1943 when Allied bombers plastered the only factory making them. Attempts to resume production failed, and resources were directed to more critical systems. But imagine if the Nazis had succeeded in deploying such an aircraft in large numbers before the war turned against them.

8 HE-100 FIGHTER

In March 1939, Luftwaffe pilot Hans Dieterle achieved an absolute average speed record of 463.9 mph, the last such speed record set before the war. His aircraft was the Heinkel He-100V8, a fighter prototype. Although possessing excellent flight characteristics (speed, dive, maneuverability, range, etc.) the He-100 never entered production. Nazi officials decided to stick with the Messerschmitt BF-109 as its primary fighter and ordered Heinkel to focus on making bombers. Aviation enthusiasts and historians disagree as to why the He-100 died: was it politics, poor decisions by Heinkel, production problems or something else? The He-100 prototypes were retired or sold to other nations, especially Japan, whose decent mid-war Kawasaki Ki-61 fighter—the only non-radial fighter Japan fielded—was based on the He-100. Why could this have been a game-changer? Because had the Nazis and Heinkel gone ahead with production of this fighter, which was supposedly superior to even the hot Focke Wulf FW-190 introduced later in the war, events such as the Battle of Britain could have turned out much differently. The He-100, for example, had much greater range than the 109 and was far superior to the Me-110, and could have easily fended off British fighters trying to get at German bombers.

7 TYPE XXI U-BOAT

The U-boats (submarines) used in World War II were superior in every way to their WWI counterparts, and the Type XXI vessel outclassed every other submarine of every navy. The Type XXI, dubbed the Elektoboote, was the first operational submarine designed to run totally submerged for extended periods—meaning far longer than the submerged operational viability of the Type VIIC, the most numerous U-boat type. The Elektroboote could stalk Allied ships with far more impunity than earlier models thanks to its greatly improved batteries and "stealth" modifications that made it difficult to detect by Allied sonar. The type's weapons systems were superior, including hydraulically loaded torpedoes and torpedoes aimed by sonar, which eliminated the need to raise the U-boat to periscope depth for attack. Between 1943 and 1945, German shipyards built 118 Type XXI boats. But only four were combat-ready by the time the Germans surrendered, and only one ever went on patrol. Boneheaded production decisions, including those by Albert Speer, and Allied bombing prevented this deadly boat from ever becoming a menace.

6 STRATEGIC BOMBERS

After its successful debut in the Spanish Civil War, the Luftwaffe set on a strategy of using only tactical bombers (light, medium, and dive bombers), eschewing the four-engine heavy bombers being developed in England and America. This concentration on highly vulnerable and lightly armed bombers meant that the Luftwaffe never had a true strategic heavy bomber. Although in possession of some four- and six-engine planes at war's start, none was truly suitable for strategic bombing. Luftwaffe attempts to finally build long-range city-killers were either disasters or abandoned. The Heinkel He-177, the only Luftwaffe strategic bomber to enter into production, was a disastrous failure. It was a flawed four-engine design featuring two engines mounted in tandem on each wing, which frequently caused fires. Hitler also demanded that massive plane be capable of dive-bombing, which was totally wacky and contributed to its serious problems. Along the same lines was the "New York bomber" program, which featured two aircraft, the Junkers Ju-290 and the Messerschmitt Me-264, with designs to bomb New York City. But the program never went beyond the prototype stage. The few models of the decent Ju-290 were used not as bombers but long-range couriers between Nazi Germany and Imperial Japan late in the war. Meanwhile, one complete Me-264, which curiously looked like the American B-29 Super Fortress, was completed and another two were under construction when the "New York bomber" program was abandoned permanently.

5 HEINKEL HE-219 "OWL" NIGHT FIGHTER

This superb, purpose-built, two-engine night fighter was the best Axis night fighter of the war, and one of the finest piston aircraft made prior to the jet age. Just one He-219 downed twenty-five Allied bombers in a matter of *days* during the prototype period; the plane was that good. While possessing excellent flight characteristics, formidable weaponry, and radar guidance, the plane was somewhat complex to build. Heinkel only built a few hundred, partially because they were ordered to concentrate on bombers. Instead, the Luftwaffe relied on modifying existing aircraft, namely Me-110s and Junkers Ju-88s. In far larger numbers, the He-219 could have brought nighttime RAF bombing operations to a close.

4 GRAF ZEPPELIN AIRCRAFT CARRIER

The Kriegsmarine (German navy) never had an aircraft carrier during WWII, but it came close. In 1935, Hitler deemed that the Kriegsmarine would build aircraft carriers. At this point in naval history, the battleship was still the primary naval vessel, and aircraft carriers something of a novelty; therefore, naval treaties concentrated on limiting battleship tonnage. In 1937, shipbuilders laid the keel for the 33,500-ton *Graf Zeppelin* and launched her the next year. However, she was never completed. Herman Goering thought that the carrier would intrude on the duties of his Luftwaffe, and Admiral Karl Doenitz championed U-boats over surface vessels. Such territorial fights and the increasing shortage of war materials led to her abandonment at 80 percent completion. The Soviets captured the *Graf Zeppelin* in 1945, but it wasn't learned until 2006 that the Soviets used her for target practice and sank her in 1947.

3 V-2 AND OTHER GUIDED WEAPONS

Germany employed many radio-controlled weapons during the latter half of the war, including the V-1 buzz bomb, a slow, primitive cruise missile that was easy to shoot down. Radio-controlled air-to-surface missiles, such as the Henschel Hs 293 guided bomb, were a hassle for Allied shipping until techs found ways to jam the signals. Of all the German radio-controlled weapons, the V-2 ballistic missile was the most successful. However, the Nazis used the V-2 primarily to terrorize London, Antwerp, and elsewhere during the last full year of the war. Much more powerful and faster than the V-1 "buzz bomb," the Hs-293 and the "Mistel" (an old bomber packed with explosives literally flown by remote to a target), the V-2 was quite difficult to shoot down and packed a powerful explosive punch. What could have happened if the Germans had used such weapons exclusively against Allied troops instead of civilians? Considering that by summer 1944 the Allies had near total air domination in the West and the Soviets were closing hard from the East, such a weapon could have proven costly to the Allies—and cheaper than sending in fighters and bombers. With a mobile launch platform and a high-speed flight, the V-2 could—*could*—have gone a long way to negating Allied air power. But almost all of the ten thousand V-2s launched directly targeted civilians.

2 STURMGEWEHR STG-44 ASSAULT RIFLE

Germany fielded many powerful weapons systems for the Wehrmacht, including the fearsome Tiger and Panther tanks and the 88-mm cannon. The Wehrmacht's small arms inventory was good, though a little unwieldy. The basic German soldier went to war equipped with the Karabiner Kar98, an old but powerful and reliable bolt-action rifle with a 5-shot cartridge. (The Kar98 is still in use!) Elite German troops, such as the paratroopers, as well as the SS and Gestapo, were often equipped with the MP-40 or 41 machine pistol/submachine gun. German armories, however, created a very powerful and versatile submachine gun *almost* akin to the famed postwar Soviet AK-47. In trained hands, the StG-44 could lay down a devastating hail of 7.92-mm bullets (the same as used by the Kar98), and provided the power of the Kar98 and up-close versatility of the MP-40. During the last year-and-a-half of the war, they proved their effectiveness, so much so that when Hitler asked his generals in July 1944 what they needed, one of them exclaimed, "More of these rifles!" However, the StG-44 came too late in the war to have any appreciable effect. East German police units used them as late as the early 1960s.

1 MESSERSCHMITT ME-262 "SWALLOW"

The Me-262 was the world's first operational jet fighter. Despite frequent engine problems, the Me-262 was a fast and deadly aircraft and outpaced almost all Allied fighters (only the P-51D Mustang could match it). It could have gone operational in the fall of 1943, when the war was still pretty much in the balance. At that time, the Luftwaffe still had not lost most of its veteran pilots and Allied escort fighters could not penetrate too far into the Reich. The Me-262 could have swept Allied bombers and fighters from the sky, giving Germany critical air dominance once more. Fortunately for the world, Hitler himself demanded that the new fighter aircraft be modified for dive-bombing use—a purpose for which it was not designed. This meddling delayed construction and deployment for more than a year. By the time the Me-262 took to the skies operationally in late 1944, it was far too late.

❋❋❋❋❋❋

TOP 10 FABULOUS NIGHT SKY OBJECTS SEEN THROUGH BINOCULARS

10 SATELLITES AND METEORS

Satellites and meteors can and are seen by the naked eye, but in light polluted skies, many are too dim to see.

Meteors: Only the very brightest of the almost constant supply of meteors are observed. While scanning the sky with your binoculars, you are almost guaranteed to see a small streak of light shooting through your field of vision. Only the light gathering power of binoculars coupled with their large field of view (compared to telescopes) reveal these tiny, random acts of celestial violence.

Satellites: Big and bright satellites are easily visible with eyes alone. Lie down and stare up an hour or two after sunset or before sunrise (the low orbit of satellites makes them invisible due to Earth's shadow in the middle of the night). You'll notice points of light moving slowly across the sky. They seem like airplanes, but the lights won't blink. Follow them for as long as you can; their altitude and path determine where in the sky they'll disappear behind the Earth's shadow. Like meteors, many satellites too dim for eyes alone are revealed through binoculars simply by looking up.

9 THE MOON

A source of wonder, romance, and reflection since man stood up and then looked up. The brightest object in the night sky is easily visible with the naked eye, but with a pair of binoculars, much detail is revealed.

The best time to view details of the moon is not necessarily during a full moon. As Galileo first noticed, the most detail is seen at the moon's terminator, the shadow line on the moon separating the visible phase from the rest of the disk. Shadows cast along the terminator illuminate detail of the mountains and valleys of the moon. Impact craters untouched by atmosphere and erosion show the violent history of the early solar system. And the moon's darker seas (mares) reveal the ancient, active geological life of lava flows long since dormant.

8 JUPITER

Or more precisely, the Galilean moons of Jupiter. Observing the planets is one job where telescopes really come into their own, but binoculars are all you need to see the four largest of Jupiter's moons. The moons are actually bright enough to see with the naked eye, but are washed-out from Jupiter's powerful glare. Your binoculars will show them as little stars grouped around the gas giant. Track their nightly waltz around the giant planet.

7 THE DOUBLE CLUSTER (NGC 884 & NGC 869)

Located in the constellation Peruses, the Double Cluster is actually two different star clusters very close together. A star cluster is a dense grouping of stars. The Double Cluster makes a fantastic binocular target because it's a comparatively large object in the night sky. It has an apparent (angular) size of 60 minutes (1 degree). A telescope's field of view is often too narrow to enjoy both clusters at the same time. Binoculars have fields of view as wide as 6 degrees or more, easily spacious enough to fit the entire Double Cluster. (Angular size in the night sky: horizon to zenith is 90 degrees; horizon to horizon—the entire visible sky dome—is 180 degrees.)

6 THE BEEHIVE CLUSTER (M44)

The Beehive, like the Double Cluster, is another open star cluster. Located 577 light years from Earth, the Beehive is found in the constellation Cancer. It was one of the first objects Galileo studied with his telescope, and makes a fantastic binocular target because of its apparent size in the night sky.

5 THE LAGOON NEBULA (M8)

Many nebulae are areas of interstellar gas condensing, via gravity, to form new stars and star systems: stellar nurseries. The Lagoon Nebula is considered one of the prettiest sites in the night sky. Find it in the constellation Sagittarius, but only during the summer in mid-northern latitudes.

4 THE ORION NEBULA (M42)

The Orion Nebula is the smudge on the Hunter's sword in the Orion constellation. Orion is the most recognizable constellation in the winter sky, and a thing of beauty in its own right. The nebula is a star factory some 1270 light years away, making it the nearest star nursery to Earth. Its apparent size in the night sky is 1 degree.

3 THE PLEIADES (M45)

Mentioned three times in the Bible, and a source of inspiration for virtually every ancient culture, the Pleiades may be my favorite binocular target, perhaps because it was my first. In my teens, I got the idea to use some binoculars skyward after I stumbled upon an old, small, cruddy pair stored away in the house. My first target was the Pleiades, and I suppose it was love at first sight.

This small (in star quantity) star cluster is also a birthplace for new stars, although the nebulosity is usually only visible in time-exposure photography. It is super-easy to find with the naked eye but dramatically different with binoculars. Its apparent size is much too large to fit into most telescope fields of view, and so again makes a choice binocular target.

2 ANDROMEDA GALAXY (M31)

The best thing about the Andromeda Galaxy? It's a galaxy! A trillion suns. Over 2.5 million light years distant. Orbited by fourteen dwarf galaxies, at least one of which (M32), and possibly another (M110) can also be seen in your binoculars at the same time. What's not to love?

Andromeda is the furthest thing you can see with the naked eye (appearing as a faint smudge in the sky). With a total apparent size of about 4 degrees, or more than 8 times the apparent size of the full moon, it makes an outstanding object for binoculars. It's usually the first thing I locate when I look up at night with a pair of binoculars.

1 THE MILKY WAY

The delicate, silvery cloud stretching across the sky on dark clear nights is our home galaxy: the Milky Way. Lazily scanning the Milky Way flat on your back on a summer night is an astronomical treat not to be missed. With binoculars, the silver cloud reveals its nature: the stars upon stars that make up our galaxy. No part of the sky is more densely packed with visible stars than the Milky Way, nor more pleasantly addictive to behold with binoculars. Be careful not to get lost in there!

CHAPTER THIRTEEN
Tips for Life

1. Top 10 Tips to Commit the Perfect Crime
2. Top 10 Prison Survival Tips
3. Top 10 Tips for Outrunning the Cops
4. Top 10 Tips for Flying Under the Radar
5. Top 10 Tips for Getting a Flight Upgrade
6. Top 10 Tips for Sounding Smarter Than You Are
7. Top 10 Tips for Winning an Argument
8. Top 10 Tips for Improving Your Cooking
9. Top 10 Tips for Self-Improvement
10. Top 10 Tips for Your First Ballet or Opera
11. Top 10 Stain Removal Tips
12. Top 10 Tips for Frugal Living
13. Top 10 Tips to Prepare for Another Depression
14. Top 10 Tips for Surviving the Streets
15. Top 10 Most Returned Gifts

TOP 10 TIPS TO COMMIT THE PERFECT CRIME

10 DNA
DNA is the surest way to prove you committed a crime. It is absolutely imperative that you do not leave any DNA behind you, and that is very difficult. The best solution to this is to commit your crime in a place likely to have a lot of DNA from strangers, for example, a park, a mall, anywhere that a lot of people tend to gather. Finding your DNA will be like finding a needle in a haystack.

9 RELATIONSHIP
The majority of crimes is committed by someone close to the victim. The police know this well and they know whom to question. Your best bet here is to pick someone randomly as the victim. This is especially true if murder is your crime of choice. Don't be tempted to commit your crime against someone you only know in passing—it must be a total stranger.

8 PROXIMITY
This ties in to number two on this list—commit the crime in another town. You don't want to travel so far that you can be connected because you took a trip, just far enough that you are outside of the main area of interest to the police. You also don't want to be on the road for hours before the crime, because you may become tired, or after the crime, because you may still be on the streets when the big investigation begins.

7 TYPE OF CRIME
Choose your crime carefully. For example, you are almost certain to get caught if you try to rob a bank. Choose a crime that can be committed in the early hours of the morning or that can be done very discreetly during the daytime.

6 EVIDENCE

Most criminals are caught because they tried to hide the crime—what they should have been doing is trying to hide any connection they have to the crime. It doesn't matter if the police know the crime happened. If your crime involves a gun or weapon of some kind, use it and drop it. Leave it at the scene. If you follow number seven this will not be a problem. If you kill someone, leave the body there. Do not touch the body at all. Do not move the body and do not try to hide the body. If you have stolen something, you need to get rid of it as quickly as possible, and if it is money, don't start spending large—you will draw attention to yourself.

5 TIMING

Timing is everything. The best time to commit a crime is in the very early hours of the day when most people are asleep. If you do follow this instruction, remember that you need to look like you are not out of place on the street. That means no full-face coverings. The selected time is important when you come to purchase your tools.

4 TOOLS

First off, you need good thick gloves. The thin ones are not good enough as they can split and it is possible to leave fingerprints if they are sufficiently thin. Do not use anything you own and do not buy brands you normally buy unless they are very generic brands. This means you need to go shopping. Shop out of town and shop in large department stores where you are less likely to be remembered. Remember: very common brands only. You must pay in cash and you must destroy any receipts, or shopping bags. After the crime is committed, destroy everything you bought as quickly as you can and don't do it in an obvious way, like having a bonfire in your backyard when you have never done so before. Wait at least one month between buying your goods and committing your crime.

3 ALIBI

It is wise to have an alibi, though not essential if you have followed all the other rules. It doesn't hurt, however. One way you can do this is to plan an out-of-town trip and book your hotel and rental car with your credit card. Sign up for a convention and attend. Try to use a hotel with no cameras. In the early hours travel to the place of your crime, commit it, and return. Enjoy the remainder of your vacation (on your credit card) and return home the next day.

2 THE GETAWAY

If you are committing the crime in the early hours, the best mode of transport is by bike. This will enable you to get off the roads if you need to and to travel quickly. You do not want to be seen on the street walking (remember, the Zodiac Killer nearly got caught this way), and you don't want to be the only car on the street at two a.m.! Take regular bike clothes and wear them. In the case of murder, if you have dumped the murder weapon you should not need to worry about evidence if you do get picked up. Wear an iPod and take a new pack of cigarettes—you can always say you were out getting smokes because you couldn't sleep.

1 AFTERMATH

First of all, do not watch the television and avoid the papers. The police can use these as tools to try to psych you out. Avoid these things for at least a month. Do not celebrate in any way—continue about your everyday life. Do not brag about your crime to anyone.

One final tip: if you do get arrested, this does not mean you have failed to commit the perfect crime. If this happens, do not speak. The police need evidence to convict you—if you have done the job right, there won't be any. Don't help the police with testimony. Remember, the court needs to find you guilty beyond a reasonable doubt.

✳✳✳✳✳✳

TOP 10 PRISON SURVIVAL TIPS

10 DO NOT GET INVOLVED WITH PUNKS

I am not talking about guys with spiked hair—I am talking about guys who become other guys' "girlfriends," usually for protection. While the short-term benefits may be appealing (protection from other prisoners), you can become a virtual slave, to be gambled or sold to other inmates and you will definitely be used and abused.

This also includes being taken under someone's wing; it will almost certainly lead to you being a victim of rape. People who offer this kind of help are either looking for a punk or are looking for someone to pimp out. You should not associate with anyone involved with punks either. Jealousy in prison can lead to murder.

9 DO NOT DISCUSS YOUR CRIME

This rule applies especially in cases of sexual crimes. Prisoners doing time for these types of crimes are the biggest targets for rape and brutality. In fact, it is virtually guaranteed if the crime involves children. If you are convicted of a child-related crime, you should probably request protective custody from the outset; this will keep you out of the main body of the prison and will probably save your life.

8 DO NOT GET INVOLVED IN GAMBLING

This is a sure way to end up dead. This is a no-win situation; you either cannot afford to pay your gambling bills or you win and make the wrong people very angry. Avoid gambling like the plague in prison. Prisoners will do anything to get what you owe them. Having said that, it is wise to learn a few card games before you enter so you can pass the time playing friendly games.

7 DO NOT COLLABORATE WITH THE GUARDS AGAINST OTHER PRISONERS

You should never tell on your fellow prisoners—if it is found out you can enter a whole new world of pain. However, don't be disrespectful to the guards; they can help to make your time go easier.

6 DO NOT BECOME INDEBTED TO ANYONE

When you first arrive, other prisoners will offer to lend you things until you get on your feet, cigarettes, for example. They will offer you a pack in exchange for two later. Absolutely do not accept this offer, it is a very common trick to get you indebted to someone. If you smoke, quit. You should wait until you have earned your own money before buying things. Basically, the rule is: never take anything from anyone in prison. This is going to get you killed or seriously hurt.

5 DON'T STARE AT ANOTHER PRISONER

Always walk with your head facing forward. All it can take is a stare that lasts one second too long for you to become the target of violence. A guy might appear to be friendly or placid one minute, but the next he can be your worst enemy.

4 DO NOT USE DRUGS

Drug use is a guaranteed road to trouble. You will become severely indebted if you become addicted and you run the risk of being caught by the guards. Drugs are readily accessible and while they may make your time seem less painful, they will almost certainly lead you into big trouble.

3 WORK OUT

Working out not only helps to pass the time, it also helps to bulk you up, making you less of a target. You should not appear weak; this means not looking at your feet while you walk. Avoid the temptation to get a tattoo—they often lead to diseases like hepatitis. You will also regret it once you are out.

2 KEEP YOUR MOUTH SHUT

Do not tell other prisoners about your private life. Do not discuss your crimes and do not discuss politics or religion. Any type of discussion that can lead to an argument is a big no-no. Don't put your business out onto the street. At the same time, respect other prisoners' privacy and don't pry into their private lives.

1 BE RESPECTFUL AND POLITE

Always be polite and respectful to other prisoners. Respect is the only thing a prisoner has and taking that away can be disastrous. Remember, if you give others your respect, they will most likely return the favor. You do not want to make enemies in prison.

✳✳✳✳✳✳

TOP 10 TIPS FOR OUTRUNNING THE COPS

10 PICK YOUR RIDE CAREFULLY

Assuming you have a choice, this tip is obvious but not at all straight-forward. You have to choose a car that suits your circumstances. You may want to choose a fast, fancy sports car, but it may draw too much attention or run out of fuel fast or become uncontrollable from the slightest brush with a pursuing car. You may then go for a heavy, sturdy vehicle, so that it handles well, can endure rugged terrain, and withstands enough damage to still make it. But one of these may be too slow, or too big for you to maneuver through traffic, and it may even flip over too easily.

So, it's not a simple decision at all; get what you think is better for your driving style and your plan. Inconspicuous cars are a good choice in general. And once you have picked your car, first and foremost, fill her up! Several chases end a few minutes after they've started just because the speedsters forgot to fill the tank before going for it. Second, be aware of how much mileage your car can get from a full tank; this may also influence your choice in cars, depending on how far you need to go. Remember that you'll be going fast, so you'll be spending more fuel.

9 HAVE A POLICE SCANNER

This one is fairly obvious if you want to dramatically increase your chances for escape. Having a police scanner while you're driving means that you pretty much know what they're planning to do to stop you, like laying spike strips and the like. It also gives you the advantage of knowing what they think you're up to. For instance, if they lose track of you, or think they know where you'll be going, you'll know right away and you'll be able to trick them by going where they don't expect you to, leaving their cruisers in the dust.

If you are really sly, you'd get a TV installed in the car too. You could check out the news channel to see what the news helicopter is broadcasting, and get even more information from the reporters on what the police are planning (which would give you an immense advantage).

8 DON'T GET OUT

This is an obvious one too, but many "fugitives" have been shown to get desperate when their car crashes, so they get out of the car and start running scared. When this happens, you know that they're done for. Unless you severely hindered your ride, don't get out. Police officers will be chasing you from all around, their aggressive dogs taking point, and the news helicopter will keep its camera sights on you. You simply won't be able to escape on foot.

There is a video of a guy who got out, then got into a house, and changed clothes, coming out calmly as if he were someone else. He almost made it, except the news helicopter crew got suspicious of a guy wearing the same shoes as the fugitive and cried foul to the cops. Try at your own risk.

7 DON'T PARK IT

There might be situations where you might need to slow down in order to maneuver or dodge obstacles. But whatever you do, don't make a full stop. The police will obviously catch up and box you in against the obstacle you were trying to avoid. By extension, don't shift to reverse unless you absolutely need to. You will need to make a full stop for starters, and obviously driving in reverse is harder. Plus, you will need to stop yet again to shift back to normal, and by that time there will be police cruisers all around you. Also, if you stop, citizens may attack you (especially if you've given them reasons to be angry at you).

6 STAY ON COURSE

This combines several tips in one, really. First, plan your route. Notice danger points, and alternate routes you can take. That way you won't be running in circles until you run out of gas. You'll know where to go, and where to detour if things get hairy.

Second, whatever you do, don't go off-road! Even if you have a vehicle suited for off-road, it's risky. You may end up sunken in hidden curbs, or simply stuck in mud. Even if you're lucky to find a clear off-road area, you'll inevitably slow down, and the cops will catch up eventually.

Also, you need to get familiarized with the turns you'll be making and how your ride handles them. It sounds pretty dumb, but many car chases have ended from the driver overshooting the turn and running into a pole he could've easily avoided otherwise.

Finally, please don't go back to your neighborhood. You may think this is a good idea because you're familiar with the area, but it's not. If it's a small neighborhood, you'll need to slow down to take turns, and there will be bigger chances for the police to seal off the area, leaving you without escape.

5 SLOW DOWN AT INTERSECTIONS

This one sounds pretty contradictory, to say the least. Why would I want to slow down if I'm being chased, for crying out loud! Actually, it's very good to slow down and look out when you're crossing intersections, whether they have stoplights or not.

The most horrible endings to police chases happen at intersections. Your car gets smashed by an eighteen-wheeler running across or you hit a Jeep making a turn and careen out of control into a row of cars stopped at a red light. Very gruesome, and you and many innocents can get hurt, and you don't want that. So, slow down, look both ways, and plan your moves accordingly. If you get a red light, you have to be extra careful.

This also applies to railroad crossings; those freight trains will literally annihilate you if you don't pay attention.

4 CHANGE CARS

This is usually risky but effective. It's certainly more effective than changing clothes or staying in a damaged or useless car. It's much more preferable to do it indoors at a public place, such as a parking garage.

Quickly get out of your car and choose a car of a different color, even if it's a similar model to yours. It's actually better if you choose a car that's similar to yours, because you're already used to your own vehicle, and you don't want to lose control of your ride just because you're not used to how it handles. Then, take your chosen vehicle out inconspicuously, and hopefully you've bedazzled the cops and the helicopters with the switch, at least for a while.

3 TAKE COVER (FROM HELICOPTERS)

This tip is critical if you want to lose the cops completely. Those helicopters overhead, be they police choppers or a local news helicopter, will be aiming their cameras at you all the time. This means that even if you've lost the police cruisers behind, they still know where you are thanks to the helicopters, and will eventually catch up to you again, unless, of course, you're able to stay out of their sights. Try going under a roof, a parking garage for example, and get out through the least obvious path. The idea is to take cover, then take unusual roads so the helicopter cameras won't know where to look when they expect you back in the clear. If you're in an area full of trees, you might get a chance to lose them, too.

But losing the helicopters doesn't mean you've won. You'll need to be conspicuous while driving and pray that they won't find you again.

2 BEWARE THE PIT MANEUVER

This is a procedure that the police are very proud of and get extensive training on. The PIT (usually meaning Pursuit Intervention Technique) Maneuver consists of a police cruiser approaching the fleeing car on one side, until the cruiser's front wheels are roughly aligned with the speeding vehicle's back wheels. Then, the police car steers sharply, hitting the trunk of the criminal's car and making it spin out, usually to 90 degrees from the road and straight into a ditch or a wall. It's very effective and very common.

So, if you see one of the pursuing police cars approaching you to one side, either fully accelerate your car (if you're not already) in order to dodge the hit, or, slow down all of a sudden, so that you hit the front of the police car first, or the cruiser only hits you innocently on the side.

1 GET TO AN AIRPORT

This is the ultimate getaway tactic, depending on the circumstances. You don't even need to buy a ticket! (Or hijack a plane either.)

What you need to do is get to the airport quickly. Once near, the helicopters won't be able to chase you anymore because it's restricted airspace for them! That's really good for starters. Then, you need to go into the airport parking area. This is the key moment: you may want to get into the airport, buy a ticket, and fly off into the sunset. But this may be hard because the police may have warned the airport and they would be looking for you all over.

Instead, you could change your car for one of the cars in the parking area, and drive out inconspicuously, leaving the police desperately looking for you at the airport! A clean and successful escape.

※※※※※※

TOP 10 TIPS FOR FLYING UNDER THE RADAR

10 LEAVE NO TRAILS

This means pay in cash—always (unless you own an anonymous credit card)—and shred any documentation you do not need (use a decent shredder that turns your paper into dust; authorities can piece together the basic type of shredded documents). Don't use your real name if possible, and definitely don't apply for credit. Your credit report is like a big map pointing right to you.

9 SECURE YOURSELF ONLINE

If you are going to be using the Internet in your secret lifestyle, you should do everything you can to secure yourself online. This means using PGP (encryption software) when e-mailing people (and using an e-mail account that cannot be traced to you directly), and, most importantly, it means saying nothing online that you would not be prepared to see on the front page of the newspaper.

8 GET AN ANONYMOUS CELL PHONE

Most countries allow you to buy prepaid cell phones that do not need to be registered to a name or address. Once you get your prepaid sim card, top it up with cash and do not give anyone the number. Use the number exclusively for making outgoing calls. If you are planning to contact someone that may be looking for you, you should discard the prepaid sim once a month and try to buy prepaid sims online that will let you call from a foreign number.

7 GIVE UP THE PERKS

In order to reduce the chances of someone finding you when you don't want to be found, you need to stop using things like frequent flyer points, ATMs (unless you have an anonymous card—see number two), cable, video store memberships, etc. For entertainment there is always the Internet, and if you are wanting to avoid having an Internet account linked to you, just download the latest music and movies from a free Internet cafe.

6 LIVE SIMPLY

The best way to remain anonymous (and therefore to be ignored by the powers that be) is to live a simple lifestyle. If you lead a flashy lifestyle, live in the best house, drive the latest Bentley, throw world famous parties, people are going to start paying attention and the taxman is going to wonder how you can afford it. In the case of tax evasion, some governments can even order you to give detailed evidence of how you have paid for your high-price consumer goods if they are unable to find a taxable source of income in your life. This can then be used as evidence of tax fraud.

5 BECOME A DIPLOMAT

For seventy-five thousand euros, you can become an official diplomat of one of two stable Southern African (but not South Africa) nations. The result is that you are exempt from tax in your country of residence from all income earned outside of the nation. Your home becomes an officially registered consulate and you receive immunity from the governmental forces. While this won't help you with anonymity, it does help you with avoidance of the law.

4 USE A MAIL DROP

A mail drop enables you to receive mail from anywhere without your real address becoming known. It can act as a complete barrier between you and companies on the Internet that you buy goods from, and can help protect you from people who are seeking information on your wealth based on your home's location and public records. Coupled with a false name and false documentation, you can virtually become a new person.

3 BECOME A PERPETUAL TOURIST

This is perhaps the best method of becoming a sovereign individual. A perpetual tourist keeps his finances in tax havens and then travels the world spending as much time as is necessary to avoid becoming an official resident anywhere. Tourists are often treated better than residents and you can choose to live in nations that are closer to your way of thinking.

2 GET AN ANONYMOUS CREDIT CARD

Anonymous credit cards are quite easy to come by on the Internet. You simply provide upfront funds and an e-mail address and you are e-mailed your card number and expiration date. When you use the card online you can give any name, address, and security code as the clearinghouse will only take into account the number and expiration date. This means that you have less security as it is easier for someone to steal your card number and use it, but you have a hundred percent total anonymity. Combined with a mail drop, you can purchase any goods you want and they can never be traced to you.

1 BUY A CAMOUFLAGE PASSPORT

Believe it or not you can actually legally have a false passport made. They are called camouflage passports and are usually passports from a country that no longer exists, such as the USSR and Rhodesia. Groups who make and supply these passports say, "a camouflage passport is designed to look realistic enough to allow a person to conceal his nationality in event of a hijacking, riot, or some similar situation where his identity may single him out as a crime victim." Additionally, you often also receive (free of charge) an accompanying driver's license and other forms of ID from the same nation as the passport to help substantiate your false identity.

✳✳✳✳✳✳

TOP 10 TIPS FOR GETTING A FLIGHT UPGRADE

10 TRAVEL ALONE

While this is not always possible, your chances of getting an upgrade are much higher if you are traveling alone. If you are traveling as part of a group, even if it is just a small family, the airline is not likely to upgrade you because it means upgrading everyone.

9 TAKE ADVANTAGE OF SPECIAL EVENTS

If you have just recently been married or are having a birthday or other celebration, be sure to tell the airline staff. They may be willing to upgrade you to make your event more special. Take a wedding certificate with you if need be.

8 BOOK A FULL PLANE

If you can, try to book yourself onto a flight that is going to have a very full economy section —this is much easier during holidays than other times of the year. You can figure out the numbers by going through a false booking on your airline's website (make sure you don't book by mistake!). If the economy class is full, the airline is more likely to try to squeeze passengers into first class rather than turn them away. In some cases, however, if they can't upgrade, they might offer travel at a later date with an upgrade or an overnight stay in a nice hotel for free. The more flexible you are, the better.

7 BE SNEAKY

When you are booking your flight through a travel agent, be extremely friendly to them. If they like you, they may be willing to mark you as a CIP (Commercially Important Passenger) or SFU (Suitable for Upgrade). The airline can ignore this information, but it is worth a try—the more effort you put into getting your upgrade, the greater your chances.

6 PICK YOUR PLANE

If it is possible, you should try to pick a flight that will be using a plane with a large first-class cabin. There are many sites on the Internet that let you see the layout of different planes and the configurations that the various airlines use. Take advantage of these. Not only are these sites useful for finding a good "upgrade" plane, but you can also pick the best seats in economy in case you don't get upgraded. I would strongly recommend using Seat Guru (www. seatguru.com); it is an excellent resource for travelers.

5 AVOID BUSINESS HOURS

Try to fly outside of business hours because the first-class cabin is likely to be full on these flights. Try flying at odd hours of the day and on the weekends.

4 BE POLITE

Be very polite to all of the staff you are dealing with at the airline. Quite often the decision about upgrades is left to the check-in staff. If they don't like you, you won't get upgraded. Smile when talking to the staff but don't be so overly friendly that you frighten them.

3 DRESS THE PART

Dress like you are a first-class passenger. You don't have to go overboard by wearing a suit and tie, but do not wear tattered jeans, dirty shoes, and a T-shirt with Che Guevara on the front, or any other obviously "non-first-class" clothing. Also, because of the unfortunate situation with terrorism at the moment, you should probably be clean-shaven.

2 JOIN THE FREQUENT FLYER PROGRAM

By joining the frequent flyer program of your airline, you are showing loyalty to the airline. In addition, you get the obvious benefits of being a member, such as free flights if you earn enough points. If your airline has different levels of membership, buy the most expensive one you are able to afford; unfortunately, money talks, but the extra cost of the program may be well worth the improved comfort on future flights.

1 ASK

A lot of people tell you not to do this, for a variety of reasons, but in my own experience, this can work. I have been given upgrades twice in the last year for asking if the airline needed volunteers. If you have followed all of the previous rules, you have a very good chance of getting the upgrade if there are seats available. Incidentally, ask very quietly—if other customers hear you get an upgrade they will ask as well—so the airline is less likely to give you one if you broadcast your request.

✳✳✳✳✳✳

TOP 10 TIPS FOR SOUNDING SMARTER THAN YOU ARE

10 LEARN A TOPIC TO DEBUNK

The majority of "hot topics" are debated by people with very little knowledge on the subject. A good example of this is global warming—the majority of people you speak to on this subject will tell you how we must change our habits to prevent global warming, but few will know what "anthropogenic global warming" is. Spend a little time learning what the real experts on these faddish topics say and you simply can't go wrong. Try to remember some of the names of authors so you can quote them.

9 IMPROVE YOUR VOCABULARY

The simplest way to do this is to subscribe to a "word-a-day" e-mail list. Remember to ensure that you memorize the correct pronunciation and spelling of the new word or phrase. Perhaps you can start with "mesonoxian" or other obscure words.

8 LEARN OBSCURE KNOWLEDGE

By developing knowledge in a very obscure area, you are very unlikely to meet someone else with the same knowledge. This means you can wax lyrical for hours and it doesn't matter how many mistakes you make; no one will know, and you will seem ultra-smart. You might, for example, spend some time studying the early Egyptian dynasties (or an interesting character like Smenkhkare) or the writings of early Christian writers. You can be sure that even the most staunch Southern Baptist fundamentalist has never heard of most of the "fathers of the Church," let alone read anything they wrote. Saint Igantius of Antioch is a good start; you can follow up with Athenagoras, Irenaeus, Origen, Novatian, and Polycarp. Great subject matter for the atheist who wishes to debate fundamentalists.

7 LEARN GENERAL KNOWLEDGE

This can be done very easily. Buy Trivial Pursuit (Genius Edition) and memorize one card before going to bed each night. In no time you will have a fount of general knowledge so immense that no one will dare debate you at Friday night drinks. The other thing you can do to improve general knowledge is to read "This Day in History" articles. Good Lord! I feel smarter just thinking about it!

6 ASK QUESTIONS

The best way to use this trick is to ask questions when you already know the answer. This is a form of irony when used in the right way; when the person you are questioning answers, you can ask a related question which will make it appear that you have taken in what they said, absorbed it, and wish to clarify an aspect of the topic. Additionally, when you are discussing a subject with someone who clearly knows less about it than you, you can ask questions that you know will make them stumble. This is particularly good if you have a large audience, as everyone will be in awe of you. Make sure you are humble when the person's weakness shows.

5 LEARN ABOUT GOOD BOOKS

SparkNotes. I repeat, SparkNotes. Use the short notes found on this website to get a broad overview of famous classic novels. You only need to learn enough to make it seem that you have read the book. For a decent classic you should be able to do this in thirty minutes or less. And, who knows, you may find that you want to read the book and gain some real intelligence.

4 WATCH MOVIES

Watch some classic movies that are both good and bad. These movies don't have to be silent movies, black and white, etc., just good and fulfilling movies. Also, watch some bad movies. Someone who can spout off one or two good movies will sound either smart or fake. But someone who can state both good and bad movies, and justify why each is classified that way, will sound intelligent.

3 LEARN QUOTES

A great writer once said, "Most people are other people. Their thoughts are someone else's opinions, their lives a mimicry, their passions a quotation." While this is amusing, it is not entirely correct when trying to appear smarter. People will be utterly in awe of you if you can quote a famous line from poetry, a great play, or a witticism by a literary master. There are a million sites on the Internet that will help you to find quotations. Learn one a day. If you wish to learn a few lines of poetry, I recommend starting with Plath, Ginsberg, or Whitman; everyone knows who they are, but few will be able to quote them. Oh, the quotation I used here is by Oscar Wilde.

2 USE WORDS YOU KNOW

Nothing makes you look more like an idiot than fumbling language. Stick to what you know! People will argue that tapes and books can teach you new words, but you still risk a terrible mistake. Learning new words can broaden your thinking and amplify your ability to communicate. However, doing so will open you up to appearing stupid, so you should stick with words that you are a hundred percent positive of their pronunciation and meaning. Even if it takes you an entire extra sentence to explain a concept that one word would have clarified instantly, it's totally worth it.

1 BE QUIET
Quite simply, the less you say, the less you can say wrong. Oh, and smile and nod knowingly.

※※※※※※

TOP 10 TIPS FOR WINNING AN ARGUMENT

10 KEEP YOUR VOICE SOFT AND STEADY
When debating, you should never raise your voice. You should remain calm at all times. The louder you talk, the louder your opponent talks, and the end result is a yelling match. And, of course, it goes without saying that you should definitely not resort to violence. You can even try to talk quieter than normal, as this can draw people in to you and can make you appear wise. A dispute is not won by the person with the loudest voice; rather, it is won by the person with the most compelling arguments.

9 GET YOUR OPPONENT ON YOUR SIDE
It is a good idea to try to get your opponent on your side by making statements that you know he agrees with; this puts you in the strong position in the debate. You don't even need to use a fact relating to your debate. You could, for example, in a debate about the existence of God, state, "I am sure you agree with me when I say that gas is overpriced." As soon as your opponent agrees, you have won a psychological battle. You are no longer the opponent—you are a comrade. This technique is so effective it is used by telemarketers all the time.

8 DON'T ATTACK

It is not a good idea to blatantly tell your opponent that he is wrong, instead, you should show that he is wrong through good counterarguments. Telling a person they are wrong merely annoys them and does nothing for your argument (at least until you can prove it), as it is a subjective comment. Be humble in the debate and show good will—not only will it make you look good if you win, it will show that you are a worthy opponent even if you lose.

7 DON'T PLAY DIRTY

Never resort to name calling, even if your opponent does. You must attack your opponent's argument, not their person. As soon as you begin to criticize your opponent, it becomes obvious that you have run out of ways to defend your view. These types of insults (ad hominem) are a sure way to lose a debate. You should be pleased if your opponent resorts to this feeble attempt to escape the real debate as it means you are close to victory.

6 DEFINE THE FUNDAMENTALS

When arguing, both parties need to agree on fundamental "truths" to begin with; if you don't, there can be no debate. What is the point of arguing that the Bible was written by God when your opponent doesn't even believe in God? You should first debate the existence of God. If you both agree that He exists, you can then debate the smaller points. If your opponent convinces you that God cannot exist, there is little point in arguing about the authorship of the Bible. This is the structure seen in the *Summa Theologica* by Saint Thomas Aquinas—he starts with the basic points, presents arguments and counterarguments, and moves on when each point is "proven" by logic.

5 STICK TO THE SUBJECT

When a person is beginning to lose an argument, it is quite common to see them try to divert the topic at hand to another, thereby hoping you will not notice their weakness and will get entangled in a whole new debate. When this happens, don't fall for it. Return to the original topic immediately. Do not give any time to other topics (no matter how tempting it may be) until you have completed the first.

4 ASK QUESTIONS

This is known as the "Socratic method." When your opponent states a "fact," probe deeper into the fact with questions that are designed to expose its flaws; these are usually "tell me more" type questions, for example, "Can you give me an example?" or "Another way of looking at this is … does this seem reasonable?" These questions will invariably lead your opponent to the truth and if they are honest, they will concede. Unfortunately, this is not always the case. I have seen frustrated people depart the debate in anger because they believe you are "trying to trick" them. But don't worry; this is a win if it happens.

3 BE SILENT

After making a strong argument, let your opponent do all the talking, especially if he lacks the facts to oppose you. He will bluster and fumble, giving you a variety of new weapons with which to attack him. This may not lead to him conceding defeat but it may lead to him walking away from the debate—a clear victory for you. Many an argument has been won by not arguing at all! As an aside, this is an excellent method for getting your own way: make your request, and when it is declined, remain silent. This usually makes the other person so nervous (as no one likes silence) that they may give in just to get out of an uncomfortable situation.

2 KNOW YOUR FACTS

Do not state that something is "true" unless you absolutely know it is; be prepared to prove it if necessary. It is incredibly annoying to debate a topic with a person who is simply making up their argument on the fly. You wouldn't like it if people did it to you, so don't do it to others. Only engage in a debate that you know you can win based on facts.

1 KNOW WHEN YOU'RE BEAT

If you have all the facts to back you up, you should be able to win your argument if your opponent is honest. But there will always be times when your opponent gets the better of you and they corner you. When this happens, be courteous and concede the win. You should always be graceful in defeat. Nothing is worse than a person who argues simply for the sake of it and absolutely will not give in, no matter how obvious their loss.

✳✳✳✳✳✳

TOP 10 TIPS FOR IMPROVING YOUR COOKING

10 THROW AWAY YOUR MICROWAVE

The microwave is good for one thing only—defrosting—and even that can be done just as easily by putting something in the refrigerator one day before you need it so it can defrost gently. Microwaves do not add to the flavor of anything they cook, whereas stovetop or oven cooking does through the caramelization of juices (which is what gives us the brown crispy outside of meat). Having a microwave in the house leads to the temptation to cut corners. I have not had a microwave for three years, and I can still cook an entire meal from scratch in less than forty minutes, and I guarantee it tastes a hell of a lot better than anything cooked in a microwave.

9 READ THE RECIPE

If you are using a recipe, read it twice from beginning to end before you start doing any cooking. So often we skim a recipe and then in our hurry (once things start to heat up) we neglect certain steps. By reading the recipe twice, you are less likely to skip a step, which can result in disaster. Having said this, I also recommend experimenting with your cooking—don't become a slave to your cookbook—but make the choices intentionally, not through forgetfulness.

8 MAKE A LIST

If you are cooking a meal with multiple components, such as a roast chicken with vegetables, it can be very helpful to write a list of what you need to do and when. You can write down specific times (I find it useful to work back from the time you want to serve). This results in a much smoother working process and you won't have people waiting for dinner to be served late.

7 USE WINE

Wine can add a lot of flavor to a meal; if you are braising meat, for example, in a pot roast, pour in some wine. The alcohol content left after cooking is not enough to make this an "adults-only" meal (on the other hand, I think children should be given wine with dinner from a very young age anyway). The general rule is to use red wine with red meat, and white with white. If you are going to pan-fry some fish, just pour in a half-cup of white wine and some herbs, and you can make a lovely meal with a ready-made sauce.

6 USE FRESH HERBS

Dried herbs have little or no flavor. This tip alone can transform bland food into masterful food. You can either grow your own herbs, or you can buy them fresh from the supermarket. The herbs you are most likely to use repeatedly (and, therefore, the best ones to grow yourself) are thyme, bay leaves, parsley (use the Italian flat leaf type—it has a lot more flavor than curly parsley), and, (to a lesser extent unless you like to do a lot of Asian cooking) cilantro. Another less-common herb that you should try if you haven't is tarragon, which has a slight aniseed flavor and is excellent with fish or chicken. Buy the French kind; the other type (Israeli) has no flavor.

5 USE PLENTY OF SALT

Forget everything you have been told about salt and health. If you want to eat good food, you need to use plenty of salt. A real pinch of salt involves using two fingers and a thumb, not the forefinger and thumb. People have been frightened off using salt by government advertisements, and it is ridiculous. The French eat a lot of salt (and butter) and they have a very low cardiac death rate compared to England, for example, which has a bizarre obsession with salt-reduced diets. When boiling pasta, make sure the water tastes like the sea. If you have never tasted seawater, it tastes like it is so salty that a mouthful would make you gag. For a very large pasta pot of water, I usually use two small handfuls of salt. When cooking vegetables in water, always add salt. Contrary to popular belief, salt in cooking water does not stop the color from leeching out of vegetables; it simply enhances their flavor. Also, if you boil your potatoes before roasting, salty water helps to give more color and crunch to the outside.

4 USE BUTTER

Butter is fundamental in good cooking. When you fry a steak, you should always fry it in butter (with a little oil added to stop the butter burning). Butter adds flavor to anything, and can also be used as a thickener (see sauce below). Do not use margarine or semi-soft butter. Always cook with unsalted butter (then you can decide exactly how much salt you want the dish to have). If you really want to improve boiled or steamed vegetables, undercook them, then add them to a pan with a big knob of butter and finish the cooking over a high heat. Add salt, pepper, and chopped parsley.

3 MAKE A SAUCE

They say that a good sauce is the difference between a cook and a chef. Sauces are extremely easy to make and you should almost always prepare a sauce to go with your meals. If you have fried meat in a frying pan, leave the heat on and pour some wine into the pan, then scrape all the bits off the bottom and cook until the wine has evaporated by half. Pour in some stock (any type will do, but do try to match the stock with the meat or use chicken for everything except fish) and cook down until it is half again. Taste it and add salt and pepper if you need to. Strain and serve. Additionally, if you want your sauce to be a little thicker, whisk in a knob of butter with the heat off.

2 USE GOOD INGREDIENTS

Fresh ingredients make all the difference. Vegetables and meat bought from small producers (such as local farms) is even better. Supermarkets have strict requirements about the appearance of food and very little concern about taste. An apple bought from the local market will always be better than anything you can buy in a supermarket. Add to that the overpacking that we see so often in chain supermarkets and you have a recipe for disaster. I guarantee you that any of your regular recipes when made with fresh ingredients and not supermarket ingredients will be a hundred times better.

1 TASTE A LOT

Tasting is the most important part of cooking. You must constantly taste what you are cooking as you cook it. This is true even of things like hamburgers. You should take a little bit of your hamburger meat and fry it, then taste it. Keep adding more salt and pepper or other ingredients and repeat the frying. When it finally tastes right, you can make your burgers. Because this is such an important part of cooking, many chefs will not cook with ingredients they do not like. Tasting early in the cooking process can save you from a disaster later on, when it is too late to recover.

✳✳✳✳✳✳

TOP 10 TIPS FOR SELF-IMPROVEMENT

10 GET OFF TO A GOOD START

This means getting up early and eating breakfast. You will have much more energy throughout the day to follow the rest of these tips if you do! If you are so inclined, you can even include a little exercise in your morning routine. If you live with other people, you can try to use this opportunity to get everyone together at the table to eat in the mornings. This is a nice way to start the day and a good way to ensure open lines of communication in a very busy household.

9 KEEP A SCHEDULE

It is a very good idea to write down the tasks you need to achieve in each day. As you complete them, check them off. You should not, however, feel like you are bound to your list. If you don't manage to do everything, it doesn't matter, move any incomplete tasks from today onto tomorrow's list. This is also a great help if you are a procrastinator.

8 TAKE A BREAK AND HAVE FUN

If you spend too much time in front of the computer, at your desk, or doing whatever it is that your occupation requires, you should take a break. This doesn't mean you have to take time off work, it just means you should try to make better use of your non-work time to do something fun. I always have difficulty pulling myself away from the computer, and as a result I don't go out as often as I should on the weekends or in the evenings. But every time I do I wonder why I haven't done it sooner. This is a good way to develop new interests and friends and to break up the monotony of everyday life.

7 BE GENEROUS

Generosity has a tendency to come back. By generosity I am not referring only to money. You can be generous with your smiles, your advice, and many other things. Always try to find a way to help others. One day you may be in great need and people you know will be more likely to come to your aid when they know that you would do the same for them. You might know someone that could use help around the home from time to time; not only are you doing a good thing by helping them out, you may also make a great new friend.

6 ACCEPT THE THINGS YOU CAN'T CHANGE

When something bad happens in our lives, we try to fix them or change them. But sometimes we can't. Often this leads to spending hours moping and falling into depression. If you can make yourself accept the things you cannot change, you will become a much happier person. Acceptance of these situations also allows us to start finding a way to cope much faster. For example, you may realize that you have only ten dollars left in your bank account that has to last the next two weeks. Instead of getting down about it, accept that you have no money and work out a way to survive on that amount. You can save yourself from wasting hours in a bad mood by just getting on with life. You will find much more serenity in life following this tip.

5 LEARN A NEW LANGUAGE

Learning another language is one of the best ways to improve your grasp on English. In my own experience, learning French in high school taught me so much more about grammar than English class ever did. In addition, when I later started studying ancient Greek, I learned a lot about the roots of English words, something I have found very useful in writing in the years since. As well as improving your knowledge of English, if you learn a living language you increase the number of places you might like to visit or make those vacations much more enjoyable by being able to speak to the natives in their own tongue.

4 BREAK THE CHAIN

If you have a lot of patterns in your life, try breaking them. Do something different every day. Let's say you always order the same meal at your regular Friday night restaurant. Why not try something else this Friday? Not only do you get to broaden your experiences of life, you open up many doors for the future. Not long ago, I would never eat Asian food or seafood. Then one day I decided that I would just try it. Seafood is now one of my favorite foods and I would hate to be without it. Because I discovered that I love Thai and Chinese food, I can eat in any restaurant I want. That first step also meant that I am now willing to try absolutely any food. My disliking of disgusting foods had a much greater impact as well; I would only vacation in countries that had foods I felt safe with. Since then I have been to Asian countries and loved it.

3 FACE THE FEAR

Every day you should do something you don't want to do or feel uncomfortable doing. This varies in degrees for everyone, but we all have little things we can start out with. For example, you may not go to the gym because you fear everyone looking at you—do it anyway! In no time you will be so much more confident that you abolish the fear entirely and can move on to the next fear, maybe even something bigger. Living a fearless life gives you a confidence that is visible to others. Instead of building walls around ourselves, we should be tearing them down.

2 FORGET GOALS—LIVE FOR THE NOW

Lists of this nature almost always tell you to set and write goals. I am going to tell you the opposite. A very wise psychotherapist once told me that if you set a goal, and achieve it, you are often left with an empty feeling because the goal is not what you thought it would be. Not only does it not satisfy, you inevitably end up missing out on so much life by striving to reach something in the future. Having said this, I don't think you should ignore the future—it is worth having some idea of what you might like to one day achieve—but don't focus all of your energy on getting it. A good example of the difference is this: I have a goal to live in France. I spend ten years trying to save up all my money so I can achieve that goal. In the meantime I am so busy scrimping and saving I can't afford to go out with friends, I can't afford to live in a nice home, and I am miserable because I am not living in France. On the other hand, if I simply decide that one day I would like to live in France, the idea is in my mind, but I continue to live and enjoy my life. In living my life, I am happy now and not focused on a distant goal. If it happens, great. If it doesn't happen, I haven't failed at anything. But who knows what wonderful things may happen in my life in the meantime? A very good fictitious example of this can be found in the film *American Beauty*.

1 DON'T PROCRASTINATE

This is one I struggle with a lot in my own life. The feeling after completing a task you would normally put off is a great high and certainly a much healthier one than some of the other highs in our lives. When you put something off, you are putting yourself into time-debt. You have to pay that debt back and almost always you end up having to do that at the most inconvenient time. By putting off writing, for example, I end up having to write at seven at night when I would rather be watching a movie and having a drink! Your life will become so much more organized if you follow this rule.

✳✳✳✳✳✳

TOP 10 TIPS FOR YOUR FIRST BALLET OR OPERA

10 WHAT TO SEE

There is a reason that the "classical" operas and ballets are classics: they're very good and worthy of being performed over and over. If you are familiar with and like the music from any particular opera or ballet, it might be a good one to start with. Or, you can simply call your nearest company or go to their website and ask them which they would recommend. Opera and ballet companies are always very happy to have new attendees, particularly since the average age of fans tend to be a bit on the older side (147 years old, to be exact). I would suggest any of the "story" ballets to begin with, such as *Swan Lake, Coppelia, Sleeping Beauty*, or, of course, *The Nutcracker*. If you feel a bit more adventurous, you can attend one of the more abstract ballets. You can also sometimes find ballets choreographed to a certain type of music, or a certain songwriter. If you know that you'll enjoy the music you're at least assured of having a pleasant evening. Be aware that most operas are quite depressing—usually at least one or two characters do not survive and in some of them none of the main characters live to the end! If you've watched enough Quentin Tarantino movies and can take the carnage, I'd recommend anything by Puccini or Carmen, because you will recognize some of the music. Or, you usually can find a more lighthearted opera, such as *The Elixir of Love, Cosi Fan Tutte*, or the *Marriage of Figaro*. Don't worry about not understanding what's happening; many operas now have OpTrans, which displays the words in English above the stage. Also, you will get a program with a plot synopsis. If you are totally undecided on opera versus ballet, choose the ballet. Ballet dancers are in excellent physical shape and almost always wear skimpy costumes displaying their lovely legs; opera singers wear circus tents. At least you'll have something to look at the ballet.

9 WHO TO GO WITH

Go with whomever you'd like to bring and whom you can drag along with you. Married couples, dating couples, platonic friends, anything goes. Opera and ballet being cultural activities, no one is going to bat an eye if you're a man and bring another guy, or a woman who brings a man twenty years younger than her, or five women who go together, or even if you go alone. I would recommend against bringing any of the following: young children who either cannot sit still or who will not understand that the woman on stage did not just really kill herself; people who fall asleep when they sit in the dark and then begin to snore; people who cannot survive for ten minutes without checking their cell phones; and people with bladder issues, unless they have an aisle seat. Oh, and please, for the love of God, do not bring people who feel compelled to sing or dance along!

8 TICKETS: WHEN TO GO, WHERE TO SIT, HOW TO GET THEM

If you were feeling a bit nervous, I'd recommend either a weeknight or a weekend matinee. These tend to be less formal. If you look online, you can usually find a seating chart of the venue with the pricing structure. Take a look at it before you call for tickets. Oddly, the most expensive sections are not necessarily the best value. I'd much prefer to sit in the first row of one of the less expensive sections than two rows ahead of that for an additional ten dollars a ticket. It's also nice to sit toward the center of the theater; it's pointless being five rows from the stage if you're in the end seat on the right and you can't see half of the performance. If you're on a budget or just don't feel like spending much money, don't be at all embarrassed by or worried about buying the least expensive tickets. You'll still be able to hear quite well, and to see the performance nicely. Also, the cheapest seats often tend to be taken up by students, so people will assume that you're an actual fan rather than someone who is just attending to see and be seen! Normally you should just be able to call the box office and they will help you purchase tickets. They can be mailed to you or you can pick them up at the box office a day or two before the performance if you're in the area. If you're buying them at the last minute, you can pick them up right before the performance at the "will call" window at the box office. If the performance you want to see is sold out, it's worth trying again in a day or two; subscribers often turn their tickets back in for resale if they cannot attend on their scheduled night. Or, you can buy them from brokers, but I'm afraid you're on your own with that. (They'll be the guys standing out front in sports team jackets with signs saying, "I need tickets." Or maybe that's for football games....) Since you will probably use your credit card to buy the tickets, you will also quickly end up on every cultural mailing list in the city. This will really impress your postman, if no one else.

7 WHAT TO WEAR

Black tie and tails for men, and evening gowns with opera gloves for ladies, of course. No, I'm completely kidding. I really think that that's the number one reason that most people are worried about going, and it's not at all a concern. Unless you're going to opening night, or possibly in Europe, you will see very few people dressed that formally. (And, of those, I think 80 percent are because the women want a chance to dress up and they've forced their men into black tie. The other 20 percent are men who want to dress up.) A jacket for men and a nice dress for women will be more than suitable. If you're attending on a weeknight, many people will not have changed from work so any range of business attire will be seen. Matinees can be even more informal; I've seen people wearing jeans. The exception is if you are bringing a little girl, particularly to *The Nutcracker*. In that case, she is required to dress in the most beautiful velvet dress available with lace trim, tiara, white tights, and whatever else little girls that know they are secretly princesses should wear.

6 WHAT TO BRING AND WHEN TO ARRIVE

Now you're looking quite elegant, so don't ruin the effect by lack of planning now. Bring opera glasses or small binoculars if you have them. Unwrapped hard candies and/or breath mints and a handkerchief or tissue are good to have as well (even if you never cough, for some reason being in a theater seems to cause choking fits). Make sure you have an umbrella if there is any chance of rain, and appropriate outerwear (and underwear!). Ladies, your purse will either be on your lap or on the floor at your feet so I would suggest not bringing that huge one that doubles as a weekend tote. Plan on how long it will take you to arrive there on time if the traffic is terrible, and then leave at least fifteen minutes before that. Everyone else is going to be arriving at the same time and will be trying to park in the same garage or get out of cabs on the same street. You do not want to rush in at the last minute, all sweaty and out of breath. Remember, you are a high-class person now; Cary Grant was never disheveled and rushed. Also, if you arrive late you will not be seated until the ushers feel it's an appropriate time to let you in. You did not go to all of this effort to spend the entire first act in the lobby watching the performance on the closed circuit television, did you?

5 UPON ARRIVAL

Here you are! Usually at the entrance doors you will be greeted, and someone will take your tickets and return the stubs. At this time they will normally tell you in which direction to go (up the stairs, to the door on the right, etc.). Since you have cleverly arrived early, you will have plenty of time to find the coatroom and the restroom. Now is also your chance to admire your fellow patrons of the arts. It will seem that everyone else knows each other and you know no one. Do not believe this. No one else knows anyone either, except the ten people who attend every performance so that they can shriek "Dahling!" across the lobby at each other just to make you feel insecure. Ignore them. In some venues you can go to the bar and preorder an intermission drink. This is quite snazzy because they will give you a number and at intermission you will come out and find your drinks nicely waiting on a table with your number on it, while the hoi polloi is fighting their way to the bar desperately trying to get a glass of wine so they can swill it and be back by the next act. You can calmly sip your drink and laugh at them. See? You're well on your way to being snooty and pretentious already!

4 TIME TO SIT

Everyone else is heading toward the seats and for some reason there has apparently been a power surge because the lights dimmed for a second and a chime-like alarm went off. This means that the performance will begin shortly. So head on in. Hopefully, an usher will be on hand at the entrance to the seating area. You will hand them your ticket stubs; they will look at them and give them back. Then they will hand you programs and lead you to your seats. They will not wipe your seats off with a cloth like they do at the stadium because you are indoors. Hence, you do not have to tip them, a courteous thank you will do. Invariably, if you are in the middle, then the people on the aisle are already sitting. If you are on the aisle, the people in the middle will arrive after you. If you are close enough to the aisle you may choose to just stand and move back into the aisle to let them in. If you are further in, generally you stand as they pass in front of you, or you may twist your knees to the side so they can pass. If you are the one coming through, face forward (toward the stage) and sidle sideways excusing yourself nonstop the entire way. All participants in this little dance are socially obliged to pretend that they are not rubbing up against and being rubbed up against random unattractive strangers. Now that you're seated, it is your chance to read your program. Read the synopsis so you know what's going on, see how long you have to wait until intermission, look to see who you know who has donated money, and complain about the fact that your health insurance company, which is supposed to be a non-profit, has enough money to donate to the arts but just raised your premiums again.

3 THE PERFORMANCE BEGINS: BASIC ETIQUETTE

The lights have dimmed, and all of a sudden people are clapping for no apparent reason. This is generally because the conductor of the orchestra has arrived. The orchestra is seated down in the front in a sort of subterranean level known as the orchestra pit. Occasionally someone on stage will fall into this pit, but that happens less often than you might think. Now the music begins. Do not talk anymore! Just because the curtain is not up yet does not mean that the performance has not started; it has! Hopefully you have turned off your cell phone, and by off, I mean off. Vibrate is not off because it will still buzz and can be heard. And just because your phone is silent does not mean that it is acceptable to send text messages or to check them. Every time you do everyone in your row will automatically glance over at the sudden flash of light from your phone. Even if you are miserable, bored, and not enjoying yourself, sit still, be quiet, and leave at intermission. If you begin having a coughing or sneezing fit, you have your hard candy ready. If it continues, at some point you will have to determine whether or not you will annoy people more by squeezing past in the middle of a performance or staying in your seat while coughing out a lung. Just remember that sound travels an incredible distance in the theater because of the lovely acoustics, so any noise you make is disturbing people six rows behind you. If for some reason you get bored, amuse yourself by glaring at people near you who do not have as much couth as you do and who are behaving badly.

2 WHEN TO APPLAUD

What an incredible performance! You're so glad that you came. You never knew that operas and ballets had such incredible stage settings, and the lights and special effects are dazzling as well. The singing or dancing seems great to you, so you want to applaud. But when? In ballet, the audience will applaud at the end of a great dance. This generally tends to be after a pas de deux, where two dancers perform together, or after a solo (one dancer). Sometimes the audience will begin to applaud during a dance, usually when the dancer can spin or leap around and around in circles for an extended period without toppling over or falling into the orchestra pit. Opera audiences are more finicky and do not applaud as often. They tend to applaud infrequently, only after particularly beautiful arias (songs) and never until they are over. Unless you are absolutely sure that it is in fact the end of the song, it's probably best to wait until the rest of the audience applauds. If you stand up and start screaming "Bravo" in the middle of "Vissi D'Arte" you will greatly irritate everyone else and humiliate yourself (especially since you should be screaming "Brava," but that's for a more advanced lesson). It is also customary to applaud at the end of each act (when the curtain falls and the house lights come up).

1 INTERMISSION

Now you're an old pro at this cultural thing, so you get a chance to enjoy yourself. Time to go and get a drink, go outside to have a cigarette, wander out to the lobby to stretch, or use the restroom. As for the restrooms, there will, of course, be a long line for the ladies room. If you are near one (and if you are a lady or even just a regular woman), it's best to rush there immediately when the lights come up, knocking over everyone in your path. Otherwise there will be a huge line, which you will spend the entire intermission standing in. If you do not get there in the beginning, wait until the end of intermission when the line is finally back down to a few people. When intermission is ending, the lights will briefly dim again and you will hear the warning chime. Return to your seat and climb over your neighbors again; you're old friends by now so it's easier this time.

❋❋❋❋❋❋

TOP 10
STAIN REMOVAL TIPS

10 BLOOD
Dry or wet, you can remove blood with hydrogen peroxide. Pour a little onto the stain and let it sit for a couple of minutes. Rinse, repeat, and it should be gone. Incidentally, this will not remove forensic evidence of blood, just the stain.

9 PEN INK
Spray hair spray onto the stain (use a lot) and let it dry. Wash as normal. Another tip for removing ink is to soak the stained article in milk overnight, then wash.

8 RED WINE
If the spill is small, pour white wine onto a cloth and dab the red wine; it works like magic. If the stain is larger, pour salt on it. Both of these tips only work if the wine is wet.

7 NICOTINE
Lemon juice should remove nicotine stains. If the stains are on your fingers, use lemon juice and pumice stone.

6 MELTED WAX
Lay brown paper over the garment and iron, moving the paper often. The paper will absorb the wax.

5 RUST
Rub with lemon juice and salt and leave in the sun. Then wash as usual.

4 GREASE
To remove grease, dab the stain with eucalyptus oil then put through a hot wash. You may need to repeat the process. Another useful tip is to rub butter into your hands if they are stained with grease. Then rinse with soapy water.

3 BLACK MARKS ON THE FLOOR

Sometimes you get black marks on the floor from the soles of shoes. A great way to remove these is to pour a little lighter fluid onto a cloth and wipe.

2 CRAYON ON WALLS

Use baking soda on a damp cloth to rub crayon stains off smooth surfaces. A more risky way is to use club soda.

1 GRASS

Grass stains can be removed by wiping the article over with club soda. Repeat until the stain is gone and wash.

❋❋❋❋❋❋

TOP 10 TIPS FOR FRUGAL LIVING

10 MAKE A BUDGET

This is essential for all lifestyles, not just frugal living. Make a budget (be completely honest with yourself) and put a special section aside to keep track of how much money you spend. Each week, try to spend a little less than the week before. This can be a lot of fun as you start competing with yourself. You will be amazed how much lower you can go week by week.

9 CANCEL UNNEEDED SERVICES

Cancel cable TV and any magazine subscriptions you have. If you are like me, the chances are that you don't read the majority of your subscriptions. I have a subscription to the *New Yorker* and on the rare occasion that I do open the latest copy, I normally just look at the cartoons! Most of the magazines that are available have websites with many of their print articles online. Use those instead.

8 SELL, SELL, SELL

Spend a weekend going through every room in your house, picking out all of the things that you don't use or need. Once you have finished rounding up all your unneeded goods, sell them on eBay. Not only will you simplify your life by decluttering, you will make some money that you can put in the bank for an occasional treat.

7 TALK TO OTHER FRUGAL PEOPLE

There are thousands of brilliant resources on the Internet for people who are interested in frugal living. In addition to websites, I strongly recommend the newsgroup misc.consumers.frugal-living, which has thousands of subscribers and a nonstop flow of useful tips and advice for frugal living.

6 SAVE ON BILLS

Run your washing machine on cold, and make sure you turn out any lights that are not in use. Another great way to save money is to turn down the thermostat on your hot water heater. Most electric and gas companies have brochures that tell you how to save money—take advantage of these. You can save a lot of money by wrapping up warm on the sofa with a good book and leaving the heat turned off.

5 SEARCH OUT FREEBIES

There are lots of freebies available that can save you a great deal of money. A Google search for free goods can bring up a lot of useful items that you would normally have to pay for. You can also try writing to some of your favorite companies and ask for samples. If you have to stay in a hotel for any reason, be sure to pack up any leftover soaps or shower items; you are paying for them as part of your hotel room bill, so you might as well get some use out of them.

4 MAKE YOUR OWN CLEANING PRODUCTS

This may sound horrifying complicated, but it is very easy to make all of your own household cleaning products. Not only is it easy, it is fun. One bar of soap can make enough washing detergent to last months! For other cleaning needs you can often use vinegar in place of the expensive items you are used to buying. Don't bother buying dryer sheets—they are totally unnecessary and cost a lot of money.

3 USE COUPONS

Check your local stores regularly for coupons or special deals. You should be careful though; don't buy something that is not essential just because it is on sale. Keep the coupons handy in case you need one at a later date.

2 SAVE ON CLOTHING

Don't buy new clothes unless you absolutely must. It also goes without saying that you should not buy big label brand clothing as it is much more expensive than regular clothes. This is also a good opportunity to develop some good old-fashioned skills like sewing; if you have clothes that are in need of repair, don't throw them away, repair them. It is not difficult to learn how to use a needle and thread.

1 EAT WELL

I say eat well because if you follow this tip, you will eat better than you have before. First off you need to stop buying any prepackaged meals. Start making your own meals—all three of them. As you get better at being frugal, you can set aside time on the weekend to bake bread and other goods; it is much cheaper to make your own bread than it is to buy bread from the shop. In addition, it tastes much better. You can also dispense with things like milk and use milk powder. Remember to buy your flour and milk powder in bulk.

※※※※※※

TOP 10 TIPS TO PREPARE FOR ANOTHER DEPRESSION

10 GET TO KNOW YOUR NEIGHBORS

It is a very good idea to get to know your neighbors well, even in times of a normal economy. Your neighbors can keep an eye on your home while you are away, they can feed the pets, and they can lend you a cup of sugar if you need one! In the event of a depression they can be even more useful: you can create a small community where you can share necessities that one may have and others lack; you can set up patrols (if the situation were so dire as to need it); and you can even have shared meals, which can help to keep waste and costs down.

9 BUY METAL

If you have a considerably large amount of money, you will probably want to consider investing some of it in metals, such as gold and silver (though these are already seeing massive price increases). Of course, if you have a fortune you probably already know this, but it doesn't hurt to remind people. In the event of a collapse of your nation's currency, you will need a backup, and precious metals have been shown in the past to be an excellent one.

8 STOCKPILE DRUGS

If you regularly take medication, try to stockpile as much as you can. In a depression you may find that you cannot afford drugs, or, in a worst-case scenario, the drug companies may go under! Additionally, store up bottles of aspirin and other common over-the-counter drugs that we all tend to use from time to time throughout the year. As you use these drugs, be sure to use the ones that are the closest to their expiry date to prolong the life of the others.

7 SAVE MONEY

Right now. Begin saving as much money as you can. Cut down on all of your expenses (except debt repayment) and save every penny. If we end up in a depression, you are going to need it. This is also a good time to start thinking about selling any items in your home that you may not need. If it becomes very likely that a depression is going to hit, sell everything non-essential, that means the TV, DVD player, stereos, etc. I would recommend that you keep your computer (preferably a laptop in case you lose your home and need to move around), as it will come in handy when the depression ends.

6 GET RID OF DEBT

You should try to get rid of as much debt as you can right now. While you can pay your mortgage now, you may not be able to in a month, and as banks are feeling the pinch, they are not going to tolerate even one missed payment. This can obviously lead very easily to you losing your home. If you think the recession now is painful, try suffering it on the streets! This is a tip to help you cope before the depression hits. If you find yourself in an untenable situation and the depression has already arrived, forget this tip and read the number one entry on this list carefully.

5 MOVE YOUR STOCKS

If you own stock, it is now a good time to consider the types of companies that are likely to do well in a depression; these are the companies you should move your stocks into. The companies most likely to survive and profit are dry food manufacturers, diaper and toilet paper manufacturers, and any company making products that are seen as essential to survive. "Comfort" and "sin" stocks like cigarettes and alcohol are also stocks that do extremely well during bad times as people rely on them to blot out their suffering.

4 LEARN A USEFUL TRADE

Some trades are more in demand during a depression than others. For example, a baker, a handyman, or an electrician should be able to find work during the worst economic downturn, but a change control facilitator may not. Invest in some good old-fashioned skills now and not only will it help you survive a depression, it may well be a complete career change for you in the future.

3 STORE UP FOOD

Right now you should be hoarding dried and canned foods. Also tablets for purifying water and other nice-to-haves like toilet paper, candles, and batteries. I know this sounds like preparations for a nuclear holocaust, but the effects could be horrifyingly similar. Keep all of your goods in a dry, clean area. I would also recommend a book on the basics of cooking, so you can convert your flour to bread and perform other culinary miracles that require nothing processed or prepackaged. This is a skill that will be invaluable whether we have a depression or not.

2 RELOCATE OR BUY AN RV

If you think you are in a job that is likely to not be needed during a depression, you should consider relocating to an area that has a lot of wildlife and land. If you lose your house, an investment in an RV now (not on credit!) could be your lifesaver. You can drive it to a new town, find a private area where you won't be disturbed, and park it while the depression rides out. Make sure you find an area where you can rely on plentiful fresh water and animals.

1 BUY A GUN

If things get so bad that people begin to steal off each other, this will come in very handy. You can use it to protect your family and belongings, as well as to kill animals for food. And if you really are in dire straits, you can use it to rob someone else! (Okay, I didn't mean that; we should all try to help each other out, not kill each other). A gun will be most useful in hunting so be sure to buy one that is practical for shooting birds and larger animals. You will also want to buy a book on how to skin, clean, and prepare wild animals for human consumption.

※※※※※※

TOP 10 TIPS FOR SURVIVING THE STREETS

10 SLEEPING BAG

A sleeping bag is necessary, preferably one made of down because it is lightweight and very compact. This is the most vital piece of equipment you will need. You can either stash the bag, or carry it with you. Carrying it with you makes you more mobile because you can sleep wherever you end up. If you can't get a good-quality down bag, double-bagging two poor-quality ones will do the job (though definitely not as well).

9 MATTING

Matting is also needed (preferably plastic and lightweight); you must keep your sleeping bag off the ground away from the damp. If you can't find or buy matting, at least make sure you put your sleeping bag on cardboard; putting it directly on the concrete will result in you feeling like you are sleeping on a block of ice. The cold can cause your back muscles to freeze up and numb and the result is that when you stretch in the night you can tear them, potentially leading to months of difficulty walking (and walking is what you need to be doing every day).

8 BACKPACKS

For your backpack, consider keeping a smaller backpack for use during the day and a larger one that you can stash. You should keep in mind that some states have "camping bans" which make it illegal to walk around the city with a large camping backpack. One homeless man was even refused service at Denny's because they "do not serve people with backpacks"—clearly discrimination against the homeless—but you need to be aware of this. A small day backpack will spare you all of these problems.

7 TOILETRIES

You will need soap, a toothbrush, and razors, at the very least, which you should keep with you in your day backpack. It is also worth trying to score a mirror of some kind; just because you are living on the street doesn't mean you can't take care of your appearance because you will certainly find life easier when dealing with non-homeless people.

6 USEFUL ITEMS

Some extra small items are very handy to have when you live on the street. For example, you will want a needle and thread to fix minor tears and loose buttons; this can save you a lot of trouble trying to find new clothes, especially in winter. You will also probably want a couple of pens or pencils (you never know when you might need these). It goes without saying that an essential item is a can opener, without one of these you limit the types of food you can buy (and canned goods are often the cheapest). You will also want a pair of scissors, which you can use for trimming your own hair, cutting your nails, and for any other task that may require the use of something sharp. A bottle opener and/or a corkscrew is also useful. And finally, a box of matches or a lighter is essential.

5 CLOTHES

Most homeless people prefer to layer their clothes. This means you wear all of your various layers of clothes during the night, but as the day progresses, you can remove each layer successively. This allows you to keep cool when you need, and warm if it gets too cold. A good pair of leg warmers is recommended for wearing under your pants. In addition, you will need a good scarf and a hooded sweatshirt.

4 HEADWEAR

In summer you will need a baseball cap to protect you from the sun. This is essential to prevent you from suffering sunstroke and even potentially getting skin cancer from overexposure. It can also help to conceal a head of hair badly in need of a cut which can be very off-putting to people you may need to deal with. In winter you will need a good warm knit hat. A lot of the body's heat escapes through the head, so this is one of the most important things you will need in winter.

3 SHOES

You absolutely must have a good quality pair of shoes, especially in winter. If you have a hole in your shoe and your socks get wet, you will have a miserable few days with wet feet; this can, of course, lead to health problems that you want to avoid. If you do not have quality shoes, forget buying beer—use all the money you can muster to get good shoes without holes. Make sure you wear socks, shoes rubbing on the skin can cause lesions. One homeless guy in the local soup kitchen had been wearing dress shoes that were ill-fitting without socks for months and his ankles were covered in festering sores which were being scraped by the shoes every time he walked. It was too late for him to do anything about it—don't let this happen to you!

2 BAGS

Plastic garbage bags are essential to life on the streets. They will be raincoats in winter, and protection from the sun in summer. You can use them to protect your matting from the wet ground. A tip for getting free bags: janitors in large buildings often keep spare bags under the garbage can for easy replacement when emptying. If you make sure you take just one or two per garbage can no one will notice and you will have a constant supply on hand. You will probably also want to keep a few smaller bags on hand just in case you have a need for them.

1 MISCELLANEOUS EXTRAS

It is very important that you travel light. You want to keep your belongings to a minimum and the items in this list cover virtually everything you will need. Having said that, you should consider carrying a few other smaller items that can be invaluable. For example, priority-mailing envelopes (free at the post office) are great for storing things and they are durable and waterproof. You may also want to keep a bottle or two to store things like coffee. Forget things like flashlights; they are heavy, the batteries run out, and they show everyone exactly where you are, and you probably want to remain fairly anonymous and blend in on the streets.

TOP 10 MOST RETURNED GIFTS

10 DUPLICATE TOYS

When you have a big family, it is a wonder this little mishap doesn't happen all the time. Yes, there are lists aplenty throughout the preceding months. However, parents and grandparents and in-laws like to go out on tangents and get kids whatever they so desire. This can, and has, resulted in gift duplications that only lead to irritated children who, so verbally, announce, "Hey, we already got this toy the other day!" I sure hope you kept the receipt.

9 HOUSEWARES

Whatever gave you the idea that I have any intention, ever, of making pressed sandwiches? Yes, I have been the ever-proud recipient of one of these useless machines that I have used precisely this many times: zero. Unfortunately, I couldn't return it since it was purchased from a store in another state. I still have it. Also, while we're at it, unless it is specifically asked for, bathroom accessories are not cool gifts since no one that I have ever seen shy of eighty-year-olds have their bathrooms decked out in lavender. No good.

8 MOVIES

Wow, how did you know I wanted my very own copy of *Mega Force*? Oh, thanks, now I can watch *Ed* as often as I want! Unless you are on an intimate-knowledge basis with your to-be gift recipient, getting a movie for him or her is a hit-or-miss prospect and chances are one of the two parties is going away thoroughly disappointed. Keep that deluxe edition of *Weekend at Bernie's Two* for your own collection.

7 VIDEO GAMES

You are treading into some seriously shark-infested waters here, pal. Now assume for a moment that your child has taken the time to not only sketch out a perfect mock-up of the video game's cover in their Christmas list but also has drawn you a map to the various locales at which said game can be purchased; maybe it's a good idea for you to follow it. He or she obviously wants this particular game enough to have politely begged you for it since Halloween, so wrapping up a copy of "Sim Paint Dry" is going to be the first rung on the rapidly building ladder of disappointment that is your parenthood.

6 MUSIC
Just because you are not a fan of modern punk or emo doesn't necessarily mean that your sullen teen isn't. Believe me, I understand, Fallout Boy and Panic at the Disco! are by far more annoying than a cat in a woodchipper, but your son or daughter is infatuated with them. If you're already nursing the head wound from the projectile that was a Billy Joel hits collection, I suggest a return trip to the mall.

5 SHOES
Sometimes your favorite aunt or stepmother goes a little bonkers and decides to pick you up a fine, new pair of sneakers for Christmas. Oh, but aren't their intentions just the sweetest? You can count the number of times on one finger you've worn Stride Rites. But, to the fashion-blind that are your relatives, these particular shoes are what are "in" and "hip." But after opening them, all your kid wants to do is kick her in the hip. Glad that receipt is taped to the box, Nana.

4 SPOUSE-INAPPROPRIATE GIFTS
So you've been married for ten years? Congratulations! You went right out and got your spouse a toaster for Christmas, huh? Nice. Don't be surprised if you find divorce papers in your stocking.

3 CLOTHING
Do you see those tattered rags all in black your kid "wears" to school? Have you even noticed, shy of just in passing, that your daughter is wearing leggings and denim miniskirts with a Green Day T-shirt? Hmm ... well, maybe that's your problem. If you are going to get your children clothes for Christmas, I'd suggest rifling through their rooms and copying exactly what you see there. Or, better yet, gift certificates to Hot Topic.

2 AGE-INAPPROPRIATE TOYS

Do you, as I do, have that loony grandmother somewhere deep in her eighties who believes that her great-grandchildren are forever two, even when some of them are six? Yeah, I thought so. Well, unfortunately, there is really not much to be done about it since the chances she even remembers your name, let alone where the receipts are, are pretty slim. Luckily, many stores will grant credit and you can then return that eighteen-month age-appropriate toy for something more fitting for your twelve-year-old.

1 SOMETHING YOU JUST PLAIN DIDN'T WANT

More often than not, you are just going to get a whole bunch of crap that you will never in a million years look at twice again not to mention even use. There is just no room in your life for an ant farm, a year-supply of various salves, or a creepy glow-in-the-dark Jesus clock. Find that receipt quick and get yourself something nice.

CHAPTER FOURTEEN

Travel

TOP 10 MOST AMAZING STREETS IN THE WORLD

10 GRAVITY HILL, VARIOUS LOCATIONS

Claim to Fame: Gravity hills appear to defy the laws of physics.

Unlike the other streets on this list, this is not a specific street but rather a variety of streets; there are, in fact, hundreds around the world. When you park your car at the foot of a gravity hill (also sometimes called magnetic hills or mystery hills), the car will appear to roll up the hill, not down. The reason for this is an optical illusion caused by the surrounding environment. The Mystery Spot in Santa Cruz, California, is a well-known gravity hill.

9 EBENEZER PLACE, SCOTLAND

Claim to Fame: World's shortest street.

Ebenezer Place is the shortest street in the world, measuring just 6.8 feet. There is just one house on the street, number 1 Ebenezer Place, which was built in 1883. The building is a hotel (Mackays) and the owner was instructed to paint a street name on its shortest side. It was officially declared a street in 1887.

8 PAN-AMERICAN HIGHWAY, THE AMERICAS

Claim to Fame: World's longest road.

The Pan-American Highway is the longest driving road in the world. It has replaced Yonge Street (in Toronto, Canada) as the longest road since changes were made to the configuration of Highway 11 and Yonge Street in the 1990s. The Pan-American Highway links the mainland nations of the Americas and is an amazing 29,800 miles long. The highway passes through fifteen nations, including the U.S., Canada, Mexico, Peru, Argentina, and El Salvador.

7 PARLIAMENT STREET, ENGLAND

Claim to Fame: World's narrowest street.

Parliament Street is in Exeter, England. It is the narrowest street in the world, measuring less than two feet at its narrowest point. It was originally called Small Street (for reasons that are obvious) but was renamed when Parliament passed an act of law that expanded the representation of the people in the House of Commons. The street dates from the 1300s and is 50 meters long.

6 ROAD TO GIZA, EGYPT
Claim to Fame: World's oldest paved road.

The Road to Giza is the world's oldest known paved road. The road is over 4600 years old and is six-and-a-half feet wide. It covered a distance of seven-and-a-half miles, connecting the quarries to the southwest of Cairo, to the quay on Lake Moeris, which connected to the Nile. The road was used to transport the enormous blocks of basalt to Giza where they were used for building (especially for paving).

5 9 DE JULIO AVENUE, ARGENTINA
Claim to Fame: World's widest street.

9 de Julio Avenue (meaning 9th of July Avenue in honor of Argentina's independence day) is the widest street in the world. It has six lanes in each direction and spans an entire city block. There is a single building that sits on the avenue (the former Ministry of Communications building) but there are many famous landmarks along the side, such as the old French Embassy, a statue of Don Quixote, and the famous obelisk and Plaza de la República.

4 LOMBARD STREET, UNITED STATES
Claim to Fame: World's crookedest street.

Lombard Street in San Francisco is famous for its bizarre hairpin turns. There are eight of the turns (called switchbacks) and the street is known as the "crookedest street in the world." The turns were added because the street would have been too steep for most vehicles (though it would still be less steep than the street in number one). The twisting section of Lombard Street is now one way, in order to make it safer and there is a parking ban in place.

3 THE MAGIC ROUNDABOUT, ENGLAND
Claim to Fame: World's worst roundabout.

Anyone who has been on the Internet for a while will recognize the Magic Roundabout; it has appeared in virtually every "funny picture" list you can find. The roundabout is a real roundabout in Swindon, England. It was built in 1972 and it includes five other smaller roundabouts. To make matters worse, you must travel counterclockwise (the reverse of the normal situation on British roundabouts) when you enter the smaller central roundabout. The Swindon Junction has been voted the worst junction in Great Britain.

2 SAVOY COURT, ENGLAND
Claim to Fame: Only street in Britain where you must drive on the right.
The British drive on the left (unlike Europe and the United States). But there is one exception to this rule: Savoy Court is the only street in Britain where cars must legally drive on the right. Apparently this dates back to the old hackney cabs—by driving on the right, the driver was able to open the backdoor without leaving the cab, allowing the passengers to alight on the sidewalk. This is allowed by a special act of Parliament.

1 STEEPEST STREET, NEW ZEALAND
Claim to Fame: Steepest street in the world.
Baldwin Street in Dunedin, New Zealand, boasts the steepest street. New Zealand has many cities built on or around mountainous and hilly areas, and Dunedin is no exception. This street (and many others in New Zealand) were designed by British town planners who had never been to the country. They simply overlaid a grid pattern on the map and had no idea that they had made impossible or ridiculous design choices. The slope on Baldwin Street has a 35 percent grade. The road is so steep that at the top it is made of concrete because the usual road surfacing material used in New Zealand (asphalt) would slide down the street in hot weather.

※※※※※※

TOP 10 MYTHICAL PLACES YOU WANT TO LIVE IN

10 CAMELOT

Reason: King Arthur lives here and you can joust all day long!
Camelot comes from legendary British tales of King Arthur, who may, or may not, have been real. In Camelot we find Arthur's famous round table where his knights get to sit around like equals and have a few beers while they discuss their latest knightly conquests. Camelot is surrounded by forests and rivers so you can get in a spot of fishing and hunting if it floats your boat. Justice and peace reign in Camelot. Oh, and the ultra-hot (in a medieval way) Guinevere lives there too!

9 GARDEN OF EDEN

Reason: No need to work, food aplenty, and everyone is naked!
Many believe Eden was a real place and just as many don't. But, the fact is, if it were real, this would be the spot to settle down! The Garden of Eden is full of trees bent over with fruit and all the animals are friendly. Not only do you get to eat until you can eat no more, you can ride lions and tigers all afternoon! Seriously, it doesn't get more awesome than that. Just watch out for the snake!

8 EL DORADO

Reason: It is a City of Gold!
El Dorado is a legendary city of gold. It is seen as a type of "Holy Grail" for each man—the thing you most seek in life is found here. Basically, whatever your fetish, you will not leave unsatisfied from this place. Better yet, it is somewhere in South America, so it shouldn't cost you much to get there!

7 COCKAIGNE

Reason: It rains cheese!
Cockaigne is a land of contraries, where all the restrictions of society are defied (abbots beaten by their monks), sexual liberty is open (nuns flipped over to show their bottoms), and food is plentiful (skies that rain cheeses). This is a place where idleness and gluttony are the principal occupations—who doesn't want that?

6 BEIMENI
Reason: You never grow old.

Beimeni is a legendary city said to be home to the fountain of youth! It is also a land of great wealth, an earthly paradise. Legend has it that Juan Ponce de León discovered Florida while he was looking for Beimeni and the fountain of youth, which is kind of ironic.

5 VALHALLA
Reason: Battle and feast daily.

Valhalla, the "afterworld" of the Vikings, is a place where all the dead warriors and gods live. Now, you have to be dead to go there, but it is worth it! Every day you get to fight against giants! But wait, it gets better. At the end of every battle you get to feast on the cosmic boar and drink beer all night long! When you finish eating the boar (Sæhrímnir) he is brought back to life so you can start eating him all over again! Oh, and the Valkyries (hot goddesses) live here too, so you are not likely to get bored.

4 AVALON
Reason: If it's good enough for Jesus, it's good enough for us!

Avalon is the place that King Arthur ended up before he died. It is also the place where King Arthur's sword (Excalibur) was made. In Avalon you can get the best apples in the world, and presumably pretty damned good cider too. When Jesus came back to life, he is said to have visited Avalon with Joseph of Arimathea (the guy who gave Jesus his tomb). I told you the apples were good.

3 SHANGRI-LA
Reason: It's a utopia.

Shangri-La is a mystical valley in the Himalayas. It is a permanently happy land, isolated from the outside world. The people who live at Shangri-La are almost immortal, living years beyond the normal lifespan. The place is so popular that the Nazis sent an expedition out to find it in 1938 Fortunately, they didn't find it!

2 CITY OF THE CAESARS
Reason: Lots of gold and diamonds—and it's magic!

Most of the descriptions of the City of the Caesars talk about the city as a prosperous and rich city full of gold, silver, and diamonds. It is described as an enchanted city that appears in certain moments. At least one description says it located in between two mountains, one of gold and another of diamonds.

1 YS

Reason: Orgies.

Ys is a mythical city built on the coast of Brittany and later swallowed by the ocean. Ys was built below sea level by Gradlon, King of Cornouaille, upon the request of his daughter Dahut, who loved the sea. It was the most beautiful and impressive city in the world. Unfortunately for the King (but fortunately for those who live there), Dahut was a bad girl and she started throwing wild parties and orgies.

✳✳✳✳✳✳

TOP 10 FASCINATING GRAVEYARDS YOU MUST SEE

10 LA RECOLETA CEMETERY, BUENOS AIRES, ARGENTINA

Always topping lists of places to visit in Buenos Aires, the Cementerio de la Recoleta is a fascinating glimpse into Argentine history. The most famous tomb is undoubtedly that of Eve Peron's, but there are many more Argentinean politicians, poets, and personalities. The cemetery is designed much like a city, with wide avenues branching off into alleyways, all lined with "houses" for individuals and families. Many are exceptionally well maintained, but there are many more that no longer have family members to maintain them and have thus fallen into disrepair. There are stories of crypts being used as maintenance closets, with cleaning supplies stored on top of coffins. Among the tombs that have been maintained, you will find many sculptures that have been declared national historic monuments, as well as a myriad of styles, from Egyptian to Gothic to Art Deco. Another interesting note: among Argentina's rich and famous deceased, you may also find a colony of feral cats that have made Cementerio de la Recoleta their home and who are often fed by the locals.

9 SAINT LOUIS CEMETERY, NEW ORLEANS, LOUISIANA

This is actually three cemeteries, each worth visiting, though Saint Louis Cemetery number one is, in my opinion, the most interesting, and the one I will be referring to. The tombs in Saint Louis are above ground, and the stone buildings are actually concealing bodies only a few feet away from the visitor. The reason for this is supposedly because

the ground water level in New Orleans is impractical for burials, though there is some dispute of this. Saint Louis number one is more than a little rundown, and a tour guide is strongly recommended. Voodoo is alive and well in New Orleans and the tomb of Voodoo Queen Marie LaVeau is supposedly located in the Glapion family crypt. When I visited, graffiti made this particular tomb hard to miss, but that was a few years ago, and I can't vouch for what it looks like now. As an aside, when I visited I did not go with a tour. Aimless wandering through the one-square block cemetery found many tombs that had been broken into, and more than a few remains scattered. This cemetery is not for the fainthearted.

8 FOREST LAWN MEMORIAL PARKS, GLENDALE AND HOLLYWOOD HILLS, LOS ANGELES, CALIFORNIA

Three places for the price of one! First, Forest Lawn: A unique entry … the creators of these parks wanted to approach the creation of a final resting place with a sunnier outlook. The result is practically a theme park for death. Traditional headstones are ditched in favor of markers set into the ground, and replicas of artwork—paintings and statuary—and famous buildings from all over the world, abound. If, for instance, you want to see the complete collection of Michelangelo's sculptures but can't afford to bounce around Europe, look no further. This cemetery contains the only complete collection in the world that is made from casts of the originals and marble from the same quarry Michelangelo used. Between Glendale and Hollywood Hills, you can find the final resting place of what may seem like most of Hollywood (and you'll find the rest at Hollywood Forever). Curiously, some of the graves are in a restricted section, among them Hollywood elite such as Humphrey Bogart, Nat King Cole, and Mary Pickford, but most are available to the public. Some of the more visited markers are those of Walt Disney, L. Frank Baum, Errol Flynn, James Stewart, Spencer Tracy, Tex Avery, Scatman Crothers, Bette Davis, Marty Feldman, Buster Keaton, Fritz Lang, Liberace, Telly Savales (buried with a lollipop!), and many, many more. Hollywood Forever is located nearby, adjacent to the north wall of Paramount Studios. It is less popular because it spent the latter part of the twentieth century being run down and financially mismanaged and was later purchased by its current owners in 1998 and refurbished. Movies are screened there in the summertime, drawing hundreds of visitors. Famous occupants include Mel Blanc, Cecille B. DeMille, Douglas Fairbanks, Douglas Fairbanks Jr., George Harrison, Johnny and Dee Dee Ramone, Rudolph Valentino, and my all-time favorite actor, Peter Lorre.

7 GREEN-WOOD CEMETERY, BROOKLYN, NEW YORK

Boasting six hundred thousand graves spread out over 478 acres, this site is a popular tourist attraction for those visiting New York City. Like Père-Lachaise in Paris, there was a campaign to promote the cemetery involving moving famous bodies there and donating monuments. Unlike Père-Lachaise, however, the plan didn't really work, and from the time it was opened in 1838 until the building of the Brooklyn Bridge in 1883 made it easier to get there, the cemetery did not get that many permanent residents. Those that did come to stay had plenty of room to do so. There are hundreds of ornate tombs for famous and non-famous residents alike, but the site still seems wide open. Most New Yorkers who made their name in the second half of the nineteenth century (a prolific chunk of time for famous New Yorkers) can be found here. There are also war memorials and monuments, including an obelisk that serves as a grave marker for 103 of the nearly 300 victims of the Brooklyn Theater Fire.

6 OLD JEWISH CEMETERY, JOSEFOV, PRAGUE, CZECH REPUBLIC

Easily the oldest cemetery on this list, with the earliest discernible headstone dating back to 1439, the Old Jewish Cemetery operated until 1787, which means it closed before most of the entries on this list had opened. The headstones bear this out, jumbled at strange angles and deeply weatherworn. Ropes divide the walkway from the headstones, and tickets can be bought to see the cemetery individually or in addition to visiting the surrounding synagogues. Interestingly, while many Jewish cemeteries were destroyed during the Holocaust, Hitler specifically requested this one remain intact, as he apparently intended to build a museum here after his assumed victory.

5 ZENTRALFRIEDHOF, SIMMERING, VIENNA, AUSTRIA

At 2.4 square kilometers, it is the second largest cemetery (after Hamburg) in Europe. It also, at 3.3 million occupants, is the largest in Europe by number interred. Conveniently, the most famous occupants of Zentralfriedhof are located in a section called the Ehrengräber. Just as Vienna is the capital of classical music, the Ehrengräber is the home of many classical musicians and composers, many of whom where moved from other cemeteries (to complete the collection, so to speak). Here you will find Ludwig Van Beethoven, Johannes Brahms, Antonio Salieri, Franz Schubert, Johann Strauss (I and II), and, interestingly, Falco (of Der Kommissar fame).

4 MERRY CEMETERY, SAPANTA, MARAMURES COUNTY, ROMANIA

A strangely joyous cemetery, Merry Cemetery contains hundreds of wooden markers brightly painted with scenes from the lives (and sometimes the demise) of the deceased, as well as poems about their lives. There is little or no weatherproofing on the markers, so the paint fades with the memories of the dearly departed.

3 PROTESTANT CEMETERY, NEAR PORTA SAN PAOLO, ROME, ITALY

This Italian cemetery is also known as the Englishman's cemetery and the Non-Catholic Cemetery, although the latter moniker applies the best. This was the place to bury those who died in and around Rome but who were not Catholic. The most recognizable feature of the cemetery is probably the Pyramid of Cestius, a small-scale, Egyptian-style pyramid built around 18 to 12 BC that is the tomb of Gaius Cestius Epulo, making it the oldest tomb in the cemetery by over a century and a half. It was incorporated into the city fortification known as the Aurelian Walls, which were, in turn, later used as a partial border to the cemetery. The first modern burials date from the mid-1700s. Its most famous residents include the poets John Keats and Percy Shelley, making it a pilgrimage site for fans of Romantic poetry. An interesting story surrounds the burial of Percy Shelley. Though he was cremated on the beach near where he drowned, his ashes (minus his heart, which would be buried with Mary Shelley years later) were to be interred here. The body of his son, William Shelley, also buried in the Protestant Cemetery, was exhumed to join his father. Unfortunately, the body exhumed was that of a five-and-a-half-foot man, not the body of a three-year-old boy. In the end, William Shelley's body was never found, and Percy Shelley was buried without him.

2 CIMETIÈRE DU PÈRE-LACHAISE, PARIS, FRANCE

Located east of Paris's city center, Père-Lachaise has become arguably the most famous cemetery in the world, boasting hundreds of thousands of visitors a year. It was not always this popular, though. When it was first opened in 1804, no one wanted to be buried there because it had no history. In a campaign to promote the cemetery, famous bodies were actually moved to Père-Lachaise, among them Molière and the famed lovers Heloise and Abelard. This unusual attention grabber worked, and Père-Lachaise became the place to go when you were done going places. There are so many famous buried in Père-Lachaise, it could make up its own list: Marcel Proust, Gertrude Stein, Jim Morrison, Oscar Wilde, Isadora Duncan, Camille Pissarro, Édith Piaf, Marcel Marceau, Ticky Holgado, Max Ernst, Colette, Frederic Chopin, Sarah Bernhardt, and Honoré de Balzac.

1 HIGHGATE CEMETERY, HIGHGATE, LONDON, U.K.

The amazing thing about Highgate Cemetery is its unusual setting in a fairly wooded area, so complex monuments and simple gravestones alike are surrounded by trees, ferns, and wildflowers. While the Friends of Highgate Cemetery, who took over maintenance of the decaying site in the late '70s to early '80s, have done much to improve conditions, the grounds, particularly in the west cemetery (available by tour only) are still rough terrain in some places, with the vegetation constantly threatening to swallow the place whole. The most famous of its monuments is by far the tomb of Karl Marx, but various other Victorian celebrities boast fascinating monuments here.

✳✳✳✳✳✳

TOP 10 DIFFERENCES BETWEEN EUROPE AND AMERICA

10 GOVERNMENT

These governments could not be any more unalike if we purposely attempted to create them so. And, as it turns out, we (the U.S.) kind of did. Not happy with the persecution the European government was dishing out to specific religious groups, the original Pilgrims who ended up on American shores would eventually pass down ideas for a new government in their new land, despite the fact that they persecuted people in equally (if not worse) ways than the nations they left behind. Here are the governmental differences spelled out as clearly as possible:

Europe: The European Parliament (Europarl or EP) is the directly elected parliamentary body of the European Union (EU). Together with the Council of the European Union (the Council), it forms the bicameral legislative branch of the Union's institutions and has been described as one of the most powerful legislatures in the world. The Parliament and Council form the highest legislative body within the Union. However, their powers as such are limited to the competencies conferred upon the European Community by member states. Hence the institution has little control over policy areas held by the states and within the other two of the three pillars of the European Union. The Parliament is composed of 785 MEPs (Member of the European Parliament), who serve the second largest democratic electorate in the world (after India) and the largest transnational democratic electorate in the world (492 million).

America: The federal government of the United States is the United States governmental body that carries out the roles assigned to the federation of individual states established by the Constitution. The federal government has three branches: the executive, legislative, and judicial. Through a system of separation of powers or "checks and balances," each of these branches has some authority to act on its own, some authority to regulate the other two branches, and has some of its own authority, in turn, regulated by the other branches. In addition, the powers of the federal government as a whole are limited by the

Constitution, which leaves a great deal of authority to the individual states. The federal government is based in the federal district of Washington, D.C., and is often referred to as "Washington."

9 TELEVISION

While Americans enjoy a mind-numbingly huge array of television stations via satellite or cable, Europe (though able to acquire said choices) also has a slew of nationally funded channels that offer them different types of programming (and in the case of the BBC in Britain, free of advertising). Since about 2000, both continents offer roughly the same when it comes to cable, satellite, and the offers of broadband with phone service and TV. The BBC and ITV are due to launch Freesat, which, unlike Freesat from Sky, will be a free-to-air system similar to Freeview. Europe, of course, features comedies and dramas specifically catered to its core audience, such as *Dr. Who* and the original *The Office*. American television companies have been known to pilfer European (usually English) programming, which then needs modification to make it more appealing to U.S. viewers. In some cases these American spinoffs have become more popular than the originals, for example, *The Office* and *Three's Company*.

8 MEAL TIMES AND ETIQUETTE

Europeans are more likely to be found eating as a family around the dinner table than many Americans who prefer the convenience of eating in front of the television. As a result, fast food chains are not as popular in places like France and Italy as they are stateside. This, however, is not true of all nations in Europe, as the English (possibly through the influence of American television programming) are also beginning to lean toward the convenience of fast food (either ready-made or ready-to-cook). Another striking difference is that in mainland Europe, supermarkets are far fewer in number than in America, as a large number of Europeans still buy their food daily from markets in their towns or city centers (again, this is probably no longer true of the United Kingdom). These markets are part of the appeal that Europe has for Americans traveling to Europe.

7 STORES

Shopping in the typical American city is a matter of walking around, going inside of whichever building one needs to explore in order to locate goods and services, and purchasing. Europe has a plethora of the "big box" stores like Wal-Mart, Target, and those similarly huge home-improvement stores like Lowe's, Home Depot, and the like. We like what we need readily available at our fingertips, and, unfortunately, this has contributed greatly to the end many of mom-and-pop stores. Grocery delivery is very common in England, while it is still only seen occasionally in the U.S. Europeans prefer the open-air shops with the amazing array of vastly different foods available in each specific location suited specifically to the item's location. The upside to this is that you get personal service; the downside is that if you get dreadful service, you have no one to complain to. It can take a lot more effort to find the items you need, as you have to go to many stores instead of one.

6 MONEY

American currency is just about as basic as it comes: Bills for anything for a dollar and over (5, 10, 20, 50, etc.), and coins for anything a quarter (25 cents) or less: dime (10), nickel (5), penny (1). For the most part and for the longest time our bills have been green with nothing more than age-old etched images of presidents and persons of historical significance, and some say hidden meanings dating back to the rise of the Freemasons and other government clubs. The member states of the European Union have adopted a universal currency called the euro (with the exception of the British, who are exempted from adopting the euro). This can be incredibly convenient when on vacation, but the adoption of the euro has caused some difficulties in nations where prices dramatically rose, such as Italy.

5 LANGUAGE

America has one language for all—American English (though some might say that Spanish is creeping in); Europe, on the other hand, has more languages than nations. As a result, most Europeans will learn at least one other language in school (this is often compulsory in mainland Europe, but not the United Kingdom). English is spoken in most major cities and in the case of some people, like the Dutch, the English in Europe can be better than the English in England. Combined with the universal currency of Europe, this really does make vacationing easier.

4 SPORTS

To Americans, nothing kills a weekend more appropriately than sitting around with some good friends, nursing a few beers, and watching your favorite sports team beat the snot out of its opponent. We here in the U.S. have five major sports: baseball, American football, basketball, hockey, and car racing. Grabbing several bowls of artery-clogging goodies, staking out a spot in a favorite chair, and yelling at the television are what sports fans are all about. We love our sports so much we've delegated entire clothing lines to them. Now in Europe, the four main spectator sports are football (soccer), cricket, rugby, and tennis. And, as we all know, our rabid attraction to our home teams rivals the beastly incorporation Europeans have with their own. In fact, I have never seen anything even remotely close to the mass of infuriated spectators rising in unison to a bad call or a loss than European sports crowds. It's just scary and has been known in the past to be deadly.

3 COOKING

American cooking, for all its variety and excitement, owes its very existence to everywhere else. Even our deep-seeded southern roots stemmed from French influence. If it can be successfully fried, we'll happily do it. If it can be mass-produced and served with french fries, we'll joyfully do that, too. We love our steaks, our hamburgers, our hot dogs, our potato and tortilla chips, and our foods smothered in gravy. Europeans have a diverse cultural history in their food and this is still obvious in every nation. It would be wrong, however, to consider European food healthier overall—this is not necessarily the case and Europeans, knowing this, tend to eat smaller portions. Virtually every aspect of French cooking involves butter and cream. Of all the European nations, England is the one with the worst reputation for food—it is expensive and usually bad. This, however, is beginning to change as more English people take an interest in redefining old English favorites (such as steak-and-kidney pudding) for the new millennium.

2 DRINKING

There is very little doubt that America's favorite alcoholic beverage has got to be beer. We love to import, export, and support the local microbrews of which there are literally thousands. We do have quite the active wine-making community as well, generally on the west coast in California, though other states produce wine as well. In Michigan, selling alcohol before noon is not only taboo, it's illegal. On Sundays you aren't allowed to purchase after five p.m., and if it's a holiday, none after two a.m. the previous day or on the holiday at all. Now, in bars and pubs, you can purchase (as long as you are inside) until two a.m.

Also, unless you want some serious trouble, you ought to be twenty-one to do so at all. Despite this high drinking-age, many kids start around sixteen or seventeen. Europeans, of course, have beer, wine, and other alcohol, but most often just different variations on the common theme. In Europe the drinking age in each country varies too, but to be on the safe side, carry your ID if you drink or purchase alcoholic beverages. Some countries list two legal ages: one to buy beer and wine and another to buy stronger spirits such as vodka, while other countries allow younger people to drink while dining in the company of adults. It seems that the laws are similar as are the concerns for underage drinking and especially drinking and driving. One major difference, however, is that many European families give their children wine with dinner (often watered down); there is much less a taboo associated with alcohol in Europe than America, which may be partly a side effect of the prohibition movement.

1 EVERYDAY LIFE

While Americans and Europeans (excluding the British) drive on the same side of the road, there are still many different rules. The most obvious is the American rule allowing cars to turn on a red light. Most of the street signs in Europe use the same international symbols. In England, there are a variety of different crosswalks with different names: a puffin crossing has the lights on the same side as the pedestrian; a toucan crossing is for pedestrians and bicycles; a Pegasus crossing allows horse riders to cross as well. There are also tiger crossings (alternating yellow and black stripes) to allow cyclists to cross without dismounting, and, of course, there's the zebra crossing. But wait—there's more. There are also pelican crossings, which are traffic-light controlled.

Power sockets in the United Kingdom differ from the rest of Europe, and both are different from American (and Japanese) sockets. European plugs generally have two circular pins for inserting into the socket (though there are variations in almost all of the nations in Europe), while British and Irish plugs have three thick rectangular pins. Also, European lights switch off in the opposite direction to American lights.

✳✳✳✳✳✳

TOP 10 UNDERRATED INTERNATIONAL DESTINATIONS

10 PUEBLA, MEXICO

Most visitors to Mexico never make it past the beaches of Cancún or Acapulco. But a few hours outside Mexico City stands the historic city of Puebla. With its beautiful colonial architecture, perfect weather, and delicious local cuisine, Puebla has a particular allure and charm. And as the place of origin for Cinco de Mayo, it's great for the history buff.

9 GDANSK, POLAND

History hasn't been too kind to this charming Baltic coastal town, which was razed to ashes during World War II. But most of the old structures have been rebuilt with great precision, and it's easy to spend hours (or days) just wandering through the pleasant historic quarter. Easily accessible by train from Berlin or Warsaw, Gdansk is definitely worth a visit.

8 QUITO, ECUADOR

Quito wraps itself around the base of Pichincha, a snow-capped volcano that provides one of the most unique backdrops of any city on earth. The historic downtown was among the first to be designated a UNICEF World Heritage Site. While you're there, take the short flight to the Galapagos to check out one of the best-preserved biospheres on the planet.

7 LISBON, PORTUGAL

Even after it adopted the euro as its national currency, Portugal remains a fairly economical destination. It boasts a rich, multicultural history, great music, and no shortage of spectacular vistas awash in brilliant Mediterranean colors. And, if that's not enough, stick around for the food.

6 GRANADA, NICARAGUA

One of the oldest colonial towns in Central America, Granada is accessible by road from Managua. Not as well kept a secret as in years past, Granada is becoming a more popular destination for tourists due to its history and relative safety. But if you go in the off-season, you should get it mostly to yourself. Don't miss out on the local coffee.

5 STELLENBOSCH, SOUTH AFRICA

South Africa is best known for its incredible wildlife reserves, and they are undoubtedly amazing. But many don't realize that South Africa produces some of the best wine in the world. Take the road from Cape Town to explore this lush, green wine country, and don't forget to grab a few bottles along the way.

4 TANGIER, MOROCCO

Long the haven for drunken ex-pat writers and other scoundrels, Tangier has undergone a period of urban renewal that is helping to shake off its reputation as "the Tijuana of the Mediterranean." You'd be hard-pressed to find water as blue as that which laps at its shores. Many visitors will find its vibrancy overwhelming, but the best way to see Tangier is to simply allow yourself to be swept away in it.

3 MONTEVIDEO, URUGUAY

Generally overlooked because of its proximity to its bustling neighbor (Buenos Aires), Montevideo has much to offer with its interesting fusion of colonial and deco architecture. And, as a smaller city, it's generally more relaxed. While you're there, go to a *parilla* and sample some of the best steak you'll ever eat.

2 HANOI, VIETNAM

Assuming you can get used to the traffic (not as easy as it sounds), Hanoi never fails to leave an impression on its guests. Hardly the place that it was thirty years ago, Hanoi is an exciting, bustling city filled with the aroma of exotic spices. Don't forget to see nearby Ha Long Bay, which may just be the single most beautiful place on earth.

1 DAKAR, SENEGAL

The stifling, chaotic maze of Dakar might be too much for some, but those who brave the humidity and mosquitoes will walk away with a truly unforgettable experience. Don't resist; let yourself be carried along by the sights and sounds. When you leave, Africa will no longer be an abstract notion or fleeting images on your TV. This is Africa at its most visceral, and I promise it will change you for the better.

✳✳✳✳✳✳

TOP 10 INTERESTING ABANDONED PLACES

10 BODIE, CALIFORNIA

Founded in 1876, Bodie is the authentic American ghost town. It started life as a small mining settlement, though it found even more fortune from nearby mines that attracted thousands. By 1880, Bodie boasted a population of almost ten thousand; such was the boom. At its peak, sixty-five saloons lined the town's main street, and there was even a Chinatown with several hundred Chinese residents.

Dwindling resources proved fatal, however, and although greatly reduced in prominence, Bodie held a permanent residency through most of the twentieth century, even after a fire ravaged much of the downtown business district in 1932. Bodie is now unpopulated. The town was designated a National Historic Landmark in 1961, and in 1962 it became Bodie State Historic Park as the few residents left moved on.

Today, Bodie is preserved in a state of arrested decay. Only a small part of the town survives. Visitors can walk the deserted streets of a town and interiors remain as they were left and stocked with goods. Bodie is open all year, but the long road that leads to it is usually closed in the winter due to heavy snowfall, so the most comfortable time to visit is during the summer months.

9 SAN ZHI, TAIWAN

More of a modern choice, this is an abandoned city in the north of Taiwan. In the area of "San Zhi," this futuristic pod village was initially built as a luxury vacation retreat for the rich. However, after numerous fatal accidents during construction, production was halted. A combination of lack of money and lack of willingness meant that work was stopped permanently, and the alien-like structures remain as if in remembrance of those lost. Indeed, rumors in the surrounding area suggest the city is now haunted by the ghosts of those who died.

After this the whole thing received the cover-up treatment. And the government, who commissioned the site in the first place, was keen to distance itself from the bizarre happenings. Thanks to this, there are no named architects. The project may never be restarted thanks to the growing legend, and there would be no value in redeveloping the area for other purposes, maybe simply because destroying homes of lonely spirits is a bad thing to do.

8 VAROSHA, CYPRUS

Varosha is in the Turkish occupied city of Famagusta in Cyprus. It was previously a modern tourist area, and flowered into one of the most luxurious holiday destinations. In 1974, however, the Turks invaded Cyprus and tore up the island. Citizens fled, expecting to be able to return to their homes within days. The Turkish military wrapped it in barbed wire and now controls it completely, allowing nobody to enter to this day, aside from themselves and UN personnel. The buildings are slowly falling apart. Though on the positive side, rare sea turtles have begun nesting on the deserted beaches.

The Annan Plan had provided for the return of Varosha to Greek Cypriot control, but after the rejection of the proposal by Greek Cypriot voters, this handover to Greek Cypriots has not materialized. That is not the end of the story, as the governments are working together to plan a complete revival of Varosha to its former beauty as currently, three concept hotel complexes have been designed by Laxia, Inc. And, by 2010, the de facto "Turkish Republic of Northern Cyprus" will apparently open Varosha to tourism once again.

7 HASHIMA ISLAND, JAPAN

Hashima Island is one among 505 uninhabited islands in the Nagasaki Prefecture of Japan about 15 kilometers from Nagasaki itself. It is also known as *Gunkan-jima* or Battleship Island, thanks to its high sea walls. It began in 1890 when a company called Mitsubishi bought the island and began a project to retrieve coal from the bottom of the sea. This attracted much attention, and in 1916 they were forced to build Japan's first large concrete building on the island—a block of apartments that would both accommodate the seas of workers and protect them from hurricanes.

In 1959, population had swelled, and boasted a density of 835 people per hectare for the whole island (1391 per hectare for the residential district)—one of the highest population densities ever recorded worldwide. As petroleum replaced coal in Japan in the 1960s, coal mines began shutting down all over the country, and Hashima's mines were no exception. In 1974 Mitsubishi officially announced the closing of the mine, and today it is empty and bare, with travel currently prohibited. The island was the location for the 2003 film *Battle Royale II* and inspired the final level of the popular Asian videogame "Killer7."

6 BALESTRINO, ITALY

Balestrino is quite a strange case in that it was extremely difficult to find any decent information on it, at least on the abandonment itself. No one is quite sure when the town was established, though records date back to before the eleventh century when Balestrino was owned by the Benedictine abbey of San Pietro dei Monti. The upper part of the town consists of a Castle (of Marquis) and the lower part a parish church (of Sant'Andrea). Records of population go back to around 1860, when around 800 to 850 people lived there, mainly farmers who took advantage of the landscape to farm olive trees.

In the late nineteenth century, the northwest coast of Italy was struck by numerous earthquakes. One of these in 1887 (magnitude 6.7) destroyed some villages in the area of Savona, and although no official records show Balestrino was affected, it coincides with much repair work and a dip in population. Finally in 1953 the town was abandoned due to "geological instability," and the remaining inhabitants (around four hundred) were moved to safer ground to the west. The derelict part of Balestrino that has stood untouched and inaccessible for fifty-plus years is currently undergoing planning for redevelopment. Today around five hundred people remain in the town's newer area, which is about a mile down the road.

5 KATOLI WORLD, TAIWAN

I thought I would break out of the abandoned residential mold and look at something inspired by Miyazaki's Oscar-winning film *Spirited Away*. Those who have seen it will know that the family stumbles across an old theme park at the start of the movie, one that was built in the eighties but has since lost popularity and been abandoned. Well this is a usual occurrence in Asia; one can find many amusement parks that have been left to rust. Here is just one of them, though one that was forced to close for something other than financial loss.

Katoli World is situated in the Dakeng Scenic area just outside of Taichung, Taiwan. Opened in the mid-'80s, it enjoyed moderate success as one of the few theme parks on the island of Taiwan to host a roller-coaster. The park was closed after a massive earthquake on September 21, 1999. Thousands of people were killed during the quake but nobody inside the park as it struck after opening hours. Large areas of the park were destroyed and it was forced to close. A place once vivid with young laughter is now slowly turning to rust.

4 CENTRALIA, PENNSYLVANIA

Jonathan Faust opened Bull's Head Tavern in Centralia in 1841, and Centralia was incorporated as a borough in 1866. The anthracite coal industry was the principal employer in the community until the 1960s, when most of the companies went out of business. An exposed vein of coal ignited in 1962 thanks to weekly garbage burning, and as a result a huge underground coal fire commenced. Attempts to extinguish the fire were unsuccessful, and it continued to burn throughout the 1960s and 1970s, with adverse health effects reported by several people due to the carbon monoxide produced.

In 1979, locals became aware of the scale of the problem when a gas station reported a fuel temperature of 172 degrees Fahrenheit. This provoked widespread attention, boosted in 1981 when a twelve-year-old almost plunged to his death, as a four-feet wide, one-hundred-and-fifty-feet deep sinkhole suddenly opened beneath his feet. In 1984, forty-two million dollars was spent on relocation, with most residents moving to the nearby Mount Carmel and Ashland. In 1992, Pennsylvania condemned all houses within the borough, meaning that of the thousand-plus residents in 1981; only a handful of people now remain, mainly priests. The fire still rages on, and according to experts could do so for another two-hundred-and-fifty years.

3 YASHIMA, JAPAN

Yashima is an imposing plateau to the northeast of Takamatsu, the second largest city on Shikoku, one of Japan's major islands. This plateau stretches out to sea. It is the site of a famous battle that took place on March 22, 1185, during the Genpei War. The top of Yashima hosts the Yashima Temple, which is a well-known Shikoku pilgrimage. This is about the only thing that does draw crowds to this strangely neglected geographical anomaly, but it wasn't always so.

During an upsurge in mid-'80s' Japanese economy, the people of Takamatsu decided that the plateau was an excellent place to encourage tourism, so took to pouring money into developing this sacred land. Six hotels were built, along with many parks and trails, even an aquarium. Though somewhere along the line people realized that Yashima plateau wasn't such an attractive opportunity, especially with views of the nearby rock quarry. Visitor numbers then dropped, as millions of yen were lost on inflated real estate deals. All the hotels and shops were forced to shut down, as was the cable car that at one point transported many to Yashima's heights.

2 PRIPYAT, UKRAINE

Pripyat is an abandoned city in the zone of alienation in northern Ukraine, Kiev Oblast, near the border with Belarus. The city population had been around fifty thousand and had been home to most of the Chernobyl nuclear power plant workers. Then the Chernobyl disaster struck in 1986 and the place was abandoned due to threat of radiation. Afterward Pripyat acted like a museum for a long time, perfectly showing a slice of Soviet life. However, at some time at the beginning of the twenty-first century, the place was looted heavily and nothing was left behind—even toilet seats were stolen.

The city will not be safe for human habitation for several years to come, and even then it will be a long time before people consider it healthy to develop once again. Before the power plant was built, concerns were voiced at its planned closeness to the city of Kiev. They had planned to build it only 15 miles away, placing the capital at risk from pollution, among other things. However, after a long debate, they decided to build Chernobyl, along with Pripyat, 62 miles away from Kiev, a choice that would in the end prove to be a wise one.

1 CRACO, ITALY

Craco is located in the Region of Basilicata and the Province of Matera, about twenty-five miles inland from the Gulf of Taranto at the instep of the "boot" of Italy. This medieval town is typical of those in the area, built up with long undulating hills all around that allow for the farming of wheat and other crops. Craco can be dated back to 1060 when the land was in the ownership of Archbishop Arnaldo, Bishop of Tricarico. This long-standing relationship with the church had much influence over the inhabitants throughout the ages.

In 1891, the population of Craco stood at well over two thousand people. Though there had been many problems, with poor agricultural conditions creating desperate times. Between 1892 and 1922 over thirteen hundred people moved from the town to North America. Poor farming added to earthquakes, landslides, and war, all of which contributed to this mass migration. Between 1959 and 1972, Craco was plagued by landslides and earthquakes. In 1963 the remaining eighteen hundred inhabitants were transferred to a nearby valley called Craco Peschiera, and the original Craco remains in a state of crumbling decay to this day.

✳✳✳✳✳✳

TOP 10 AMAZING LATIN AMERICAN VACATIONS

10 PETEN REGION, GUATEMALA

Take one of the direct international flights into Flores to explore this wondrous region. From the cobblestone streets of colonial Flores to the imposing Mayan ruins of Tikal, Peten offers an affordable and safe alternative for visitors to Guatemala. On a steamy summer day, you can dip into the cool waters of Lake Peten Itza or tour the caves of Ak'tun Kan. And make sure you take away some of the great local habanero chile salsa, unless you're just too afraid of it.

9 SALAR DE UYUNI, BOLIVIA

The world's largest salt flat is located in Bolivia, and it offers one of the most unique landscapes on the planet. The Salar de Uyuni covers over 7500 miles, and the salt is over thirty-two feet thick in the center, creating in effect a salt tundra. In summer, the salt planes are a completely flat and bone-dry expanse, but in the wet season, it is covered with a thin sheet of water that is still drivable. Rent a Land Rover for a camping trip, or stay in a hotel that's completely made of salt! Definitely for the more seasoned trekker, but a truly unforgettable experience. You'll probably never walk on the moon, but in Uyuni, you'll come pretty close.

8 BOCAS DEL TORO, PANAMA

If you're like me and passionately detest the hordes of tourists one associates with Costa Rica or other destinations, Panama might be a great alternative for you. Bocas del Toro is a small archipelago on the country's western coast. Remote and difficult to access even today, the region's indigenous and

West African cultures have flourished over the centuries, and one usually hears more English or Creole than Spanish here. Check out nearby Red Frog Beach for a quiet getaway, or take in some great snorkeling in the reefs. Stay too long and you're likely to stay for good.

7 JALISCO STATE, MEXICO

If there is such a thing as a perfect climate, you'll likely find it in Jalisco. Most come to Jalisco for the beaches of Puerto Vallarta, and it is undoubtedly a beautiful place. But if that's not your thing, stay in the historic center of Guadalajara for some great food, music, and museums—Old Mexico at its finest. Or tour the Jose Cuervo distillery for some free samples. You can also find less-crowded beaches like Barra de Navidad, La Manzanilla, or San Patricio. Jalisco has much to offer, and you could easily spend weeks wandering around without even leaving the state.

6 RIO DE JANEIRO, BRAZIL

Founded in the sixteenth century as a fortification against French pirates stalking the Portuguese trade routes, Rio has become one of those places whose very name conjures images of steamy tropical nights, sensual Latin rhythms, and beautiful, scantily-clad women. And that's pretty accurate. Take in the Carnival atmosphere of the *cidade maravilhosa* along Impanema or Copacabana Beach, or a panoramic flight around Sugarloaf Mountain in a helicopter (well worth it). Sadly, Rio does have a reputation for crime, and you should take certain precautions while visiting, but don't let it keep you away.

5 TORRES DEL PAINE, CHILE

At the southern tip of the New World lies Torres del Paine National Park, in Patagonian Chile. Visiting here might leave you with the impression that you have reached the end of the earth, and that you'd be crazy to go one step further for fear of falling into some infinite abyss. In other words, it is way down there. The park is home to lakes, vast glaciers, and mountains massive and sheer. It's certainly a must-do for the outdoorsman, but it offers something else, not easily explained in a travel brochure. Somewhere between the deafening silence in the air, the mighty rocks crowned with mist and snow, and the eternal and inexorable march of the glacial ice, you will feel as though you have borne witness to the dawn of creation itself, and it's extraordinary.

4 BUENOS AIRES, ARGENTINA

Tango, Madonna, and escaped Nazis. That's the extent of most people's knowledge of this sprawling Argentine metropolis. Nevermind the quintessentially European feel of the place or its affordability, world-class restaurants, nightlife, wine, and art. Nevermind the flourishing rock/hip-hop music scene, the internationally renowned fashion industry, or the cultural diversity born from being the capital of a nation of immigrants. Nevermind you can fly there directly from the U.S., Europe, and Australia for a reasonable price. Madonna? Who's that?

3 GALAPAGOS ISLANDS, ECUADOR

The Galapagos Archipelago was claimed by the newly independent Republic of Ecuador in 1832. Three years later, some egghead named Darwin visited the islands and came up with some universally popular scientific theories. Come to the Galapagos and it's easy to see why he chose this spot. Giant tortoises, sea lions, penguins, albatrosses, and countless other species rarely seen anywhere else can all be witnessed in this relatively small nineteen-island chain. Arrange your trip early, as restrictions to the delicate biosphere are understandably tight. And make sure you spend a few days there to help the local economy.

2 JAU NATIONAL PARK, BRAZIL

Amazonia—vast beyond comprehension, remote, and tragically delicate. Spanning Brazil, Colombia, Ecuador, Venezuela, Bolivia, Peru, Suriname, Guyana, and French Guiana, the Amazon is one of the last frontiers, and it's disappearing at a staggering rate. There are many points of entry to the region, and one of the best is located near Manaus in Brazil's Amazonas state. Follow a straight-line road 124 miles to Jau National Park, a designated UNESCO World Heritage Site. Tropical, constantly wet (it is a rain forest), and home to myriad species of dolphins, fish, birds, crocodiles, turtles, monkeys, jaguars, tapirs, and insects, the park can be explored by boat for the adventurous or by foot for the suicidal. Fall asleep in a hammock to the calls of the wild, and be grateful to have glimpsed the splendor of this ecological treasure before it's gone forever.

1 MACHU PICCHU, PERU

The Empire of the Inca once ruled supreme across the inhospitable mountains of Peru. Remarkably, they constructed entire stone cities without the need for cement and built sprawling networks of roads along the spine of the Andes still passable today. The most famous is the Camino del Inca, or the Inca Trail. Hire a guide to take you on the four-day journey from Cuzco to Machu Picchu, once a great mountain stronghold of the Inca. If the altitude gets to you, chew on some coca leaves (yes, it's legal; no, it's not cocaine) while you take in some of the most breathtaking vistas the Western Hemisphere has to offer. Passing through the Sun Gate as the morning fog slowly fades over the spectral city, long before the tour buses arrive from Cuzco, you might feel as though Machu Picchu has been waiting hundreds of years just for you.

About the Editor

Jamie Frater was born in 1974 in Naenae, a suburb of Lower Hutt, New Zealand. He studied postgraduate music at the Royal College of Music in London, after which, due to an insatiable desire to share fascinating, obscure, and bizarre facts, he created Listverse.com where he presents a new top-ten list every day. He has been a guest speaker on numerous national radio and television stations in the United States and Great Britain. Jamie now writes full-time for his California-based website from his home, which he shares with his partner of seven years and his pet Bengal cat, Dexter.